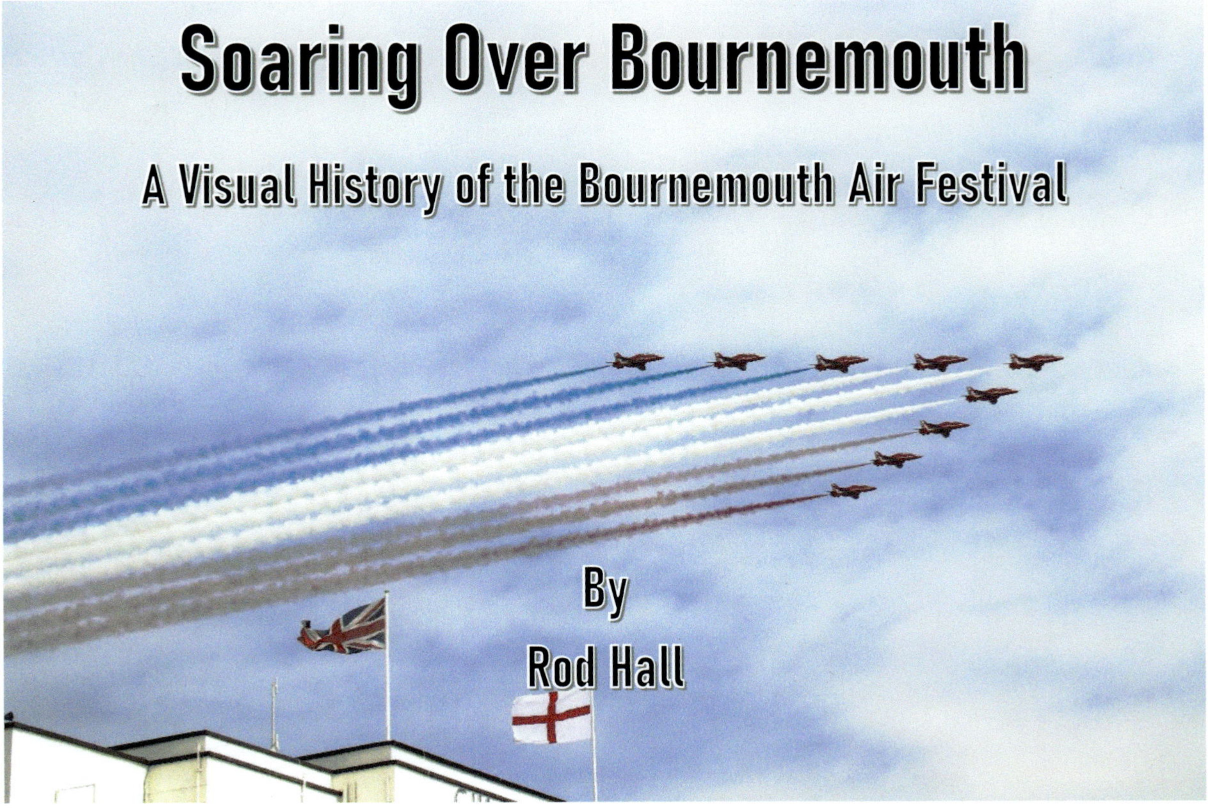
Soaring Over Bournemouth
A Visual History of the Bournemouth Air Festival
By
Rod Hall

Contents

Introduction

My name is Rod Hall. As a keen enthusiast of aviation photography, I have been fascinated with planes since childhood. My journey began by visiting RAF bases near my hometown of New Costessey, Norfolk. In the early 1990s, I spent most school holidays photographing aircraft taking off and landing at the end of the runway at RAF Coltishall. One of my favourite subjects was the Sepecat Jaguar, a versatile jet used for ground attack, close air support, and reconnaissance. I was able to capture many images of the Jaguar during multiple deployments in the Gulf War.

I was fortunate to have supportive parents who nurtured my aviation hobby. They regularly took me to RAF Coltishall so I could indulge my passion for planes while getting thrillingly close to the runway. My parents secretly enjoyed those outings too. The only difference between my early film photography days and digital photography today is that technology has evolved. Gone are the days of anticipation waiting to see if shots on 35mm film turned out, replaced now by instant digital gratification. Sadly RAF Coltishall closed in 2006, ending the station's long, distinguished history as a vital fighter base.

I have decided to publish a book capturing my memories of the Bournemouth Air Festival through my photography before the event's potential end in 2024. Attending every festival since moving to the South Coast, I aim to share the incredible aircraft displays enjoyed by attendees over the years. My book will remind veteran viewers of past highlights while introducing younger generations to the air show and the aircraft that make it so spectacular.

I captured all the photos in this publication, and they are also available for purchase as larger prints at rodhall-photography.picfair.com. As I put this together, I enjoyed rediscovering some of the amazing aircraft and pilots we've welcomed to the Air Festivals over the years, and I hope you enjoy the content as much as I have enjoyed putting it all together.

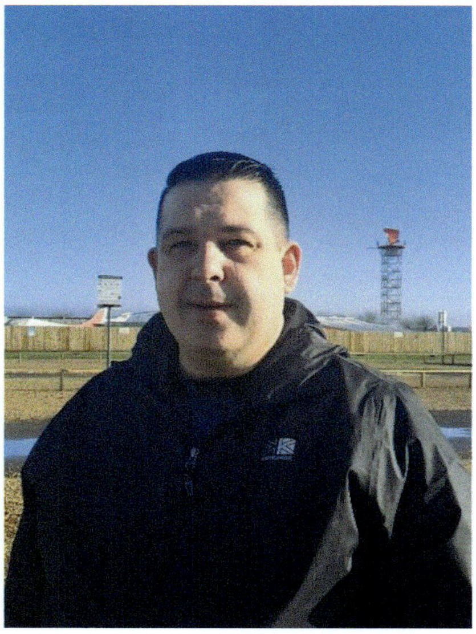

I hope you enjoy my photographic memories of the Bournemouth Air Festival over the years, as much as I have loved reliving the memories.

Rod Hall

Bournemouth Air Festival – A Brief History

The Bournemouth Air Festival is currently an annual aviation extravaganza, it has become a prominent event on the British airshow calendar, captivating audiences with breathtaking aerobatic displays and highlighting the rich history of aviation. The festival is free to visit, and the festival site is 1.5 miles long between Bournemouth and Boscombe piers. The RAF Village is on the East Overcliff. The Royal Navy village, with the Army and Royal Marines conduct demonstrations on the beach with vehicles, have-a-go equipment, and personnel to speak to. Over the years this event has evolved into a four-day celebration of aviation excellence, drawing aviation enthusiasts and the public alike.

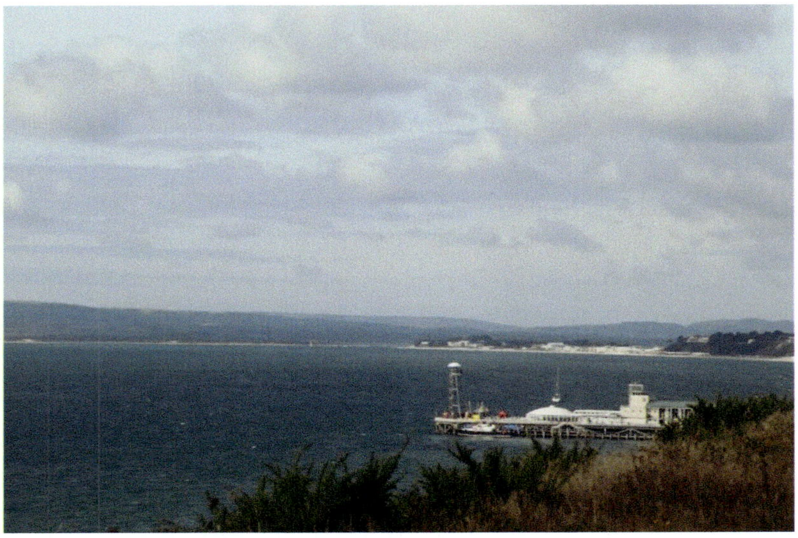

Inception and Early Years (2008-2010)

The Bournemouth Air Festival took flight in 2008, making its debut as a one-day event. Organised by the Bournemouth Tourism and Bournemouth Borough Council, the festival aimed to boost tourism, promote the local economy, and offer a spectacular experience for both residents and visitors. The inaugural year featured a lineup of aerobatic displays, military demonstrations, and parachute displays, setting the stage for future editions.

The success of the first year prompted organisers to expand the festival, turning it into a four-day event in subsequent years. By 2009, the Bournemouth Air Festival had firmly established itself as a major highlight on the UK airshow circuit, attracting large crowds with its diverse program of aerial displays and ground-based entertainment.

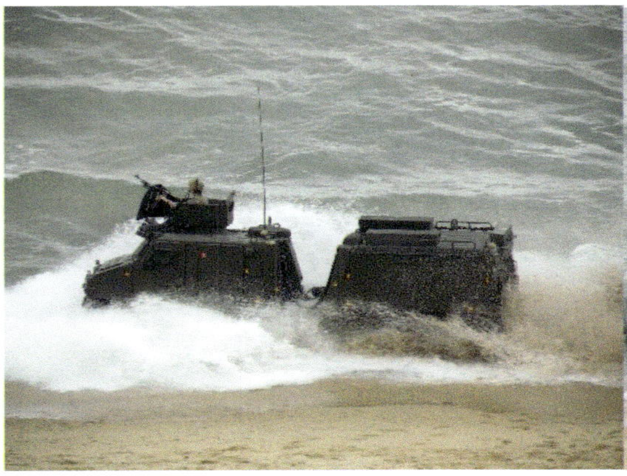
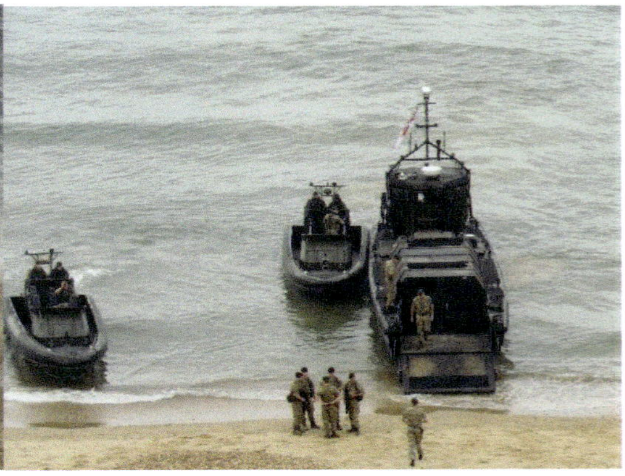

Growing Popularity and International Participation (2011-2015)

As the festival continued to gain momentum, attracting aviation enthusiasts and families alike, organisers began to secure participation from renowned international display teams and military aircraft. The inclusion of iconic aircraft such as the Red Arrows, the Royal Air Force's aerobatic display team, added prestige to the event and drew larger crowds.

Throughout these years, the Bournemouth Air Festival diversified its offerings, incorporating not only military displays but also civilian aerobatic teams, historic aircraft, and entertainment on the ground. The festival's success was reflected in increasing attendance numbers, establishing it as a must-see event for aviation enthusiasts from across the country.

Innovation and Special Features (2016-2019)

In a bid to continually enhance the festival experience, organisers introduced innovative features, including night air displays, fireworks, and music concerts. The introduction of twilight and night displays illuminated the Bournemouth skies with mesmerising aerobatic performances set against the backdrop of fireworks, providing a unique and thrilling spectacle for spectators.

Additionally, the festival expanded its offerings on the ground, featuring interactive exhibitions, family-friendly activities, and food festivals, creating a well-rounded experience for attendees of all ages. The festival's commitment to innovation and variety contributed to its sustained popularity and success.

Challenges and Adaptation (2020-2022)

The Bournemouth Air Festival faced unprecedented challenges in 2020 and 2021 due to the global COVID-19 pandemic. The restrictions and uncertainties surrounding large gatherings forced organisers to cancel or modify the event, disrupting the annual tradition. Despite these challenges, the organisers adapted by exploring virtual alternatives, including online displays and engagement to keep the spirit of the festival alive during the challenging times.

The Future of the Air Festival

There is uncertainty concerning the future of the Bournemouth Air Festival, after another record-breaking year in 2023 the currently Bournemouth, Christchurch and Poole Council are struggling to fund the event and looking for sponsors to come forward to continue its success. This uncertainty has already seen the 2024 Air Festival being cut back to a three-day event (Thursday to Saturday)

Aircraft of the World Wars

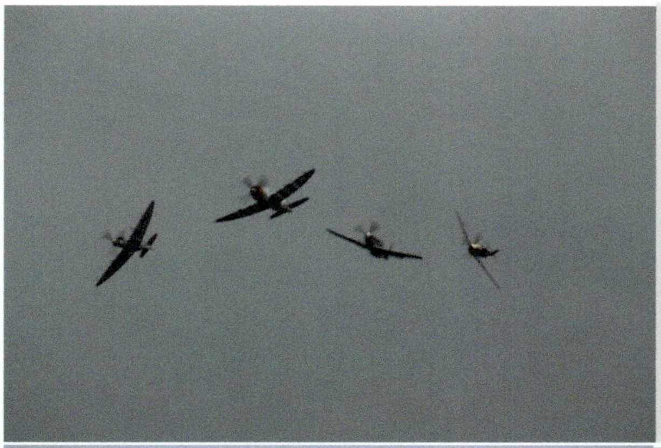

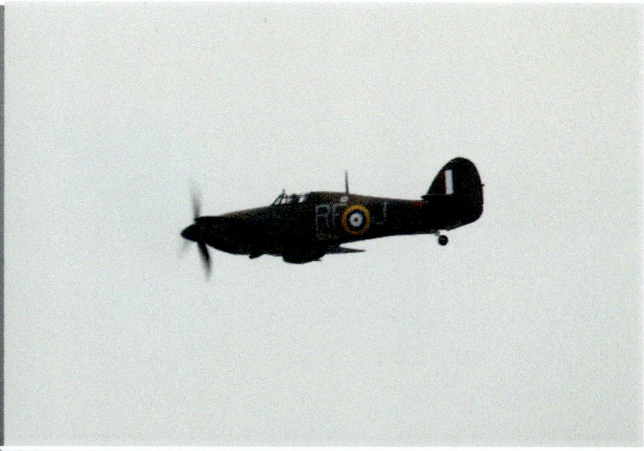

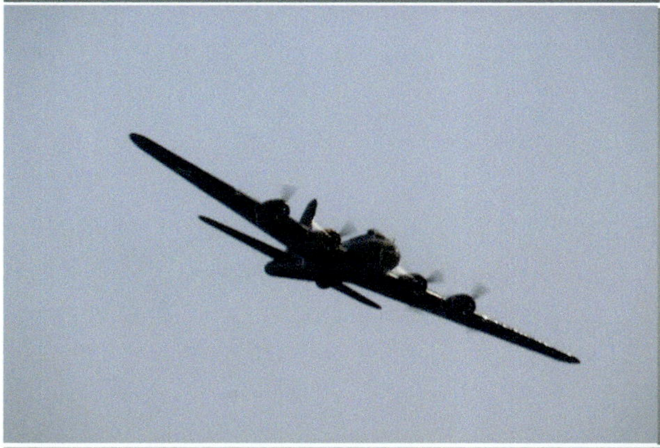

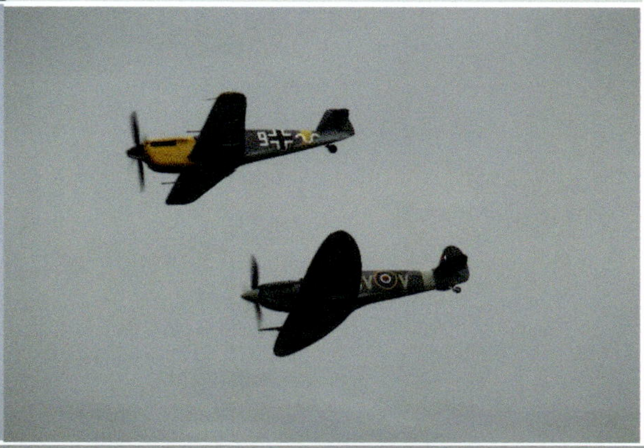

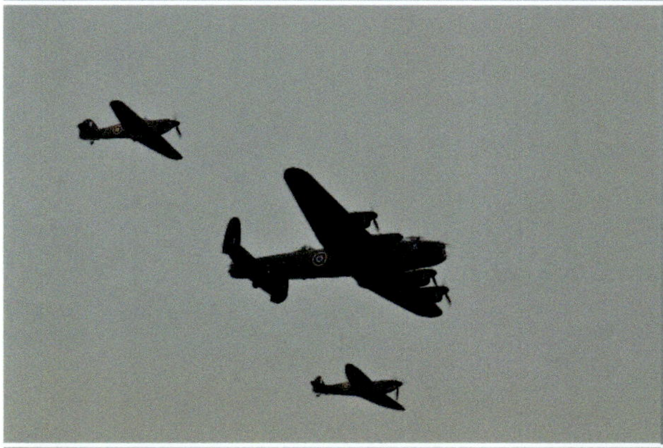

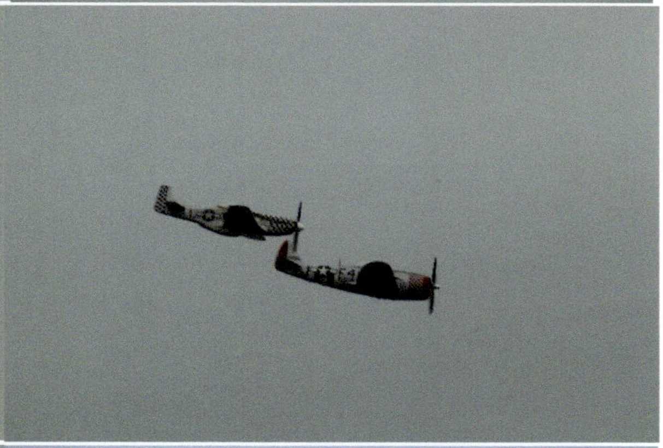

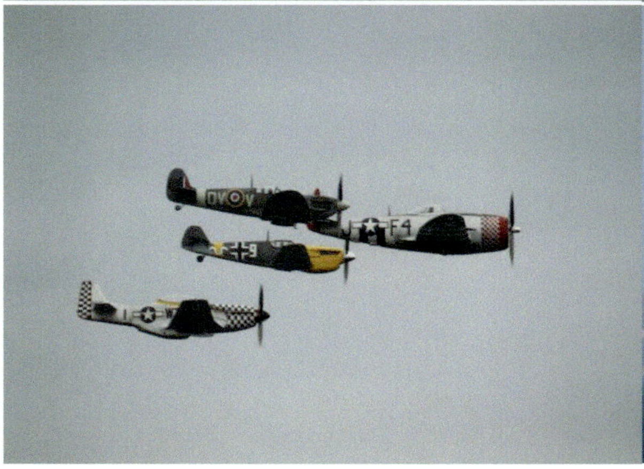

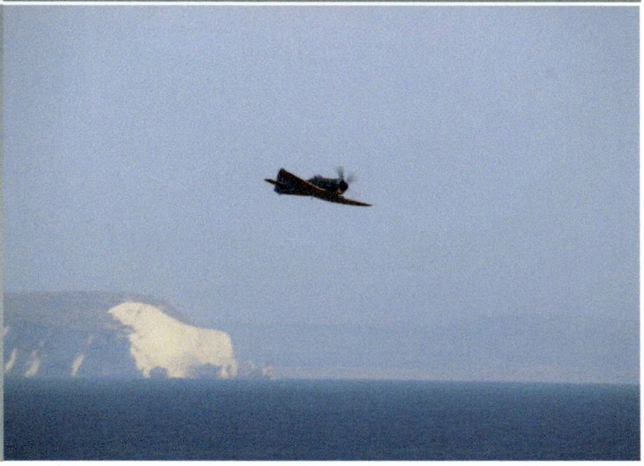

Battle of Britian Memorial Flight

Introduction

The Battle of Britain Memorial Flight (BBMF) serves as a poignant homage to the bravery and valour of the Royal Air Force (RAF) during a critical chapter of World War II. Founded with the mission of safeguarding and honouring Britain's aviation legacy, the BBMF stands as a solemn reminder, showcasing legendary aircraft pivotal in the Battle of Britain.

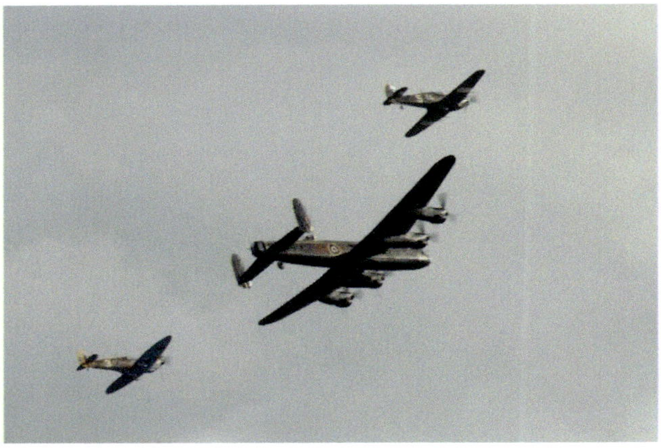

Formation and Purpose

Established in 1957 to mark the 17th anniversary of the Battle of Britain, the Battle of Britain Memorial Flight (BBMF) was created to commemorate the bravery and resilience of RAF pilots who defended British airspace against the German Luftwaffe in 1940. Its main goal was to obtain and preserve aircraft that played key roles in the Battle of Britain and other major World War II air campaigns.

Central to the BBMF's purpose are its meticulously restored and maintained historical aircraft, including the renowned Supermarine Spitfire, Hawker Hurricane, and Avro Lancaster, which represented the three vital aircraft types in the Battle of Britain. These iconic planes honour the valour of the past and serve as flying memorials, taking part in airshows, ceremonies, and flypasts throughout the United Kingdom.

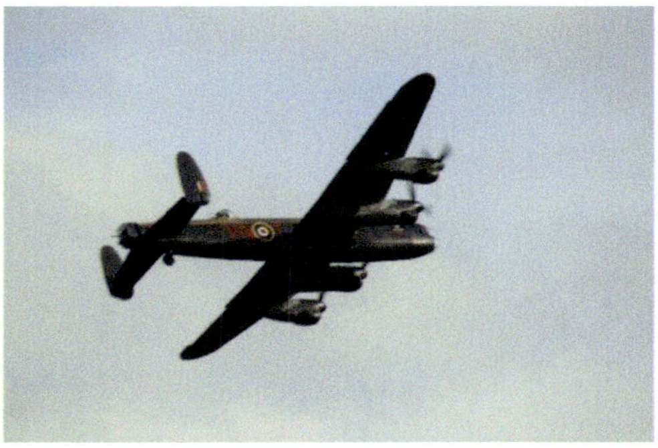

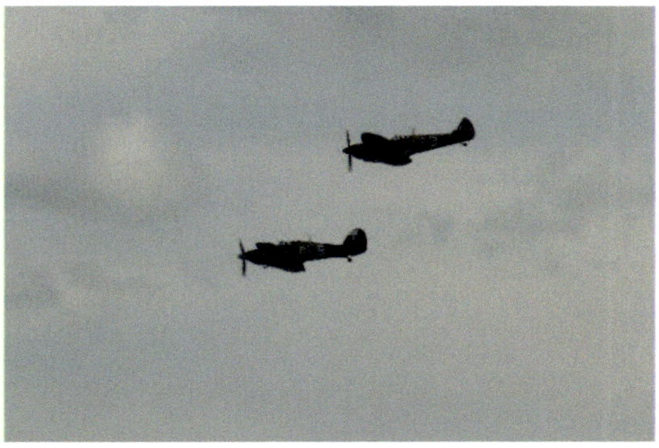

Restoration and Maintenance

A dedicated team of engineers, technicians, and support staff lovingly preserve these historic aircraft. Meticulous restoration and maintenance keep the vintage planes soaring decades after their initial service. The BBMF's authenticity and accuracy shine through in the meticulous attention to detail given each aircraft under its care.

Commemorative Role

The Battle of Britain Memorial Flight (BBMF) plays a vital role in honouring significant events and anniversaries, commemorating the sacrifices made by the RAF during World War II. Through ceremonial flypasts at national events and participation in remembrance services, the flight helps preserve the nation's collective memory and pay tribute to the velour of the "Few" - the RAF pilots who defended Britain in its darkest hour.

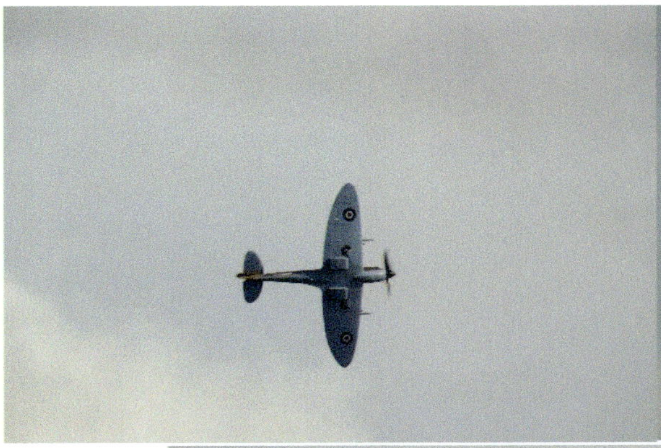

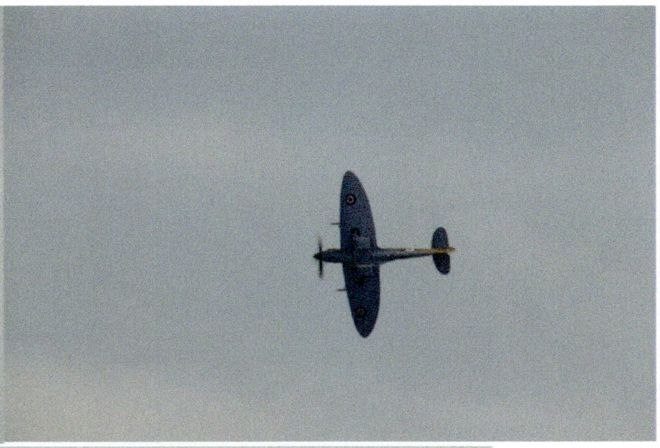

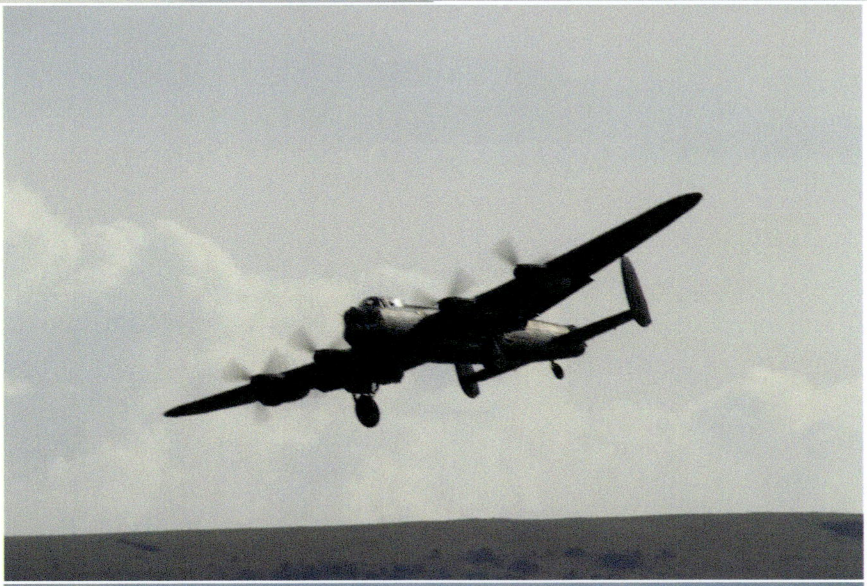

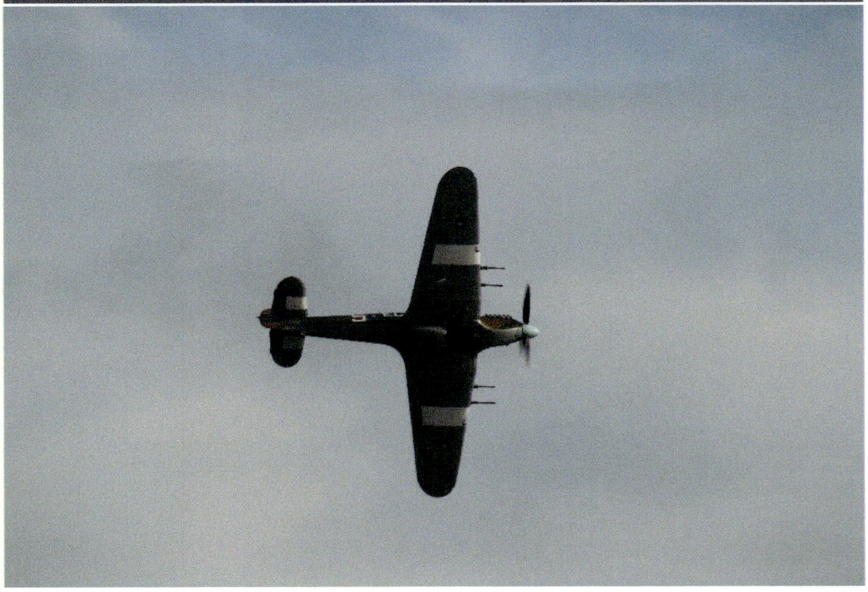

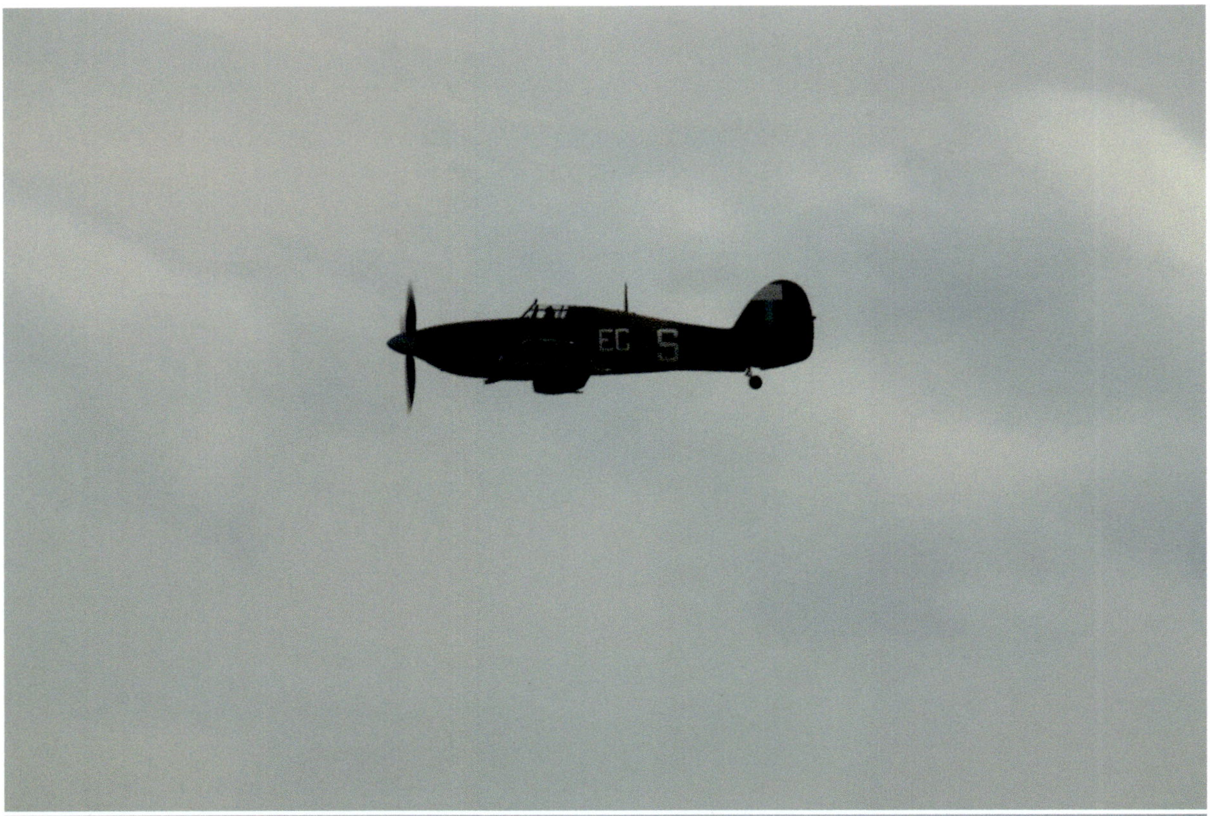
EG S
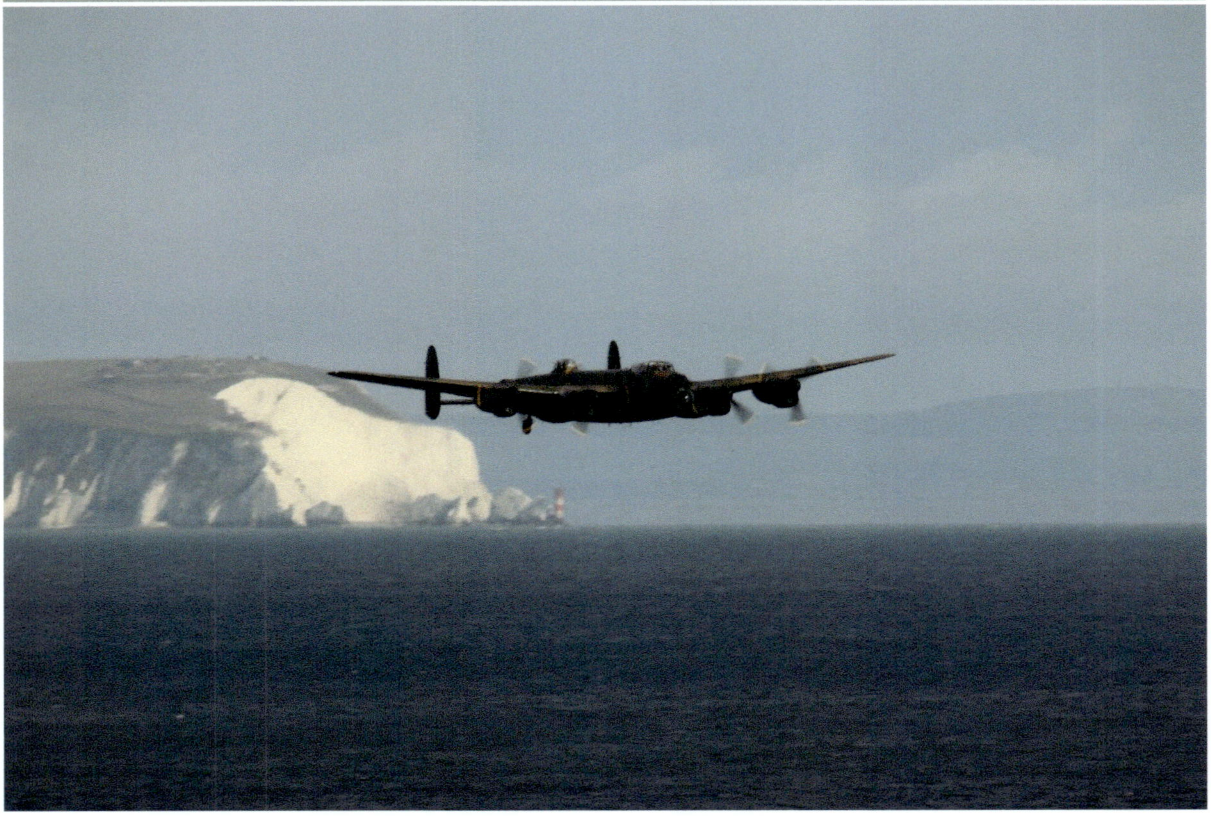

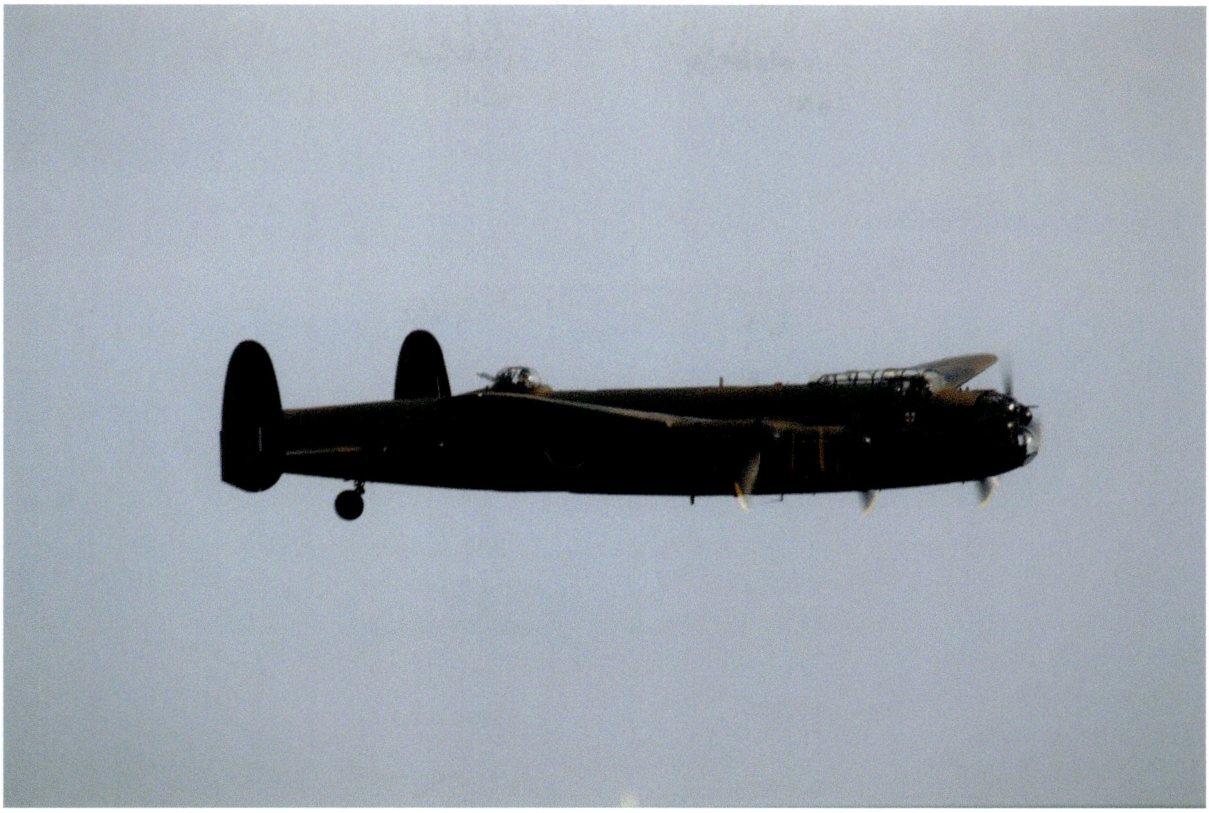

Public Engagement and Education

The Battle of Britain Memorial Flight honours the past while engaging people today. Beyond commemorations, it actively connects with the public through airshows, open houses, and educational programs. These events allow people of all ages to experience the flight's historic aircraft in action and learn about the courage and resolve of RAF personnel during World War II's critical moments.

As the BBMF continues its mission of remembrance, its legacy endures as a testament to the bravery and resilience of those who served. By preserving and displaying its historic fleet, the flight ensures future generations can witness living history and appreciate the sacrifices that secured today's freedoms. The BBMF remains a soaring tribute to the RAF's indomitable spirit and the nation it defended.

The BBMF (Battle of Britain Memorial Flight) has been present for nearly every Air Festival, a welcome sight in the skies over the years. The distinctive grumble of their Merlin engines produces a unique sound that everyone can identify. Only adverse weather has kept the BBMF from flying these delicate aircraft, which we must preserve for future generations. While the BBMF Trio normally consists of the Lancaster, Spitfire, and Hurricane, the Dakota has joined the Spitfire and Hurricane when the Lancaster was unable to fly.

Avro Lancaster

The Avro Lancaster, designed and built by the British aircraft manufacturer Avro, was one of the most famous and successful bombers used by the Royal Air Force (RAF) during World War II. The plane played a crucial role in various bombing campaigns, especially the strategic bombing offensive against Nazi Germany.

The Lancaster was developed from the Avro Manchester, which had proven to be underpowered and unreliable. The Lancaster addressed these issues by replacing the Manchester's unreliable engines with more powerful Rolls-Royce Merlin engines. This redesign significantly improved the aircraft's performance and reliability.

Avro received an initial contract for 1,070 Lancasters, the majority of which were constructed at Avro's Chadderton factory near Oldham, Lancashire during the war years. The Lancasters were test-flown from Woodford Aerodrome in Cheshire. Due to the wartime demand exceeding Avro's production capacity, the Lancaster Aircraft Group was formed, comprising several companies that either performed primary assembly of Lancasters or produced subsections and components for other group members.

The Lancaster bomber was also produced overseas. In early 1942, it was decided that Canada should manufacture the aircraft, with Victory Aircraft building it in Malton, Ontario. Of later Lancaster variants, only the Canadian-built Lancaster B X was made in large numbers, totalling 430 units. The early Canadian models were like their British counterparts, except for using Packard-built Merlin engines, American instruments, and electrical systems. Notably, in August 1942, a British Lancaster B.I flew to Canada as the first example to make a transatlantic crossing, serving as the pattern aircraft for Canadian production.

The Lancaster bomber had a key design feature: its 33-foot (10 meter) long bomb bay with no obstructions, which initially allowed it to carry the heavy 4,000-pound (1,800 kg) "Cookie" blast bomb. Later, bulged doors were added to 30 percent of the B.I models, enabling them to carry even larger 8,000-pound (3,600 kg) and 12,000-pound (5,400 kg) "Cookie" bombs. It played a vital role in many strategic bombing missions, most famously the "Dambusters" raid of May 1943 when Lancasters deployed Barnes Wallis' innovative "bouncing bombs" to strike Ruhr Valley dams.

The Lancaster's operational career boasts impressive statistics, but it is important to note that the average age of the seven-man crew was just 22 years old. These young men endured extreme danger and discomfort, with many demonstrating remarkable courage as they persevered in flying missions despite the low odds of survival. Indeed, Bomber Command suffered the highest casualty rate of any British military branch in World War II.

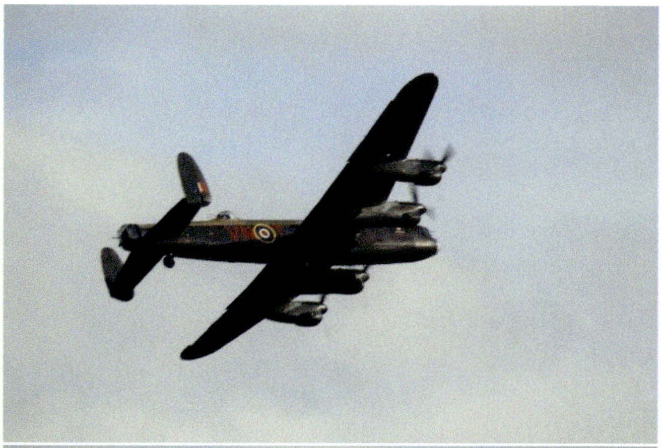

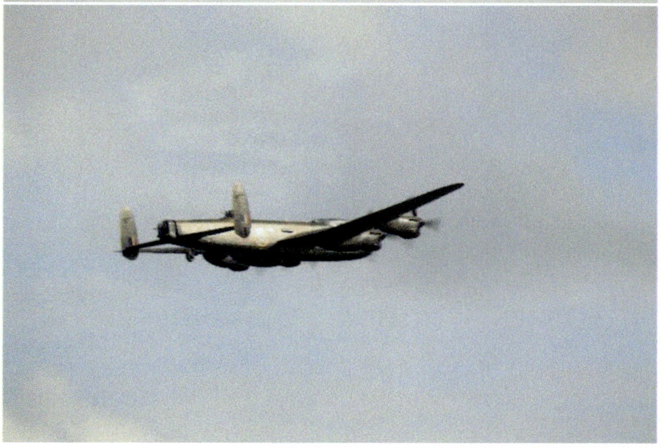

Quick Facts

- The prototype Lancaster flew for the first time on January 9, 1941
- The Lancaster had a crew of seven: pilot, flight engineer, navigator, bomb aimer, wireless operator, mid-upper gunner, and rear gunner
- It had a maximum bomb capacity of around 14,000 pounds (6,350 kg)
- Powered by four Rolls-Royce Merlin engines
- Range of approximately 2,530 miles (4,070 km)
- Over 7,300 Lancasters were built during World War II

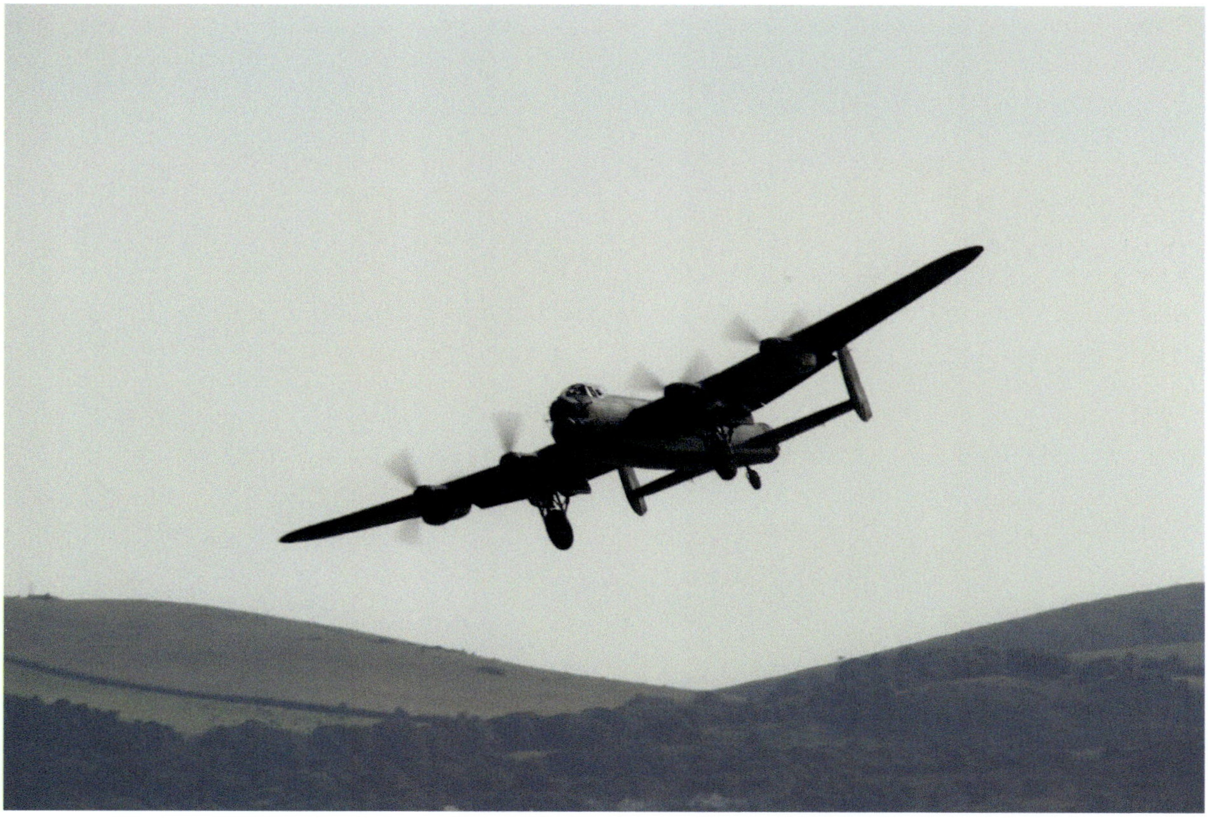

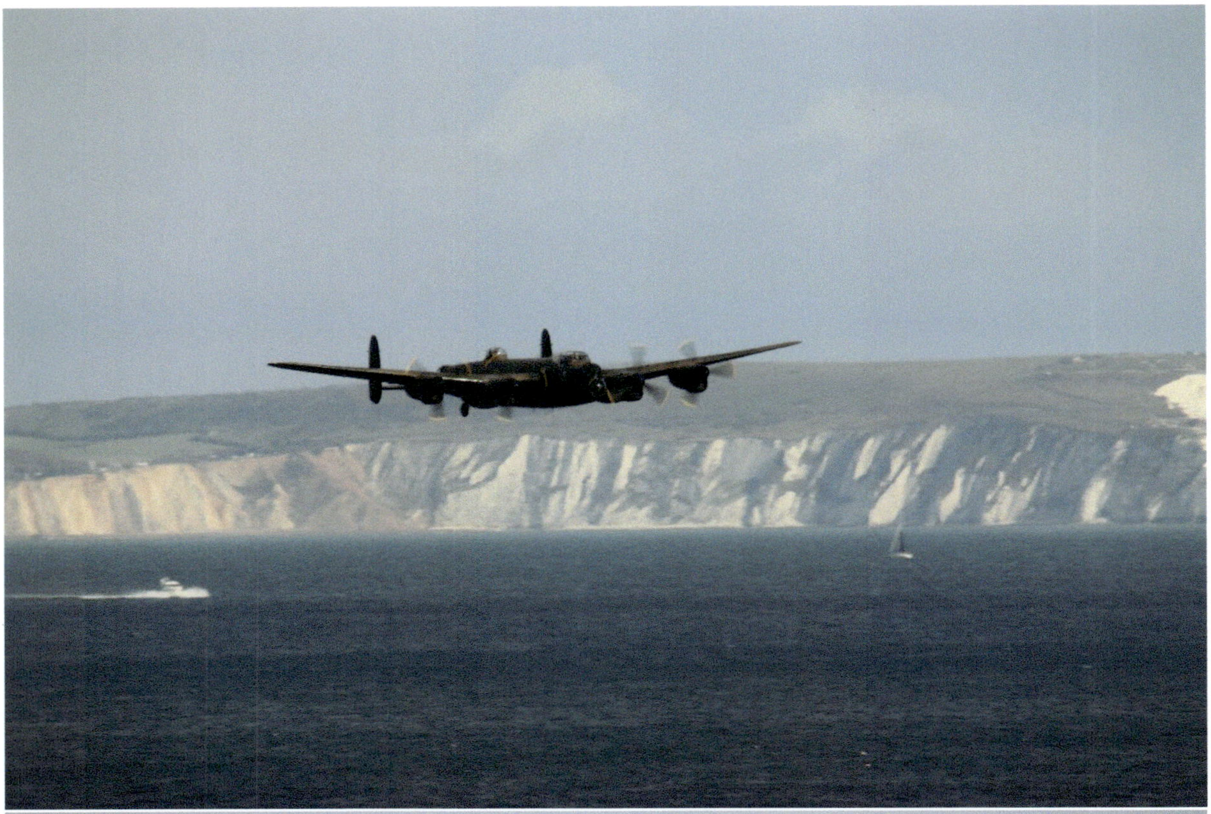

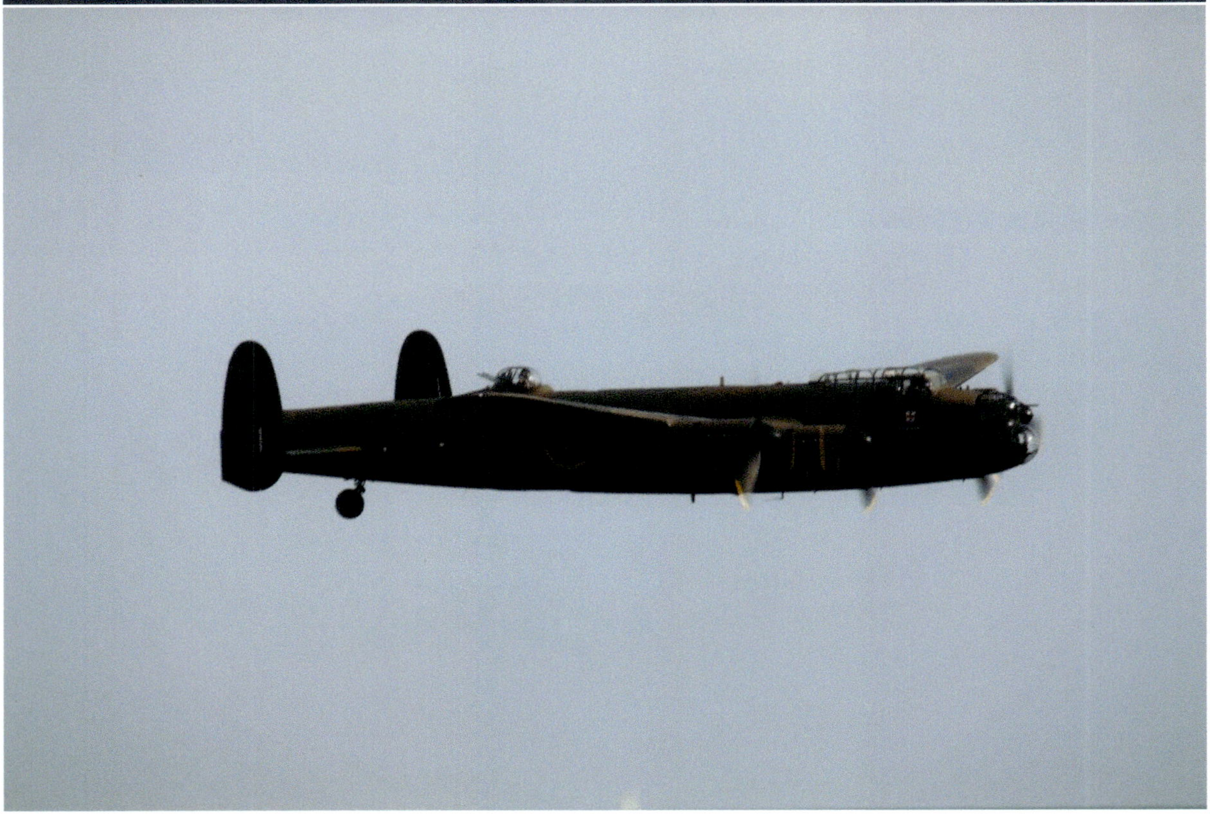

Supermarine Spitfire

The iconic Supermarine Spitfire became a symbol of courage, innovation, and British resolve during World War II, capturing the hearts and minds of the nation. Designed by R.J. Mitchell, this legendary fighter aircraft played a pivotal role in Britain's heroic defence against the Luftwaffe onslaught during the Battle of Britain.

The sleek and graceful Spitfire epitomized the height of aviation technology when it was created. Its elliptical wings, praised for aesthetics, enabled exceptional performance through agile and stable flight. Powered by the Rolls-Royce Merlin, the Spitfire had the optimal mix of speed, manoeuvrability, and firepower to be a formidable aerial combatant.

During the Battle of Britain, the Spitfire and Hawker Hurricane planes served as the backbone of the RAF's defence against the German Luftwaffe's unrelenting assaults. The brave Spitfire pilots, known as "The Few," engaged in fierce dogfights high above the English Channel and southern England, foiling the enemy's efforts to dominate the skies. Their velour and expertise, paired with the Spitfire's exceptional performance, proved vital in shifting the momentum of the battle in the Allies' Favor.

Another variant was The Supermarine Spitfire Griffin, pairing the timeless elegance of the classic Spitfire airframe with the brute force of the Rolls-Royce Griffon powerplant. Forged in the fires of World War II, this ultimate Spitfire variant stands as a monument to British aeronautical mastery. Powered by the mighty Rolls-Royce Griffon engine, the Spitfire Griffon soared to new heights. This liquid-cooled 12-cylinder engine, renowned for its formidable power and distinctive growl, gave the Spitfire unmatched speed and agility. With its superior horsepower and torque, the Griffon transformed the Spitfire into a dominant force in the skies, able to outmanoeuvre and outpace adversaries with ease.

Going beyond its wartime exploits, the Spitfire continued serving with distinction throughout the conflict in various theaters of war, including North Africa, the Mediterranean, and the Pacific. The plane's adaptability enabled it to excel not only in air superiority roles but also in reconnaissance, ground-attack, and even naval operations.

The Spitfire's legend endured through history after remaining in service with numerous air forces following the war. Even today, the iconic sight and sound of a Spitfire in flight evoke nostalgia and reverence for the era of sacrifice and velour it represents. A poignant symbol of enduring gallantry and freedom, the handful of Spitfires still flying are a testament to the aircraft's lasting legacy.

Quick Facts

- Early Spitfires were powered by the Rolls-Royce Merlin engine, Later variants, such as the Mk IX, featured different engines, including the Rolls-Royce Griffon
- The Spitfire was armed with eight .303-inch Browning machine guns
- The prototype, known as the Supermarine Type 300, first flew on March 5, 1936
- The Spitfire was known for its exceptional speed and agility

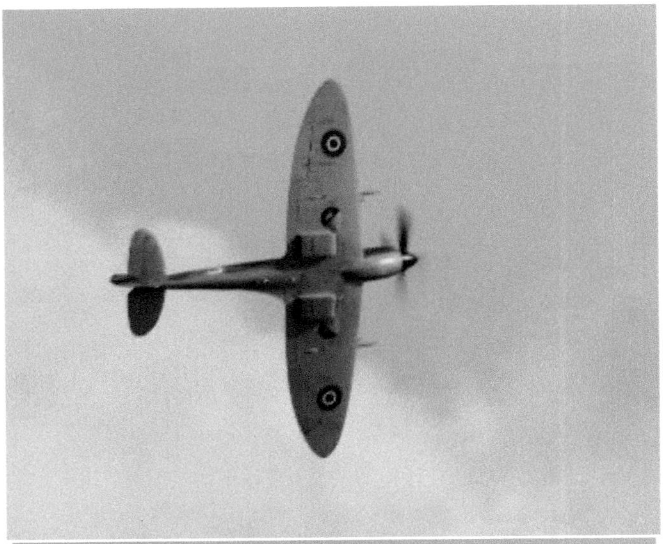

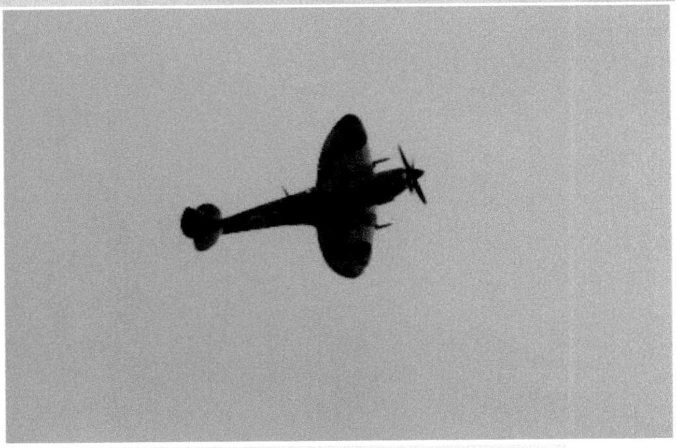

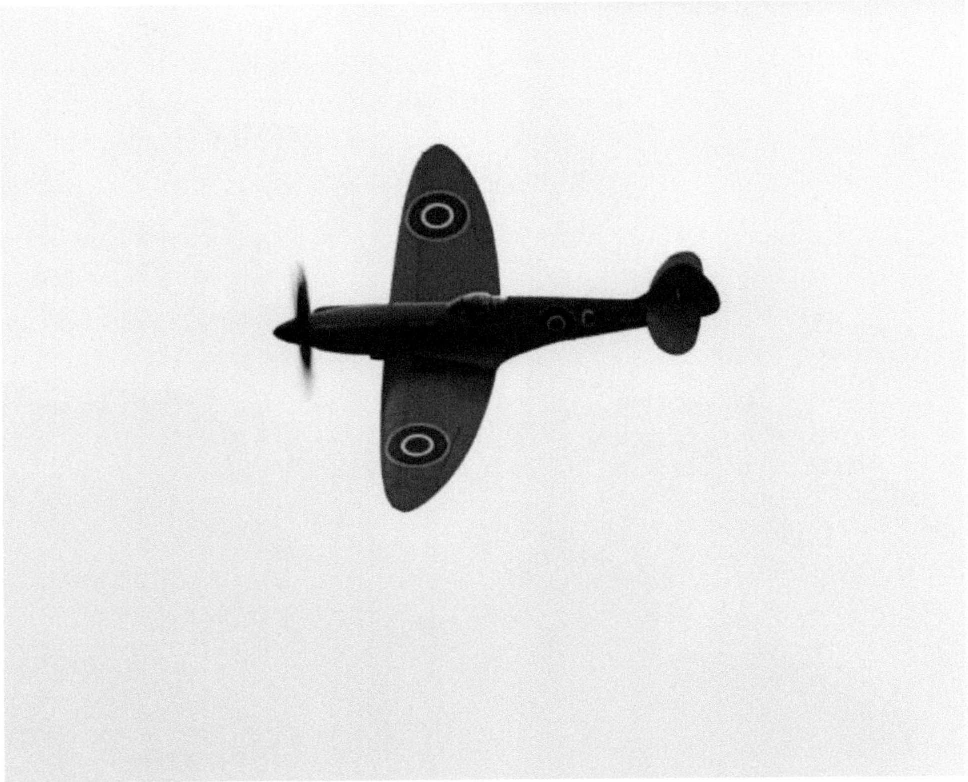

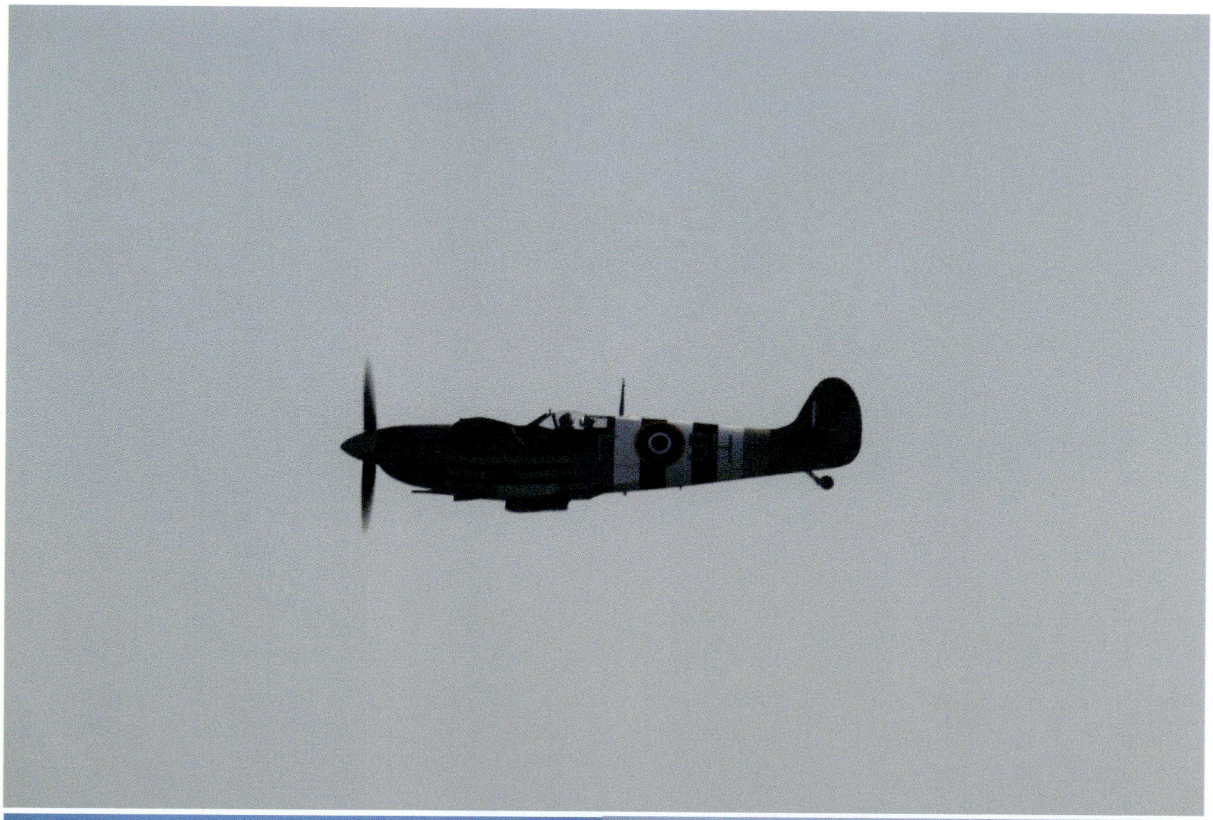

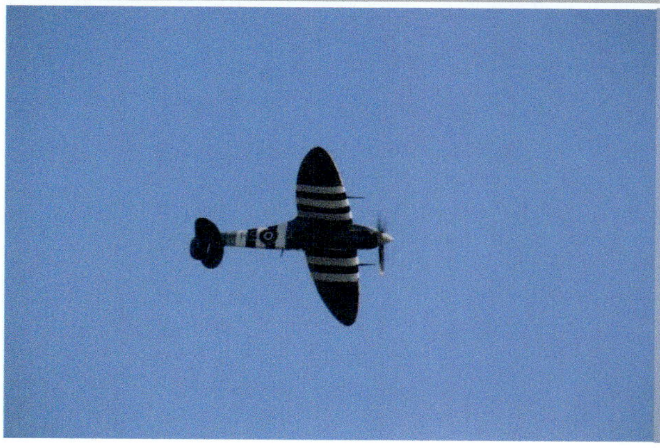

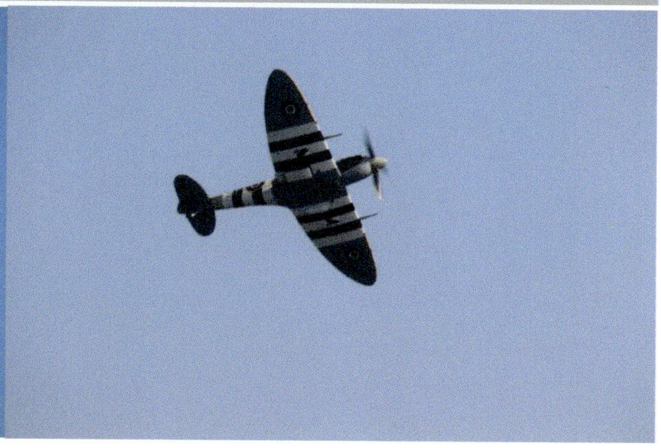

- The Spitfire went through various marks and variants, each introducing improvements in performance, armament, and capabilities. Notable marks include the Mk I, Mk V, Mk IX, and Mk XIV

- The Spitfire gained legendary status during the Battle of Britain, where it, along with the Hawker Hurricane, played a critical role in defeating the German Luftwaffe and preventing a German invasion.

Hawker Hurricane

The Hawker Hurricane, designed by Sir Sydney Camm, served as a resilient defender of Britain during World War II. With its rugged silhouette, this iconic fighter plane helped protect the skies against Axis forces. With its distinctive single-wing design and robust construction, the Hurricane showcased British ingenuity and engineering excellence. Powered by the potent Rolls-Royce Merlin engine, the fighter plane combined impressive speed, agility, and firepower, making it a formidable force in aerial combat.

During the pivotal Battle of Britain, the Hurricane faced its baptism of fire as the fate of nations hung in the balance. Rising to meet the Luftwaffe's onslaught amidst the tumultuous skies, Hurricanes engaged in fierce dogfights over the English Channel and England's green fields. With its exceptional manoeuvrability and heavy armament, the Hurricane proved instrumental in repelling the enemy attack, earning the admiration and gratitude of an embattled nation.

The Hurricane's contributions stretched far beyond the Battle of Britain. Serving with distinction from the deserts of North Africa to the jungles of Southeast Asia, this aircraft proved itself a reliable workhorse for Allied air forces across the globe. Engaging enemy fighters, supporting ground troops, and intercepting bombers, the Hurricane repeatedly demonstrated its mettle in battle.

Though often overshadowed by the more glamorous Spitfire, the Hurricane's importance in World War II cannot be overstated. Ruggedly durable and easy to maintain, the Hurricane was beloved by pilots and ground crews alike, ensuring its effectiveness throughout the war. By 1945, Hurricanes had destroyed thousands of enemy aircraft, cementing their legacy as one of the most successful fighter planes of the conflict.

In the decades since, the Hawker Hurricane has stood as an enduring symbol of courage, resilience, and sacrifice. Preserved in museums and flown at airshows worldwide, this iconic fighter plane serves as a tangible reminder of the bravery and determination of those who flew and maintained the Hurricanes in defence of freedom. As its distinctive silhouette once again graces the skies, the Hurricane continues to inspire awe and admiration, a testament to the indomitable spirit of the men and women who made these legendary aircraft part of history.

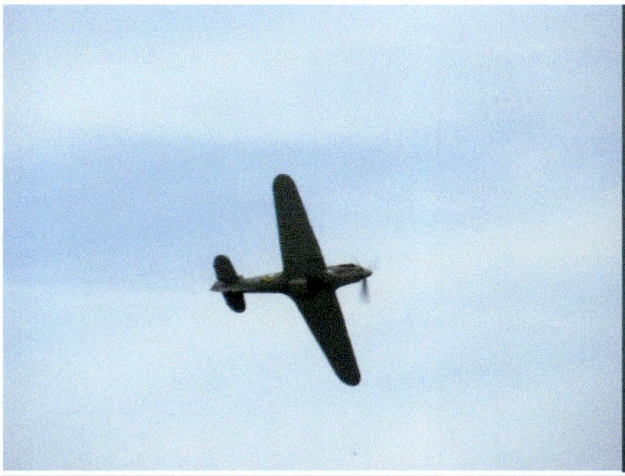
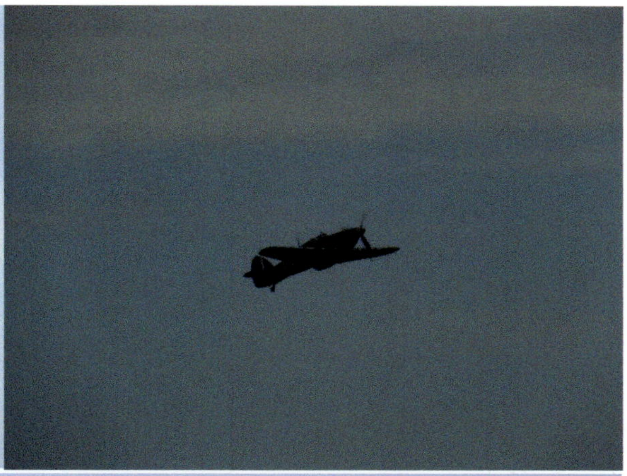
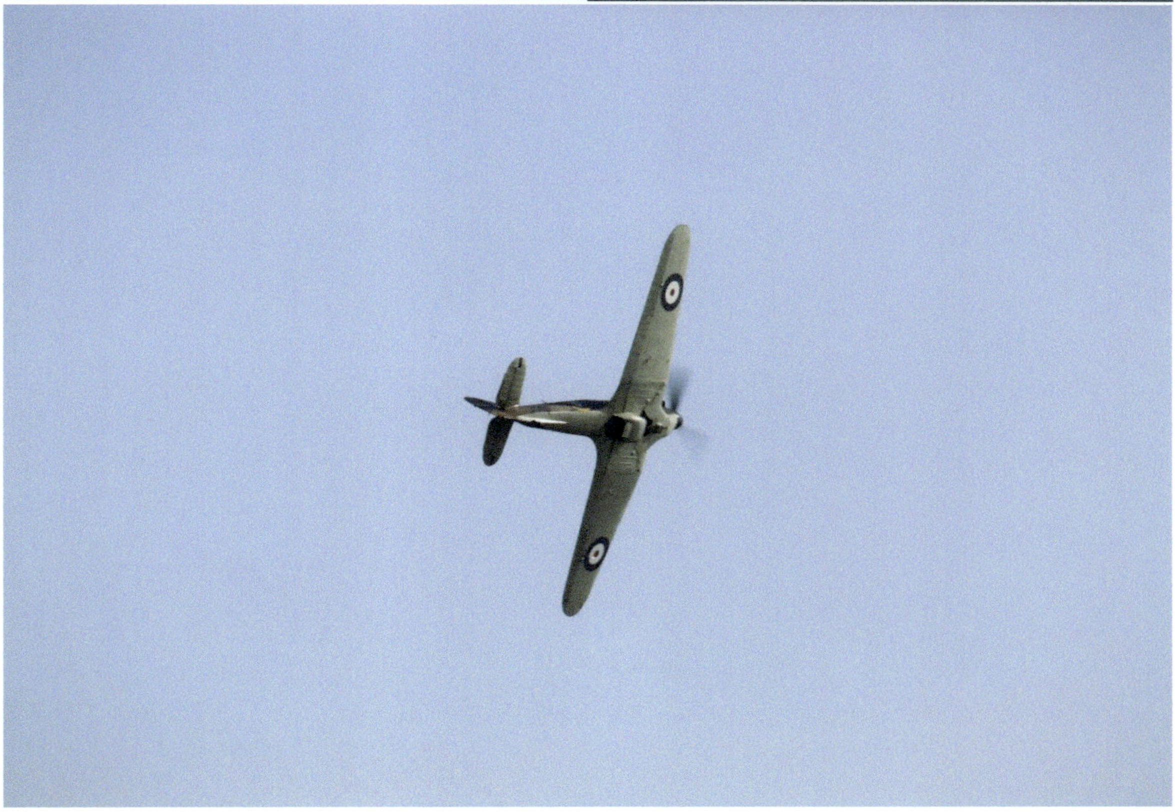

Quick Facts

- The Hawker Hurricane was designed by Sydney Camm and first flew on November 6, 1935
- The Hurricane was powered by the Rolls-Royce Merlin engine, the same engine that powered the Supermarine Spitfire
- Early versions of the Hurricane were armed with eight .303-inch Browning machine guns with later variants featuring 20mm Hispano cannons
- The versatility of the Hurricane not only saw it as an air superiority fighter but also a force in ground attack and bomber escort roles
- Over 14,000 Hurricanes were produced during the war, making it one of the most produced aircraft of its time

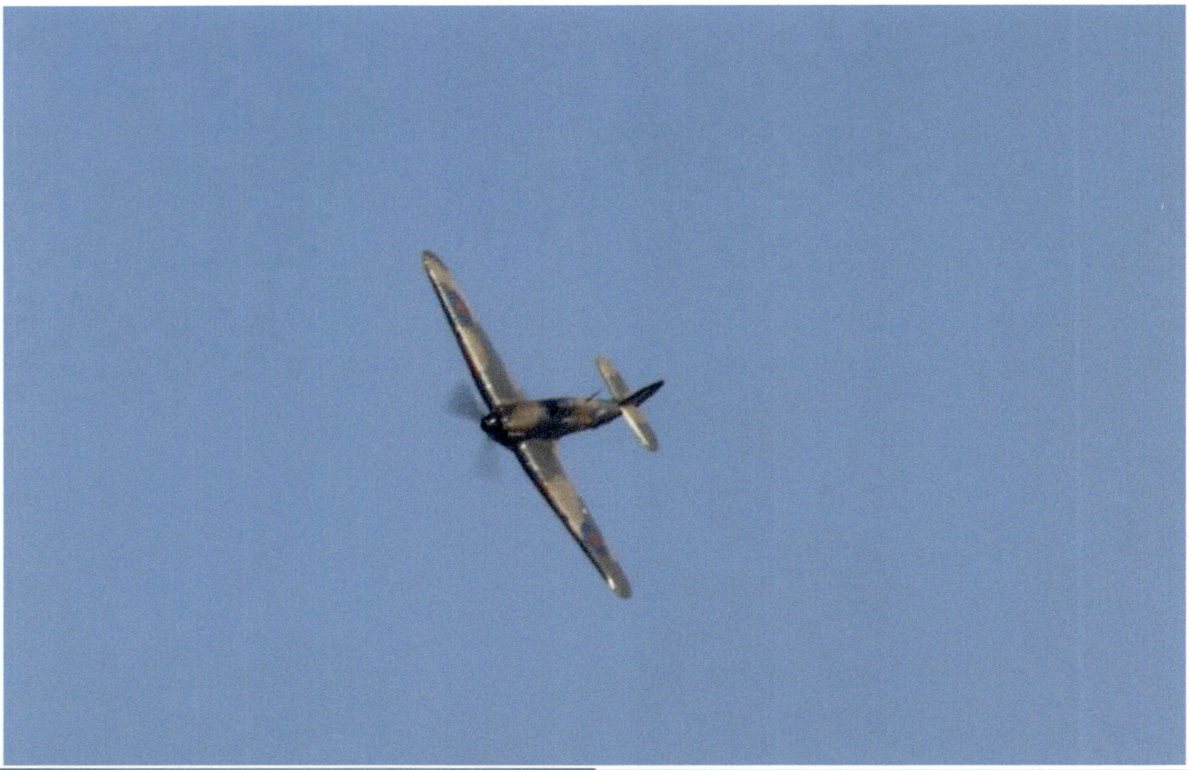

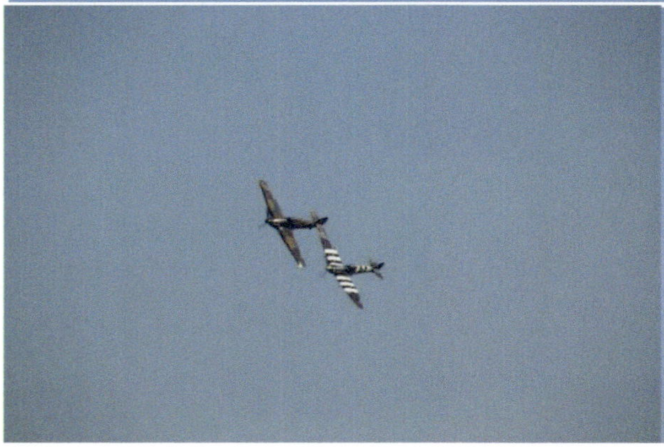

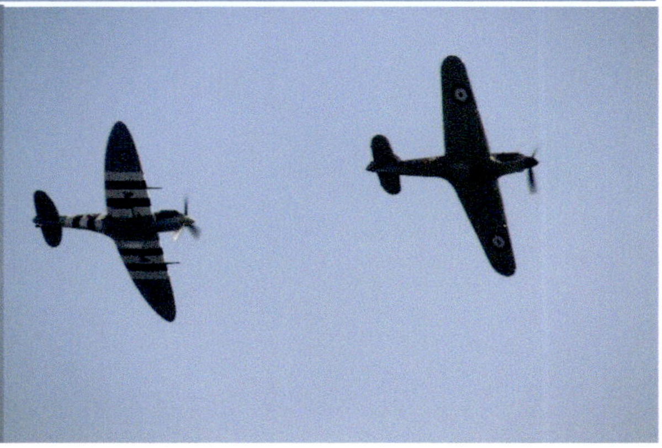

Great War Display Team

The Bournemouth Air Festival has welcomed the "Great War Display Team" on a couple of occasions, these are an aerobatic display team that specialises in flying replica World War I aircraft. This team aims to recreate the aerial combat and manoeuvres of the Great War era, providing audiences with a glimpse into the aviation history of World War I

Aircraft and Historical Reenactment

The Great War Display Team performs with replica World War I-era aircraft, often built with modern materials and engines for safety and reliability. Typical planes in their air shows include replicas of iconic World War I fighters like the Sopwith Camel, Royal Aircraft Factory SE5a, and Fokker Dr.I Triplane.

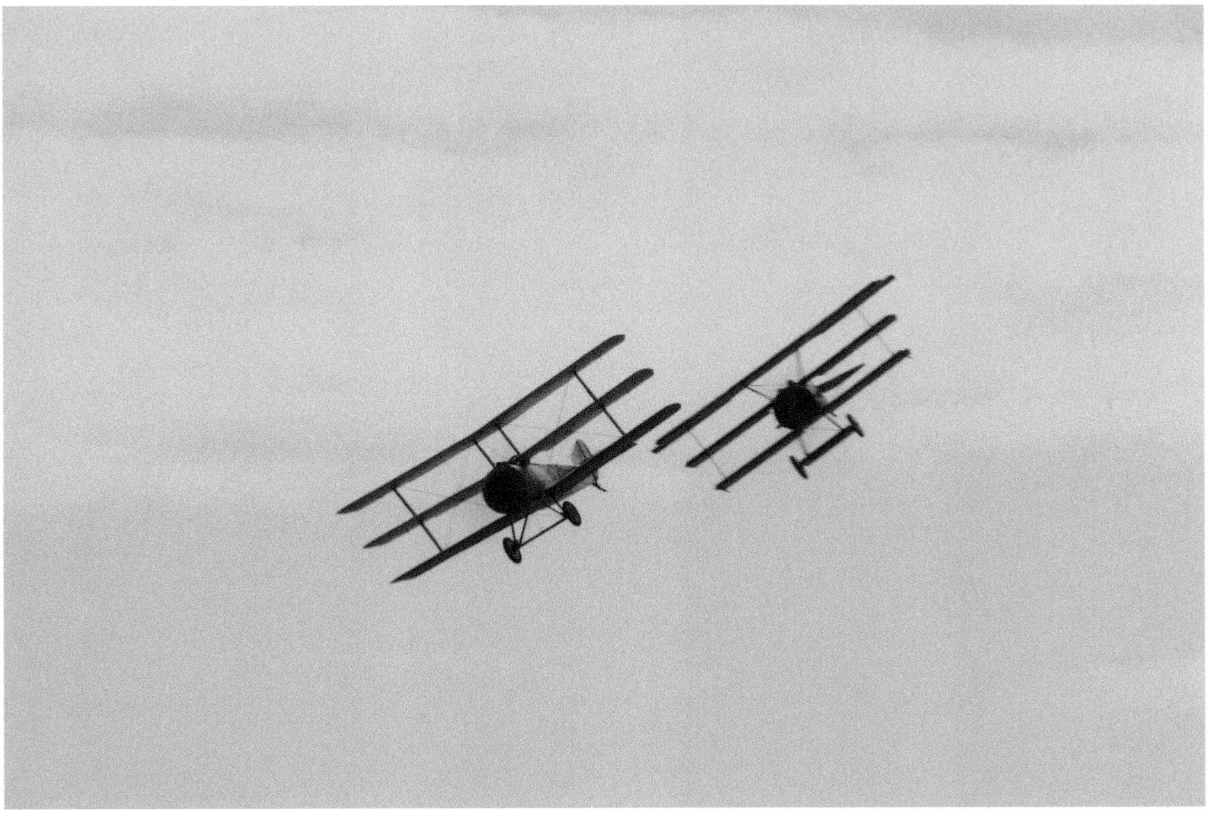

The primary goal of the Great War Display Team is to reenact historical air battles and highlight the aerial tactics employed during World War I. Pilots may wear period-appropriate uniforms, and the team strives to recreate the atmosphere of early aviation combat.

The team participates in airshows and aviation events, offering audiences a unique and nostalgic experience of witnessing World War I-style dogfights and aerobatics.

Performances often involve simulated dogfights, formation flying, and solo aerobatic displays, displaying the agility and characteristics of the replica aircraft.

Educational Outreach

In addition to airshow performances, the Great War Display Team may engage in educational outreach programs, providing information about the historical context, aircraft, and the pilots of World War I.

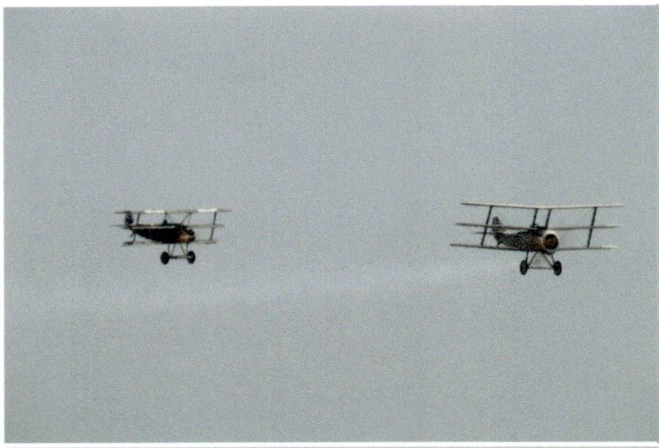
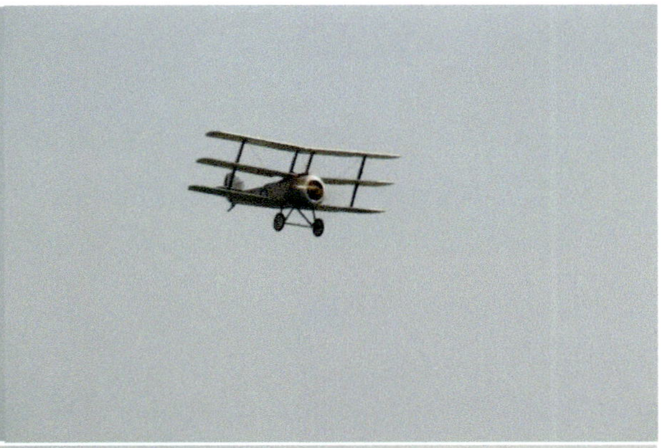
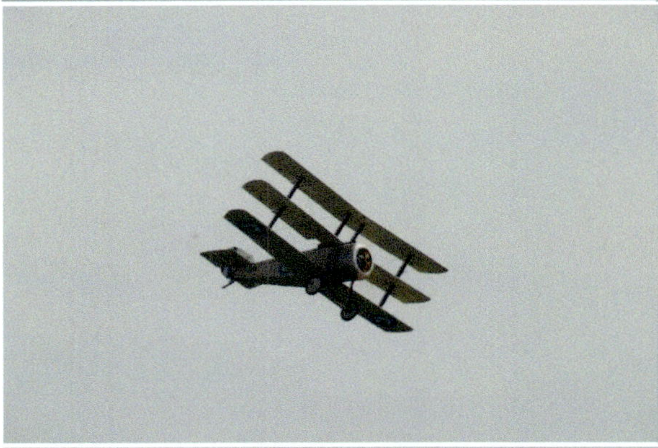
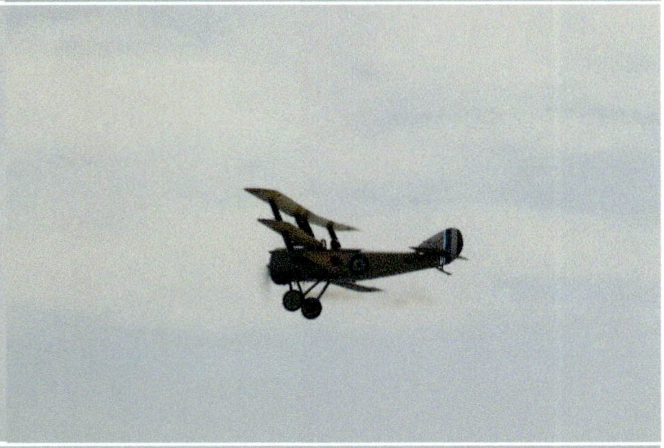
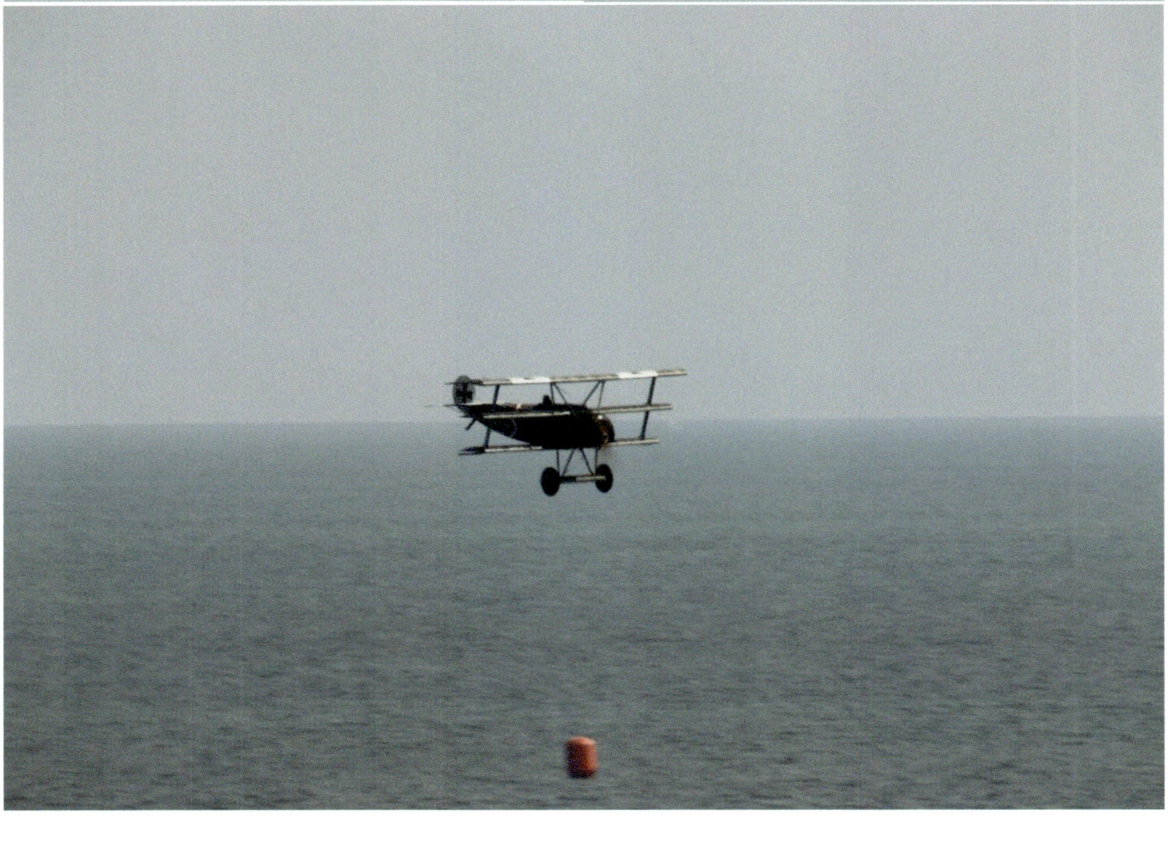

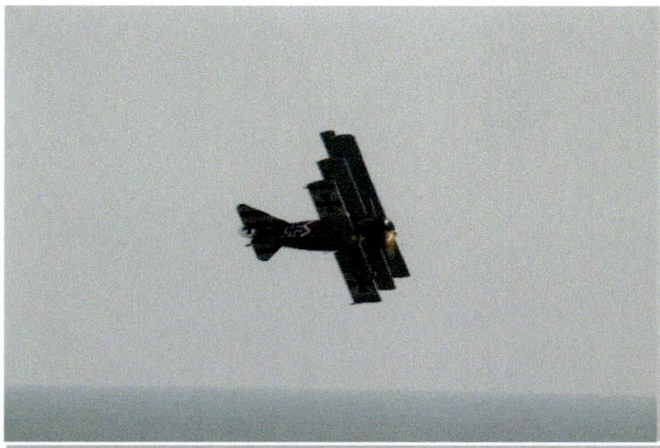

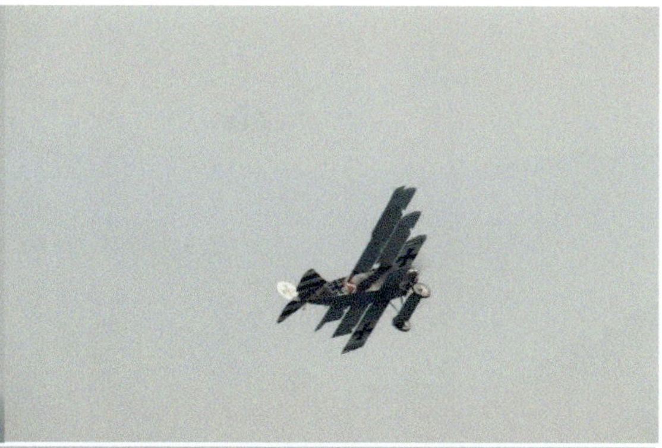

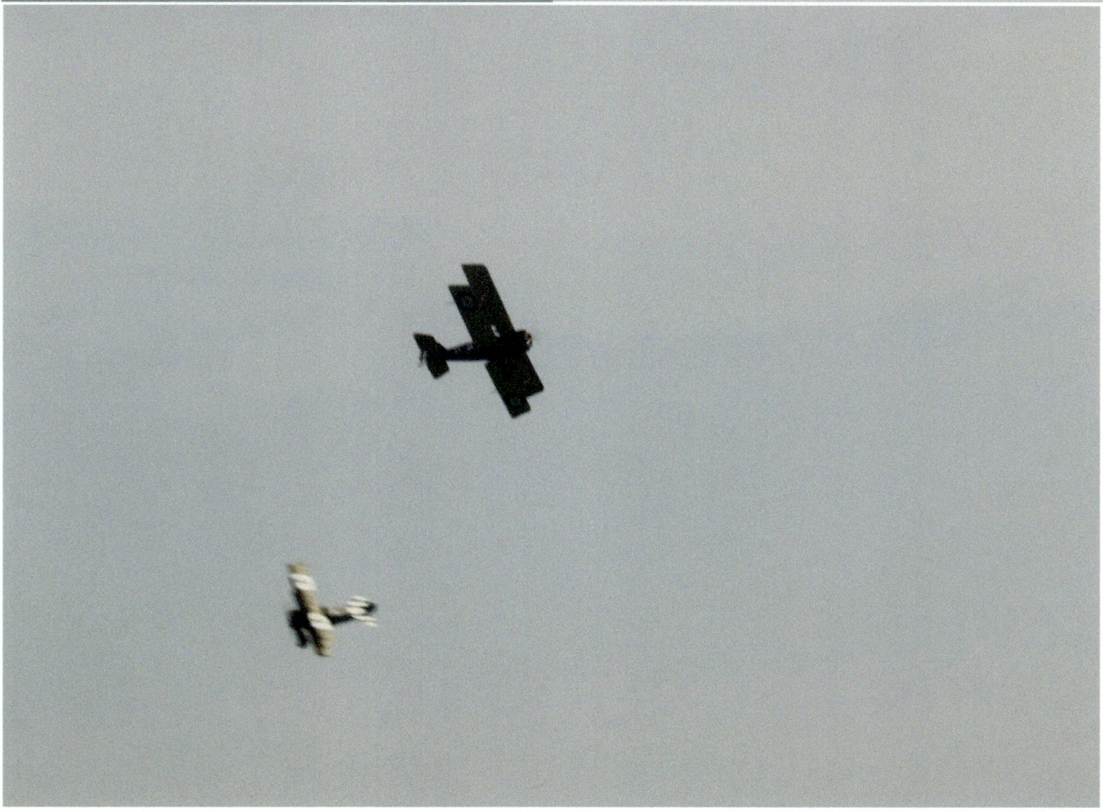

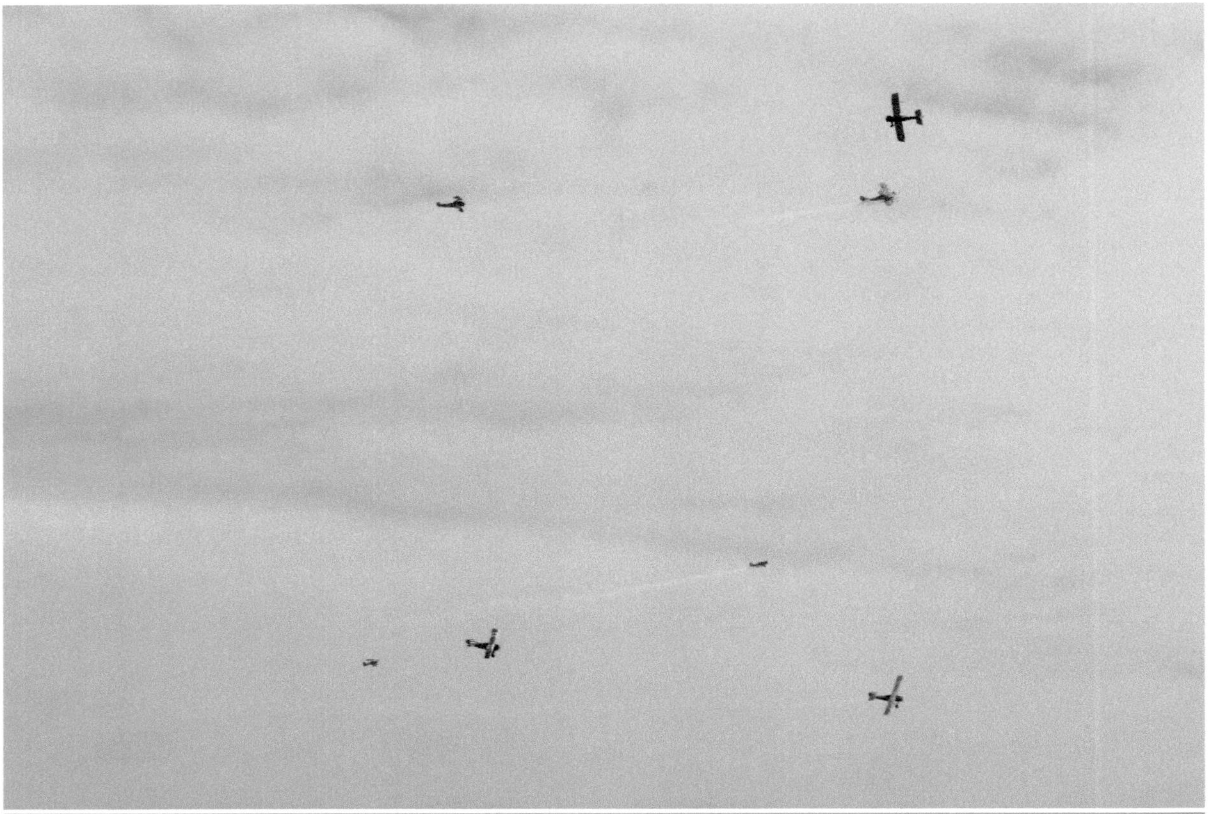

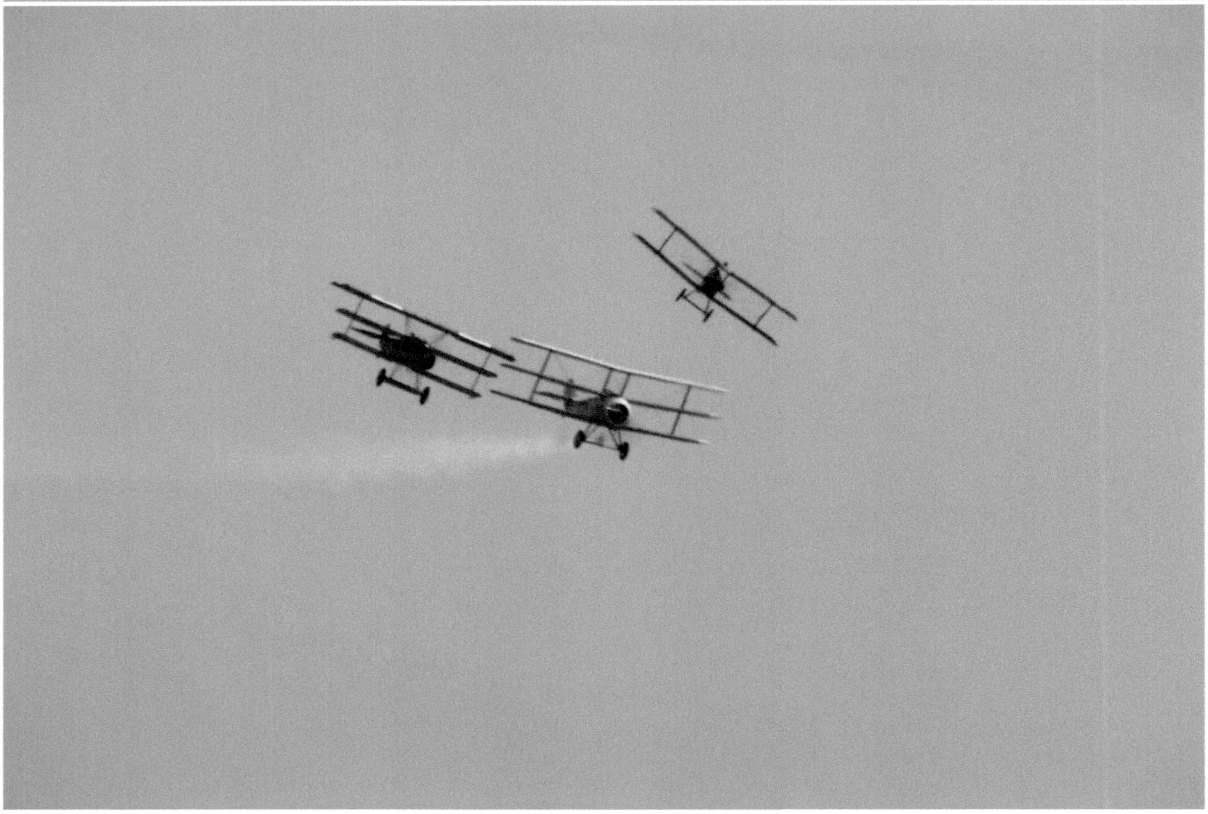

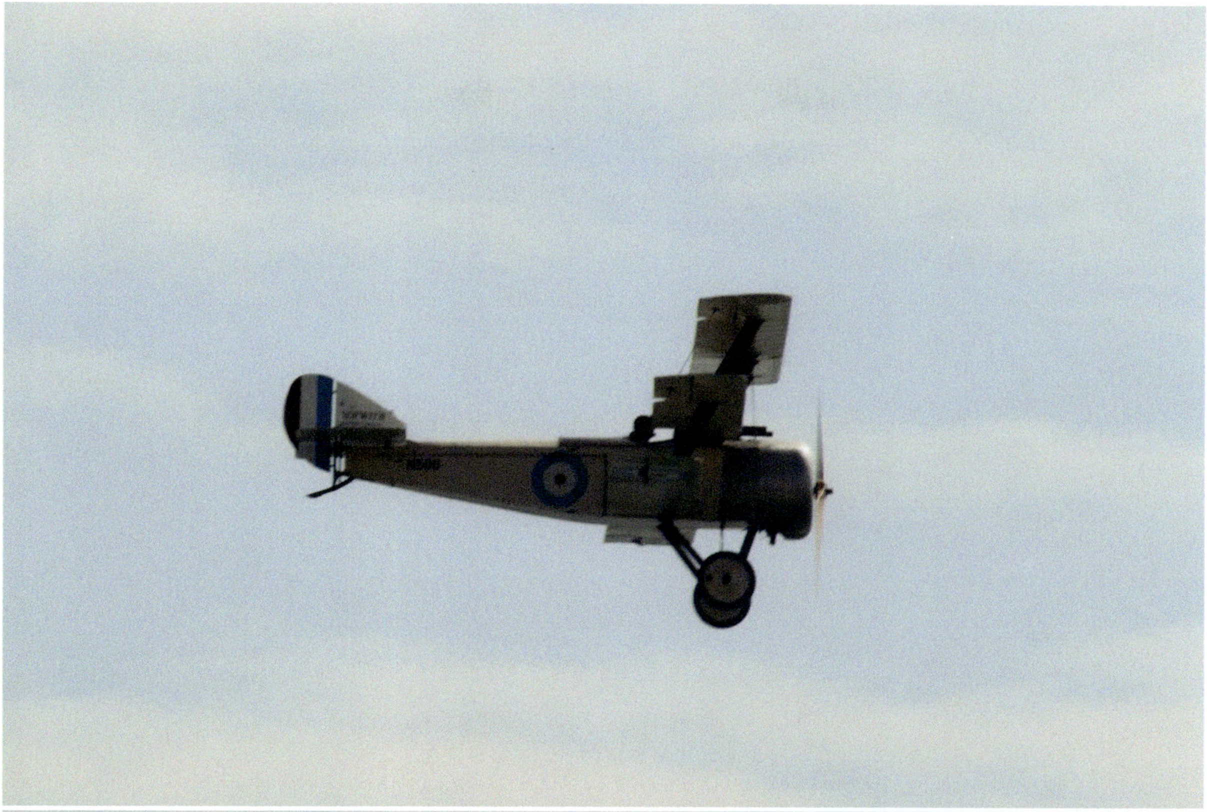

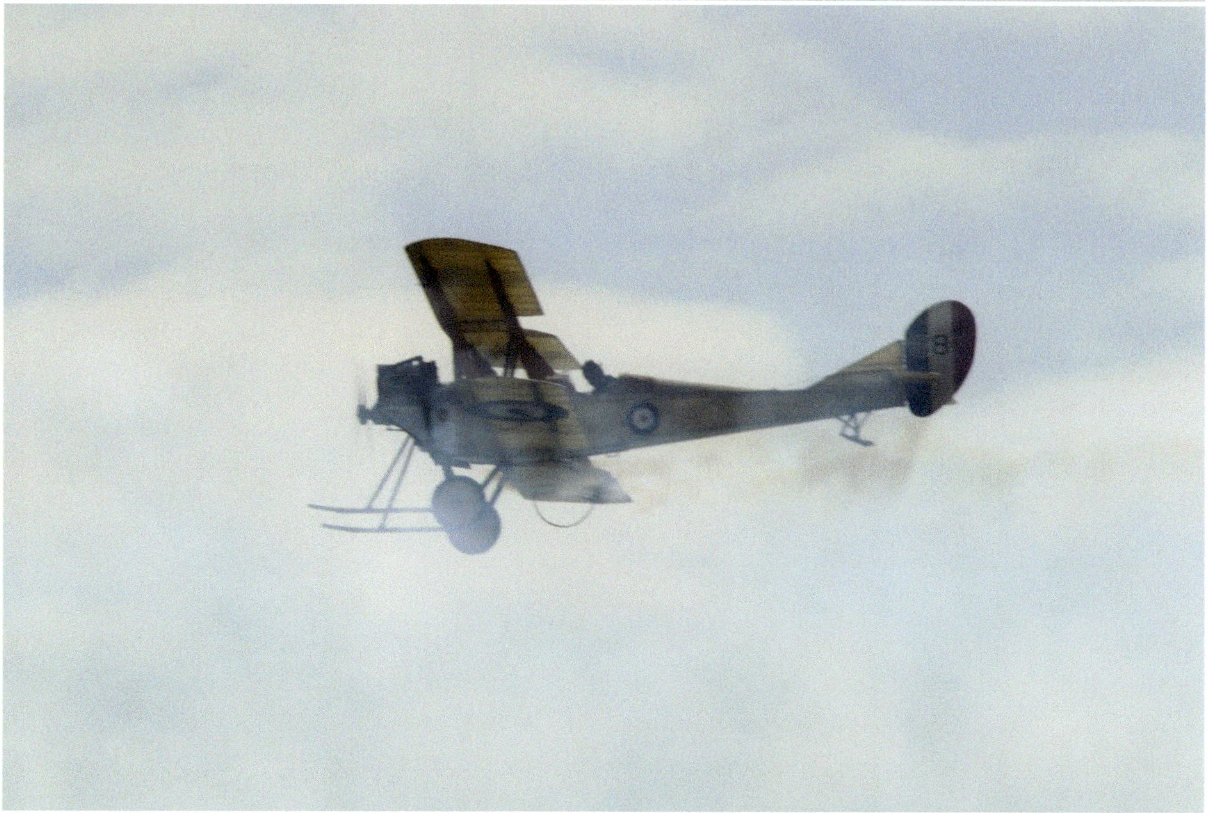

Fairey Swordfish

A relic of the biplane era, the Fairey Swordfish torpedo bomber emerged as an unlikely hero for the British during World War II. Designed in the early 1930s as a reconnaissance and torpedo platform, the Swordfish was already outdated when it entered service. However, the sturdy biplane proved its merit through vital contributions to naval battles, cementing its iconic status in aviation history.

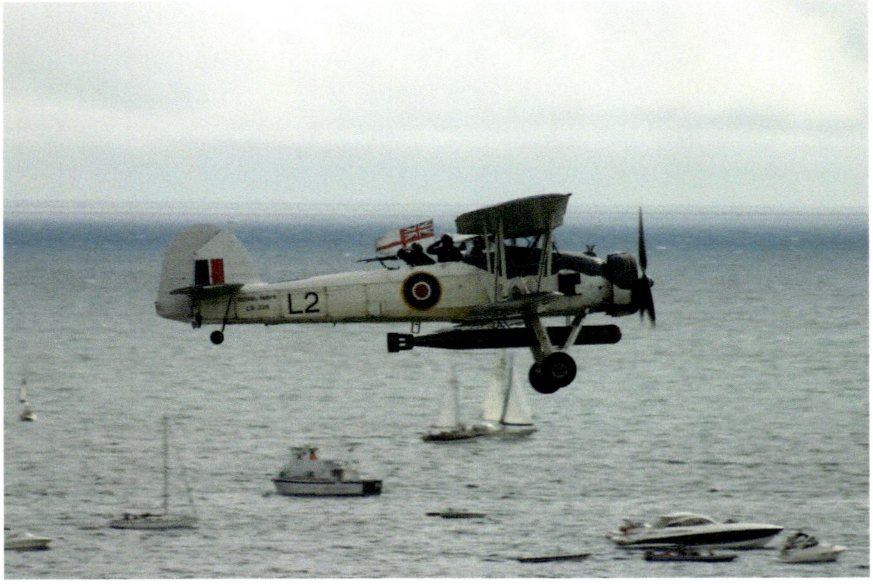

Taking to the skies for the first time on April 17, 1934, the Swordfish prototype demonstrated promise that led the Royal Navy to adopt it in 1936. Initially employed for reconnaissance missions, the Swordfish later made its mark as a formidable torpedo bomber.

Role in World War II

The Swordfish torpedo bomber gained widespread recognition for its contributions during World War II. It played a vital role in multiple naval operations, most notably anti-submarine warfare and torpedo strikes on enemy vessels. The Swordfish is perhaps best known for helping sink the German battleship Bismarck in May 1941.

Operation Taranto

The Swordfish torpedo bomber was instrumental in several key Royal Navy missions during World War II, most famously the daring nighttime aerial attack on the Italian fleet at Taranto in November 1940. Launched from British aircraft carriers, the outdated but versatile Swordfish biplanes succeeded in crippling three Italian battleships with aerial torpedoes. This audacious strike demonstrated the Swordfish's potential as a torpedo bomber, thanks to qualities like its slow speed and high manoeuvrability that enabled precision attacks on naval targets. Though considered obsolescent, the Swordfish's ability to carry torpedoes, mines, and other ordnance made it a versatile asset that altered naval warfare by proving the effectiveness of carrier-based torpedo bombing.

Post-War Service and Retirement

After World War II, the Swordfish aircraft continued serving in various roles like anti-submarine warfare and training, but as more modern planes came about, the Swordfish gradually phased out of frontline duty. This iconic biplane retired from active Royal Navy service in 1945.

The Fairey Swordfish biplane achieved iconic status and remarkable successes during World War II, cementing its place in aviation history. Despite its slow speed and apparent obsolescence, the Swordfish excelled as a torpedo bomber, pulling off daring feats like crippling the German battleship Bismarck. Its wartime exploits highlighted the Swordfish's versatility and helped shape naval aviation tactics during a pivotal era. Even today, the Swordfish remains one of the most memorable and influential biplanes of the war.

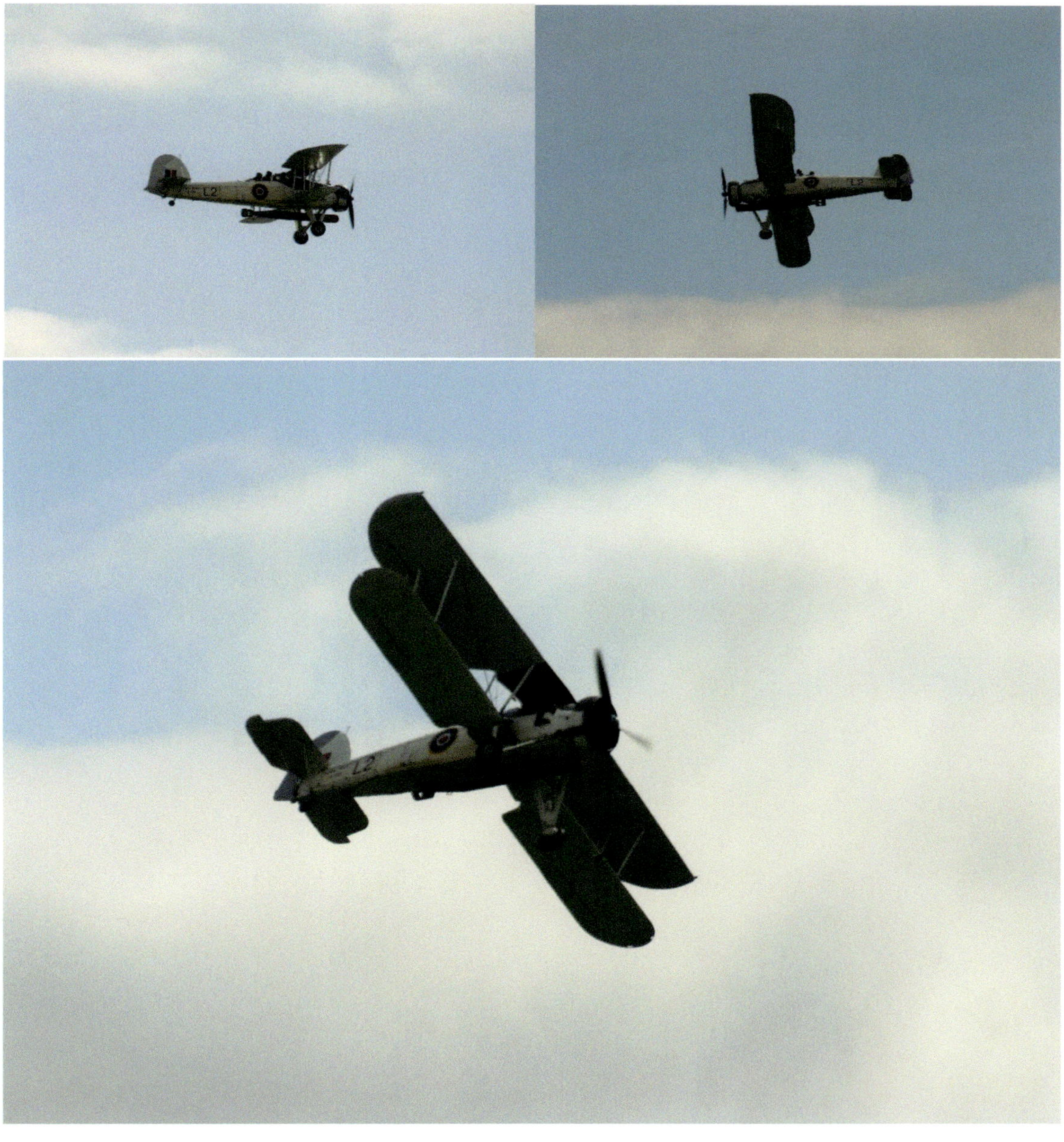

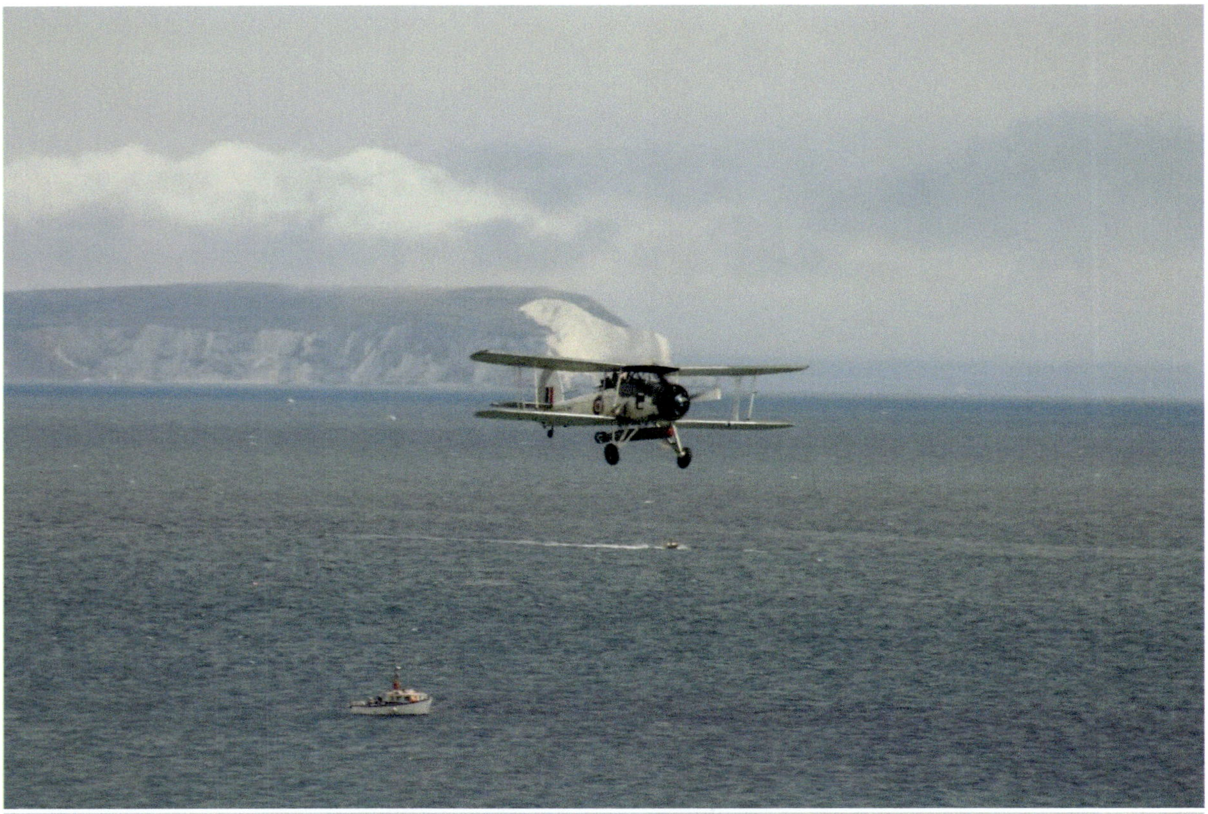

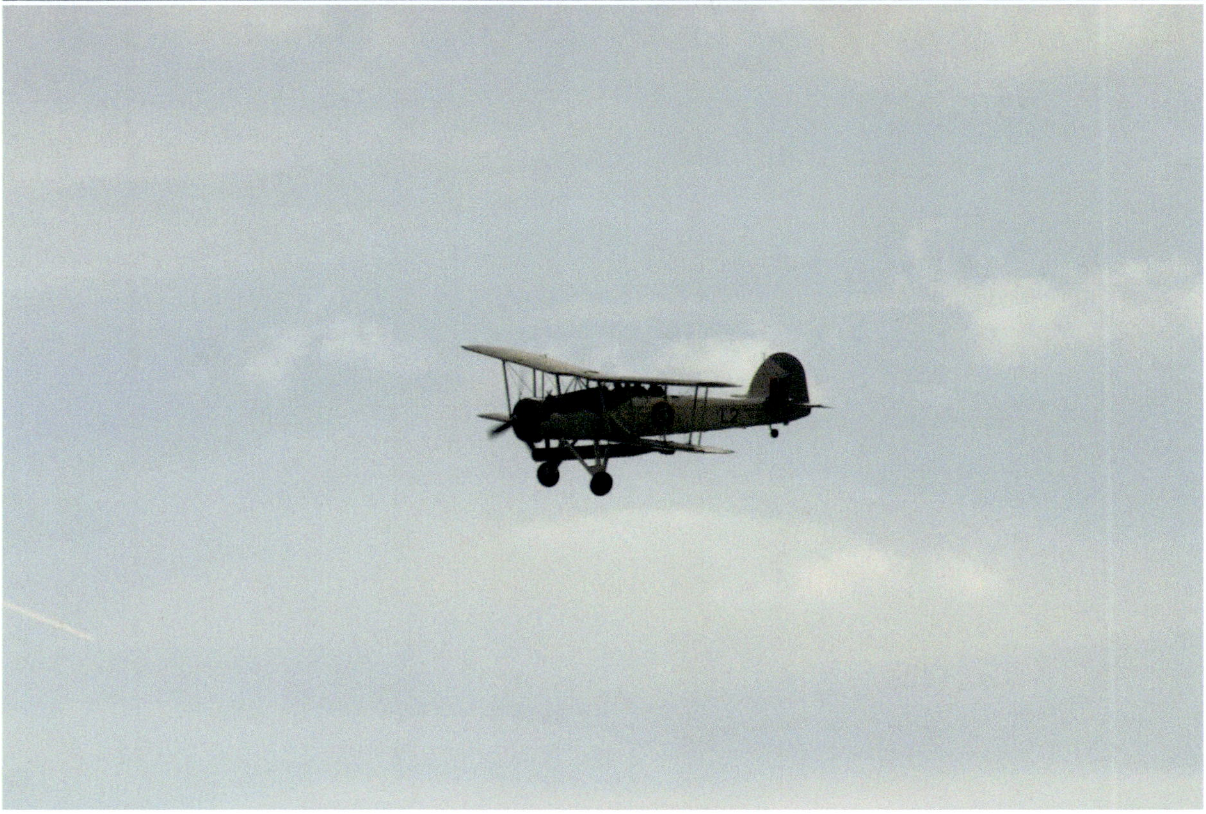

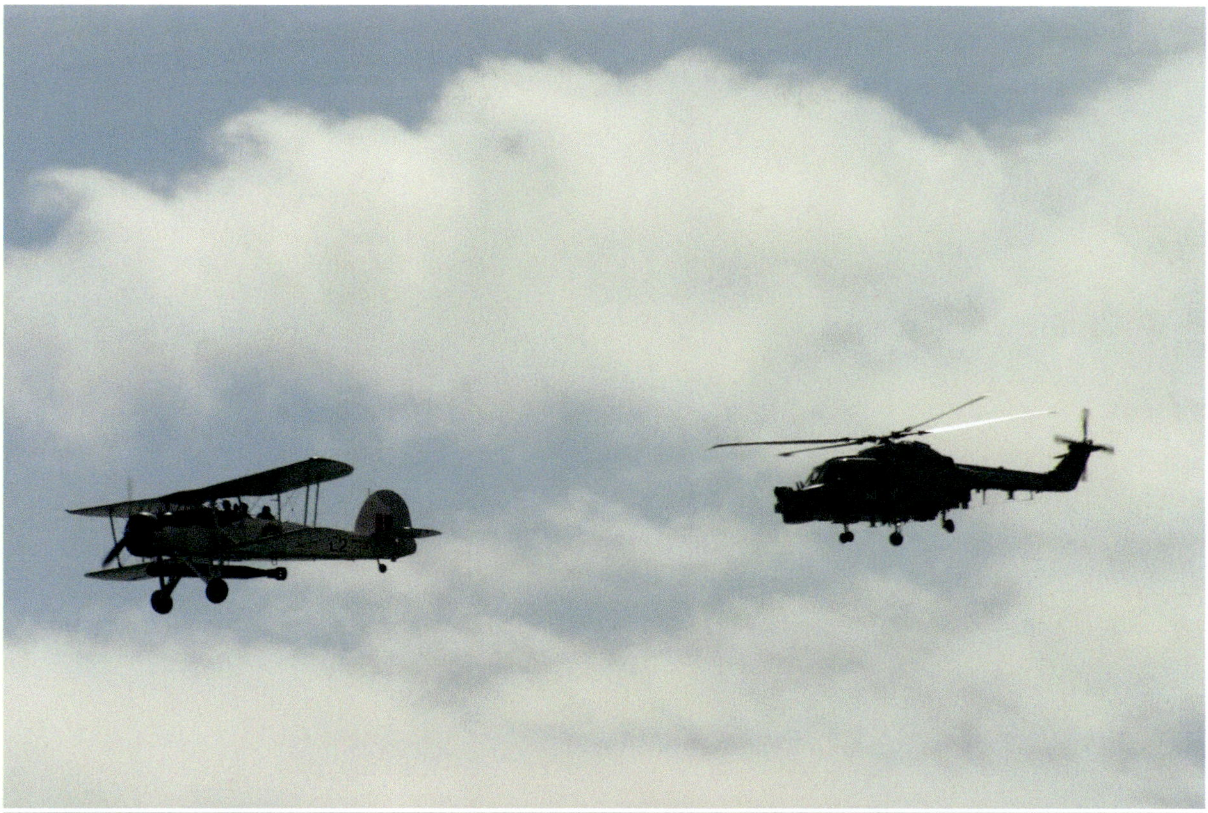
L2

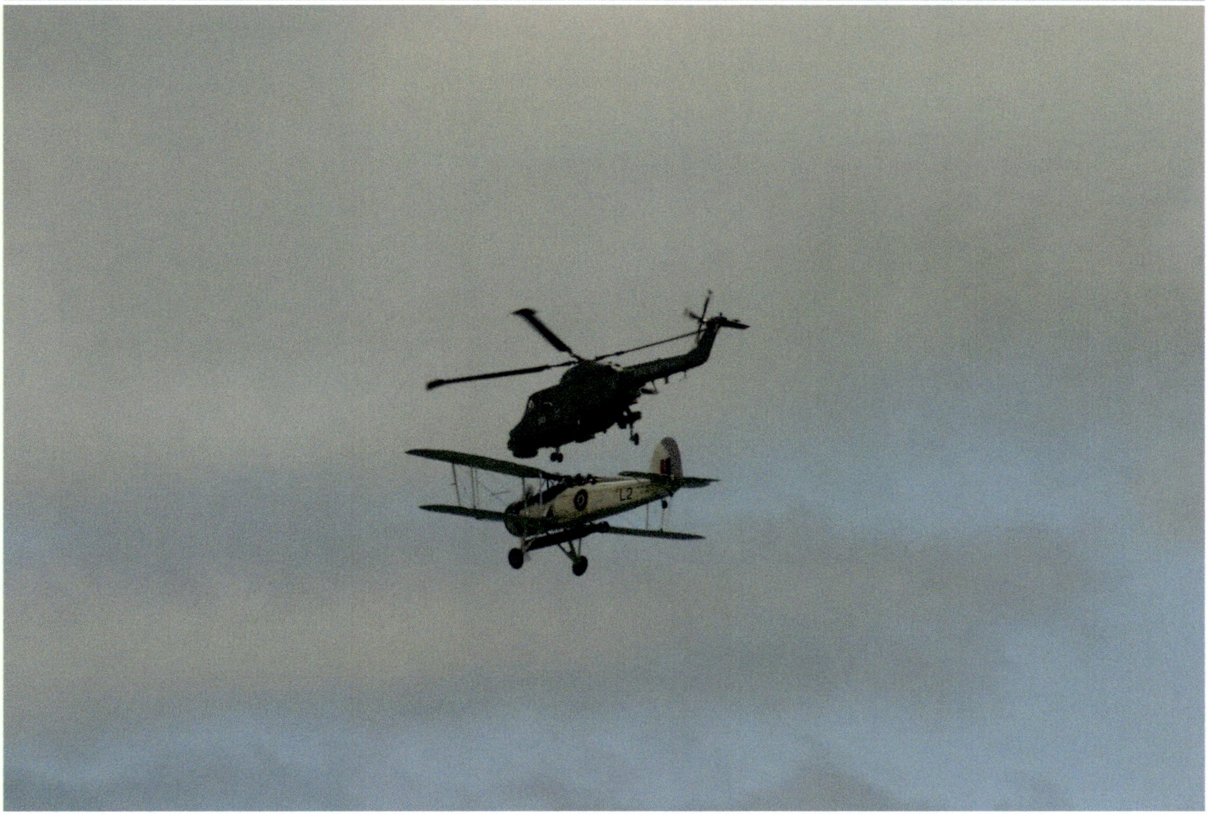
L2

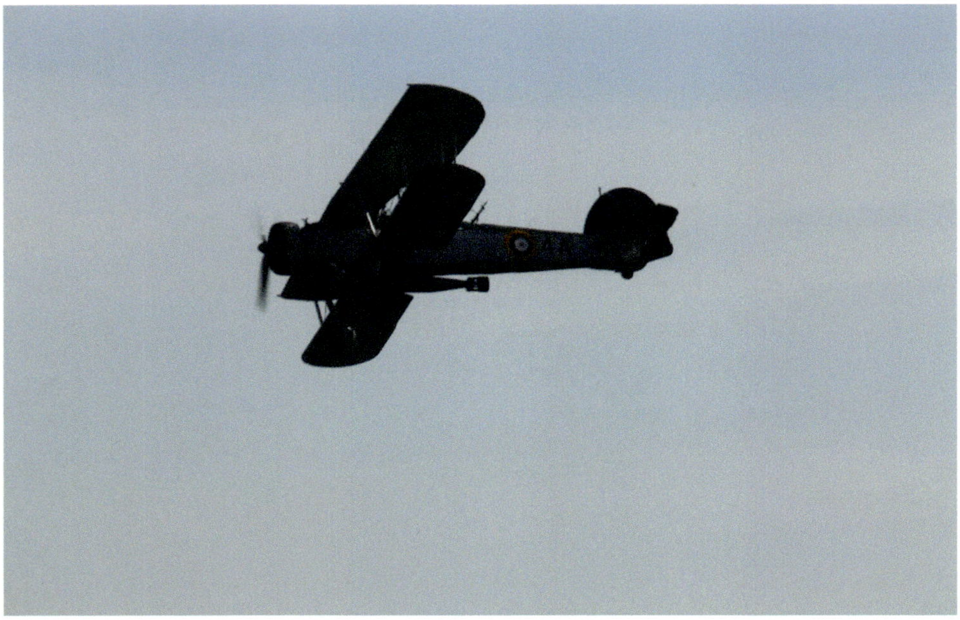

Quick Facts

- The prototype Swordfish first flew on April 17, 1934
- The Swordfish was known for its slow speed and exceptional manoeuvrability, the biplane design contributed to its agility in flight
- The Swordfish was powered by a Bristol Pegasus XII air-cooled radial engine providing approximately 690 horsepower
- The Swordfish was designed to carry torpedoes, and this was its primary role. The torpedo, typically a 1,610 lb (730 kg) aerial torpedo, was carried underneath the fuselage and released during an attack run against naval targets
- The Swordfish could carry bombs for different types of missions, carrying a variety of bomb sizes, including 250 lb and 500 lb bombs

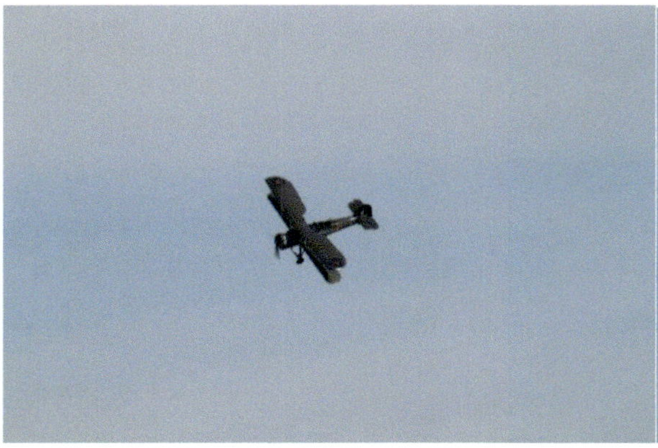

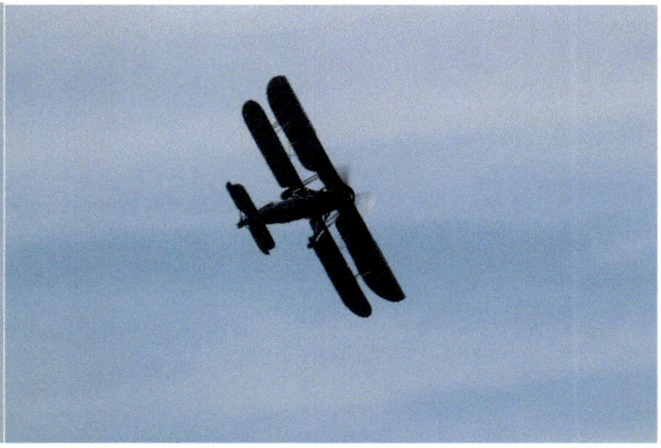

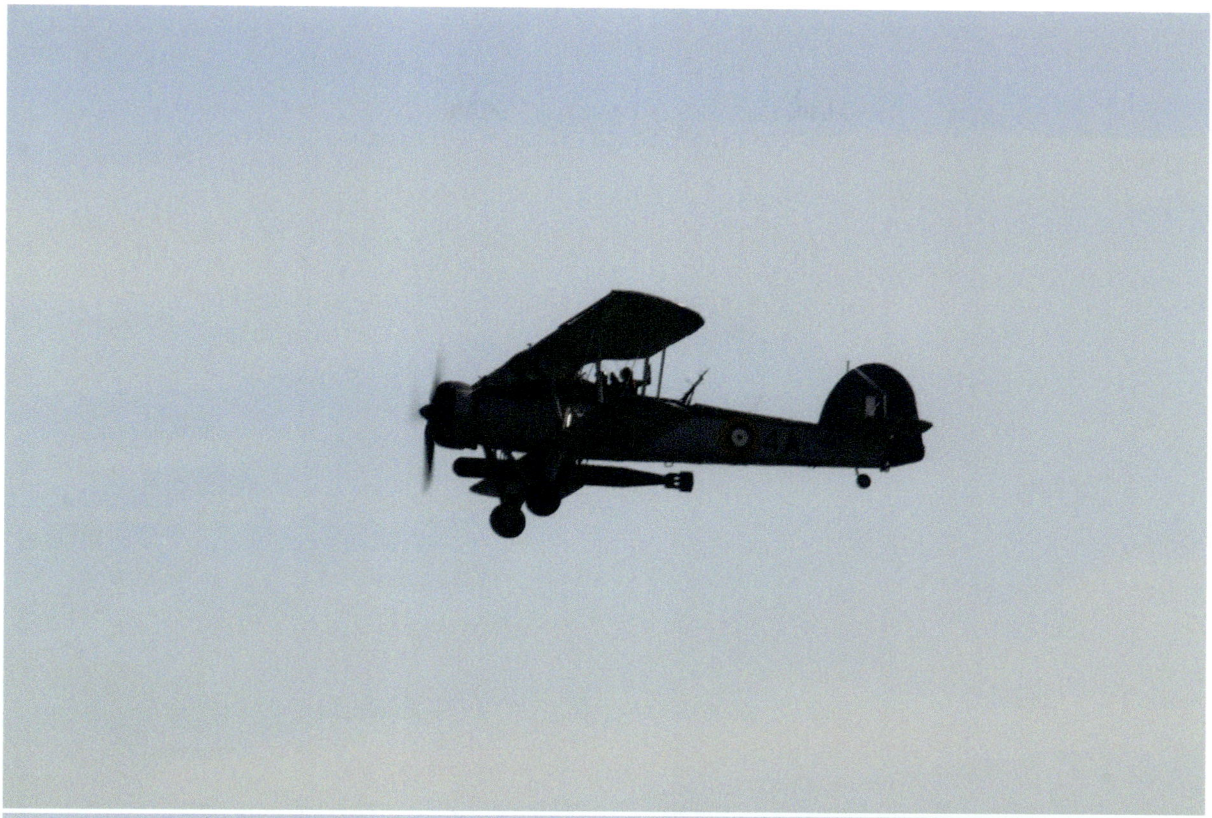

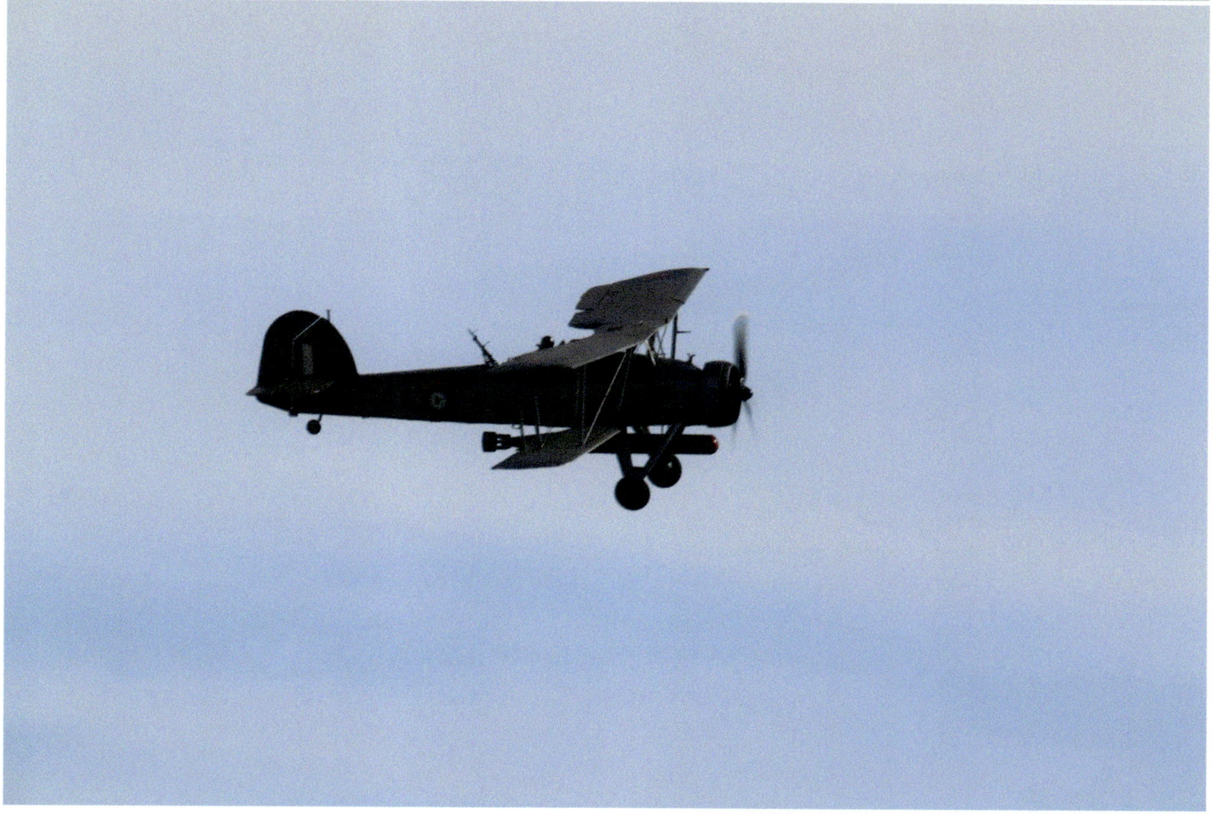

P-47 Thunderbolt

Under the guidance of Alexander Kartveli, the design team at Republic Aviation spearheaded the development of the P-47 Thunderbolt in the early 1940s in response to a requirement from the United States Army Air Corps for a high-speed, high-altitude interceptor aircraft cantered around the powerful Pratt & Whitney R-2800 Double Wasp radial engine.

The P-47 was renowned for its robust construction, engineered to withstand extensive battle damage and bring pilots home safely. With eight potent .50-caliber machine guns, the P-47 excelled in air combat. Its substantial bomb payload also made it effective for ground attack, highlighting the aircraft's versatility on the battlefield.

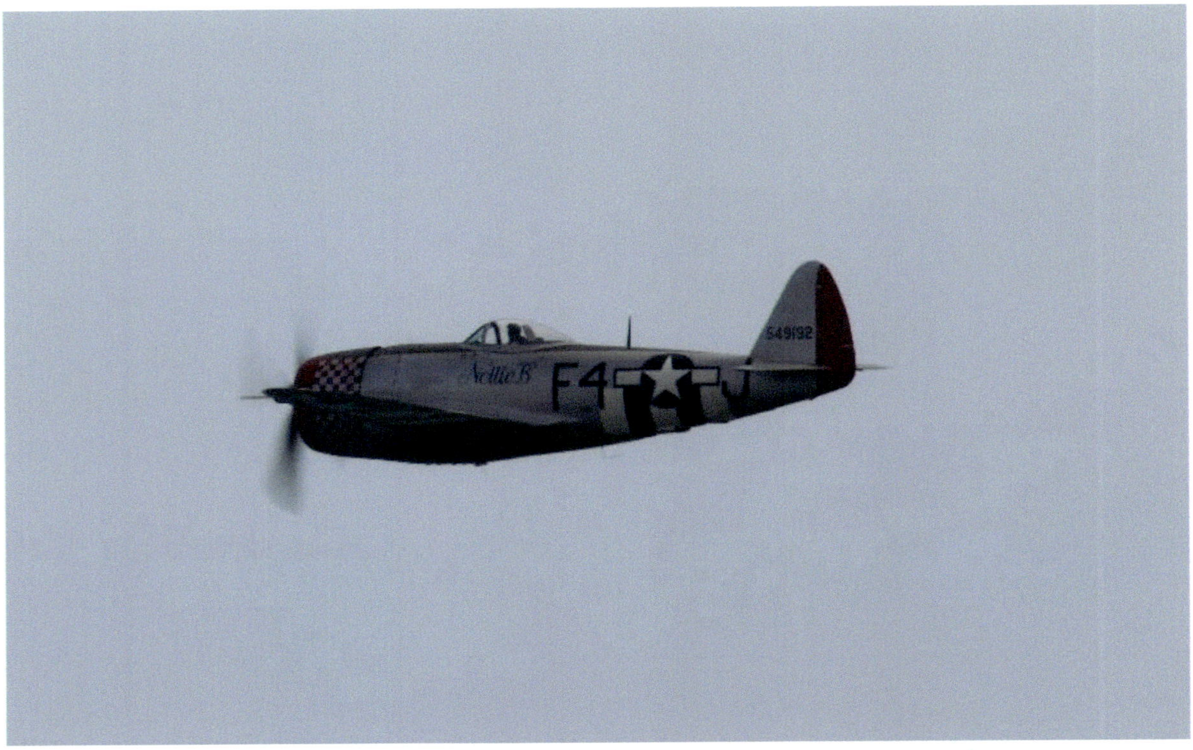

Operational History

Initially conceived as a high-altitude interceptor, the P-47 Thunderbolt entered service with the U.S. Army Air Forces in 1942 and swiftly became a mainstay fighter aircraft across various theaters during World War II. Remarkably adaptable, the Thunderbolt, the heaviest single-engine fighter used in the war, was utilized for diverse missions including bomber escort, ground attack, and strafing.

The P-47 gained widespread praise in the European Theater of Operations as a key escort fighter for American bombers like the B-17 Flying Fortress and B-24 Liberator. It played a vital role in achieving air superiority over Nazi-occupied Europe. In addition to its fighter role, the P-47 demonstrated exceptional skill in ground-attack missions. Its large bomb load capacity and precision strike ability provided crucial support for ground forces.

Post-War Service

The P-47 Thunderbolt played a vital role during and after World War II. This rugged, reliable aircraft served in the U.S. Air Force as a fighter-bomber and tactical reconnaissance plane post-war. Nicknamed "Jug" for its distinct jug-like shape, the P-47 left a lasting legacy for its durability, firepower, and contribution to achieving air supremacy over Europe. Its popularity among pilots and instrumental support of Allied ground forces cemented its status as a World War II icon. Though few remain airworthy today, the Thunderbolt connection to aviation history lives on at airshows where these warbirds still impress crowds with their impressive capabilities.

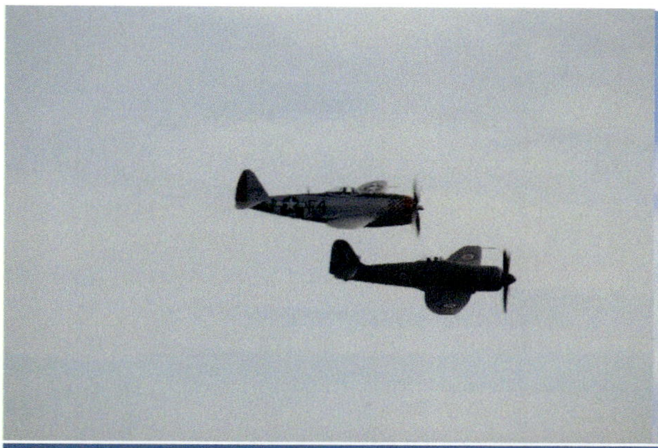

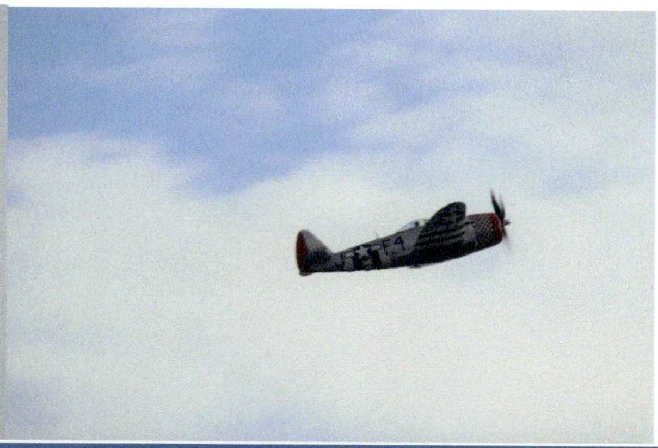

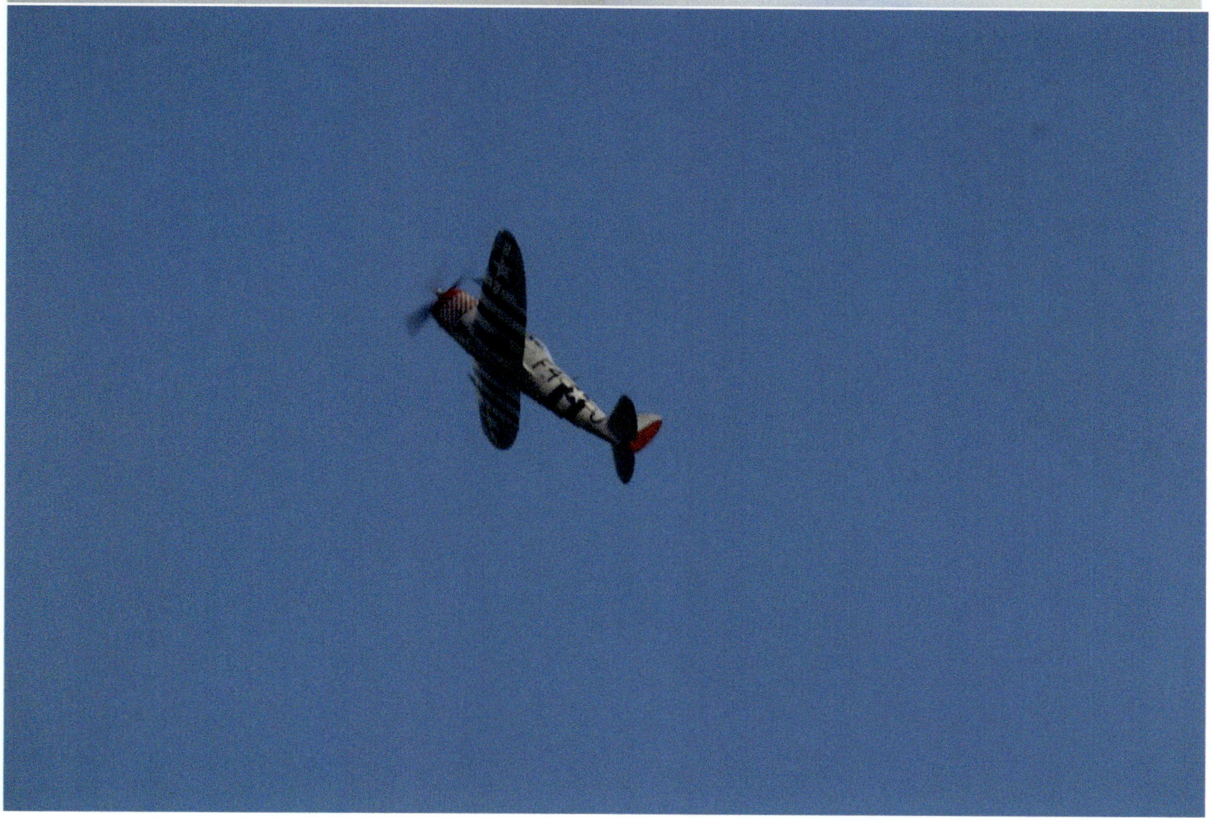

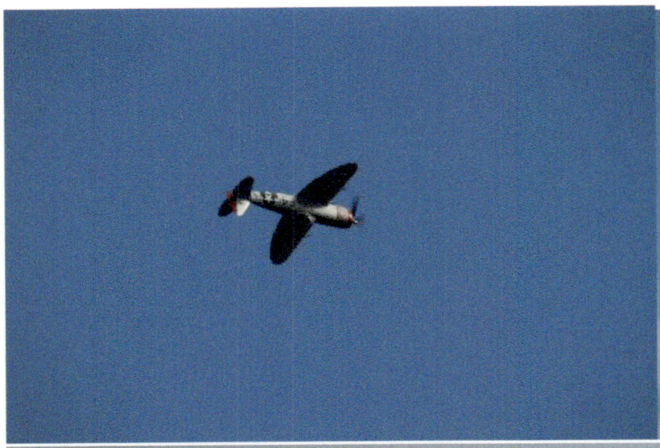
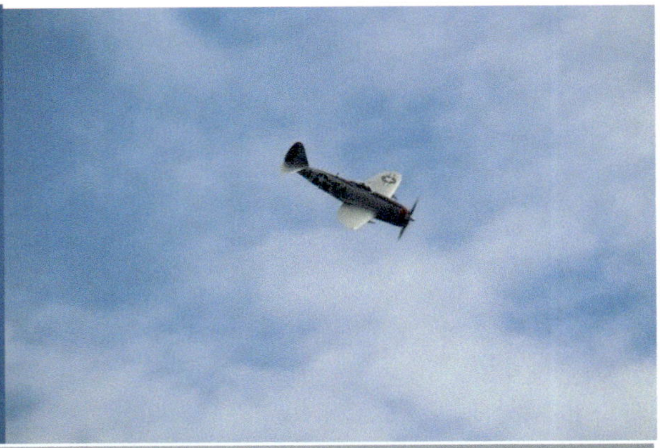
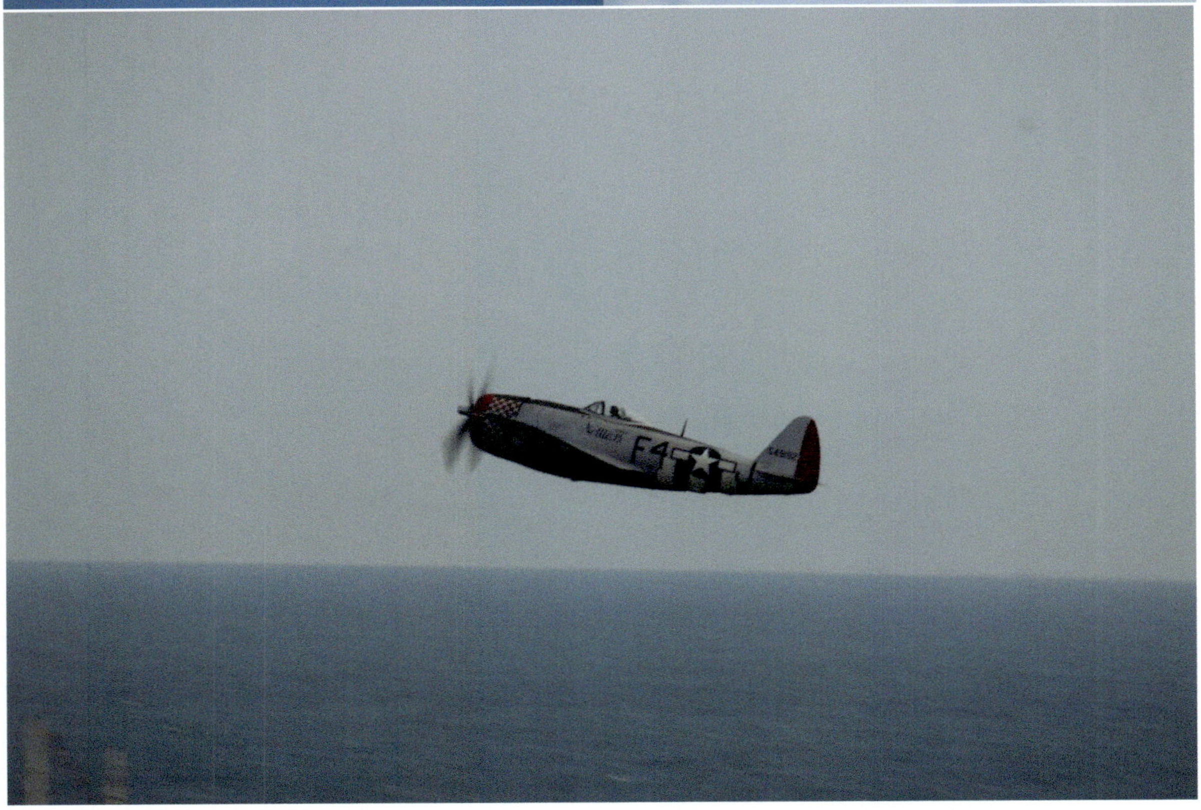

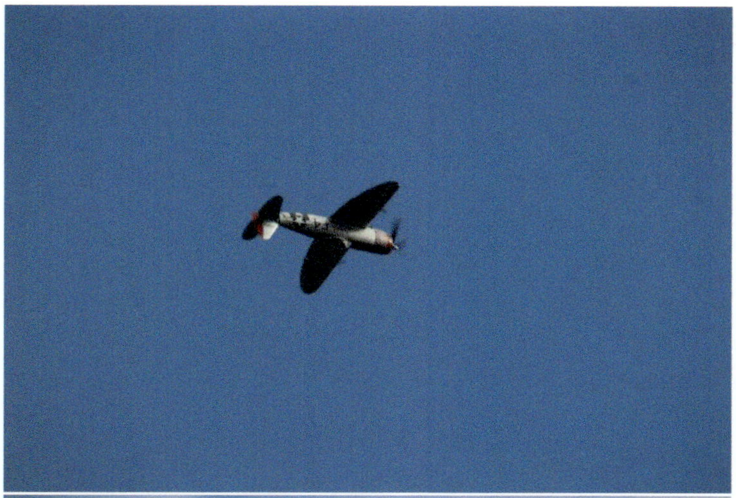

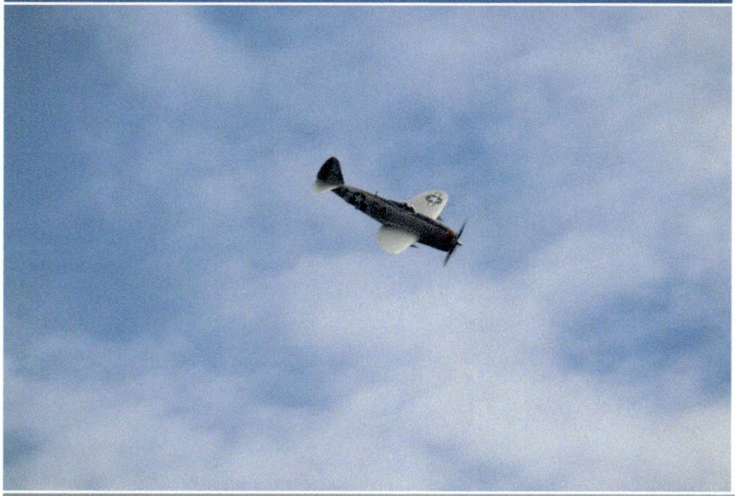

Quick Facts

- The prototype P-47 took its first flight on May 6, 1941
- The P-47 was one of the largest and heaviest single-engine fighter aircraft of World War II
- The Thunderbolt was powered by a Pratt & Whitney R-2800 Double Wasp radial engine with a top speed of over 400 mph
- The P-47 was heavily armed, typically carrying eight .50 calibre Browning M2 machine guns and was able to carry bombs, rockets, or external fuel tanks under its wings
- The Thunderbolt had a relatively long range, which was essential for escorting bomber missions into enemy territory

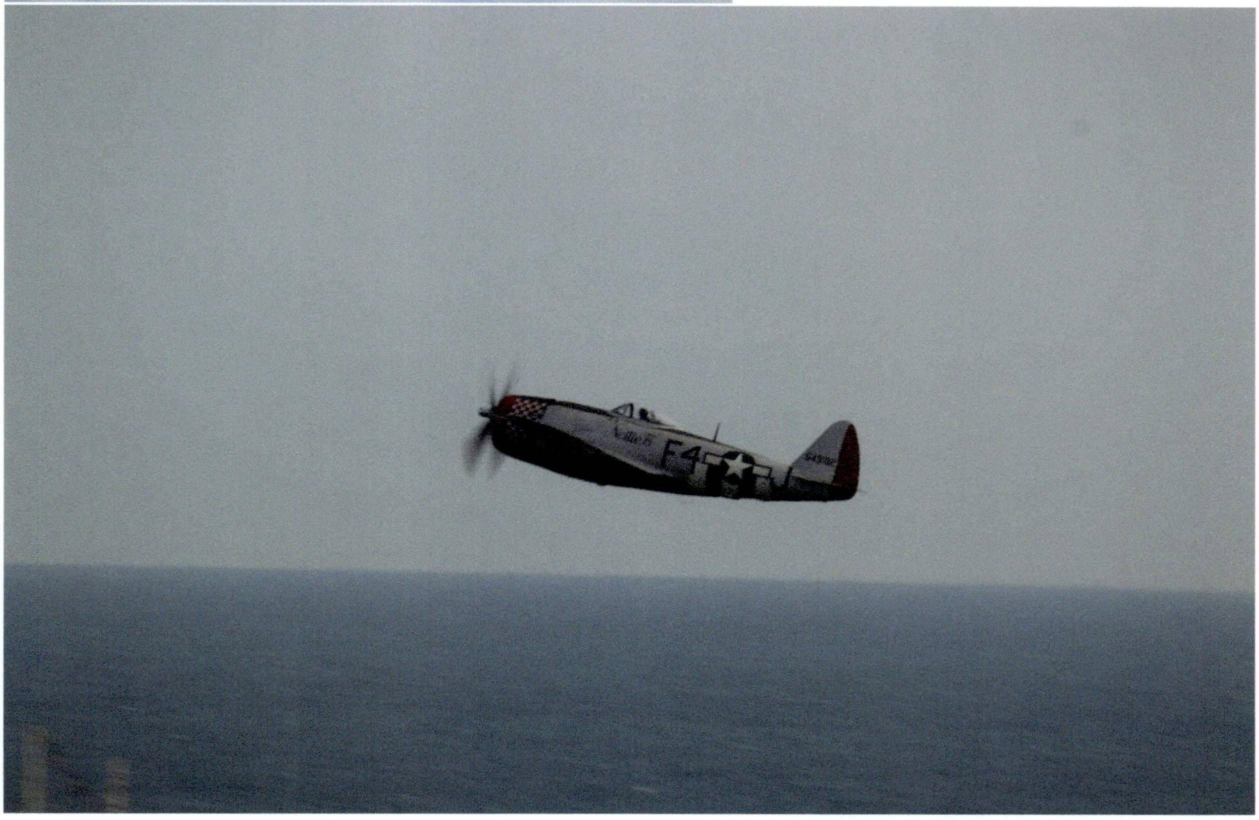

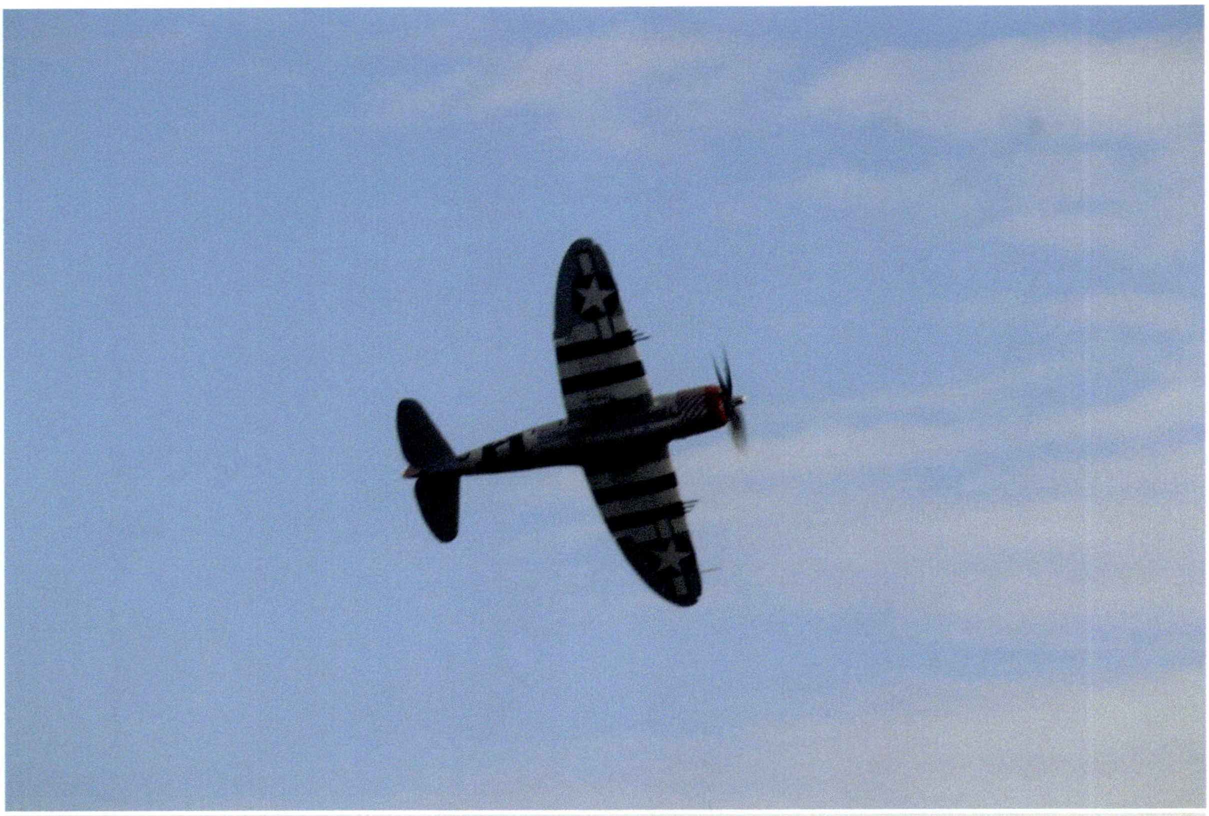

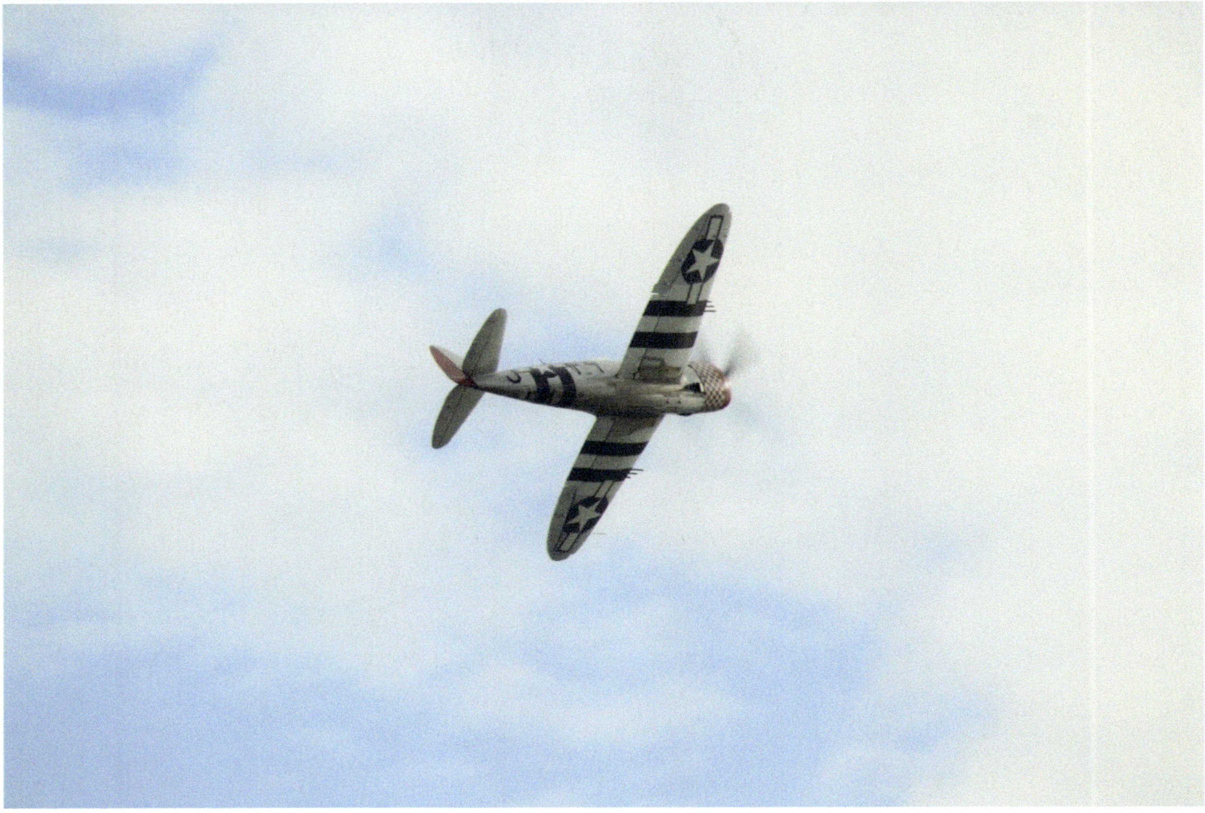

P-51 Mustang

Designed and built by North American Aviation to meet a British specification for a long-range fighter plane, the P-51 Mustang first took flight on October 26, 1940, as the NA-73X prototype. The aircraft's laminar-flow wing and efficient radiator placement were some of the innovative features that enabled its exceptional performance.

The initial Mustang variants, powered by the Allison V-1710 engine, struggled at high altitudes. However, the P-51B and P-51C models, equipped with the British Rolls-Royce Merlin engine, transformed the aircraft's performance.

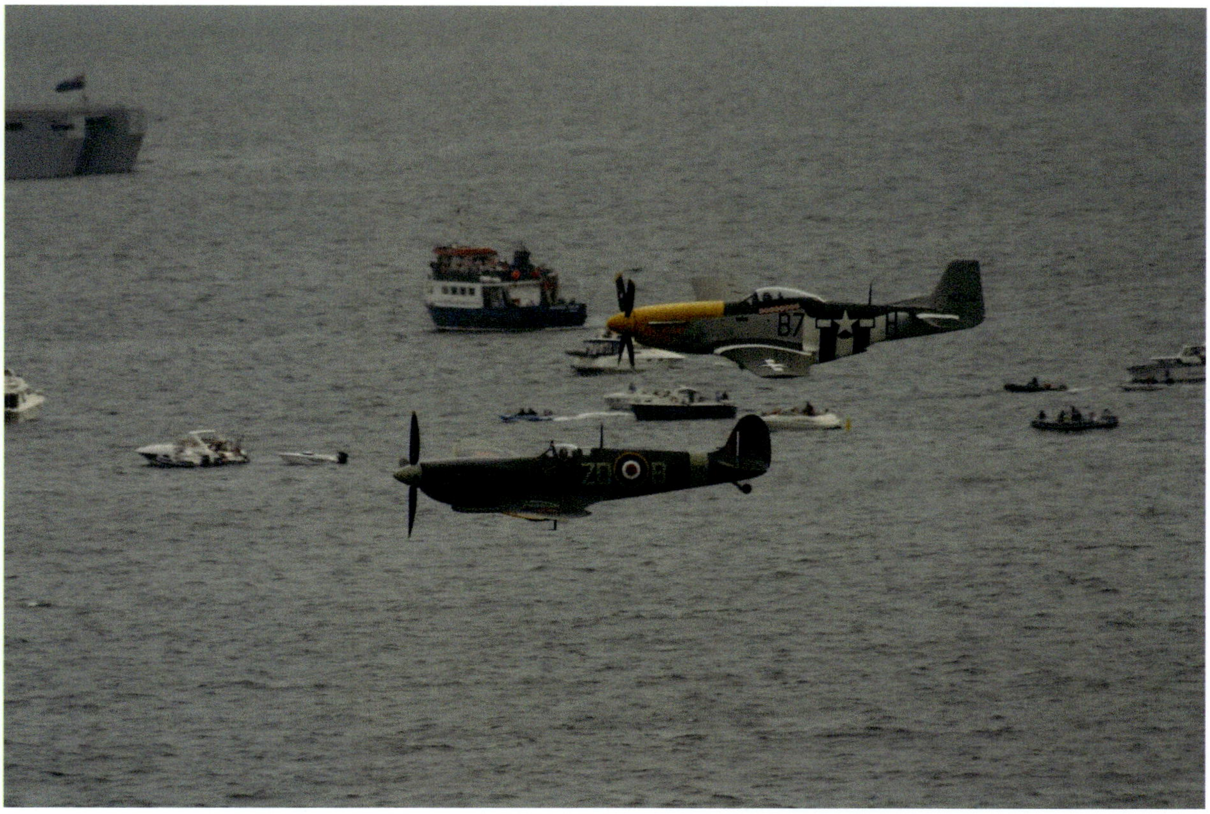

Escort Fighter Role

The P-51 Mustang's long-range capabilities and external fuel tanks made it an ideal and effective escort for Allied bombers on deep penetration raids into German territory during World War II. With drop tanks extending its range, the agile P-51 could accompany bombers all the way to distant targets and back, offering vital protection against enemy fighters. Renowned for superiority in air combat, the P-51 played a pivotal role in reducing bomber losses and helping the Allies gain control of the skies over Europe in the war's final years.

Merlin Engine and Performance

The P-51 Mustang, equipped with the powerful Rolls-Royce Merlin engine, became one of the most effective fighter aircraft of World War II. With a top speed over 430 mph, exceptional manoeuvrability, and superb high-altitude performance, the P-51D model, distinguished by its teardrop canopy, was an aviation icon that helped secure Allied air superiority.

Variants and Post-War Service

The P-51 Mustang, an iconic World War II fighter plane, saw numerous variants produced, including reconnaissance models and those outfitted with additional weaponry. After the war ended, the agile and versatile P-51 remained in service with air forces around the world, seeing action in the Korean War. Additionally, many were later converted for civilian use, becoming a popular choice for air racing enthusiasts.

With its long-range capabilities, high speed, and agile manoeuvring, the P-51 Mustang proved to be one of the most effective fighter planes of World War II, making vital contributions to Allied air operations. Even after the war ended, the Mustang remained a beloved symbol of aviation prowess, cherished by pilots and airplane aficionados alike for its outstanding performance.

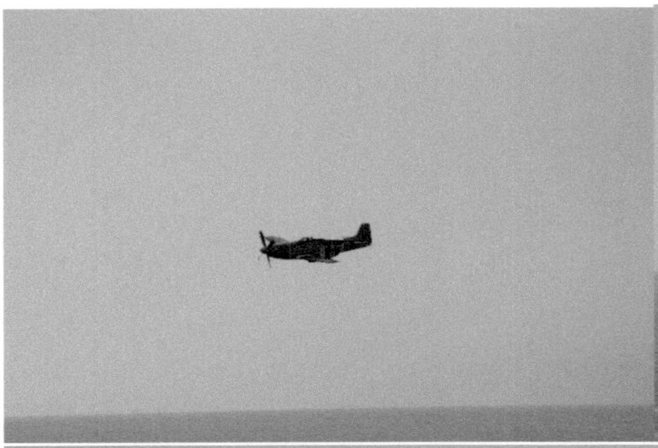

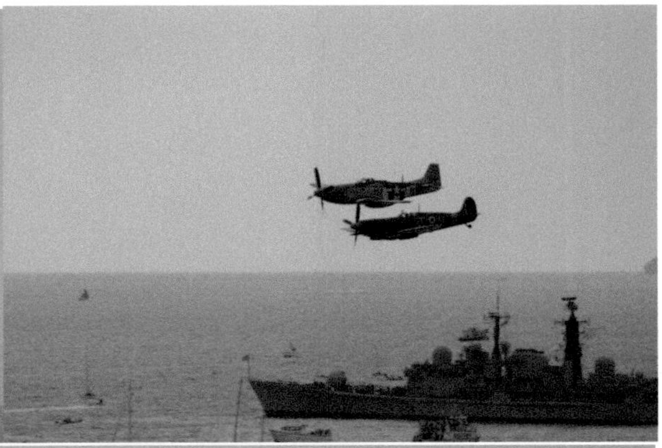

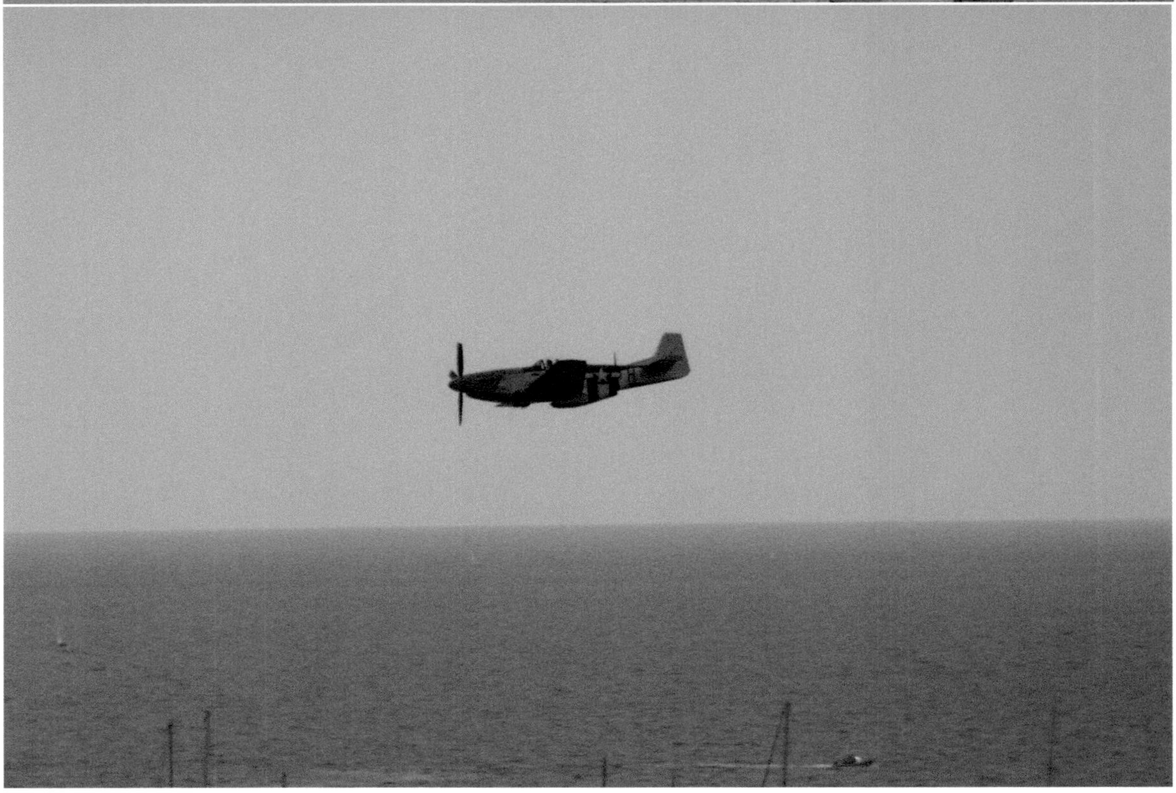

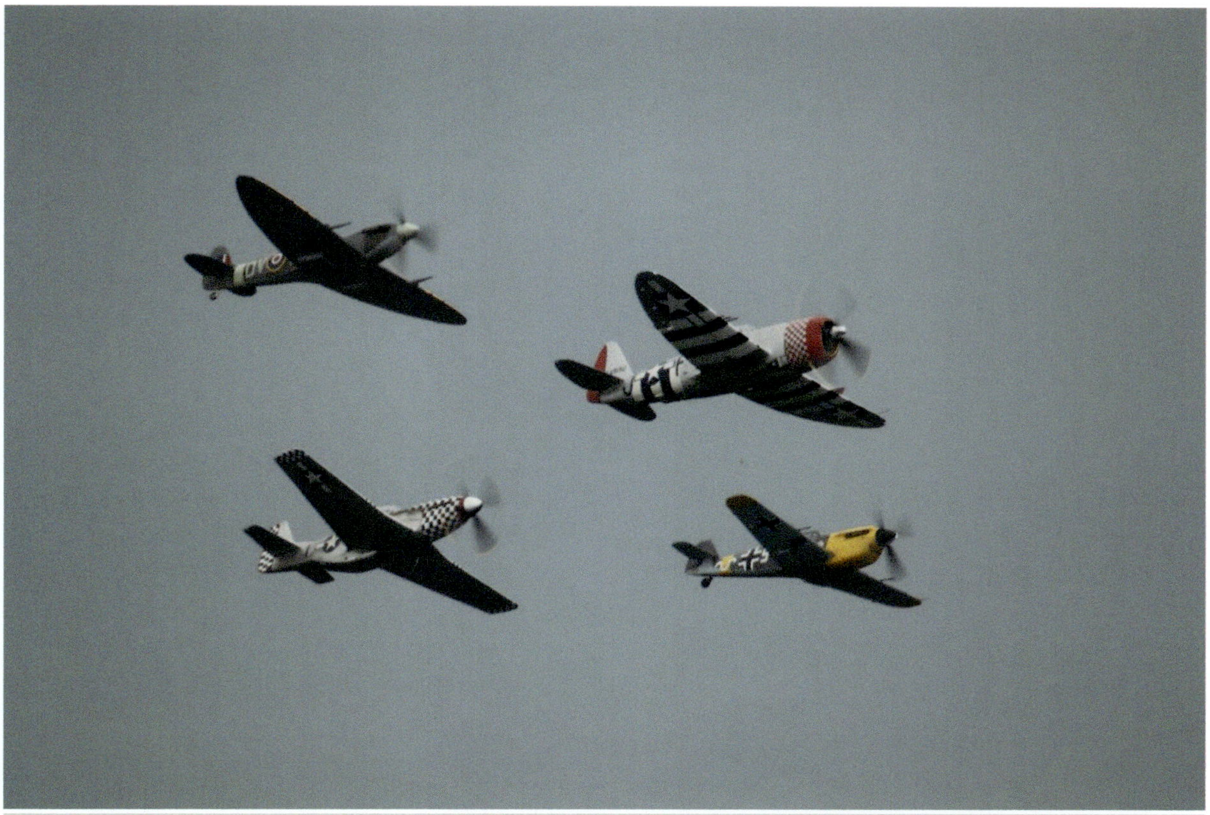

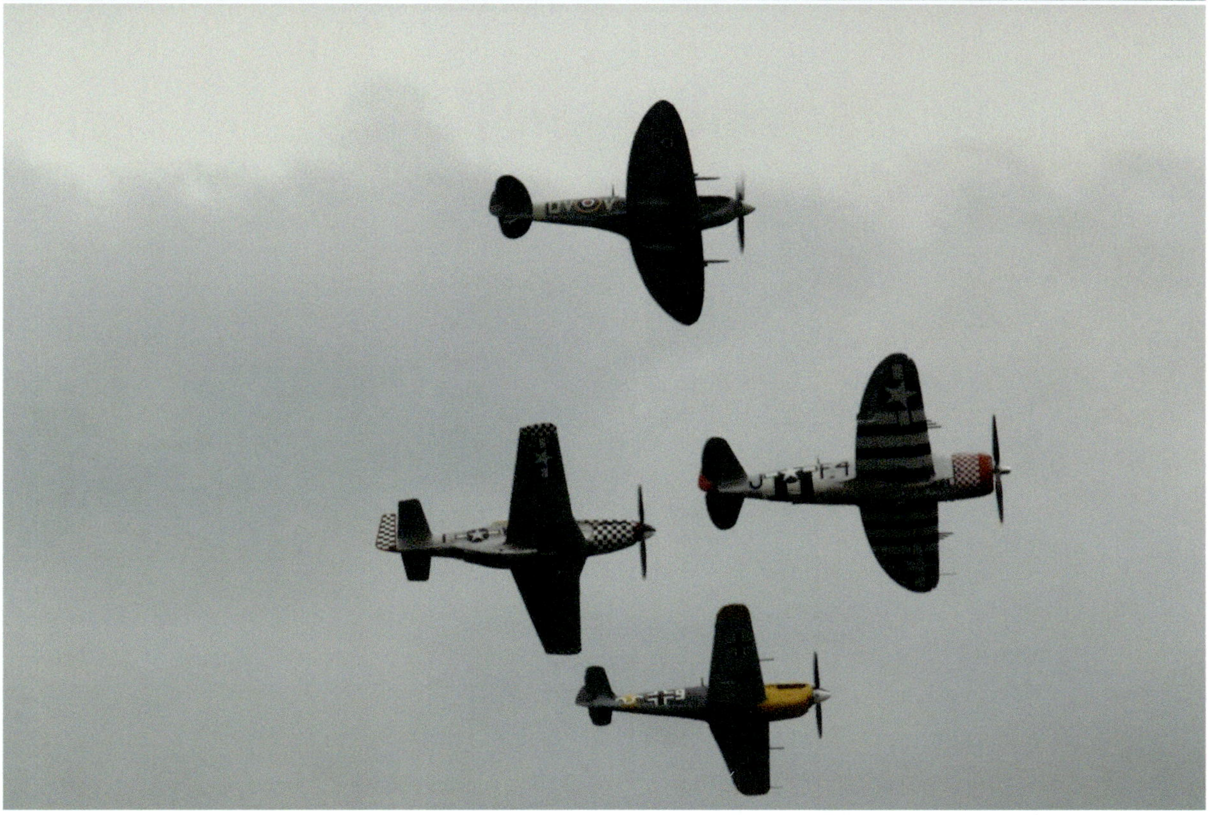

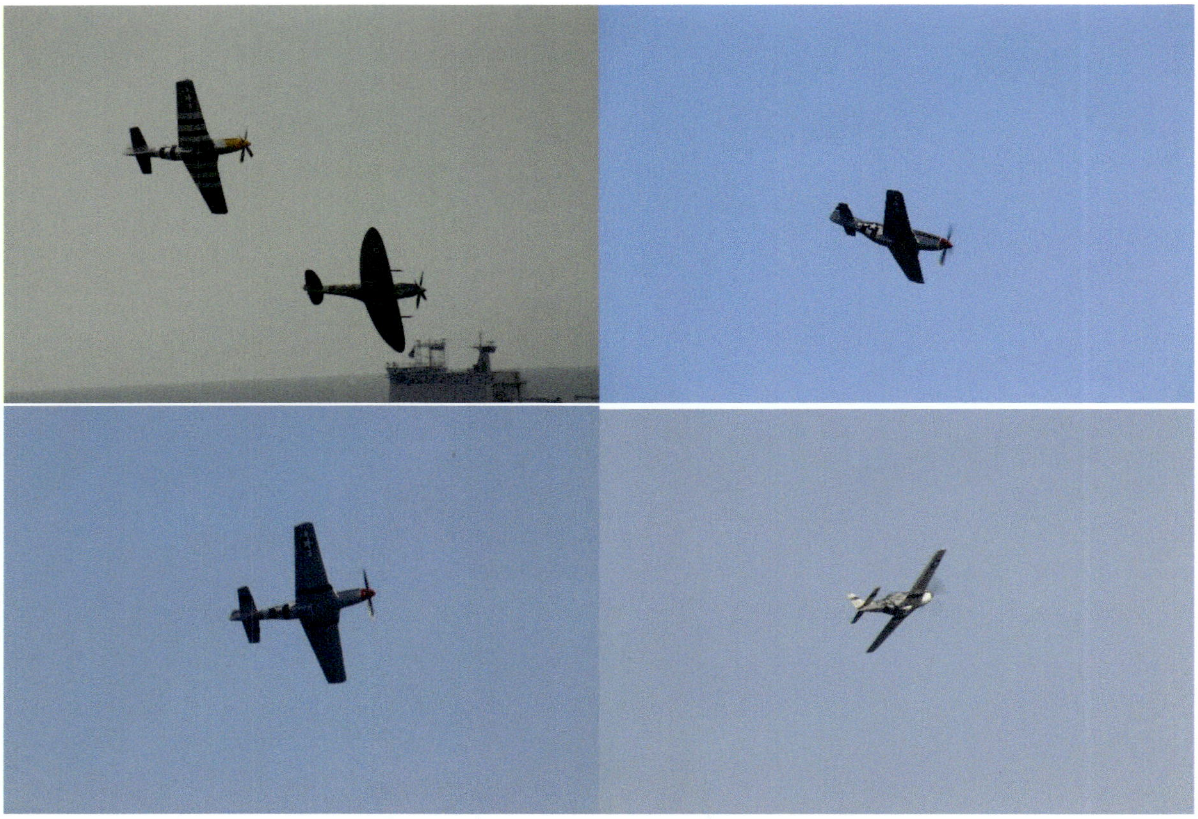

Quick Facts

- The prototype P-51 Mustang made its first flight on October 26, 1940
- The P-51 Mustang gained its first success when it was equipped with the Rolls-Royce Merlin engine, turning it into a high-performance long-range fighter. The Rolls-Royce Merlin engine gave the P-51 exceptional speed and altitude capabilities, making it one of the fastest and most versatile fighters of its time
- The P-51 is best known for its role as a long-range escort fighter for Allied bombers, such as the B-17 Flying Fortress, during daylight bombing raids over Germany
- The P-51D variant, with its external fuel tanks, had an extended range of over 1,600 miles
- The P-51 was typically armed with six .50 calibre Browning M2 machine guns. Some models had provisions for adding rockets or bombs

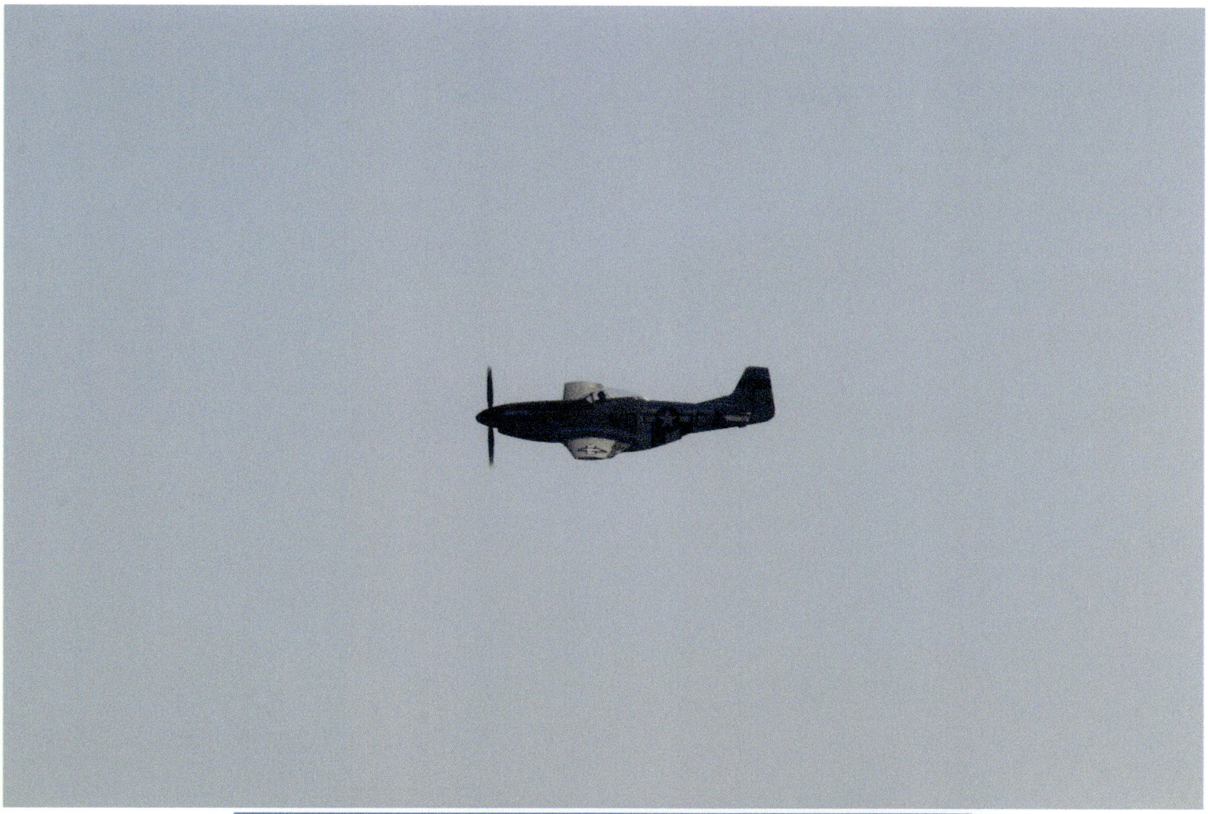

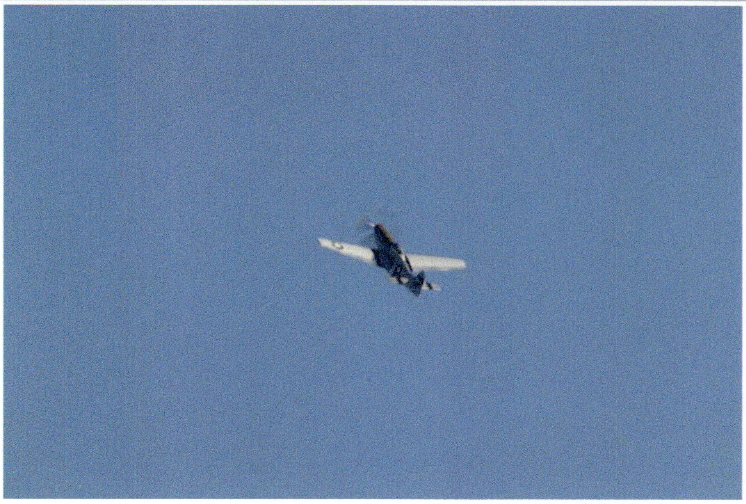

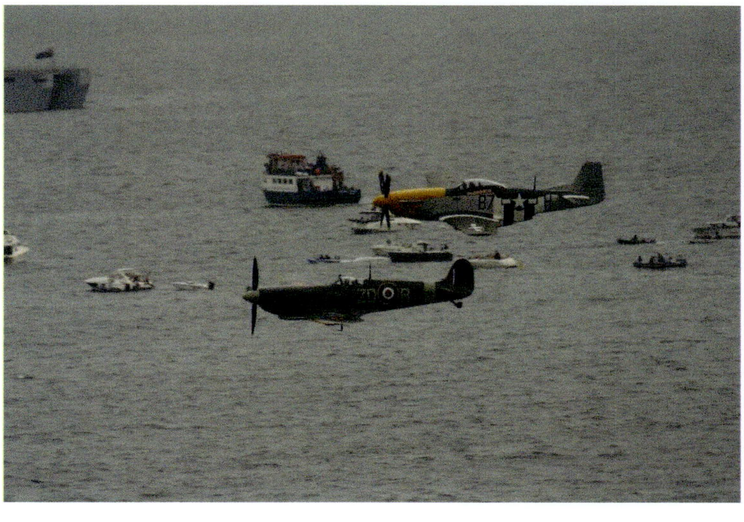

Boeing B-17 Flying Fortress – Sally B

The Boeing B-17G Flying Fortress "Sally B" is a legendary American bomber that was crucial in World War II. As one of the few remaining airworthy B-17s, she is now based in the United Kingdom. This is a brief history of "Sally B."

The Boeing B-17 Flying Fortress was designed in the 1930s as a heavy bomber for the United States Army Air Corps. The final production model, the B-17G variant represented by "Sally B," featured several improvements over earlier versions, including additional defensive weapons.

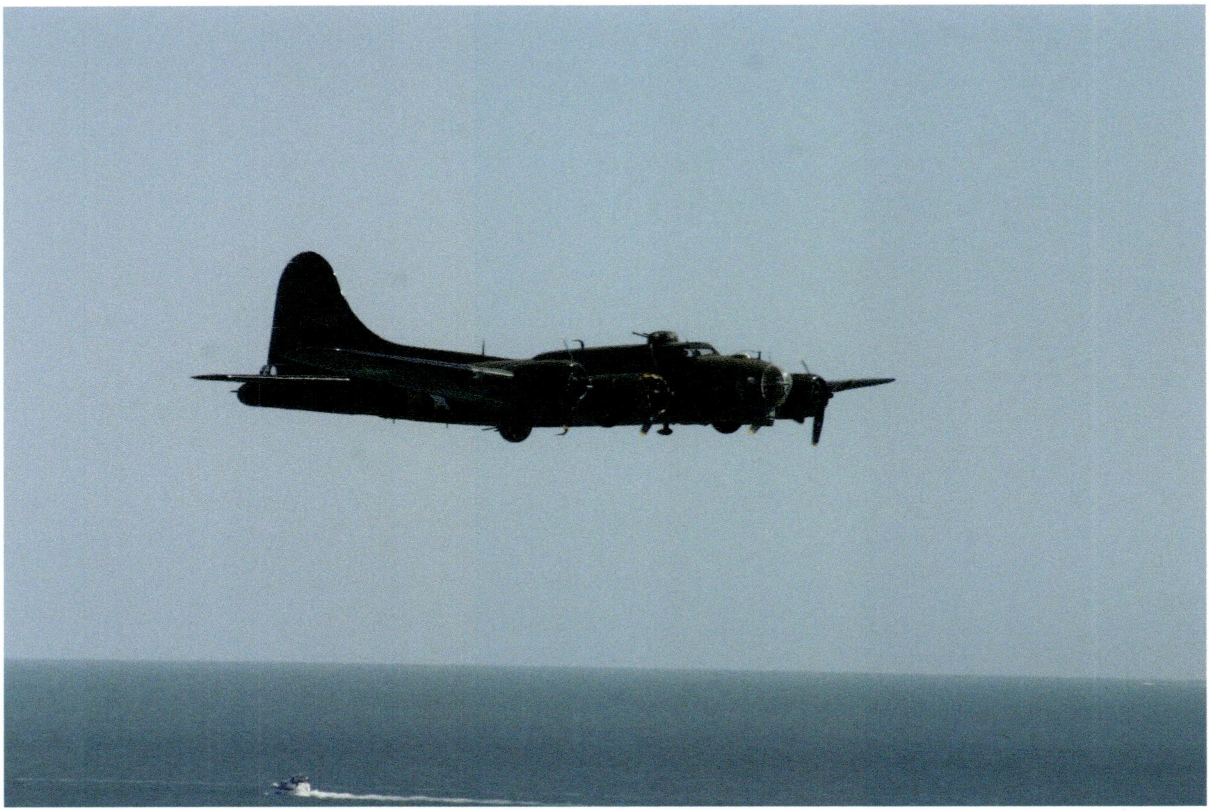

Operational History

"Sally B" was built by the Vega Aircraft Corporation in Burbank, California in 1945, but the U.S. Army Air Forces did not use the aircraft for combat in World War II. Instead, the plane served in air-sea rescue and training roles before the military sold it as surplus in 1946.

After the war, the B-17 bomber "Sally B" passed through various owners and uses, even serving as a firefighting aircraft at one point. In the 1970s, the plane was acquired by the Scandinavian Historic Flight in Sweden, where it was meticulously restored to its original wartime configuration.

Move to the UK

In 1982, British businessman Ted White purchased the aircraft "Sally B" and transported it to the United Kingdom, where he established the Sally B Support Club to finance the plane's upkeep and use. "Sally B" was so named in honour of White's late wife, Elly Sallingboe.

To make Sally B airworthy again, she underwent extensive restoration work. This included repairing and replacing various components, obtaining original or replica machine guns for the defensive armament, and restoring the interior to its wartime configuration.

Airshow Performances

Since its restoration, the B-17 bomber "Sally B" has become a prominent and beloved participant in airshows and aviation events across Europe, serving as a flying memorial to the men who flew and maintained B-17s during World War II. Its presence at these events allows audiences to witness firsthand the majesty and historical significance of the iconic aircraft.

The Sally B Support Club continues to play a crucial role in fundraising and supporting the ongoing maintenance and operation of "Sally B," a B-17 bomber operated by B-17 Preservation Ltd. The goal is to keep this iconic World War II aircraft airworthy so that future generations can experience the sights and sounds of "Sally B" firsthand.

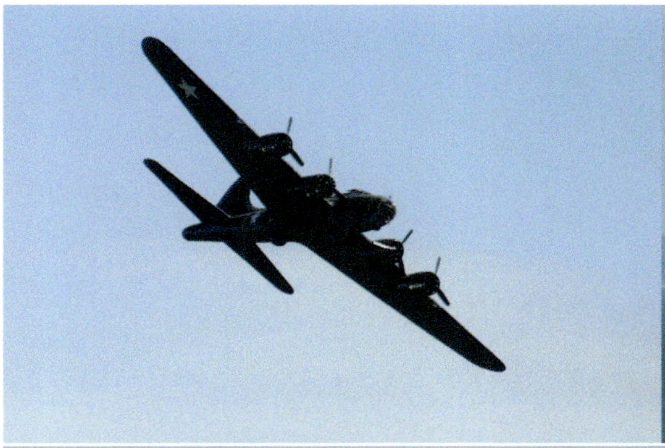

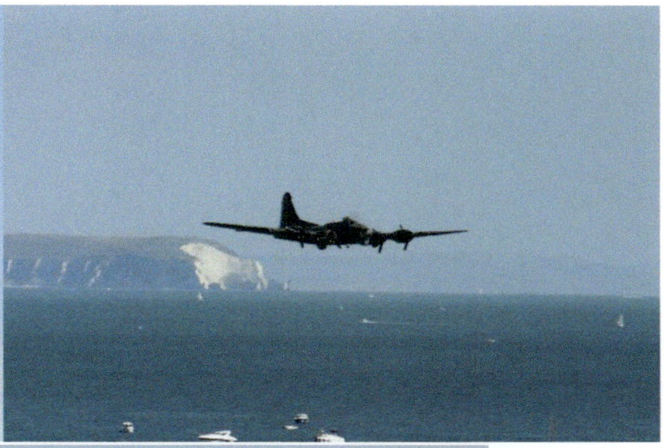

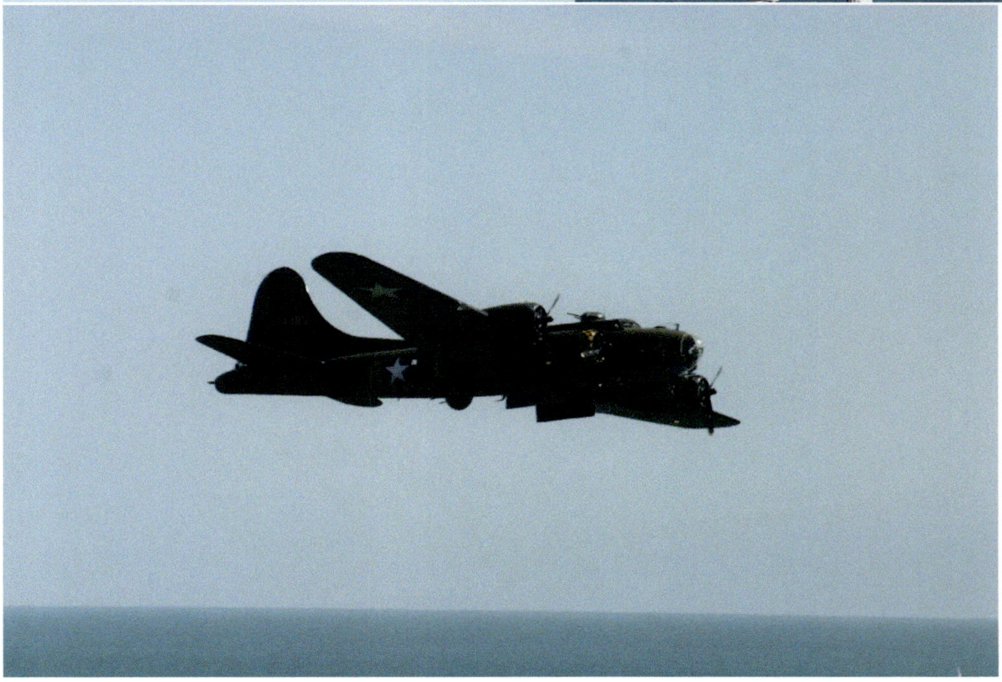

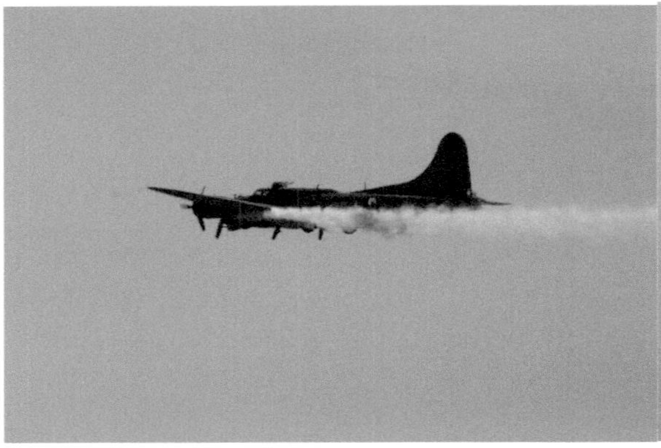

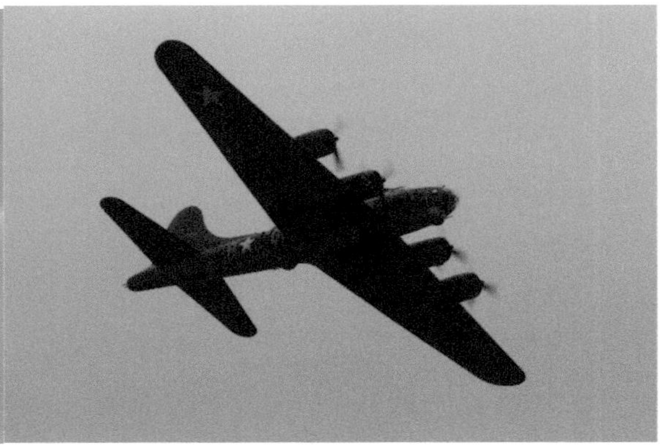

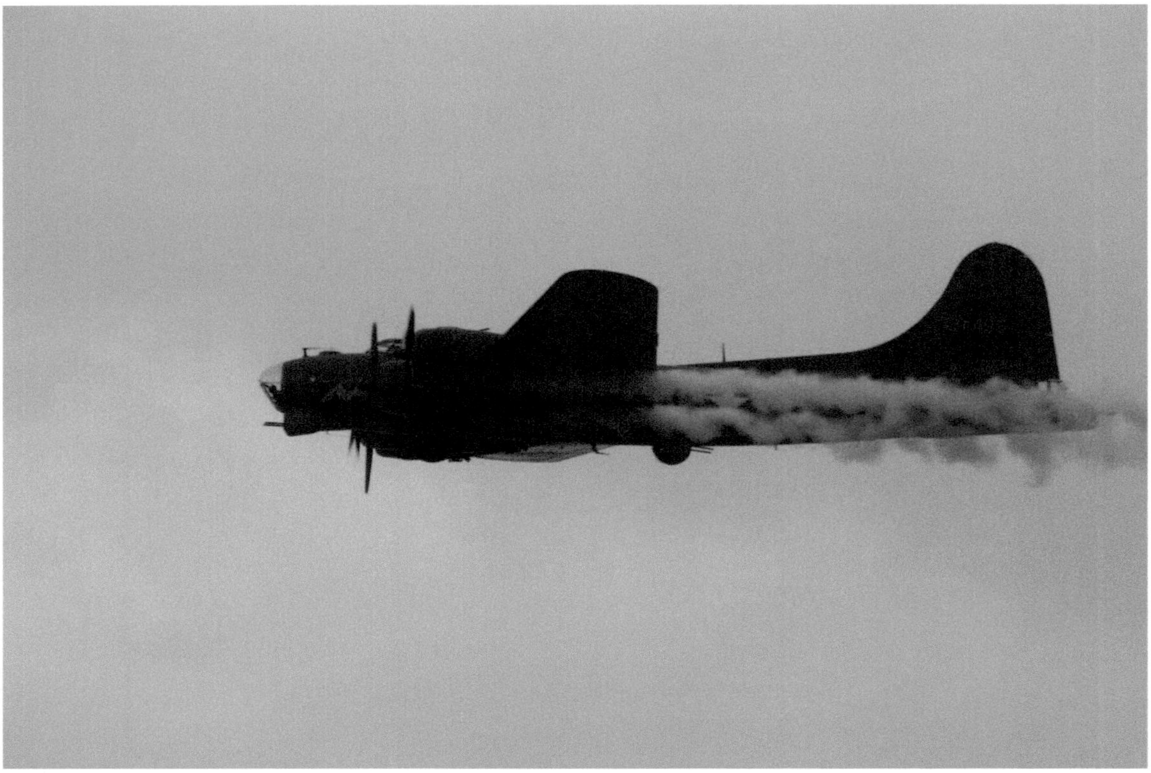

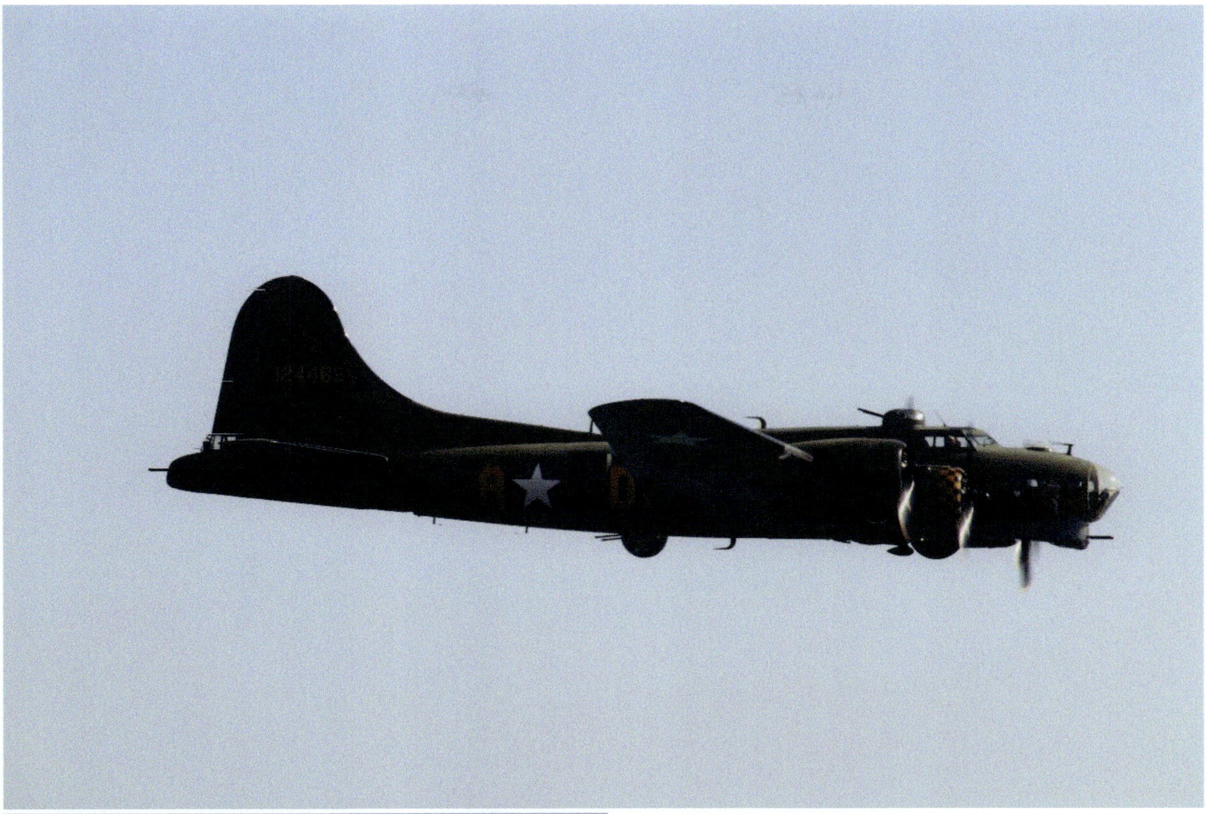

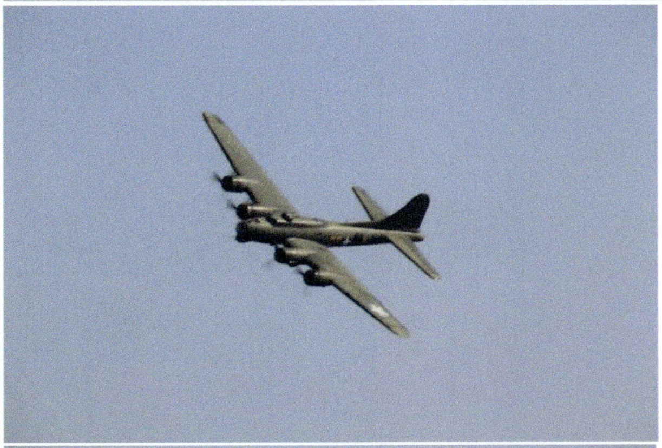

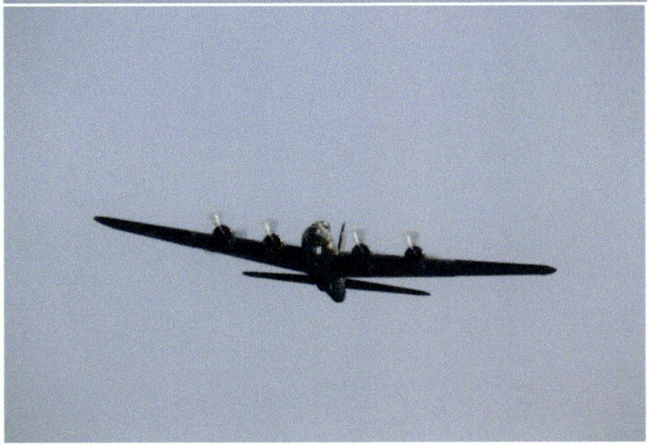

Quick Facts

Power: Four Wright R-18200-97 Cyclone radial engines,

Performance: Max speed 287 mph at 25,000 ft.
Cruising speed 150 mph at 5,000 ft.
Service ceiling 35,600 ft.
Range, 2,000 miles with 6,000 lbs of bombs.

Weights: Empty - 36,135 lb. Gross - 65,500 lb.

Dimensions: Wing span 103 ft 9 in.
Length 74 ft 4 in.
Height 19 ft 2 in.

The prototype, known as the Model 299, first flew on July 28, 1935

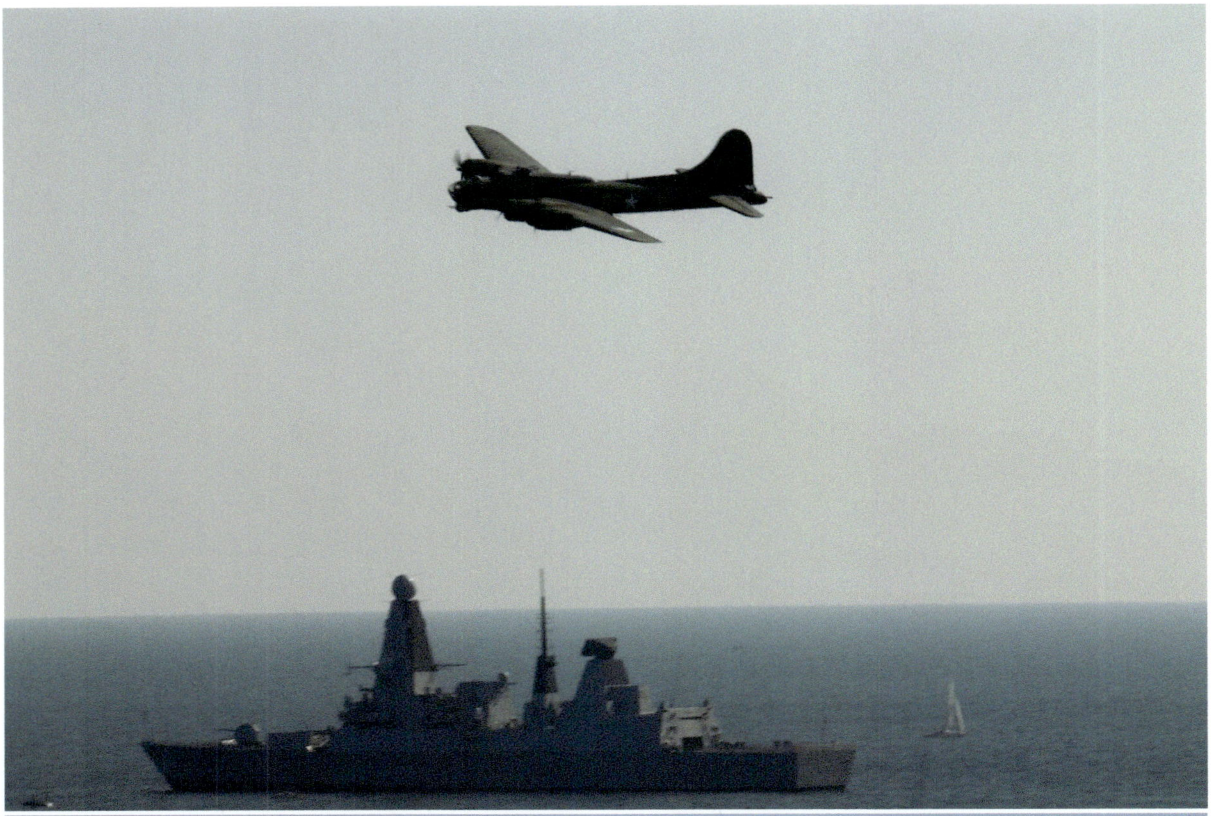

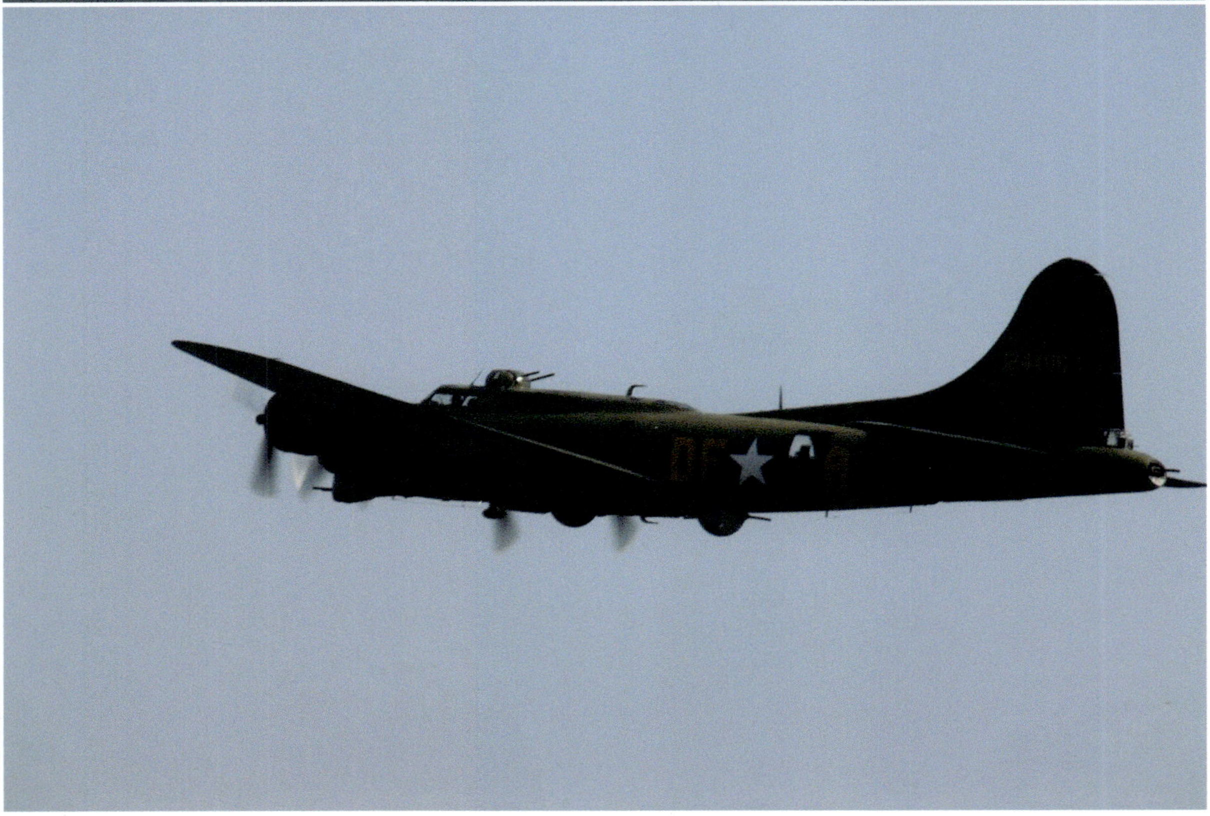

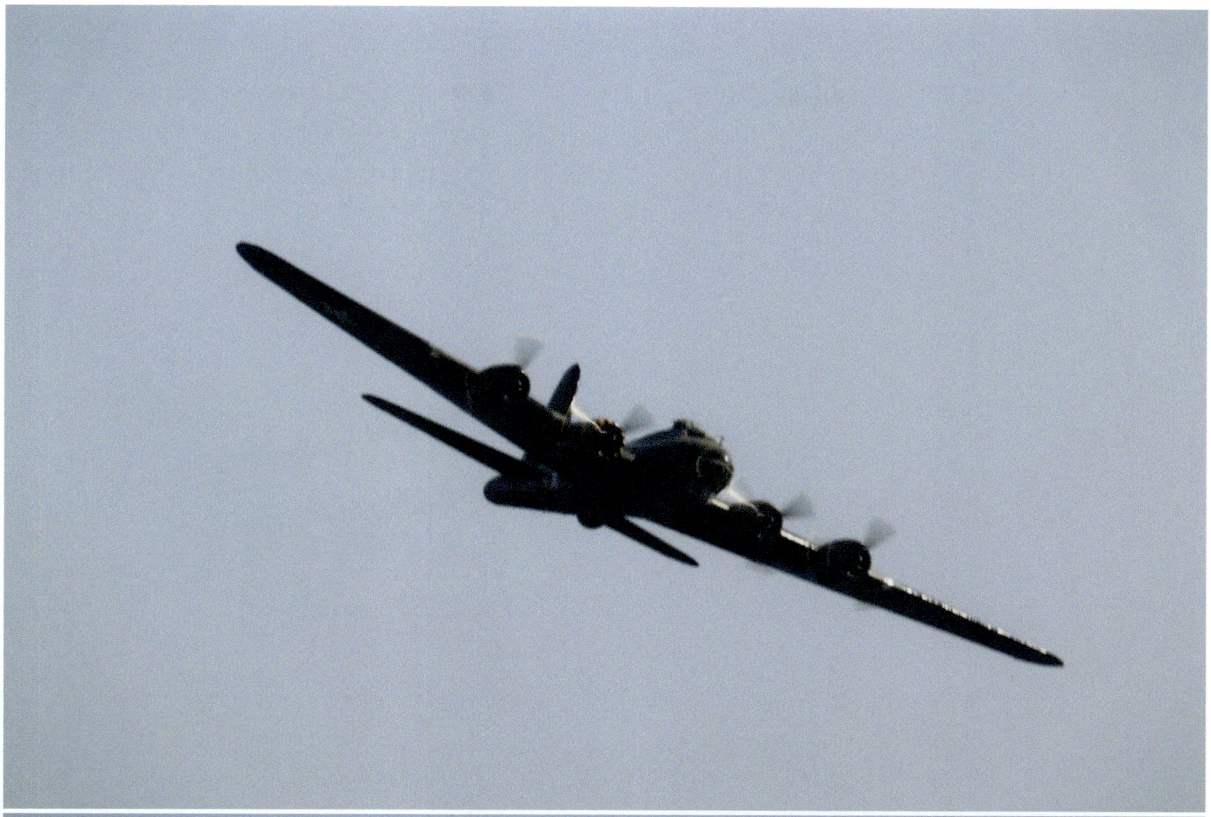

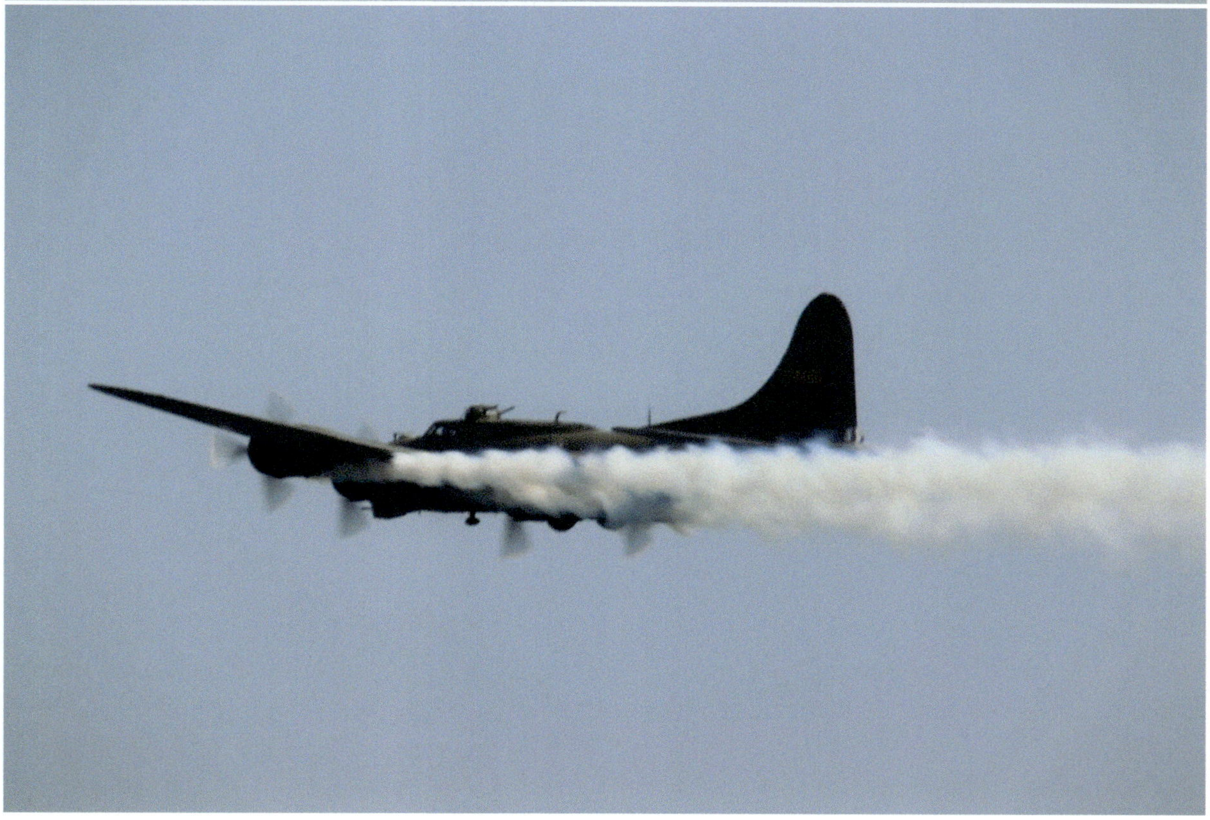

Catalina

Designed by Consolidated Aircraft Corporation in the 1930s to satisfy a U.S. Navy requirement for a long-range patrol bomber and reconnaissance aircraft, the PBY Catalina took flight for the first time in March 1935 when the prototype, dubbed XP3Y-1, made its inaugural test flight. The design proved successful, and the aircraft entered production as the PBY-1.

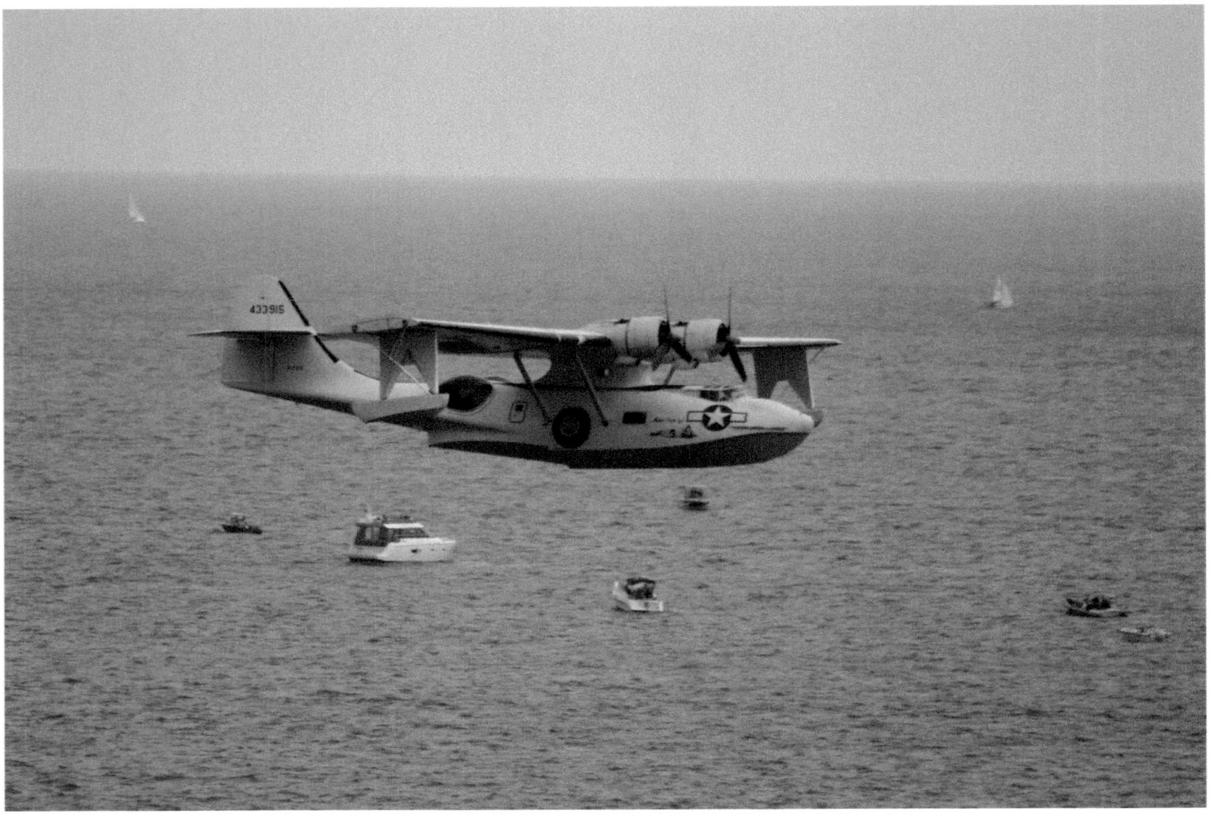

Design and Features

With its distinctive gull-wing design, the versatile Catalina was a high-wing, twin-engine monoplane renowned for its long range and ability to operate from both land and water. Typically crewed by 7 to 10 members and equipped with radar technology for anti-submarine warfare, the aircraft was adaptable to many roles.

Military Service

During World War II, the versatile PBY Catalina was one of the most widely used multi-role aircraft, serving in the U.S. Navy, Royal Air Force, Royal Canadian Air Force, and other Allied forces in numerous capacities including maritime patrol, anti-submarine warfare, search and rescue, convoy escort, and reconnaissance. With its long range and endurance, the Catalina had a major impact across the Pacific theatre, conducting vital reconnaissance and patrols while also contributing to the Allied victory at the pivotal Battle of Midway.

The Consolidated PBY Catalina flying boat played a pivotal role in the Battle of the Atlantic with its extensive anti-submarine patrols and attacks against German U-boats. Its exceptional range and endurance made the Catalina ideally suited for patrolling the vast expanses of ocean.

Although the Catalina was slow and ungainly, Allied forces used the aircraft in a wide variety of roles for which it was never intended. Most notably, PBYs saved hundreds of downed aircrew by performing air-sea rescues. Catalina airmen affectionately called their plane the "Cat" during combat and "Dumbo" during rescue missions.

Search and Rescue

The aircraft's amphibious capabilities, allowing it to land on water, enabled the Catalina to earn a reputation for effectiveness in search and rescue missions to recover downed aircrews or shipwreck survivors.

After the heavy cruiser Indianapolis was sunk during World War II, a PBY Catalina flown by LCDR Adrian Marks rescued 56 sailors in high seas. With no room left inside, the crew tied sailors to the aircraft's wings, transforming the plane into a lifeboat that shielded them from exposure and shark attacks until rescue ships arrived. For decades after the war ended, Catalinas continued serving in search and rescue operations.

Post-War Era:

Many surplus Catalinas were sold to civilian operators after the war. Some were converted for civilian use, including firefighting, cargo transport, and aerial survey missions.

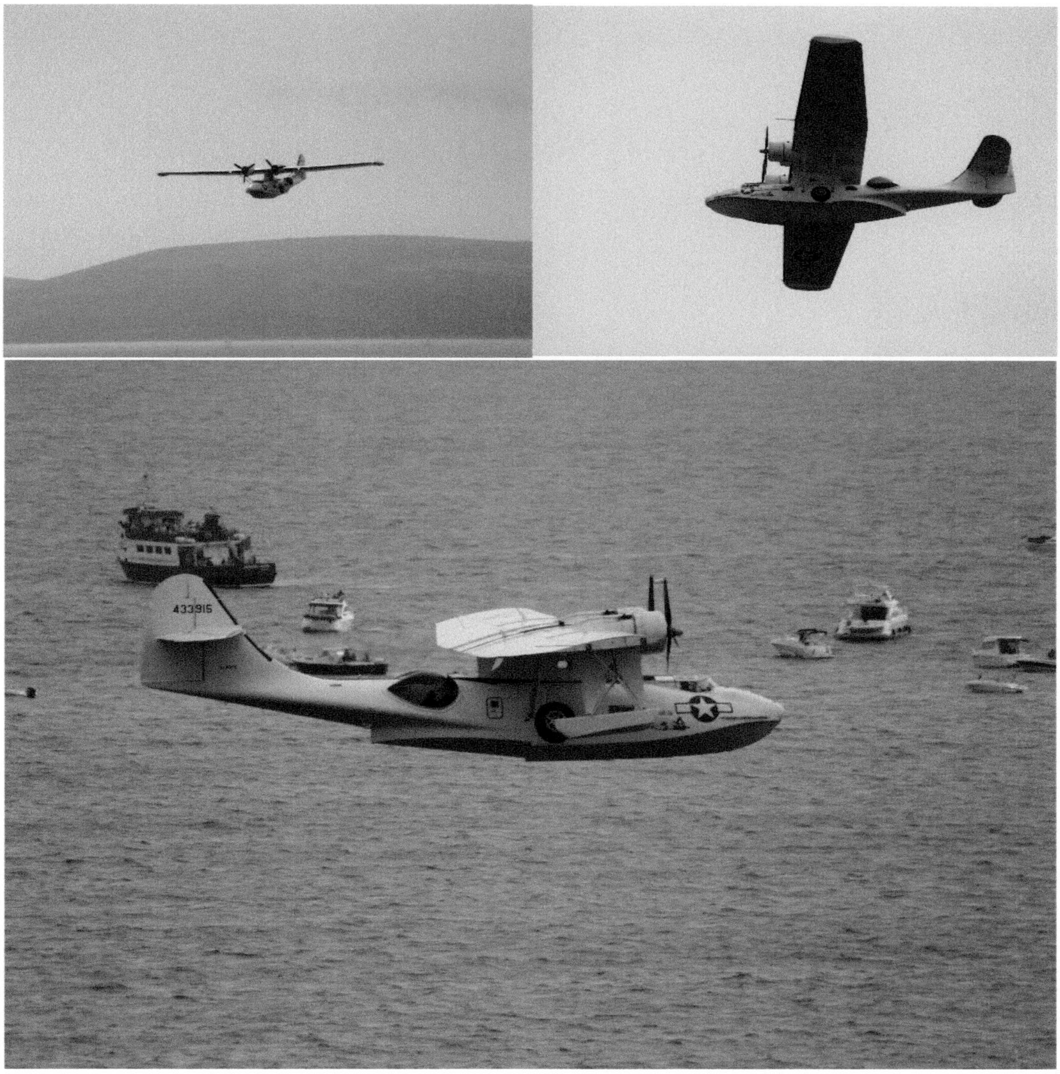

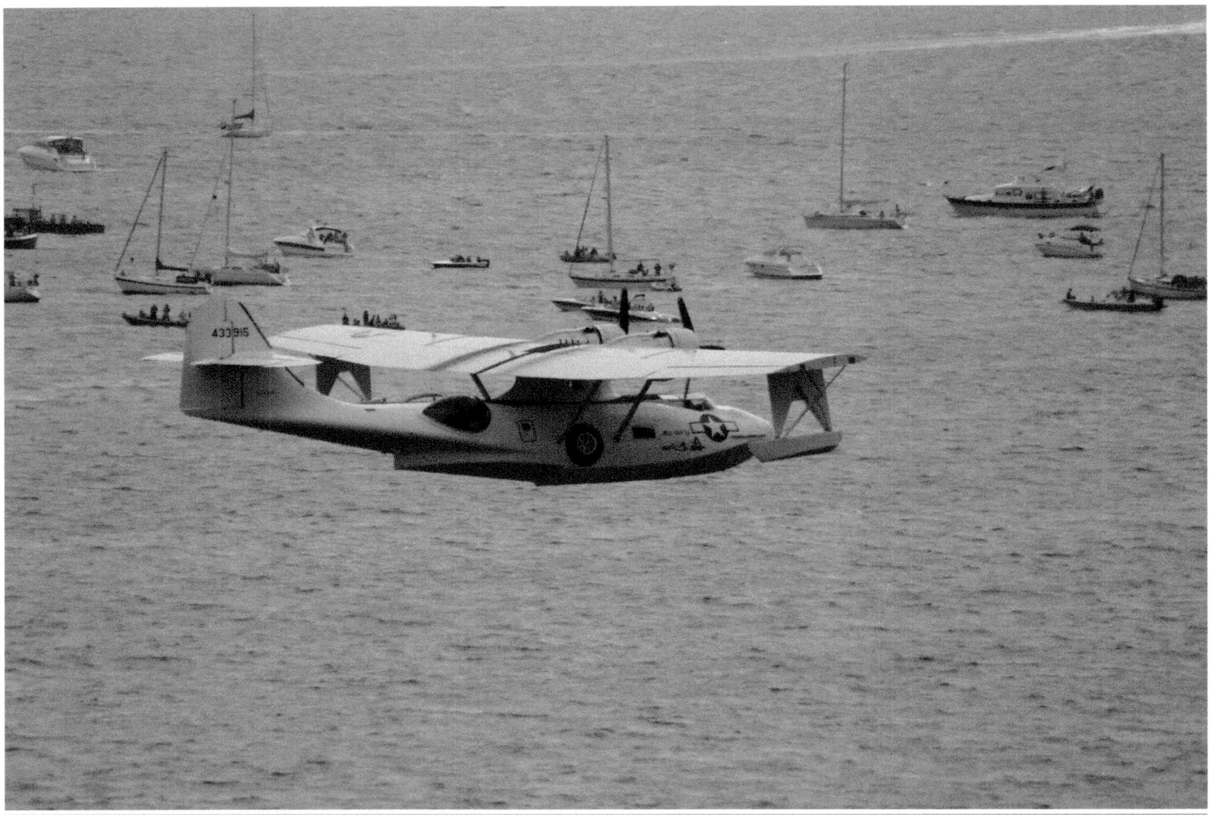
433915

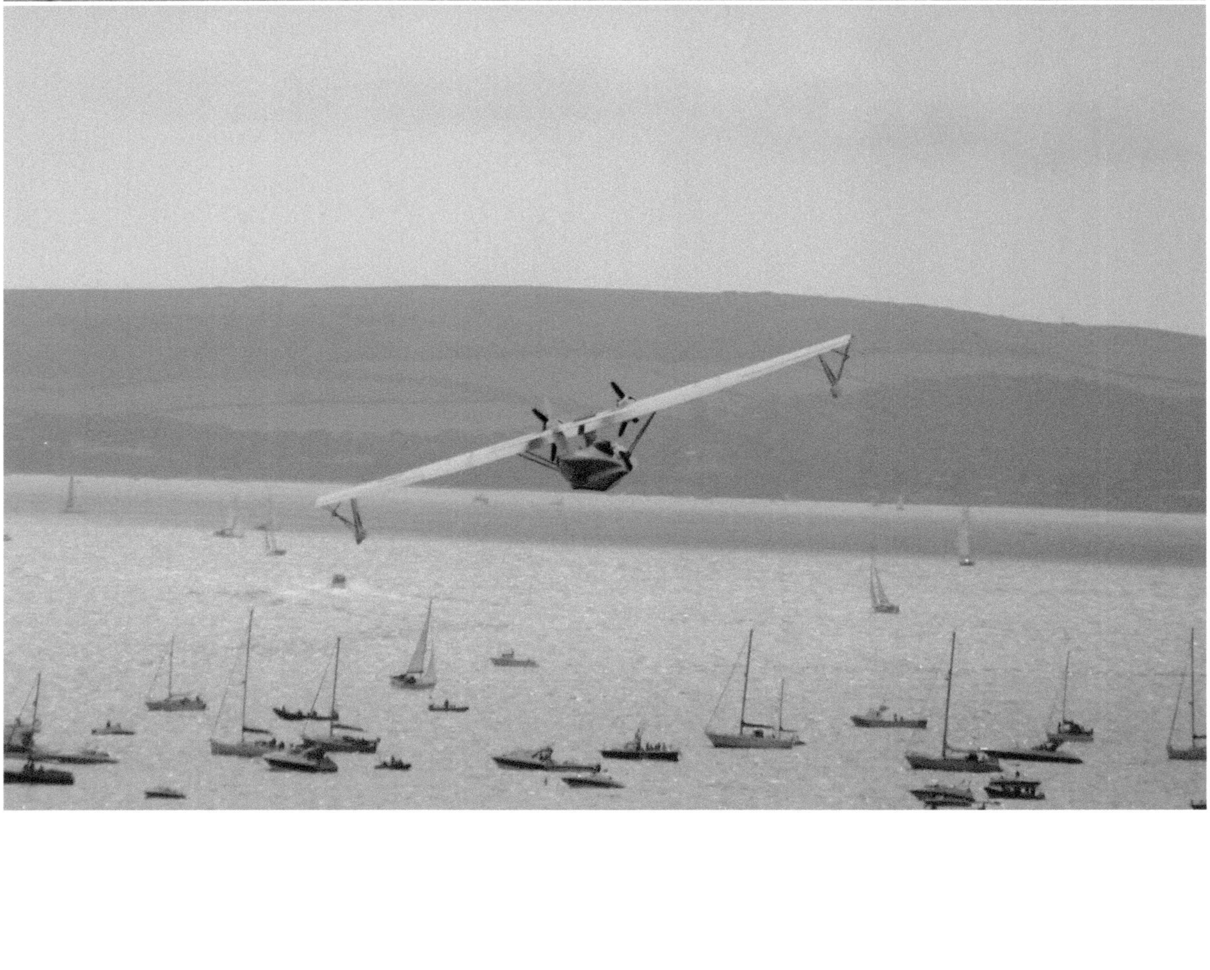

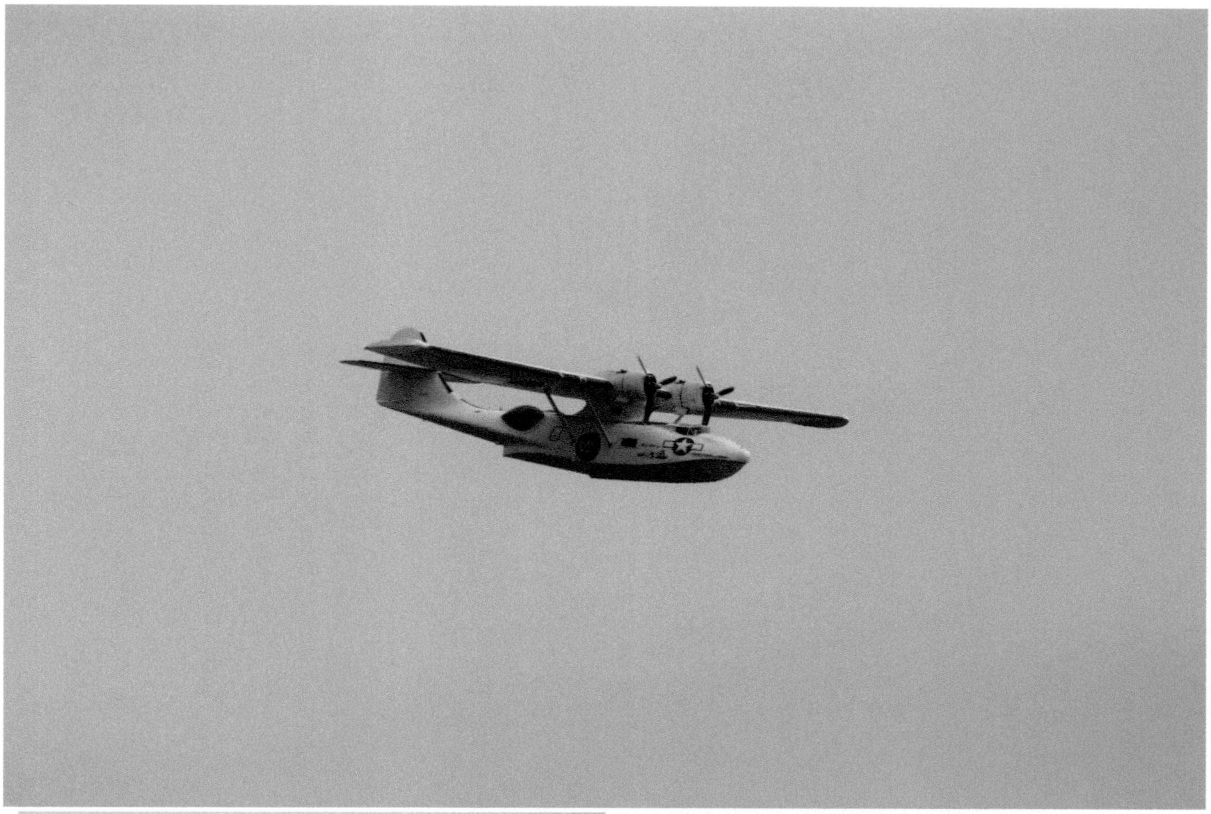

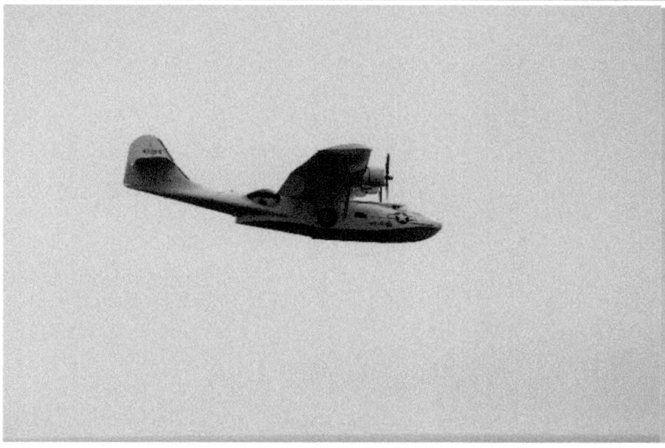

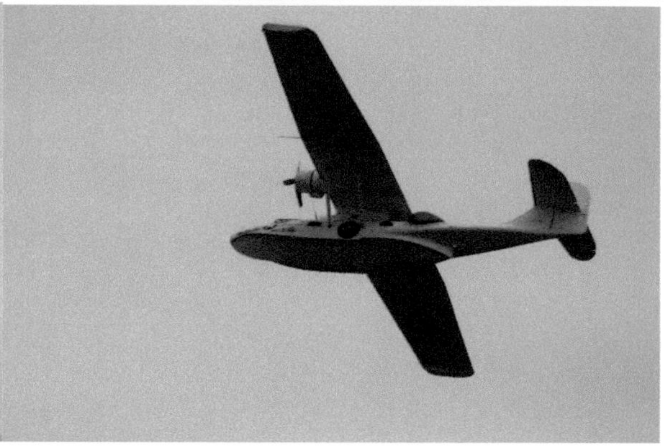

Quick Facts

- The Consolidated Model 28, more commonly known as the PBY Catalina, is a flying boat and amphibious aircraft that was produced in the 1930s and 1940s with the first flight on 21st March 1935
- Range: 4,030 km
- Top speed: 314 km/h
- Engine type: Pratt & Whitney R-1830 Twin Wasp
- Cruise speed: 200 km/h
- Wingspan: 32 m

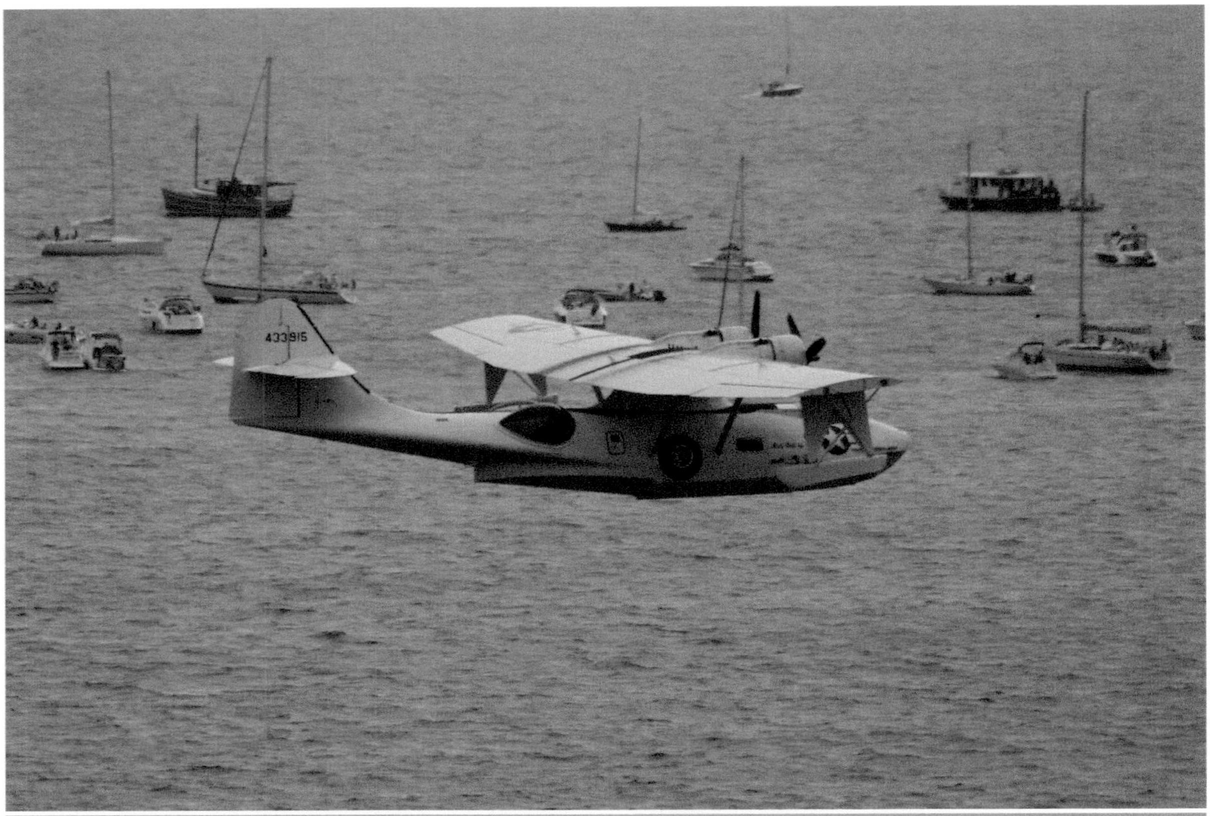
433915

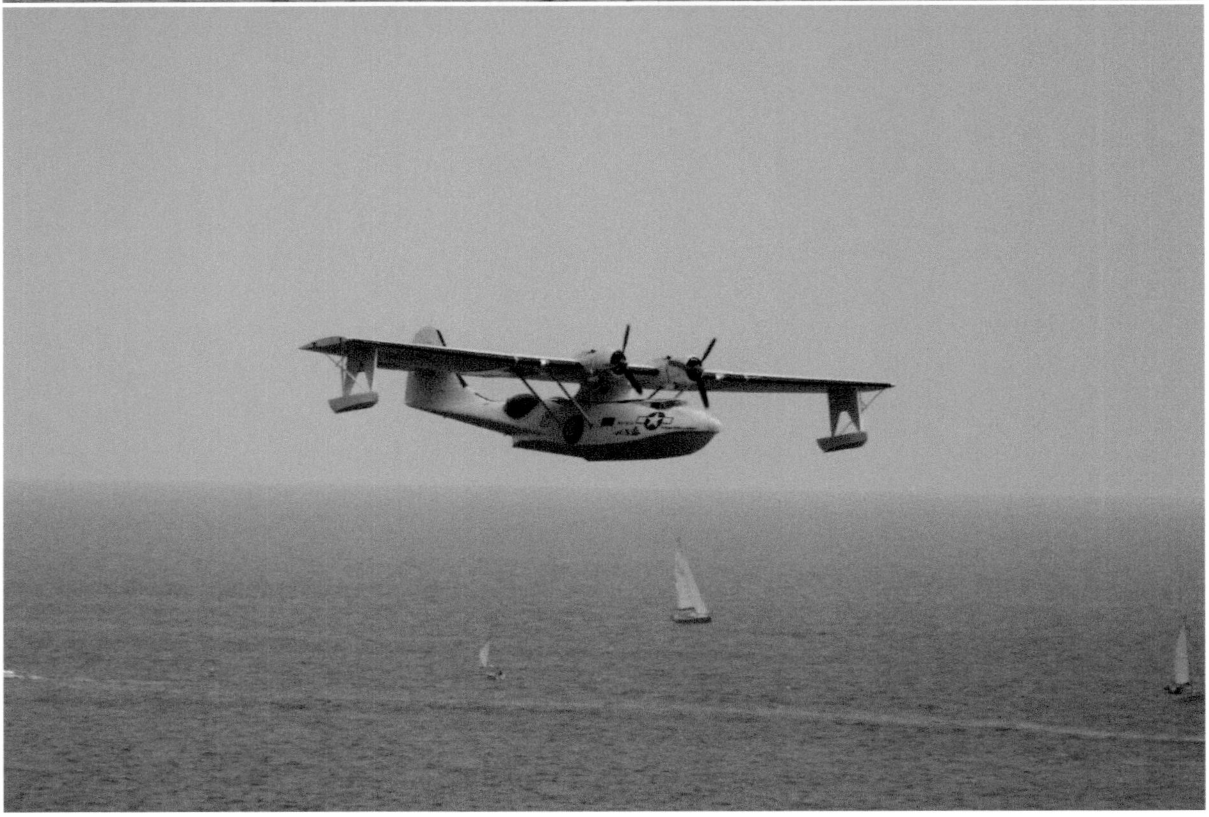

Messerschmitt Bf 109

The iconic Messerschmitt Bf 109 fighter plane, often simply called the Me 109, was designed by Willy Messerschmitt and Robert Lusser and became one of the Luftwaffe's most widely used aircraft during World War II, playing a major role in air battles throughout the conflict.

Development and Design:

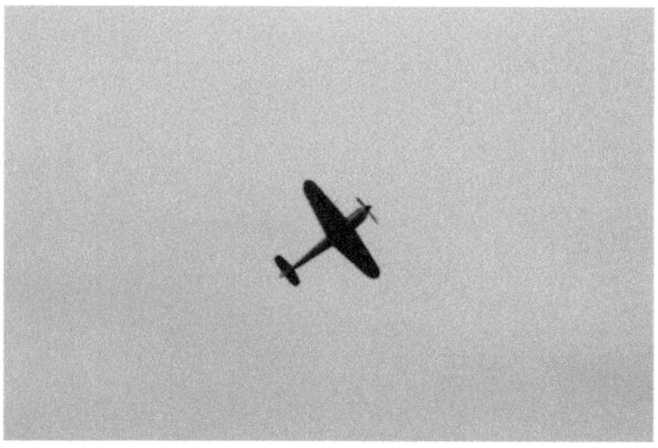

The Messerschmitt Bf 109 fighter aircraft originated in the mid-1930s when the German Luftwaffe called for a modern monoplane fighter plane. The first prototype, designated Bf 109V-1, took flight in 1935. Further refinements led to the production model Bf 109B, which entered Luftwaffe service in 1937.

Variants:

The Bf 109 fighter plane had many variants and upgrades over the course of its production, with the Bf 109E (Emil) and Bf 109F (Friedrich) models playing major roles in the early years of World War II.

Performance:

The Bf 109 was known for its excellent speed, agility, and climb rate. Its performance, especially in the early years of the war, often gave the Luftwaffe an edge over its adversaries.

Armament:

The aircraft was armed with a changing combination of machine guns and cannons as it evolved through different versions over time, transitioning to more powerful armaments in the later models.

Role in World War II:

The Bf 109 played a crucial role in the Spanish Civil War and the early stages of World War II, particularly during the Blitzkrieg campaigns in Poland and France.

The Bf 109 proved to be a highly adaptable aircraft that served in multiple campaigns throughout World War II. Its airframe was modified for various roles, including fighter-bomber, reconnaissance, and high-altitude interceptor missions on the Eastern Front against the Soviet Union and in the North African theatre.

The Bf 109 encountered increasing limitations as the war progressed and more advanced Allied aircraft emerged, including restricted fuel capacity and narrow landing gear that hindered the aging design.

The Bf 109 achieved great success early in the war, but later faced fierce competition from more advanced Allied aircraft like the P-51 Mustang and Supermarine Spitfire. However, the Bf 109's critical contributions in the early war years remain undeniable.

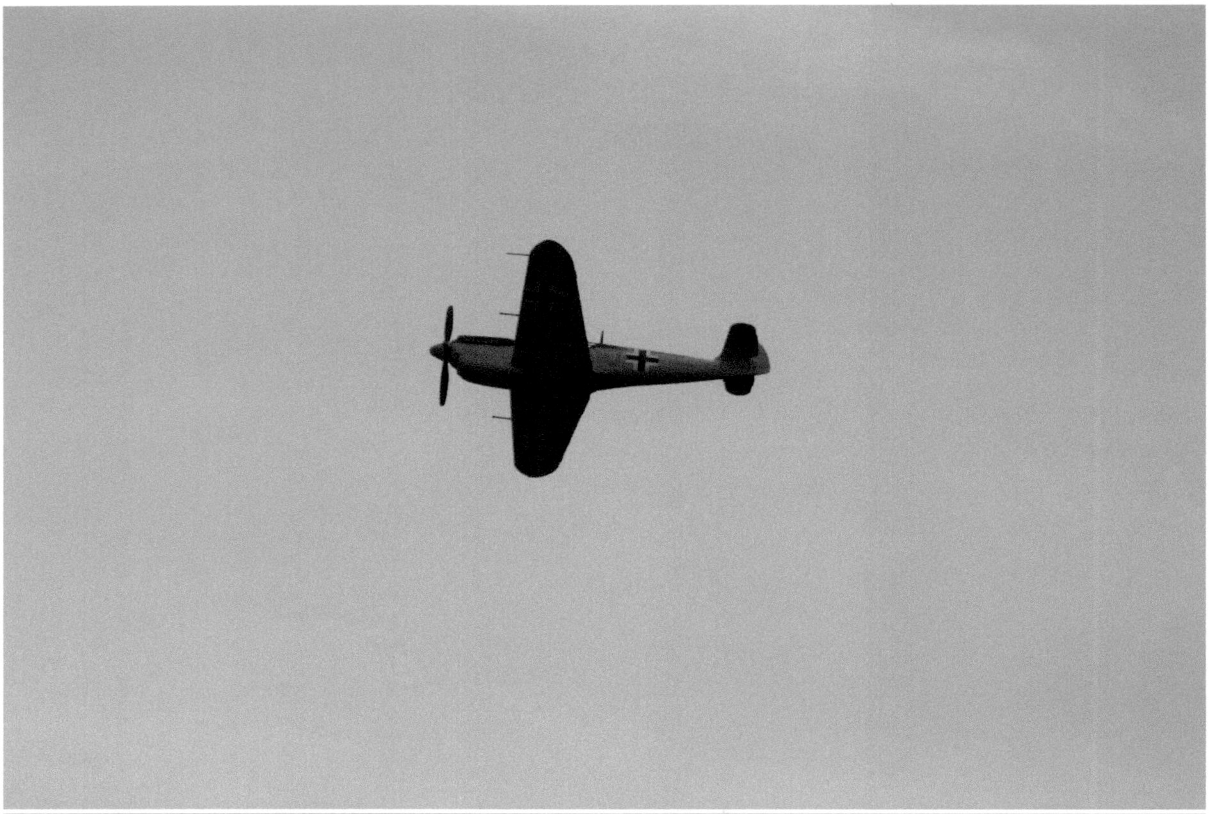

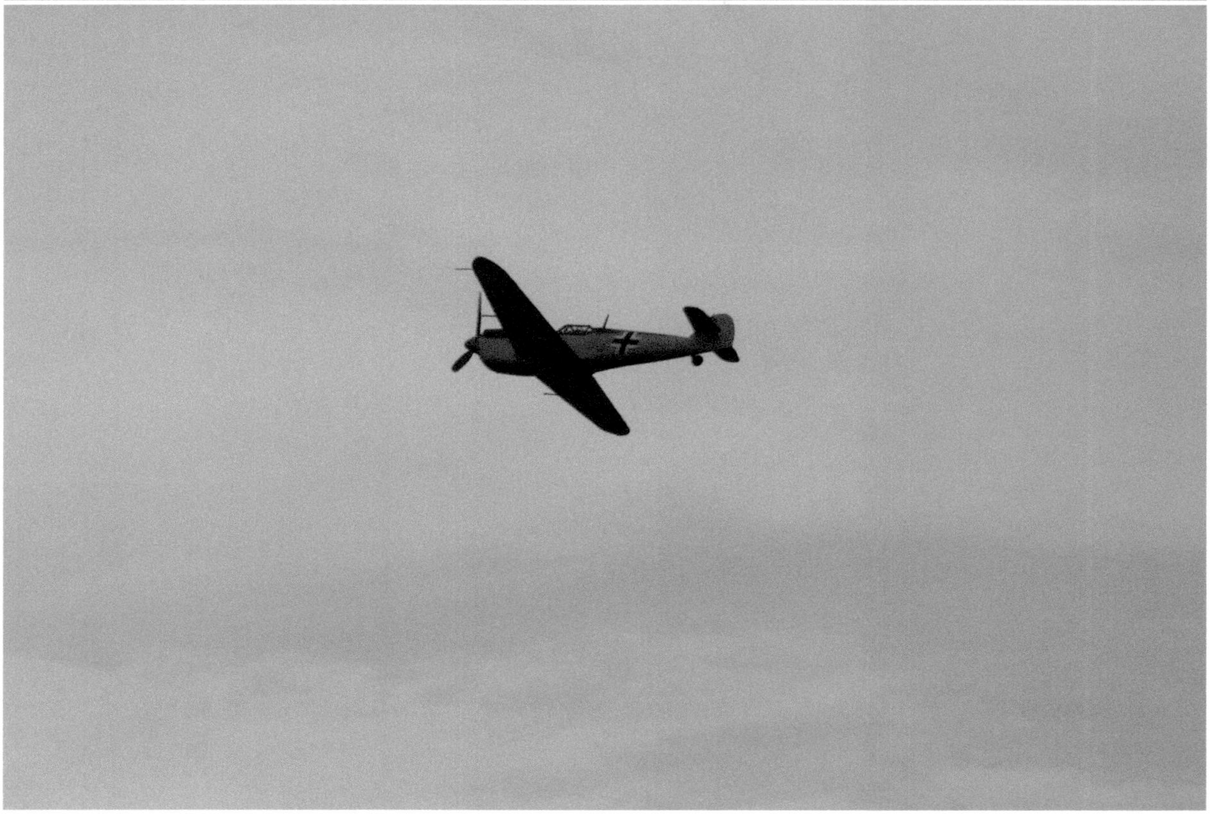

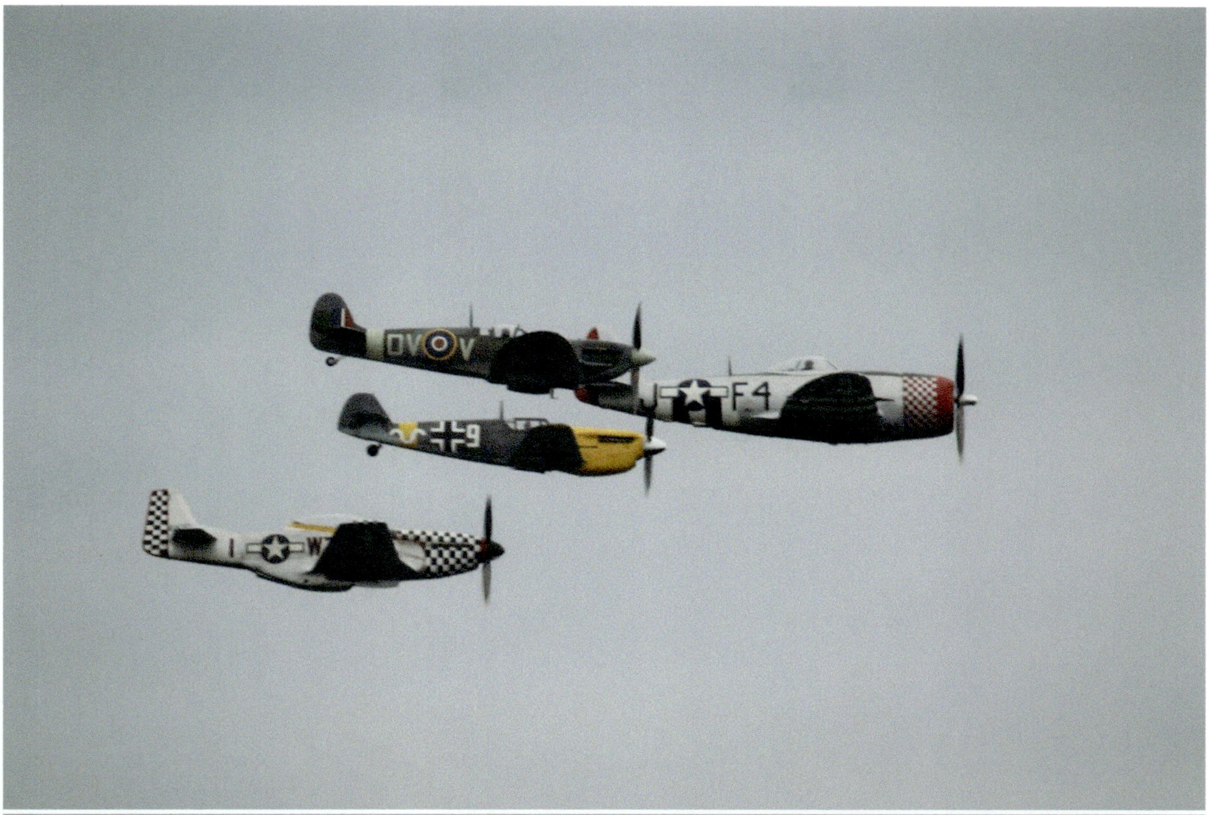
DV
V
F4
9

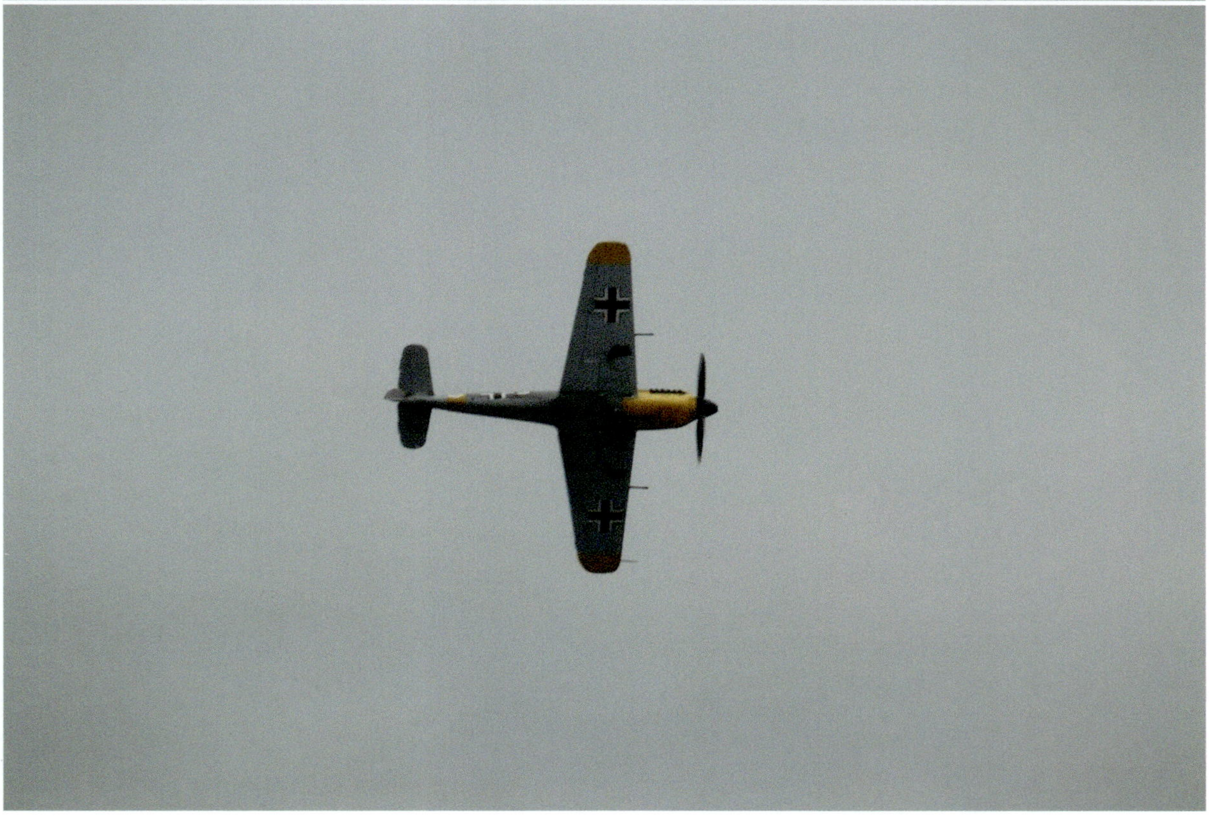

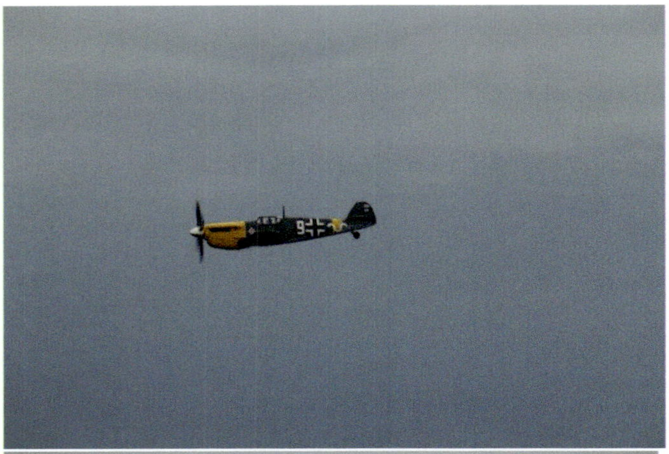

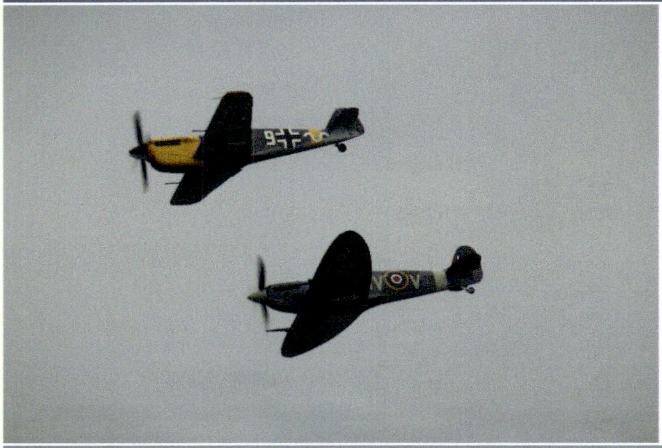

Quick Facts

Crew: 1

Length: 8.95 m (29 ft 4 in)

Wingspan: 9.925 m (32 ft 7 in)

Height: 2.6 m (8 ft 6 in)

Wing area: 16.05 m2 (172.8 sq ft)

Empty weight: 2,247 kg (4,954 lb)

Gross weight: 3,148 kg (6,940 lb)

Max takeoff weight: 3,400 kg (7,496 lb)

Powerplant: 1 × Daimler-Benz DB 605A-1 V-12 inverted liquid-cooled piston engine 1,475 PS

Maximum speed: 530 km/h (330 mph, 290 kn) at sea level

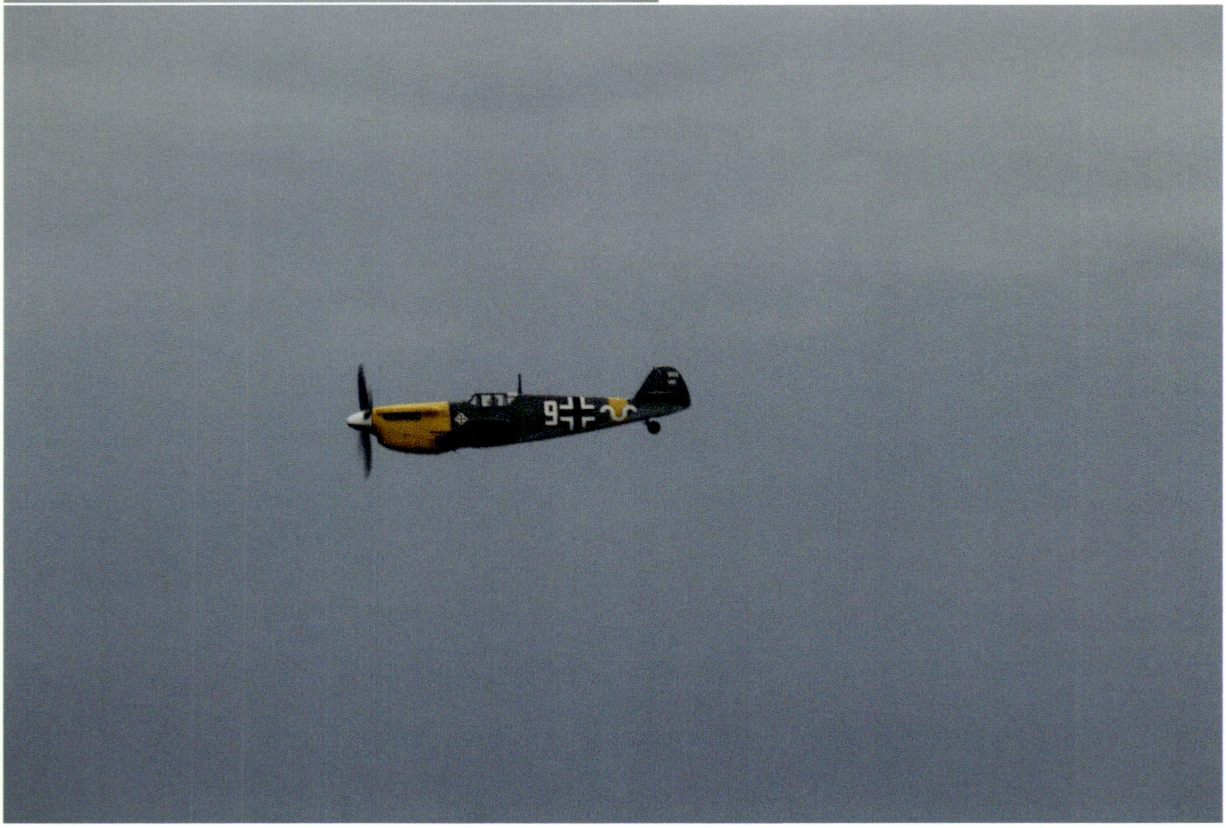

Dakota

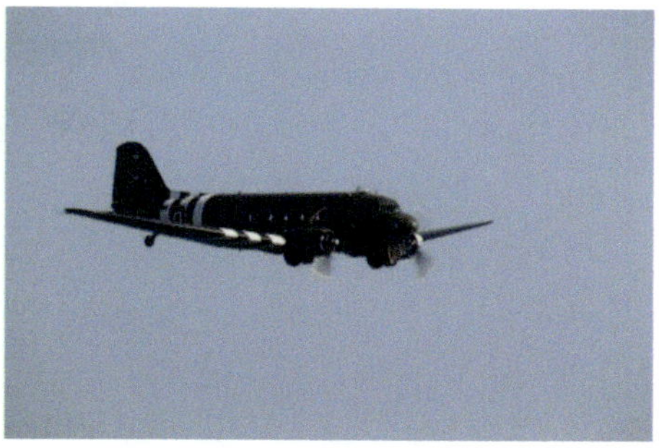

The Douglas C-47 Skytrain, known as the Dakota, was a military transport aircraft developed from the Douglas DC-3 commercial airliner. The C-47 played a crucial role during World War II and in post-war military and civilian operations.

Development:

The twin-engine propeller-driven Douglas DC-3 airliner was so successful that it spawned the C-47 military transport aircraft. The United States Army Air Forces (USAAF) developed this versatile version to meet their need for a capable transport plane.

Role and Operations:

The C-47 played a vital role during World War II by transporting troops, cargo, and wounded soldiers, as well as carrying paratroopers and towing gliders. Most notably, the aircraft was instrumental in major airborne operations like the D-Day landings at Normandy, the Allied invasion of Sicily, and the Battle of Arnhem.

Design and Features:

Keeping most of the DC-3's design, the C-47 featured key modifications that adapted it for military use, including a reinforced floor, cargo doors, and the capacity to carry paratroopers.

Powerplant:

The C-47 was powered by two Pratt & Whitney R-1830-92 Twin Wasp radial engines, providing a cruising speed of around 160 to 200 mph (260 to 320 km/h).

Global Service:

The C-47 Skytrain/Dakota, extensively used by the USAAF and Allied air forces during and after World War II, became one of history's most widely used transport aircraft. Its Dakota variant was commonly employed by the Royal Air Force and other Commonwealth nations. This reliable and versatile aircraft continued military service long after the war, seeing use in various conflicts. It also found civilian roles in cargo and passenger transport. Remaining a symbol of Allied airborne operations in World War II, many C-47s are still preserved and flown by units and museums worldwide today. The Dakota's storied reliability, versatility and wartime contributions have cemented its place in aviation history.

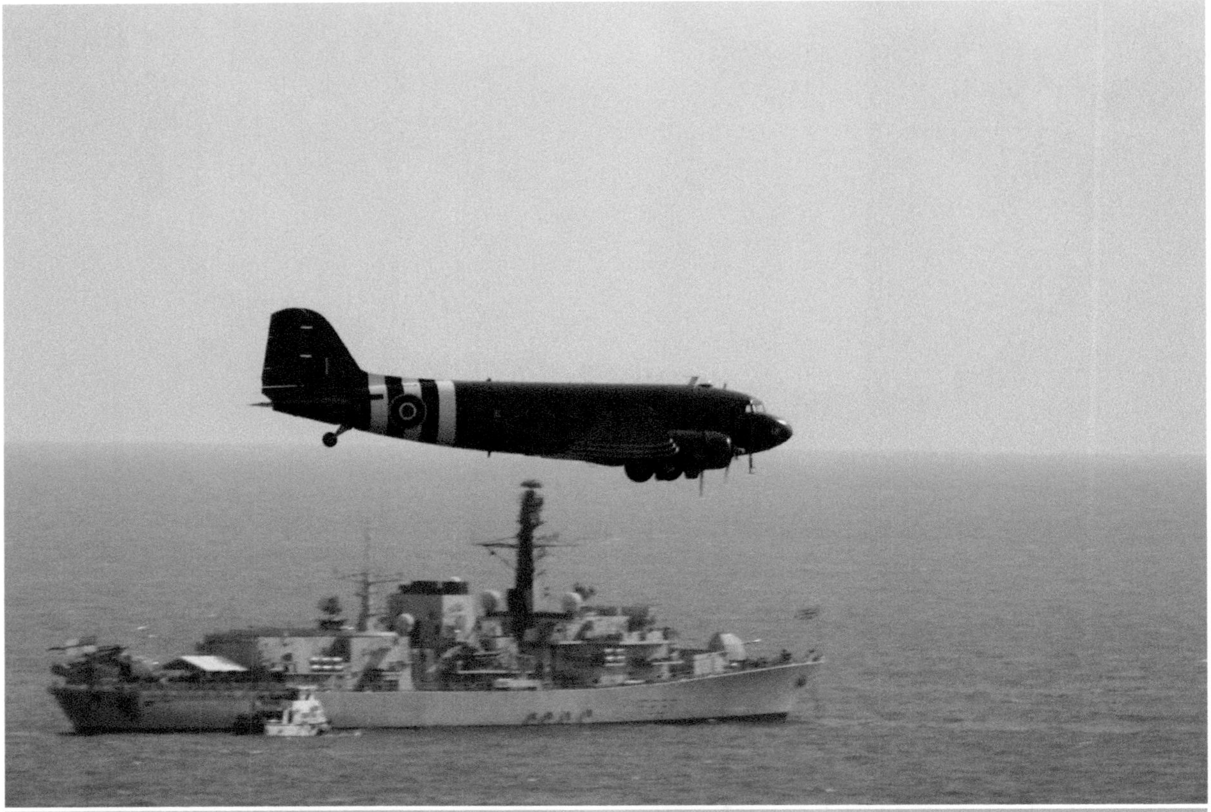

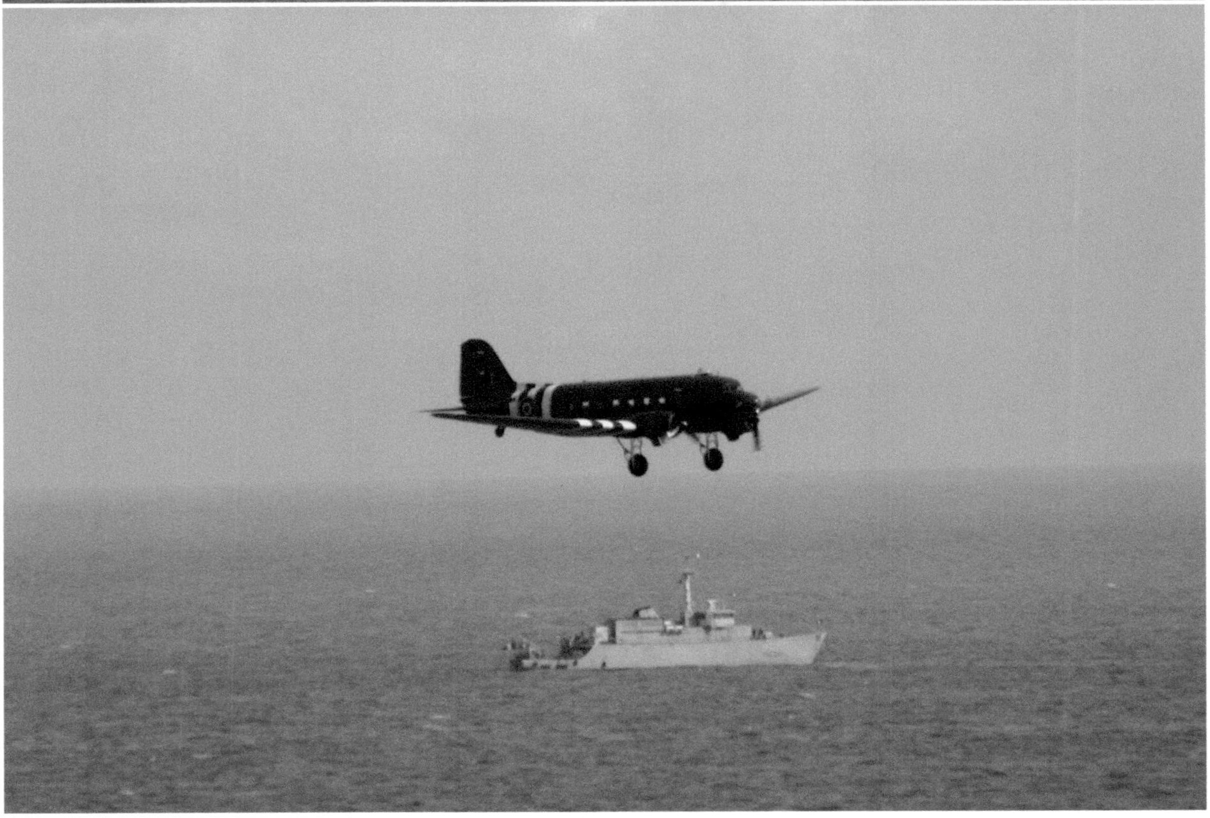

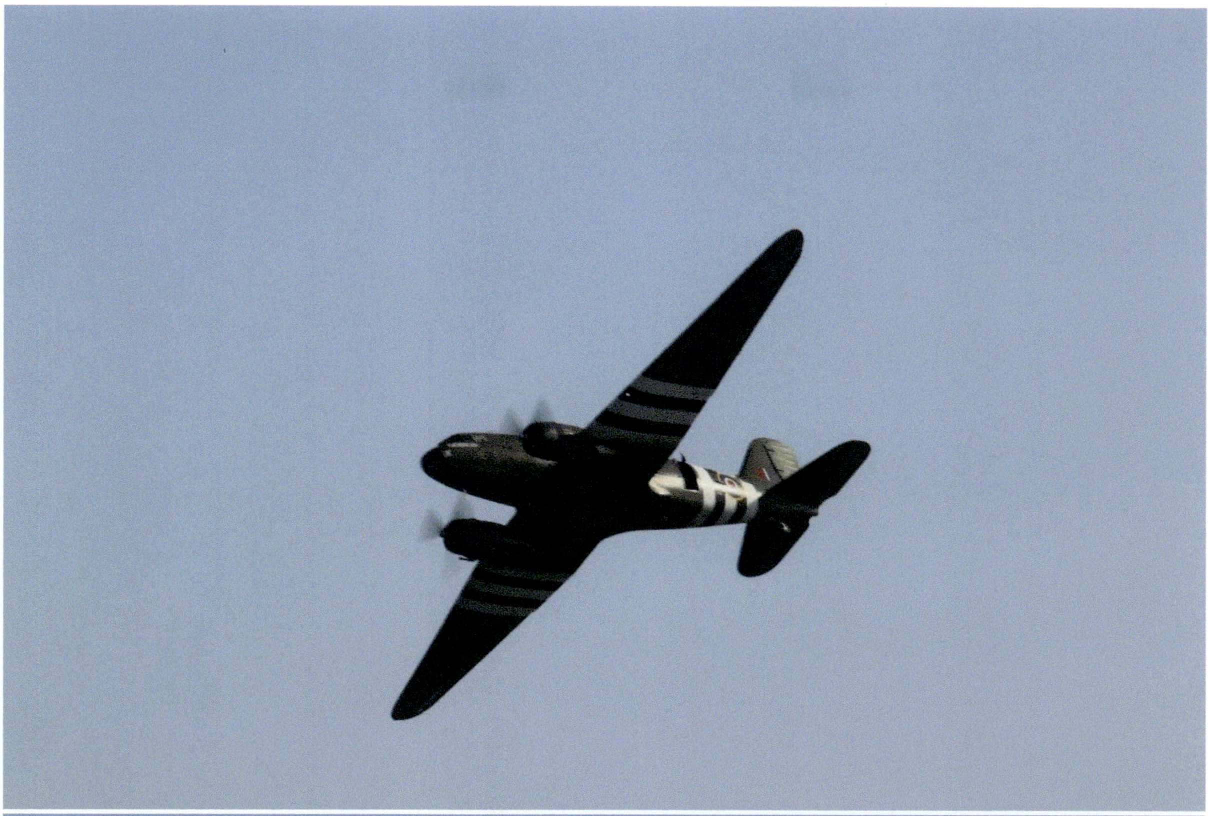

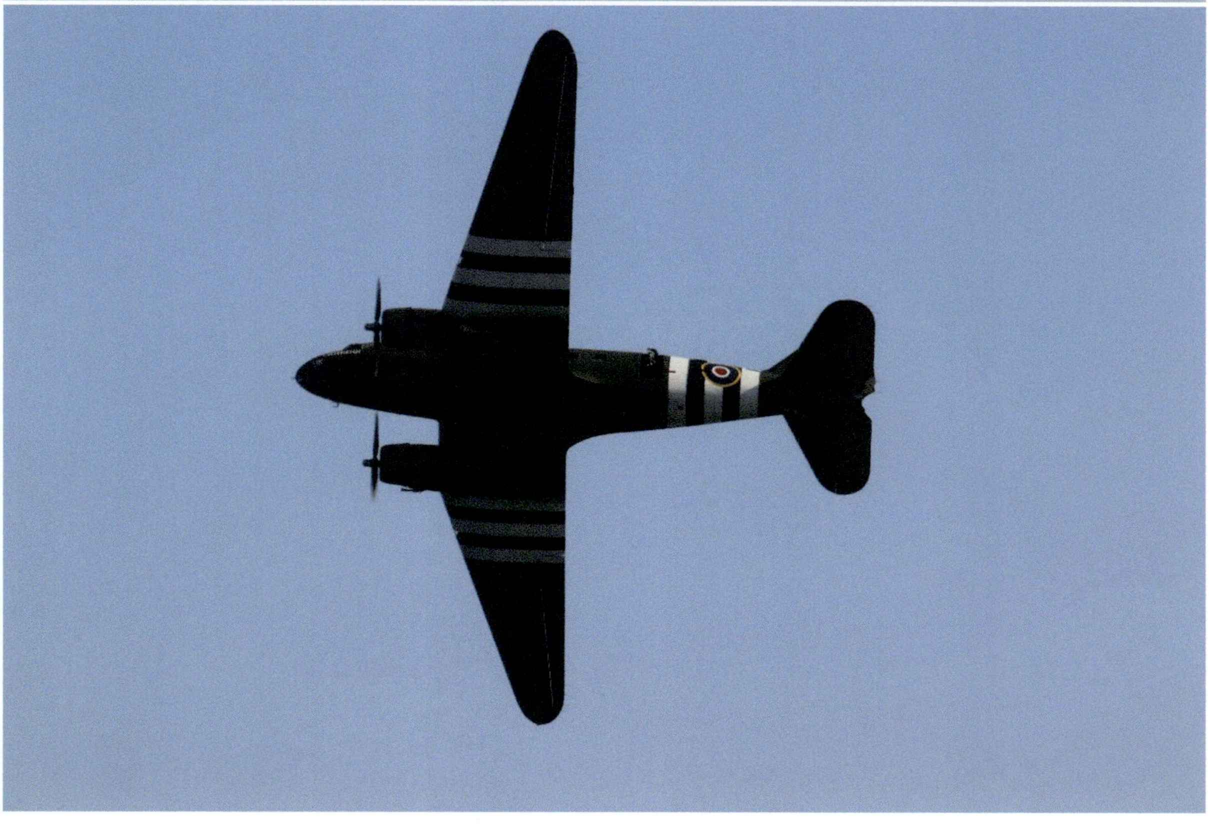

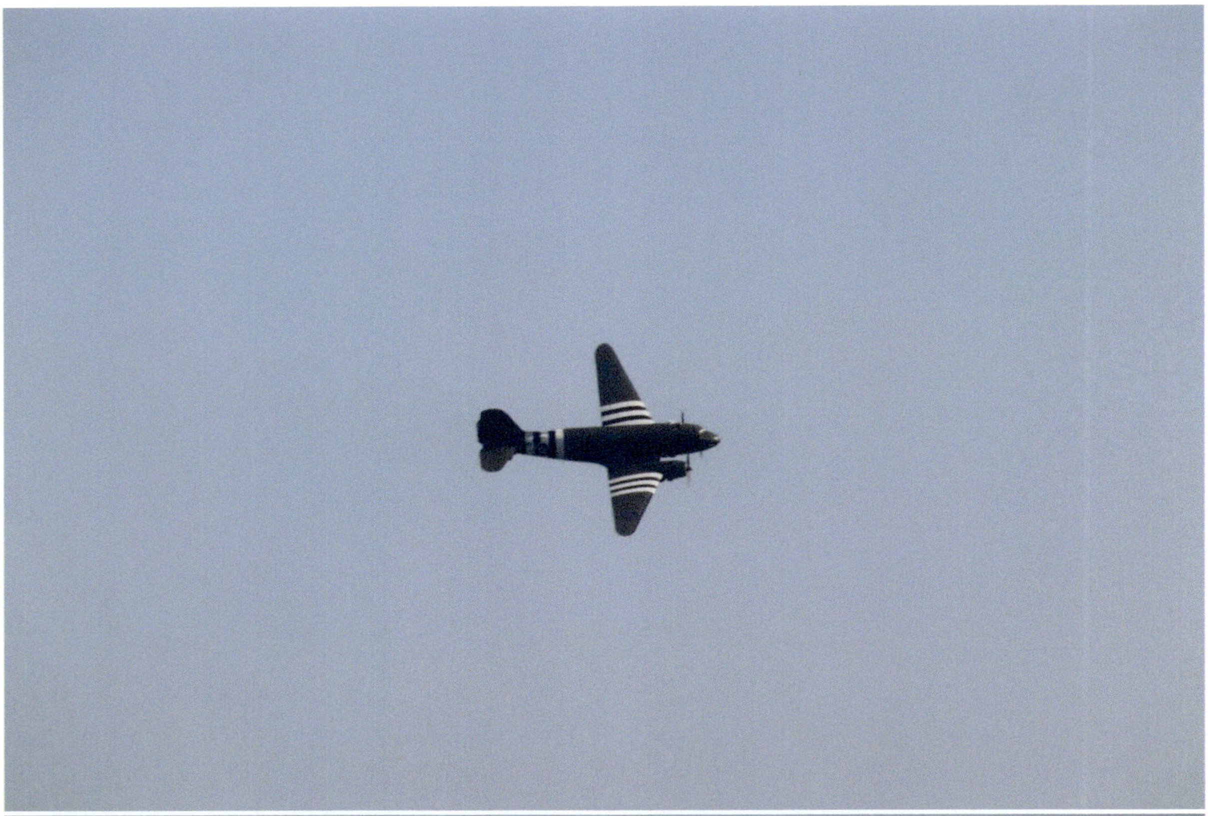

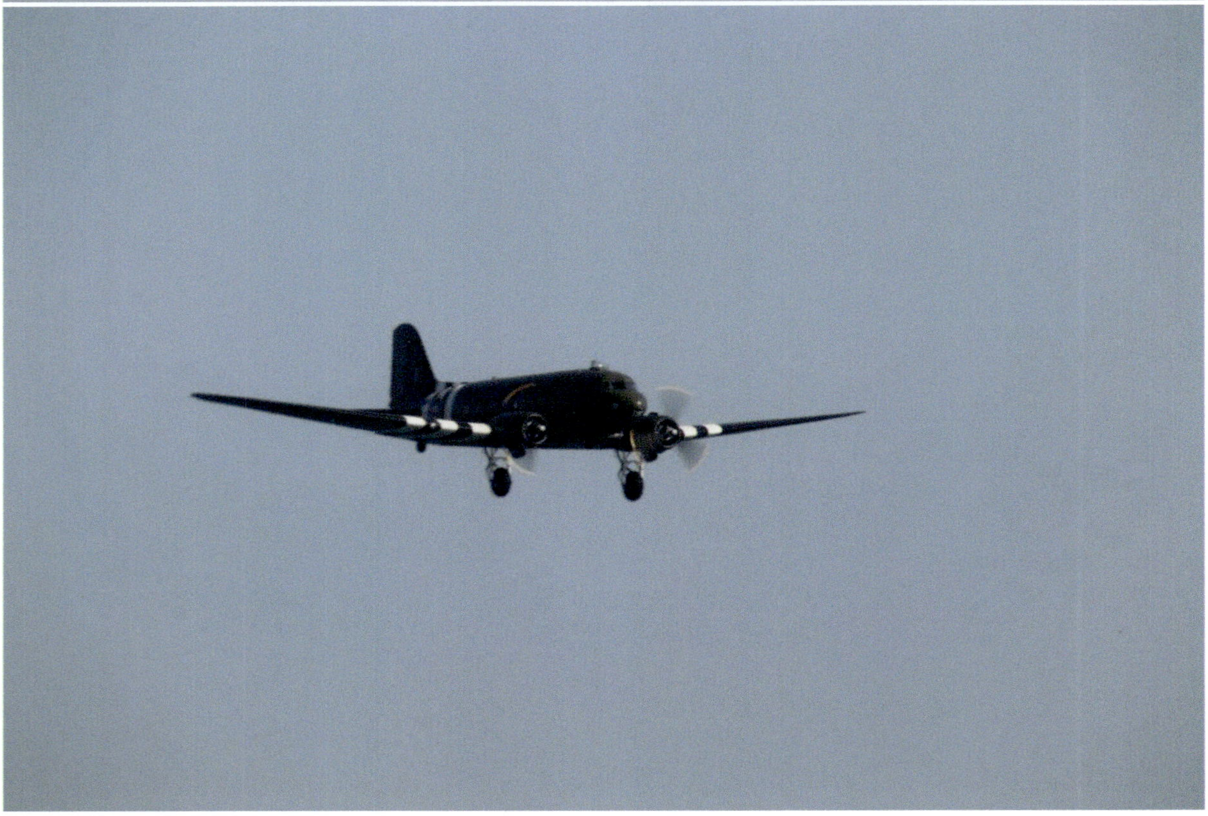

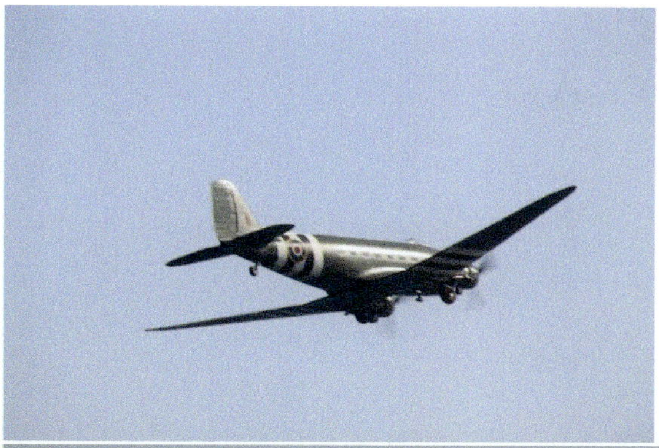

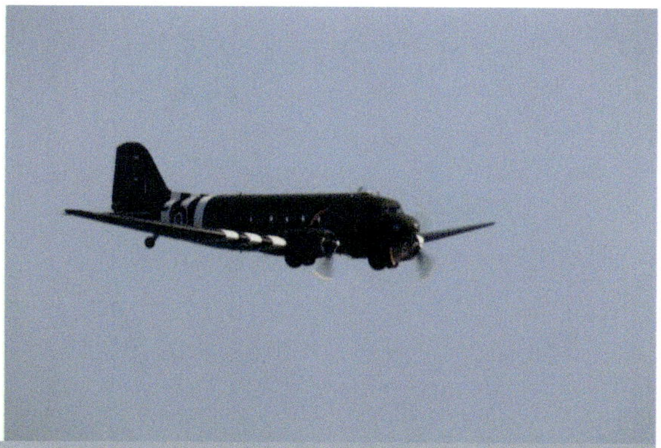

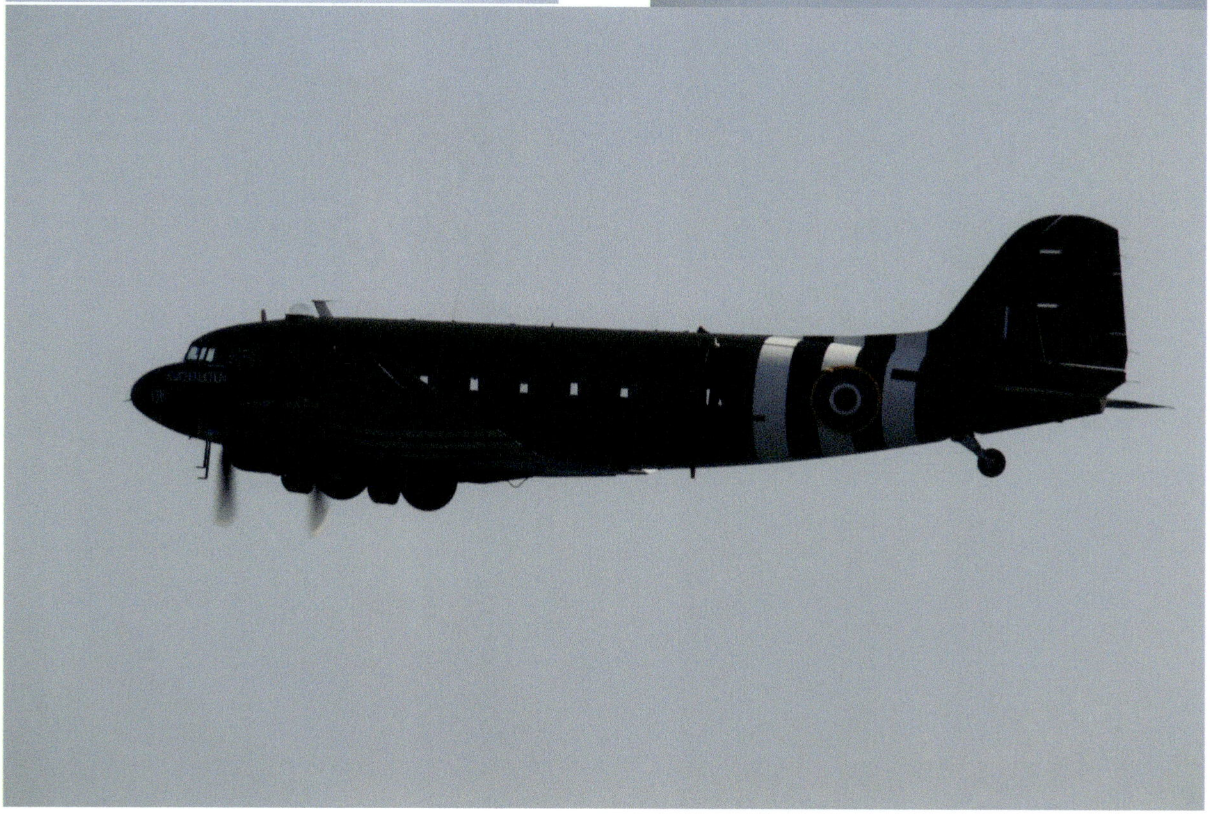

Quick Facts

Engine type: Pratt & Whitney R-1830 Twin Wasp

Top speed: 370 km/h

Range: 2,575 km

Wingspan: 29 m

Cruise speed: 258 km/h

Manufacturer: Douglas Aircraft Company

Weight: 8,255 kg

B-25 Mitchell

Introduced in 1941, the iconic North American B-25 Mitchell medium bomber remains one of the most famous American aircraft of World War II. Named after Brigadier General William "Billy" Mitchell, an aviation pioneer, the B-25 saw combat service with Allied air forces in every theatre of the war. Remarkably, many B-25s remained in operation for over 40 years after the war ended.

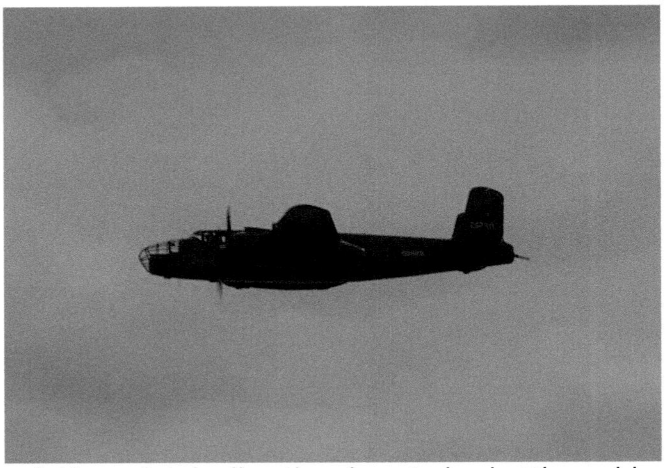

The B-25 earned a reputation as an aircraft that was safe and easy to fly. Even if one engine failed, pilots could make 60-degree banking turns toward the dead engine while maintaining control at speeds as low as 145 mph (230 km/h). However, pilots had to be careful to maintain directional control using the rudder if an engine failed at low speeds after take-off. Attempting turns with the ailerons alone risked a sudden loss of control.

The Royal Air Force acquired nearly 900 Mitchell B-25 bombers, deploying them in 1943 to replace aircraft like the Douglas Bostons, Lockheed Venturas, and Vickers Wellingtons. On January 22, 1943, the Mitchell officially entered active RAF service, initially conducting bombing missions over occupied Europe. After D-Day, the RAF and French Air Force used Mitchells to support Allied operations, moving squadrons to forward bases in Europe. The United States Army Air Forces also flew B-25 Mitchells in combat missions across Europe during World War II.

On January 22, 1943, six aircraft from No. 180 Squadron RAF utilized the Mitchell II for the inaugural RAF operation, attacking oil installations in Ghent. After the European invasion, during which 2 Group joined the Second Tactical Air Force, the four Mitchell squadrons relocated from bases in France and Belgium to support Allied ground forces. In April 1945, No. 342 (Lorraine) Squadron of the French Air Force augmented the British Mitchell squadrons.

Beyond No. 2 Group, the B-25 was also utilized by various secondary RAF units both within the United Kingdom and overseas. When No. 305 (Polish) Squadron transitioned from Bomber Command, it operated Mitchell IIs from September to December 1943 before switching to the de Havilland Mosquito.

The Royal Netherlands Historical Flight made a memorable debut at the 2016 Bournemouth Air Festival when they flew their B25 Mitchell bomber. With its distinctive sound and impressive aerial agility, the remarkable aircraft captivated audiences as the skilled Dutch crew demonstrated their flying expertise.

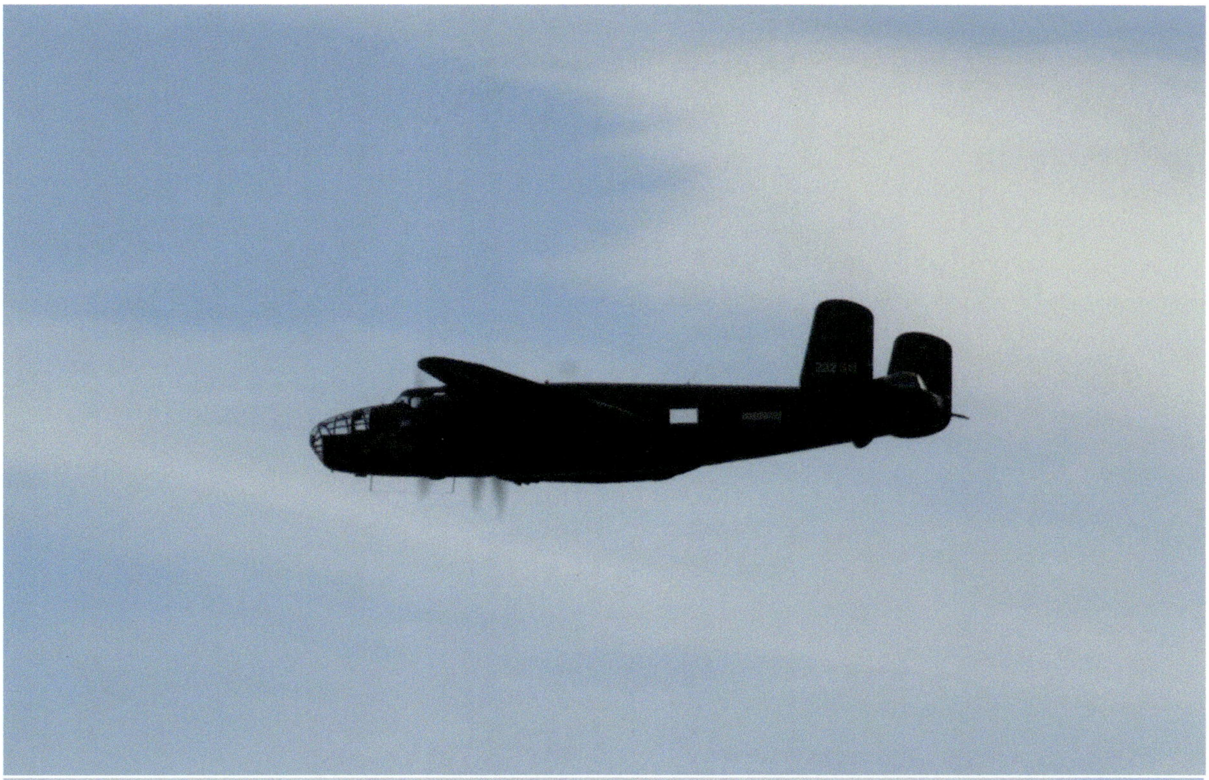

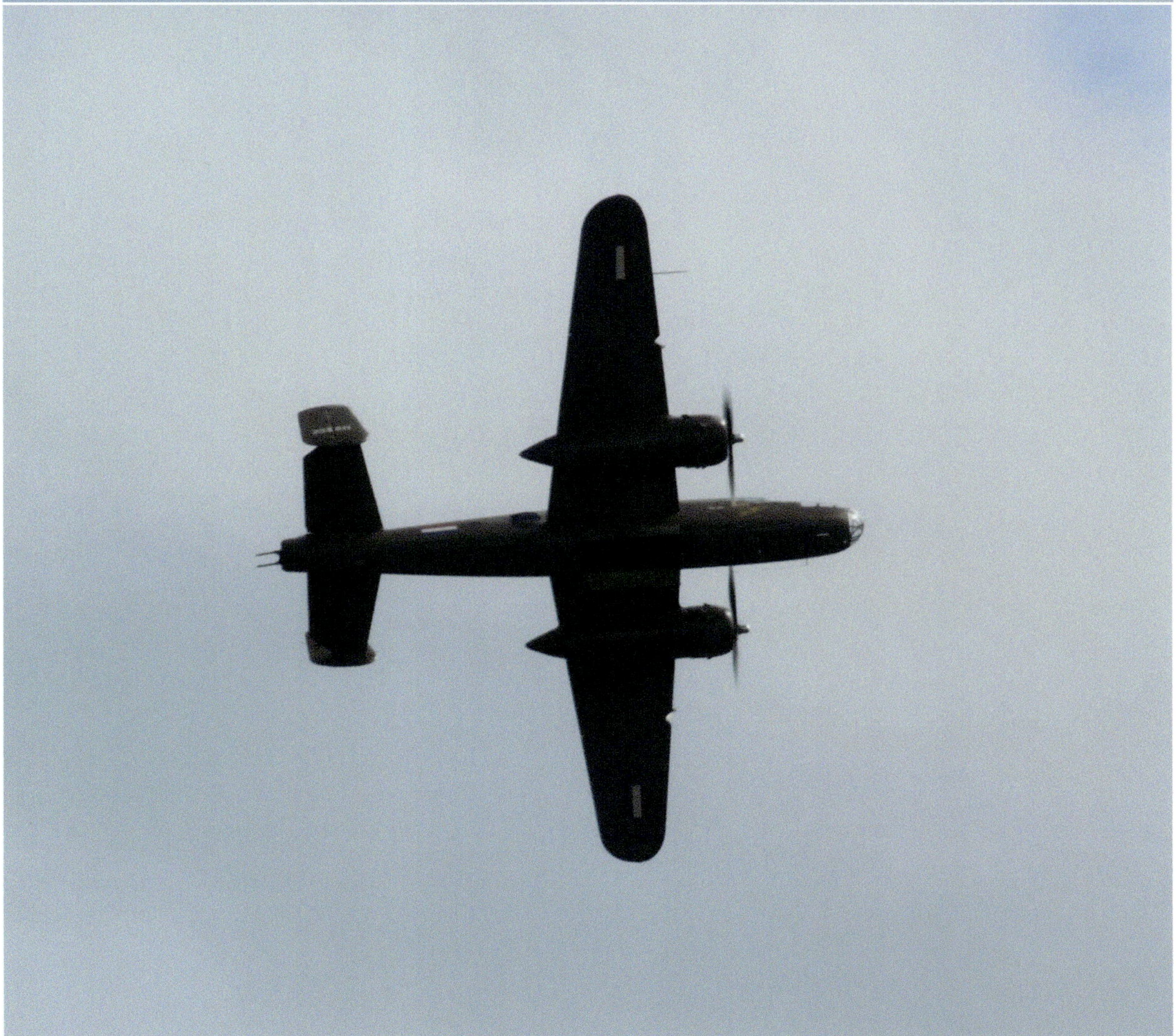

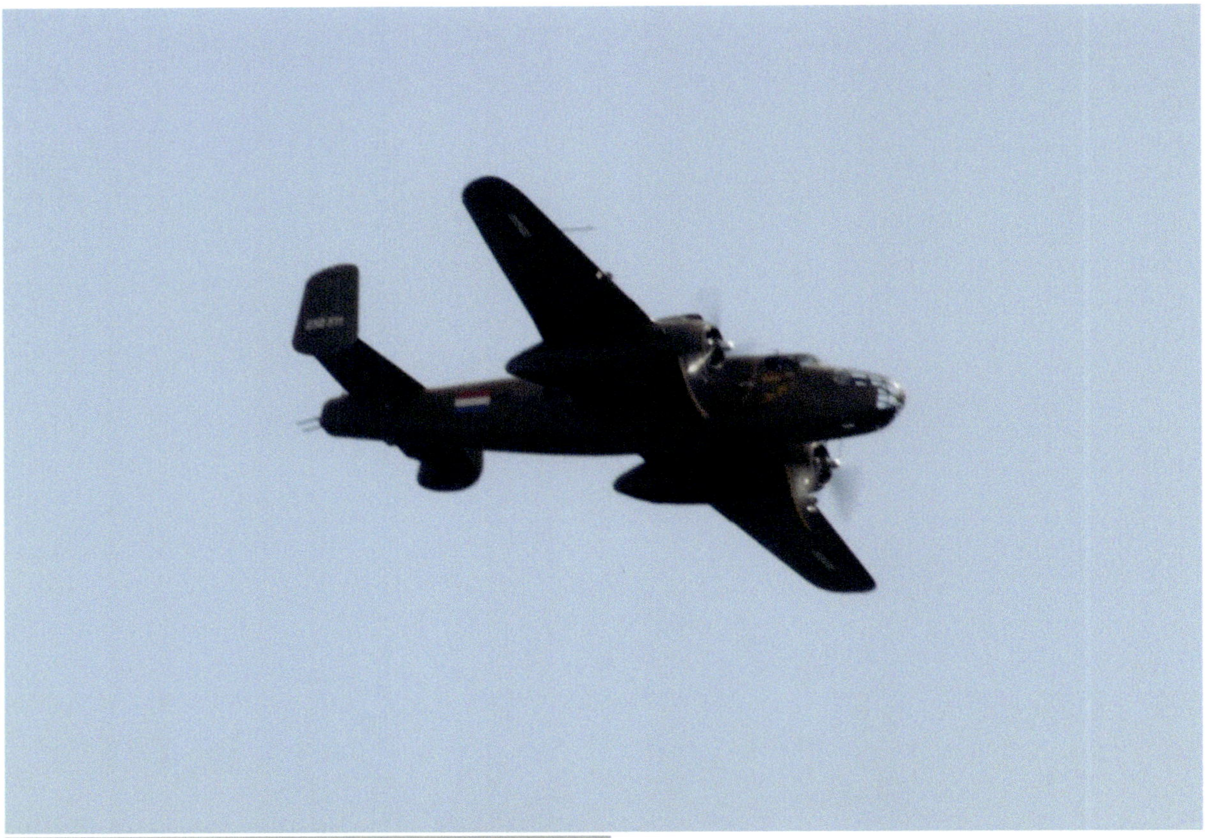

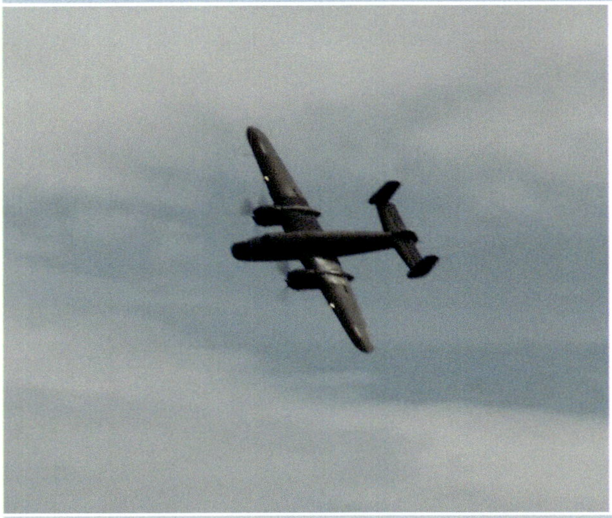

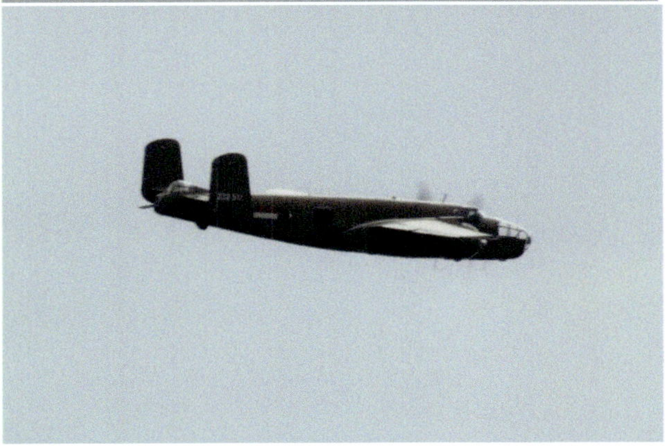

Quick Facts

General

Crew: 5 (one pilot, navigator/bombardier, turret gunner/engineer, radio operator/waist gunner, tail gunner)

Length: 52 ft 11 in (16.13 m)

Wingspan: 67 ft 7 in (20.60 m)

Height: 16 ft 4 in (4.98 m)

Performance

Maximum speed: 272 mph

Cruise speed: 230 mph

Range: 1,350 mi

Armament

Guns: 12–18 × .50 in (12.7 mm) machine guns and 75 mm (2.95 in) T13E1 cannon

Hardpoints: 2,000 lb (900 kg) ventral shackles

Bombs: 3,000 lb (1,360 kg) bombs

Bristol Blenheim

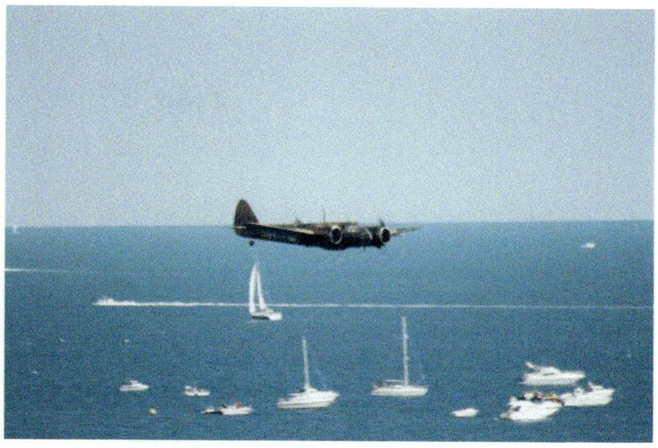

The Bristol Blenheim, a British light bomber aircraft, was designed and built by the Bristol Aeroplane Company and played a vital role in the early phases of World War II, seeing extensive service in the late 1930s and early 1940s.

Development:

The prototype of the Bristol Blenheim, a high-speed bomber designed by Frank Barnwell and his team at the Bristol Aeroplane Company to meet a specification issued by the British Air Ministry in the early 1930s, made its maiden flight on April 12, 1935.

Design and Features:

Designed for speed, the sleek and streamlined Blenheim was a twin-engine, low-wing monoplane with a three-person crew consisting of a pilot, navigator/bombardier, and radio operator/gunner.

Powerplant:

The Bristol Blenheim was a twin-engine, all-metal medium bomber aircraft with high performance capabilities. Powered by a pair of air-cooled Bristol Mercury VIII radial engines, each producing 860 horsepower, the Blenheim had controllable-pitch, three-bladed propellers on both engines. The engines featured both manual and electric starting systems.

Armament:

The aircraft was armed with a single forward-firing .303 in (7.7 mm) Browning machine gun mounted outboard of the port engine and originally a .303 in (7.7 mm) Lewis Gun in a semi-retracting dorsal turret that fired to the rear. This Lewis Gun was replaced in 1939 by the more modern .303 in (7.7 mm) Vickers VGO machine gun. The plane could carry a 1,000 lb (450 kg) bomb load in an internal bomb bay located in the fuselage's centre section.

Role in World War II:

In September 1939, the month World War II began, 11 squadrons of the RAF's Blenheim Mk I bombers were stationed overseas in places like Egypt, Aden, Iraq, India, and Singapore. At home, two more squadrons had the Mk I. Meanwhile, other RAF squadrons were transitioning to or had already received the superior Blenheim Mk IV; 168 of these updated bombers were in service when the war started.

However, as the war progressed, advances in enemy fighters exposed vulnerabilities in the Blenheim: its lack of adequate defence and armour made it susceptible to attack. While the Blenheim played a vital role early in World War II, its weaknesses led to its withdrawal from frontline duty in Western Europe by 1941. The bomber continued serving in other capacities like training and target towing until war's end.

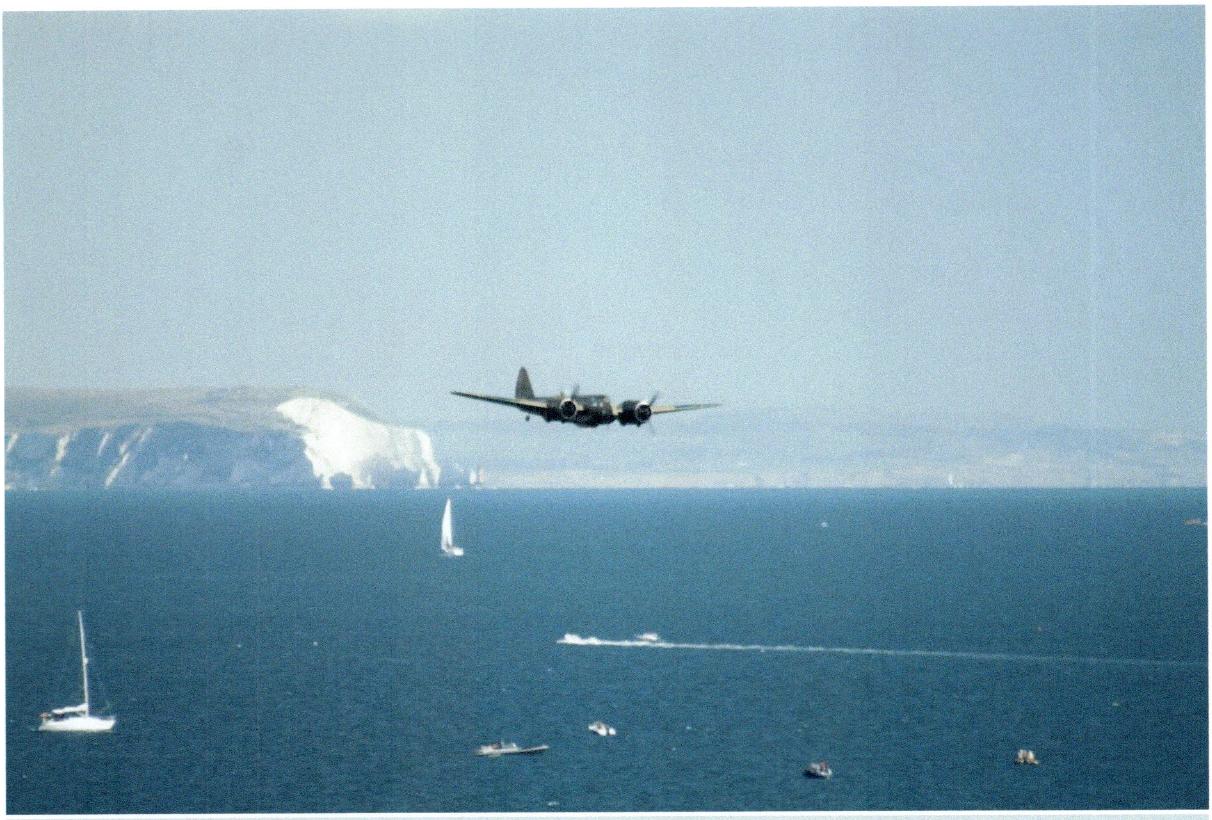

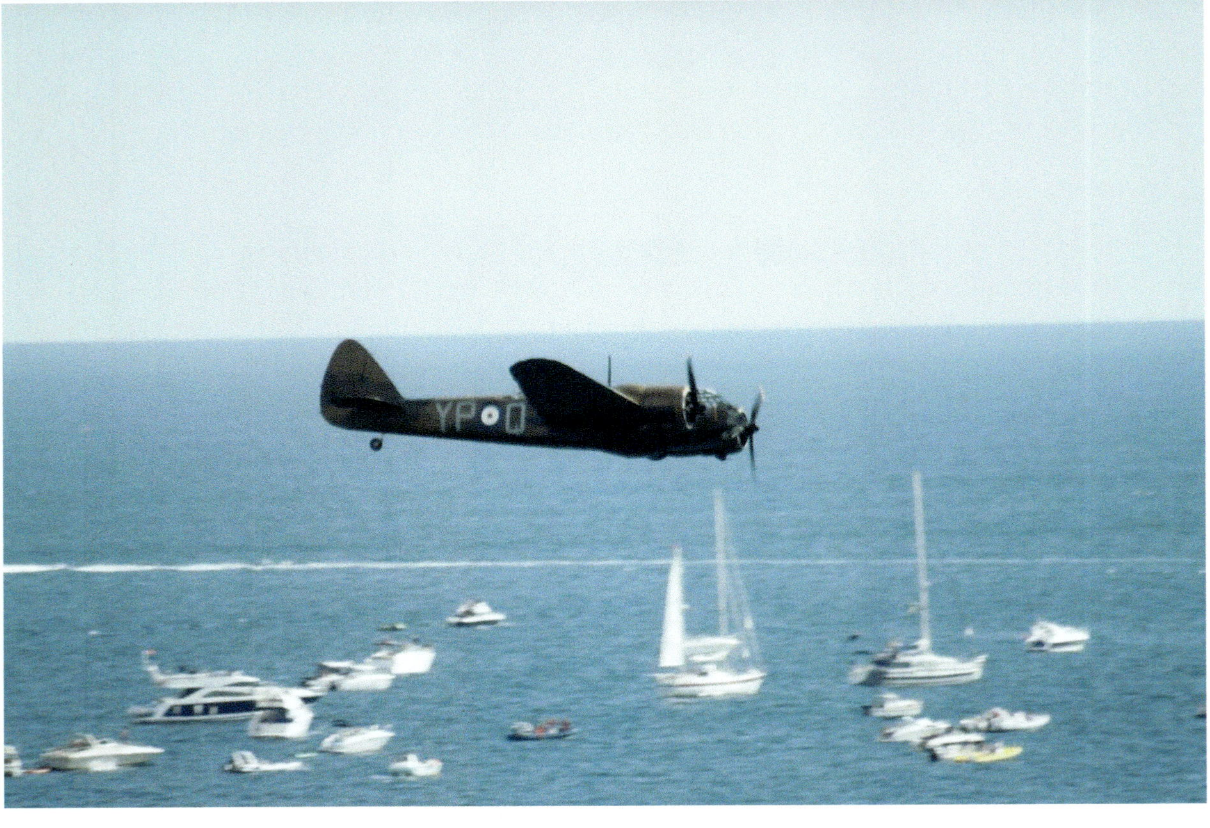
YP

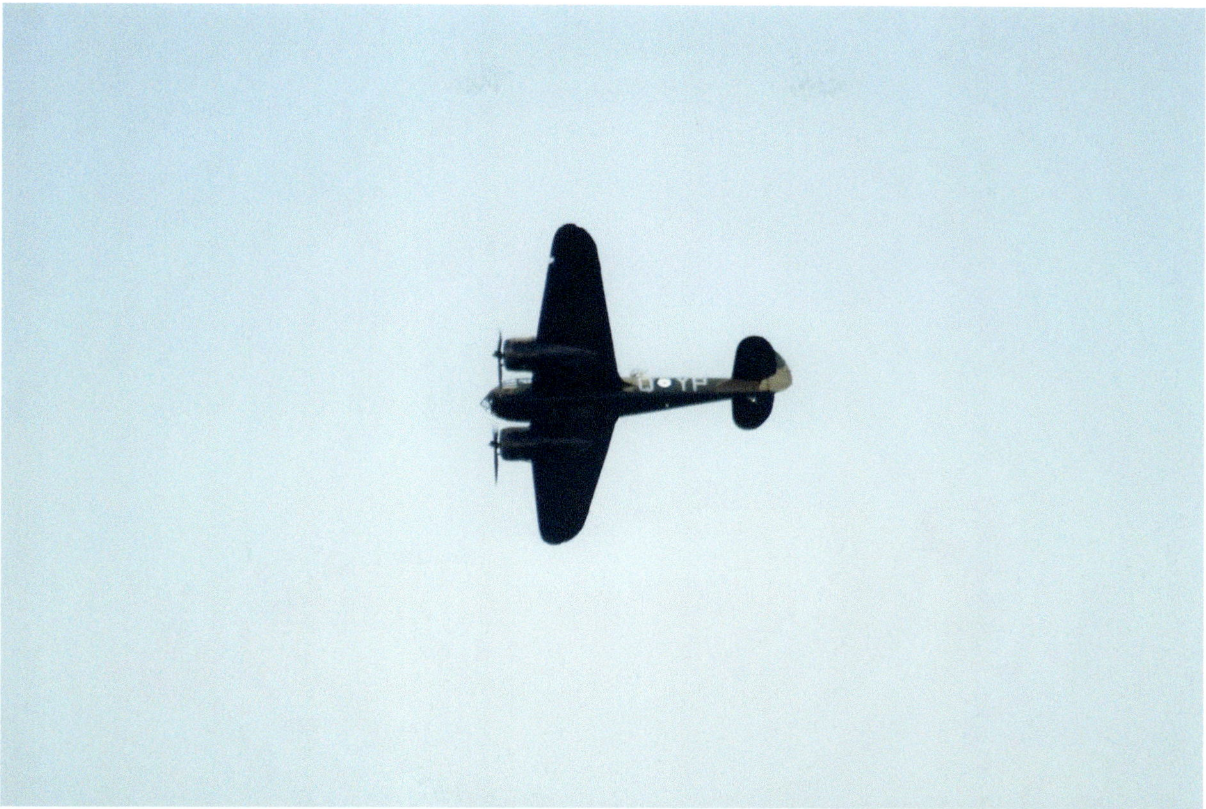

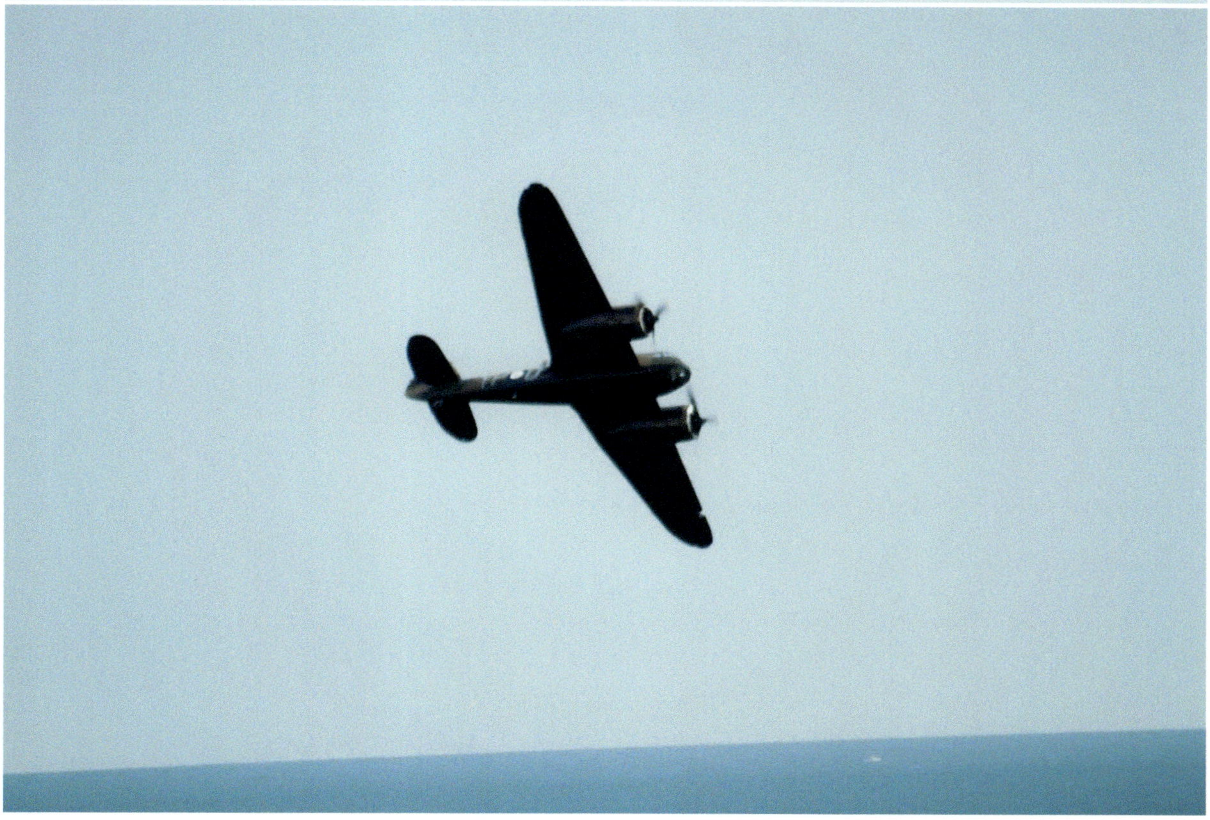

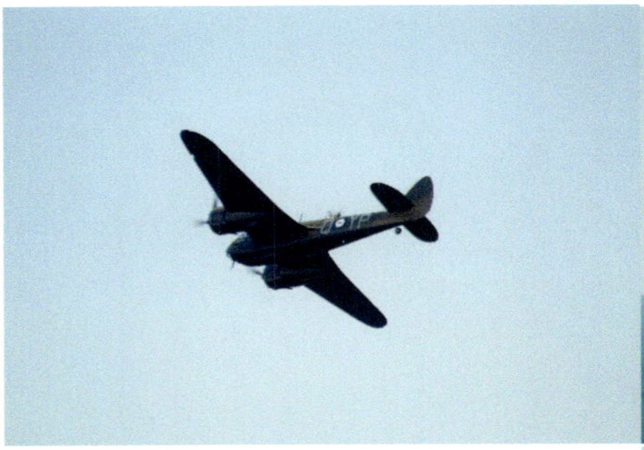
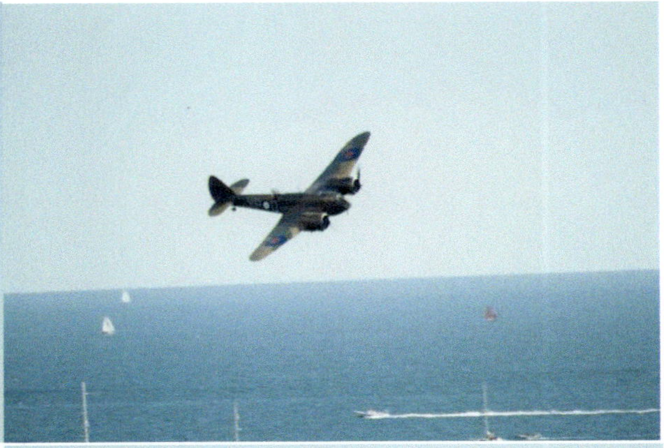
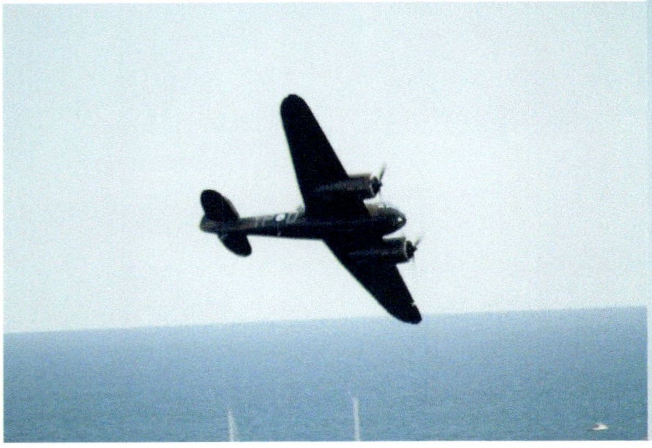
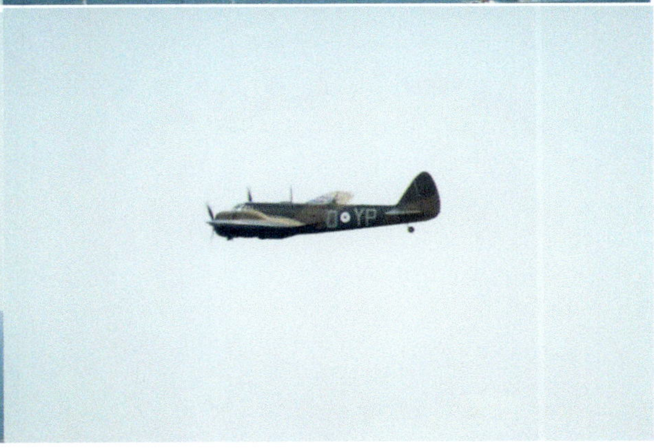

Quick Facts

Role: Light bomber, Night fighter, Aerial reconnaissance

Manufacturer: Bristol Aeroplane Company

Designer: Frank Barnwell

First flight: 12 April 1935

Introduction: 1937

Retired: 1944 (United Kingdom)1958 (Finland)

Primary users: Royal Air Force, Royal Canadian Air Force, Finnish Air Force, Royal Yugoslav Air Force

Number built: 4,422

Variants: Bristol Beaufort, Bristol Fairchild Bolingbroke

Hawker Sea Fury

Design:

The Royal Air Force initiated development of the Sea Fury in 1943 to meet wartime requirements, originally naming the aircraft simply Fury. However, as the Second World War neared its end, the RAF cancelled their order. The Royal Navy then took interest in the Sea Fury as a replacement for the obsolete and stop-gap aircraft being used by the Fleet Air Arm. Despite the RAF cancellation, development continued, and the Sea Fury entered operational service with the Royal Navy in 1947.

The Sea Fury originated from the venerable Hawker Fury, a land-based fighter plane. However, it was modified with distinct adaptations to meet the demands of naval aviation, including ingeniously engineered folding wings that enabled it to efficiently share the confined deck space of aircraft carriers. These adaptations highlighted the Sea Fury's versatility and were key to its success as a naval fighter aircraft.

The Hawker Sea Fury was an evolutionary successor to the successful Hawker Typhoon and Tempest fighters and fighter-bombers of World War II. Its fuselage closely resembled the Tempest but was fully monocoque, and the elevated cockpit gave the pilot superior all-around visibility.

Power and Precision:

The Bristol Centaurus XVI radial engine, a 2,500 horsepower technological marvel, propelled the Sea Fury fighter to unparalleled speeds and endowed it with a thunderous presence. Generating immense power, this engine enabled the Sea Fury to reach top speeds approaching 460 mph, making it one of the fastest piston-engine fighters of its era.

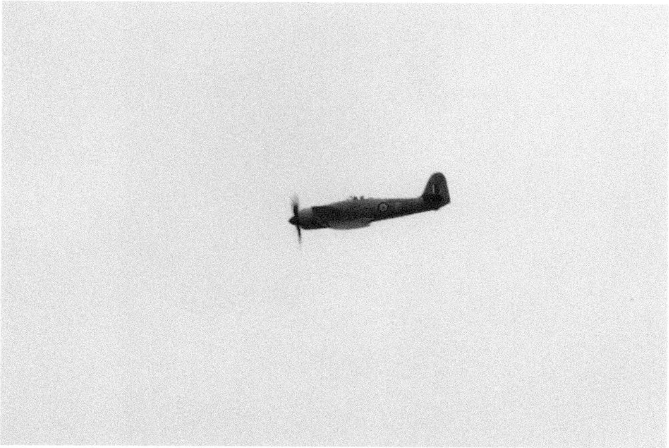

In pursuit of excellence, a Sea Fury etched its name into aviation history books on November 21, 1951, when a modified version broke the world airspeed record for piston-engine aircraft by streaking across the sky at the breathtaking speed of 805.04 km/h (499.04 mph).

Operational History:

In February 1947, 778 Naval Air Squadron became the first unit of the Fleet Air Arm to receive the Sea Fury fighter aircraft, with deliveries going to the squadron's Intensive Flying Development Unit. 787 Squadron, the Naval Air Fighting Development Squadron, later received Sea Furies in May of that year.

The Fleet Air Arm issued Sea Furies to Squadrons 736, 738, 759 and 778. The Sea Fury FB.11, a fighter-bomber variant, followed the F Mk X and eventually 650 aircraft were produced. Until 1953, the Sea Fury remained the primary fighter-bomber for the Fleet Air Arm.

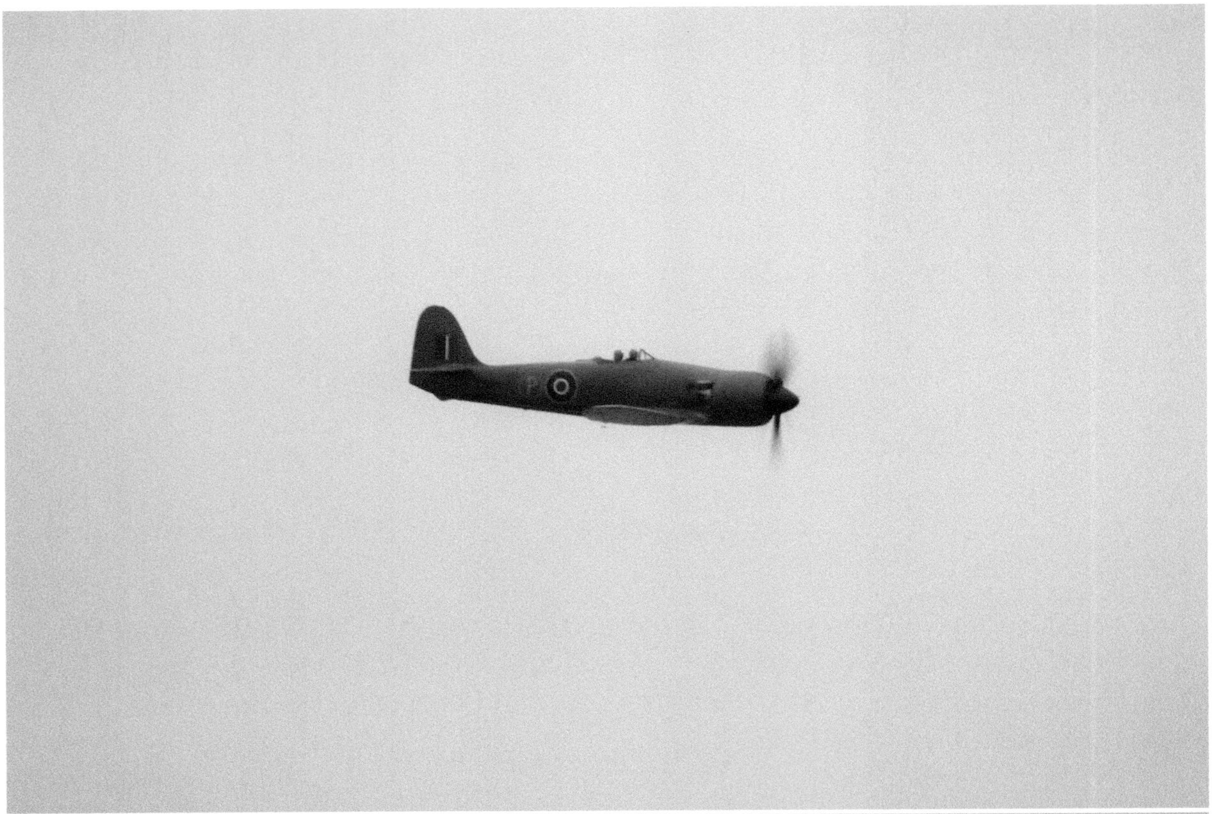

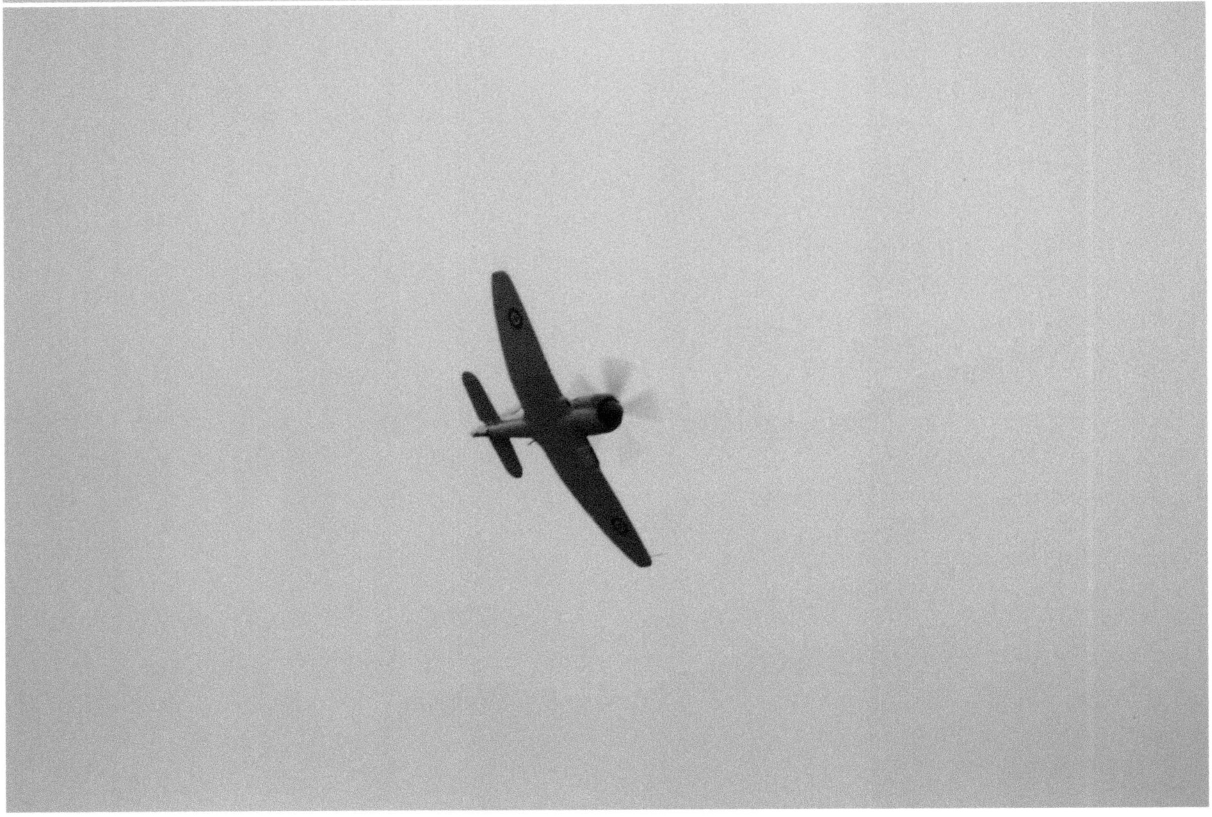

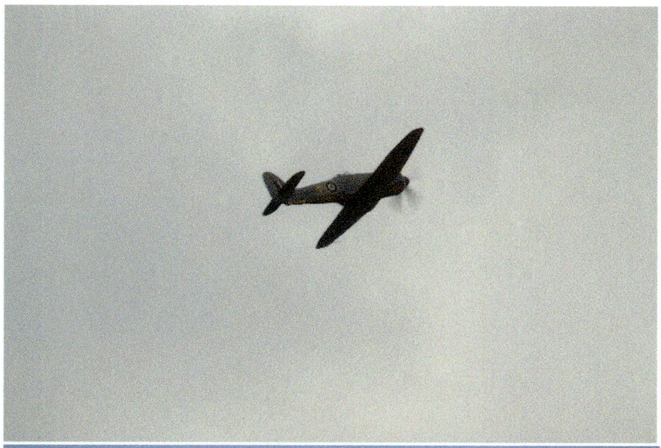

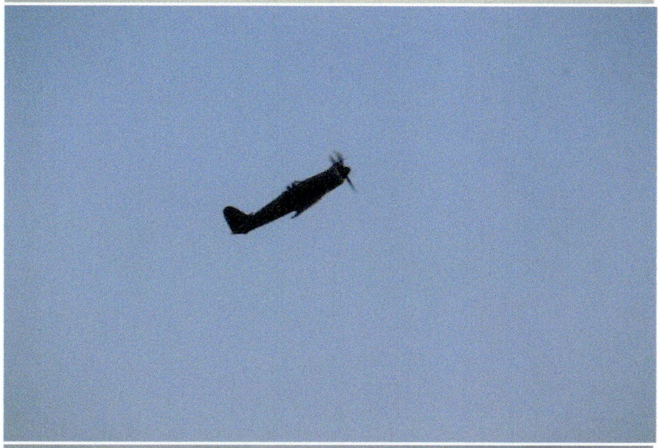

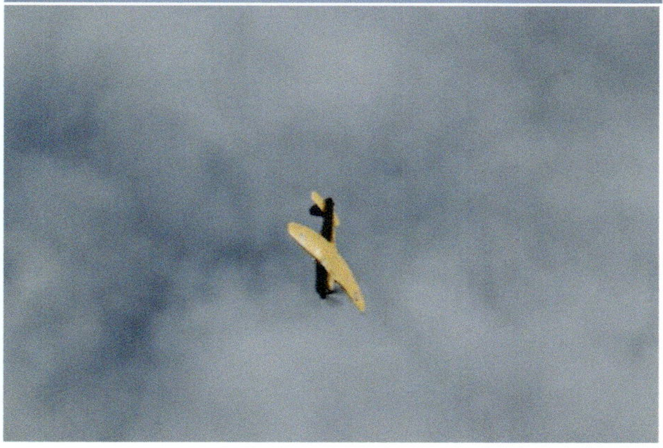

Quick Facts

General Details

Crew: 1

Length: 34 ft 8 in (10.57 m)

Wingspan: 38 ft 4.75 in (11.7031 m)

Height: 15 ft 10.5 in (4.839 m)

Powerplant: 1 × Bristol Centaurus 18 18-cylinder air-cooled radial piston engine, 2,480 hp (1,850 kW) for take-off

Propellers: 5-bladed constant-speed propeller

Performance

Maximum speed: 460 mph (740 km/h, 400 kn) at 18,000 ft (5,500 m)

Range: 780 mi (1,260 km, 680 nmi)

Ferry range: 904 mi (1,455 km, 786 nmi) with two drop tanks

Armament

Guns: 4 × 20 mm (0.79 in) Hispano Mk V autocannon

Rockets: Up to 16 × 3 inch rockets

Bombs: 2,000 lb (910 kg) of bombs

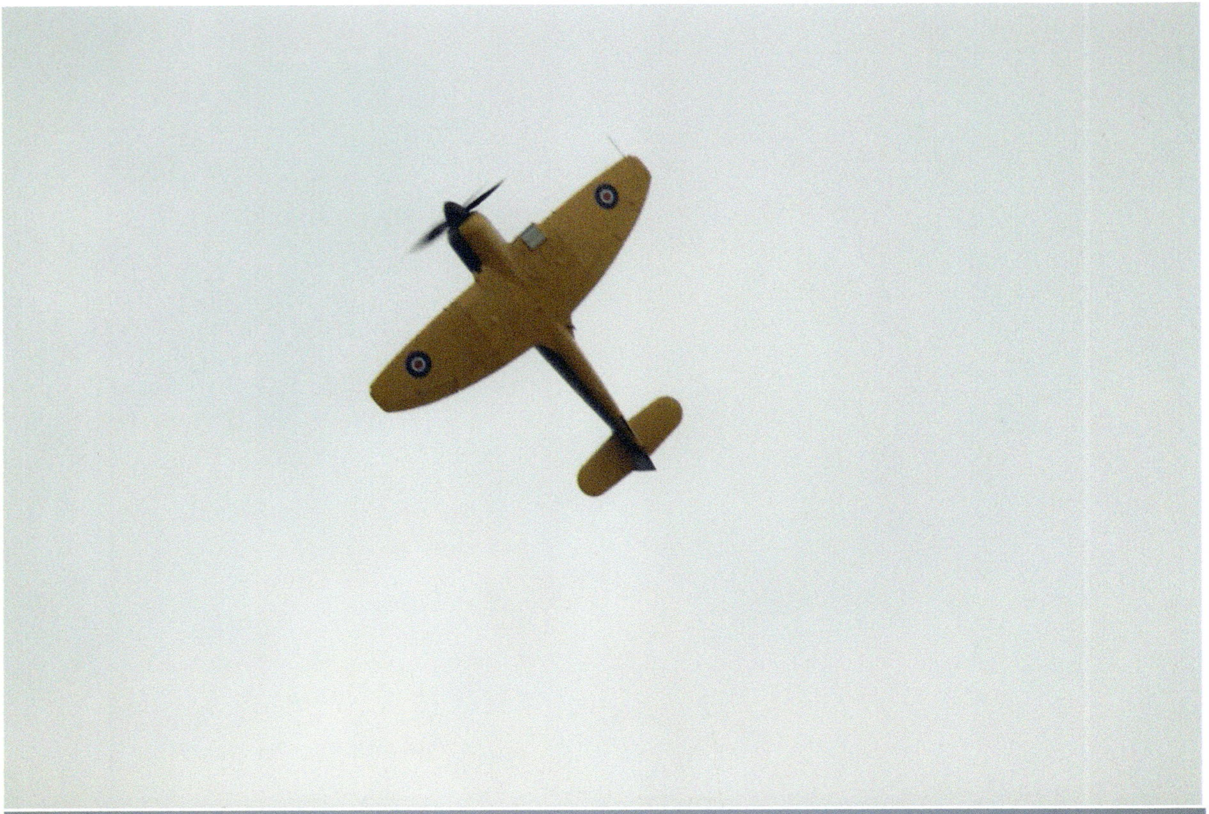

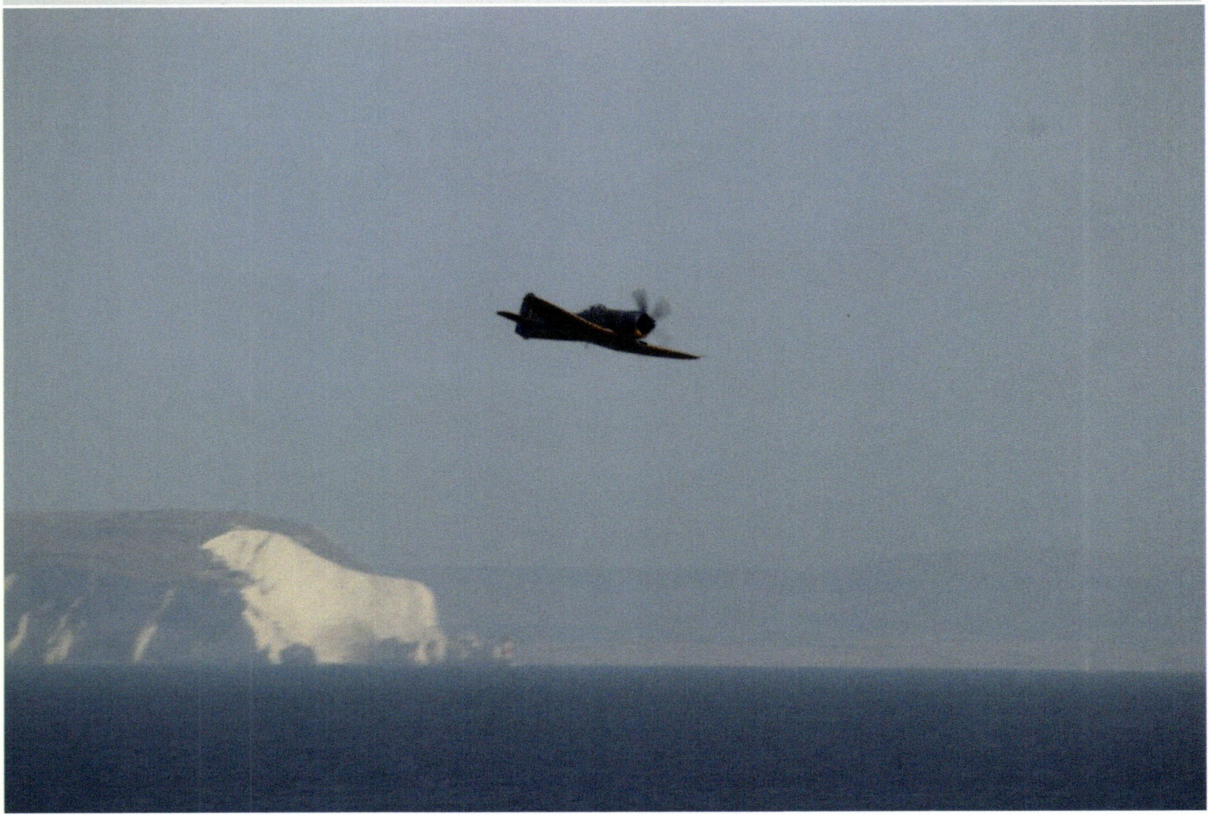

Fixed Wing and Display Teams

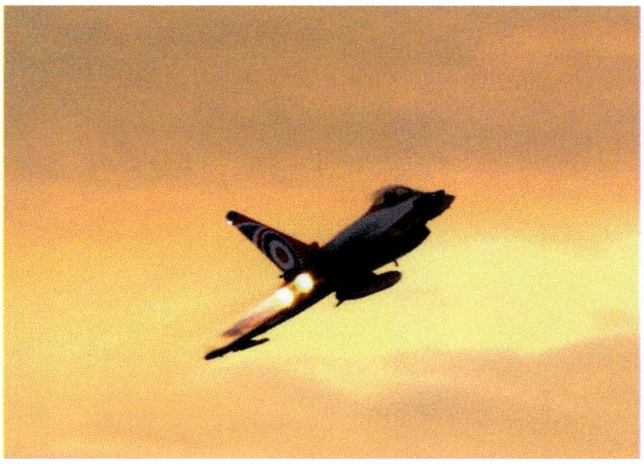

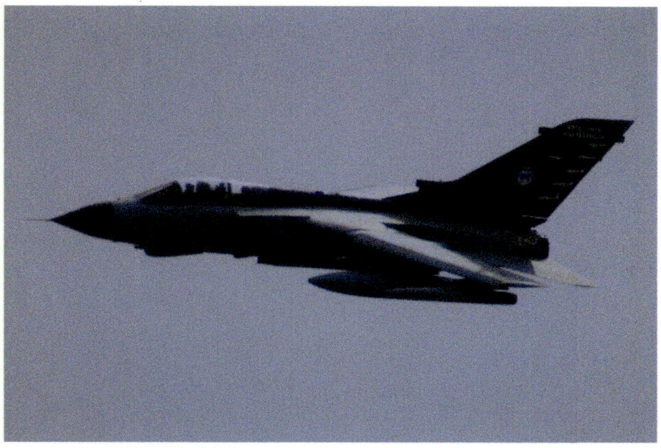

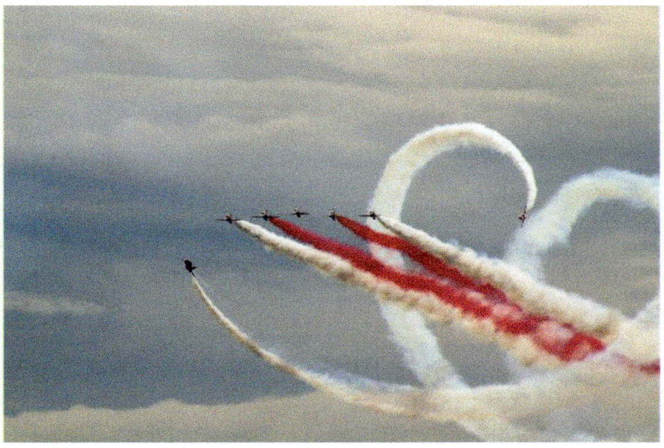

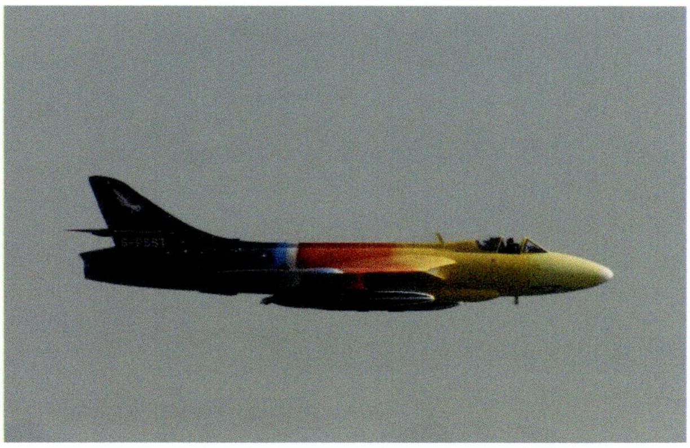

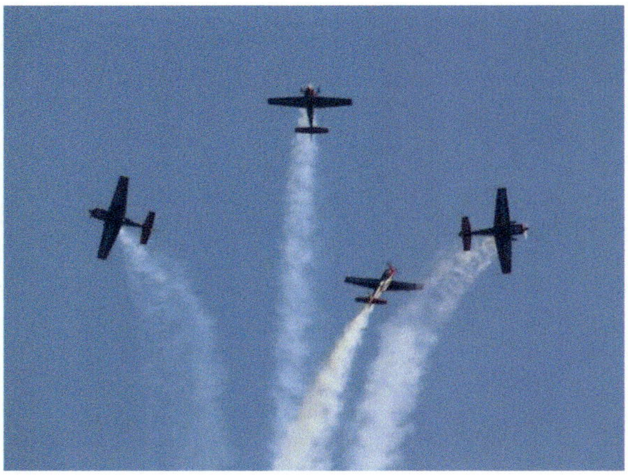

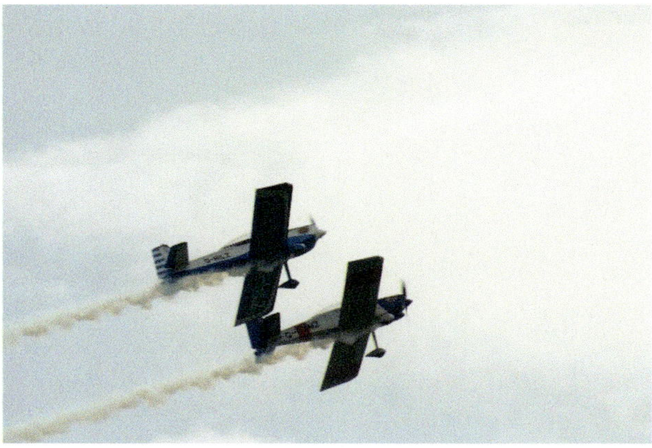

Grob Tutor

The Grob Tutor has been in service with the Royal Air Force since 2001 as part of the UK Military Flying Training System. This tandem-seat, low-wing monoplane is a basic training aircraft designed for effective communication between instructor and student during elementary flying training, featuring side-by-side seating.

The Tutor has a composite airframe and fixed tricycle landing gear and is powered by a single Lycoming AEIO-540-D4A5 piston engine. With a cruising speed of around 120 knots and a service ceiling of 19,000 feet, the Tutor's 3.5 hour endurance enables training in manoeuvres, instrument flight, navigation, and basic aerobatics.

The Tutor plays an essential role in the RAF's training program by providing pilot training to university students in University Air Squadrons and flying experiences to cadets in Air Experience Flights. Known for its sustainability and cost-effectiveness, the Tutor introduces aspiring aviators to the fundamentals of flying before they advance to more complex aircraft, making it a cornerstone of early aviation training.

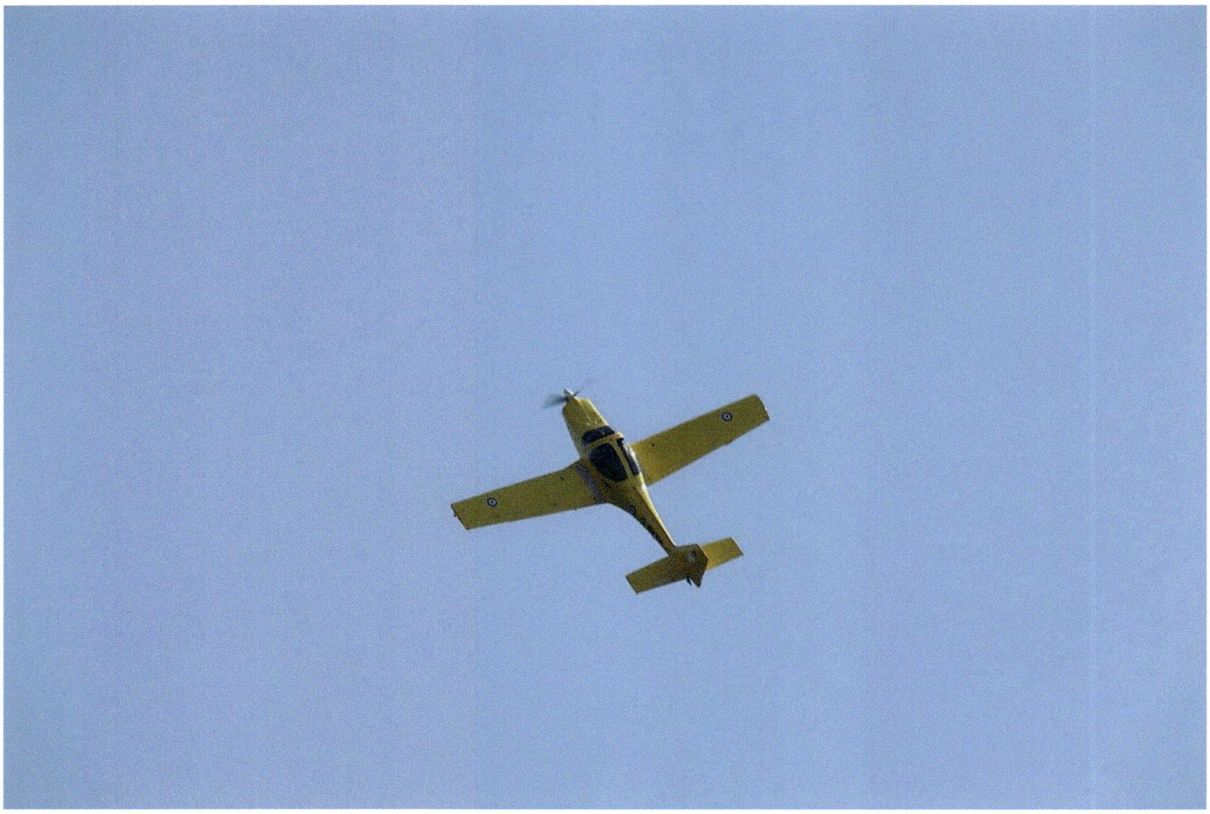

The RAF Tutor Display Team is a specialised aerobatic unit within the Royal Air Force that showcases the capabilities of the Grob Tutor training aircraft. The team performs precision aerial manoeuvres and formations, including loops, rolls, spins, and low passes, at Air Festivals like the one held in Bournemouth. Their carefully choreographed routine demonstrates the Tutor's agility and dynamic performance while adhering to strict safety standards.

Formation and Purpose:

The RAF Tutor Display Team was established to promote the RAF and its training program by performing exhilarating aerobatic displays for the public, demonstrating the agility, precision, and handling of the Tutor aircraft. Consisting of highly-skilled RAF instructors with specialised aerobatic training, the team's pilots are chosen for their instructional flying proficiency, aerobatic abilities, and public engagement skills.

Airshow Performances:

The team performs in airshows at home and abroad, giving spectators a firsthand look at the RAF's training and its pilots' prowess. These exhilarating displays promote public engagement and recruitment by sparking interest in aviation and the RAF.

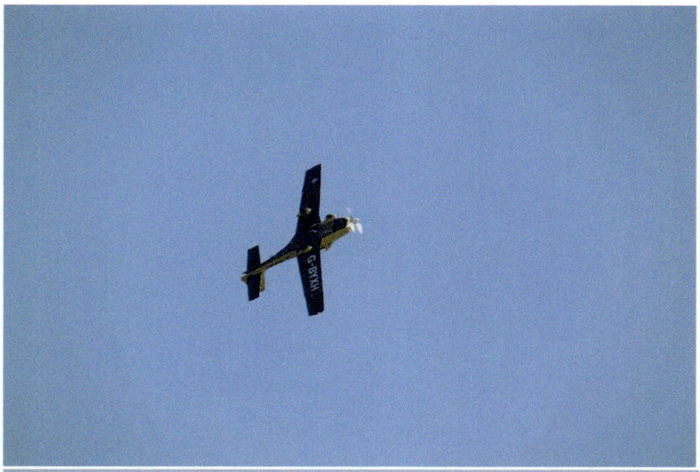

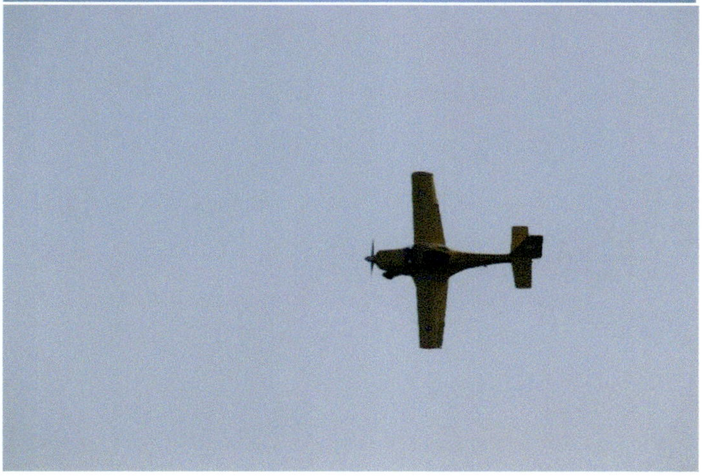

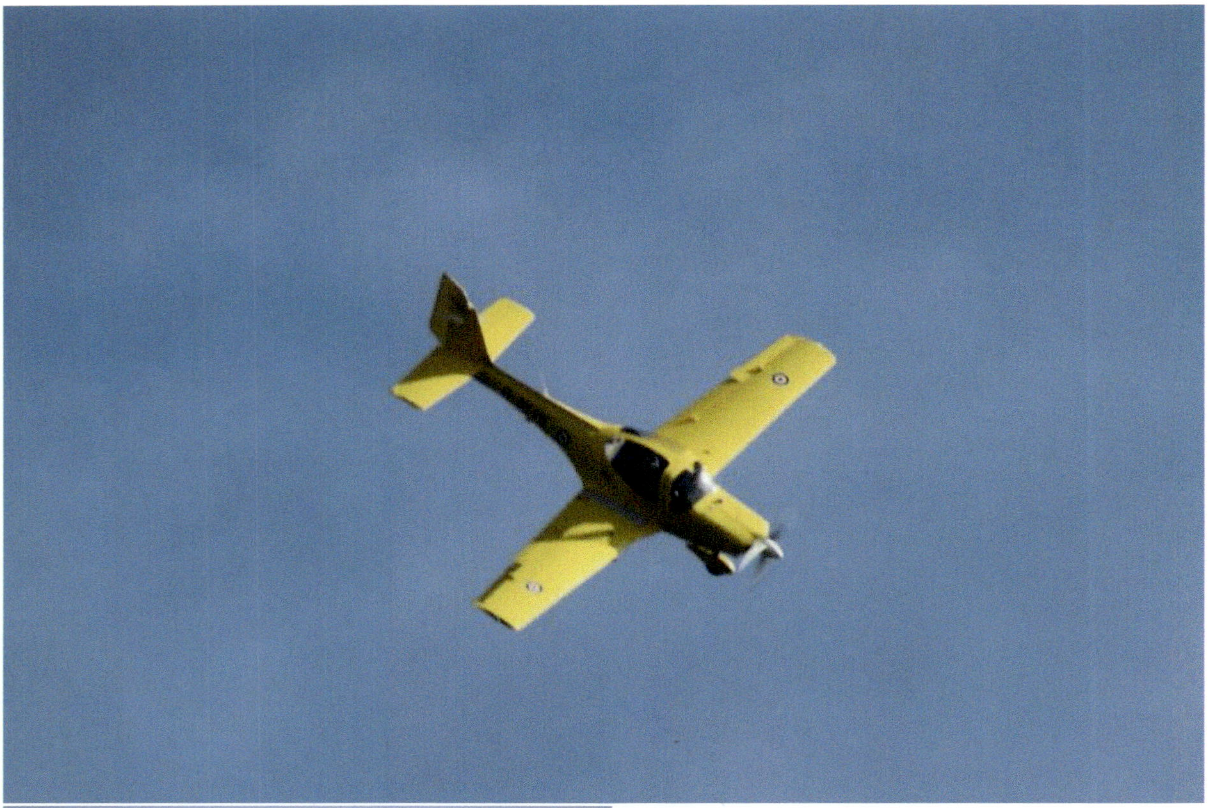

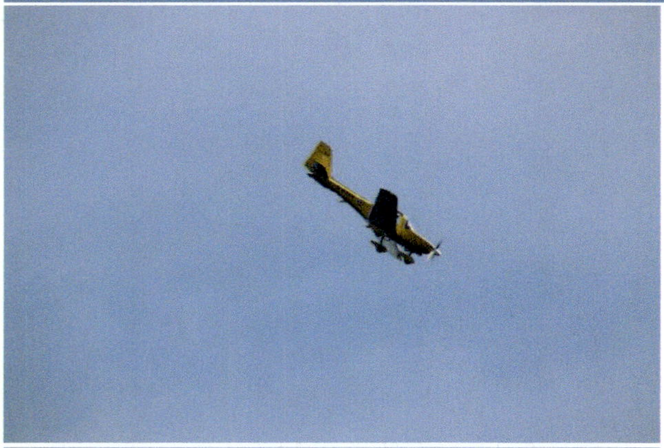

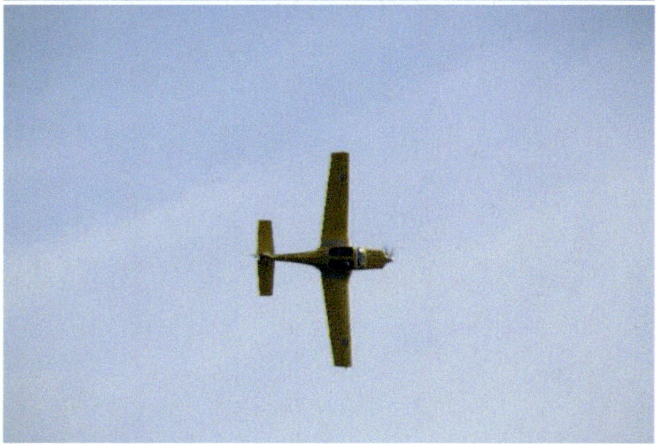

Quick Facts

Length: 7.79 m (25 ft 7 in)

Wingspan: 10.00 m (32 ft 10 in)

Empty weight: 670 kg (1,477 lb)

Max take-off weight: 990 kg (2,183 lb)

Fuel capacity: 143 L (31 imp gal; 38 US gal)

Powerplant: 1 × Lycoming AEIO-360-B1F/B 4-cylinder air-cooled horizontally opposed piston engine, 130 kW (180 hp)

Maximum speed: 250 km/h (160 mph, 130 kn)

Cruise speed: 178 km/h (111 mph, 96 kn)

Stall speed: 91 km/h (57 mph, 49 kn)

Range: 1,150 km (710 mi, 620 nmi)

Service ceiling: 6,095 m (20,000 ft)

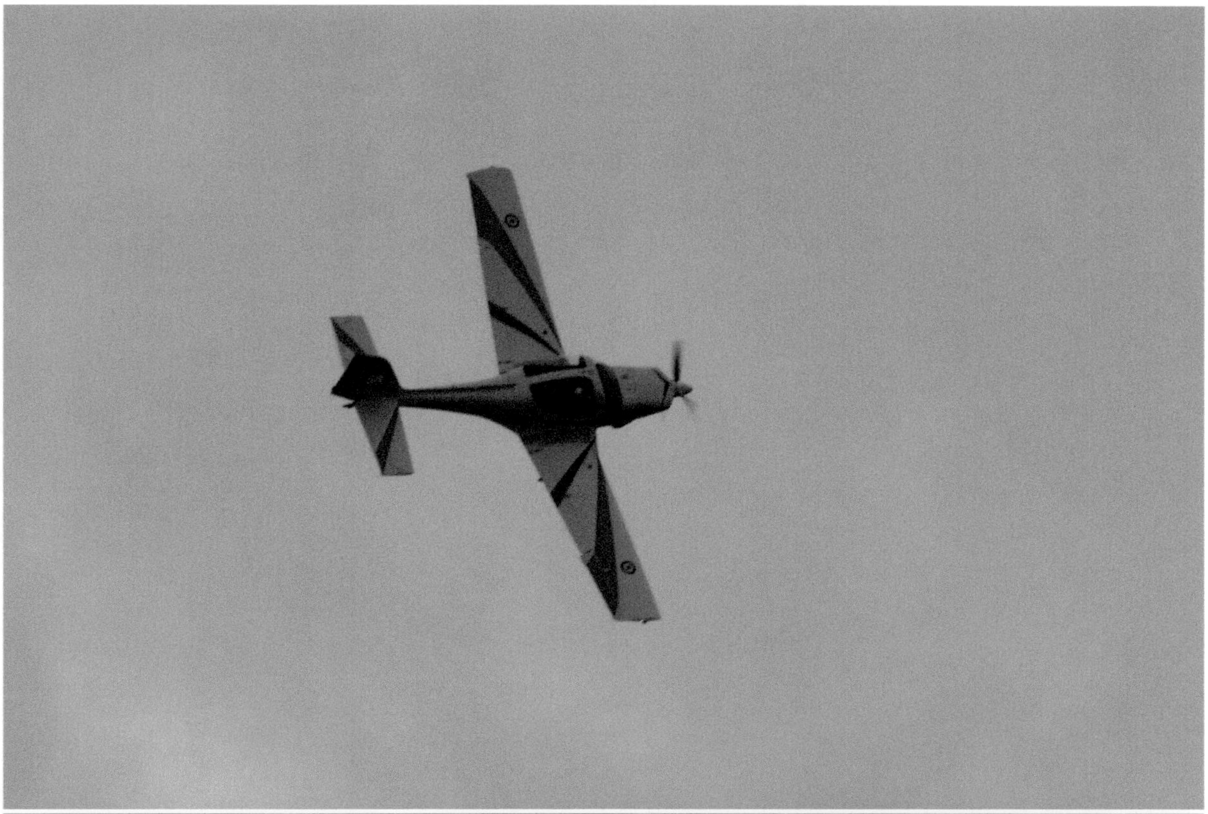

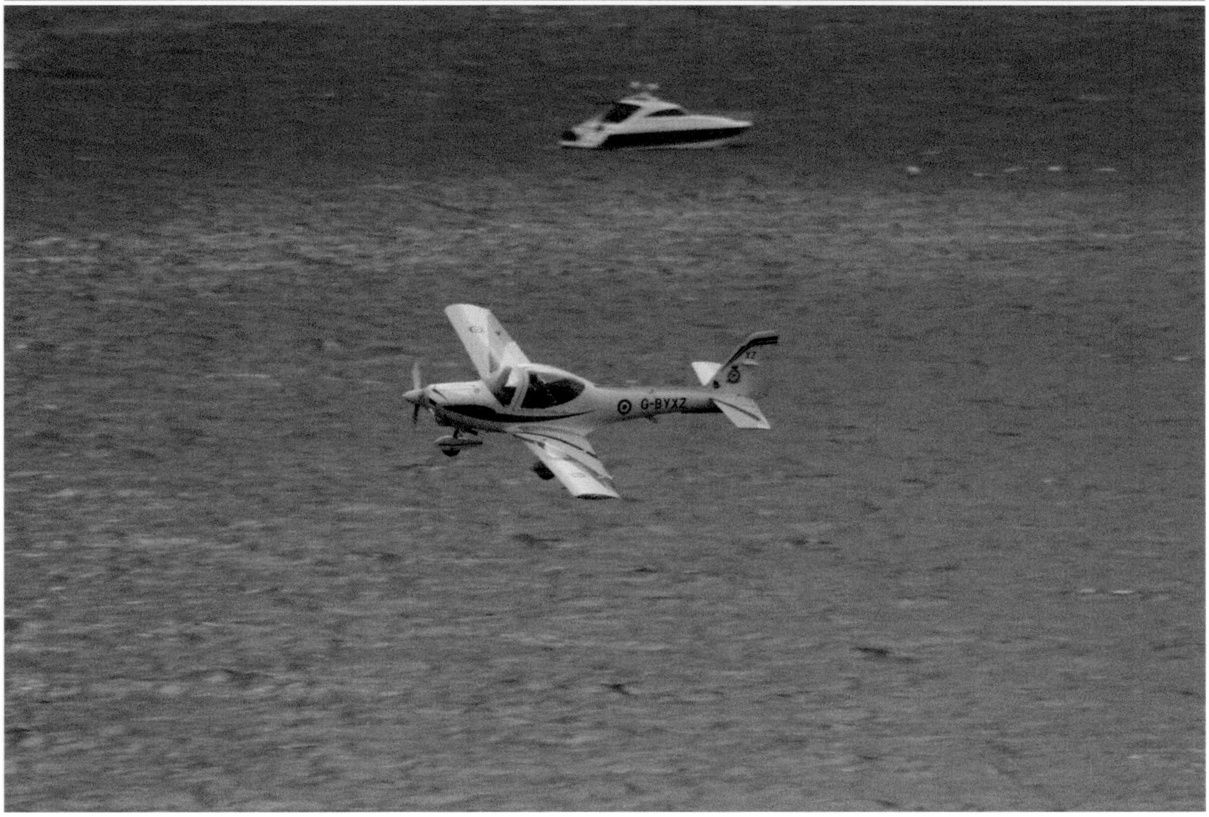
G-BYXZ

Short Tucano T1

The Short Tucano is a two-seat turboprop basic trainer originally designed by Embraer in Brazil. Short Brothers in Belfast, Northern Ireland, produced the aircraft under license as the Short Tucano. The prototype first flew in Brazil on February 14, 1986 before being delivered to Short Brothers to modify per Royal Air Force requirements. Short Brothers' first Tucano flew on December 30, 1986, and deliveries to the RAF began in June 1988, continuing through 1995 when the final example was completed.

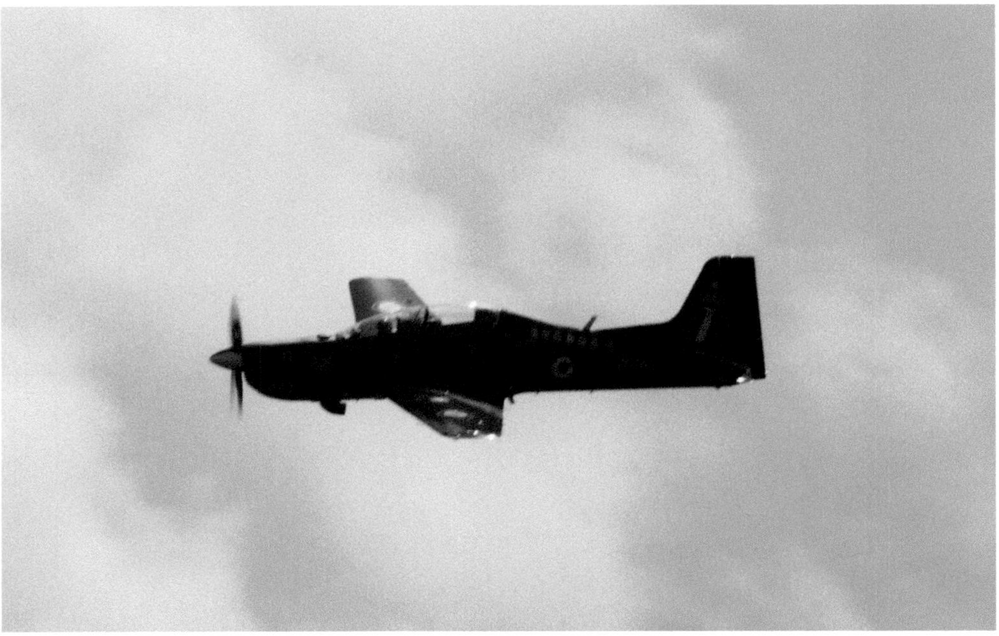

The RAF replaced the BAC Jet Provost with the Short Tucano as its basic trainer aircraft, preparing student pilots before they advanced to the Hawk T1. Upon its introduction, the Tucano proved to be about 70% cheaper to operate than the Jet Provost it succeeded.

The Tucano offered a step up in performance compared to its predecessor, featuring a turboprop engine and more modern avionics systems. This allowed trainees to experience a platform with characteristics closer to those of contemporary fast jets.

In addition to teaching basic flying skills, the Tucano trained pilots in various mission scenarios, including low-altitude flight, aerobatics, formation flying, and navigation. The aircraft also provided weapons system training.

The Tucano, used in the RAF's training program, was eventually replaced by the newer Beechcraft T-6 Texan II. This turboprop aircraft was specifically designed for primary and basic flight training.

Serving the RAF for years, the Tucano has made major contributions to the training and growth of generations of fast jet pilots, equipping them with the vital skills for flying sophisticated fighter and strike aircraft in the Royal Air Force.

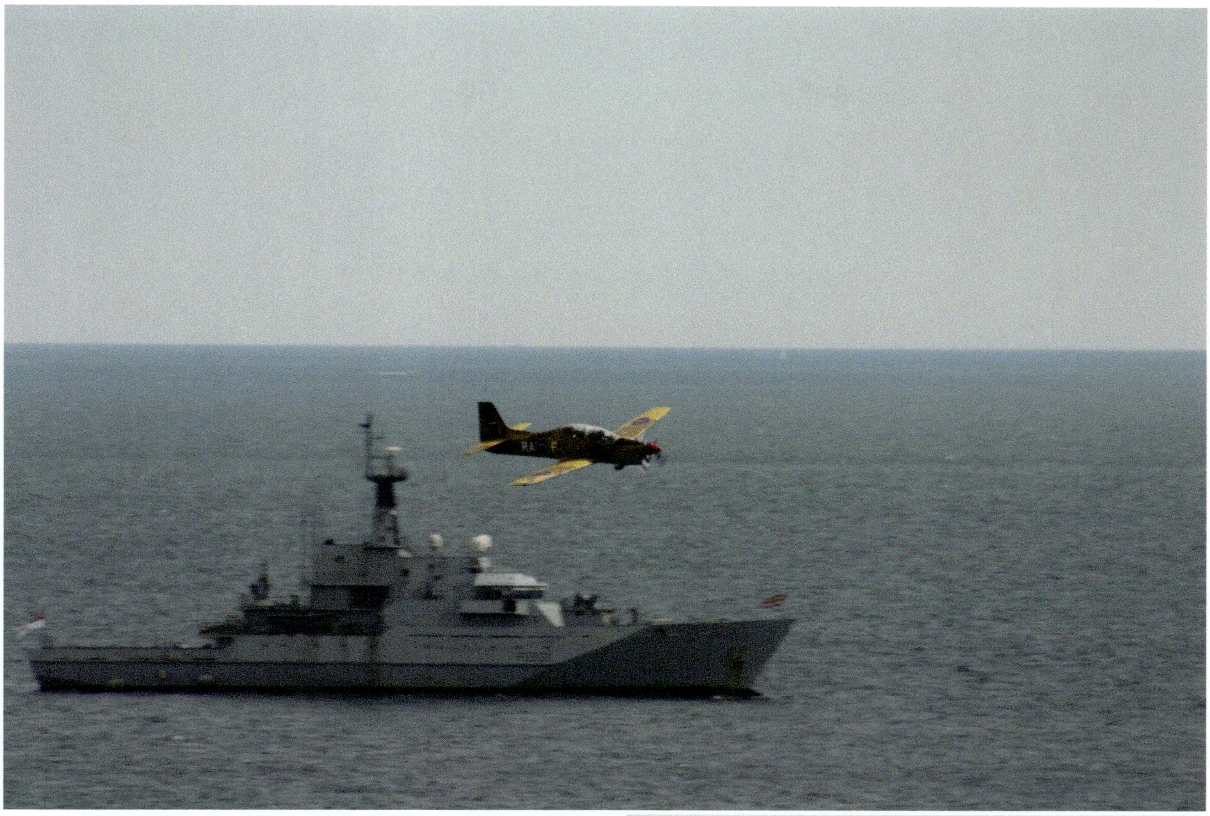

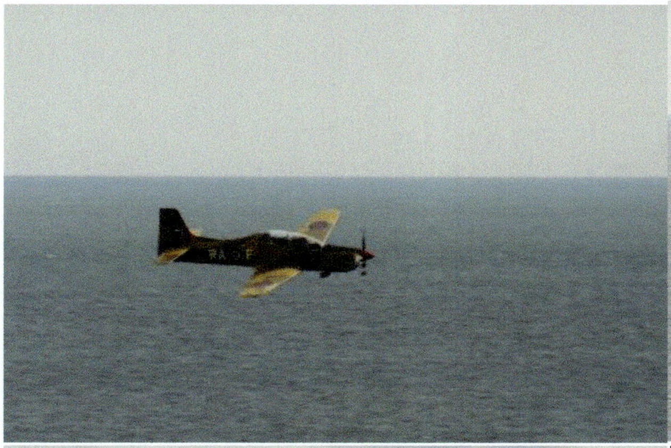

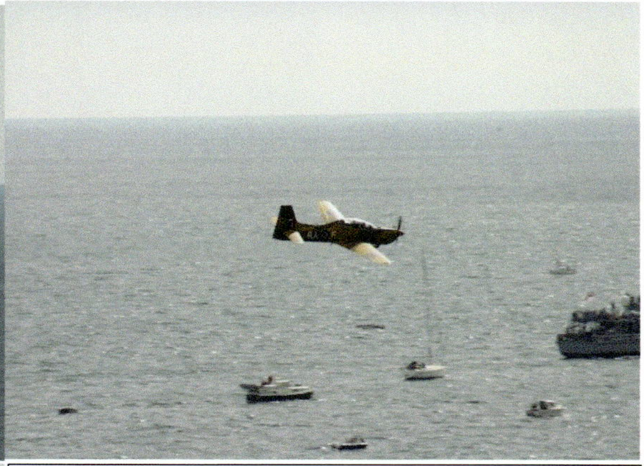

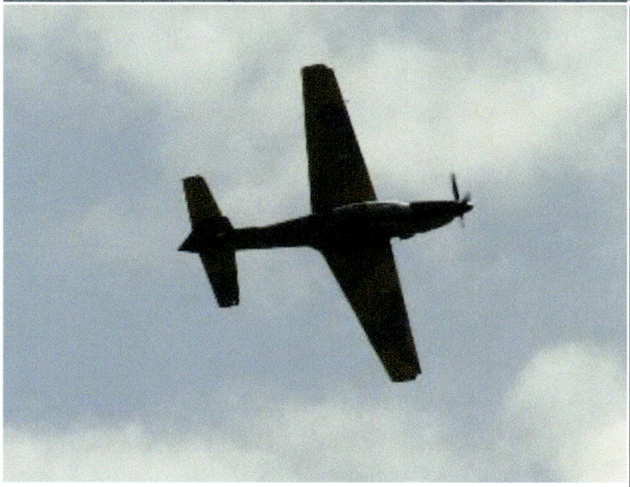

Quick Facts

Role: Trainer aircraft

National origin: United Kingdom

Manufacturer: Short Brothers

First flight: 14 February 1986

Introduction: 1989

Retired: 2019 (Royal Air Force)

Produced: 1986–1995

Number built: 160

BAE Systems Hawk

The BAE Systems Hawk is a British single-engine, jet-powered aircraft initially produced by Hawker Siddeley and subsequently by British Aerospace and BAE Systems. It serves primarily as an advanced trainer aircraft but has also been used as a low-cost combat jet.

The Hawk jet trainer was developed in the 1960s by British Aircraft Corporation, now known as BAE Systems, in response to various air forces' need for a modern, cost-effective advanced training aircraft. The first prototype took flight in 1974, demonstrating the aircraft's capabilities for providing jet-powered training.

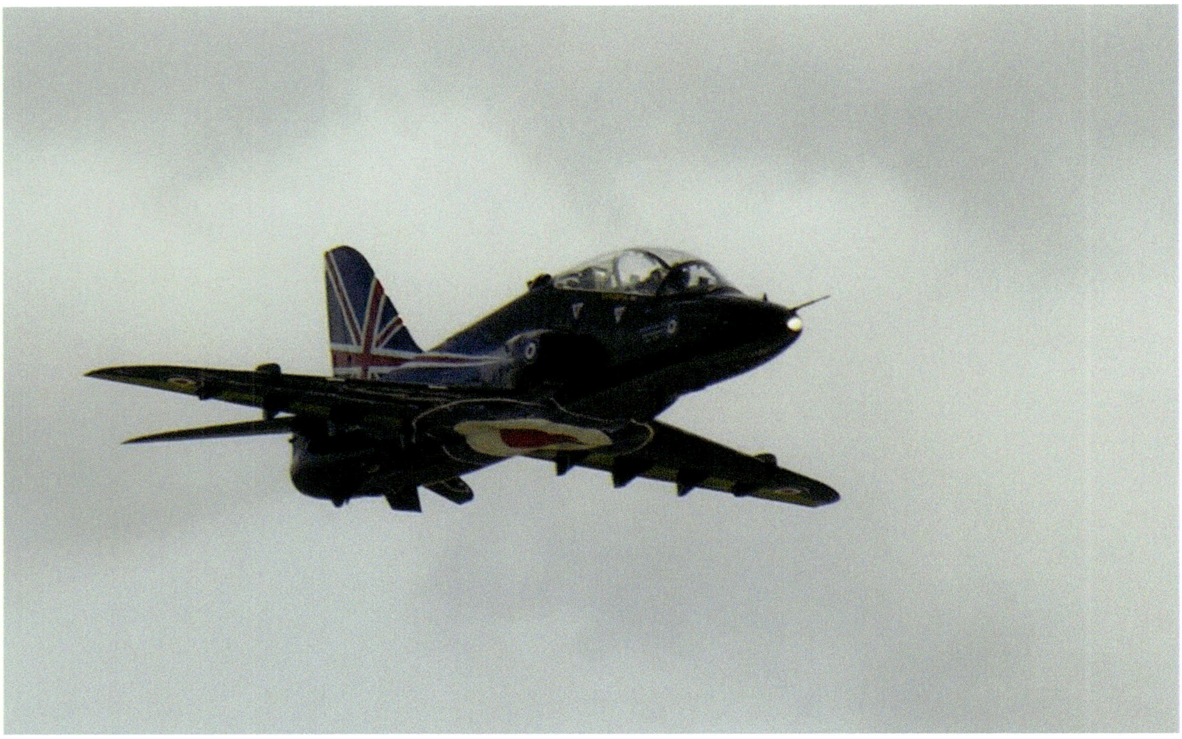

The Hawk trainer jet, designed by BAE Systems, balances agility and stability with its sleek, single-engine design. This tandem, subsonic aircraft simulates the performance of high-speed fighter jets to train pilots. Equipped with sophisticated avionics, navigation systems, and simulated weapons, the Hawk provides comprehensive training for the operational scenarios of advanced fighters. RAF Valley in Wales serves as the home base for RAF training and transitioning on the Hawk.

On 22 December 2004, the Ministry of Defence awarded BAE Systems a contract to develop an advanced Hawk model, the Mk. 128 (also called Hawk T2), for the RAF and Royal Navy. The Hawk Mk. 128 features a glass cockpit that replaces conventional instrumentation, more closely resembling modern fighter jets like the Eurofighter Typhoon, the RAF's new mainstay aircraft.

The Hawk aircraft is an ideal training platform due to its performance capabilities. It can reach supersonic speeds exceeding Mach 1, allowing it to simulate a wide range of flight conditions that prepare trainees for high-performance combat aircraft. The Hawk's aerobatic manoeuvrability and ability to mimic combat scenarios thoroughly test trainees' skills.

The Hawk became most famous after being adopted in 1979 by the Red Arrows aerobatic team, who continue to use the aircraft for flight demonstrations today.

The Bournemouth Air Festival has seen many Hawk jet displays over the years in different liveries, the most striking being the full Union Jack Hawk in 2012. The festival has also featured displays by the Hawk Demo Role team, who demonstrated ground attack manoeuvres with two Hawk aircraft.

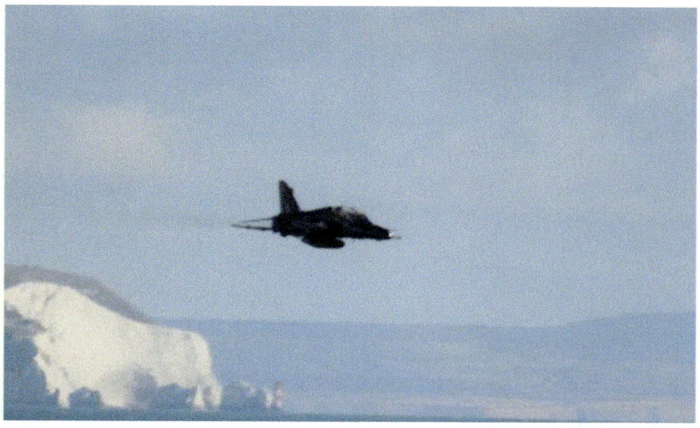

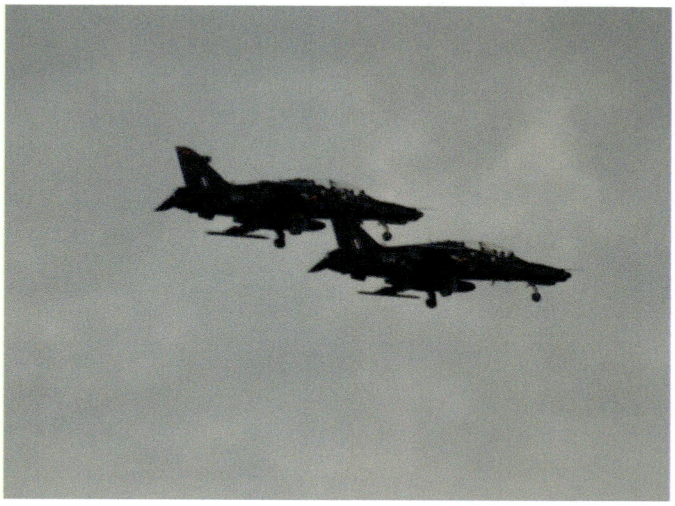

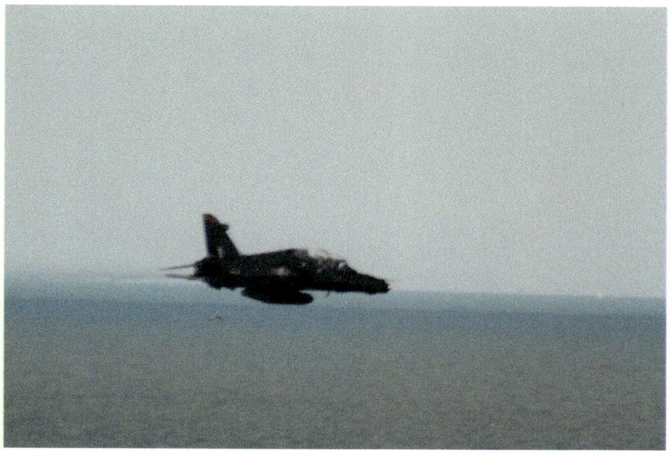

Quick Facts

General

Crew: 2: student, instructor

Lengt**h:** 12.43 m (40 ft 9 in)

Wingspan: 9.94 m (32 ft 7 in)

Height: 3.98 m (13 ft 1 in)

Wing area: 16.70 m2 (179.64 ft2)

Max take-off weight: 9,100 kg (20,000 lb)

Powerplant: 1× Rolls-Royce Turbomeca Adour Mk. 951 turbofan with FADEC, 29 kN (6,500 lbf) 29 kN

Performance

Maximum speed: Mach 0.84 (1,028 km/h, 639 mph, 555 kn) at altitude

Range: 2,520 km (1,360 nmi, 1,565 mi)

Service ceiling: 13,565 m (44,500 ft)

Rate of climb: 47 m/s (9,300 ft/min)

Armament

1× 30 mm ADEN cannon, in centreline pod

Up to 6,800 lb (3,085 kg) of weapons on five hardpoints, including:

4× AIM-9 Sidewinder or ASRAAM or A-Darter on wing pylons and wingtip rails

2x Umbani or Al Tariq

1,500 lb (680 kg), limited to one centreline and two wing pylons (Hawk T1)

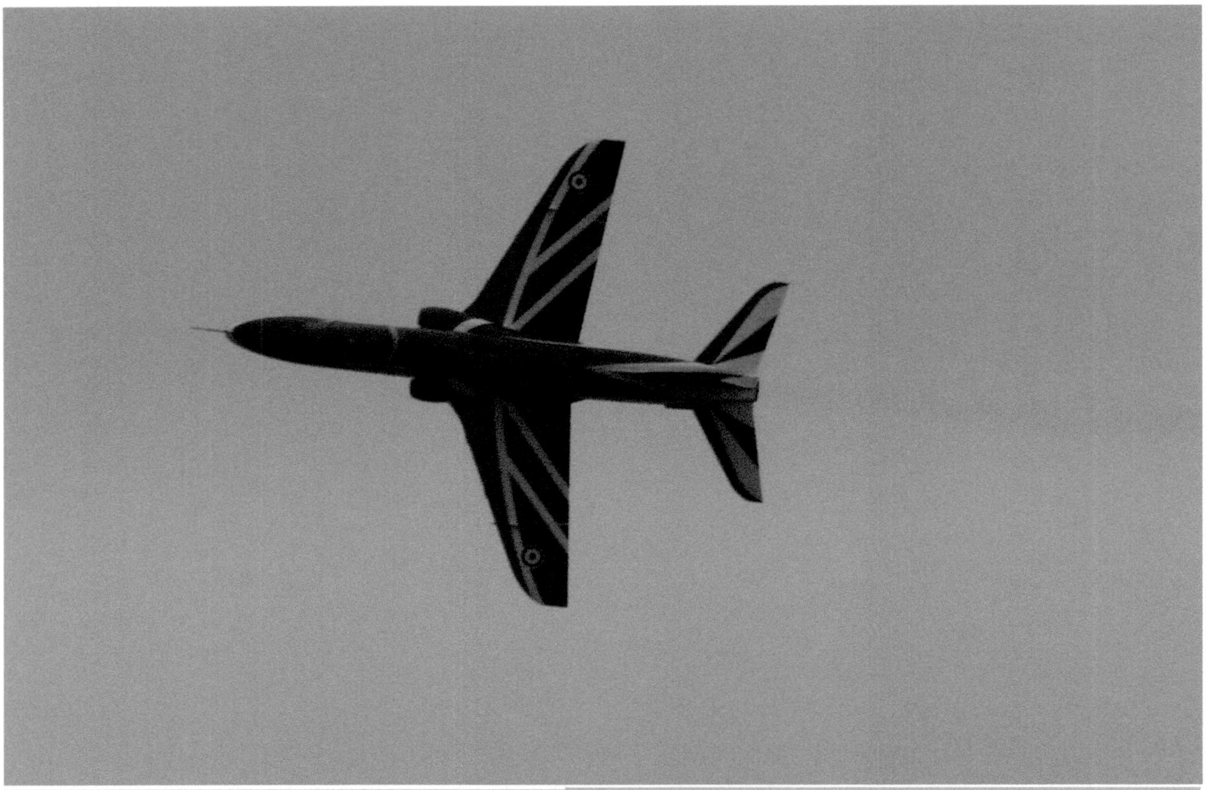

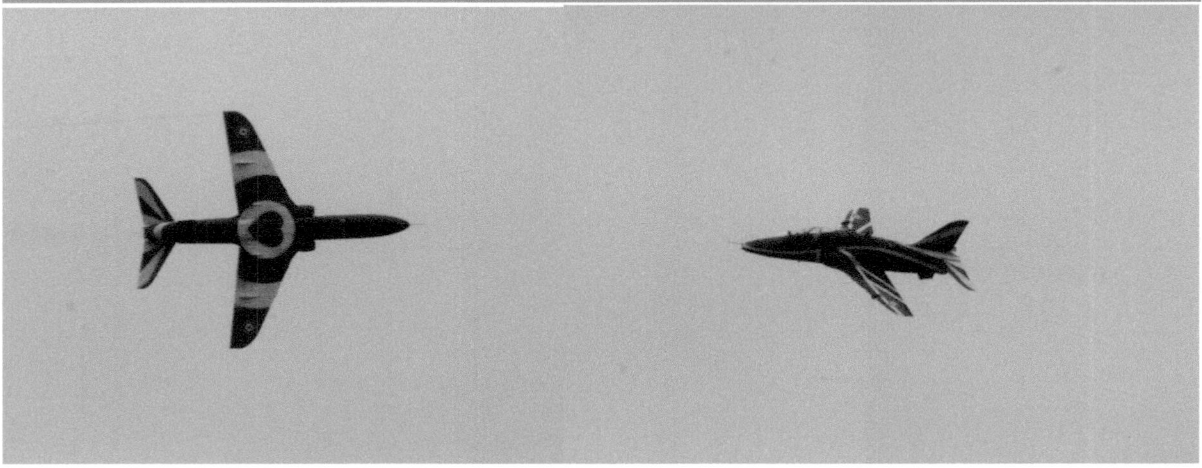

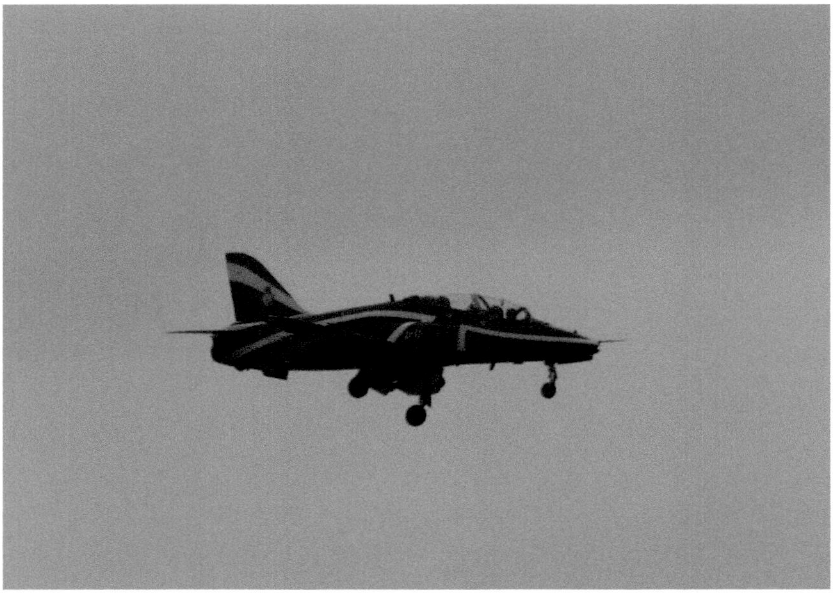

BAC Jet Provost

The BAC Jet Provost played an integral role in aviation history as the pioneering jet trainer developed by the British Aircraft Corporation, originally designed by Hunting Aircraft in the 1950s to meet the Royal Air Force's need for a jet-powered replacement for its piston-engine trainers. The Jet Provost was crucial in training generations of military pilots and spearheaded the evolution of jet trainers. The first prototype, named the Hunting Percival P.84 Jet Provost, took flight in June 1954 powered by the Armstrong Siddeley Viper turbojet engine.

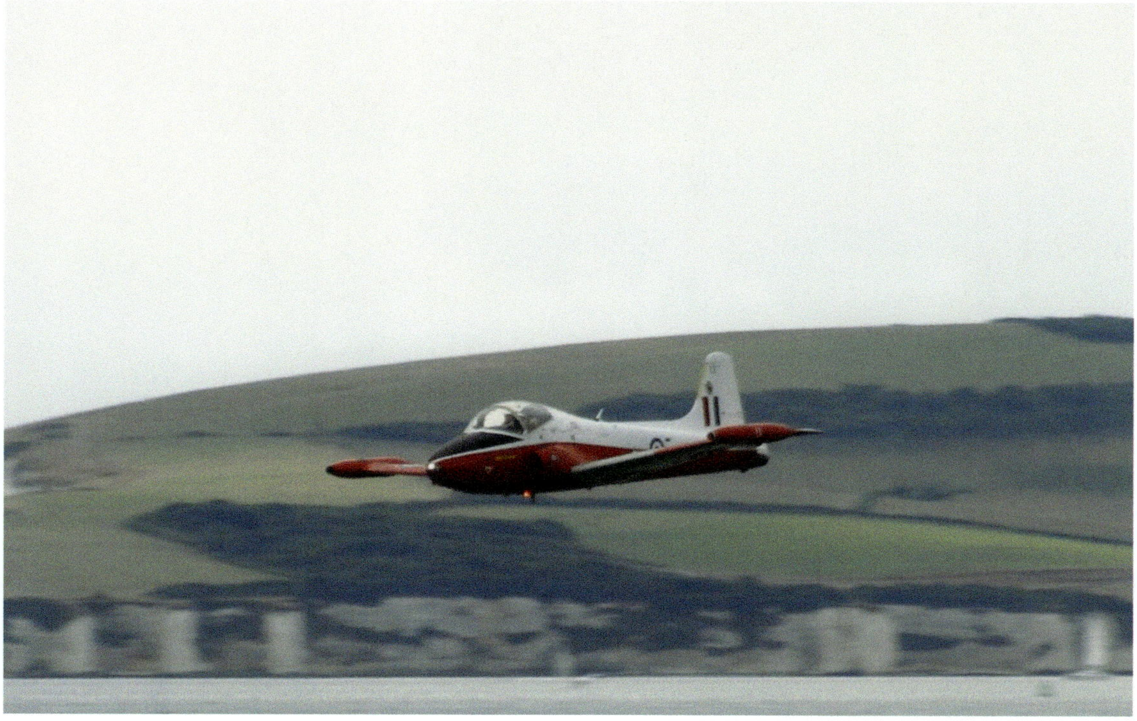

The Jet Provost was designed for jet training with a tandem seat configuration that allowed the instructor and trainee to sit side-by-side in a well-laid-out cockpit. Featuring a metal airframe and low wings, it was powered by a rear-mounted Viper engine that provided the necessary thrust for jet propulsion. With a focus on simple and maintainable design, the Jet Provost was an ideal jet trainer for novice pilots.

Though not a high-performance jet fighter, the Jet Provost provided sufficient speed and agility to serve its purpose as a jet-powered trainer aircraft. It allowed trainees to experience jet flight's unique challenges like greater speed, different handling, and jet engine use. With performance well-matched to basic training needs, the Jet Provost gave pilots their first taste of jet aviation.

The Jet Provost underwent numerous upgrades and modifications over the years. For instance, the T.4 and T.5 variants featured avionics, systems, and performance enhancements. The Jet Provost also served as the foundation for developing the Strikemaster, a light attack aircraft intended for export.

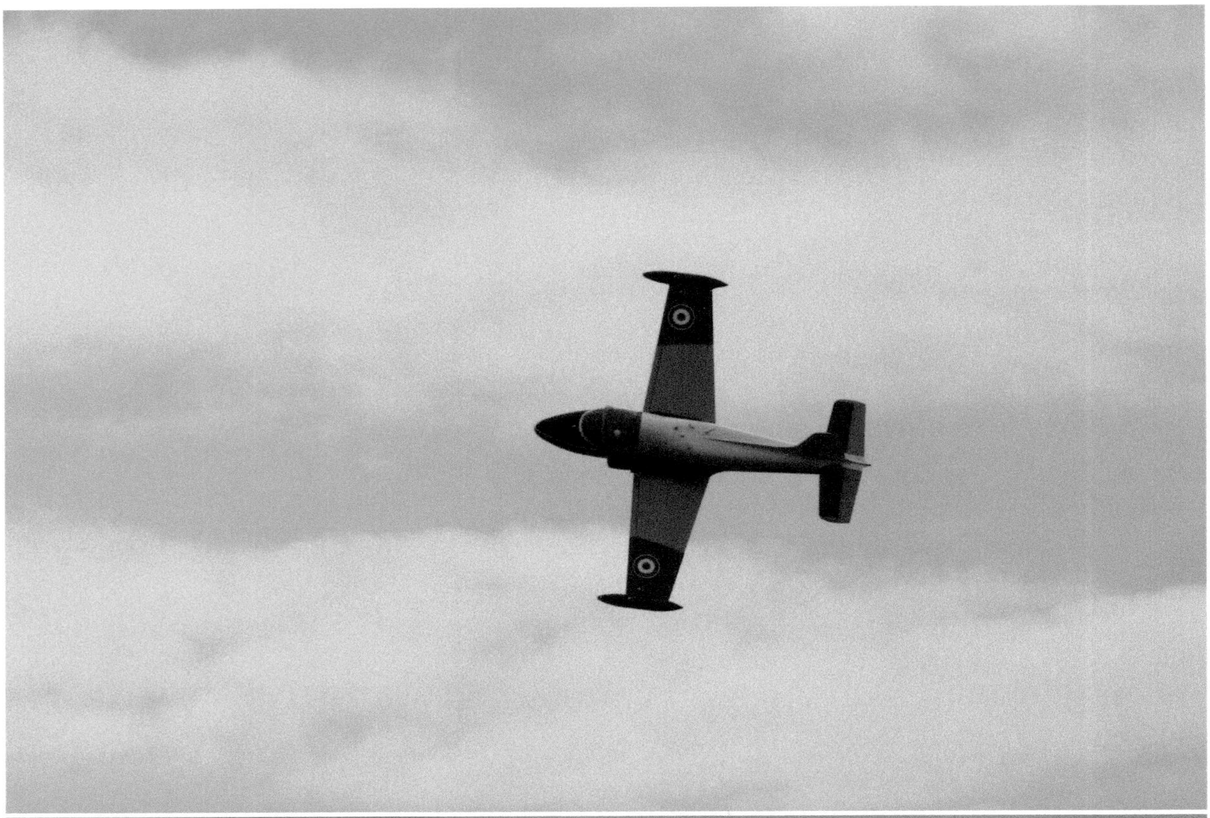

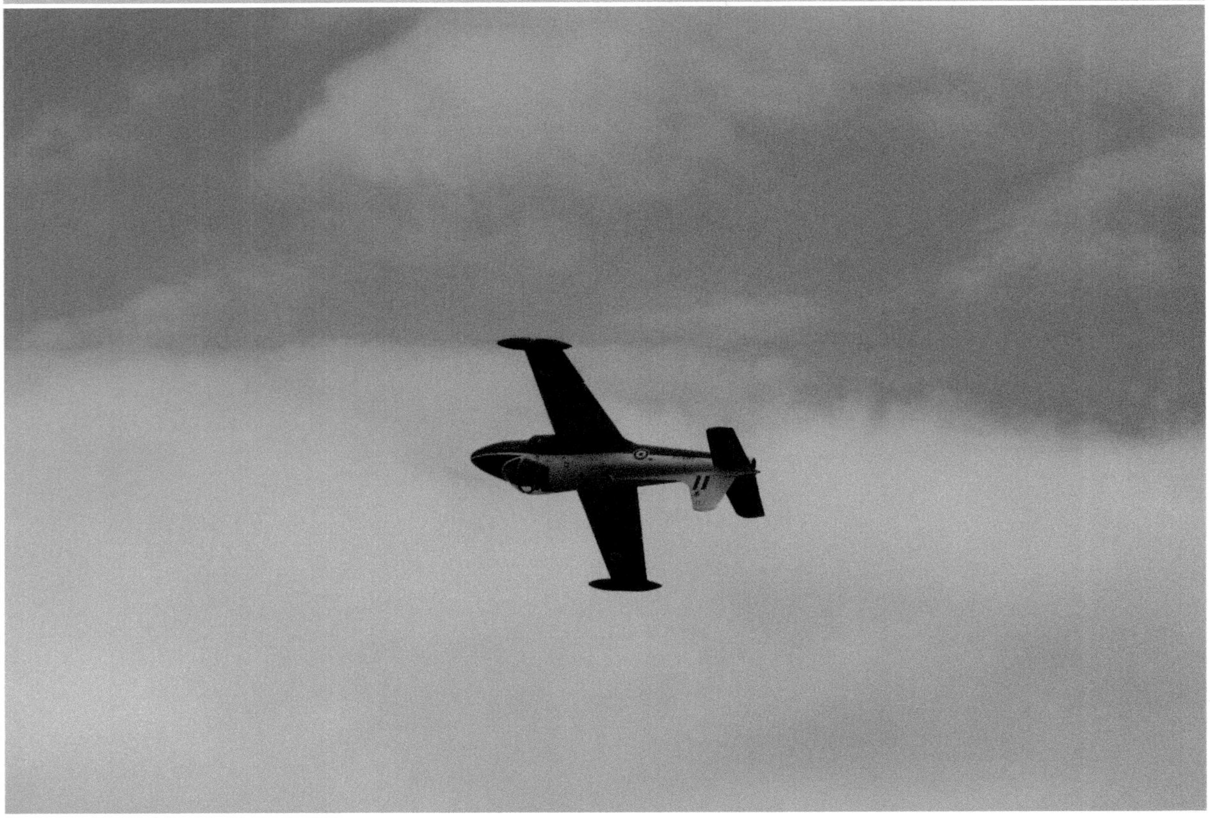

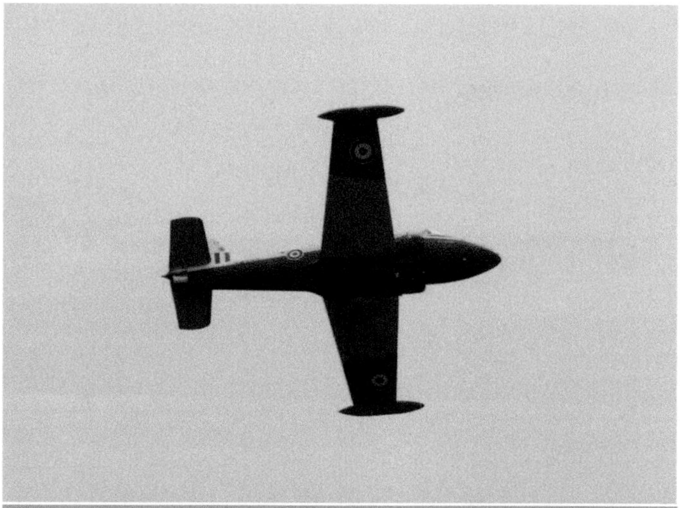
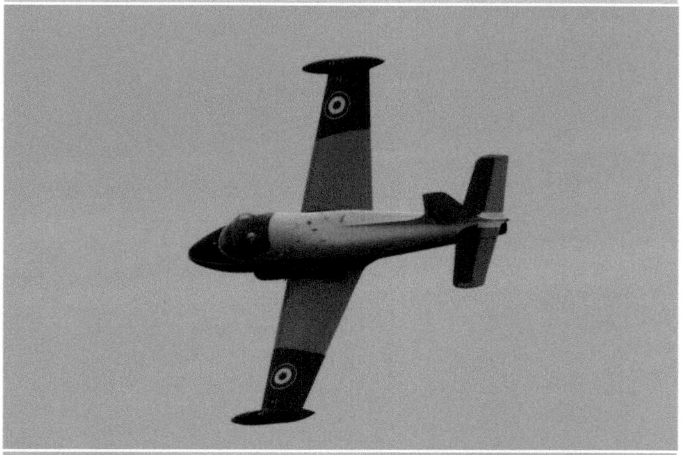
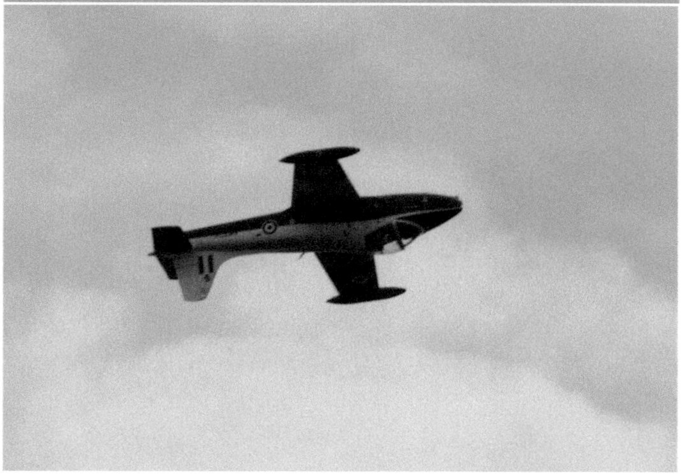

Quick Facts

General characteristics

Crew: 2

Length: 34 ft 0 in (10.36 m)

Wingspan: 35 ft 4 in (10.77 m)

Height: 10 ft 2 in (3.10 m)

Gross weight: 6,989 lb (3,170 kg)

Max take-off weight: 9,200 lb (4,173 kg)

Powerplant: 1 × Armstrong Siddeley Viper turbojet engine, 1,700 lbf (7.6 kN) with thrust of 2,500 lbf

Performance

Maximum speed: 382 kn (440 mph, 707 km/h) at 25,000 ft (7,620 m)

Range: 780 nmi (900 mi, 1,440 km) with tip tanks.

Service ceiling: 36,750 ft (11,200 m)

Rate of climb: 4,000 ft/min (20 m/s)

Strikemaster

The Strikemaster aircraft evolved from the Jet Provost to meet the need for an affordable, adaptable light attack and counterinsurgency plane. Like the Jet Provost, the Strikemaster had side-by-side seating for an instructor and trainee or a pilot and weapons officer. The Strikemaster featured upgrades in avionics, extra hardpoints for armaments, and more powerful engines compared to its predecessor.

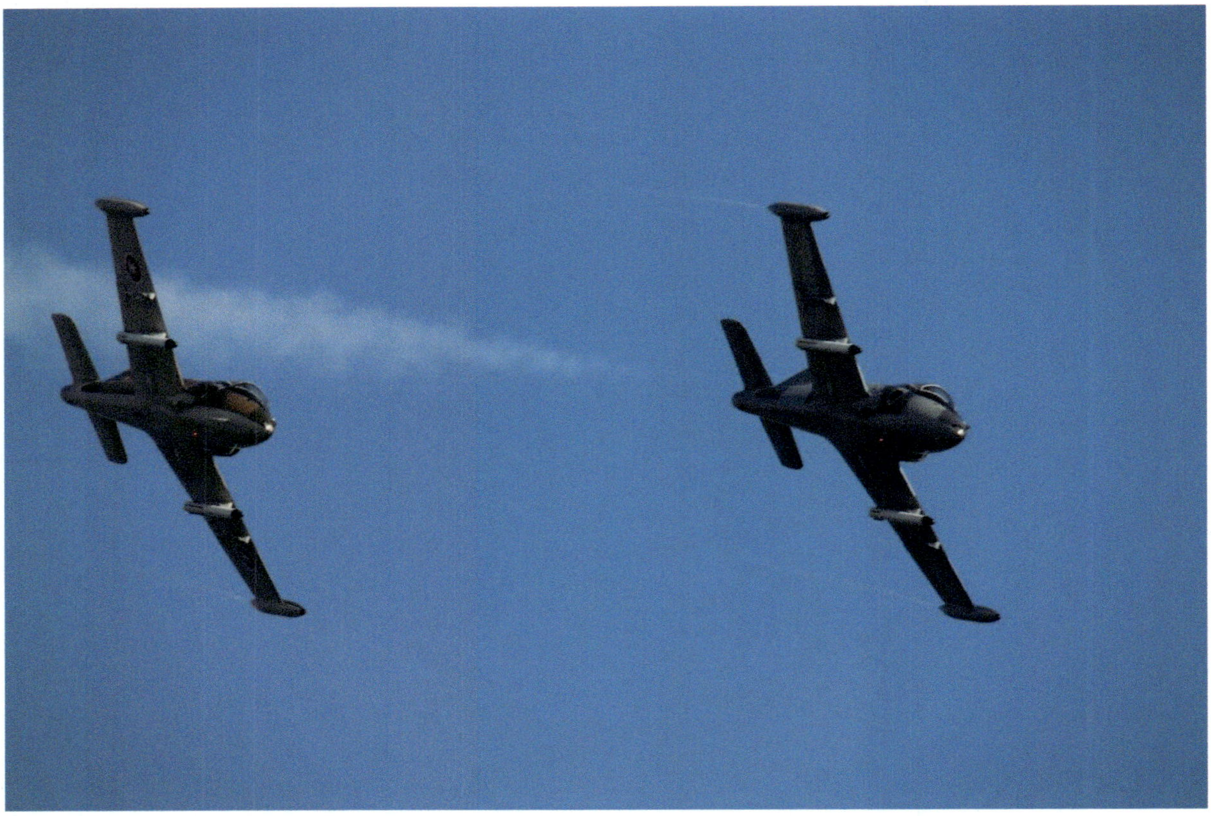

Roles and Capabilities:

Light Attack: Designed chiefly for light attack and ground-attack missions, the Strikemaster featured hardpoints under its wings that could carry a versatile array of munitions, including rockets, bombs, and gun pods.

Counter-Insurgency: Ideal for counter-insurgency missions, the aircraft could deliver close air support to ground troops and execute precise strikes on targets in asymmetric warfare.

Training: The Strikemaster was primarily an attack aircraft but retained the training abilities of its predecessor, the Jet Provost. Powered by a Bristol Siddeley Viper turbojet, the agile Strikemaster could reach speeds around 500 knots and altitudes up to 40,000 feet. This combination of agility and high speed for its class allowed it to excel as both a trainer for pilots transitioning to advanced fighters and as an attack platform.

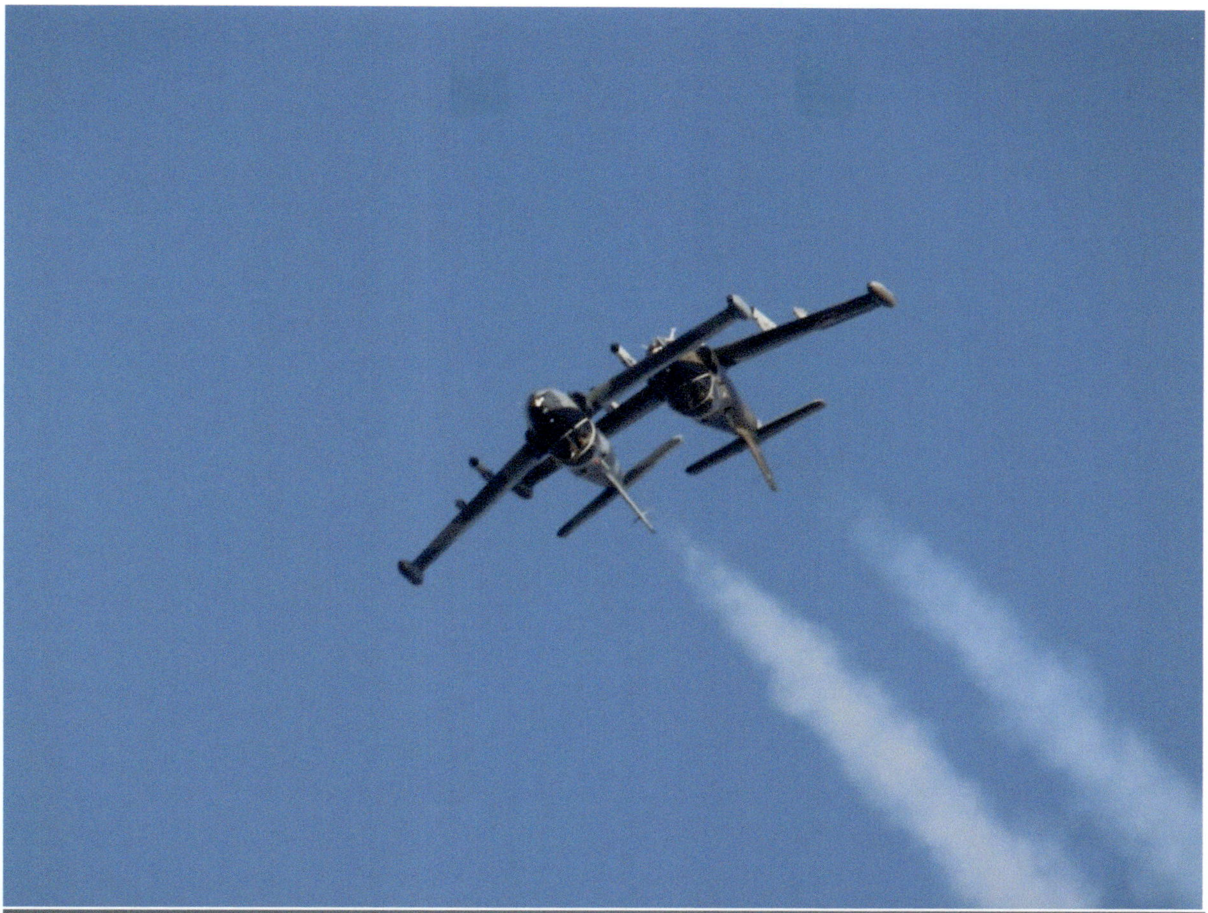

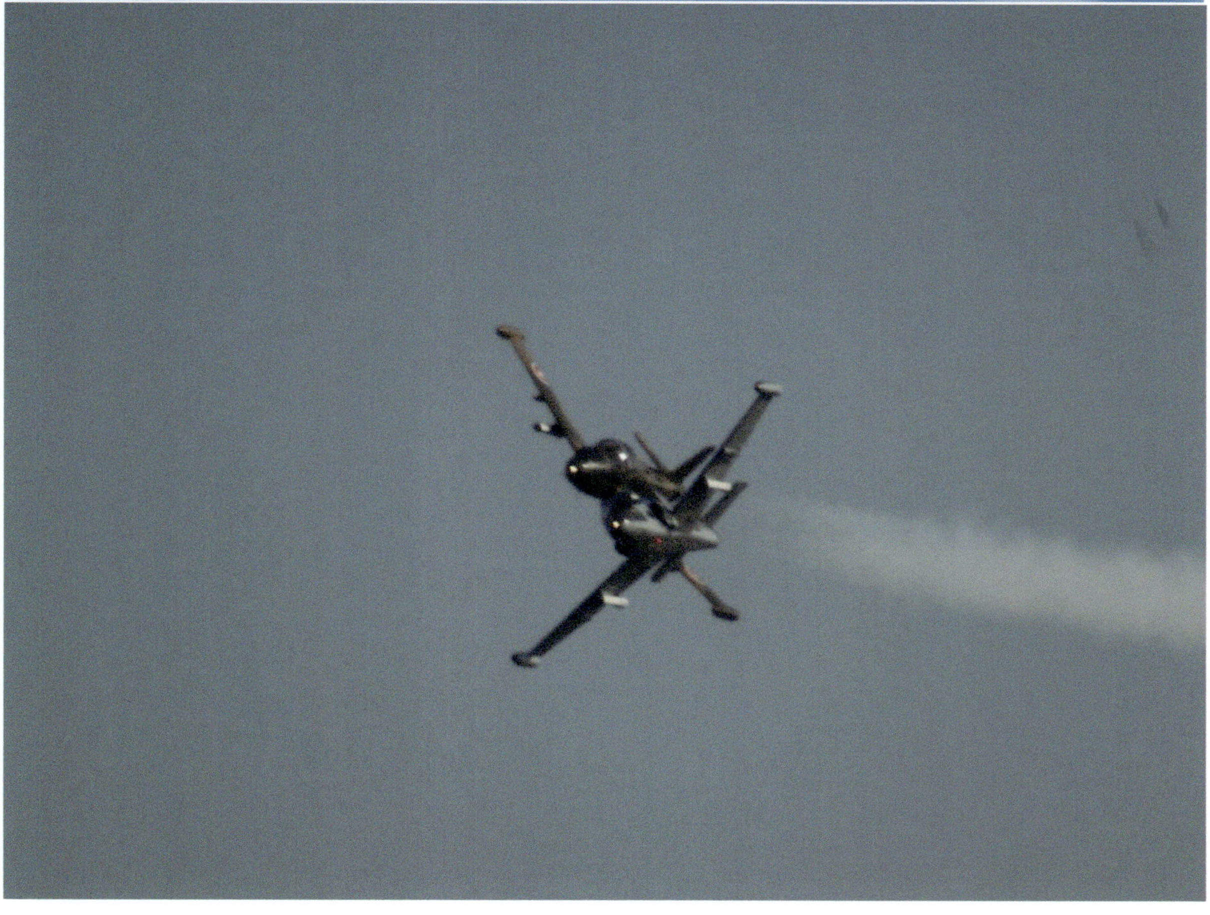

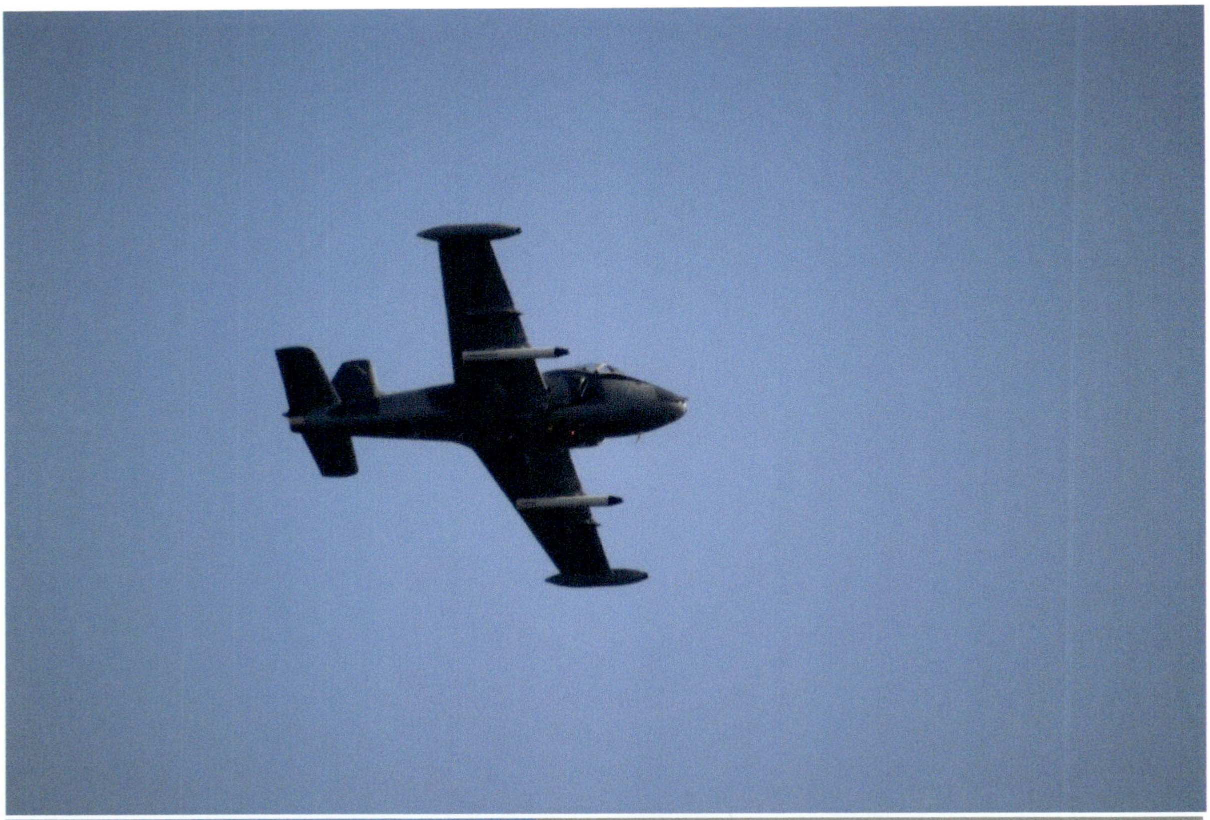

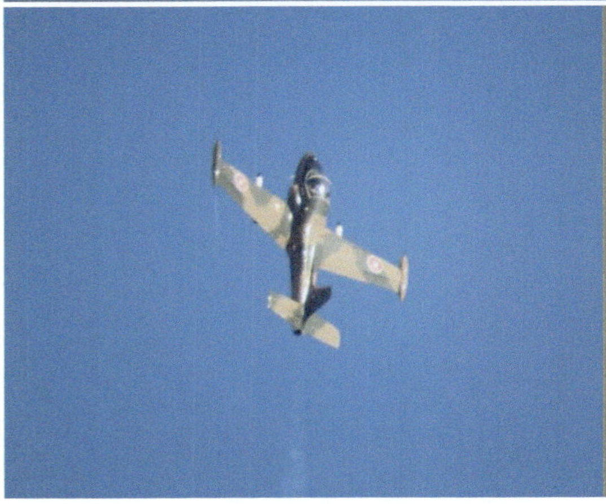

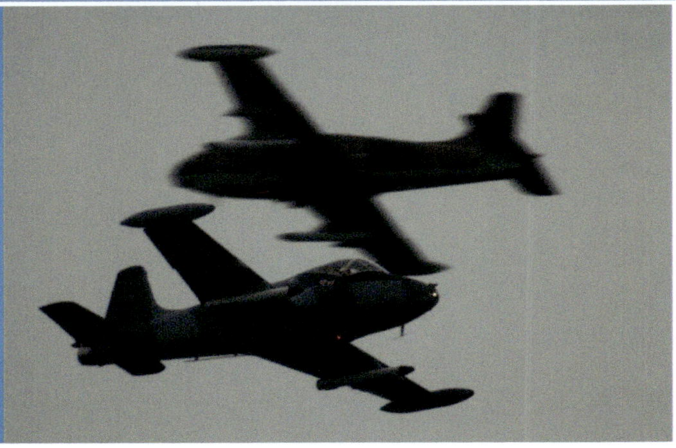

Quick Facts

Crew: 2

Length: 33 ft 8+1⁄2 in (10.274 m)

Wingspan: 36 ft 10 in (11.23 m)

Height: 10 ft 11+1⁄2 in (3.340 m)

Fuel capacity: 366 imp gal (440 US gal; 1,660 L) total including tip tanks

Powerplant: 1 × Rolls-Royce Viper Mk.535 turbojet, 3,140 lbf (14.0 kN) thrust

Guns: 2× 7.62 mm machine guns with 550 rounds each

Hardpoints: 4 (2 per wing) with a capacity of 3,000 lb (1,400 kg) of bombs

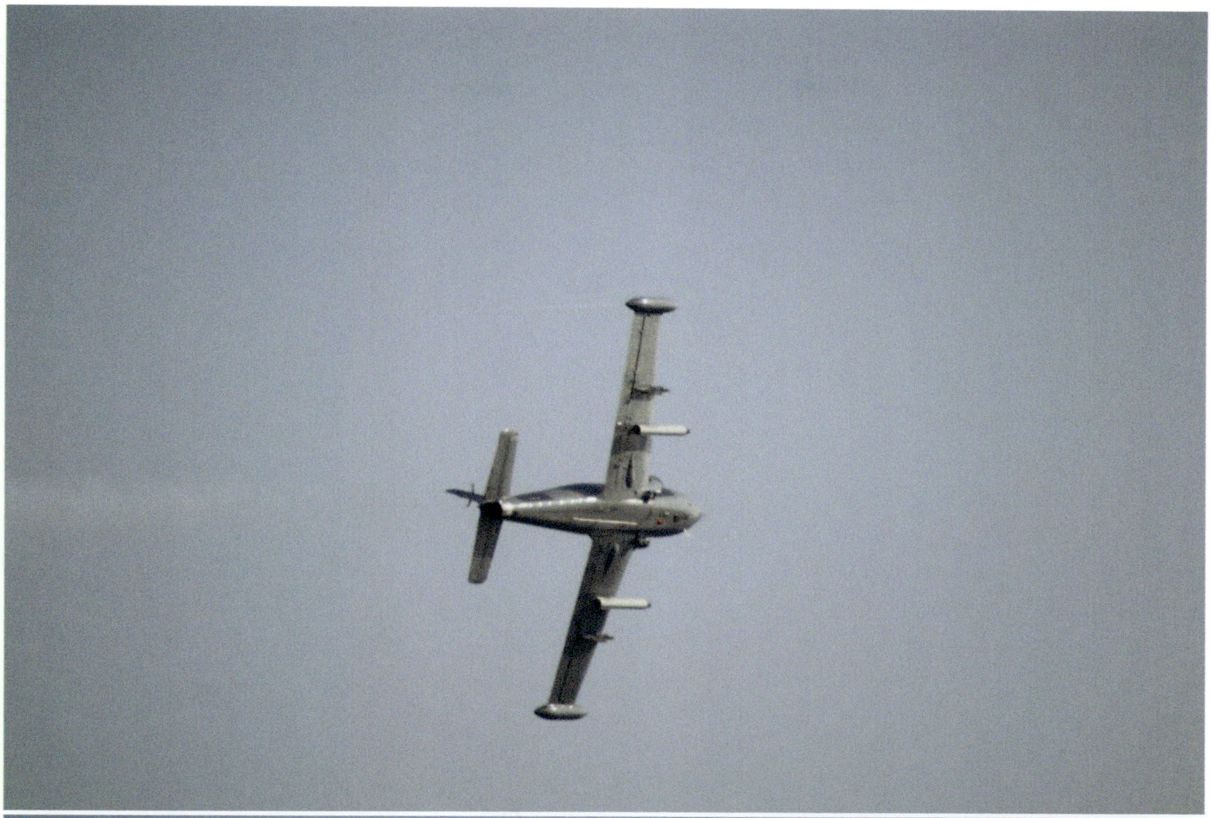

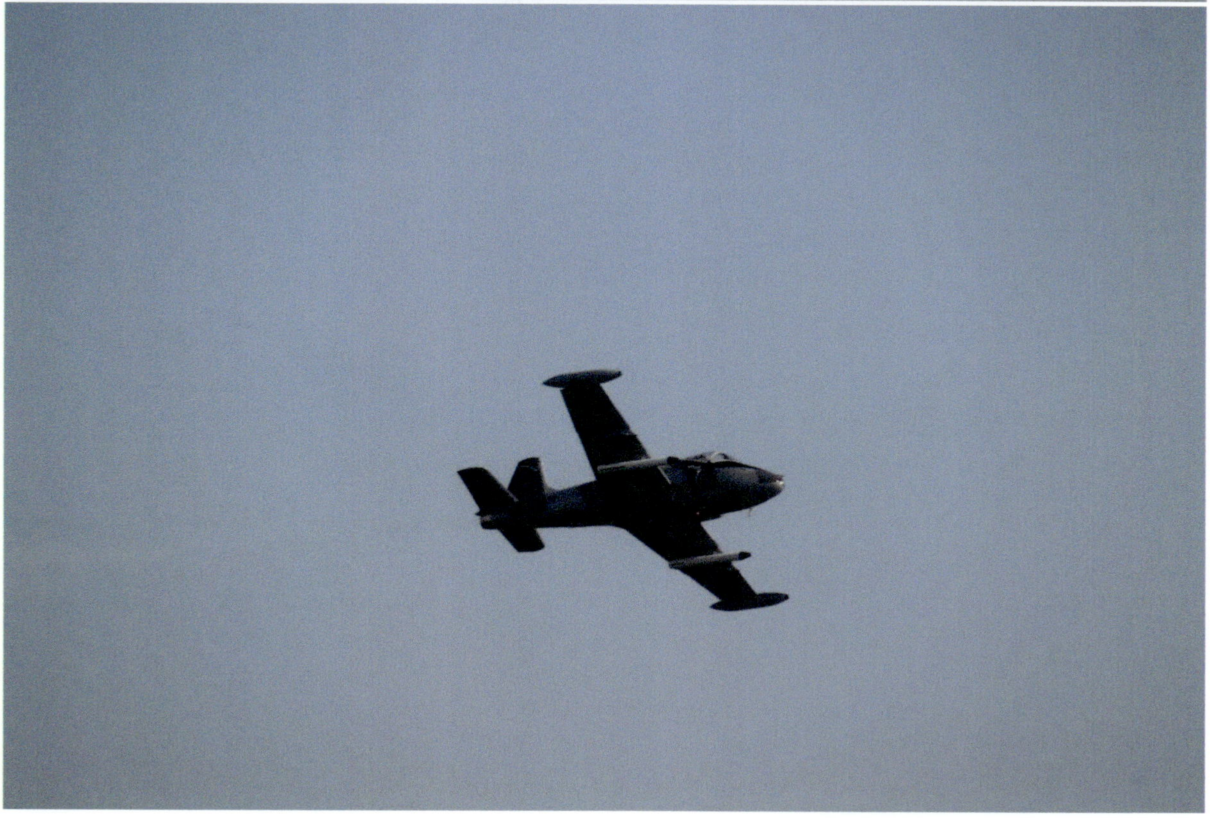

YAK-50

To meet the needs of sports pilots and aerobatic enthusiasts, the Soviet Yakovlev Design Bureau developed the single-seat Yak-50 in the late 1970s as an unlimited aerobatic competition aircraft that improved upon the earlier Yak-18 aerobatic model with advanced aerodynamic capabilities enabling complex manoeuvres.

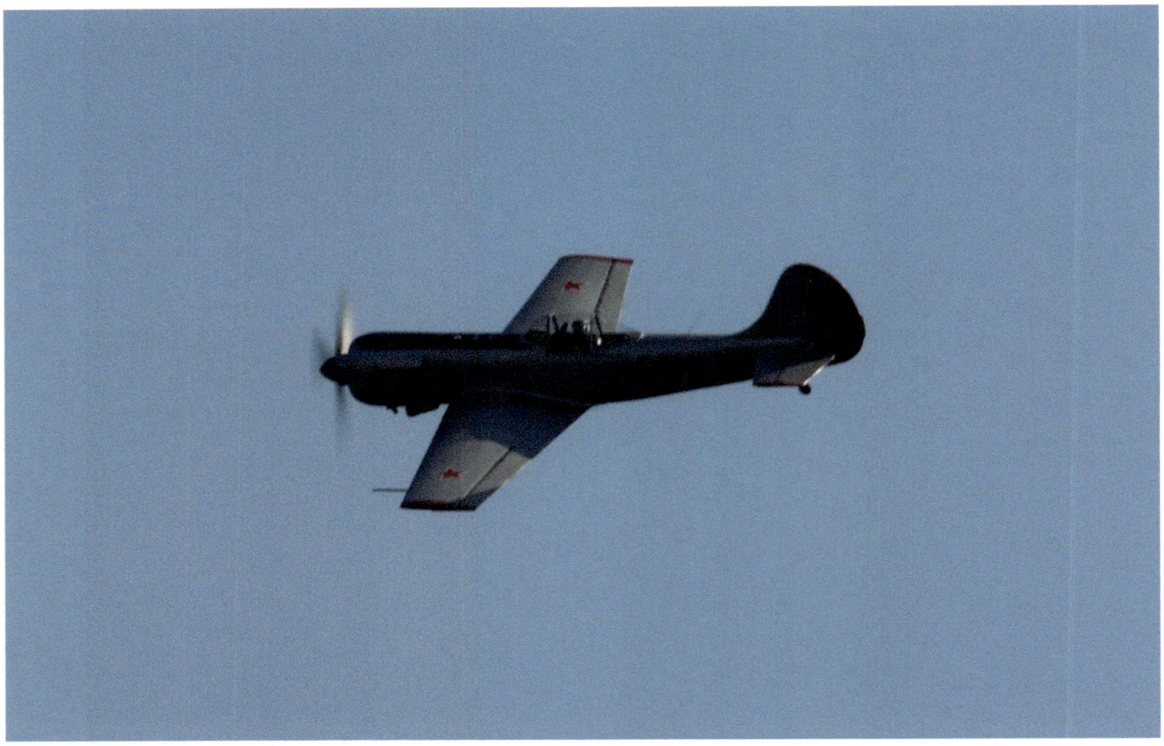

With a supercharged Vedeneyev M14P engine producing 360 to 450 horsepower, the Yak-50 has excellent handling thanks to its high power-to-weight ratio. Its robust yet agile airframe has powered it to two World Aerobatic Champion titles. The aircraft uses compressed air to operate the landing gear, brakes, and engine starter. The engine connects to the propeller through a reduction gearbox.

The design of the cockpit provides the pilot with good visibility, which is essential during most aerobatic displays, the Yak-50 has also been utilised as a military trainer by several countries.

The six-plane Yakovlev Aerobatic Display Team performs precision formation flying in their Yak-50 aircraft during airshows across the UK. Based at Henstridge Airfield in Somerset, they have frequently flown over Bournemouth, most recently with a solo routine in 2023.

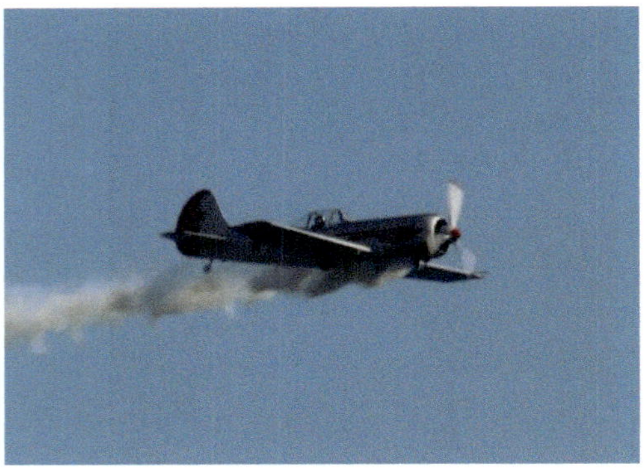

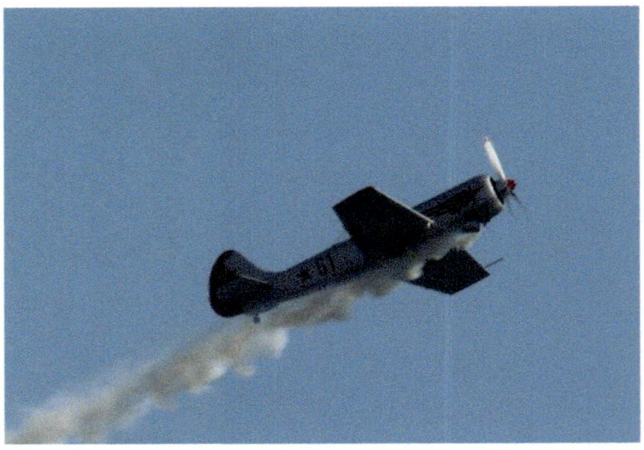

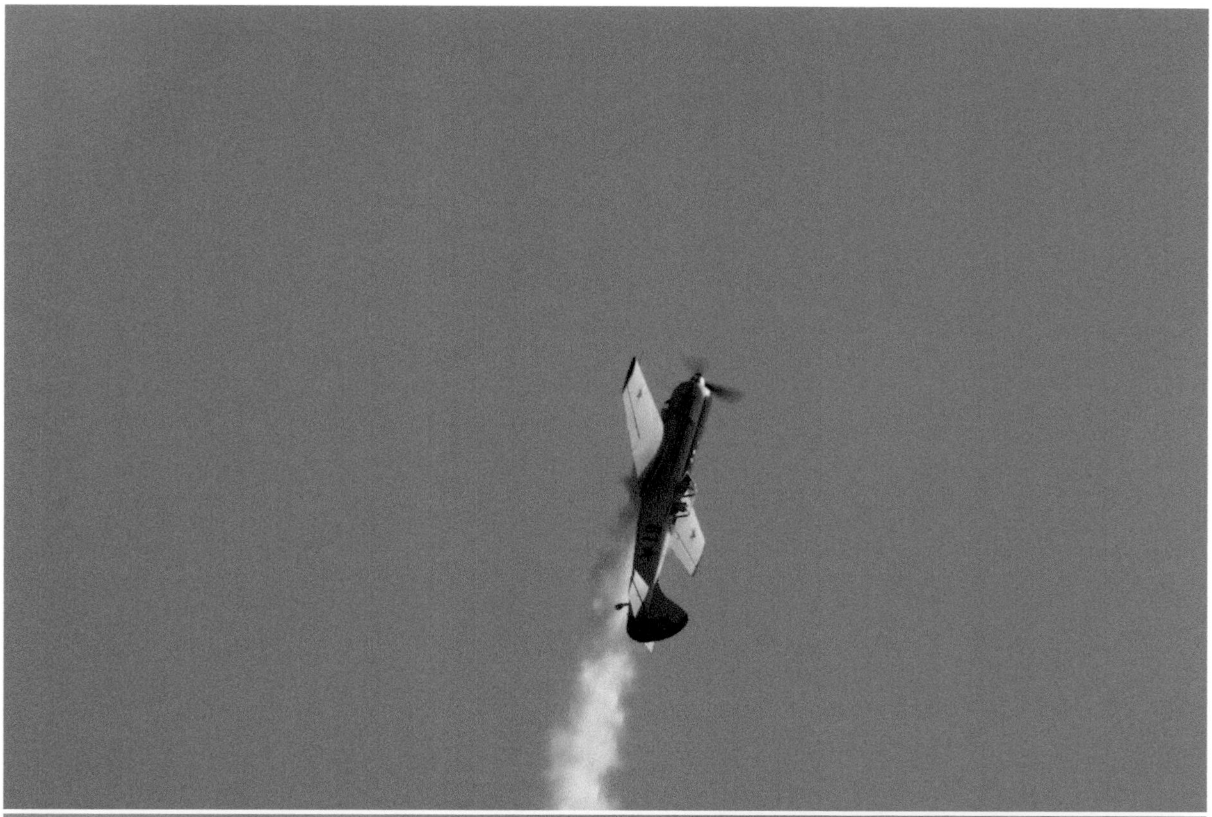

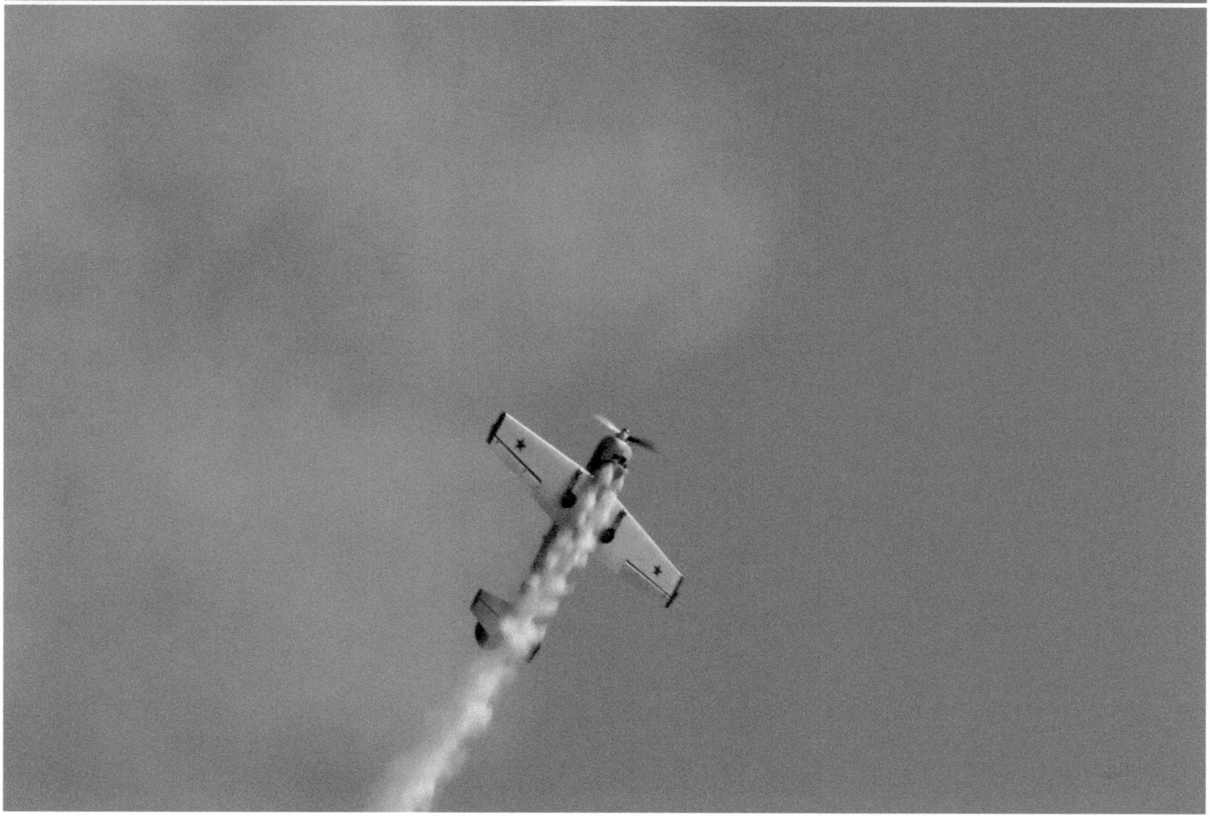

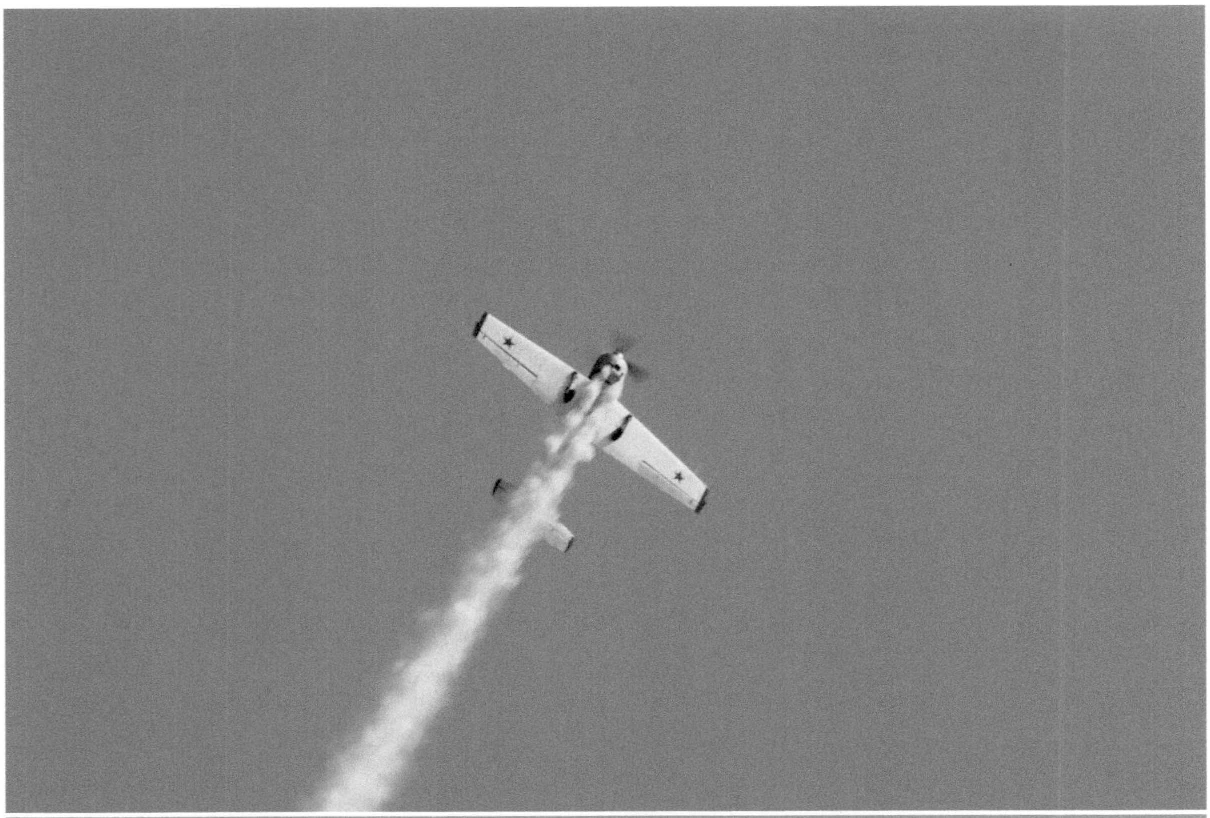

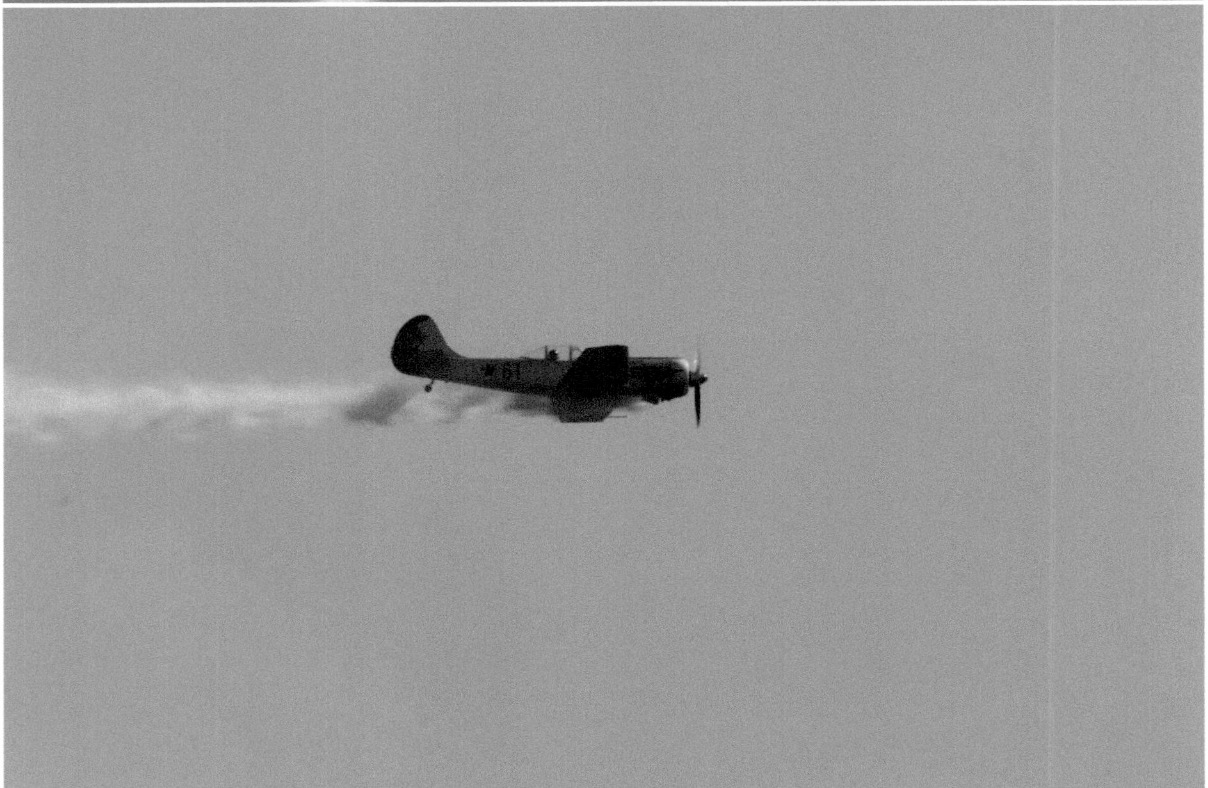

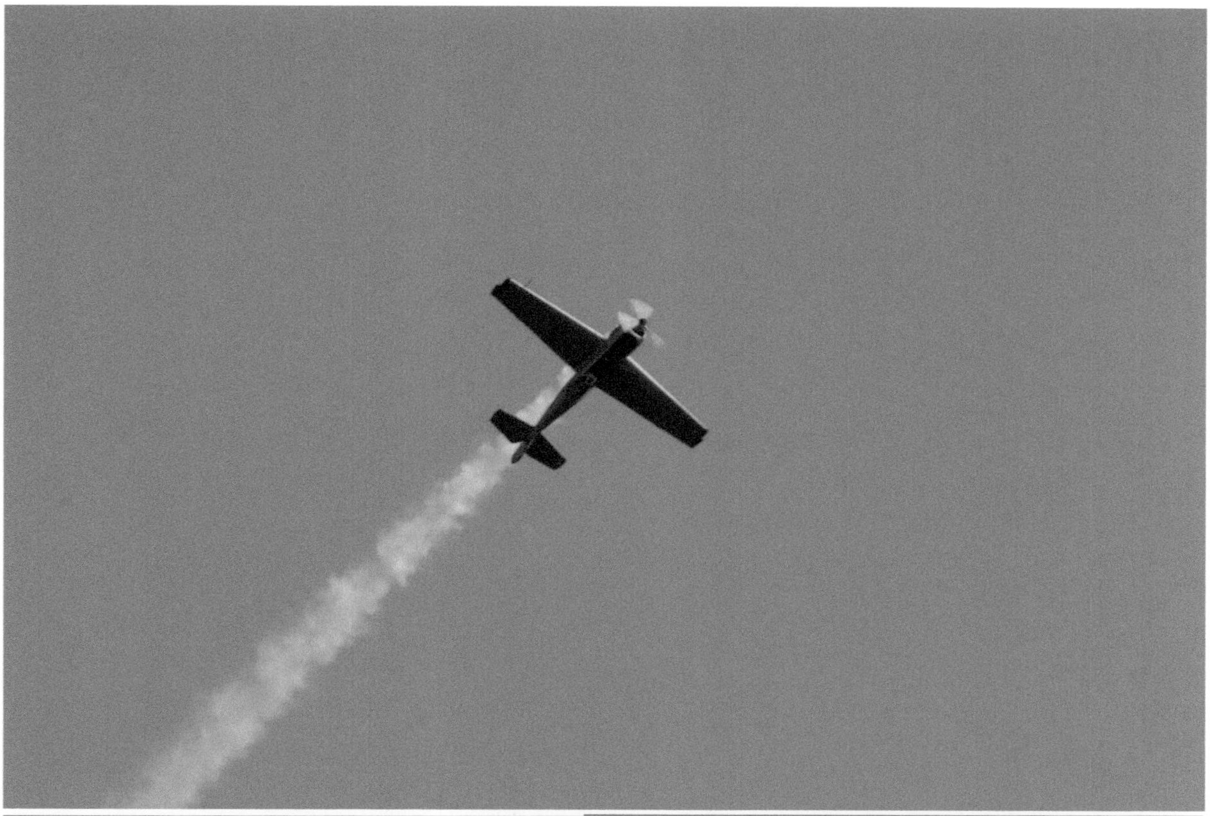

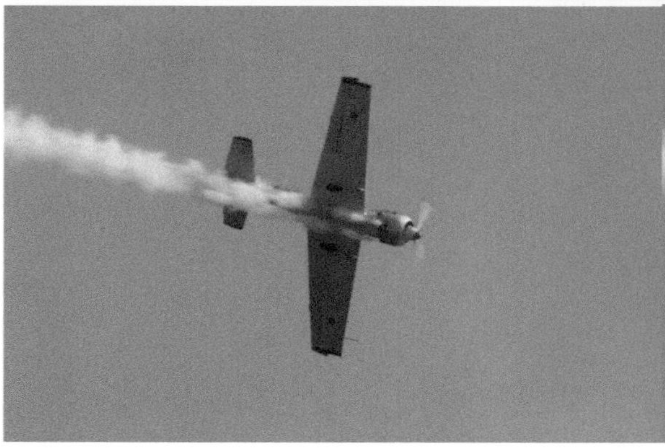

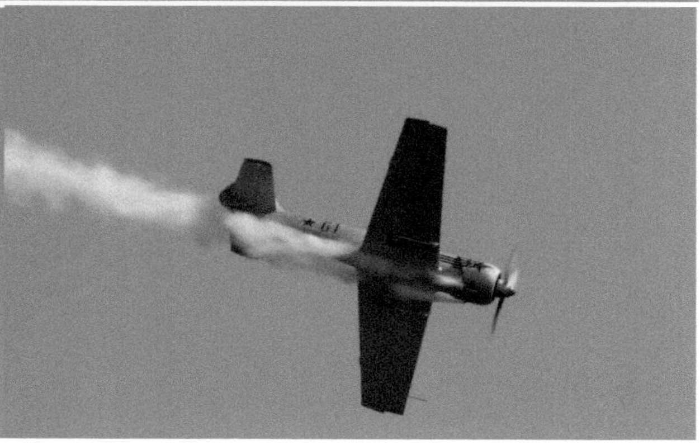

Quick Facts

Crew: 1

Length: 7.8 m (25 ft 7 in)

Wingspan: 9.5 m (31 ft 2 in)

Height: 3.2 m (10 ft 6 in)

Maximum speed: 400 km/h (250 mph, 220 kn)

Range: 500 km (310 mi, 270 nmi)

Service ceiling: 4,000 m (13,000 ft)

Take-off run: 100 m (328 ft)

Landing run: 250 m (820 ft)

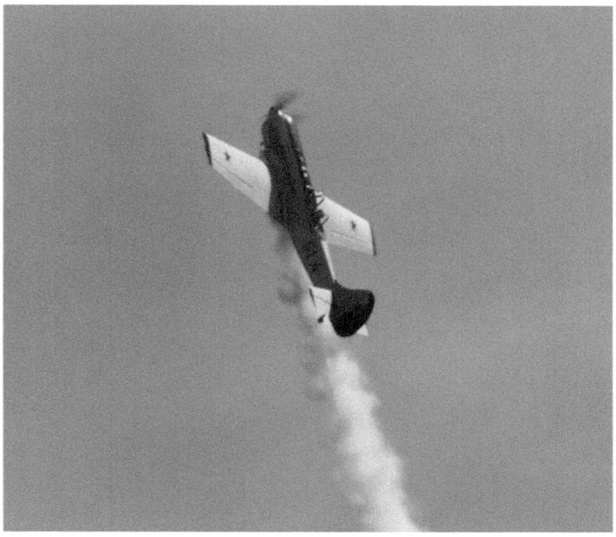

Jet Pitts

The Pitts Special, designed by Curtis Pitts, is a lightweight aerobatic biplane that has been a dominate force in the world of aerobatic competition since its first flight in 1944. Through the 1960s and 1970s, the Pitts biplanes were unrivalled in the top levels of competition. Even today, they remain highly competitive aircraft in the lower aerobatic categories, having racked up countless wins over the decades.

Curtis Pitts began designing a single-seat aerobatic biplane in 1943-1944. After the prototype first flew in September 1944, the design was continuously refined. However, the current Pitts S-2 maintains key similarities to the original prototype in both concept and design.

Former RAF Tornado pilot Richard Goodwin has amazed crowds at the Bournemouth Air Festival by flying his own Pitts Special aircraft, call signs G-EWIZ and G-JPIT. G-JPIT is most well known for being outfitted with a Lynx jet engine.

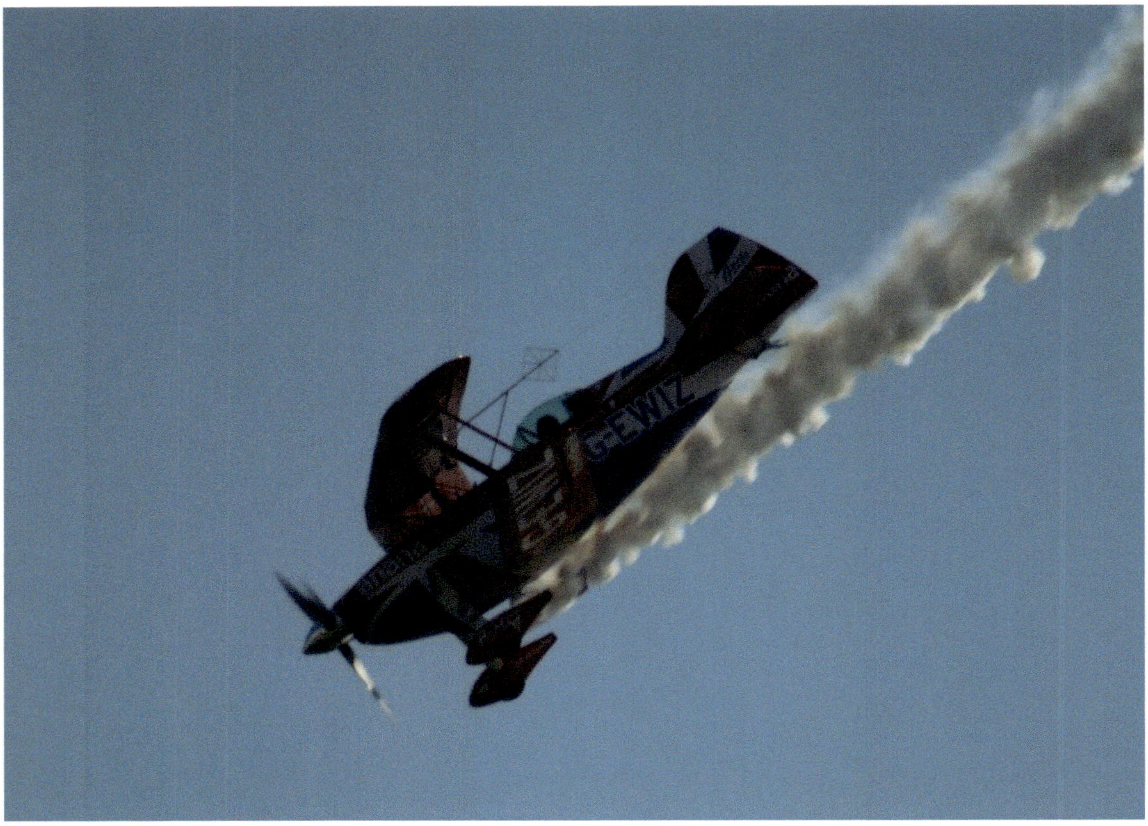

The Pitts S-2S features a robust Lycoming AEIO-540-D4A5 engine that delivers abundant power for dynamic aerobatics. Its lightweight build and symmetrical wings allow exceptional agility to execute a broad range of manoeuvres.

Richard Goodwin's aerobatic display in the Pitts S-2S biplane is a thrilling spectacle. He performs a series of precision manoeuvres including loops, rolls, spins, hammerheads, snap rolls, and inverted flight. The aircraft's nimble design enables both classic and modern aerobatic sequences, showcasing Goodwin's skills.

Most famously in 2023, Richard Goodwin re-engineered his Pitts Special biplane to include two ATM Lynx jet engines holstered on either side of the fuselage. Further modifications to the wing structure enabled the plane to hover like a Harrier jet. With these powerful additions, Goodwin's 2023 Pitts Special thundered across the airshow like an RAF Tornado.

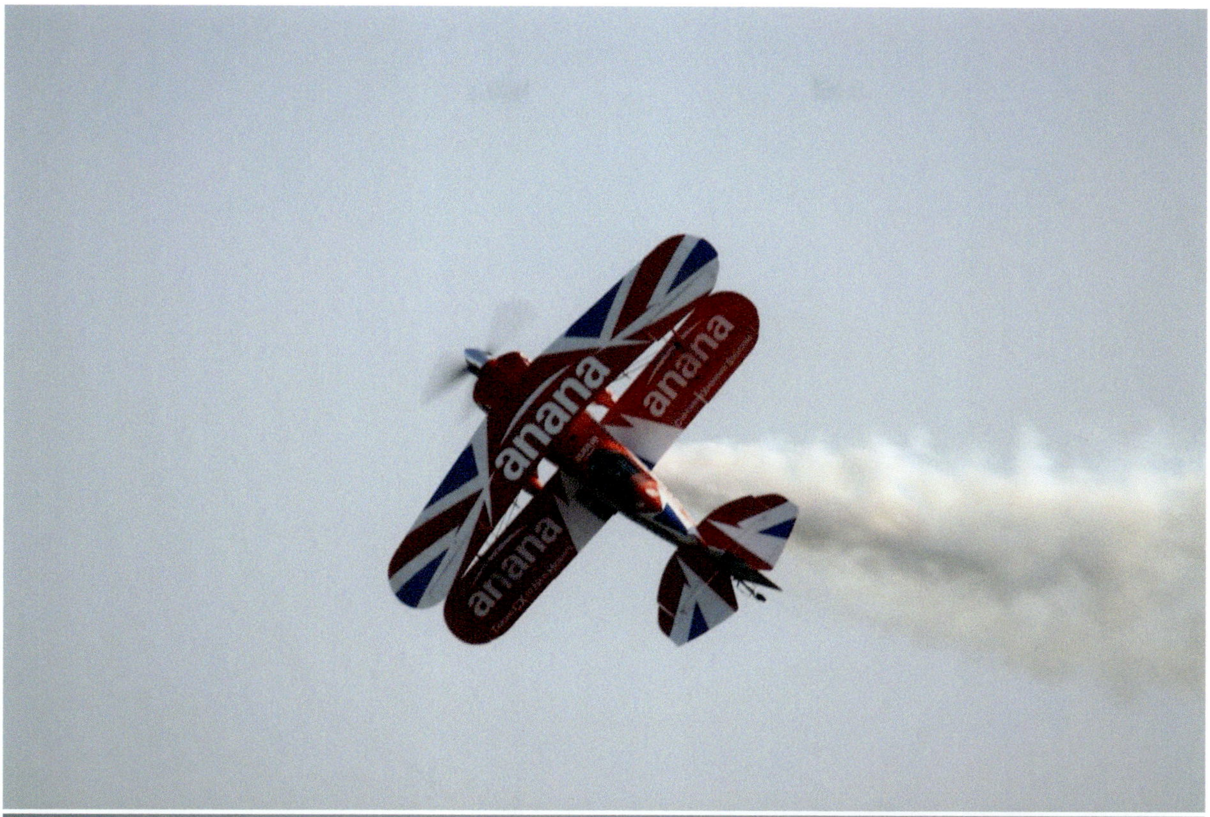
anana
anana
anana
anana

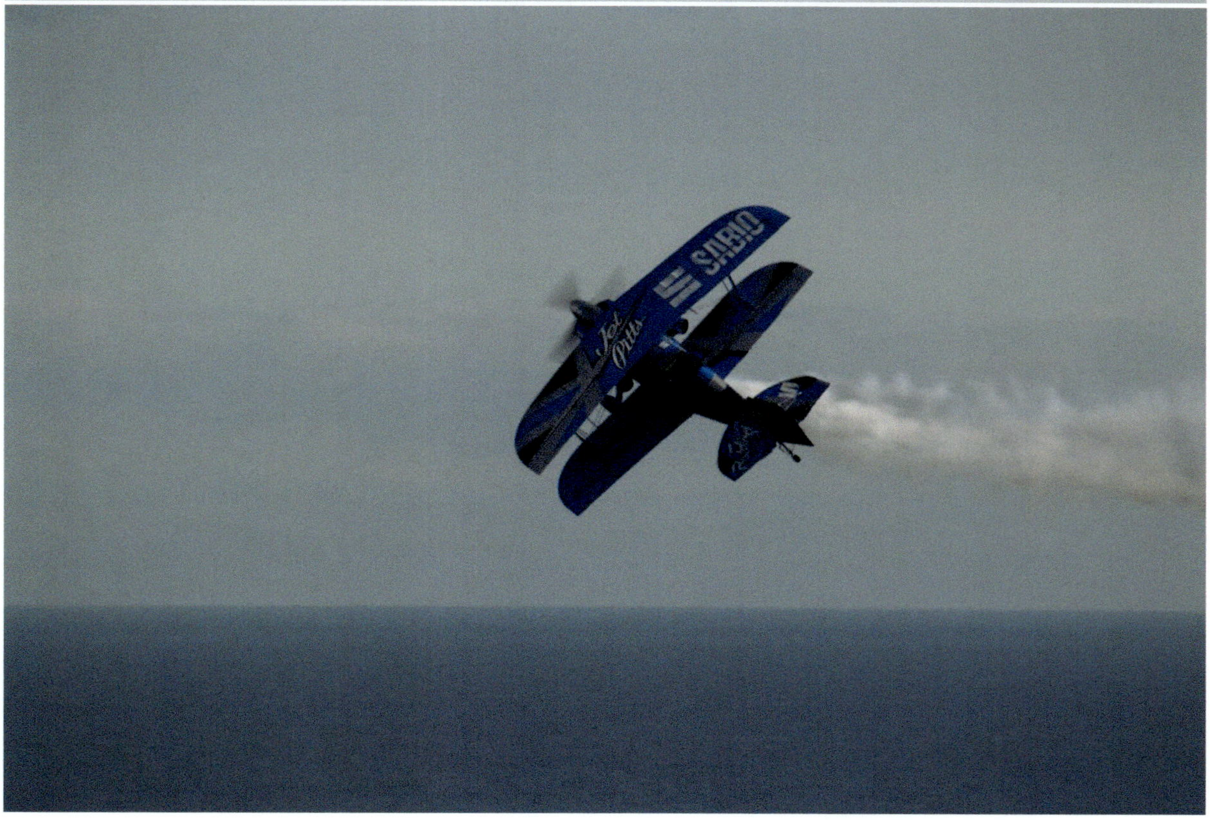
SABIO

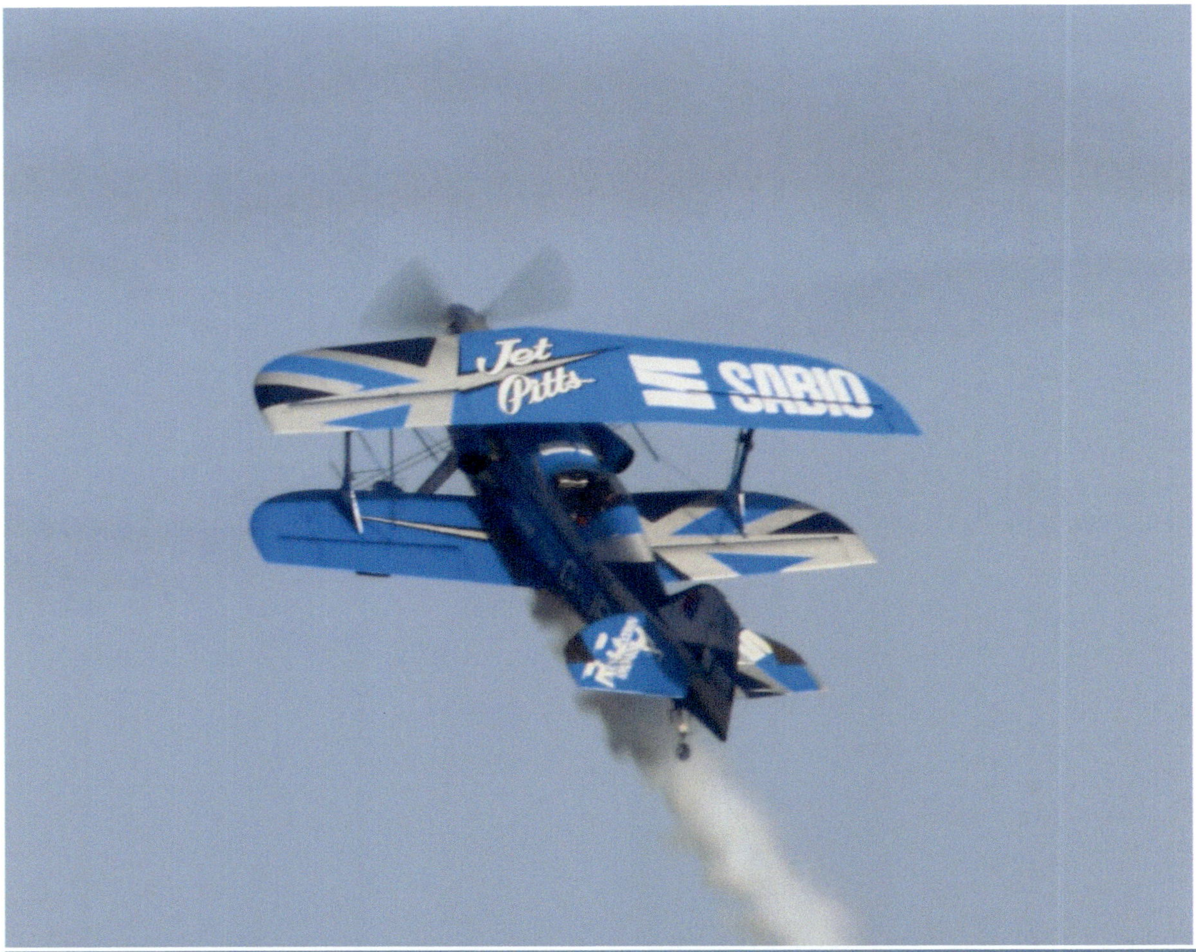
Jet
Pitts
SABIO

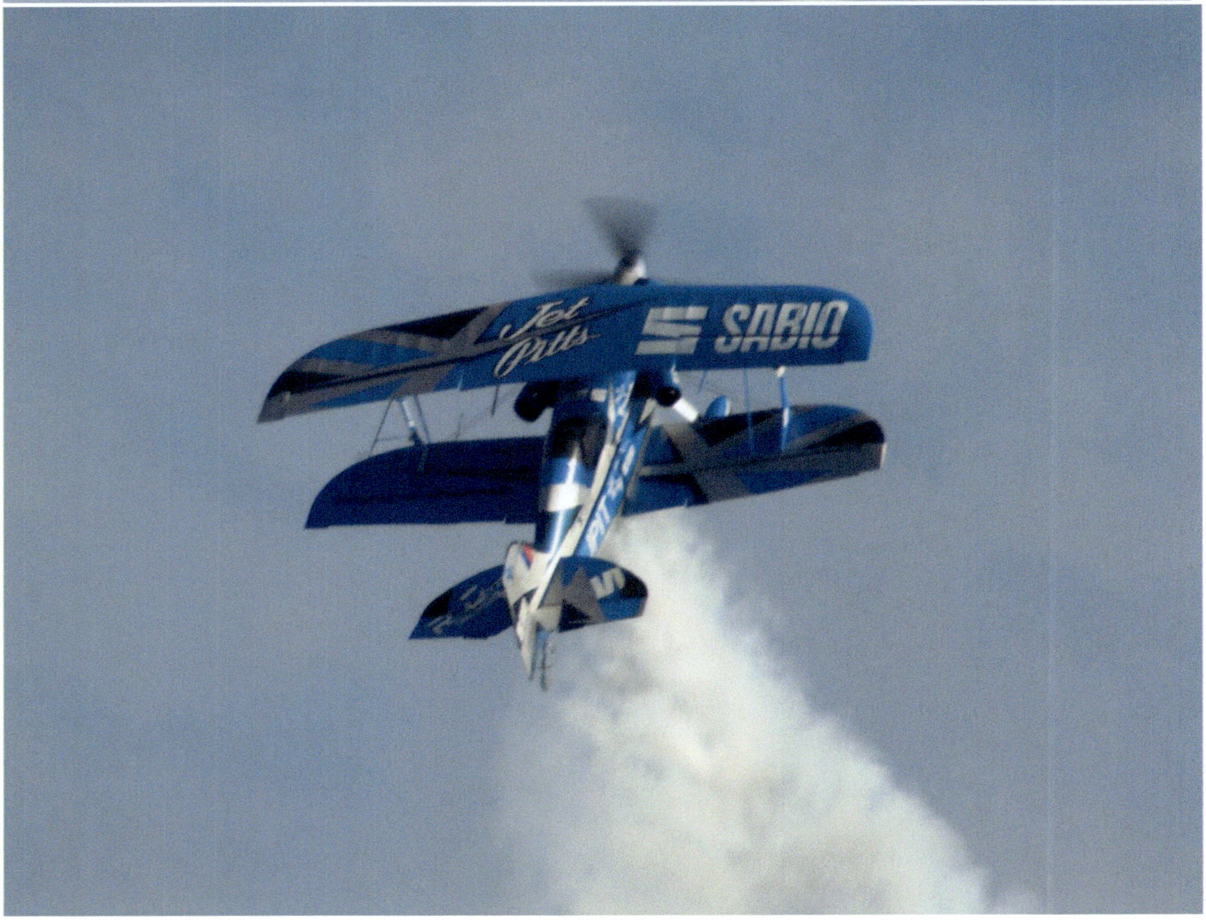
Jet
Pitts
SABIO

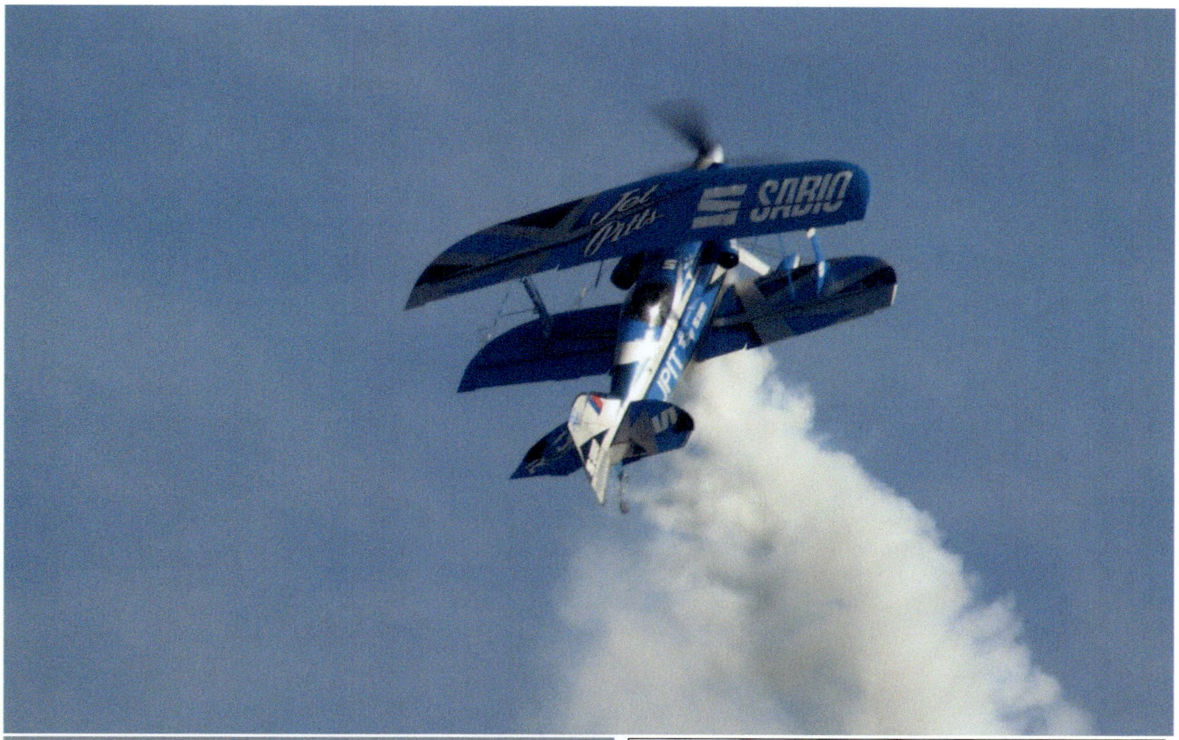

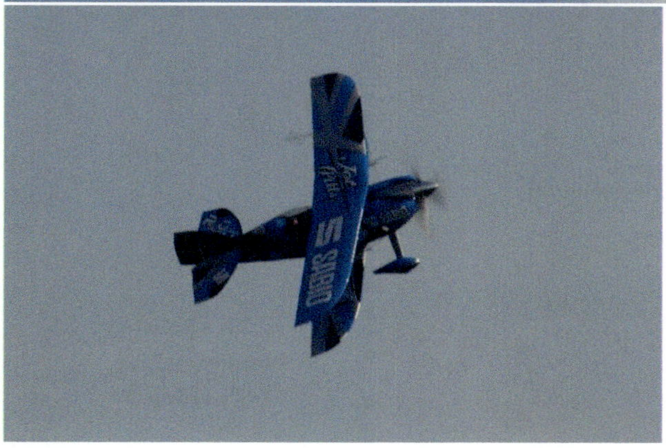

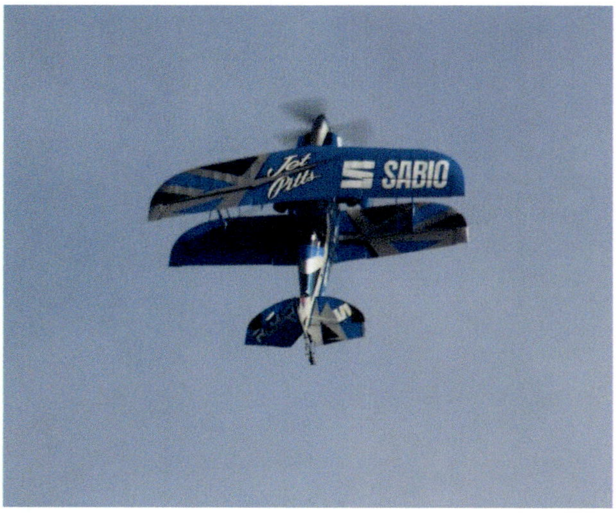

Quick Facts

Length: 18 ft 9 in (5.72 m)

Upper wingspan: 20 ft 0 in (6.10 m)

Lower wingspan: 19 ft 0 in (5.79 m)

Height: 6 ft 7+1⁄2 in (2.019 m)

Wing area: 125.0 sq ft (11.61 m2)

Cruise speed: 152 kn (175 mph, 282 km/h) (max. cruise)

Stall speed: 52 kn (60 mph, 96 km/h)

Range: 277 nmi (319 mi, 513 km) (55% power)

Service ceiling: 21,000 ft (6,400 m)

Rate of climb: 2,700 ft/min (14 m/s)

Bronco

Intended for counter-insurgency missions, the American-made North American Rockwell OV-10 Bronco is a twin-turboprop light attack and observation aircraft developed in the 1960s. With its ability to loiter for over three hours while carrying up to 3,200 pounds of weapons or equipment like paratroopers and stretchers, forward air control was one of the Bronco's primary duties.

After a 20-year career, the Bronco was finally replaced in 1991 by Pilatus PC-9s and IAI Westwinds. Upon retirement, the German Broncos were sent to various Luftwaffe museums and technical schools.

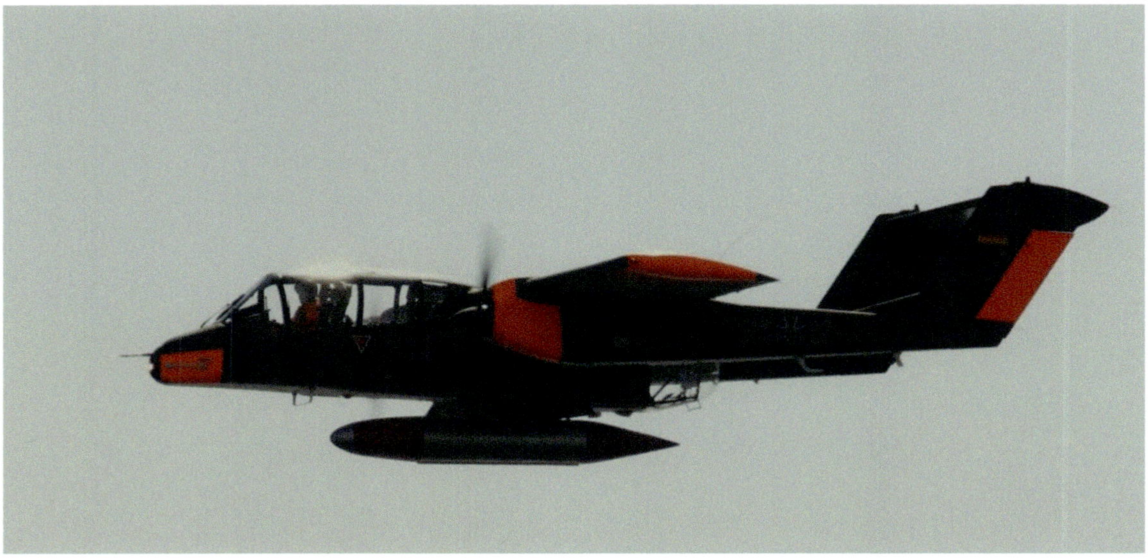

The concept aircraft was designed to operate from makeshift forward air bases using roads as runways, traveling at very slow to medium subsonic speeds with much longer loiter times than a pure jet. Efficient turboprop engines, which offer better performance than piston engines, would enable the longer loiter times. Weapons were to be mounted on the aircraft's centreline to allow for accurate aiming without adjusting for range.

The visually distinctive OV-10 has a central nacelle housing the pilots and cargo, and twin booms containing twin turboprop engines. Connecting the twin booms is a horizontal stabilizer that gives the aircraft its unique look. This twin-boom design allows the OV-10 to perform short take-offs and landings without catapults or arresting wires, even on aircraft carriers and amphibious assault ships. Further enabling operations from forward bases, the aircraft can take off and land on unimproved sites. The OV-10's versatile design supports effective missions launched from remote makeshift airfields.

The 2023 Air Festival was the debut of the OV-10B variant at Bournemouth. Originally produced for Germany to use as a target tug in the late 1960s, eighteen aircraft were delivered equipped with target towing equipment inside the fuselage. To enable visibility for the rear seat installed in the cargo bay, a transparent plastic dome replaced the rear cargo door.

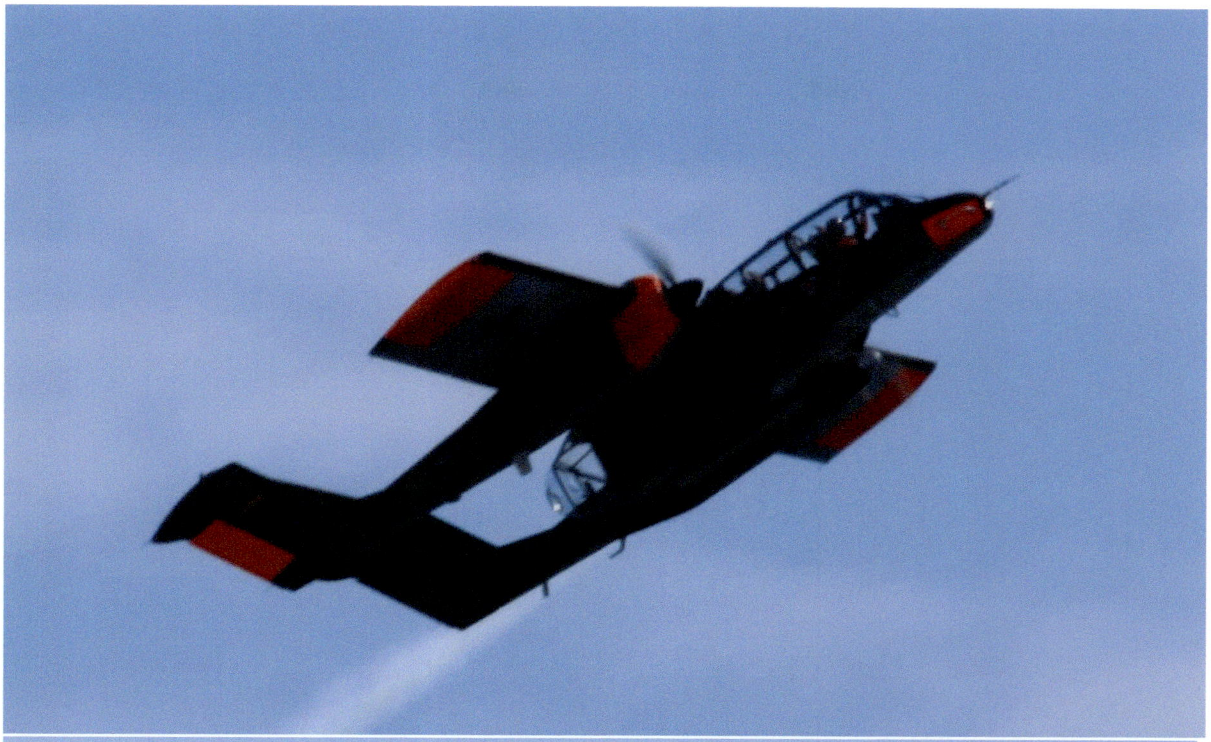

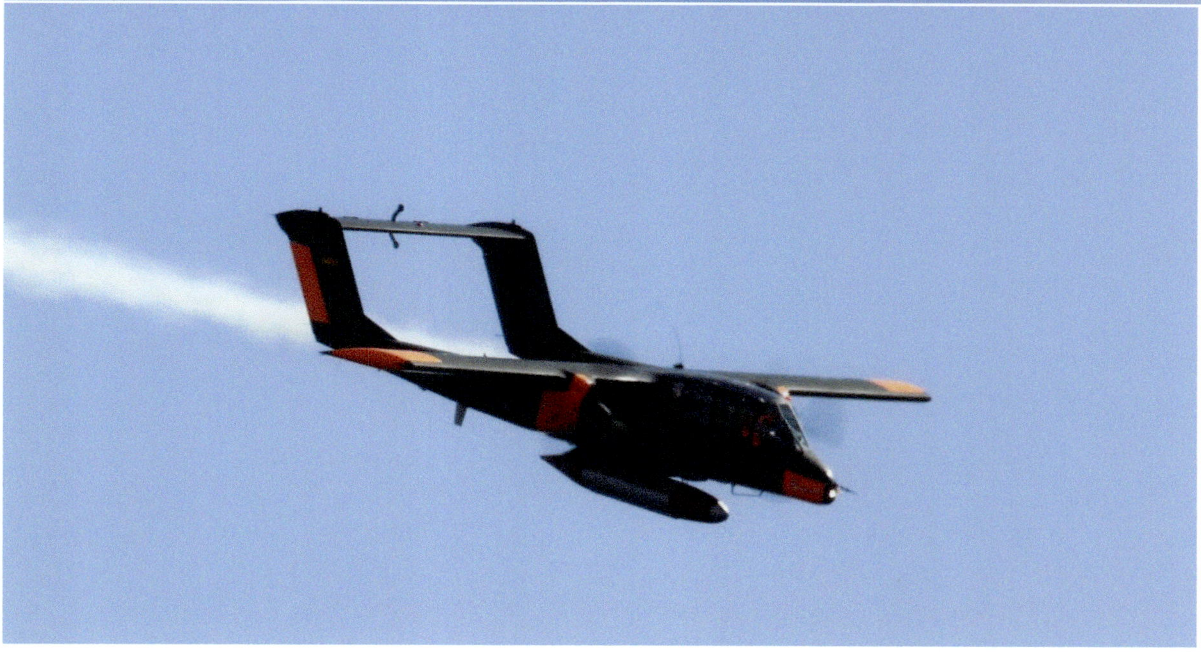

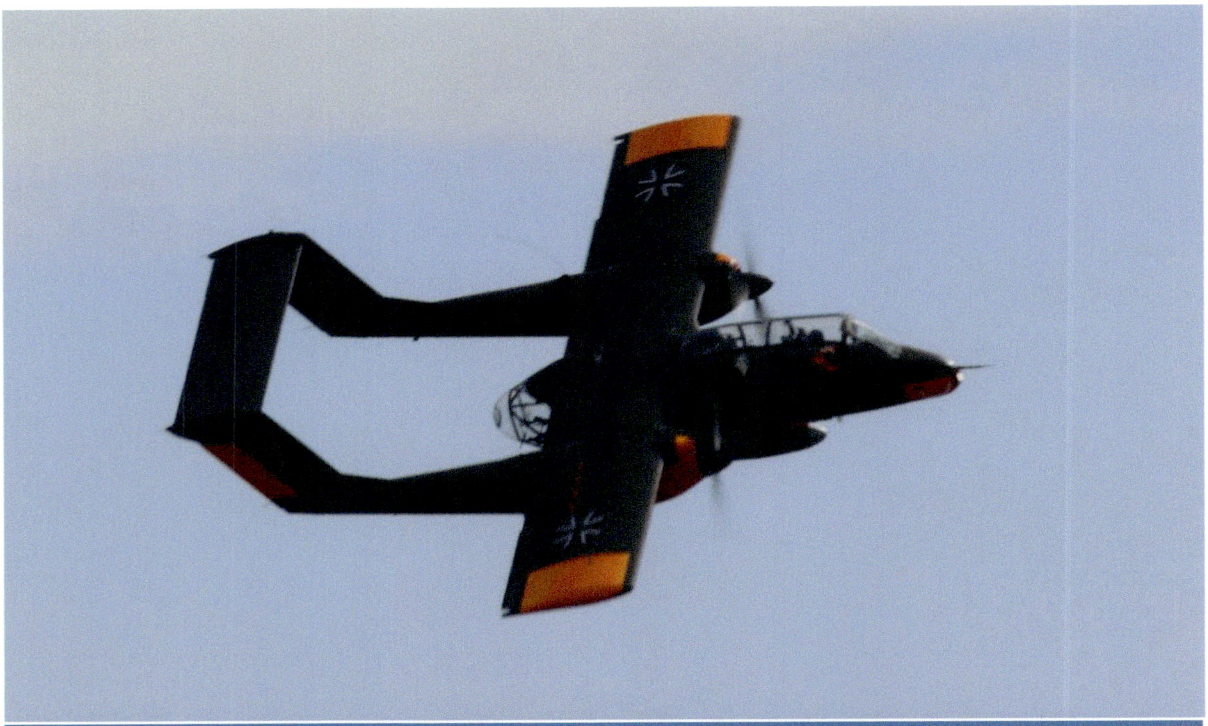

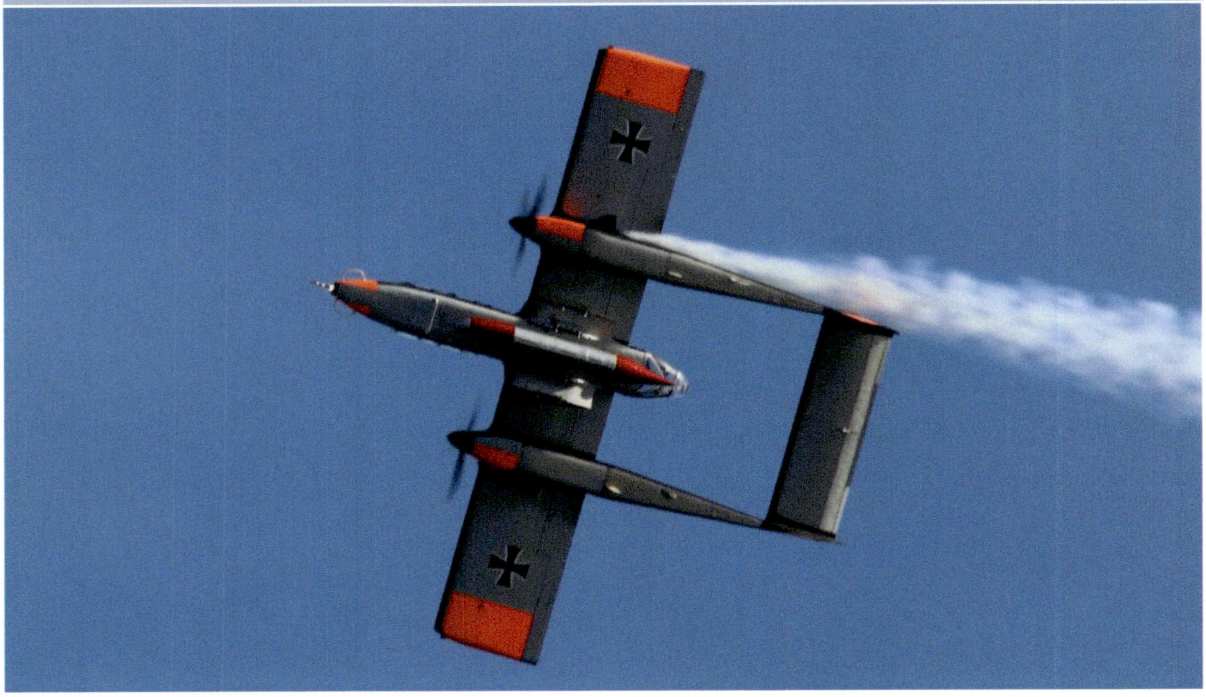

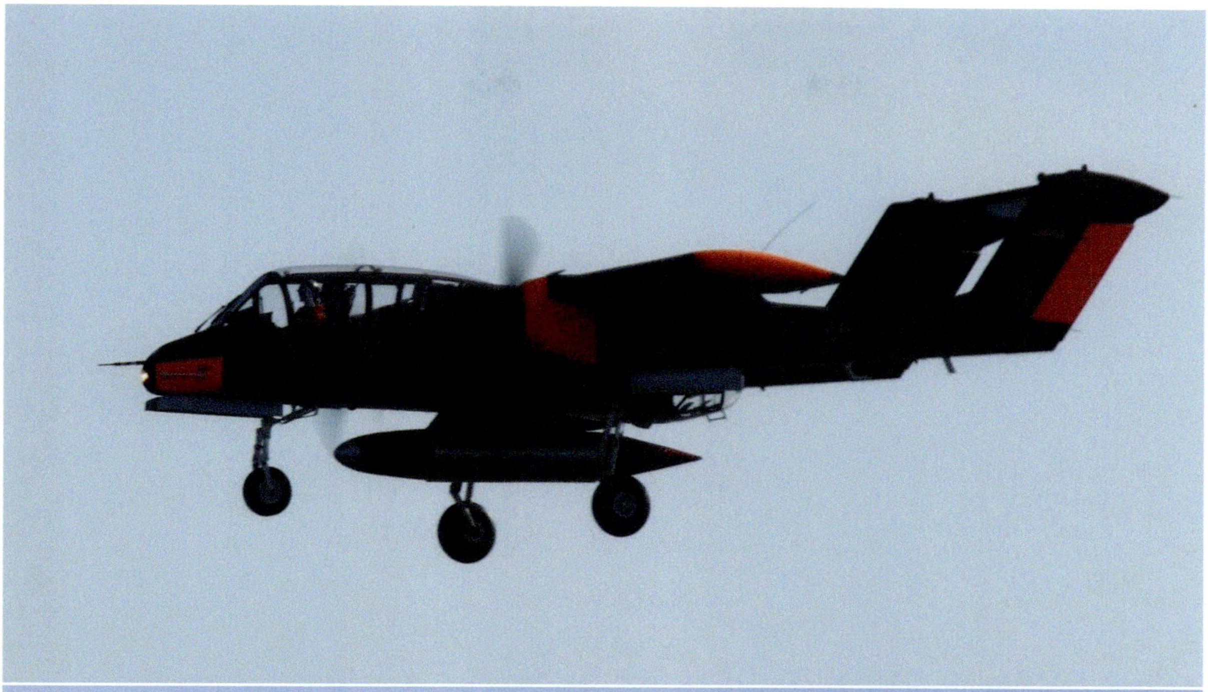

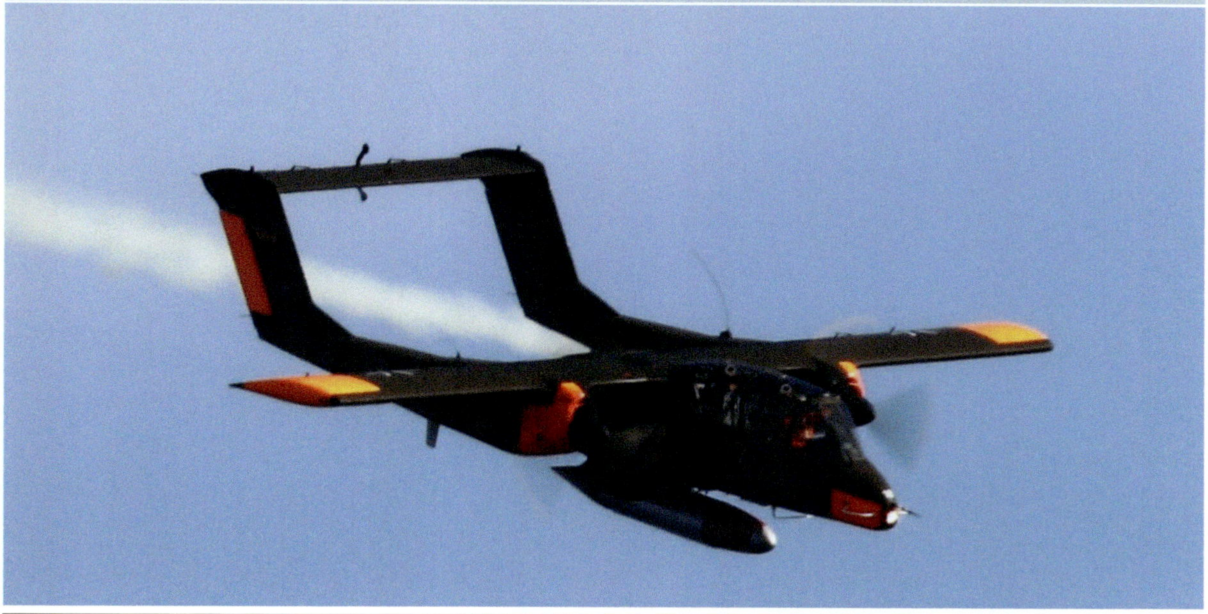

Quick Facts

Length: 44 ft 0 in (13.41 m)

Wingspan: 40 ft 0 in (12.19 m)

Height: 15 ft 2 in (4.62 m)

Maximum speed: 250 kn (290 mph, 460 km/h) at sea level

Combat range: 198 nmi (228 mi, 367 km)

Guns: 1 × 20 mm (0.79 in) M197 electric cannon or 4 × 7.62×51 mm M60C machine guns

Rockets: Tube launchers for 2.75 in (70 mm) FFARs/WAFARs or launchers for 5 in (127 mm) FFARs or WAFARs

Missiles: AIM-9 Sidewinder on wings only

Bombs: up to 500 lb (227 kg)

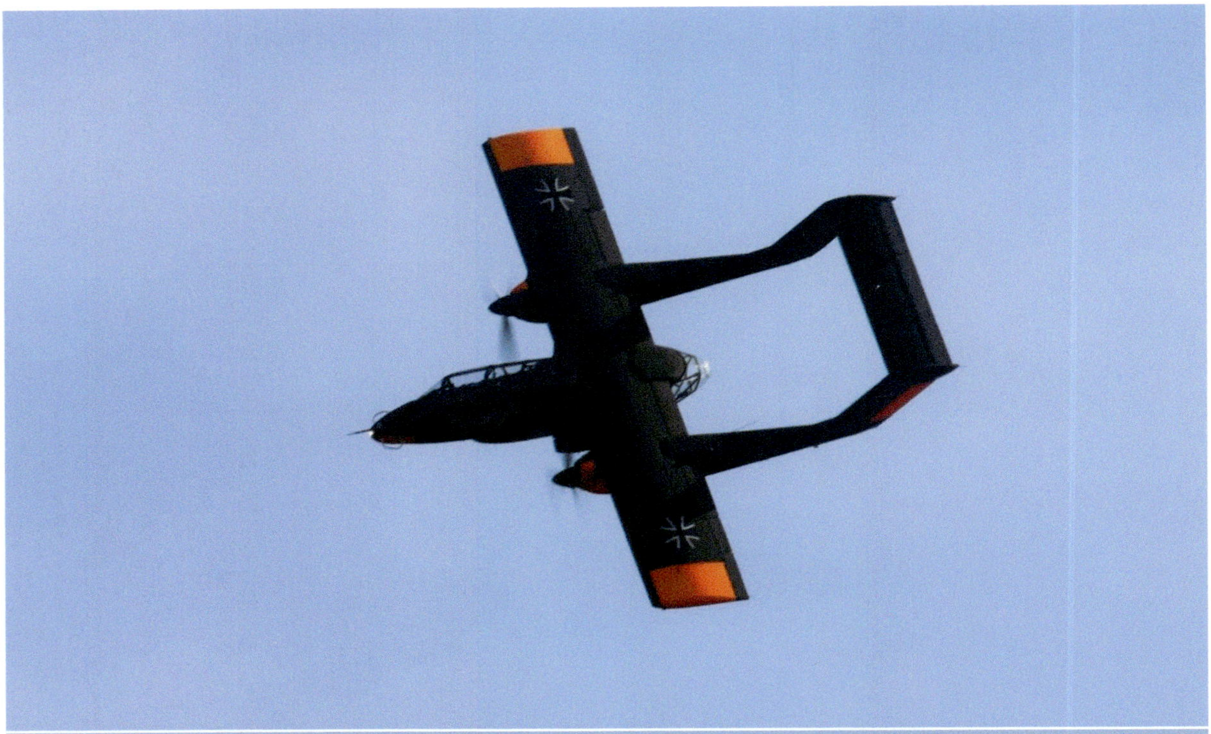

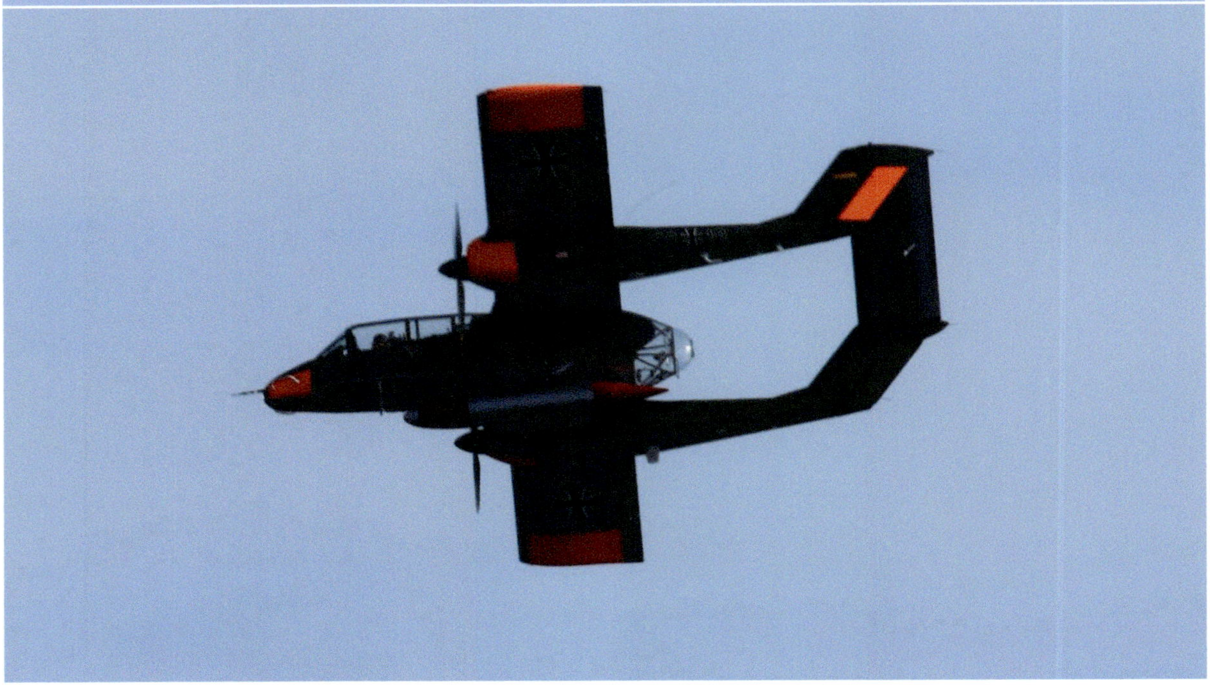

Starlings Aerobatic Display Team

Formed in 2021, The Starlings made their debut at the 2023 Bournemouth Air Festival. The team is comprised of British Aerobatic Champions Tom Cassells and Michael Pickin, who together boast over 50 years of aerobatic experience at airshows and competitions worldwide as solo performers and in formations. Tom, a current Display Authorisation Evaluator, and Michael, the youngest ever British Aerobatic Champion, pilot the latest Extra NG from Germany and the classic, championship-winning Cap 232. Both aerobatic aircraft are capable of unlimited manoeuvres, with roll rates exceeding 420 degrees per second and +10G/-10G pulls.

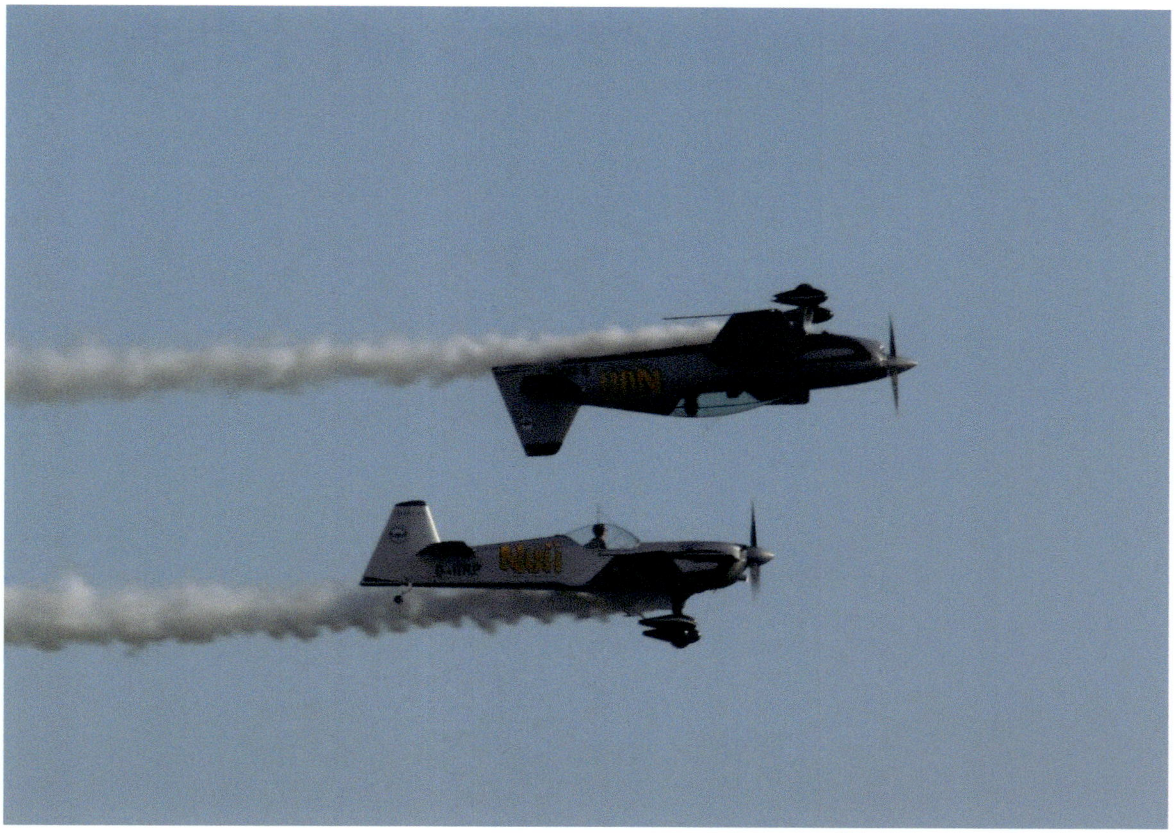

Extra NG

The NG is a low-wing, two-seat monoplane made of carbon fibre. Its cantilevered wings sit below the fuselage with a fixed landing gear, tail wheel, and enclosed tandem cockpit (passenger in front, pilot in rear). The aircraft is powered by a Textron-Lycoming AEIO-580-B1A engine turning a three or four-blade propeller.

Cap 232

The Cap 232 was based on the Cap 230 design developed for the French Air Force in 1985, which featured an all-wooden wing and fuselage. Over the years, Cap improved on the 230 with the 231 and 231Ex models. This evolution culminated in the 232, which combines a lightweight yet sturdy wooden fuselage with a newly designed carbon fibre wing. This updated design enables a roll rate exceeding 420 degrees per second, while the Lycoming AEIO-540 300hp engine allows climb rates surpassing 3,300 feet per minute.

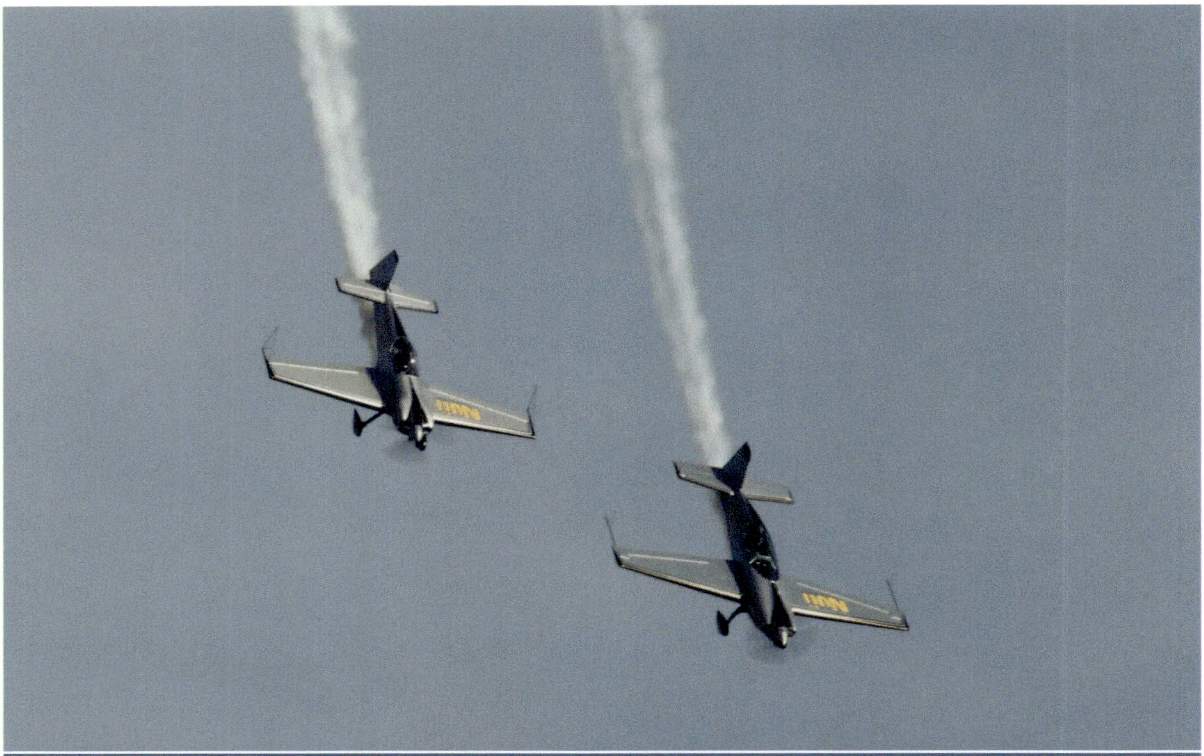

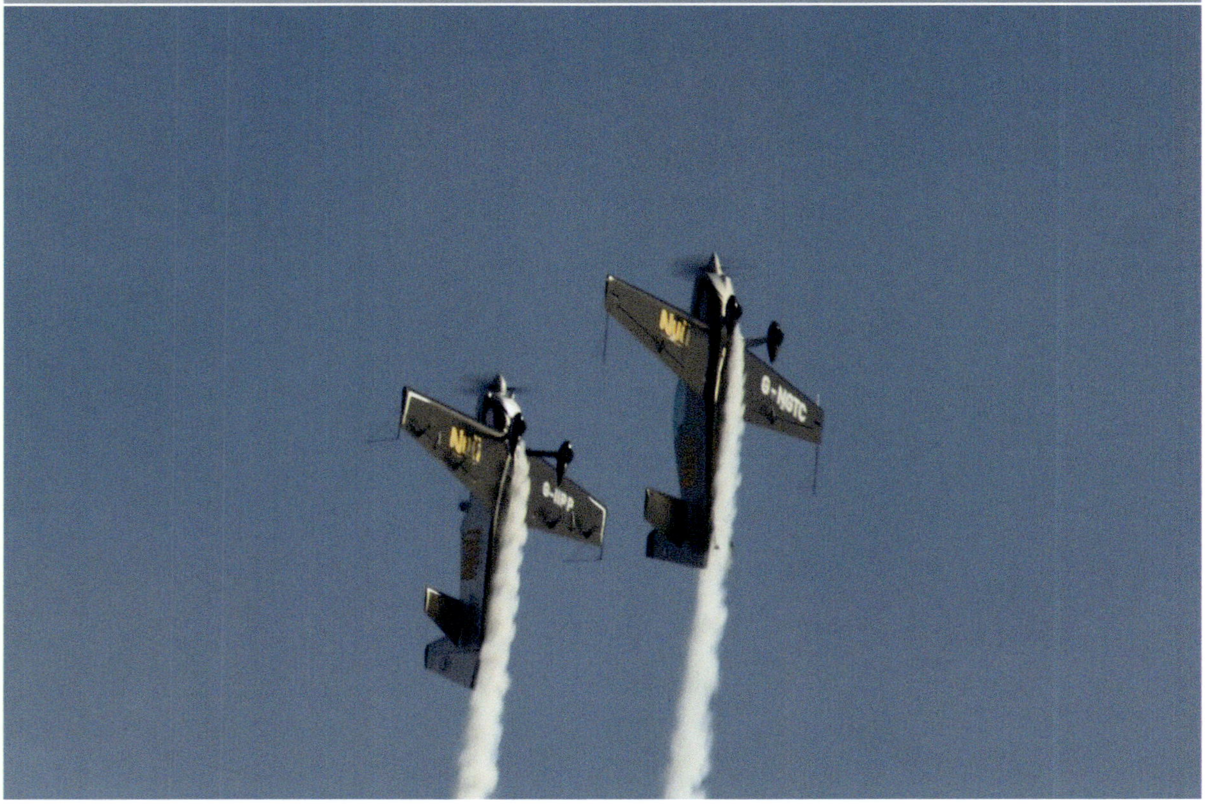

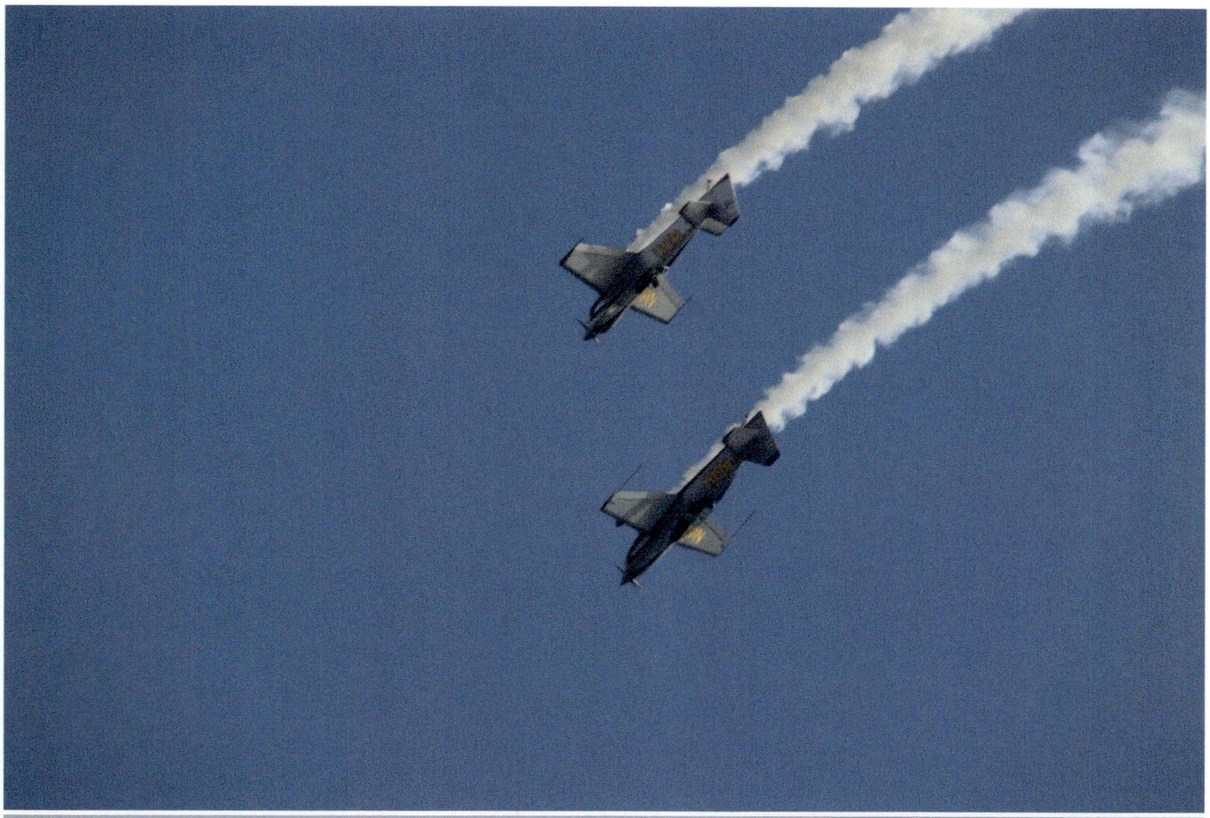

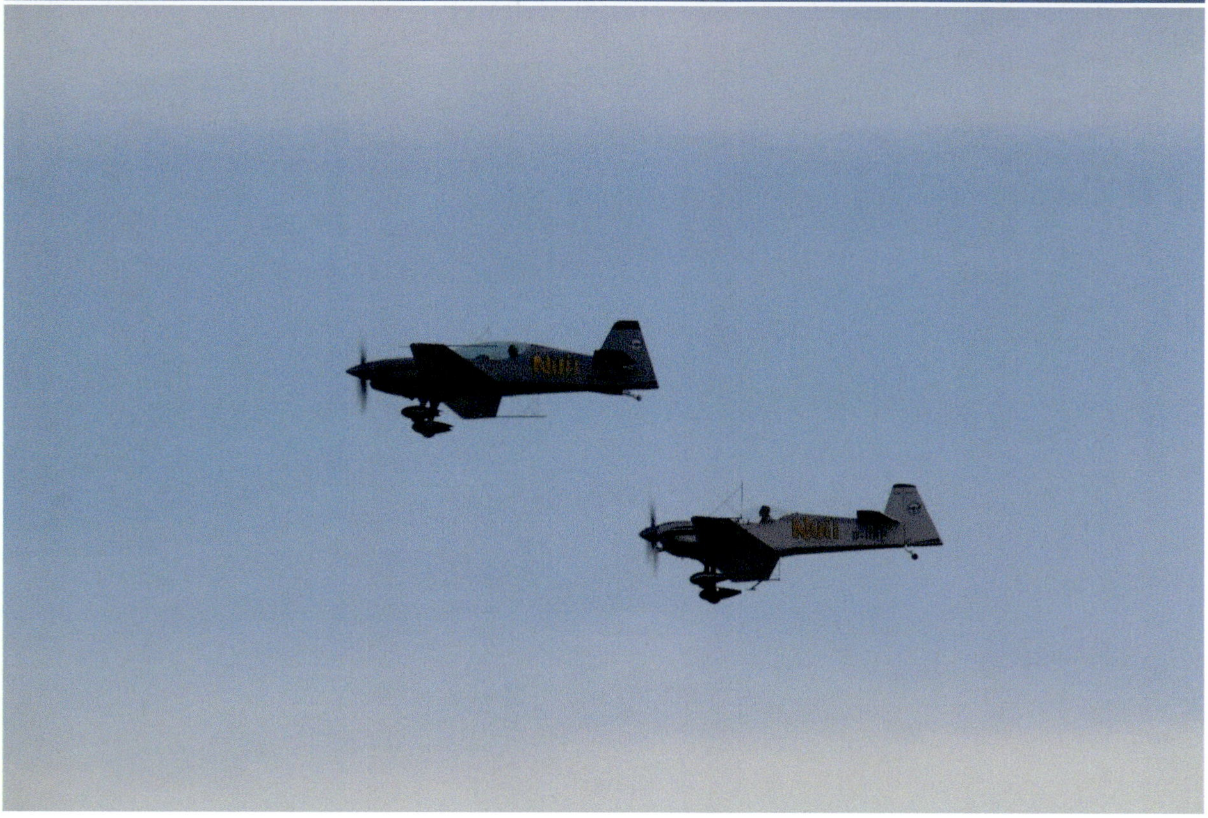

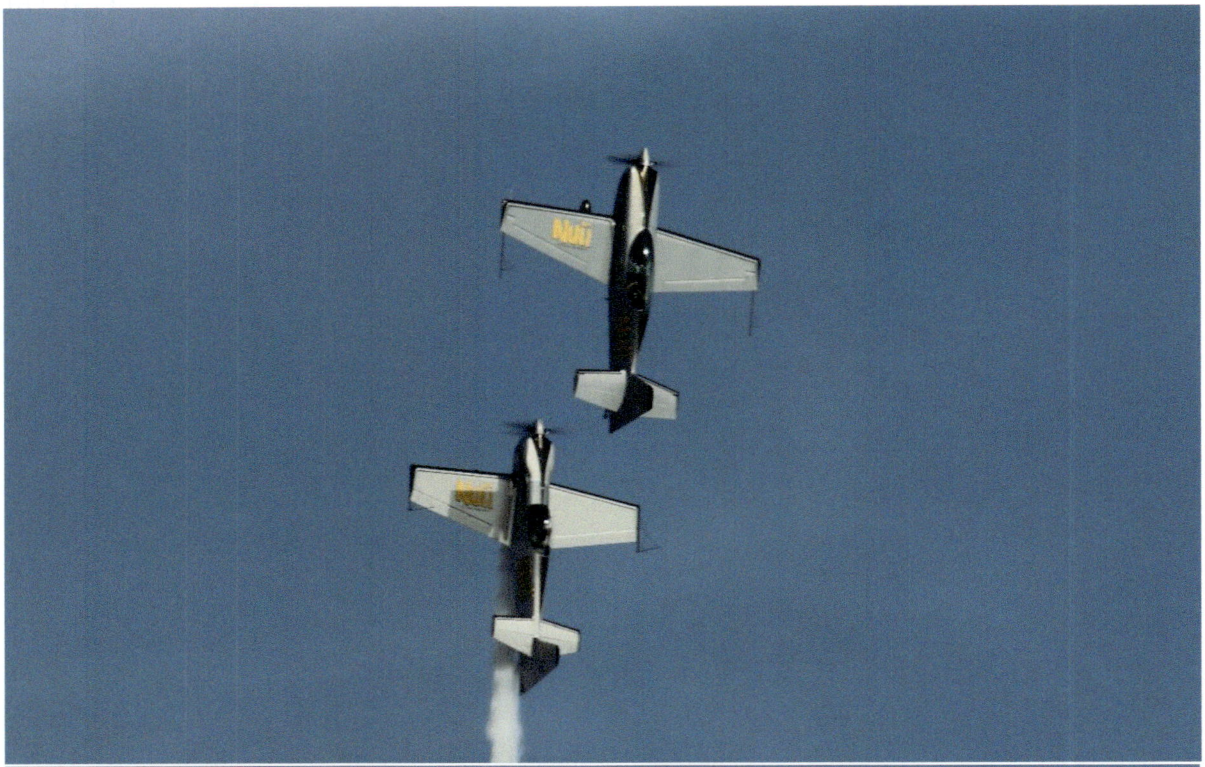

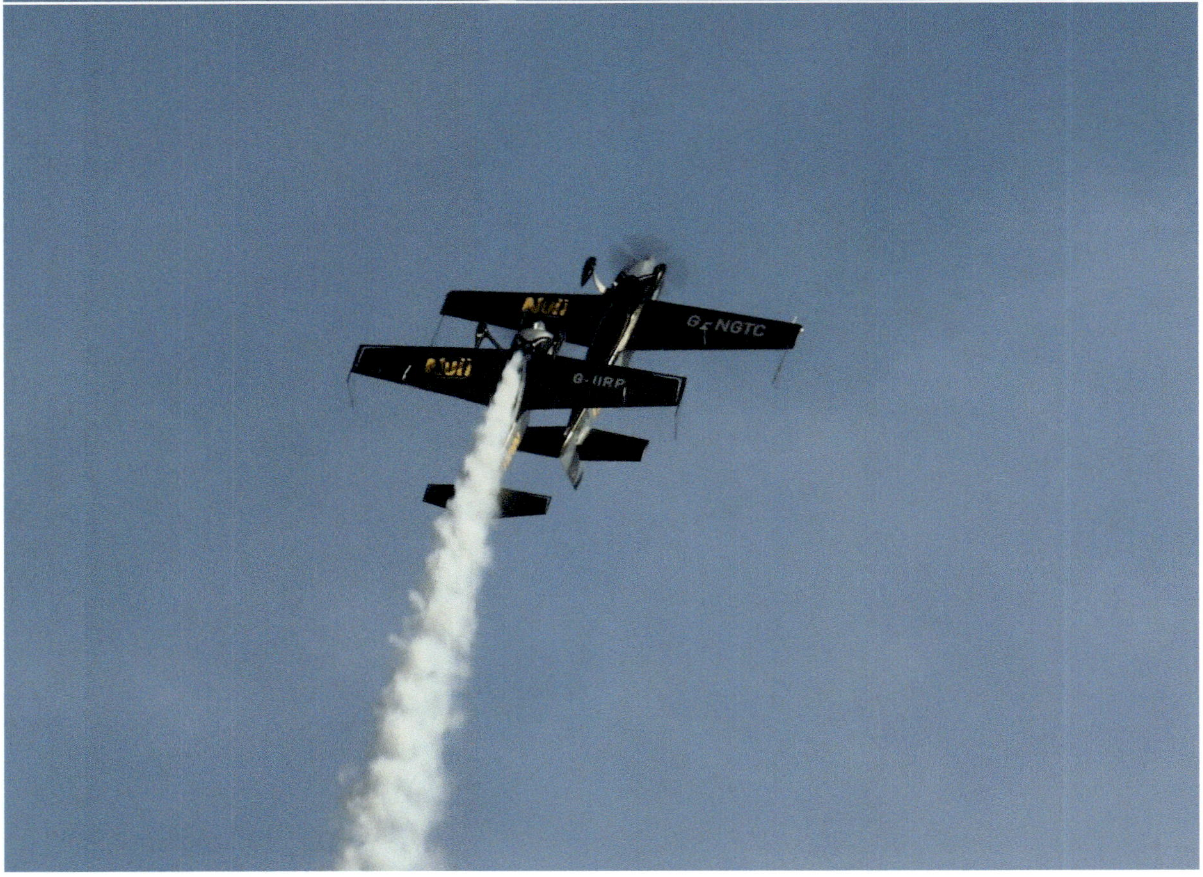
G-NGTC
G-IIRP

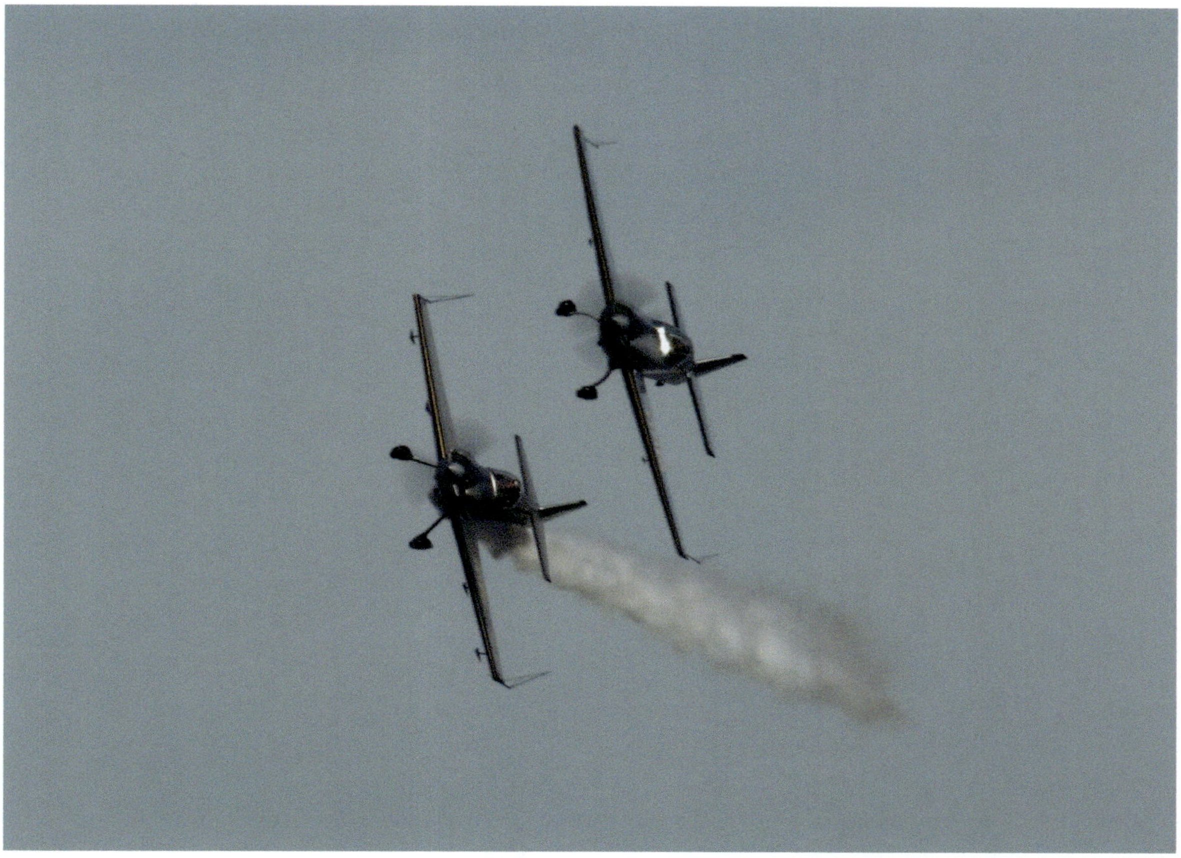

Quick Facts – Extra NG

Crew: 2

Length: 7.1 m (23 ft 4 in)

Wingspan: 8.0 m (26 ft 3 in) 8.3m with optional wingtips

Height: 2.52 m (8 ft 3 in)

Fuel capacity: 196 litres

Powerplant: 1 × Textron-Lycoming AEIO-580-B1A , 235 kW (315 hp) at 2700 RPM

Quick Facts – Cap 232

Crew: One Pilot

Wingspan: 7.4 m

Length: 6.75 m

Height: 1.9 m

Powerplant: Lycoming AEIO-540-A1E 300hp

Max speed: 405 kph

Endurance: approx 3 1/2 hrs

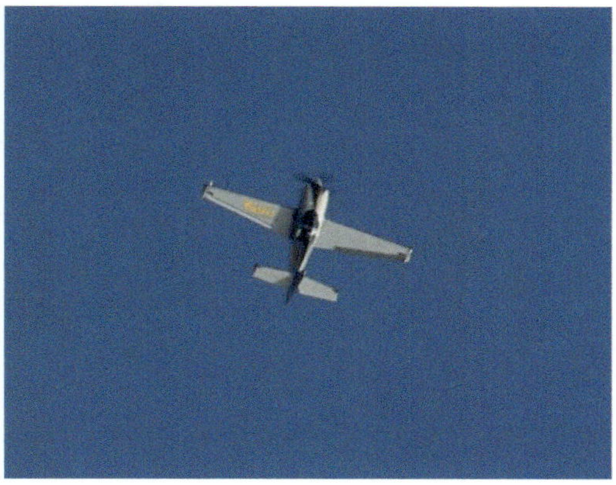

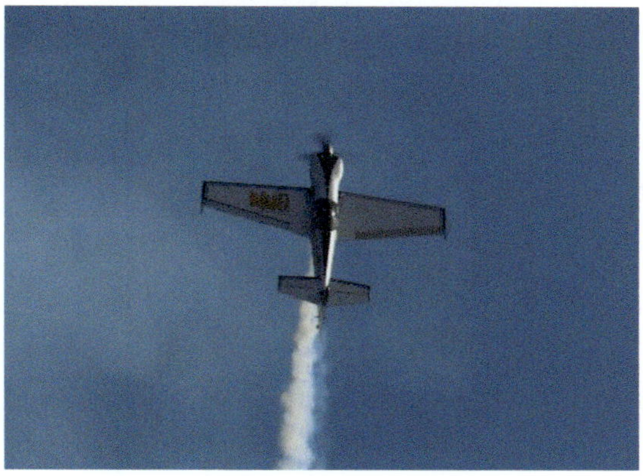

Patrouille REVA

In 1983, Réal Weber, a former air force pilot, decided to build his own aircraft inspired by the "Variez" drawings. Two years later, he created the one-of-a-kind aerobatics aircraft called the "Acroez." Weber's initial plan was to perform solo aerobatics, but growing public interest led him to be joined by two other retired French Air Force pilots. Together in 1992, they formed the aerobatic demonstration team called Patrouille REVA.

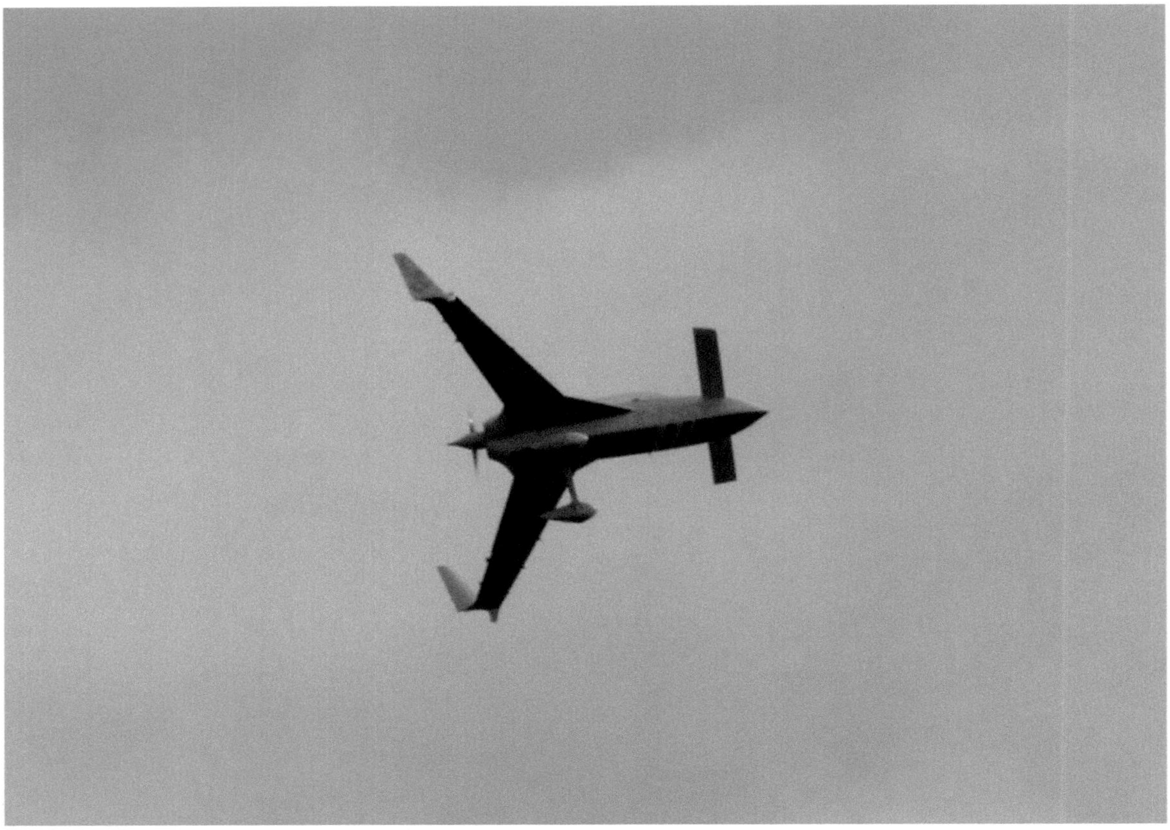

The Patrouille REVA aerobatic team demonstrated their skills in two unique aircraft - a Rutan LongEZ and VariEZ - designed by Burt Rutan, maker of SpaceShipOne. With a top speed of 315 km/h and fuel consumption as low as 25l/h, these distinctive planes performed a 16-figure aerobatic routine, ending with a heart shape. Trails of white smoke accentuated the dazzling manoeuvres.

The Long-EZ aircraft features a canard front wing, swept main wings with wingtip rudders, and a rear-mounted pusher propeller driven by a Lycoming aircraft engine. The landing gear consists of fixed main wheels with aerodynamic spats and a retractable nosewheel. The Long-EZ was a larger redesign of the earlier VariEZ model, allowing the use of more widely available Lycoming powerplants rather than the hard-to-find Volkswagen or small Continental engines the VariEZ was originally designed for. Changes from the VariEZ include a larger main wing with less sweep and a modified Eppler 1230 aerofoil, larger strakes for more fuel and baggage capacity, and a slightly wider cabin.

After almost 30 years of performing continuous airshow flying across Europe, the Patrouille REVA civilian aerobatics team, one of the most unique and respected in its field, has been disbanded. The team had performed at the 2013 and 2015 Bournemouth Air Festivals, but unfortunately, due to the disbanding, aviation enthusiasts will no longer have the opportunity to see this distinctive group grace the skies during the airshow season.

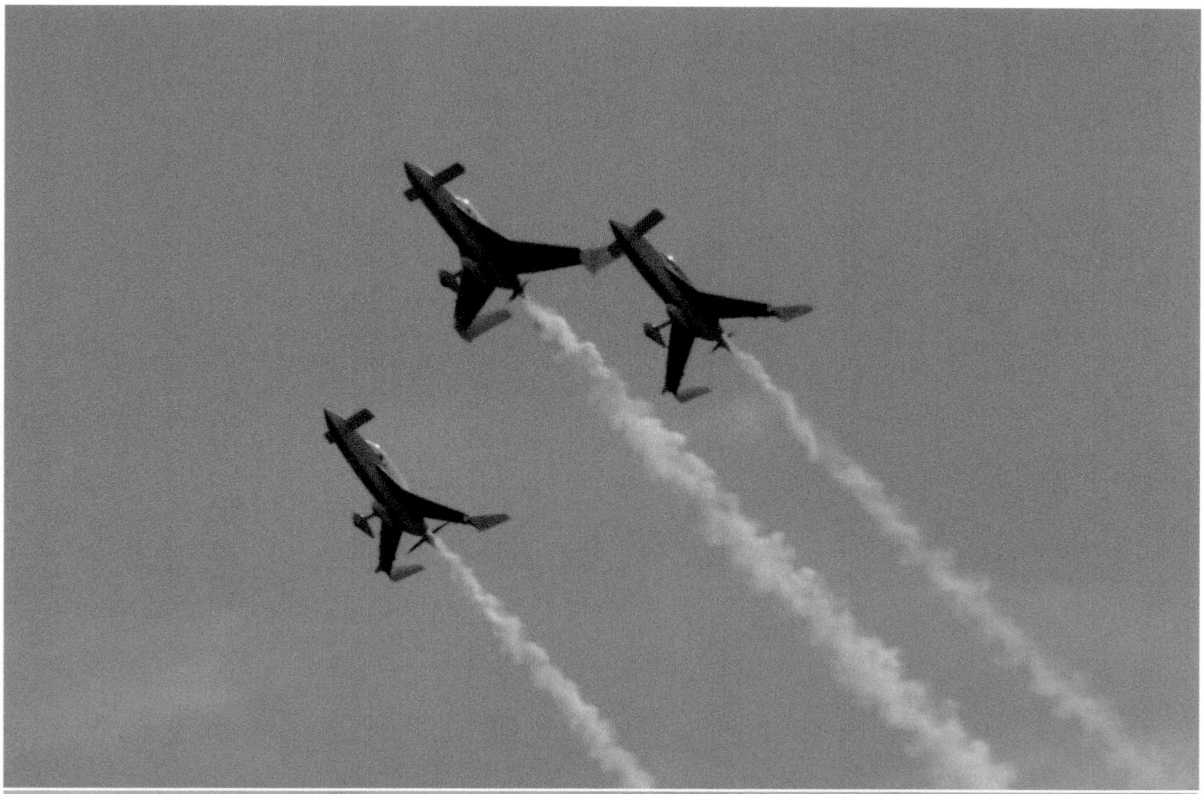

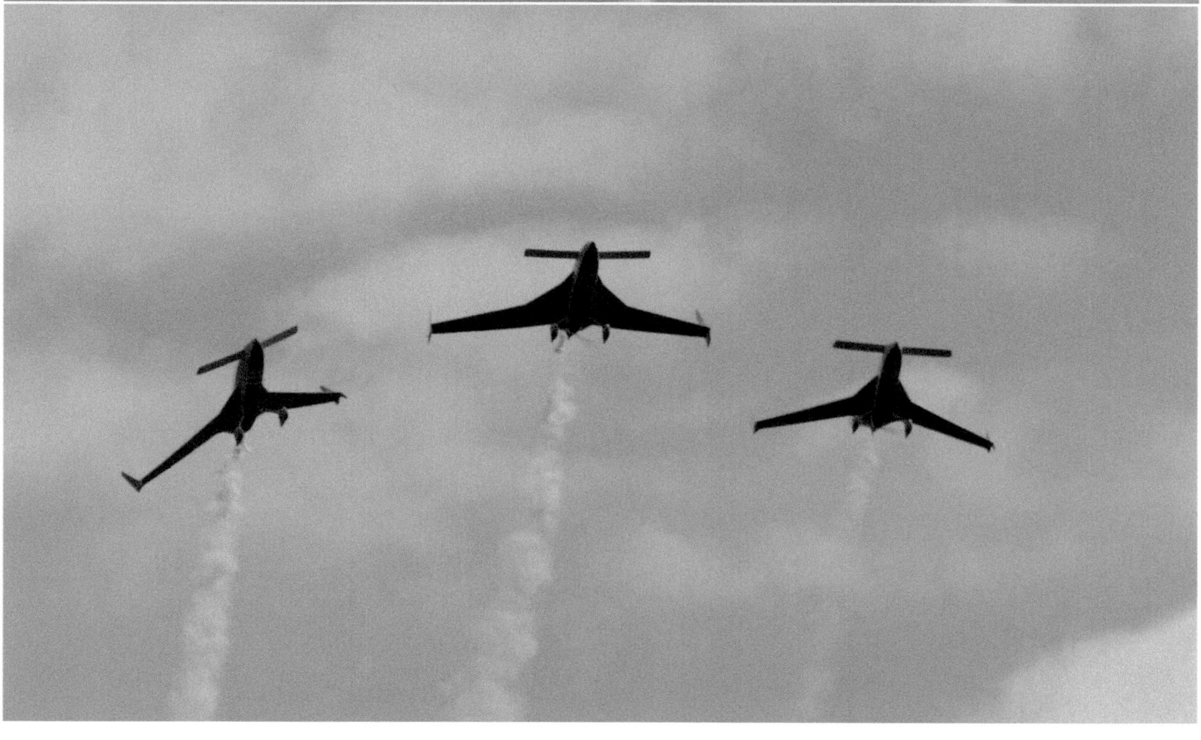

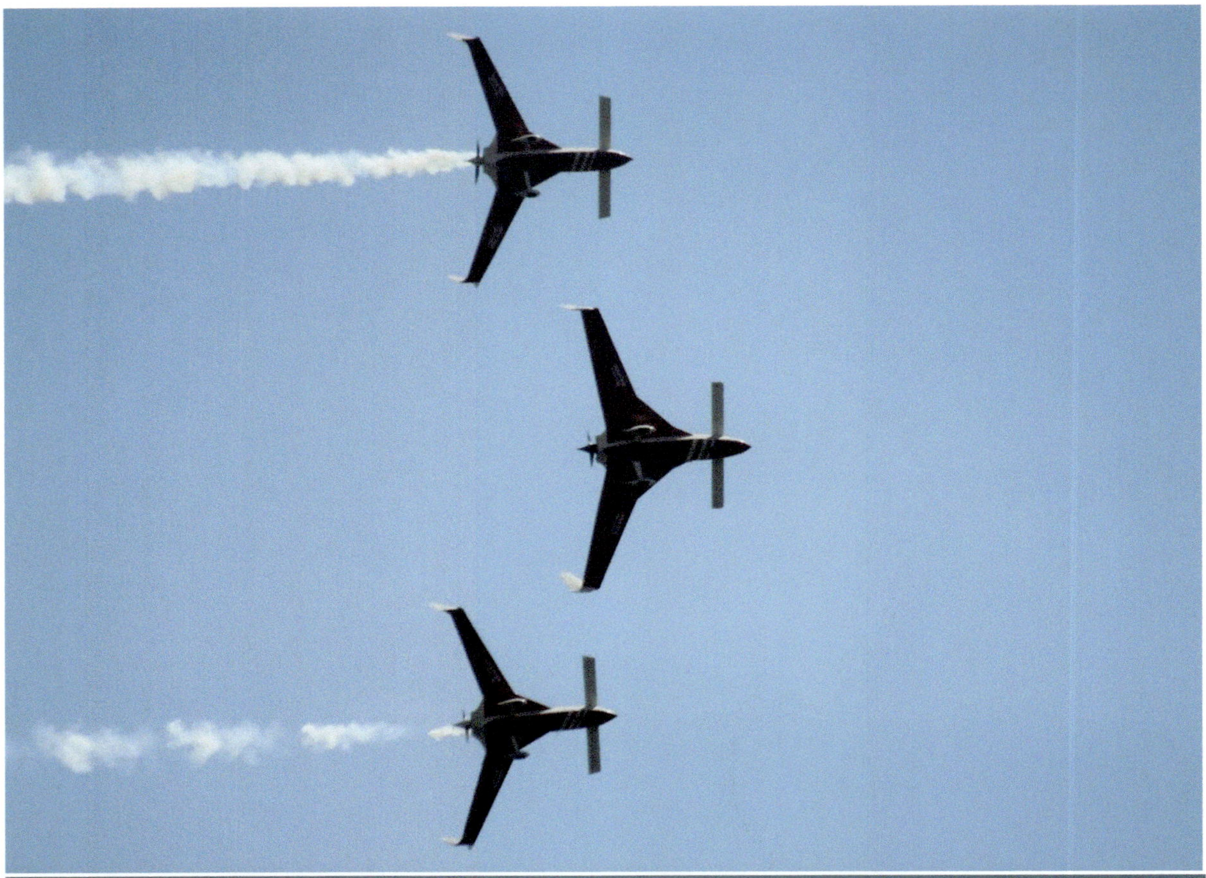

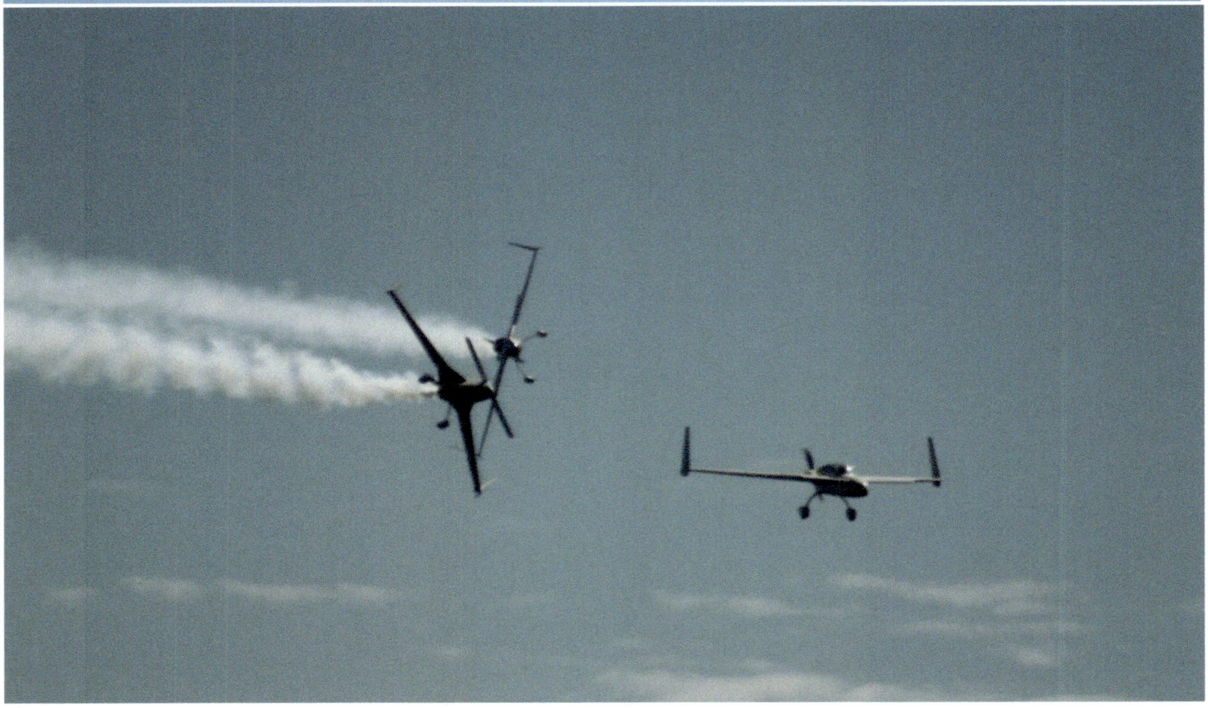

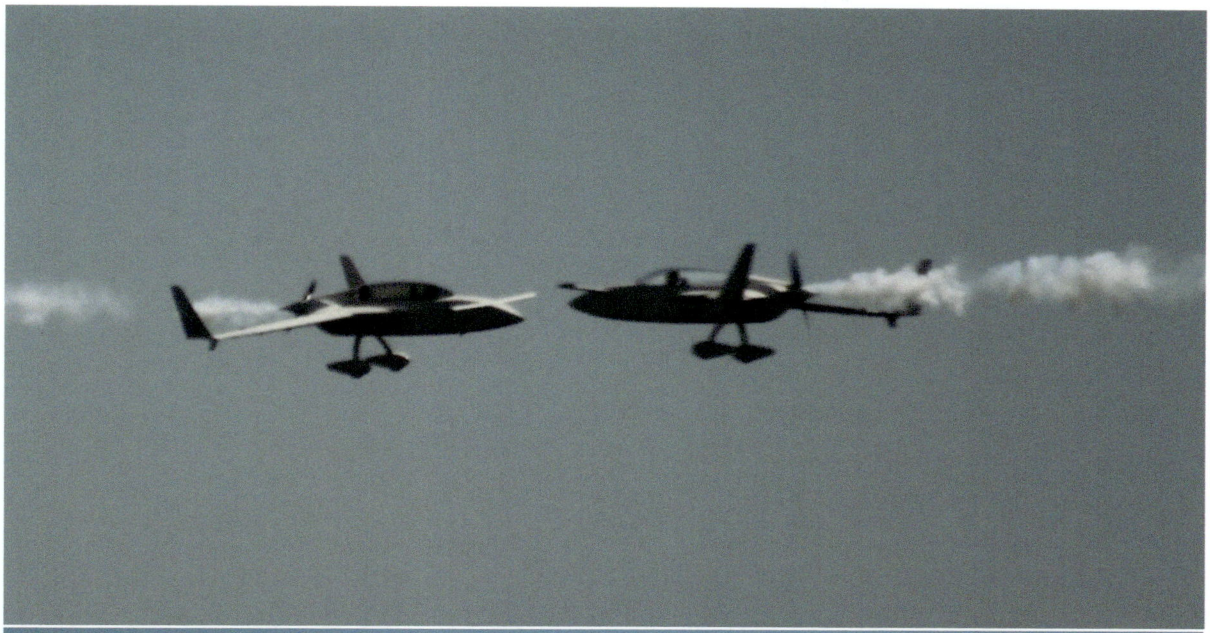

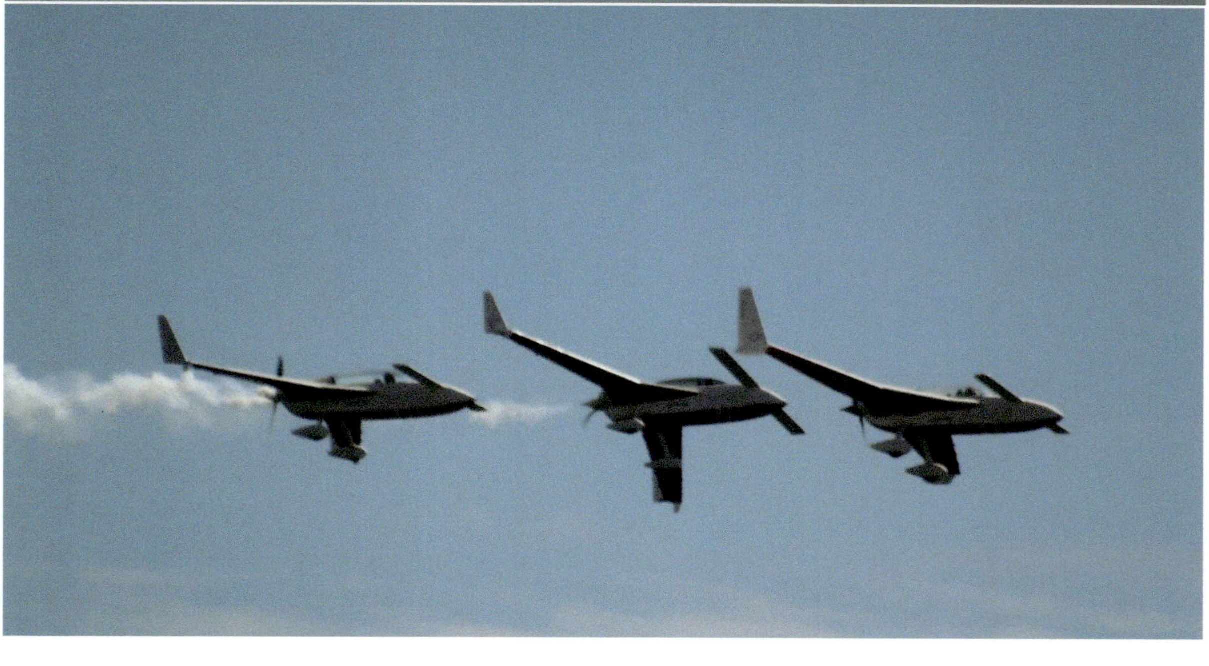

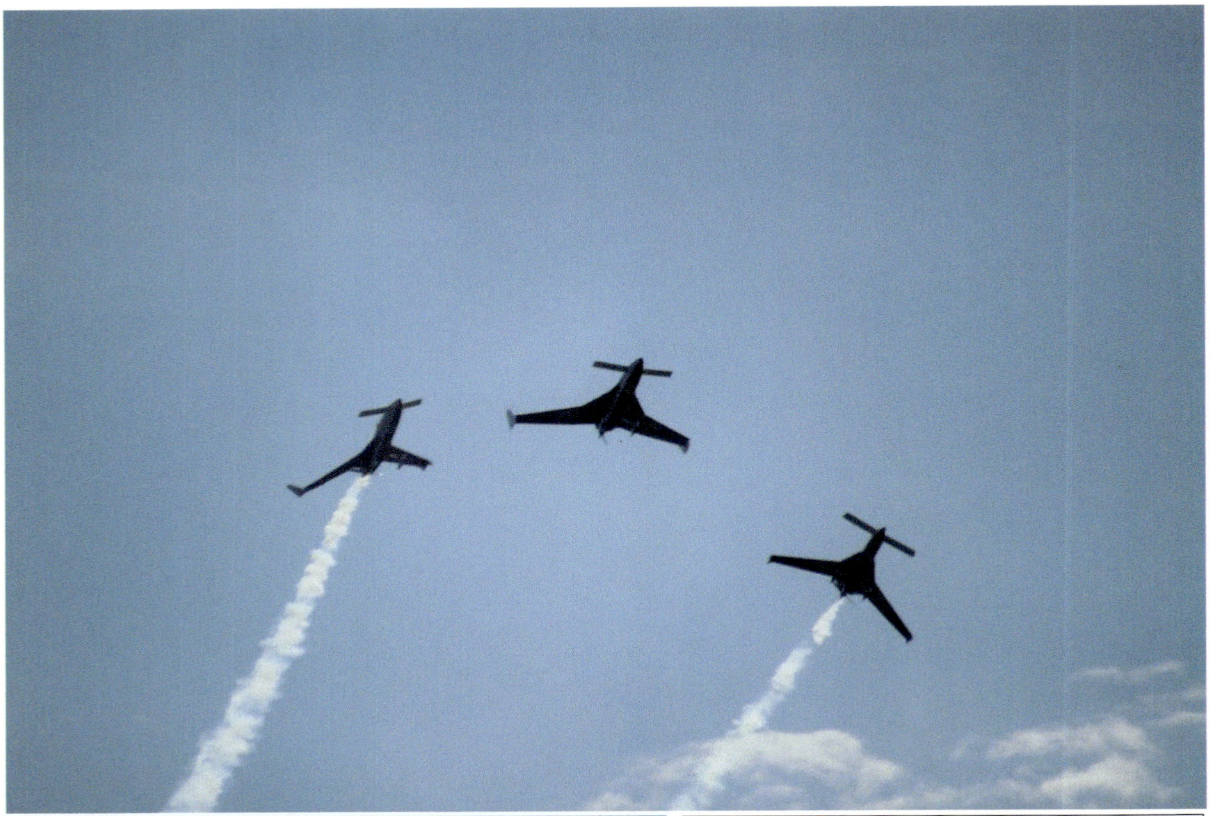

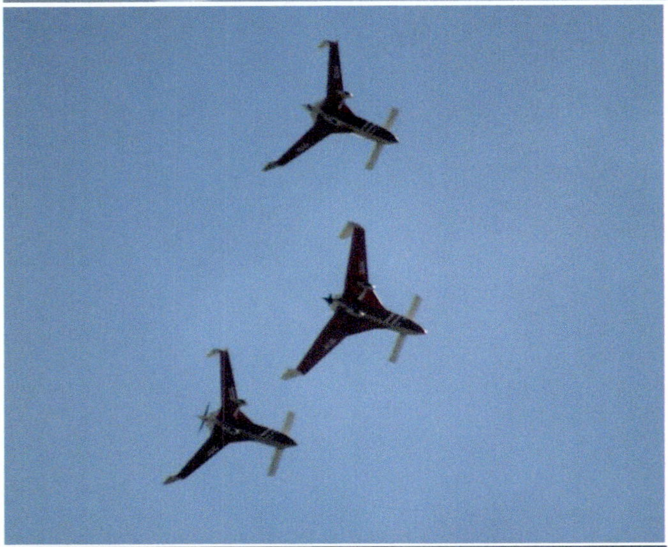

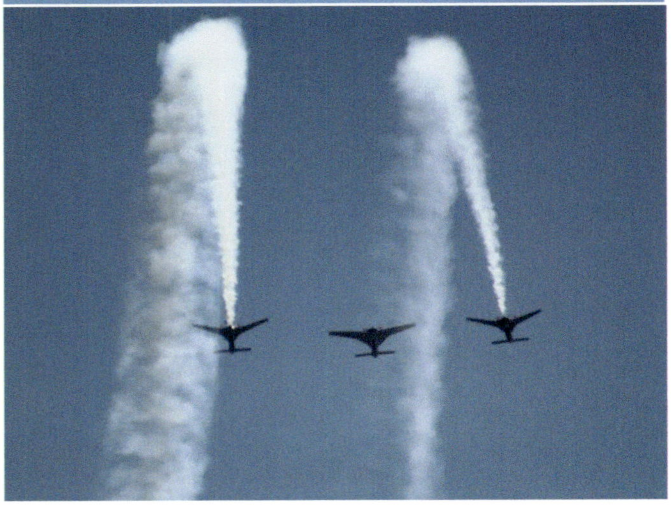

Quick Facts

General

Crew: 1 pilot

Capacity: 1 passenger

Length: 16 ft 10 in (5.12 m)

Wingspan: 26 ft 1 in (7.96 m)

Height: 7 ft 10 in (2.40 m)

Fuel capacity: 52 US Gal (197 L)

Powerplant: 1 × Lycoming O-235 air-cooled flat-four engine, 115 hp

Performance

Maximum speed: 185 mph (298 km/h, 161 kn) (max cruise)

Cruise speed: 144 mph (232 km/h, 125 kn) (40% power)

Range: 2,010 mi (3,230 km, 1,750 nmi)

Service ceiling: 27,000 ft

Fireflies – Van RV-4

The Fireflies perform in two Van's RV4s, the most successful line of build-it-yourself kit planes in the world. With impressive all-around capabilities, the fast, agile, and fun RV-4 feels like a natural extension of the pilot's body. Over the years, the RV-4 has competed in various performance events, from the National Championship Air Races to numerous aerobatic competitions.

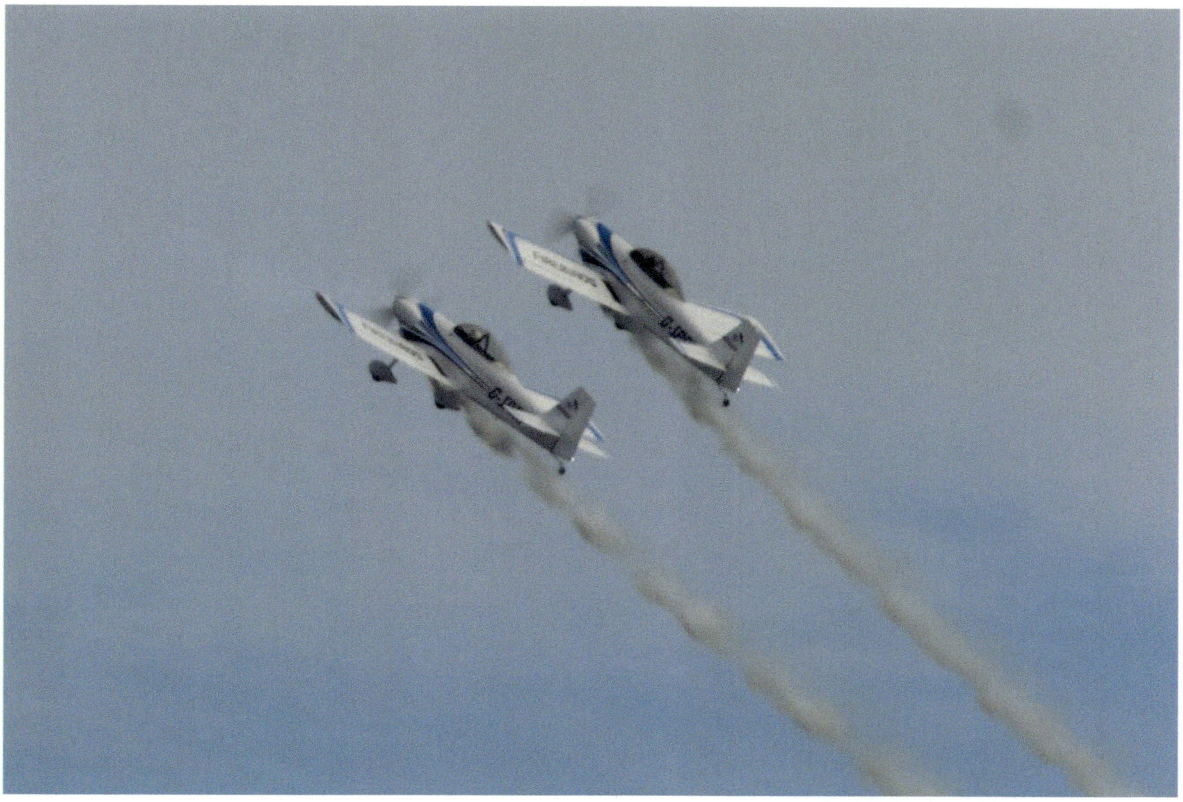

The two-seat RV-4 light aircraft accommodates a modest yet functional amount of baggage. While the cockpit is cozy, the seats remain comfortable. The kit includes a control stick for the rear passenger to participate in flying the plane, which is piloted solely from the front seat. The RV-4 is designed for 150-160 horsepower engines, though powerplants ranging from 125 hp to 180 hp can be readily installed and perform well.

The RV-4 is also an excellent cross-country aircraft, with many couples routinely using it as their long-distance travel machine. Its ability to land at small airports allows them to reach their intended destinations directly, rather than only the nearest major airport.

The Fireflies Display Team has frequently graced the Bournemouth Air Festival with their daytime aerobatic displays, which include close formations, opposition manoeuvres, and synchronized routines that fill the sky with white smoke. Their twilight pyrotechnic show, complete with wingtip pyrotechnics and coloured LED lights along the fuselage, makes the aircraft stand out dramatically against the night sky and has become a perennial favourite of the Twilight Displays over the years.

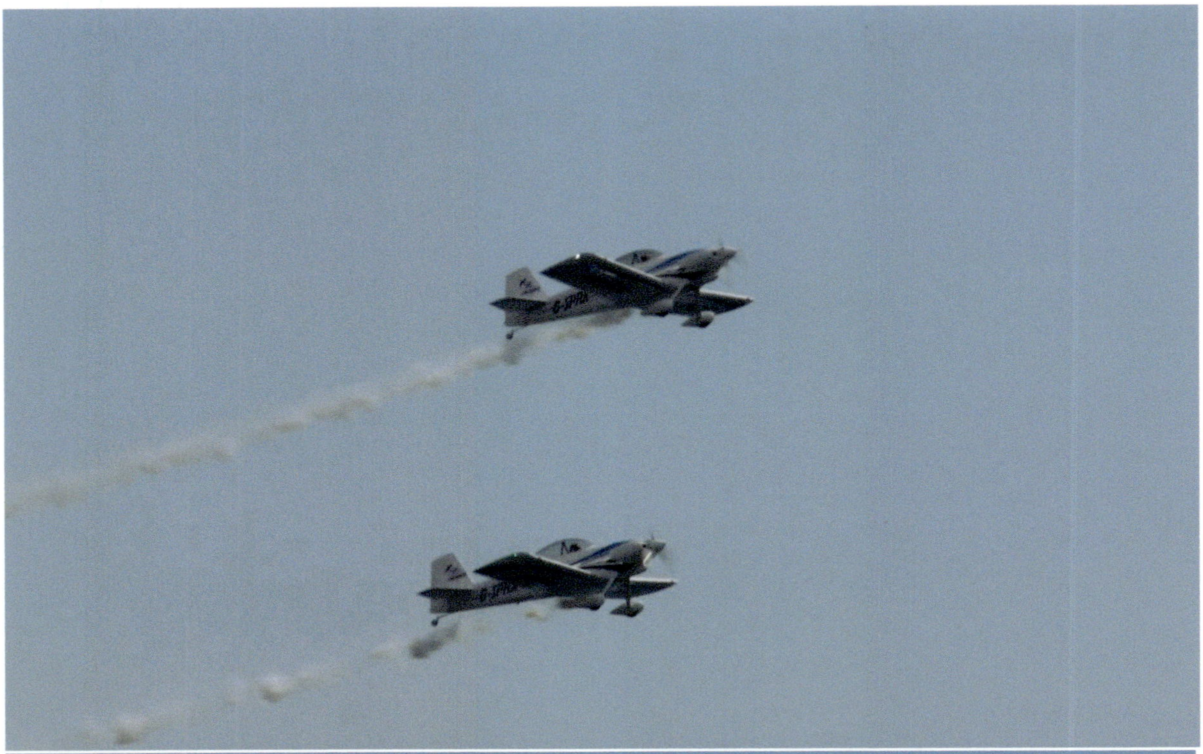

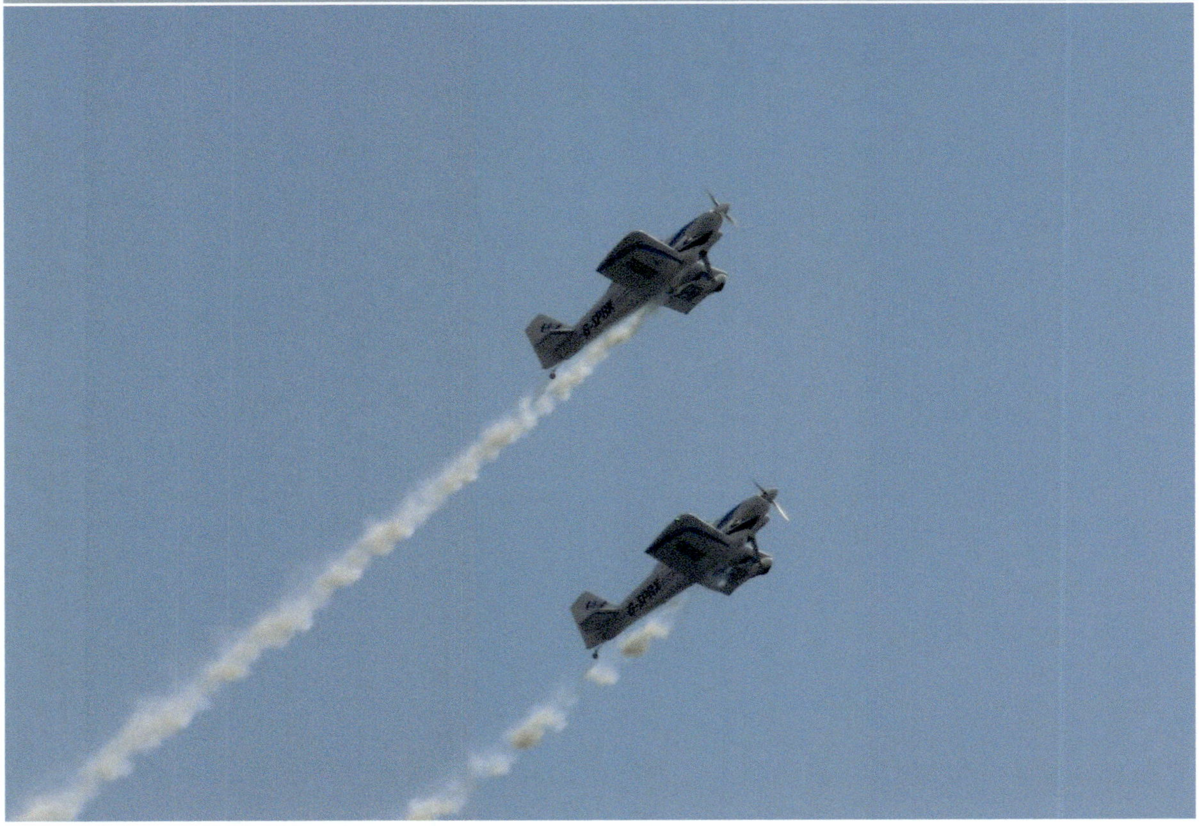

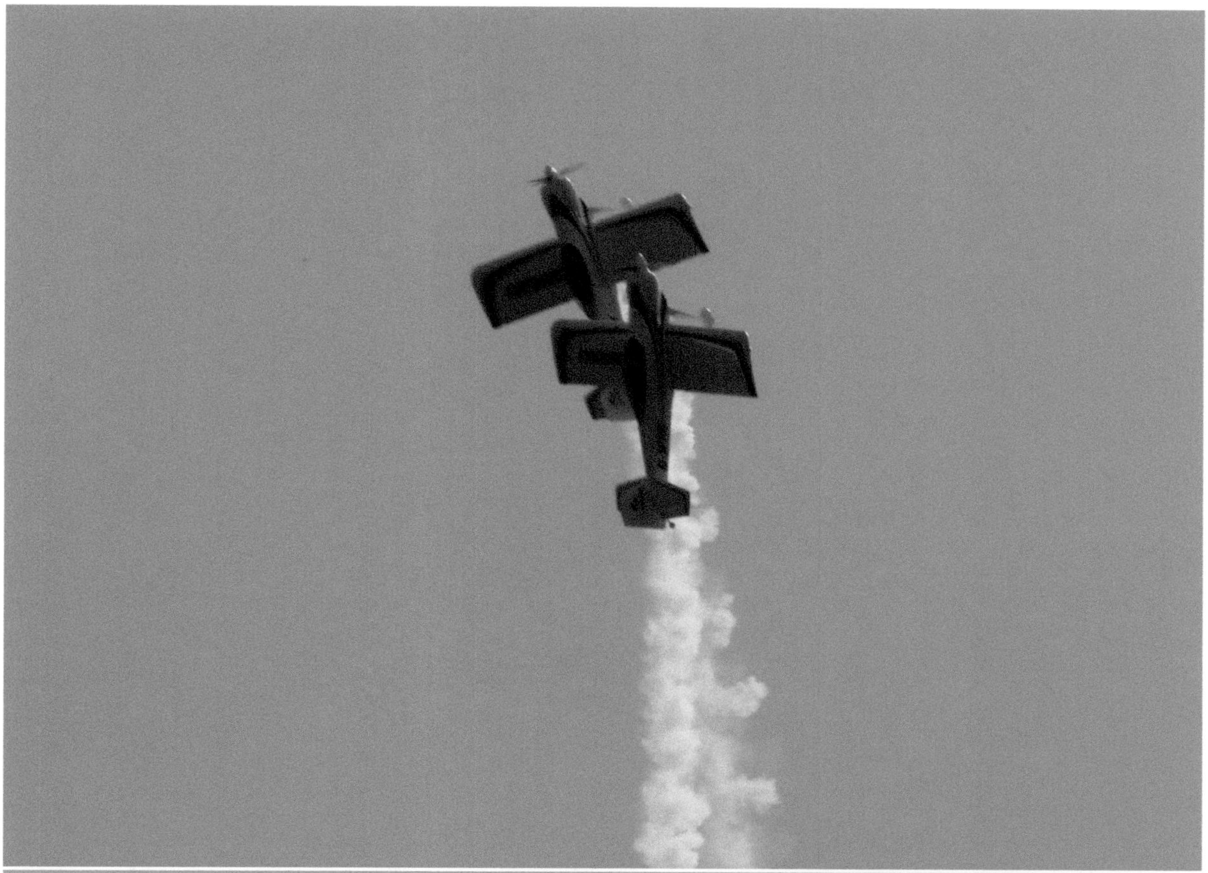

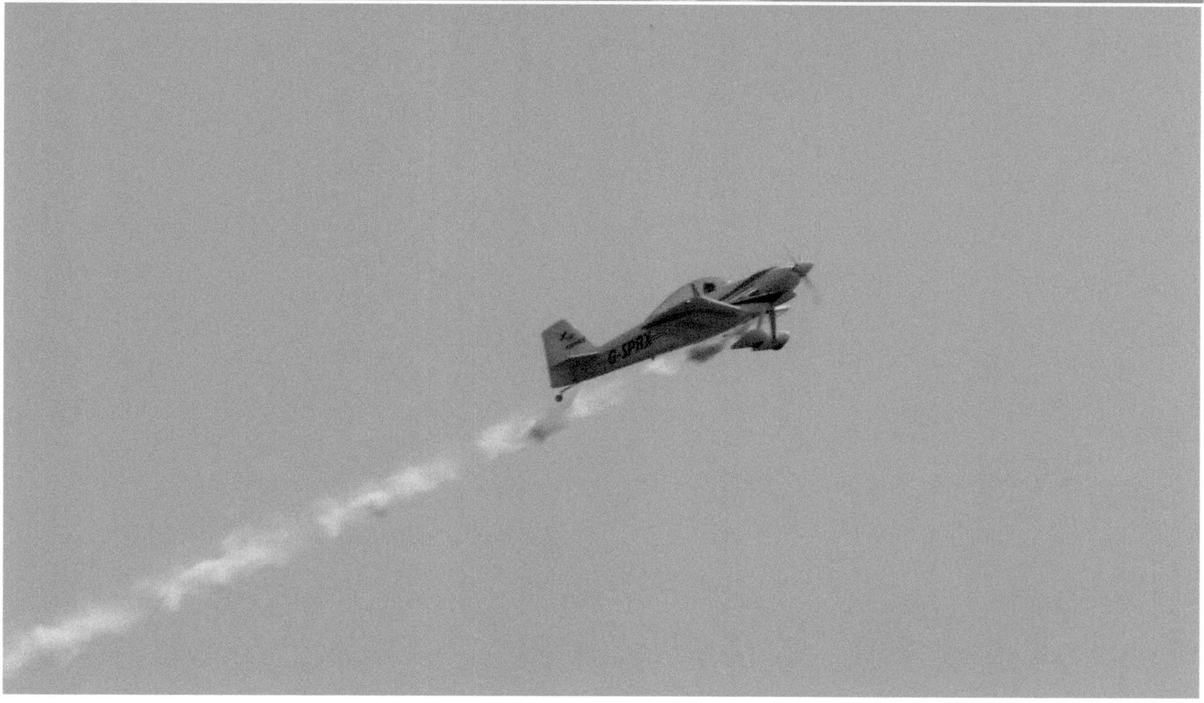

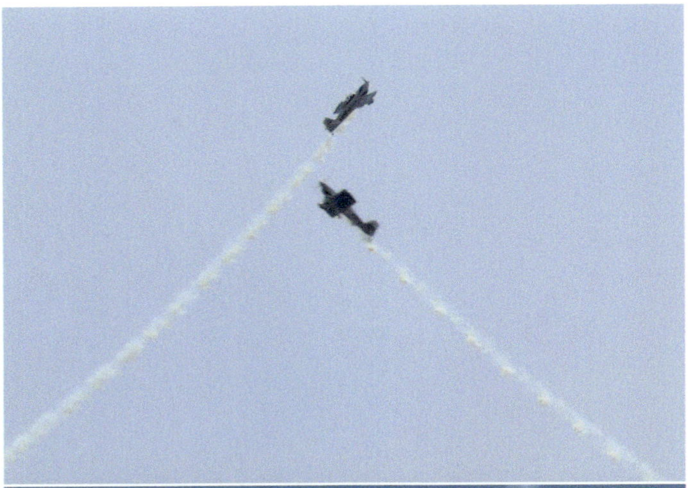

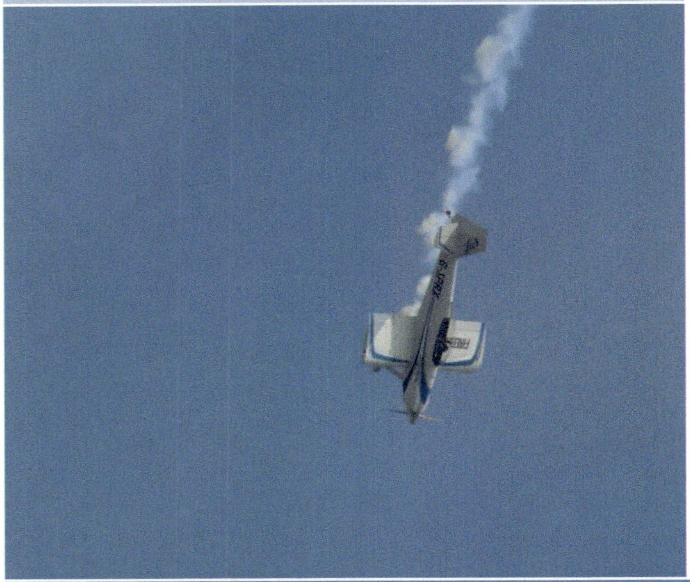

Quick Facts

Seats: 2

Wingspan: 23ft

Length: 20ft 4in

Height: 5ft 5in

Engine: 150 – 180 hp

Propeller: Fixed or Constant-Speed

Top Speed: 213 mph

Stall Speed: 48 mph

Baggage: 50 lbs

The Van RV-4 is a self-build aircraft

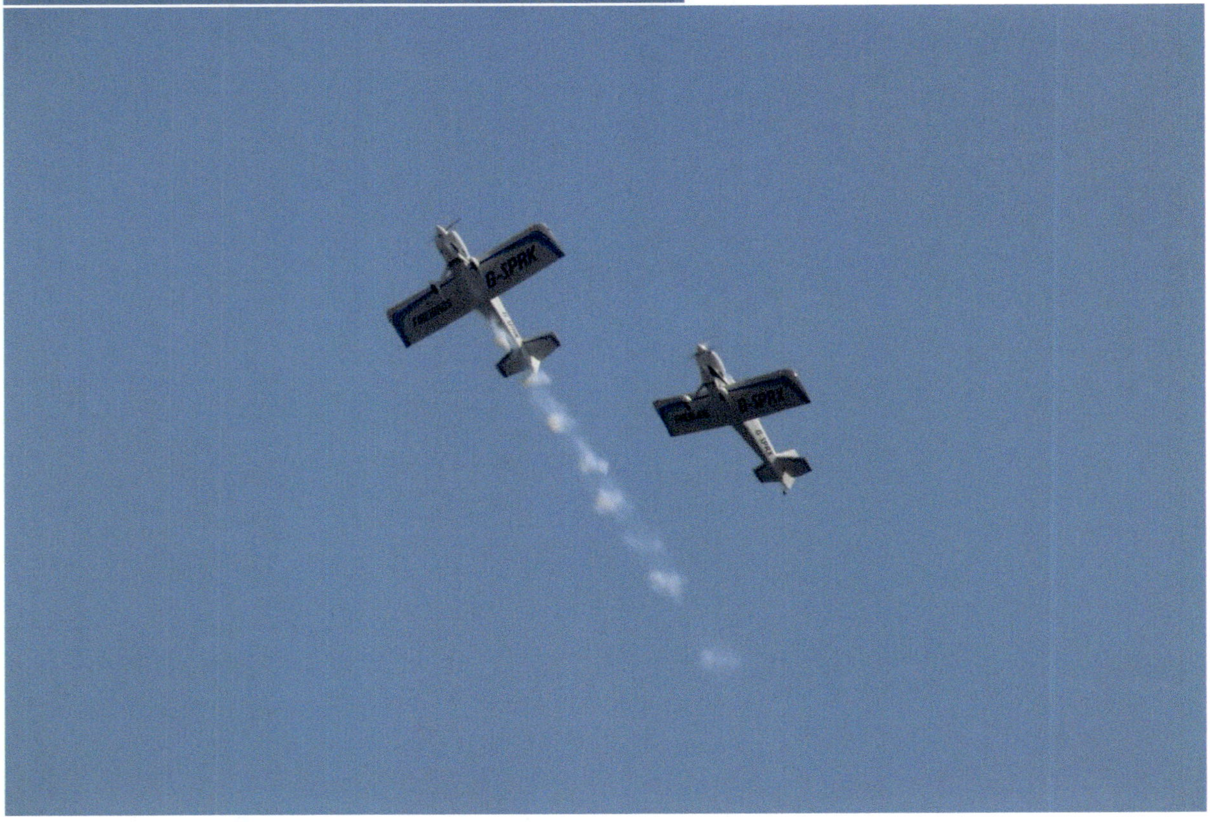

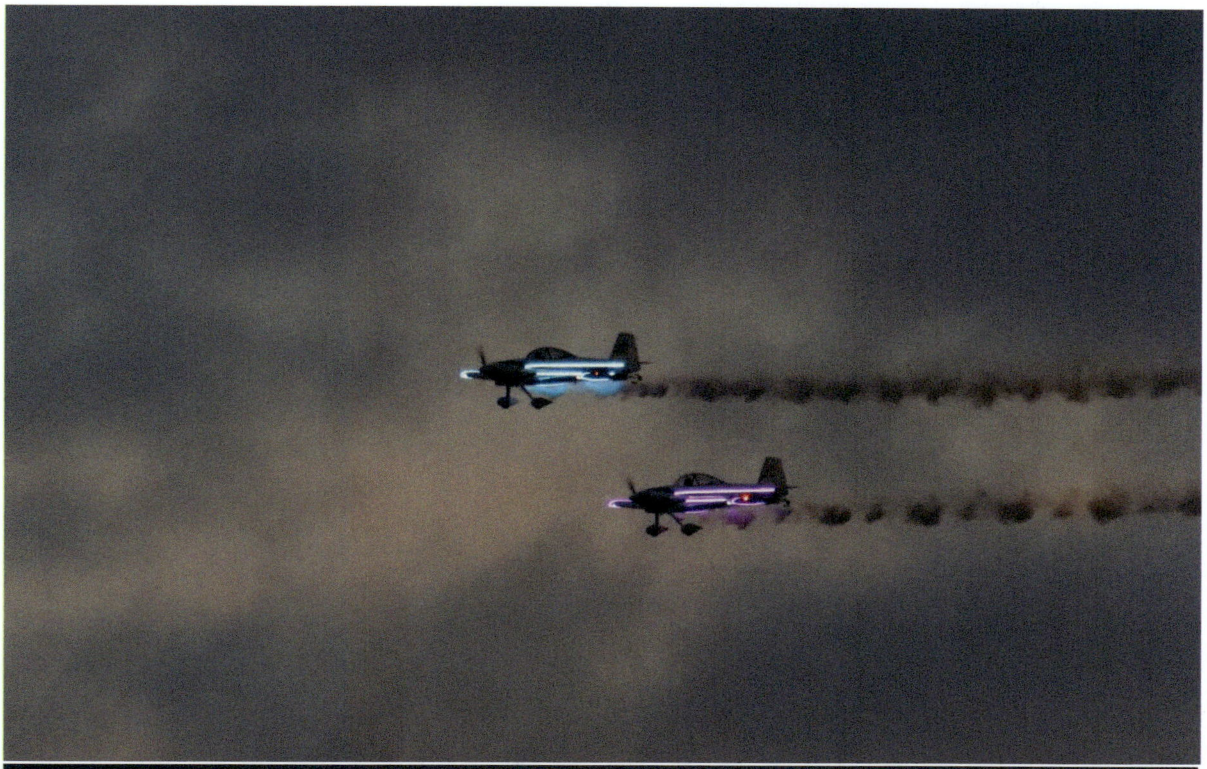

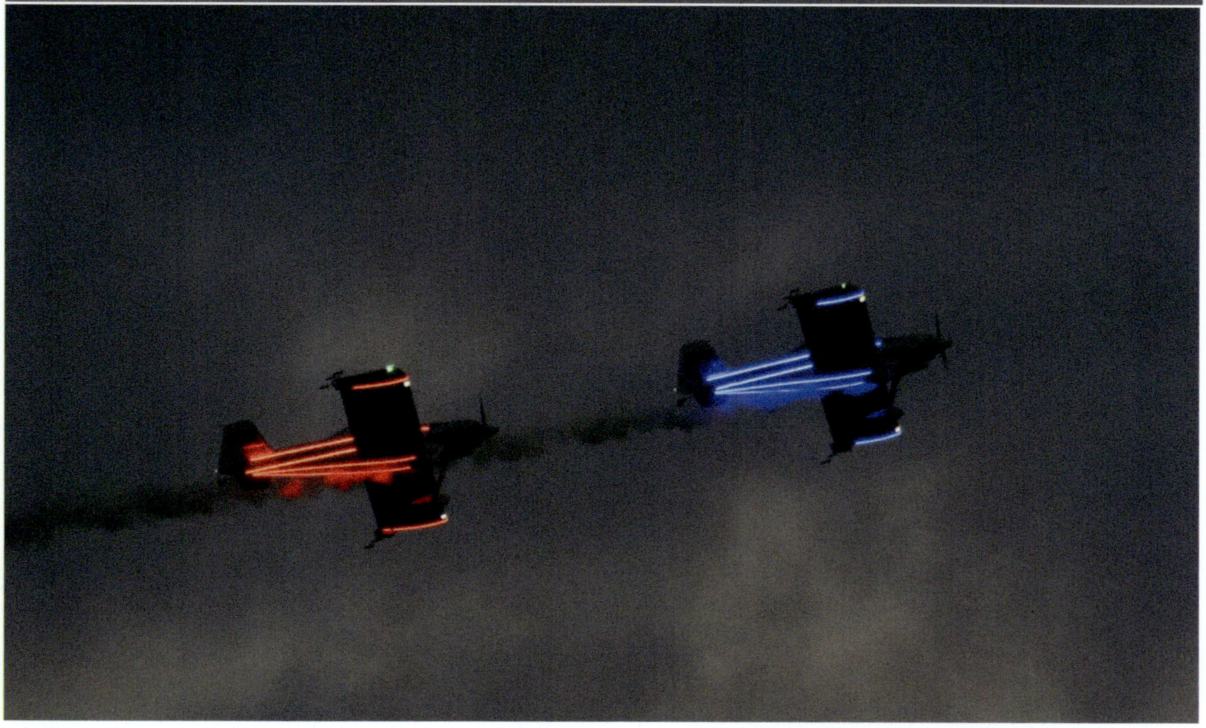

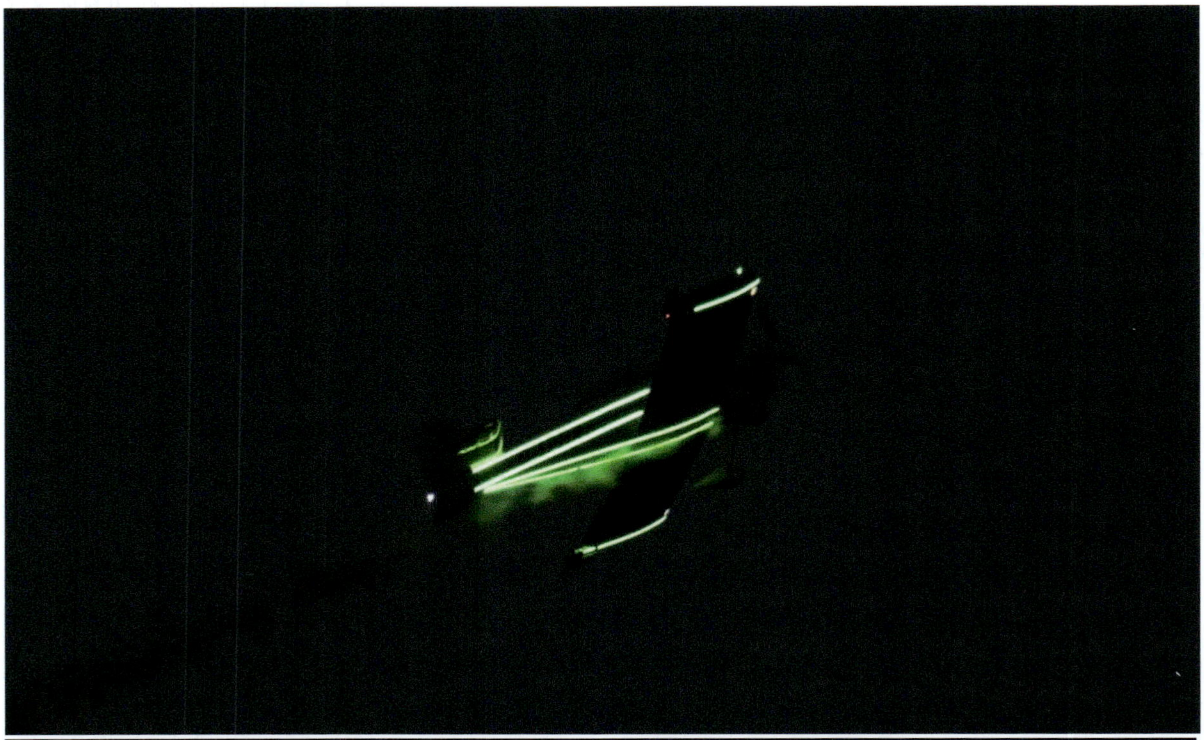

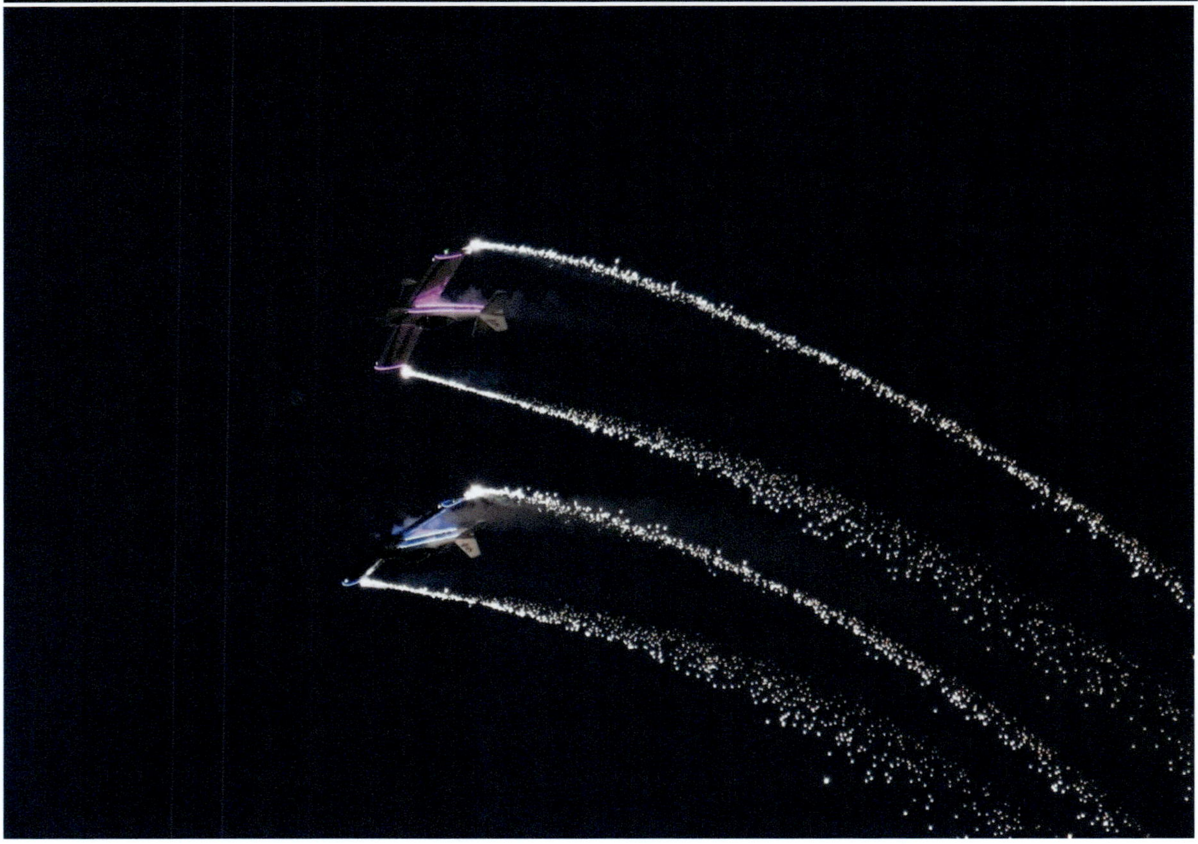

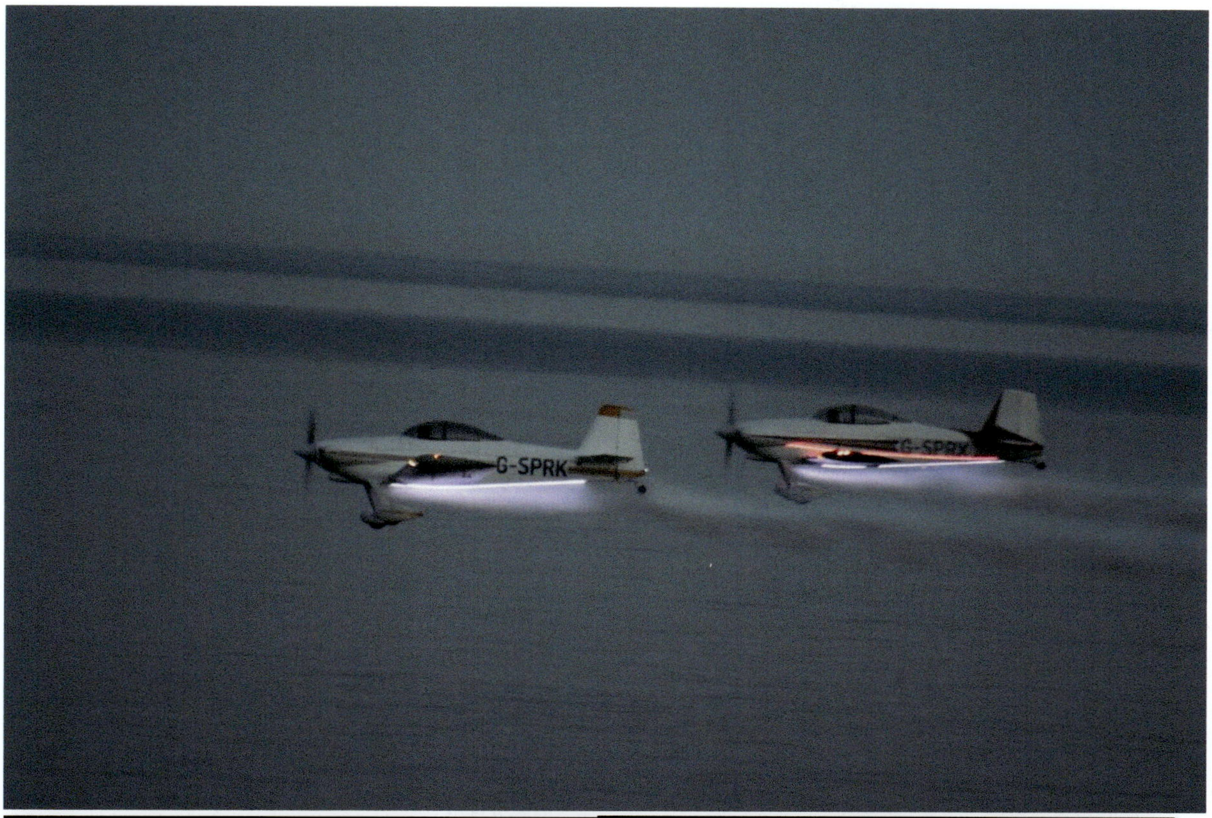
G-SPRK

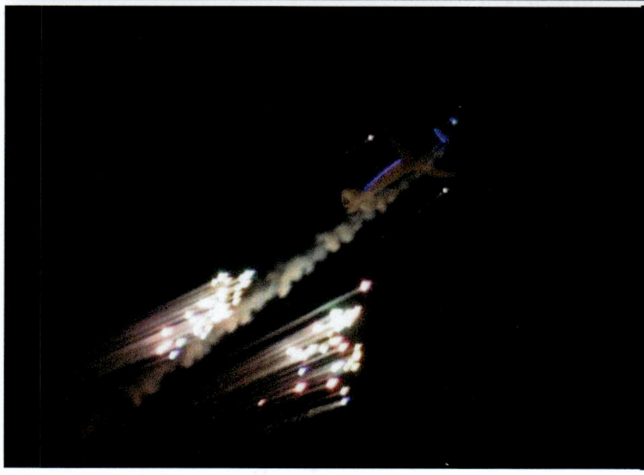

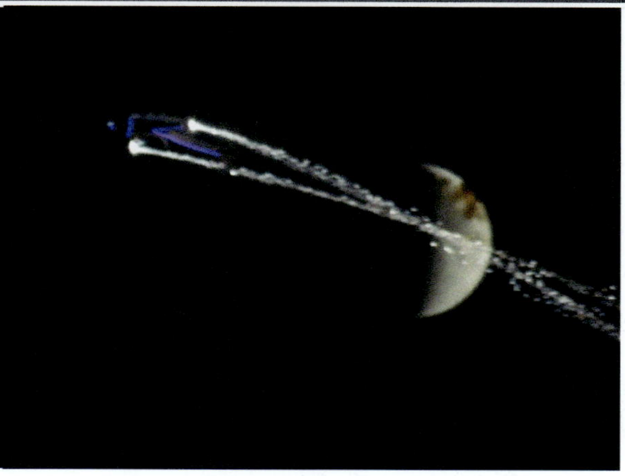

AeroSuperBatics Wing Walkers

The AeroSuperBatics Wing Walking Team has performed at the Air Festival for several years, utilizing the Boeing-Stearman biplane. The Stearman Model 75, an American biplane formerly used as a military trainer aircraft, was built in the thousands in the United States during the 1930s and 1940s, with at least 10,626 units produced.

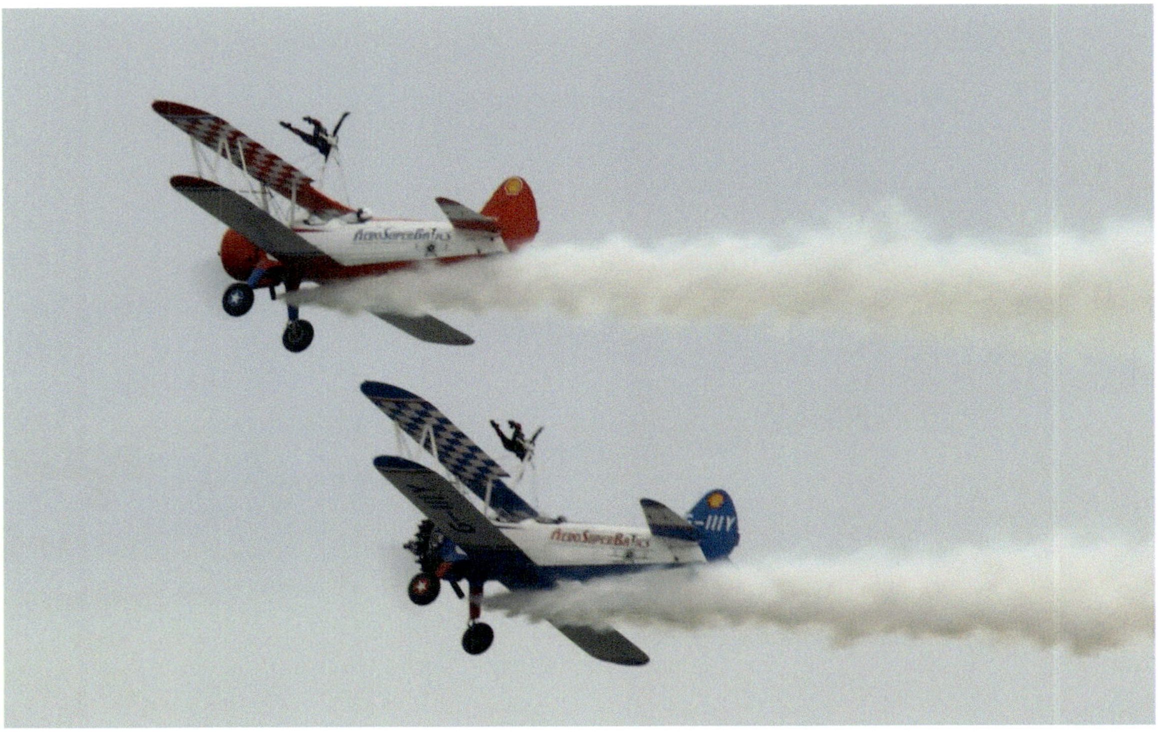

After World War II ended, thousands of surplus Steadman military planes were auctioned off to civilians and former pilots. Many Steadmans were modified for crop-dusting by replacing the front cockpit with a hopper to hold pesticides or fertilizers. Additional spray equipment like pumps, bars, and nozzles were mounted below the lower wings. A popular approved modification to improve take-off weight and climb performance was installing a larger Pratt & Whitney R-985 Wasp Junior engine and constant-speed propeller.

AeroSuperBatics operates four modified Boeing-Stearman Model 75 biplanes. The original 220 horsepower Continental radial engines were replaced with 450 horsepower Pratt & Whitney R-985-AN14B "Junior Wasp" engines, each with 985 cubic inches (16 litres) displacement. These new engines drive Hamilton Standard 2D30/6101A-12 constant speed propellers. Currently, AeroSuperBatics employs five male pilots and six female wing walkers.

The AeroSuperBatics Wing Walking Team was most well-known for its bright orange Breitling-sponsored aircraft that wowed crowds. In 2022, the planes returned to an unsponsored livery, as shown above. Notoriously, in September 2021, one of the biplanes crashed into the sea near the Sandbanks Ferry in Poole Harbour after suffering an irreparable engine failure. Fortunately, both the pilot and wing walker survived the incident.

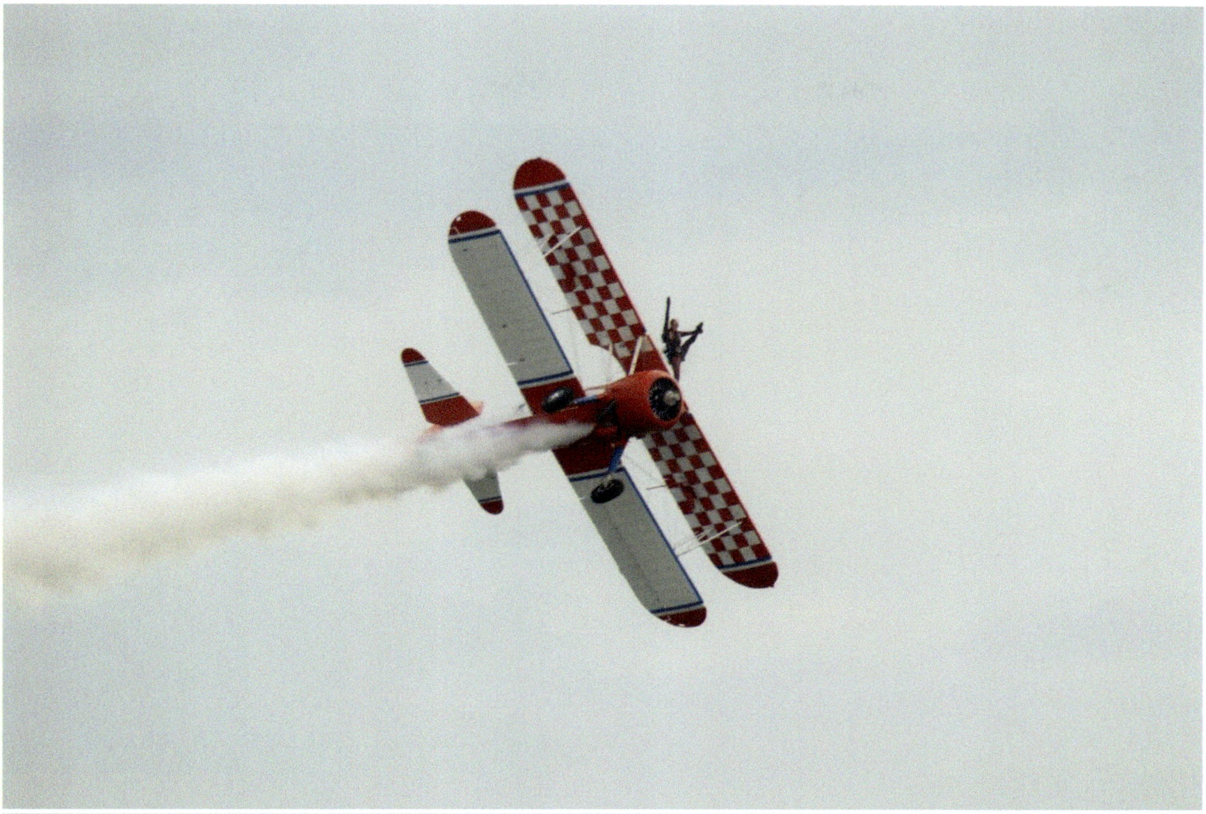

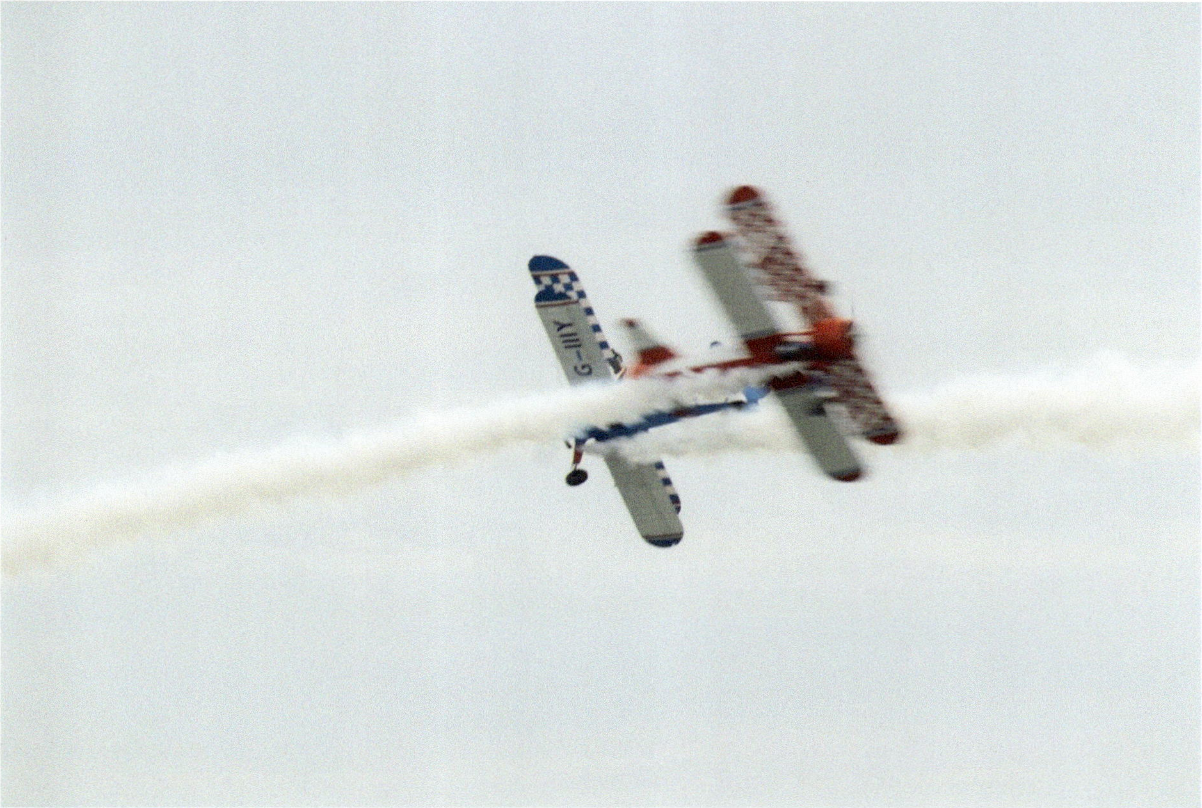
G-IIIY

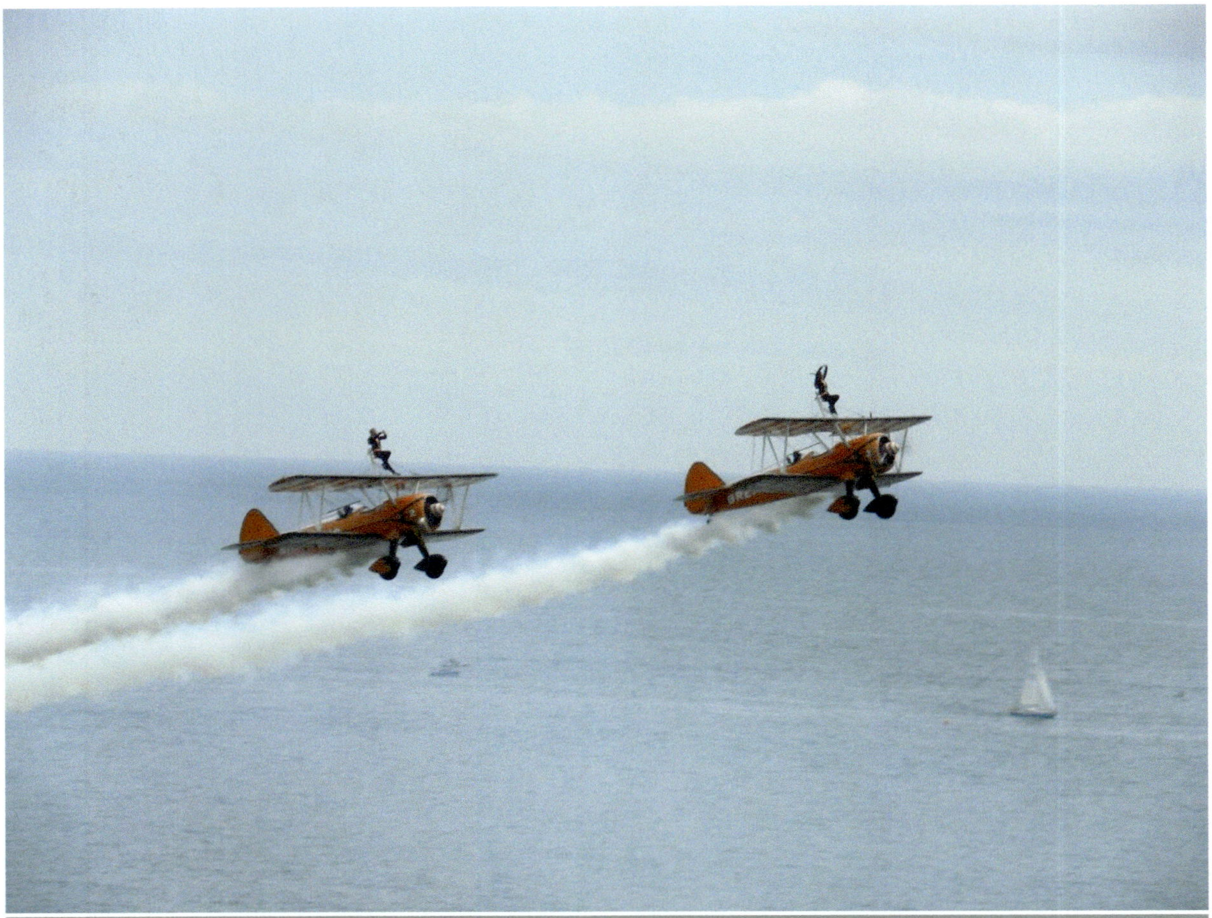

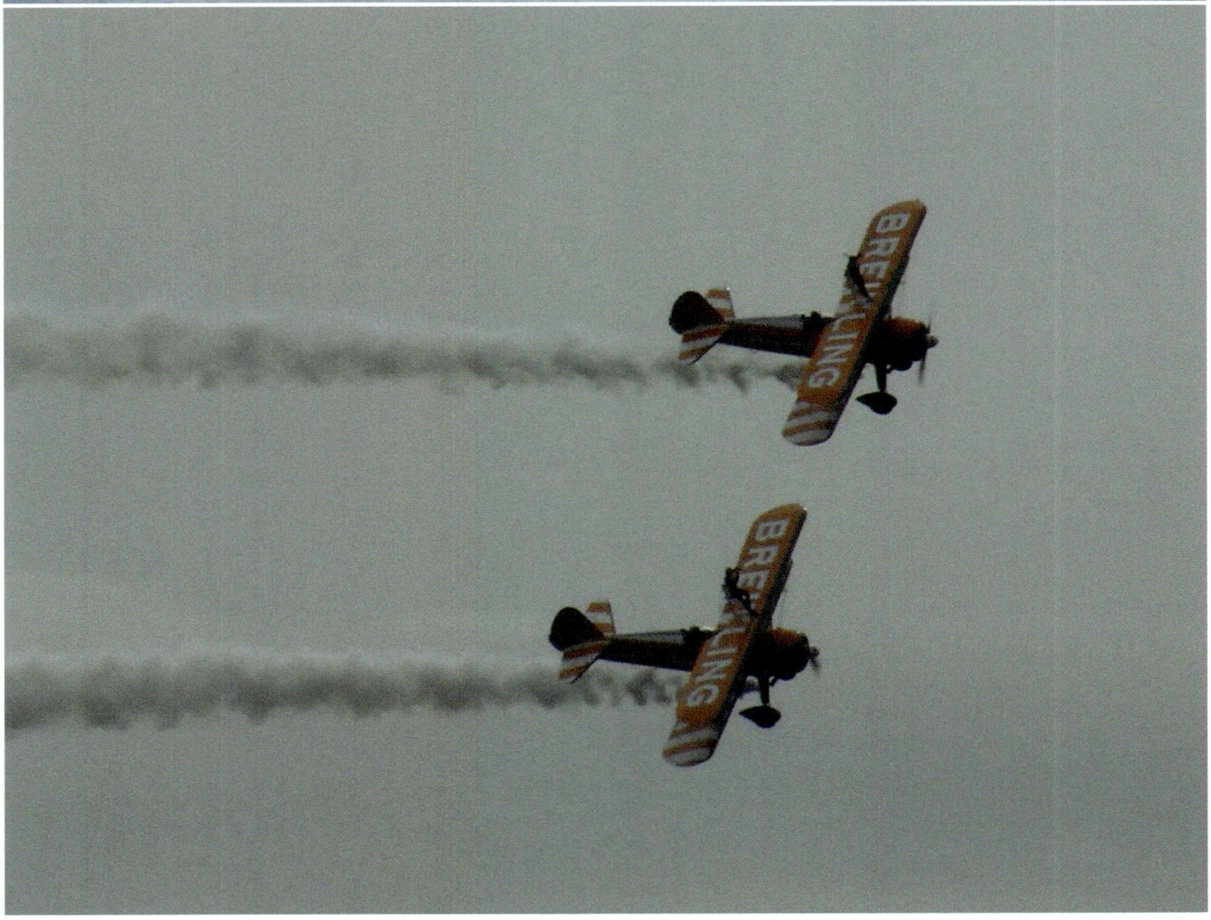

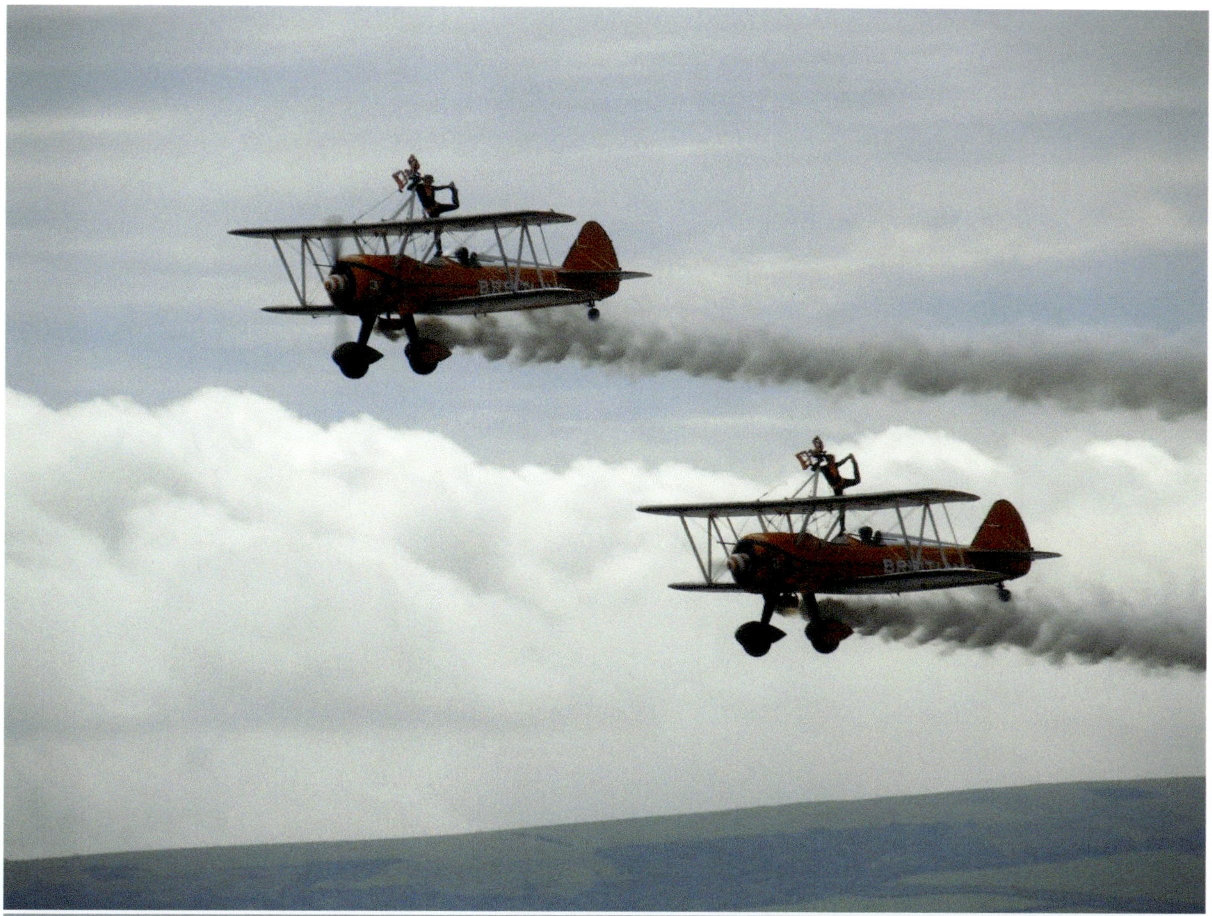

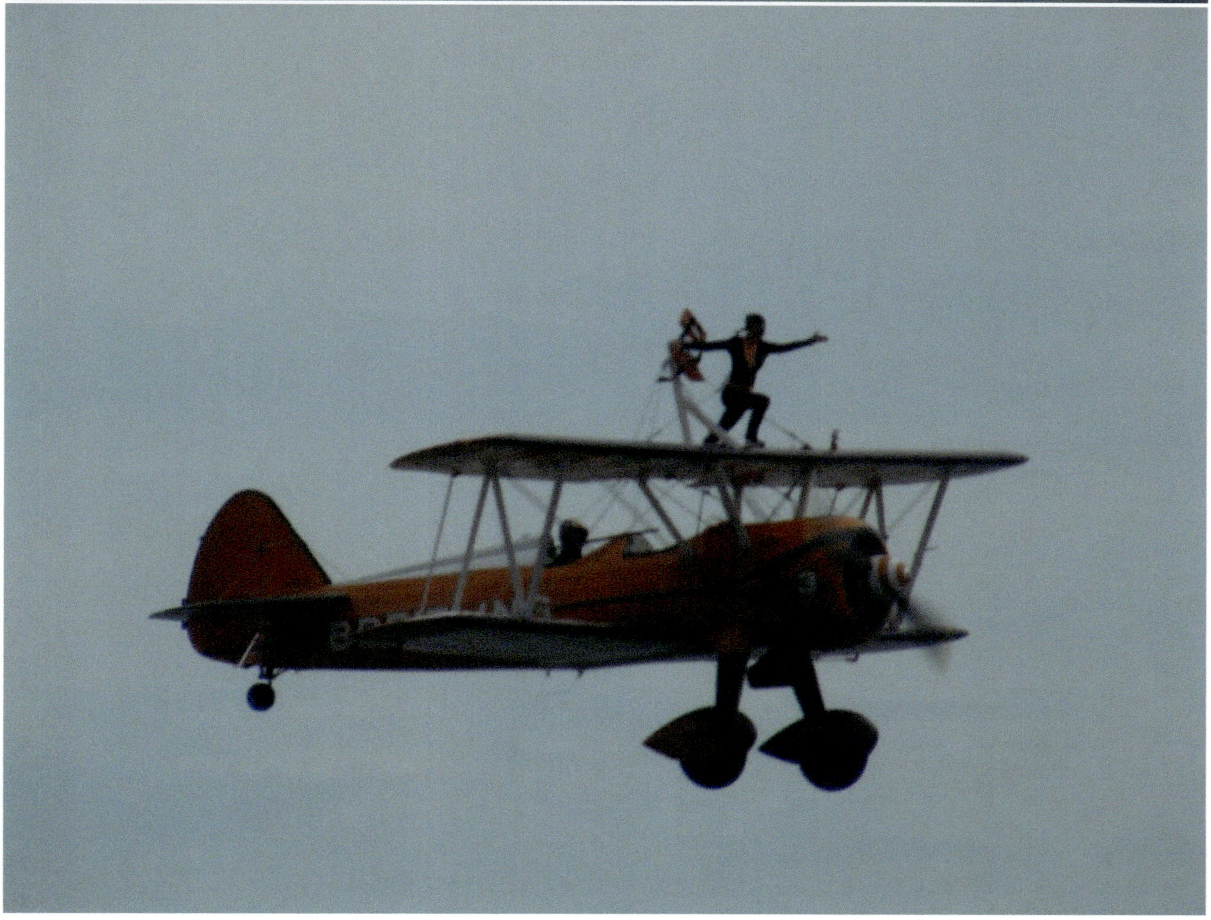

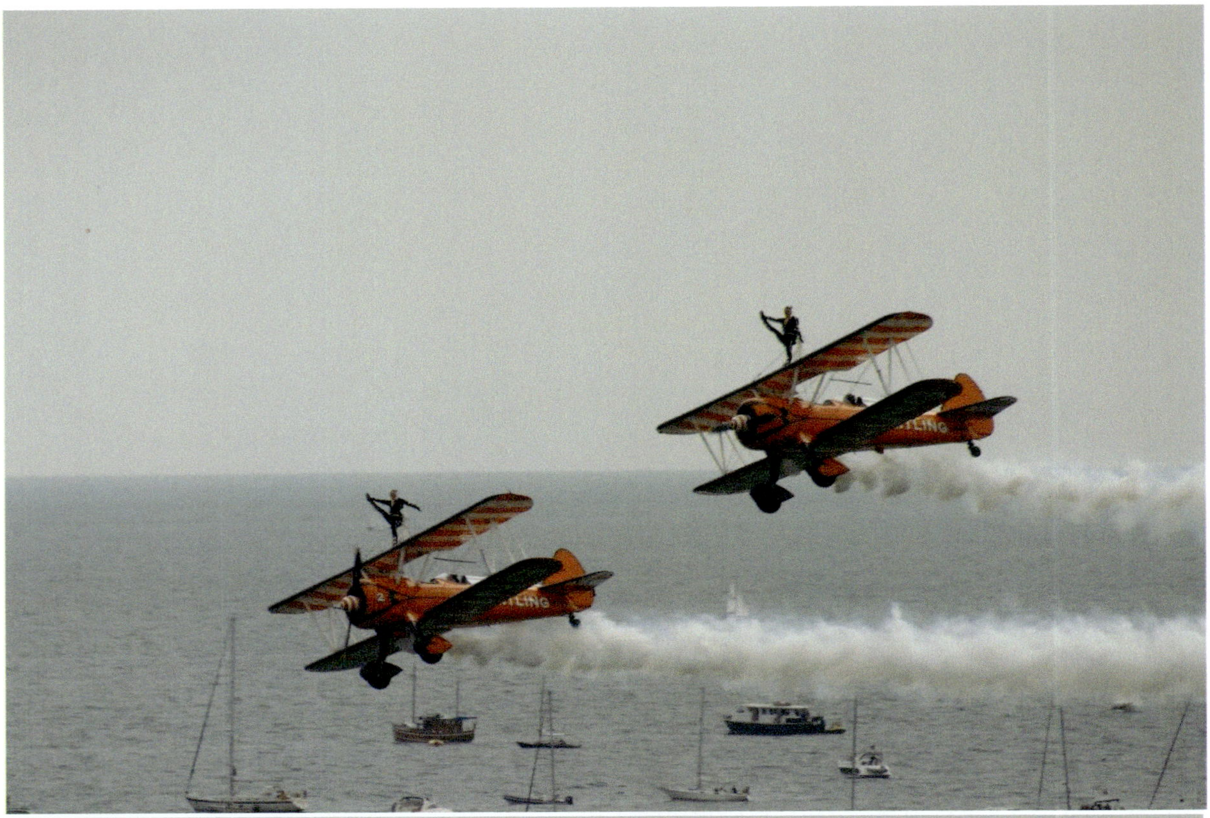

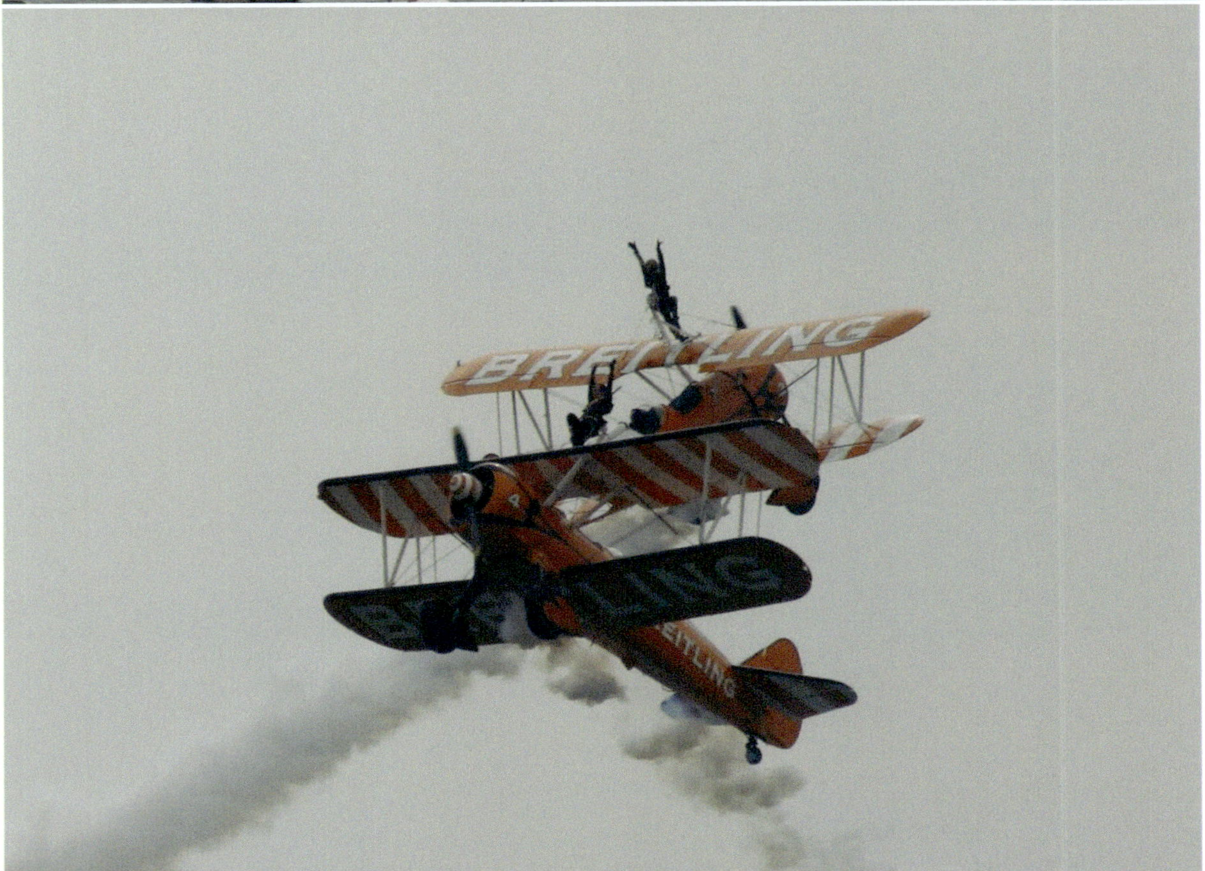

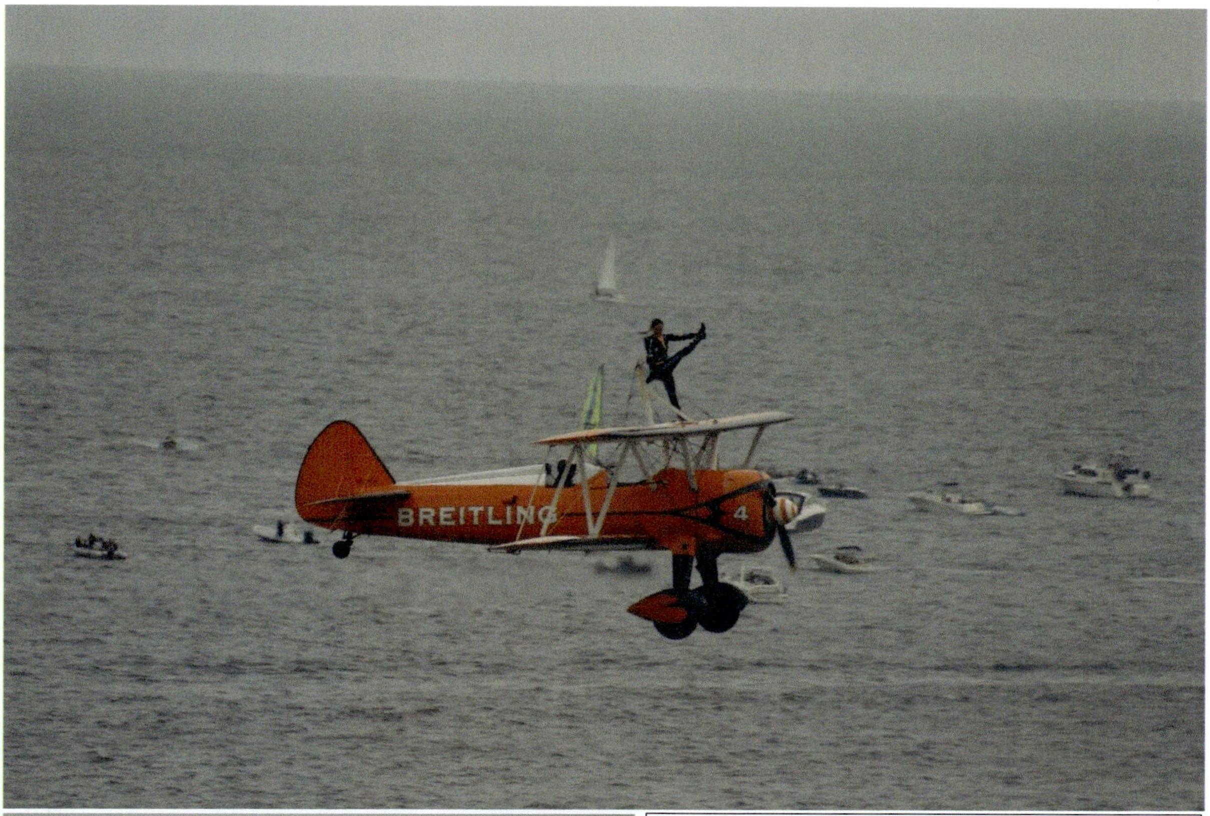

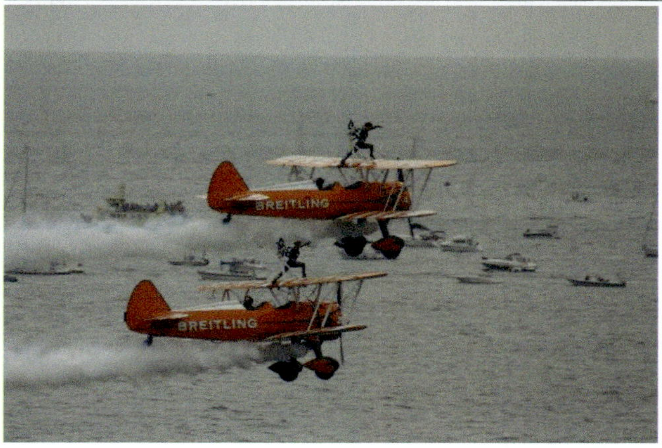

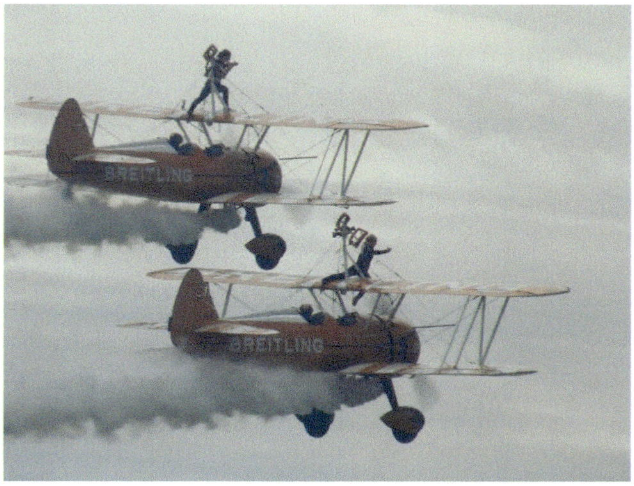

Quick Facts

General

Crew: 2

Length: 24 ft 9 in (7.54 m)

Wingspan: 32 ft 2 in (9.80 m)

Height: 9 ft 8 in (2.95 m)

Powerplant: 1 × Continental R-670-5 7-cylinder air-cooled radial piston engine, 220 hp

Propellers: 2-bladed fixed-pitch propeller

Performance

Maximum speed: 124 mph (200 km/h, 108 kn)

Cruise speed: 96 mph (154 km/h, 83 kn)

Service ceiling: 13,200 ft

The Blades Display Team

In the dynamic world of aerobatic displays, the Blades Display Team stands out for their precision, skill, and unparalleled mastery of the skies. Based at the Sywell Aerodrome in Northamptonshire, the Blades have been described as "the world's only aerobatic airline" since passengers can experience their aerobatic routines firsthand. As the only full-time civilian aerobatic team in the United Kingdom, their performances showcase unmatched talent.

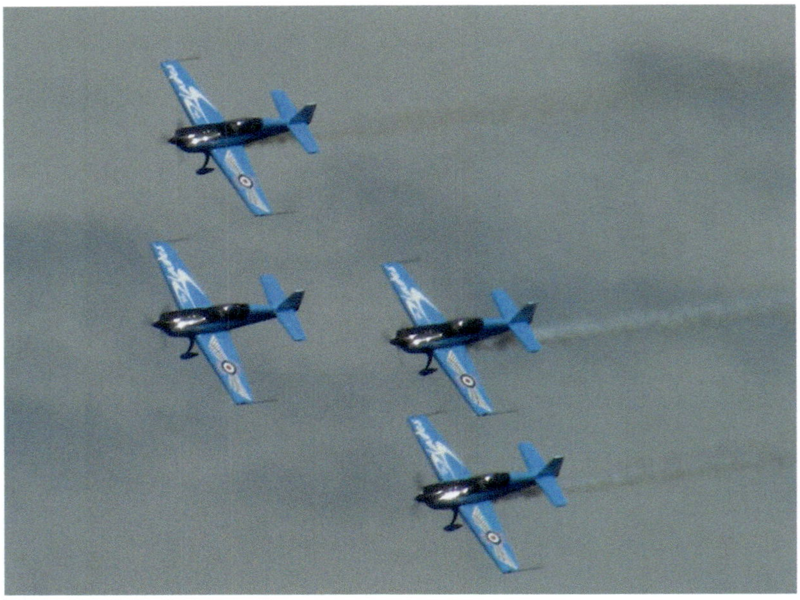

The team was founded in 2005 by Andy Offer, a former leader of the Red Arrows, and Chris Norton, a Royal Air Force wing commander. There are eight pilots including five full-time display performers. All the pilots were former members of the Royal Air Force, and the aerobatic team all flew with the Red Arrows. They hold the world record for formation looping having completed 26 consecutive loops.

The team flew four Extra 300LPs and one Extra 330SC. The Extra 330SC was used for solo parts of the performances. These two-seat propeller planes were used for four-aircraft displays and corporate flying events where passengers could ride along. Originally painted orange and black, the aircraft were later changed to light blue and black. By 2013, they had switched back to orange and black. In addition to aerobatic displays and commercial work, The Blades supported the Royal Air Forces Association, a charity assisting RAF personnel.

The Extra 300, a monoplane with a welded steel tube fuselage covered in aluminium and fabric, has its design based on the early 1980s Extra 230, which had a wooden wing. The Extra 300's wing contains a carbon fibre composite spar and carbon composite skins, while its fixed taildragger landing gear has composite main legs and fiberglass wheel pants. Powering the aircraft is a 300 horsepower, fuel-injected Lycoming AEIO-540 engine.

The Extra 300 is structurally reinforced to withstand forces of ±10 G with one person aboard and ±8 G with two people. The Extra 300LP is a lighter version of the 300L, redesigned to enhance manoeuvrability in aerobatic competitions and airshows.

The Extra 330SC is a single-seat aircraft designed specifically for unlimited category competition, featuring a Lycoming AEIO-580 engine and improved roll rate and ease of roll stops.

Unfortunately, the 2022 display season marked the last year that The Blades' unmistakable Extra 300 engines roared across Bournemouth's skyline. This came after the team announced that year would be their final season, a decision driven mainly by the continued decline of the air show circuit as more events were lost each year.

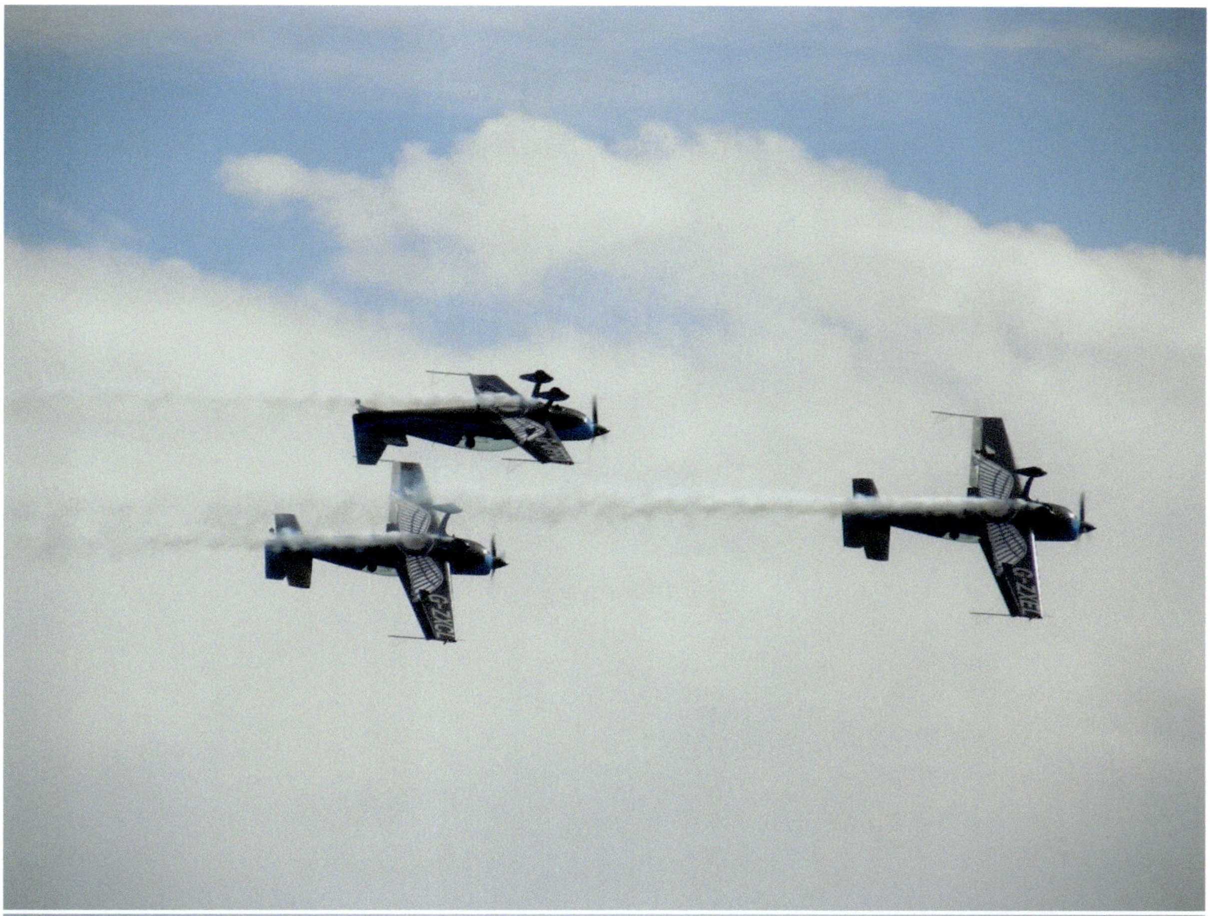

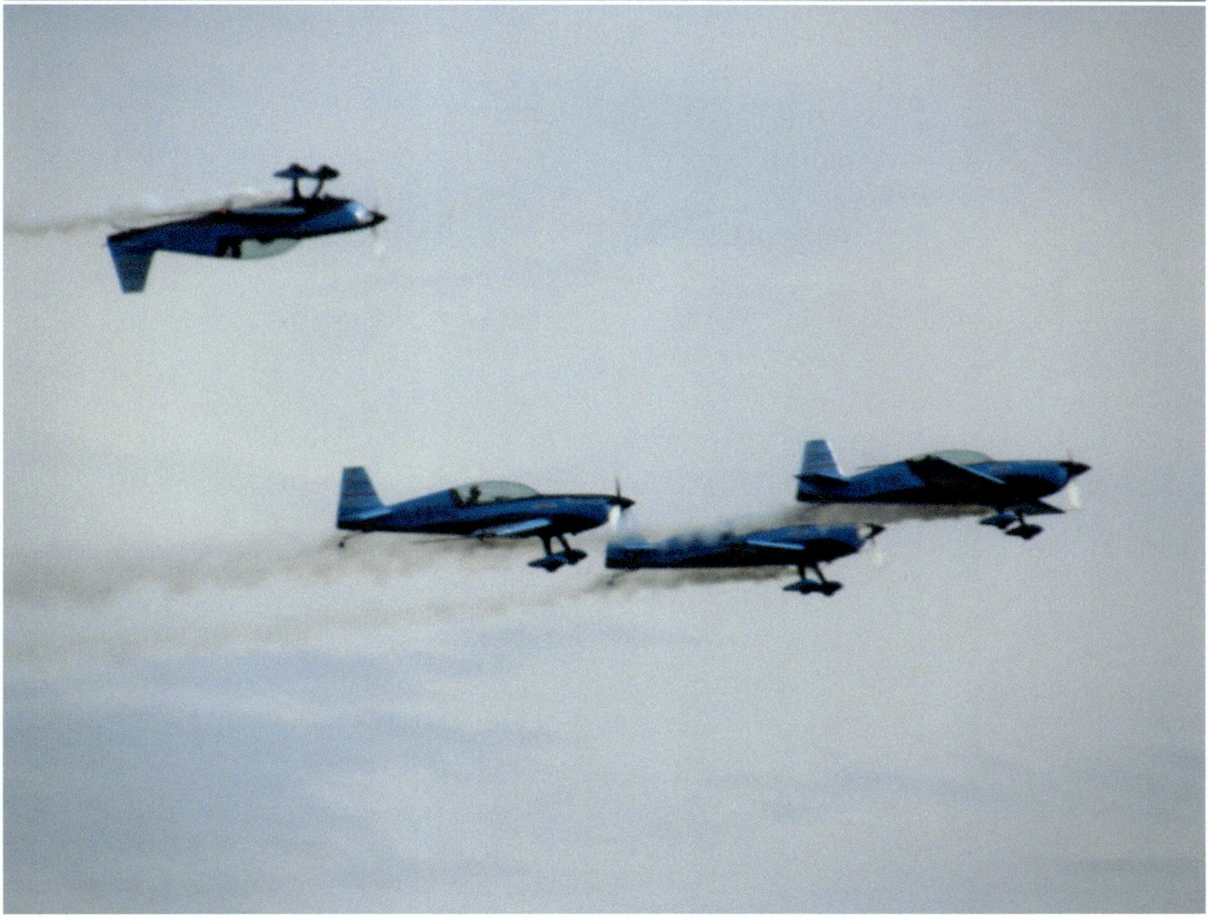

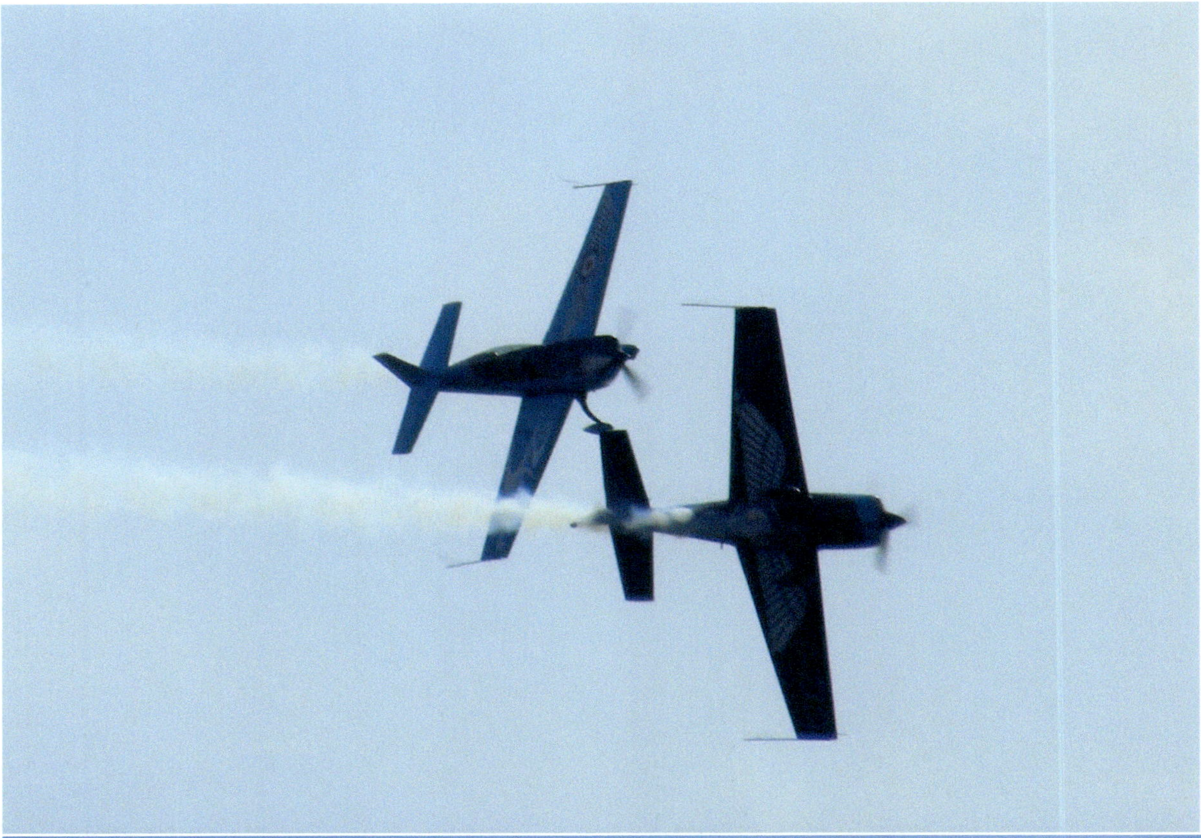

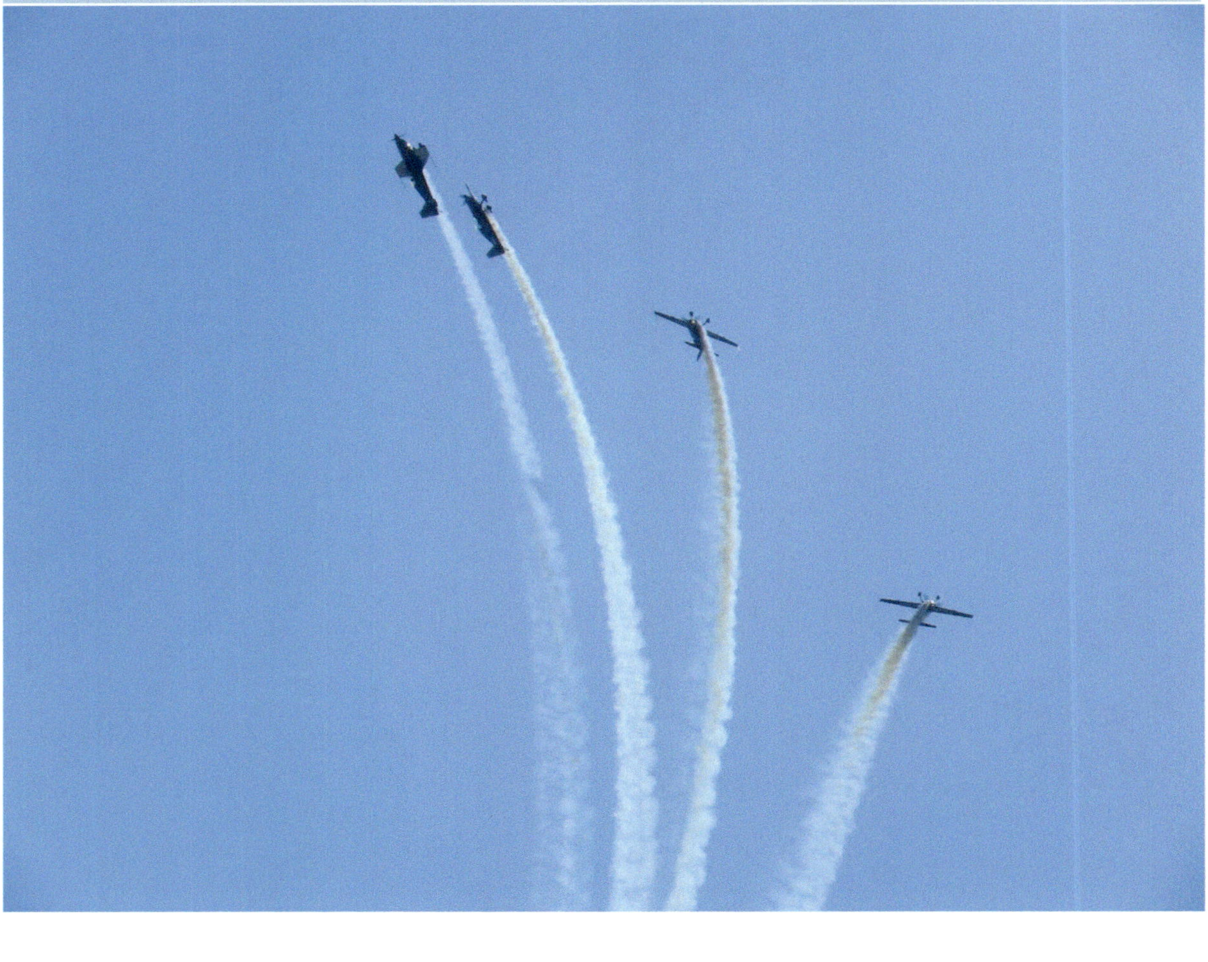

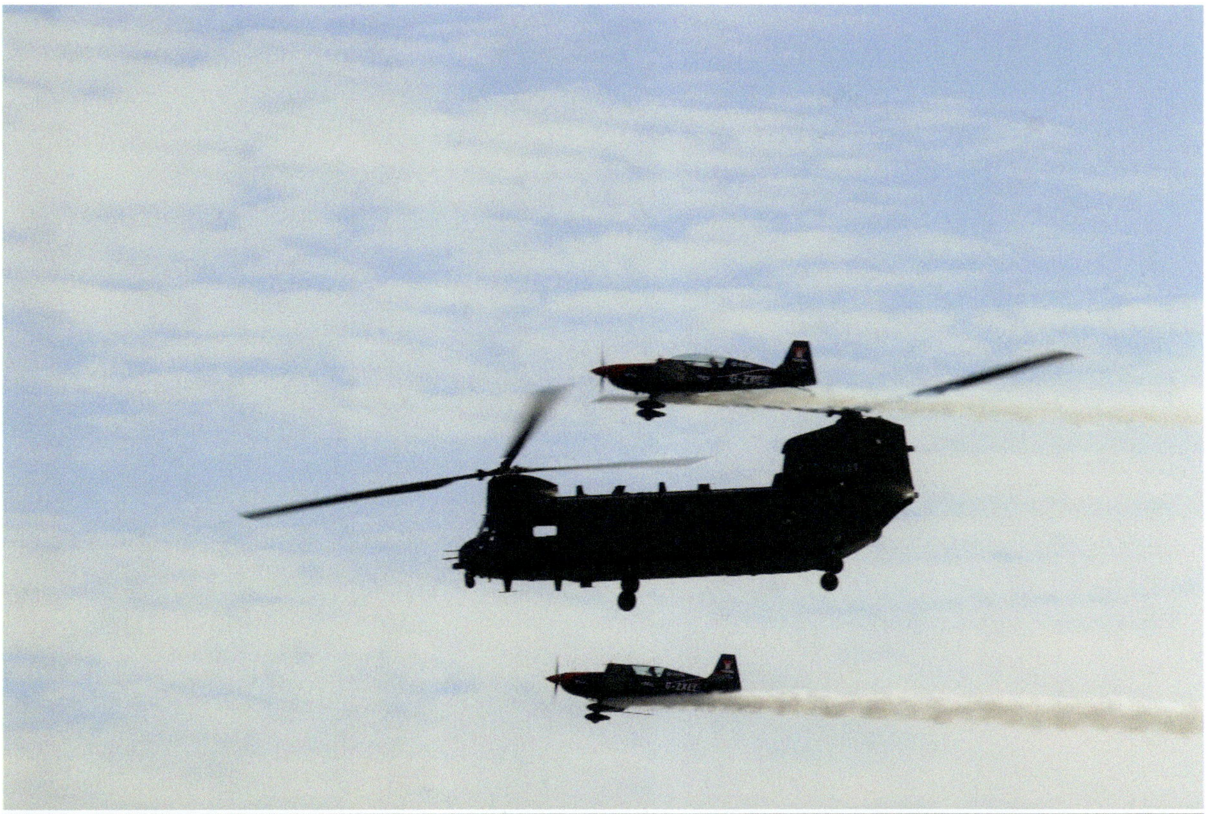

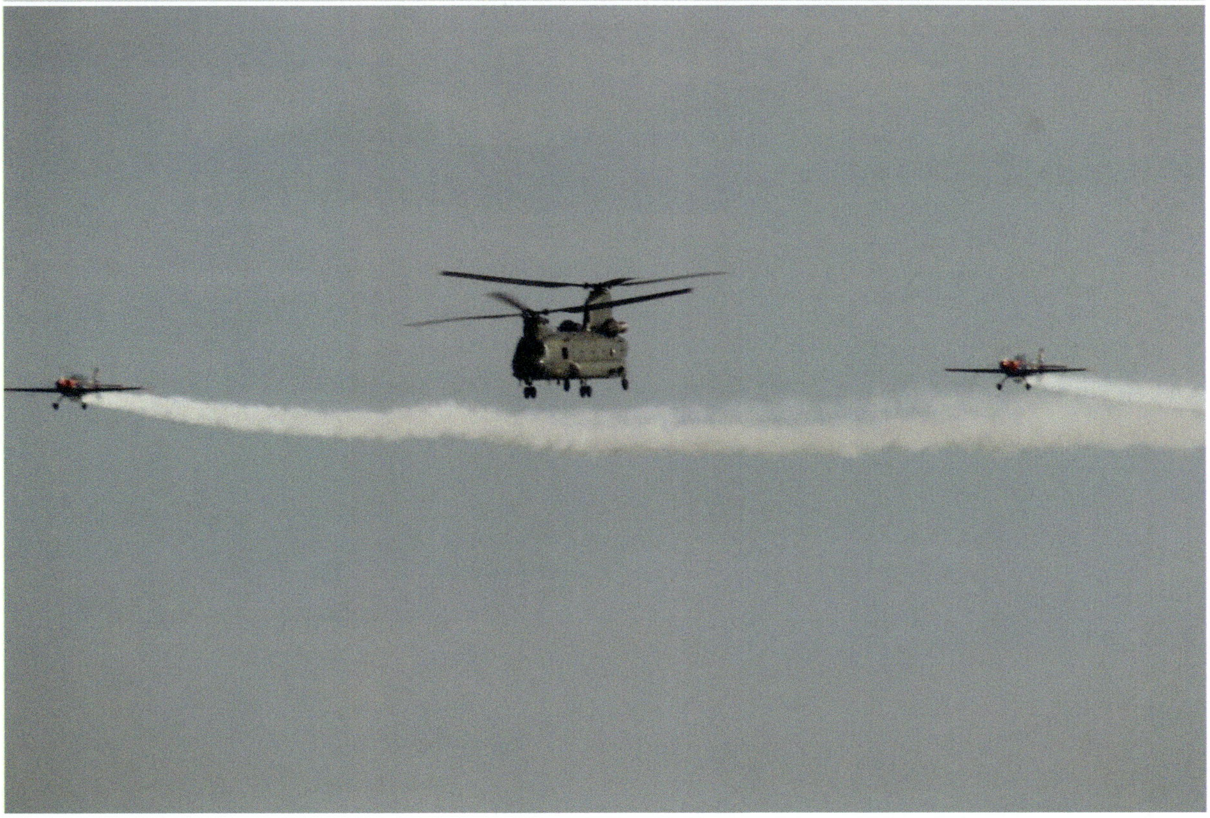

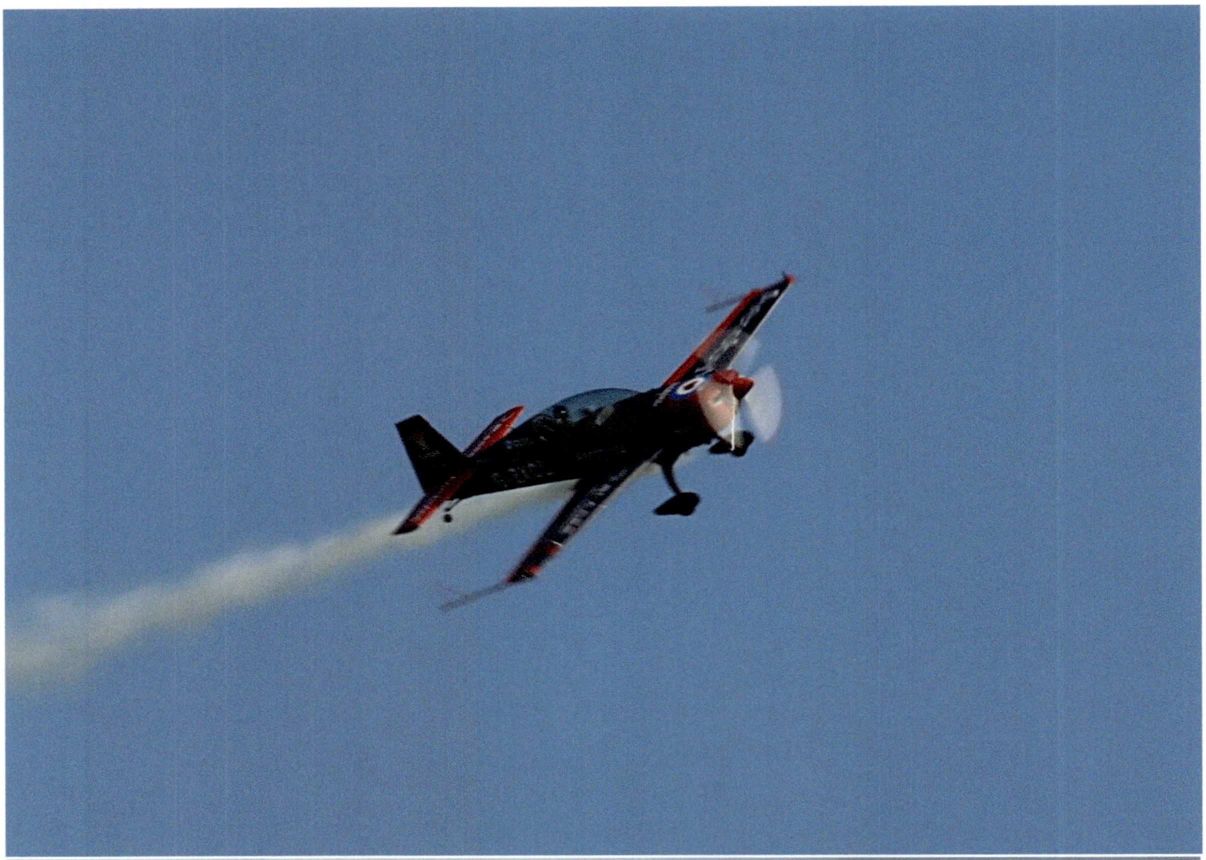

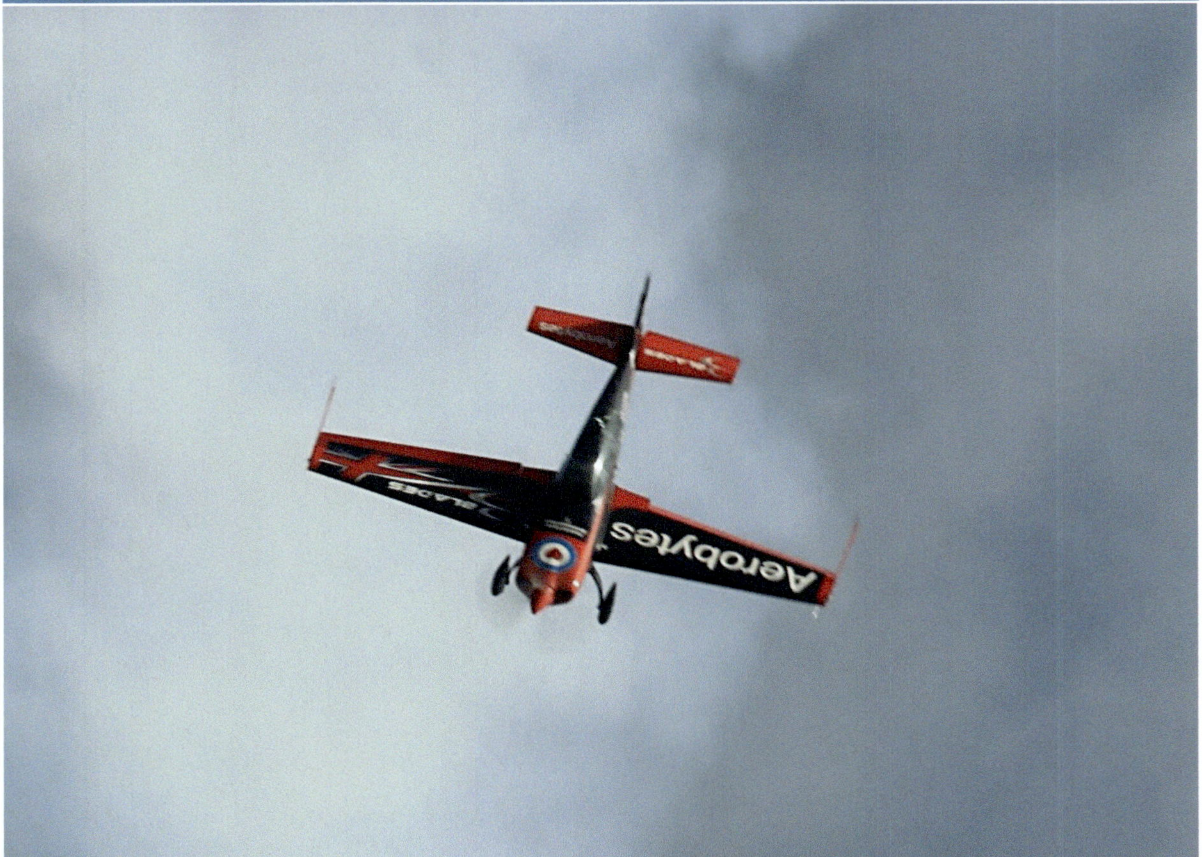
Aerobytes

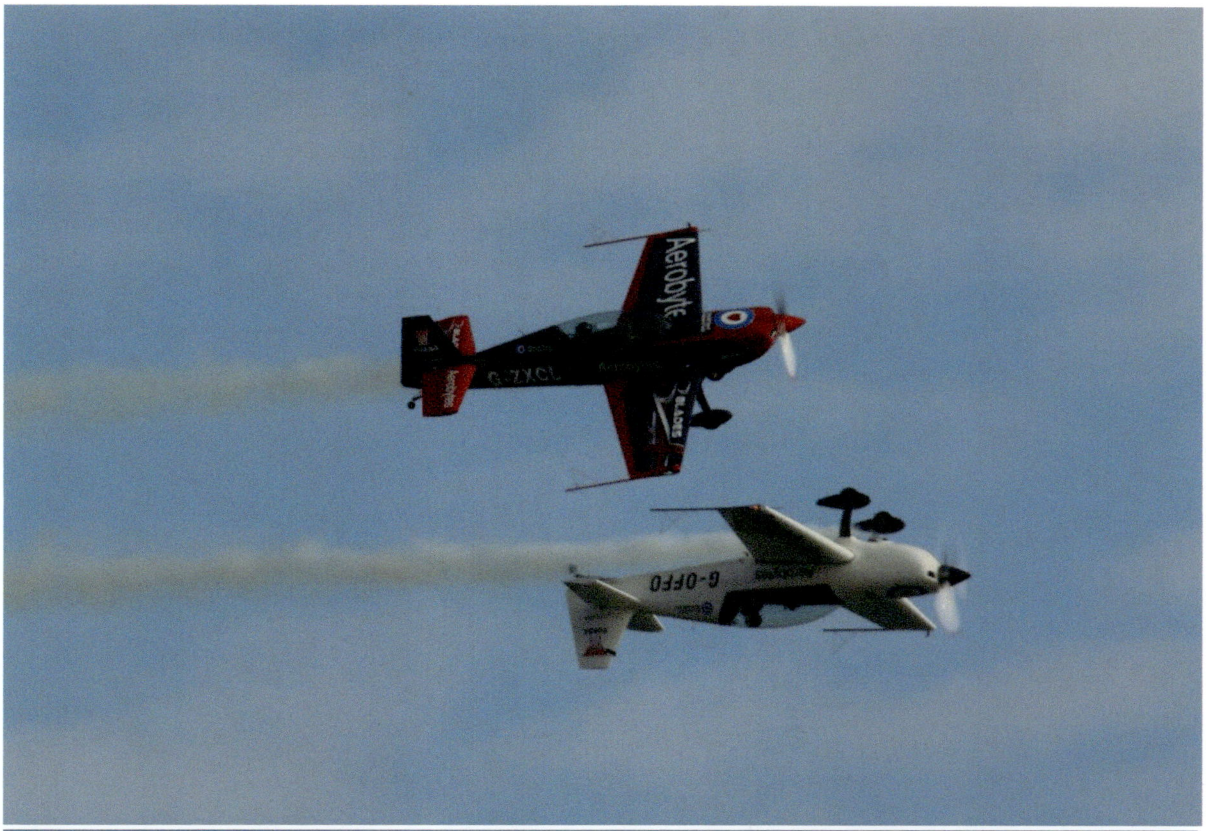
G-ZXCL

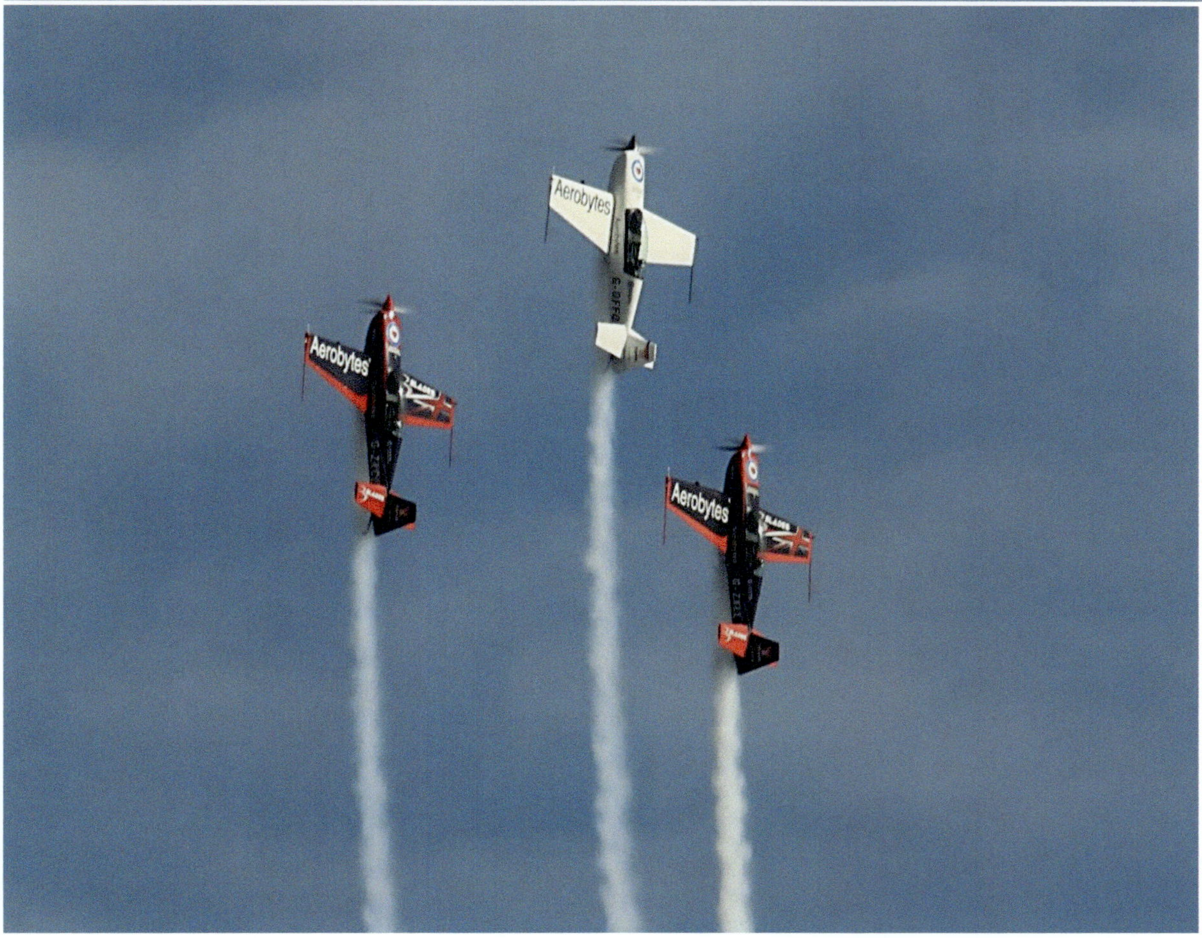
Aerobytes
Aerobytes
Aerobytes

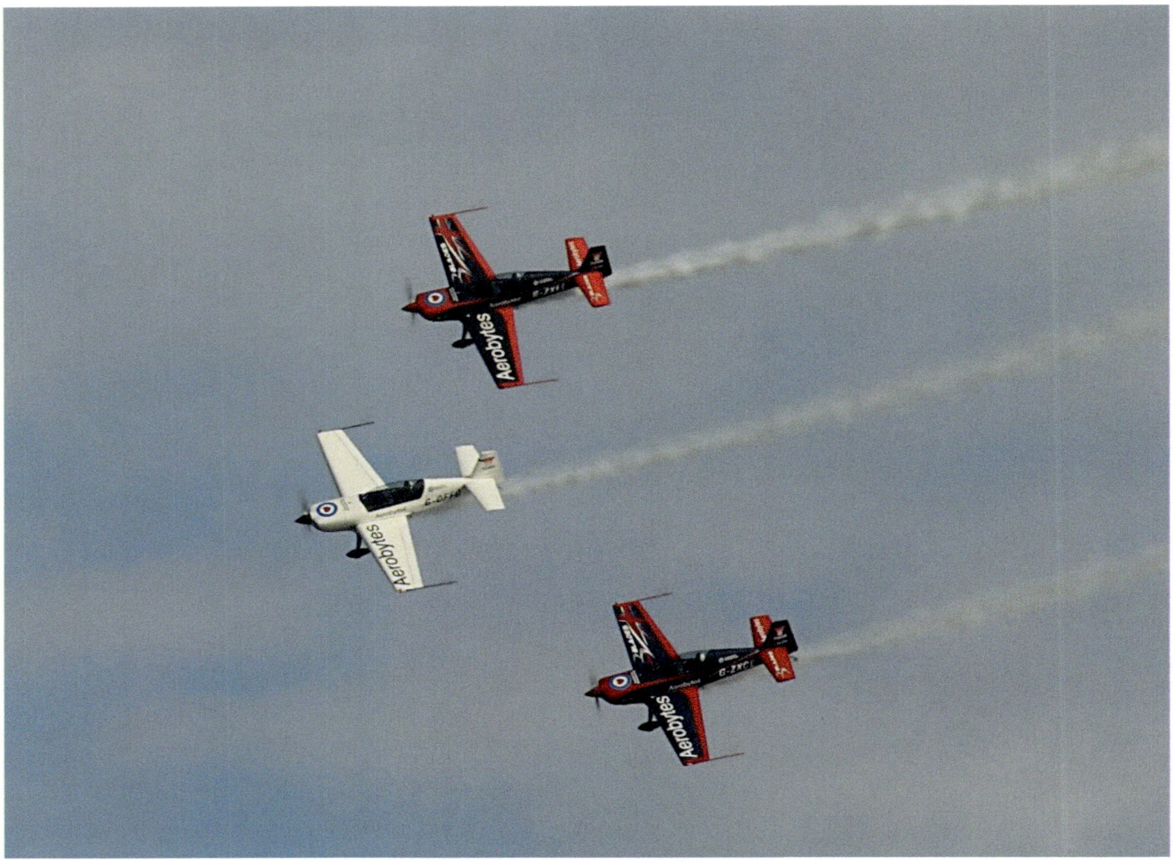

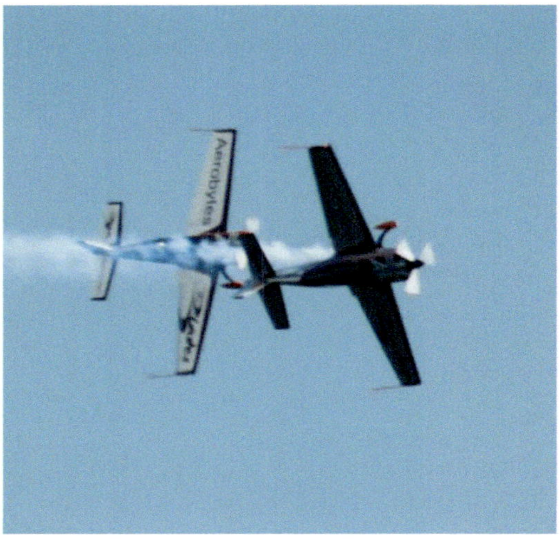

Quick Facts

General

Crew: 1 or 2

Length: 7.01 m (23 ft 0 in)

Wingspan: 8 m (26 ft 3 in)

Height: 2.6 m (8 ft 6 in)

Powerplant: 1 × Lycoming AEIO-580-B1A 6-cylinder air-cooled horizontally-opposed piston engine, 235 kW (315 hp)

Propellers: 3-bladed Muehlbauer MTV 9-B-C/C198-25

Performance

Cruise speed: 380 km/h (236 mph, 205 kn) TAS

Stall speed: 110 km/h (69 mph, 60 kn) at 820 kg / 1,808 lbs

g limits: +10/-10g at 820 kg / 1,808 lbs

Matadors Aerobatic Team

The Matadors Aerobatic Team has made a few visits to the Bournemouth Air Festival, showcasing their close formations of loops and turns. In 2015, the team flew XtremeAir planes featuring Red Bull livery.

XtremeAir, a German aircraft manufacturer, produces high-performance aerobatic and sport aircraft. Specializing in advanced, lightweight, and agile designs ideal for aerobatics and air sports, the company is known for crafting aircraft well-suited for competitive flying. One notable model is the XA42 aerobatic aircraft.

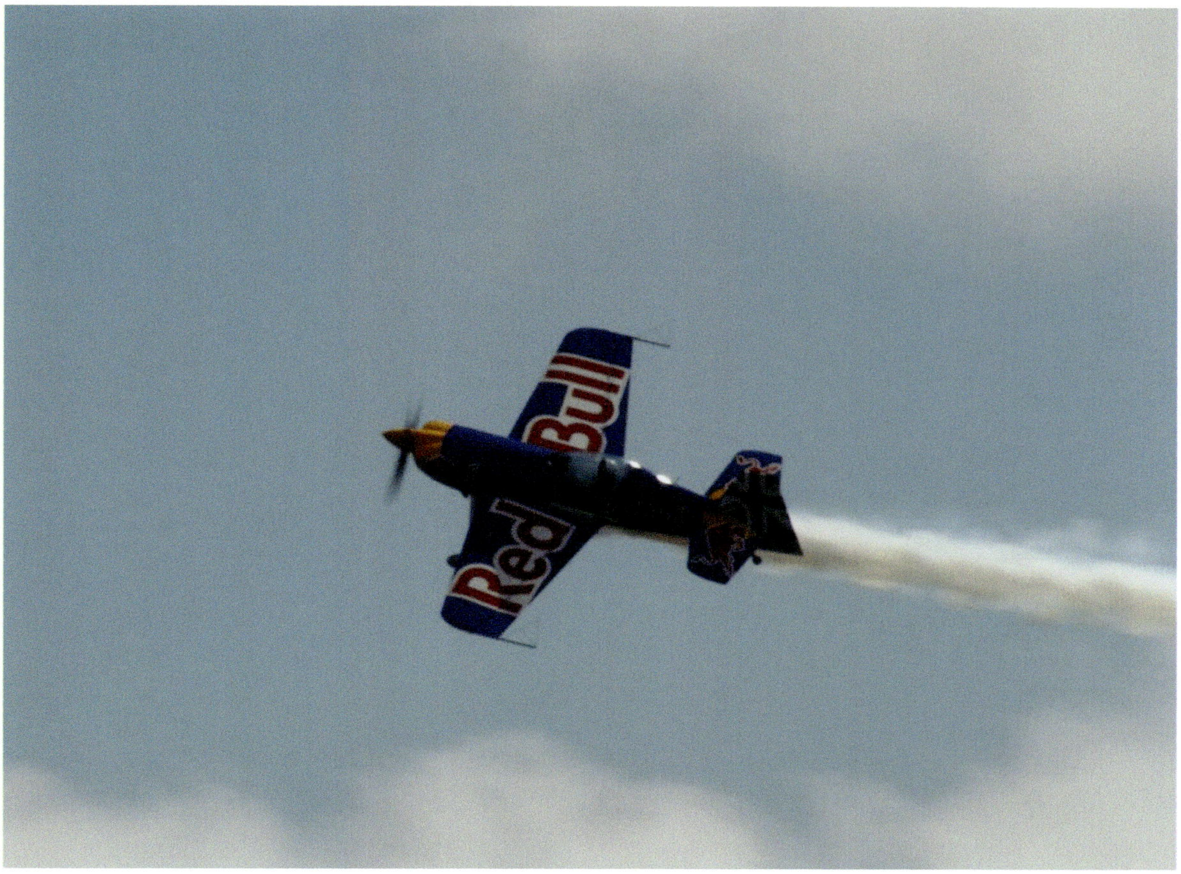

The XA42 is a lightweight, single-seat monoplane renowned for its exceptional manoeuvrability and responsiveness, making it the top choice of aerobatic pilots. Specifically designed for unlimited aerobatics, its carbon-fibre construction and powerful engine allow the aircraft to perform an extensive range of rolls, loops, spins, and inverted flight with ease. The XA42's unmatched agility and high power-to-weight ratio push the limits of competitive aerobatic capability.

The XA42 usually uses a Lycoming AEIO-580-B1A piston engine, which provides plenty of power for aerobatic manoeuvres. This engine is carefully chosen to meet the aerobatic needs of the aircraft.

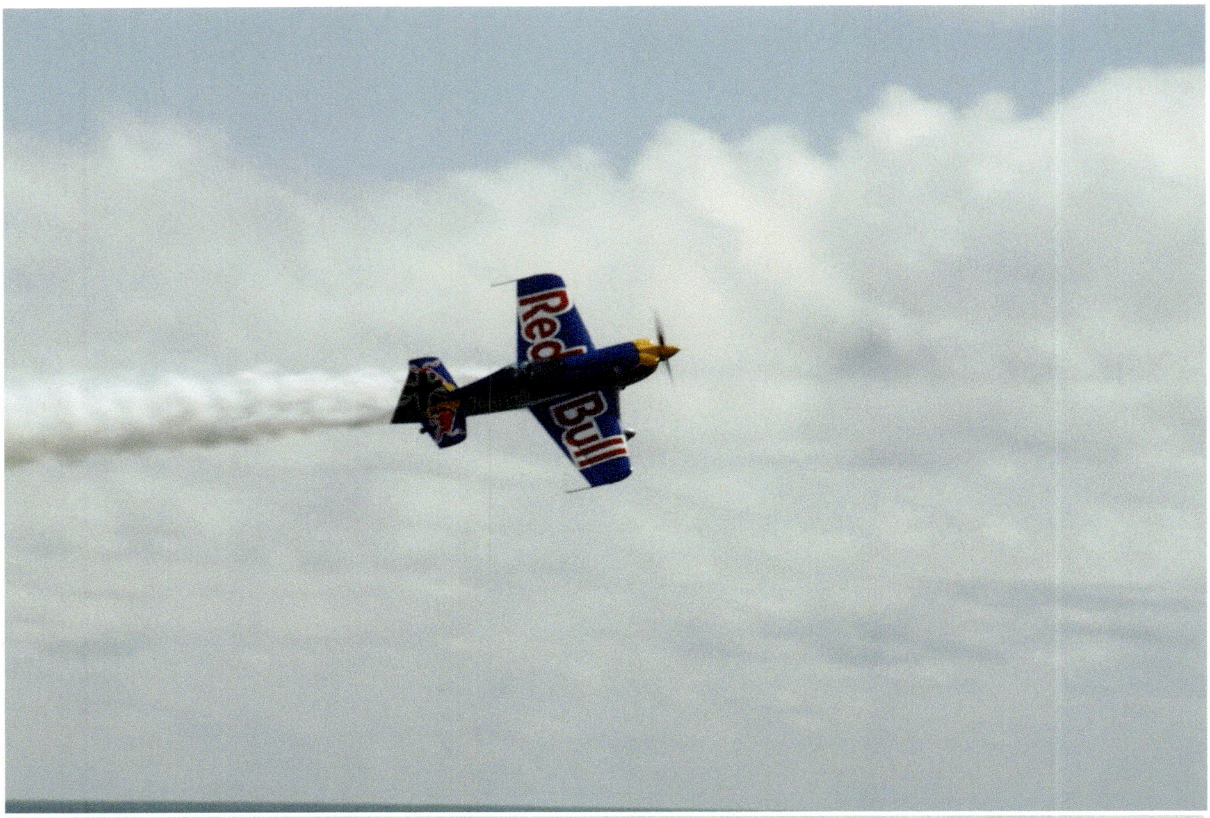
Red
Bull
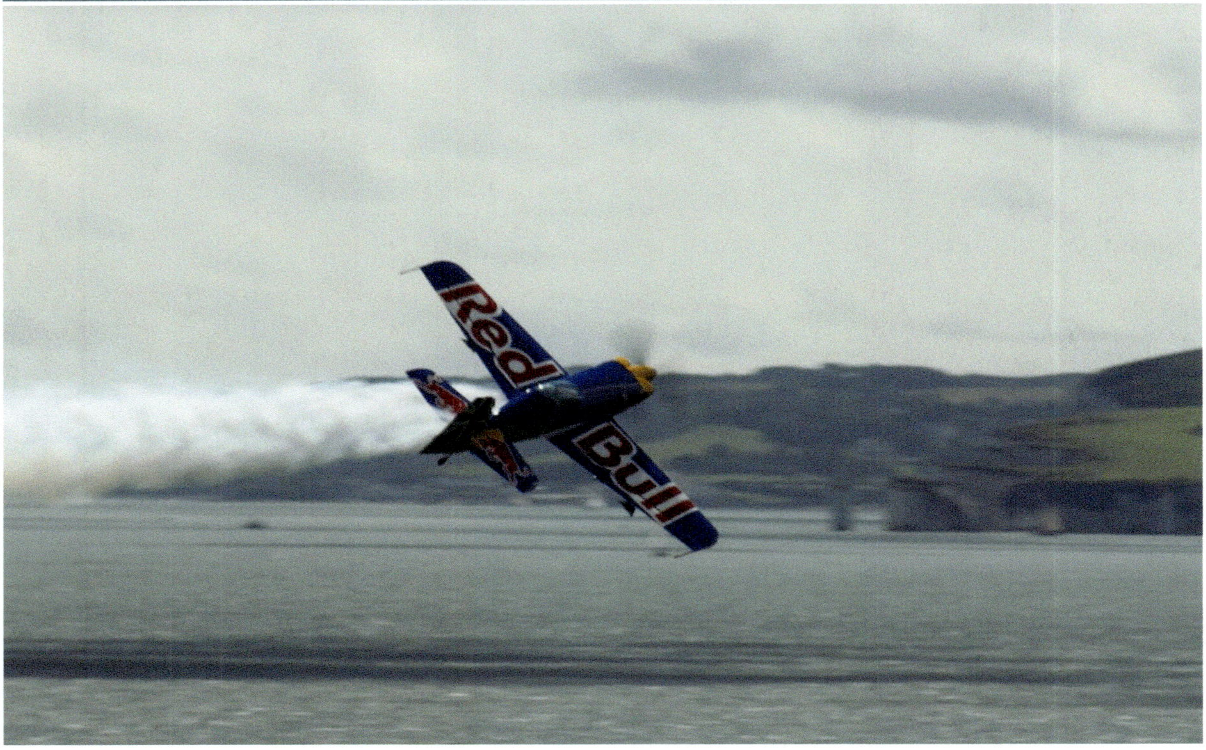
Red
Bull

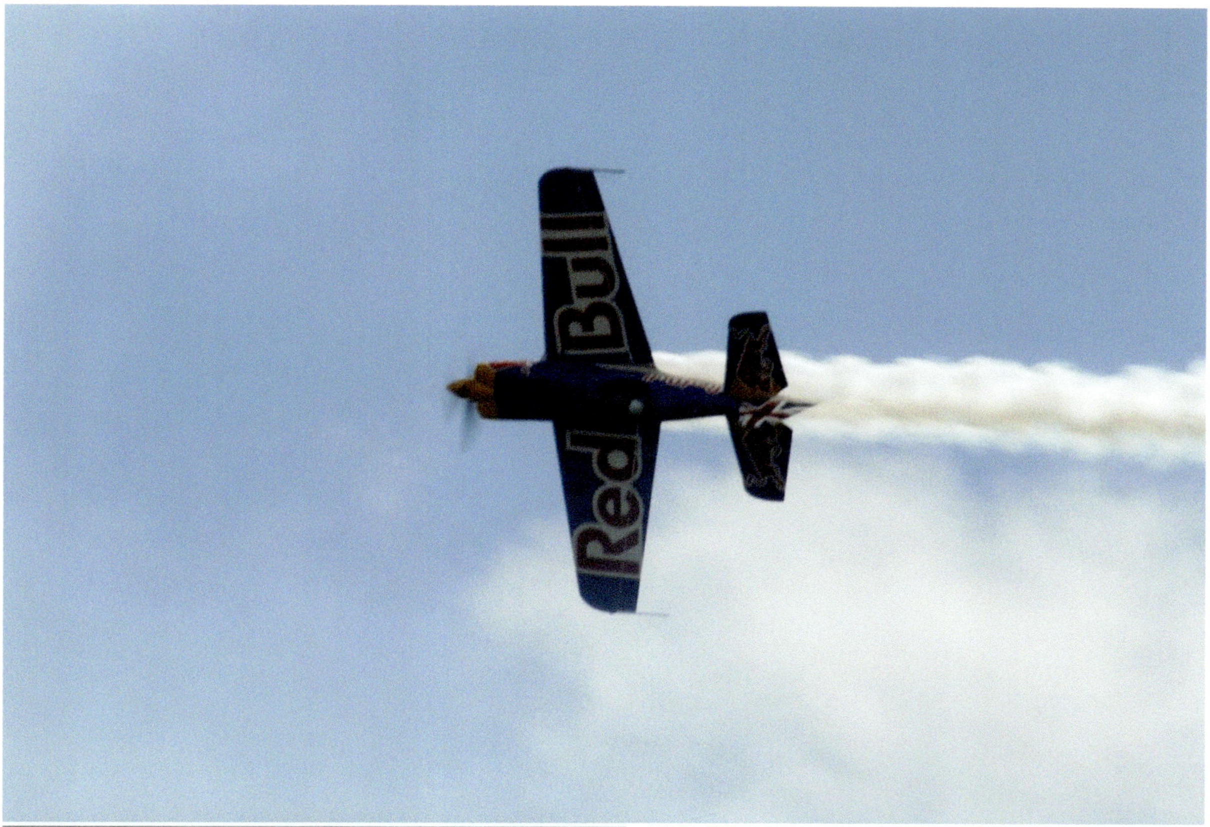

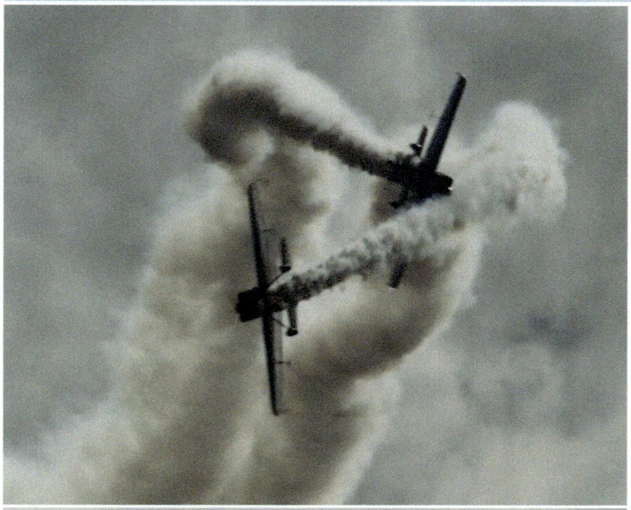

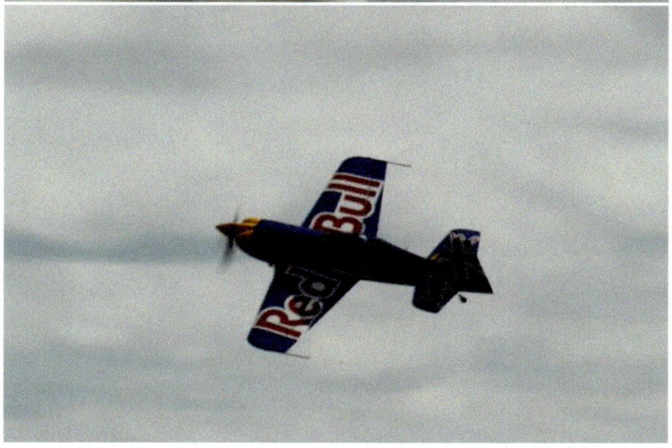

Quick Facts

General

Crew: one

Length: 6.30 m (20 ft 8 in)

Wingspan: 7.50 m (24 ft 7 in)

Height: 2.3 m (7 ft 7 in)

Powerplant: 1 × Lycoming IO-580 six cylinder, air-cooled, four stroke aircraft engine, 235 kW (315 hp)

Propellers: 3-bladed constant speed

Performance

Maximum speed: 390 km/h (240 mph)

Cruise speed: 345 km/h (214 mph)

Stall speed: 94 km/h (58 mph)

g limits: +/-10

Rate of climb: 20.7 m/s

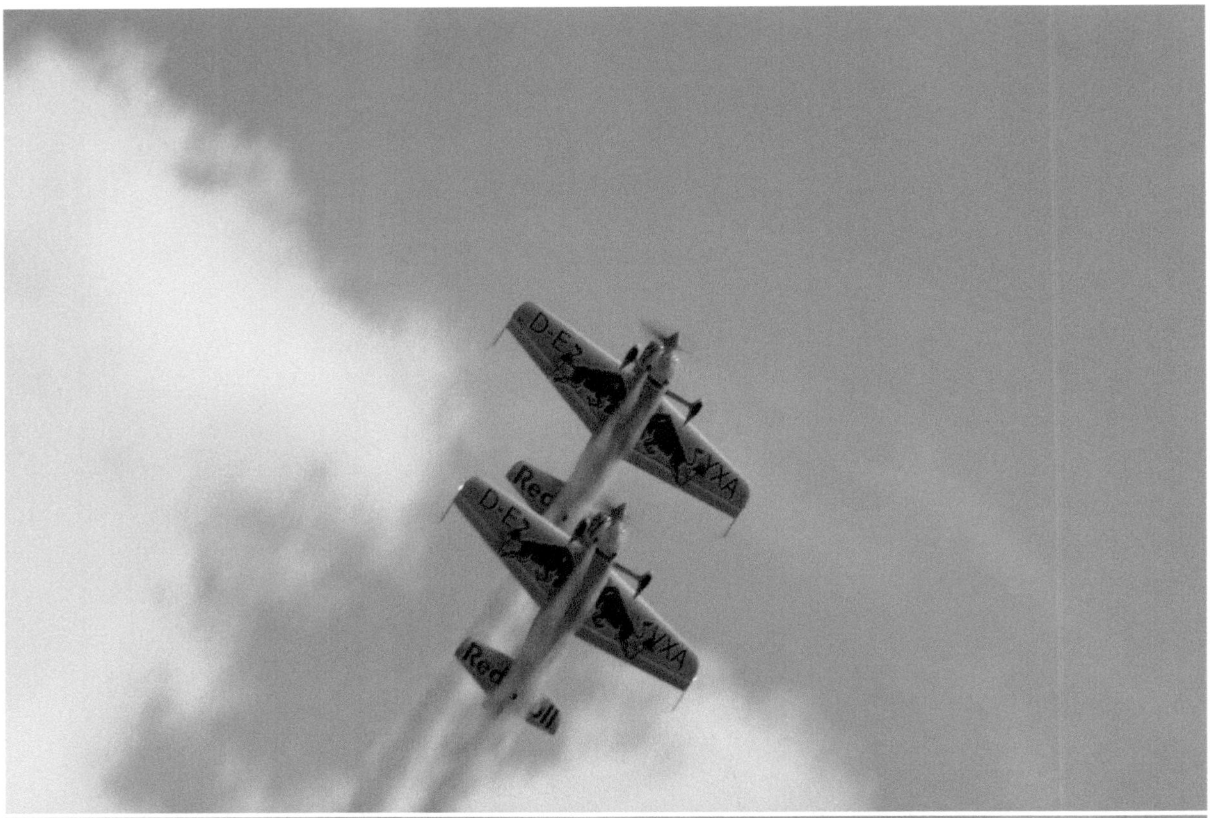

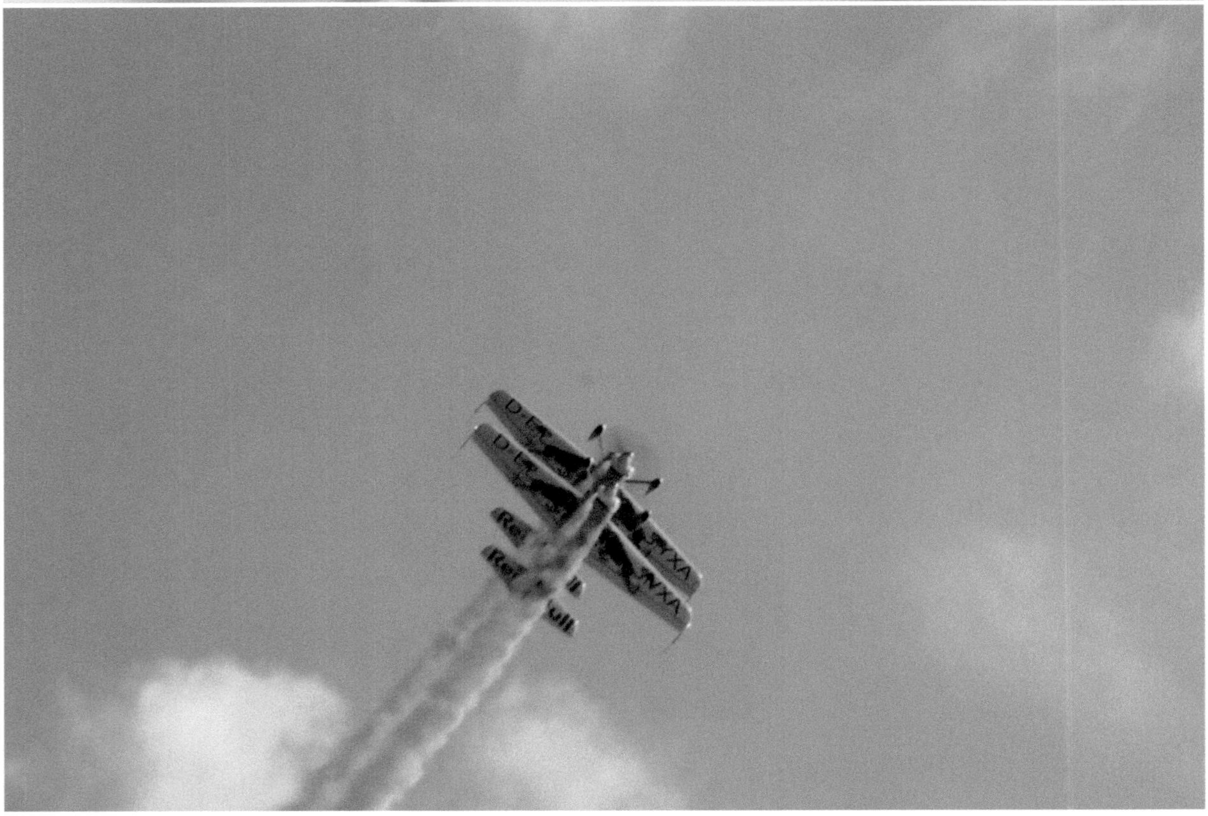

RV8tors

The aerobatic team RV8Tors wows audiences across the United Kingdom with high-flying stunts and manoeuvres in their fleet of nimble Van's RV-8 kit planes. Performing at airshows and aviation events, the skilled pilot's loop, roll, and tumble their agile aircraft through breathtaking aerobatic displays.

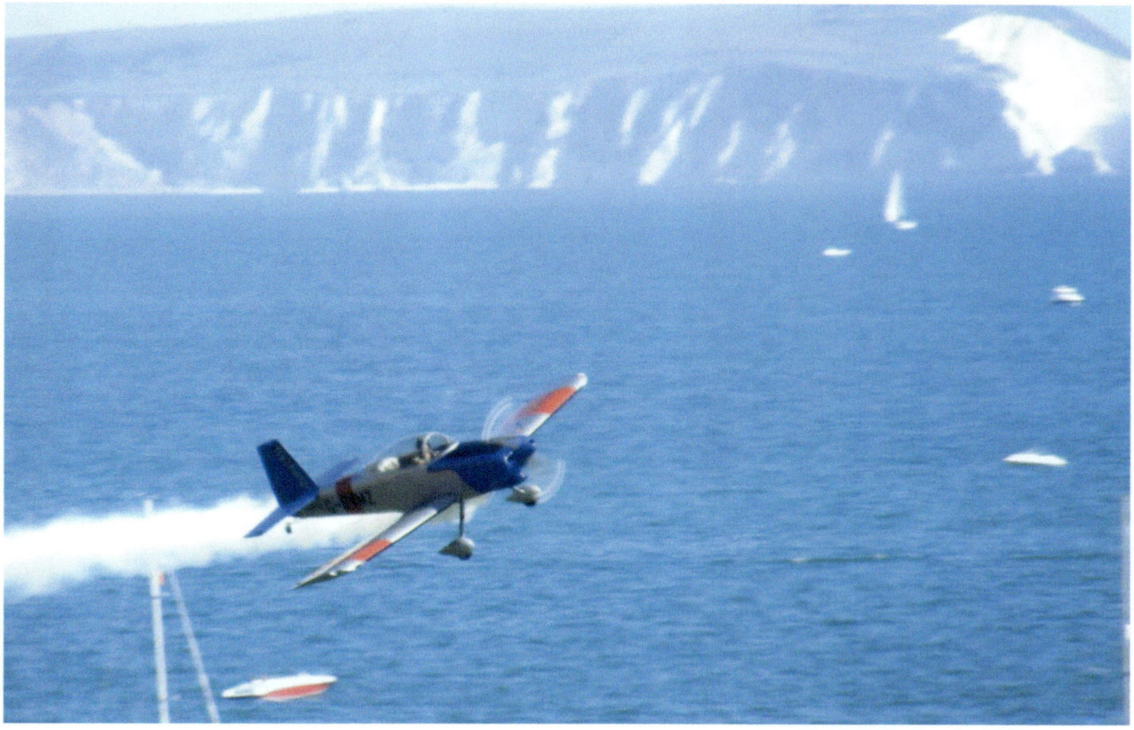

The popular RV-8 aircraft, designed by Richard Van Grunsven and built by Van's Aircraft, is a two-seat, low-wing monoplane known for its performance, handling, and versatility. As a kit-built experimental/homebuilt aircraft with tandem seating, the RV-8 falls into a category of aircraft that can be assembled by aviation enthusiasts.

The RV-8 is renowned for its outstanding performance, blending speed, agility, and fuel efficiency. Builders can choose from a variety of powerful engines, including various Lycoming models and other manufacturers, allowing great flexibility based on preferences and needs.

Due to its popularity and reputation as a high-performing homebuilt aircraft, the RV-8 has become a common sight at airshows, fly-ins, and aviation events. Representing the success of the homebuilt aircraft movement, the RV-8 offers performance and features comparable to factory-built planes while allowing builders to take pride in their craftsmanship and customize their planes during construction.

During the 2011 Bournemouth Air Festival, The RV8tors aerobatic team performed in partnership with Fly2Help, a Kemble-based charity running a competition to win a flight alongside Spitfire IXT SM520. To promote the competition, the Spitfire flew in formation with the aerobatic team.

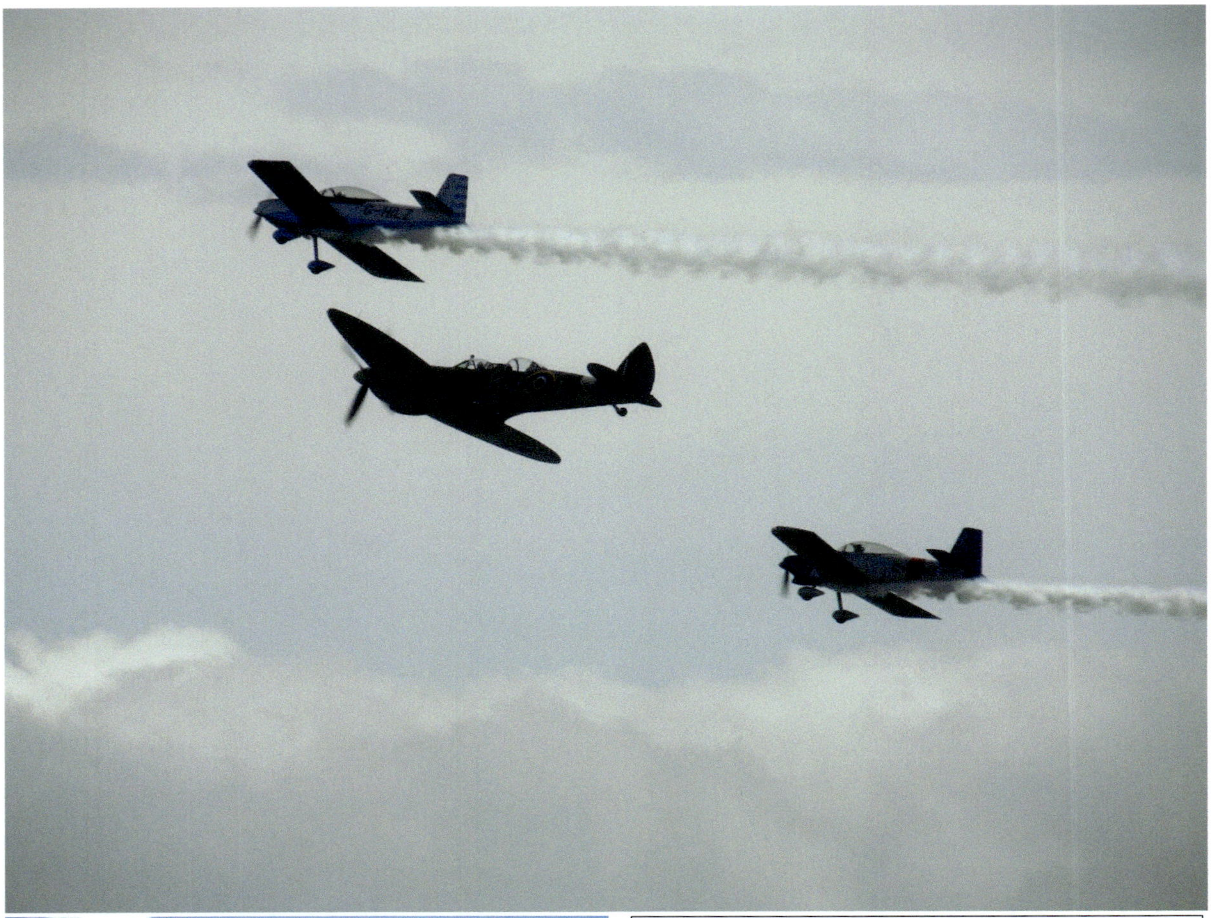

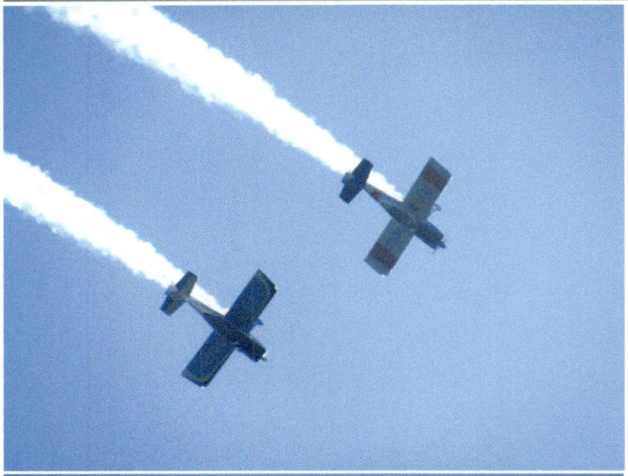

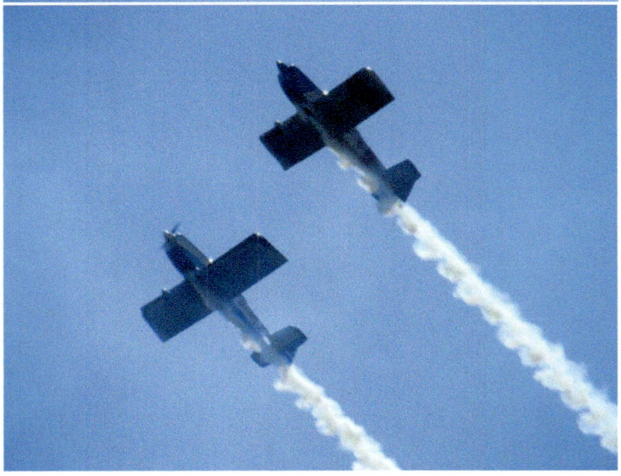

Quick Facts

General

Crew: one

Capacity: one passenger

Length: 21 ft 0 in (6.40 m)

Wingspan: 24 ft 0 in (7.32 m)

Height: 5 ft 7 in (1.70 m)

Powerplant: 1 × Lycoming IO-360 four cylinder, horizontally opposed piston aircraft engine with fuel injection, 200 hp

Performance

Maximum speed: 221 mph (356 km)

Cruise speed: 210 mph (340 km/h)

Stall speed: 58 mph (93 km)

Range: 940 mi

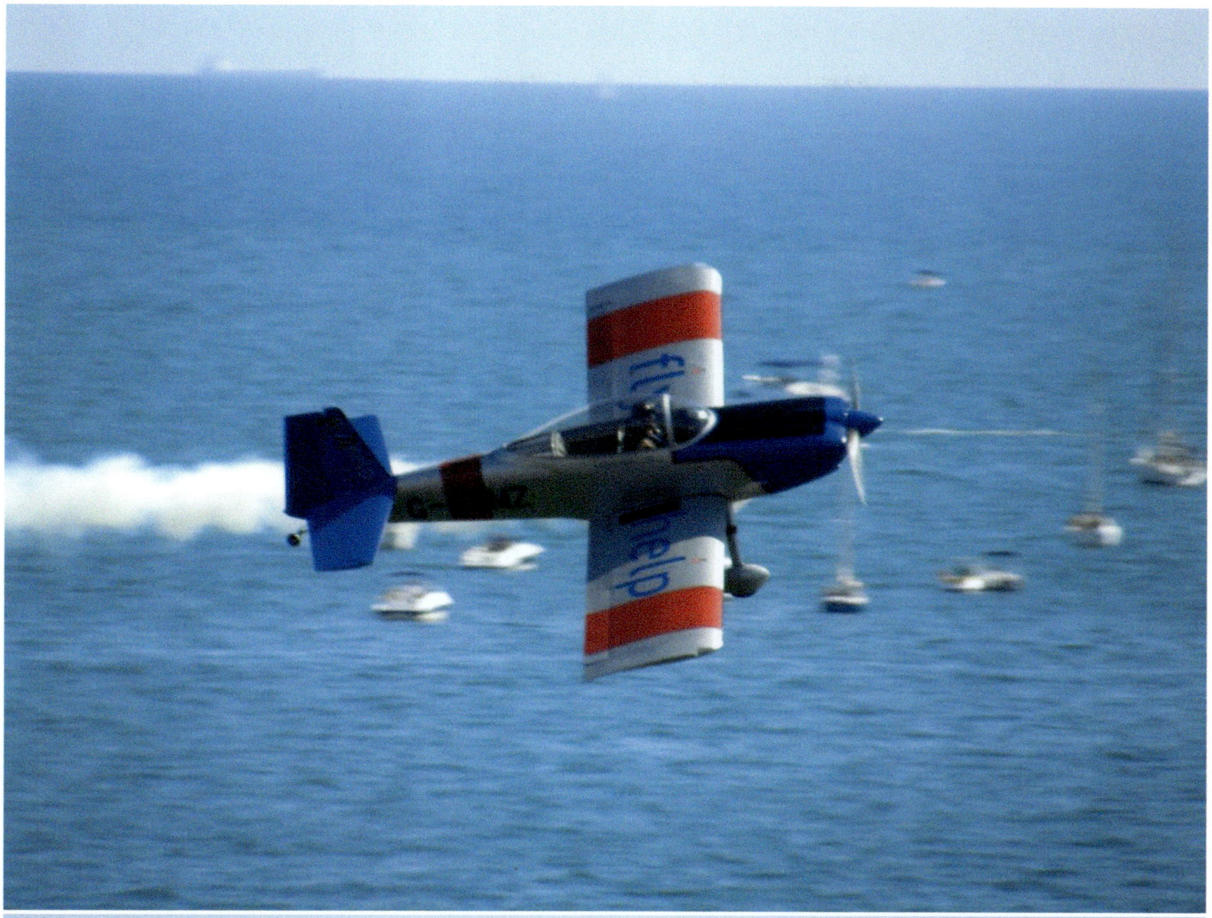
help

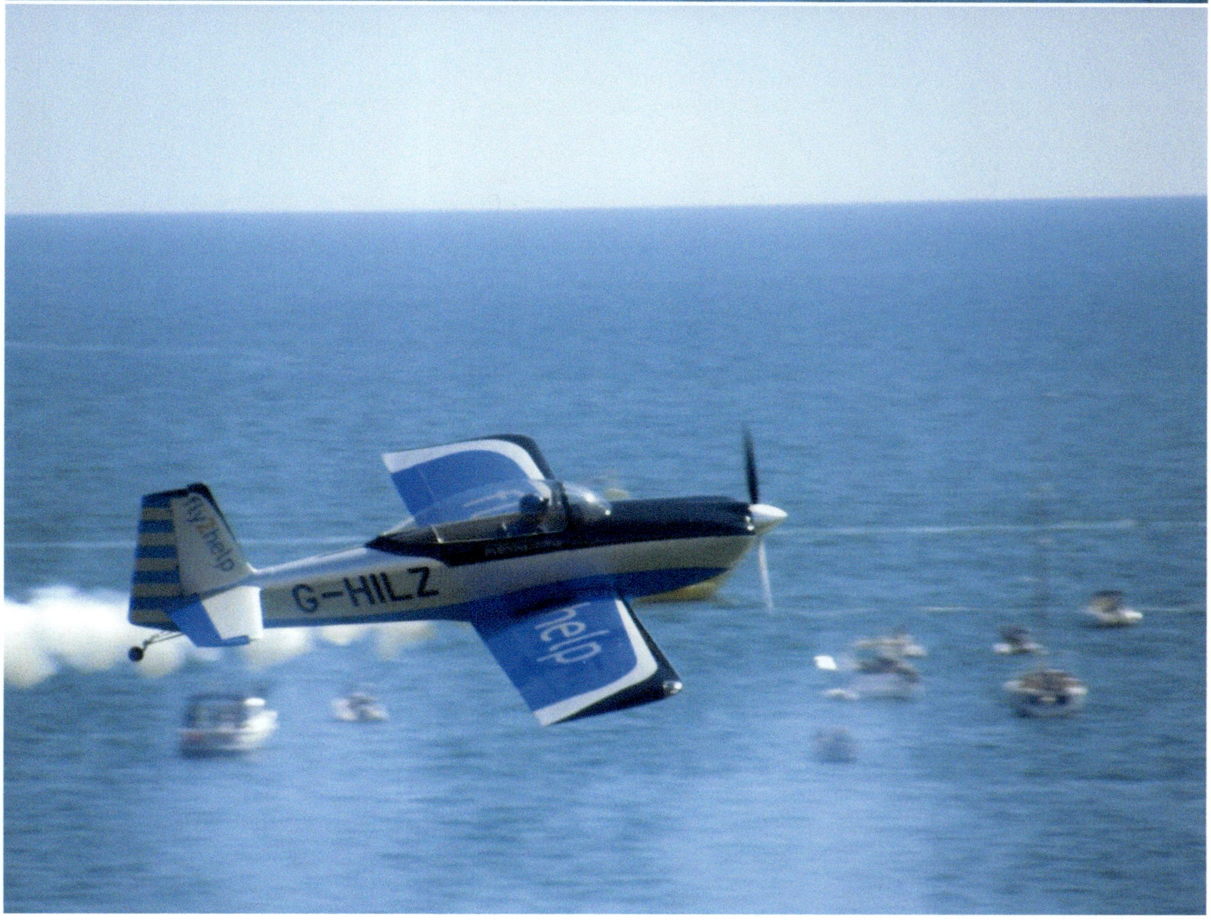
G-HILZ
help

Gerald Cooper Aerobatics

Gerald Cooper, an internationally acclaimed aerobatic pilot, aims to bring greater recognition to the art of sport aerobatics through his flying. Holder of numerous international medals and national championship titles, Cooper continues to amaze audiences with his creative freestyle routines that highlight the precision and skill required in high-level competition aerobatics. Flying his XtremeAir XA41 monoplane, Cooper made history by becoming the first British pilot ever to win gold in the Unlimited class at the European Freestyle Aerobatic Championship, defeating 21 of Europe's best aerobatic pilots in Slovakia.

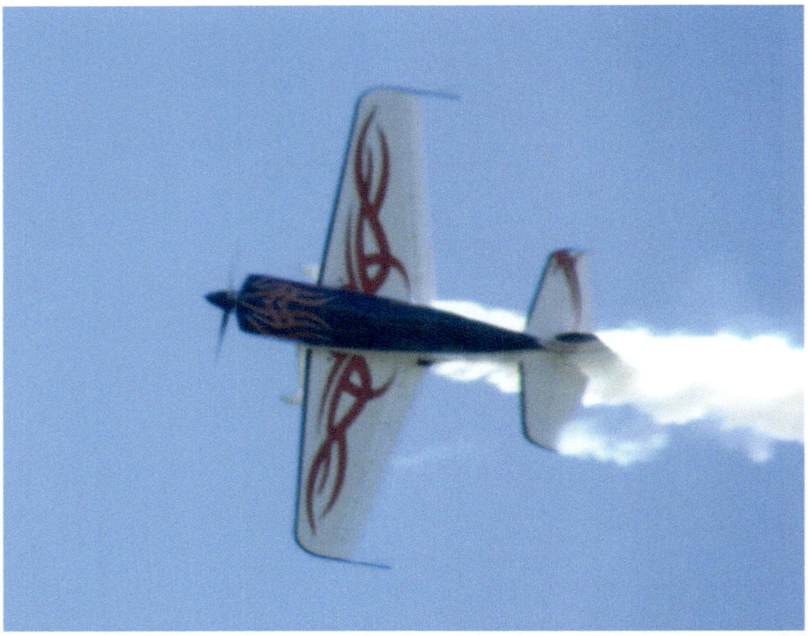

Gerald's dazzling freestyle routine shows off the outstanding abilities of his new carbon fibre airplane, the Xtreme Air XA41. With its excellent power-to-weight ratio, the aircraft enables Gerald to perform gravity-defying manoeuvres.

Gerald impressed the judges at the 2012 Royal Naval Air Squadron Yeovilton Air Show so much that they awarded him Best Fixed Wing Display, a testament to his unique aerobatic aptitude outshining some of the world's best air display pilots, including the RAF Red Arrows and Saudi Hawks.

Since beginning competitive flying in 2000, Gerald has won a number of international medals and is considered a top contender in future world competitions. Some of his accomplishments include:

- Gold medallist – Freestyle European Aerobatic Championship 2012
- British National Aerobatic Champion – 2009, 2010, 2011, 2012
- Currently ranked 7th in the world for competition aerobatics
- Best Fixed Wing Air Display, RNAS Yeovilton Air Show 2012
- Bronze medallist – FAI China Challenge 2011
- Silver medallist – FAI Desert Challenge 2010
- Bronze medallist – World Air Games 2009

Gerald Cooper is a crowd-pleaser at The Bournemouth Air Festival, pushing his aircraft to the limits with daring manoeuvres including a steep vertical climb that brings the plane to a standstill in the sky before stall turning into his next trick.

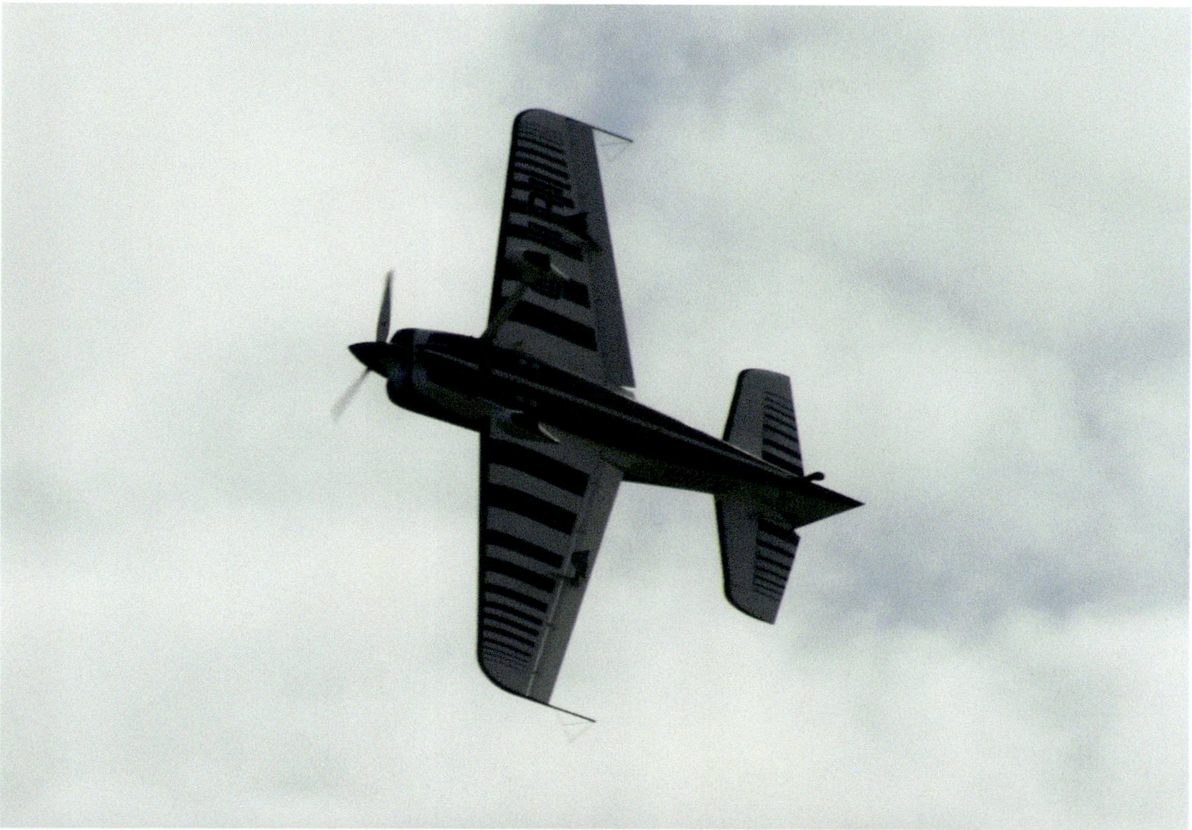

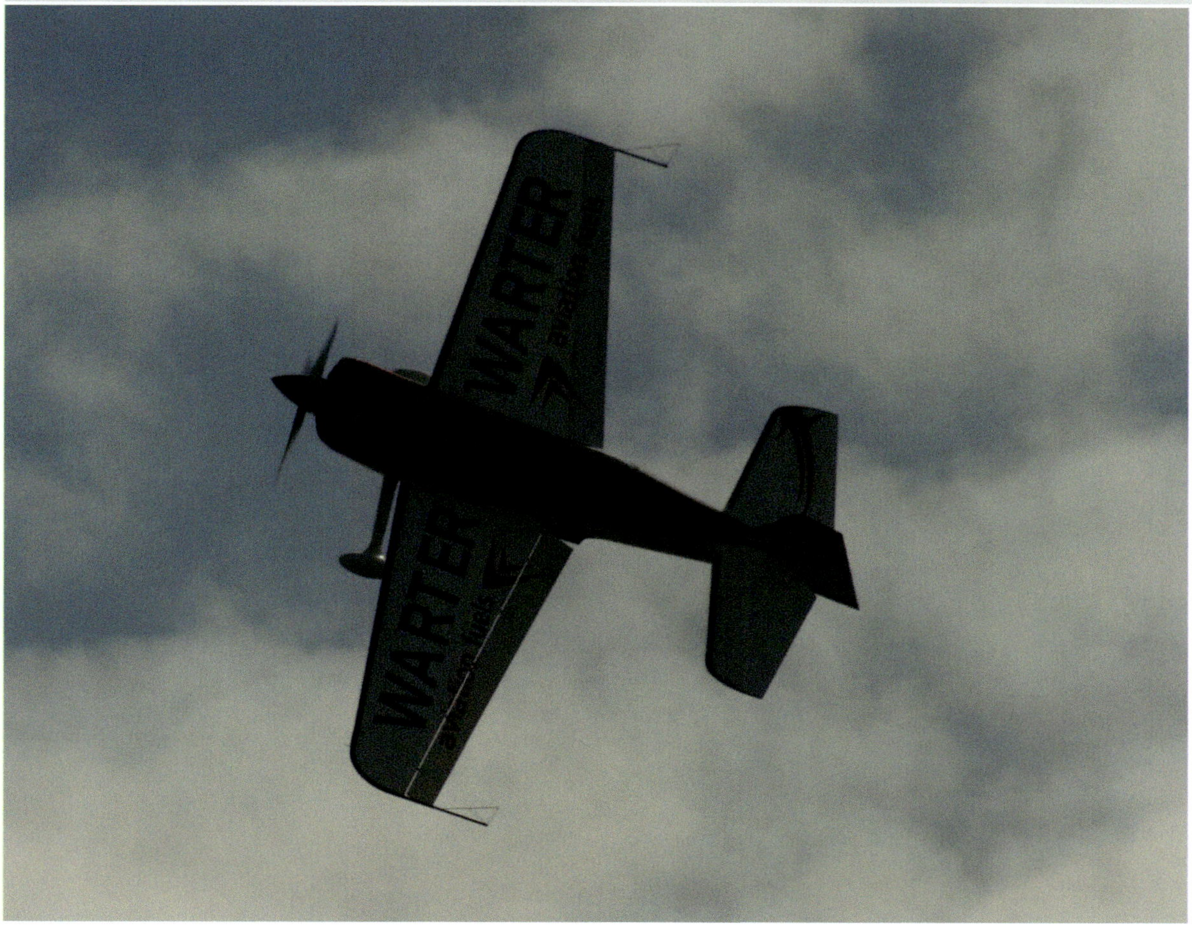
WARTER
WARTER
WARTER
WARTER

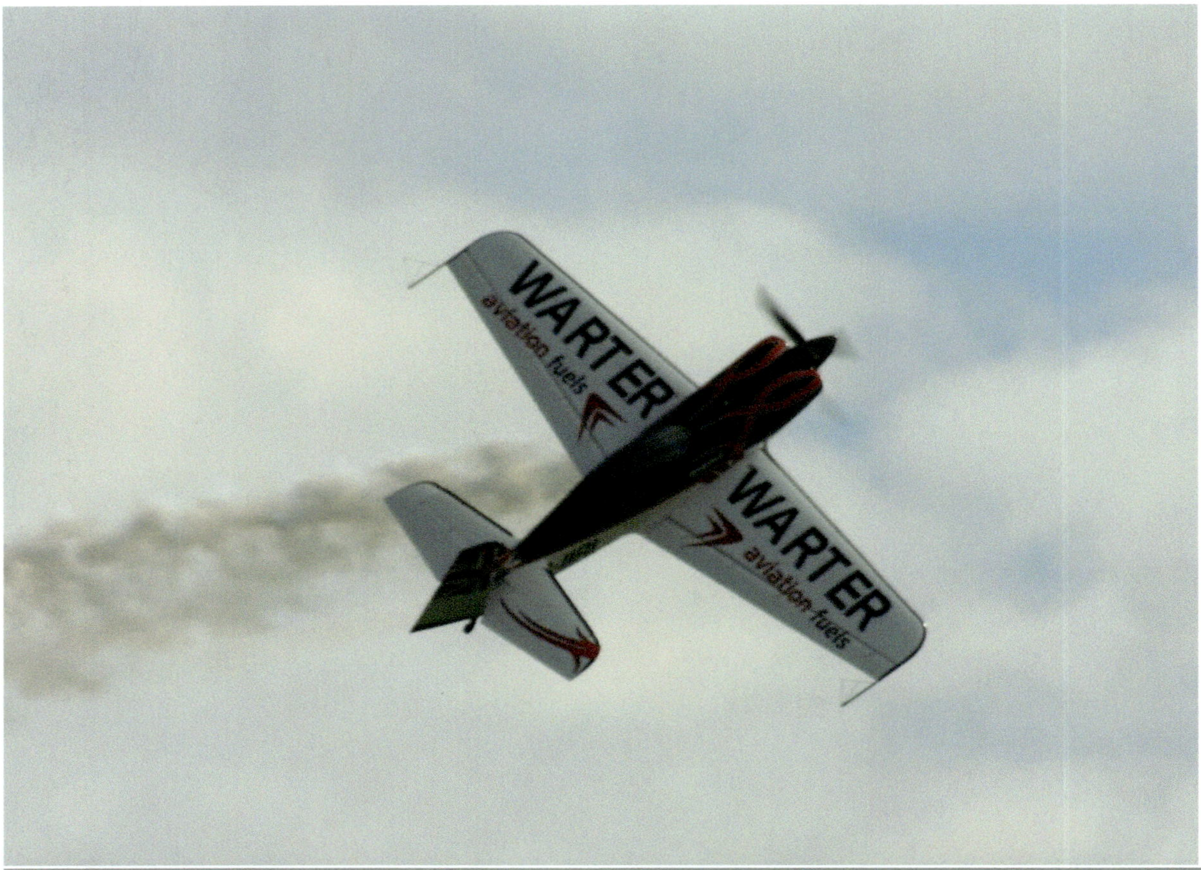
WARTER
aviation fuels
WARTER
aviation fuels

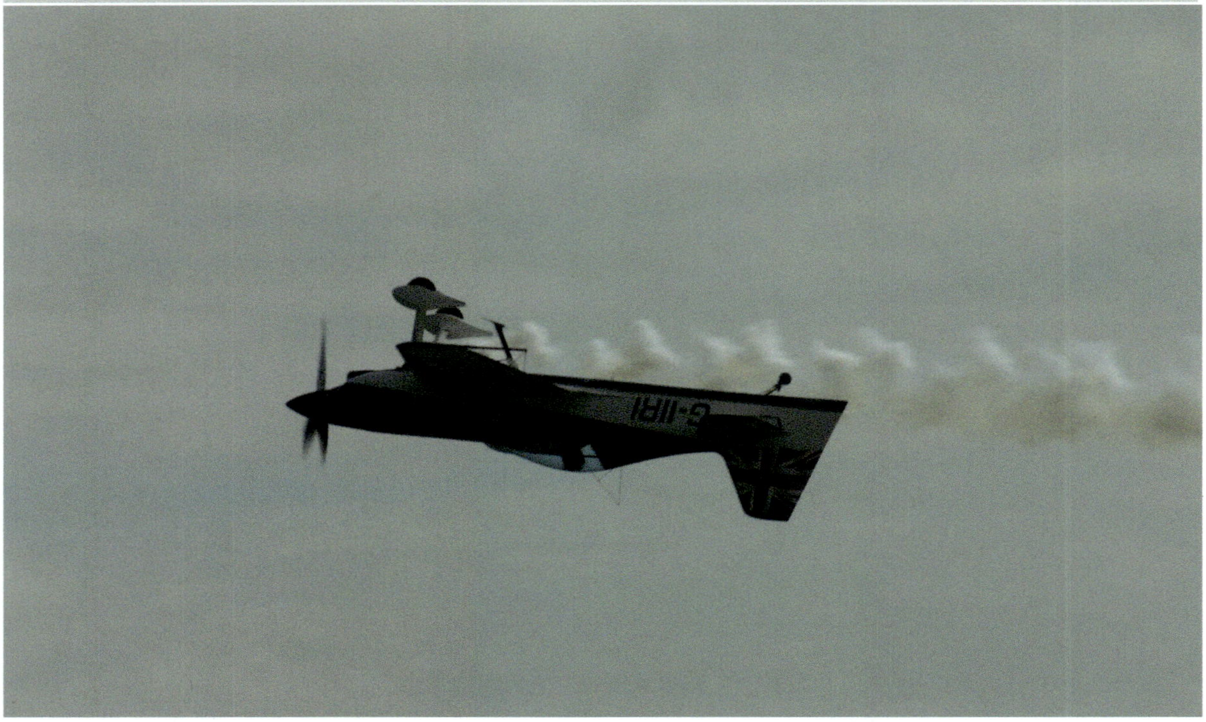

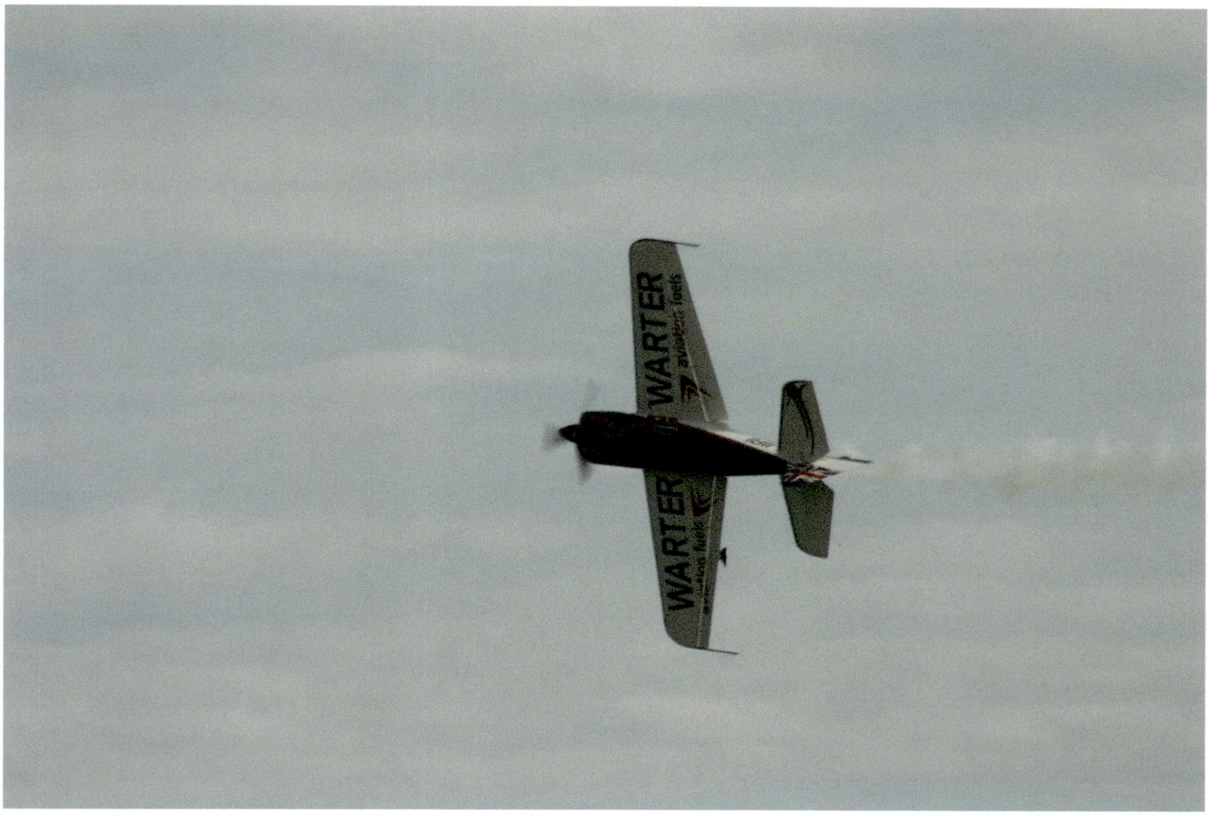
WARTER
aviation fuels
WARTER

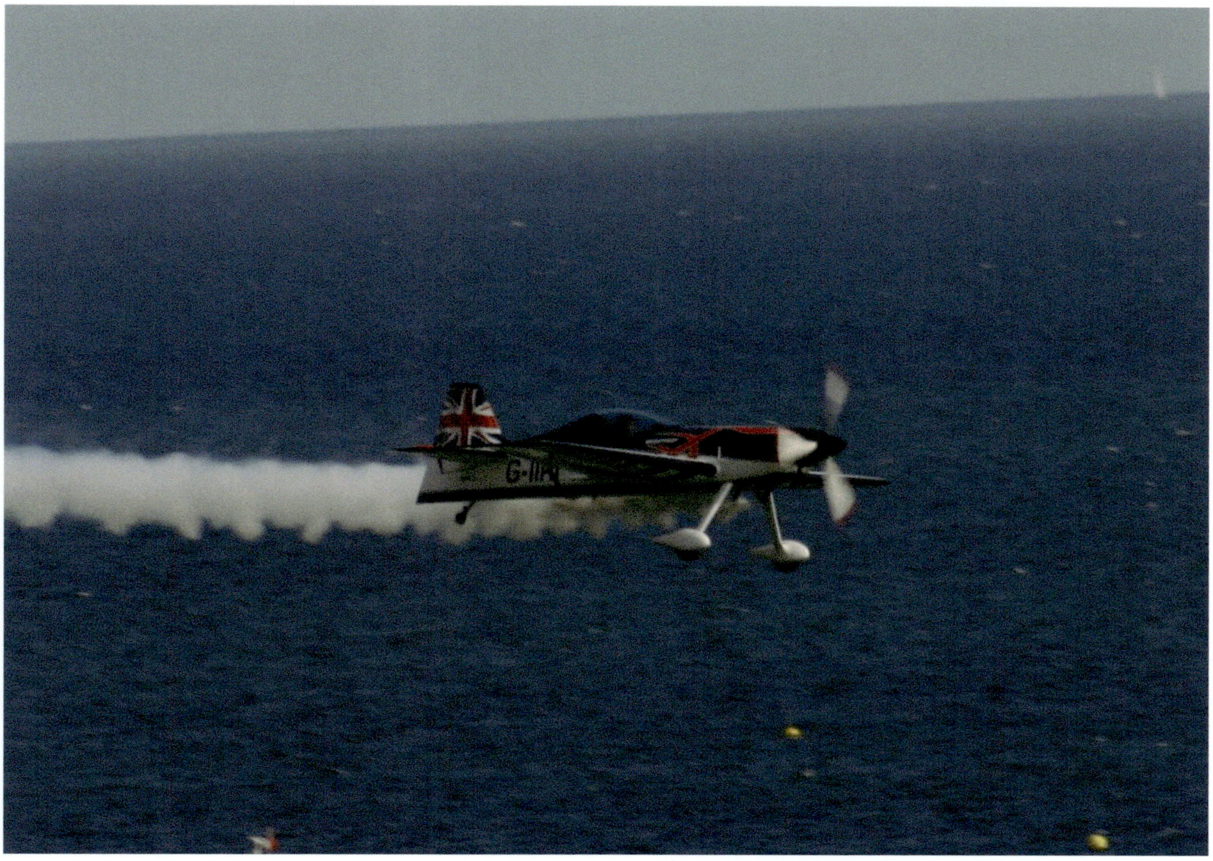

de Havilland Vampire

The de Havilland Vampire was the second jet fighter produced for the Royal Air Force after the Gloster Meteor, and the first British jet aircraft powered by a single engine. Developed and built by the de Havilland Aircraft Company, the Vampire served as an important milestone in British jet aviation.

During World War II in 1941, the British began developing the experimental Vampire aircraft to exploit the innovative jet propulsion technology. After design studies, de Havilland decided on a single-engine, twin-boom layout powered by the Halford H.1 turbojet engine (later called the Goblin). By May 1944, the RAF chose the Vampire as an interceptor. Within months after the war's end in 1946, the Vampire entered operational service with the RAF.

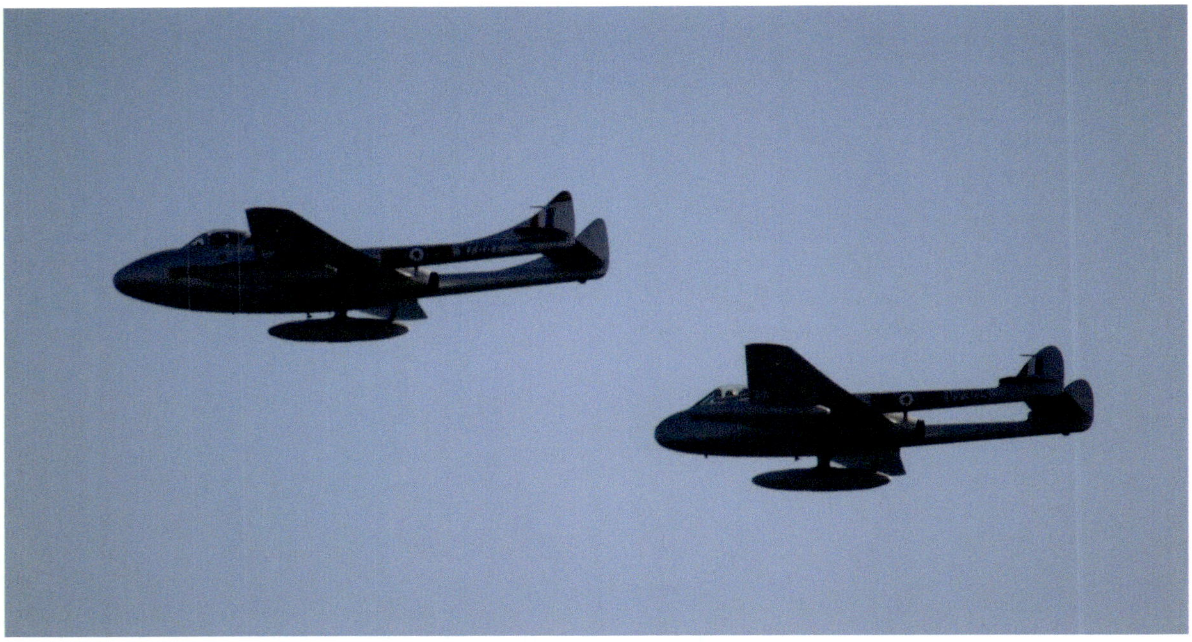

The Norwegian Air Force Historical Squadron brought two de Havilland Vampires, the FB52 and T55, to the Bournemouth Air Festivals of 2017 and 2018, wowing crowds with their close formation flying and aerobatic manoeuvres that showed off the aircrafts' agility.

The de Havilland Vampire FB52 was an export variant of the Mk 6 model, with 101 units built, 36 of which were exported to Norway and served in the Norwegian Air Force from 1949 to 1957. The "FB" in its designation stood for "Fighter-Bomber," indicating the aircraft was designed primarily for ground attack and strike missions, yet remained equipped for air-to-air duties as well. The typical FB52 featured four 20mm Hispano Mk.V cannons and could carry a range of bombs, rockets, and other ordnance on wing-mounted pylons to fulfil its ground attack role.

The de Havilland Vampire T55 was the export version of the DH 115, a trainer aircraft used by the Royal Air Force under the designation T.11. In total, 216 T55s were exported, with six going to Norway where they served from 1952 to 1955. The "T" in the designation indicates these aircraft were trainers, used to teach pilots the Vampire's capabilities before transitioning them to front-line squadrons. Though the Vampire FB52 fighter-bomber and T55 trainer models had distinct roles, their specifications were nearly identical.

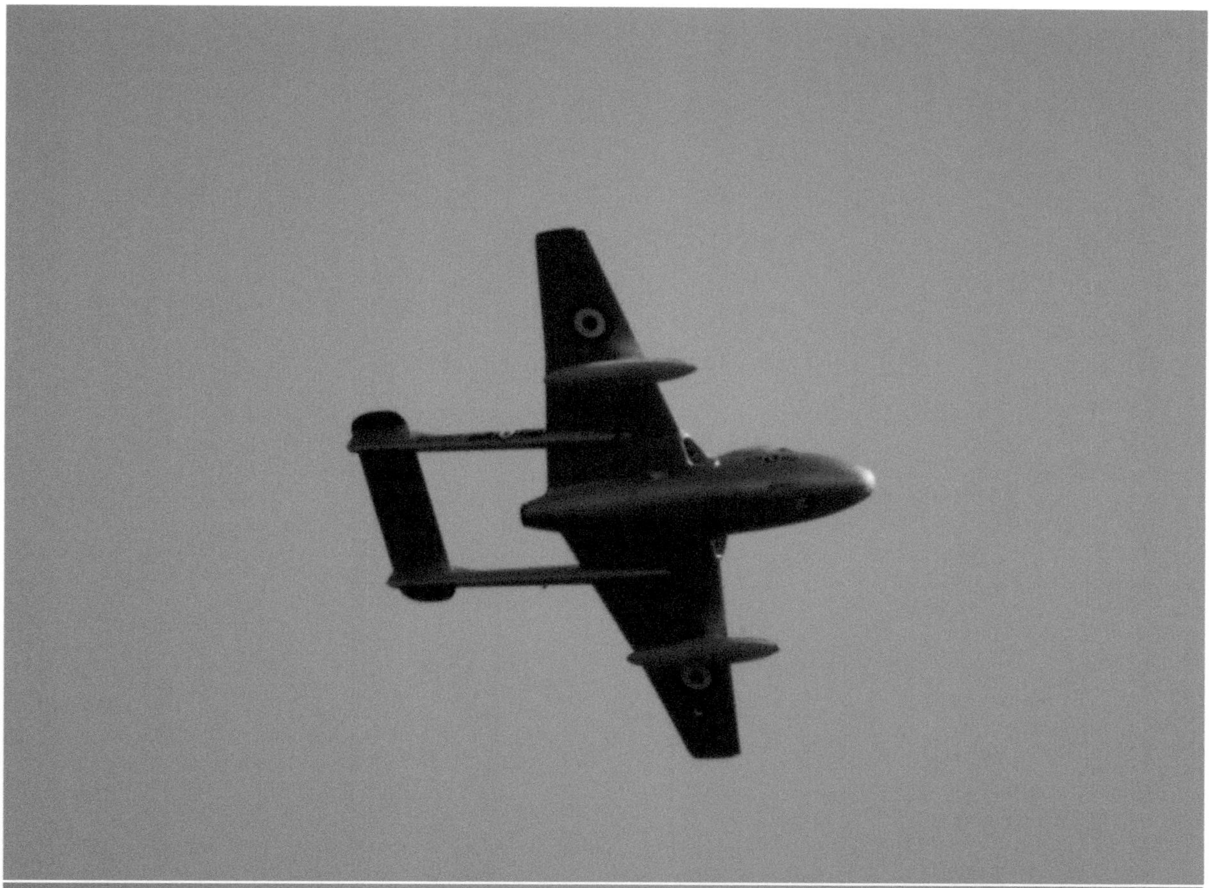

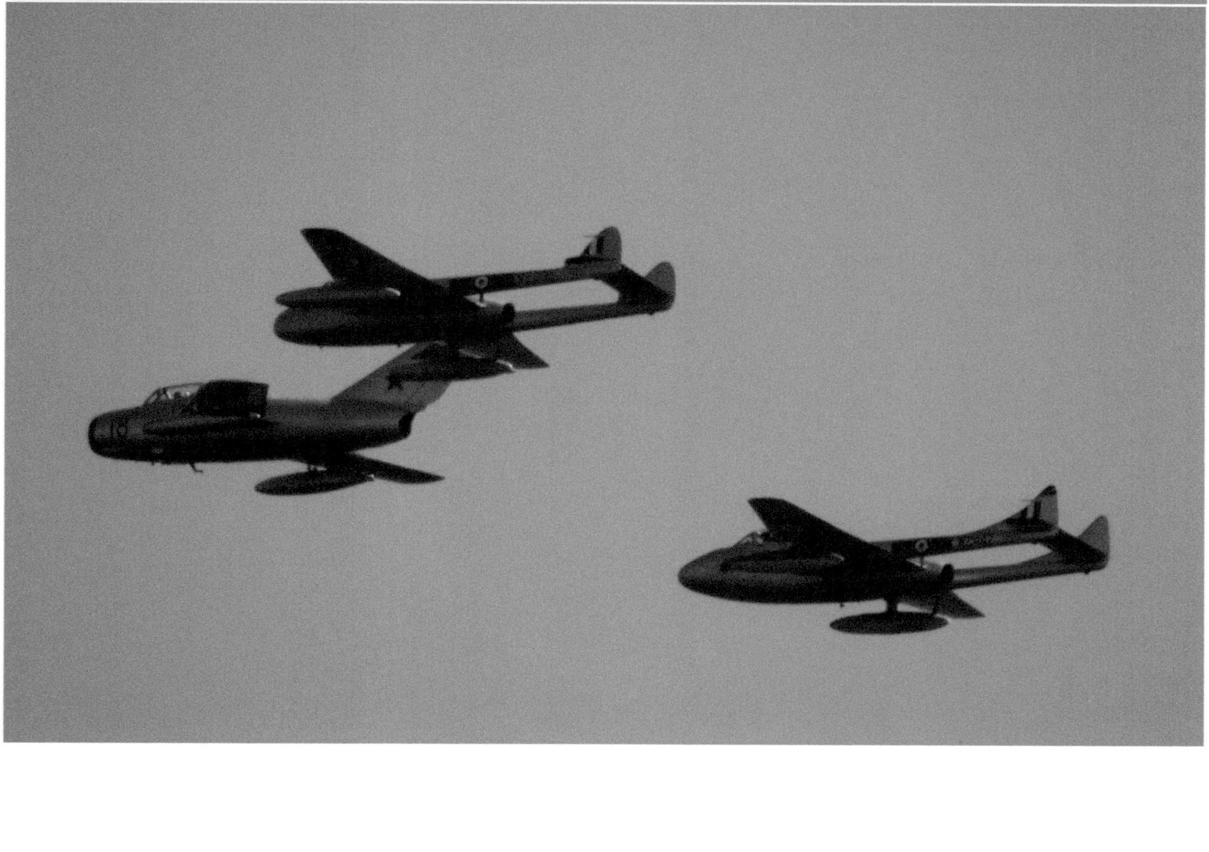

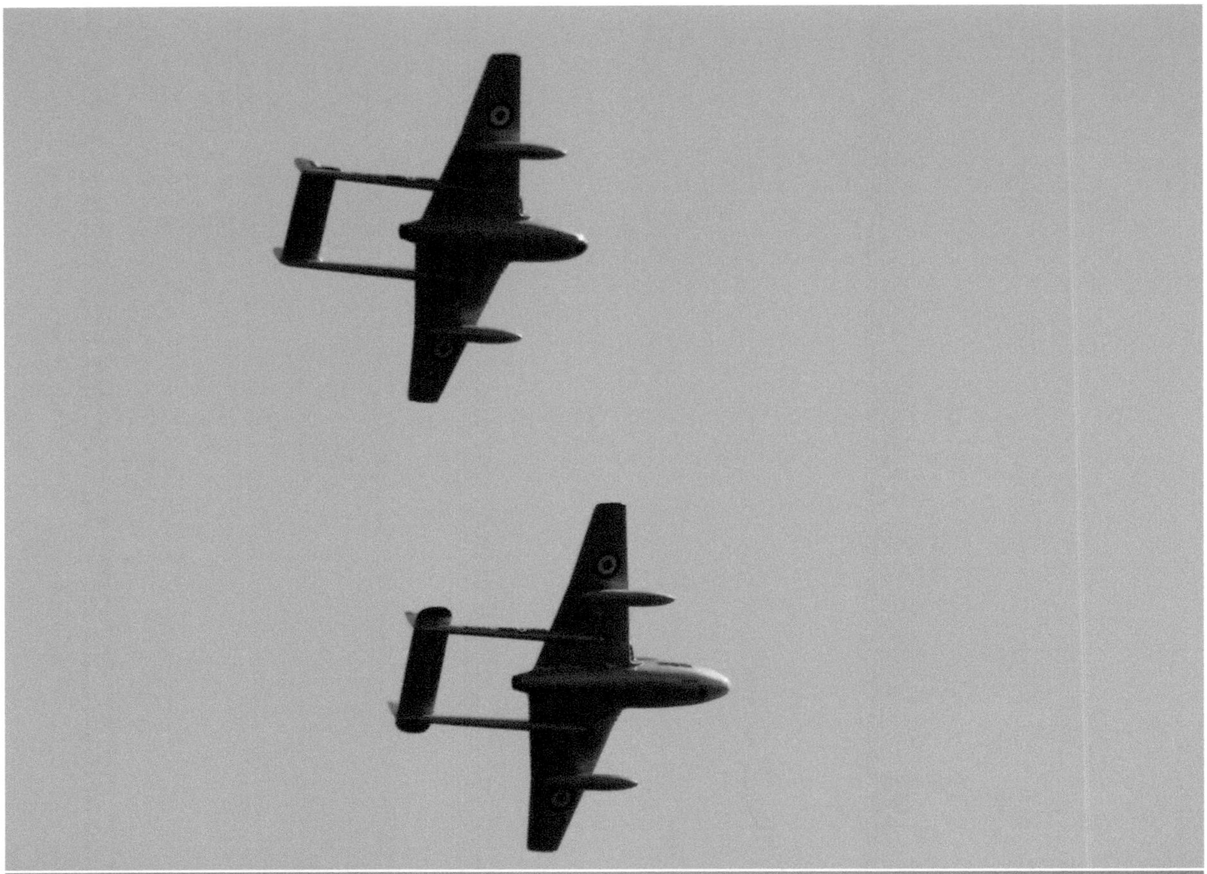

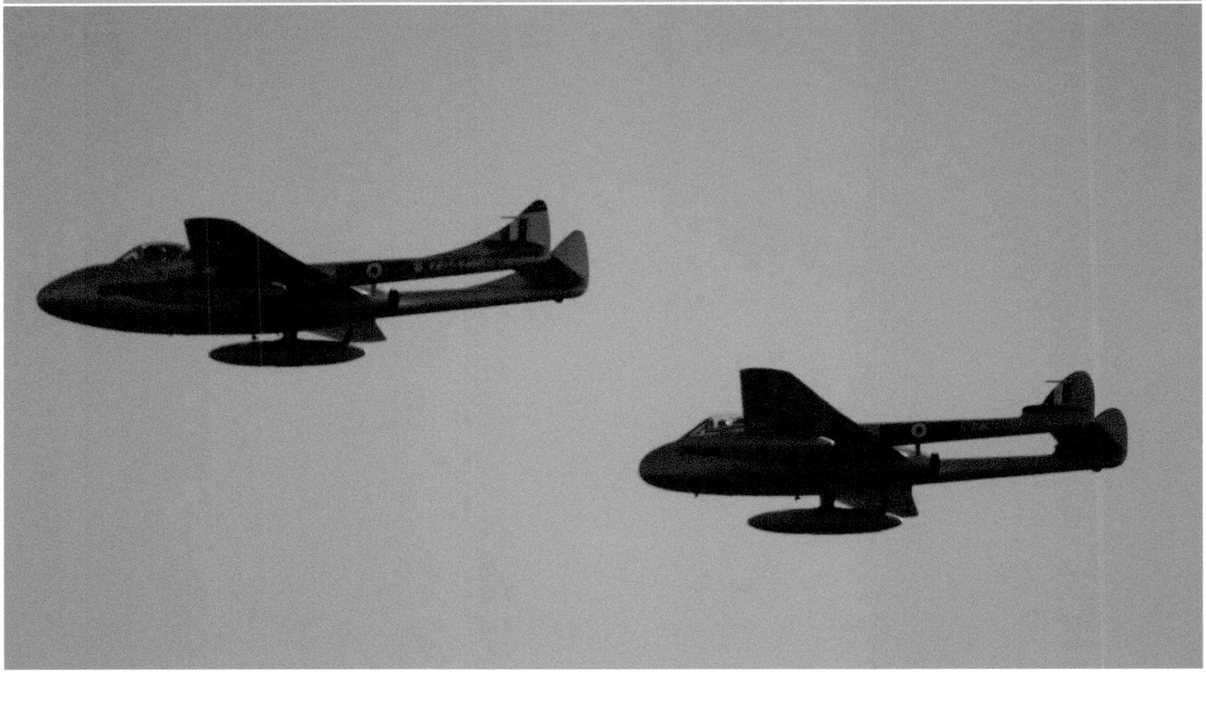

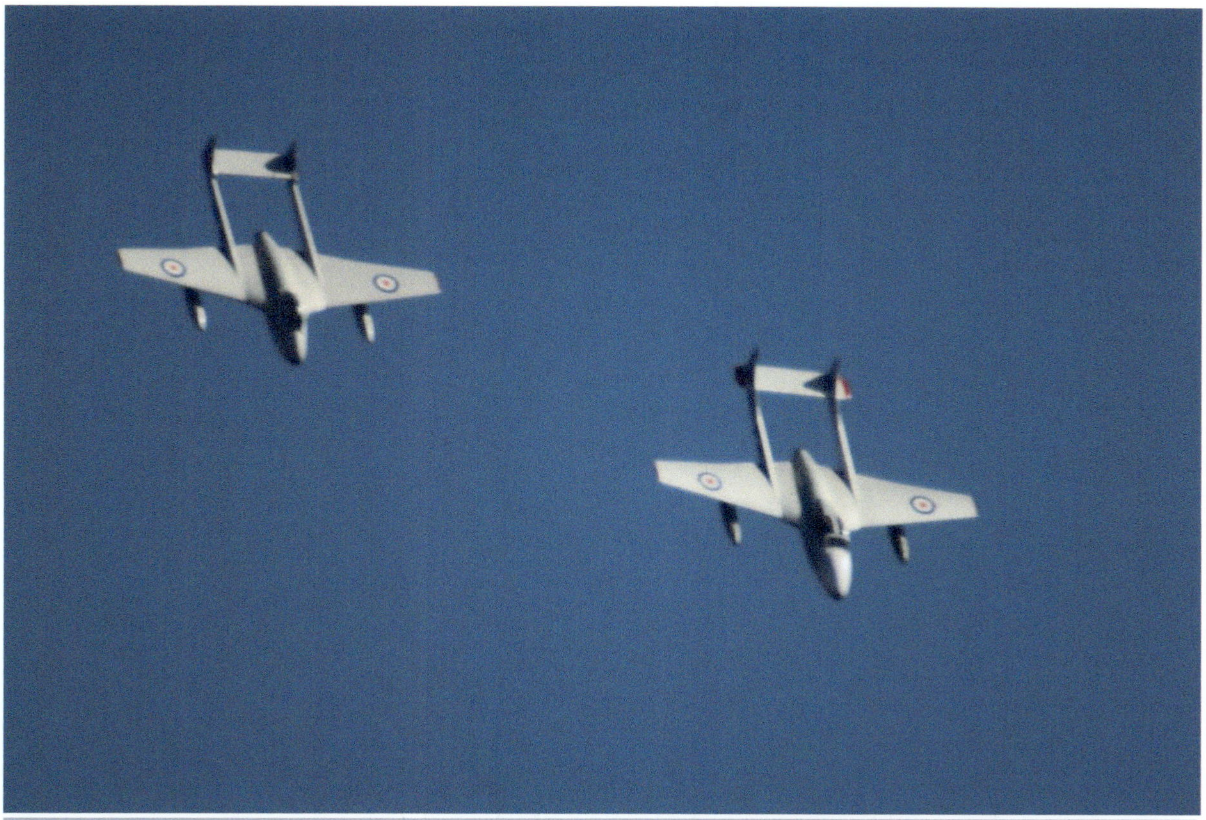

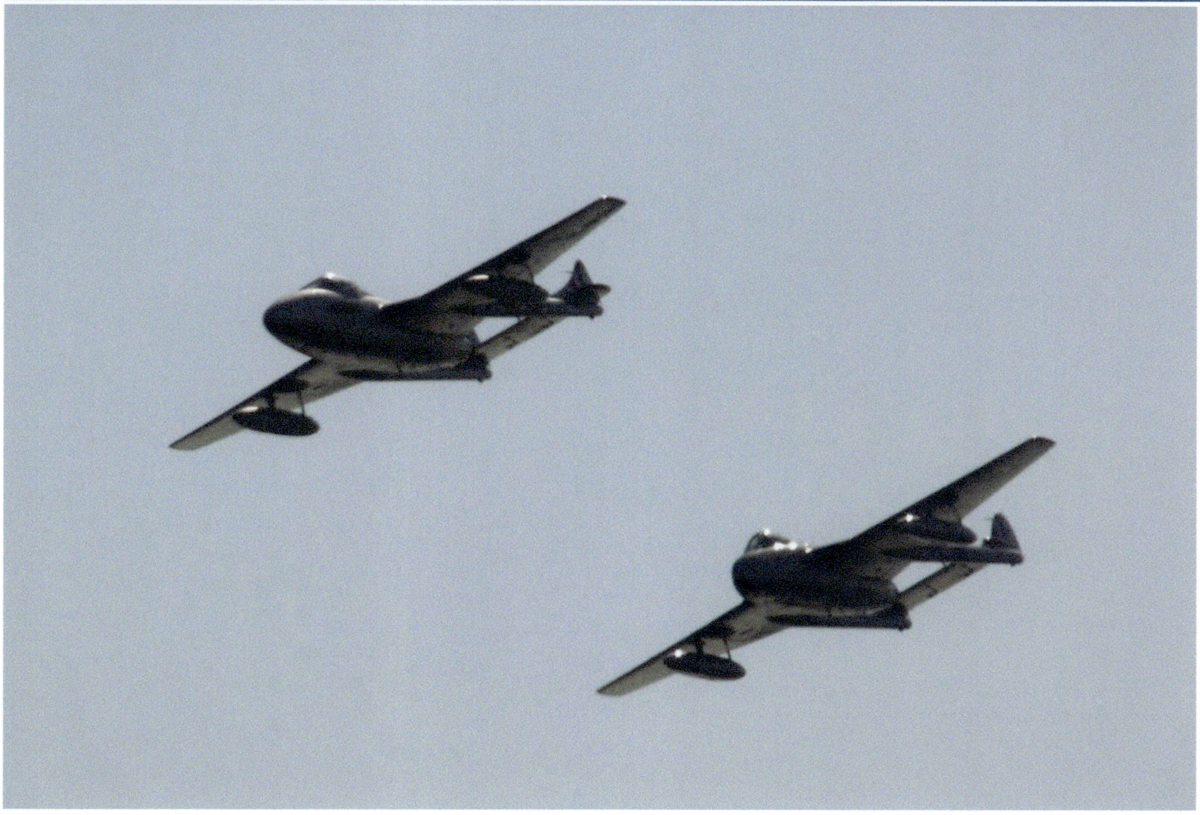

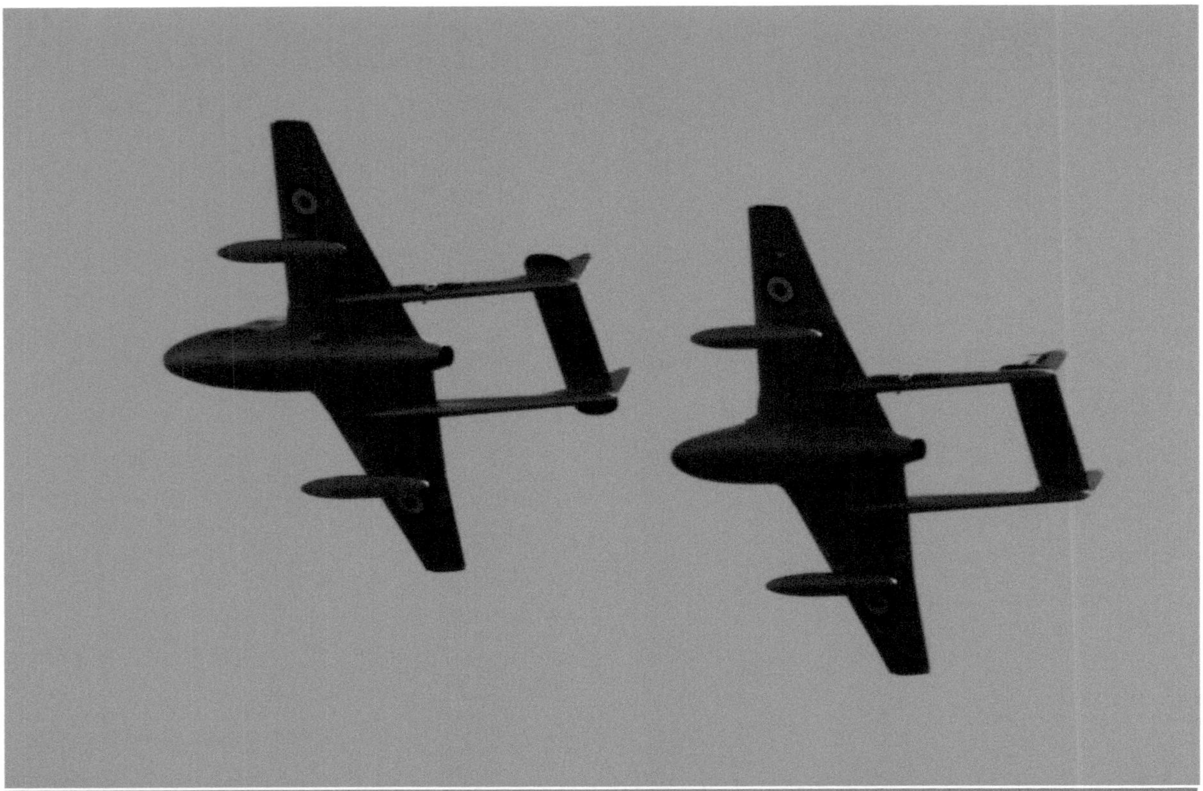

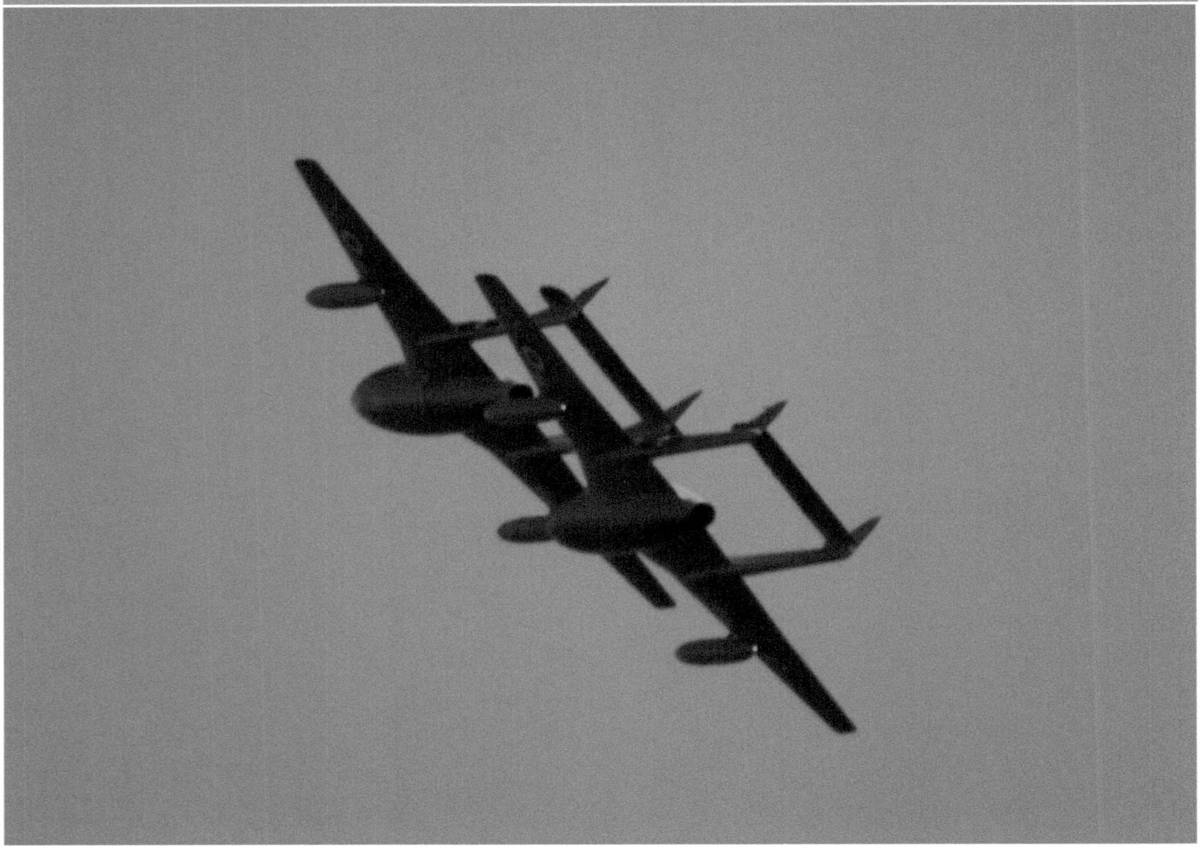

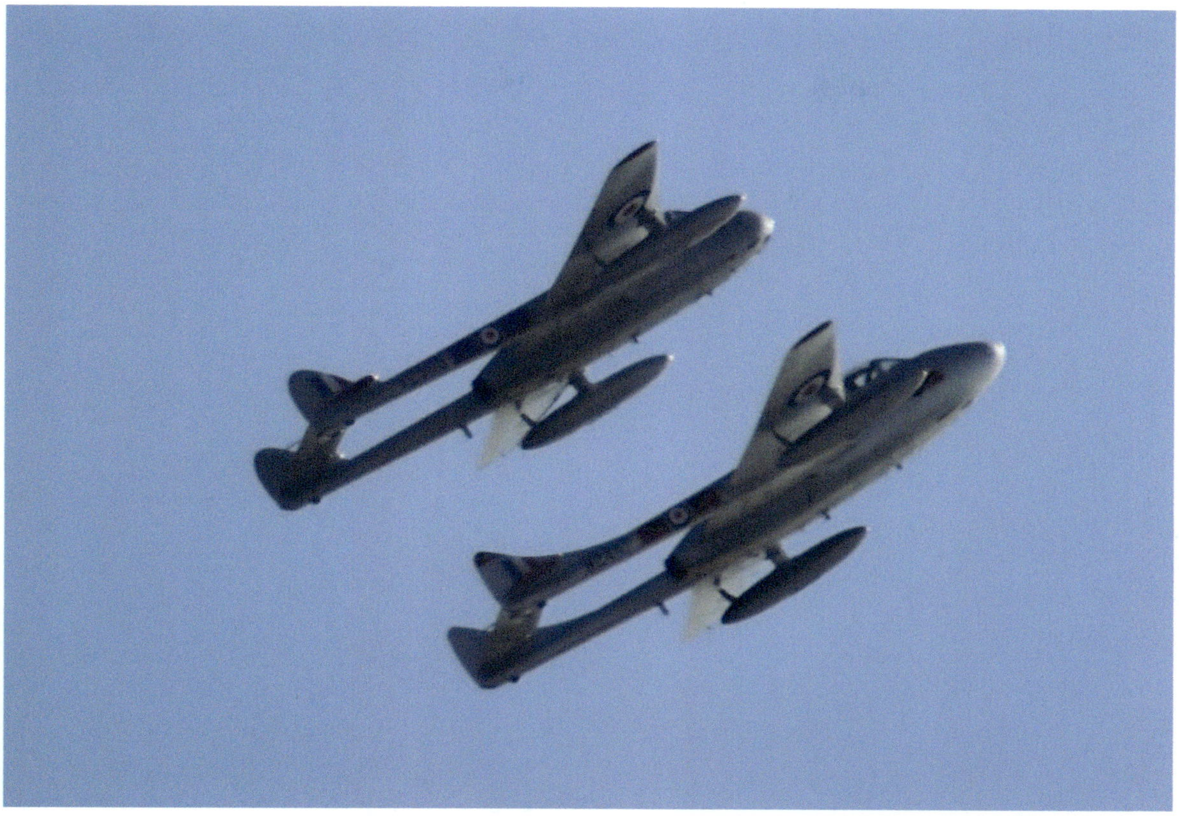

Quick Facts – FB52

General

Crew: 1

Length: 30 ft 9 in (9.37 m)

Wingspan: 38 ft (11.58 m)

Height: 8 ft 10 in (2.69 m)

Powerplant: 1×de Havilland Goblin 3 centrifugal turbojet, 3,350 lbf

Performance

Maximum speed: 548 mph (882 km/h)

Range: 1,220 mi (1,960 km)

Service ceiling: 42,800 ft (13,045 m)

Armament

Guns: 4 × 20 mm (0.79 in) Hispano Mk.V cannons

Rockets: 8 × 3-inch "60 lb" rockets

Bombs: 2 × 500 lb (225 kg) bombs or two drop-tanks

Quick Facts – T55

General

Crew: 1

Length: 30 ft 9 in (9.37 m)

Wingspan: 38 ft (11.58 m)

Height: 8 ft 10 in (2.69 m)

Powerplant: 1 × de Havilland Goblin 35 centrifugal turbojet, 3,500 lbf

Performance

Maximum speed: 548 mph (882 km/h)

Range: 1,220 mi (1,960 km)

Service ceiling: 42,800 ft (13,045 m)

Armament

Guns: 4 × 20 mm (0.79 in) Hispano Mk.V cannons

Rockets: 8 × 3-inch "60 lb" rockets

Bombs: 2 × 500 lb (225 kg) bombs or two drop-tanks

MiG-15

The MiG-15 was a revolutionary swept-wing jet fighter developed by Mikoyan-Gurevich for the Soviet Union. One of the first successful swept-wing jet fighters able to achieve high transonic speeds, the MiG-15 outclassed straight-winged jets during the Korean War, relegating them to ground-attack roles. Believed to be one of the most mass-produced jets in history, over 13,000 MiG-15s were manufactured.

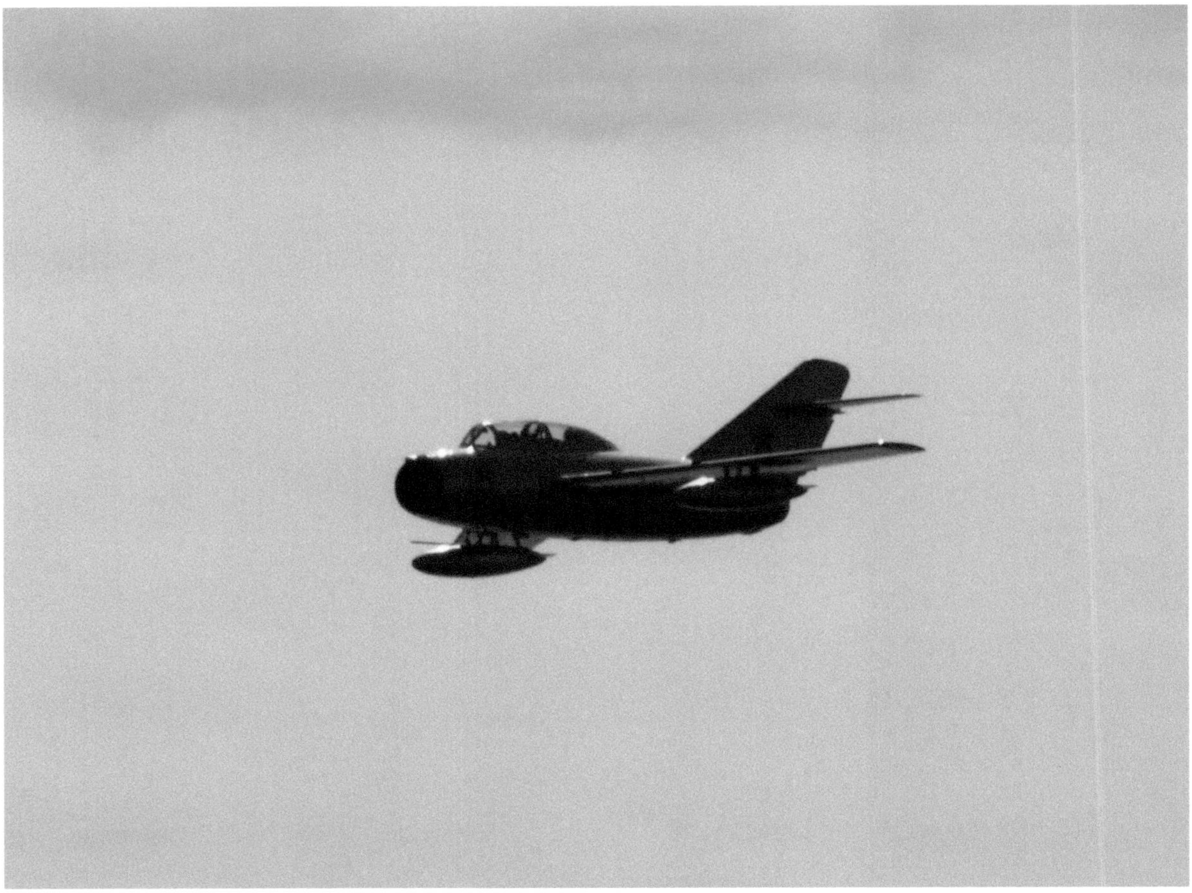

The MiG-15 was a highly versatile fighter jet used primarily as a day fighter by the Soviet Union in the early Cold War period. In addition to air combat missions, it served in various roles including as an interceptor, ground attacker, and reconnaissance aircraft. The standard armament on the MiG-15 consisted of one 37mm and two 23mm cannons. With a top speed of approximately 670 mph (1,080 km/h) and a service ceiling of about 51,000 feet (15,500 m), it was one of the most advanced and capable fighters of its time. Considered highly influential, the MiG-15 played a major role in the technological and strategic evolution of jet fighter design during the 1950s.

The MiG-15 on display at the Bournemouth Air Festival belongs to the Norwegian Air Force Historical Squadron. In 2018, it performed flybys with the Vampires, and in 2019, it partnered with the Canadair T-33 Silver Star. The aircraft is painted as "RED 18" in honour of Russian cosmonaut Yuri Gagarin, who flew the MiG-15 as a fighter pilot before becoming the first human to journey into outer space in 1961. Stationed near the Norwegian border just 40 km from Kirkenes, Gagarin gained experience with the MiG-15 that paved the way for his history-making space flight. This particular aircraft at the festival is a two-seat MiG-15 trainer version.

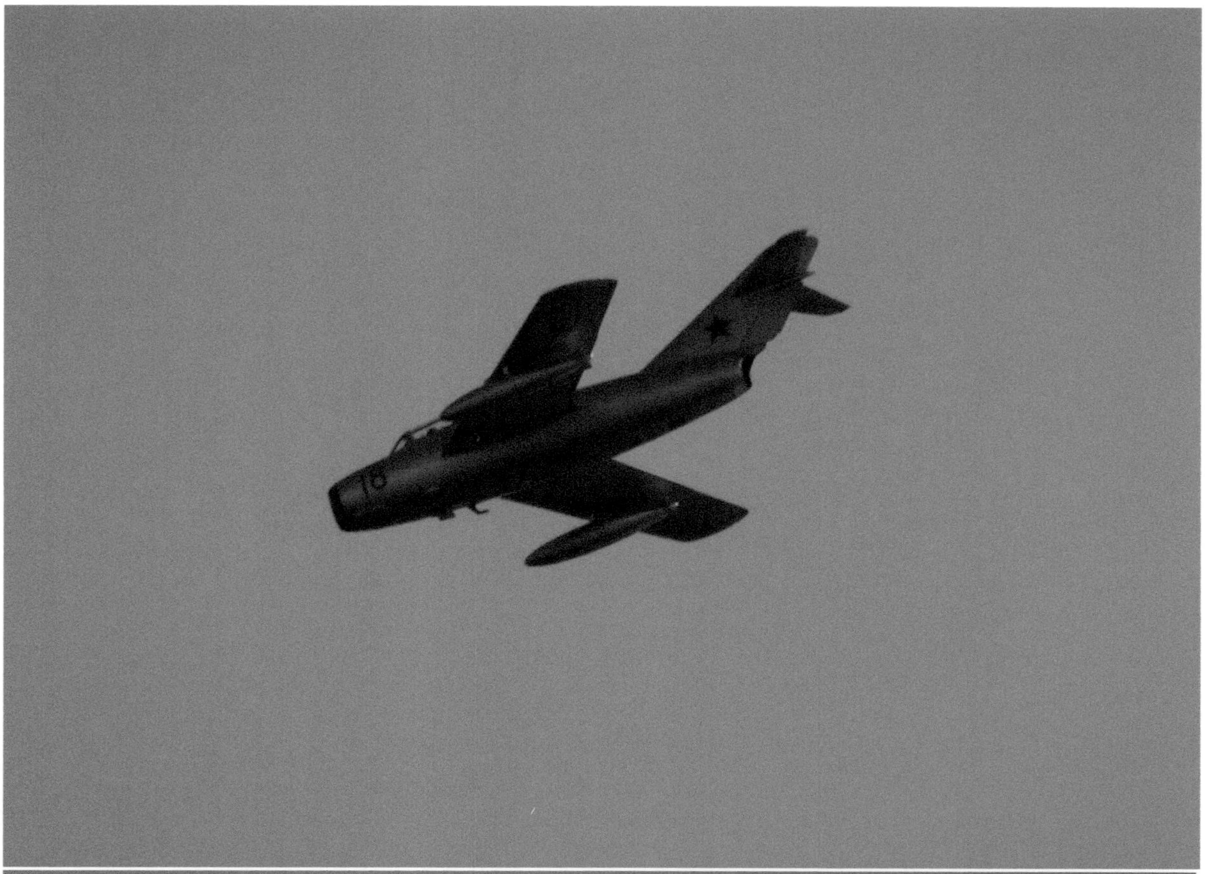

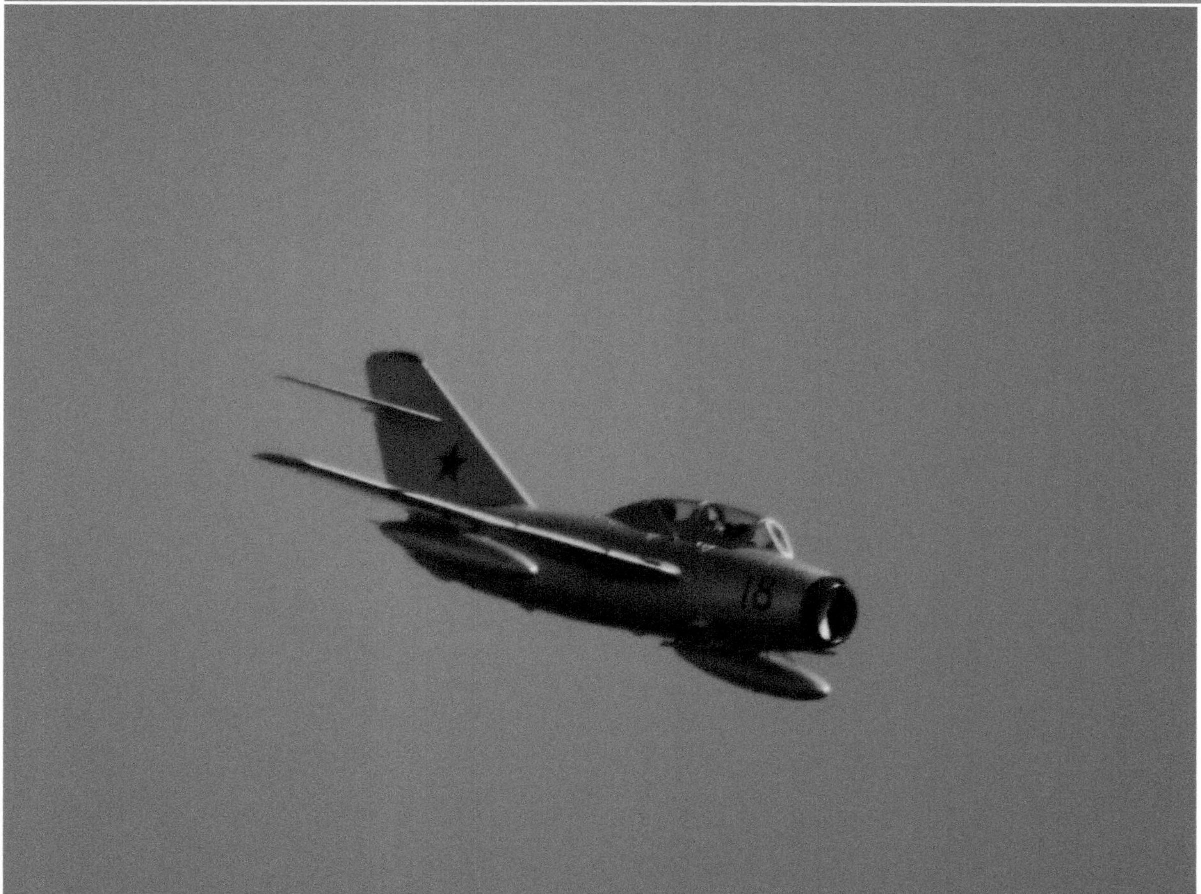

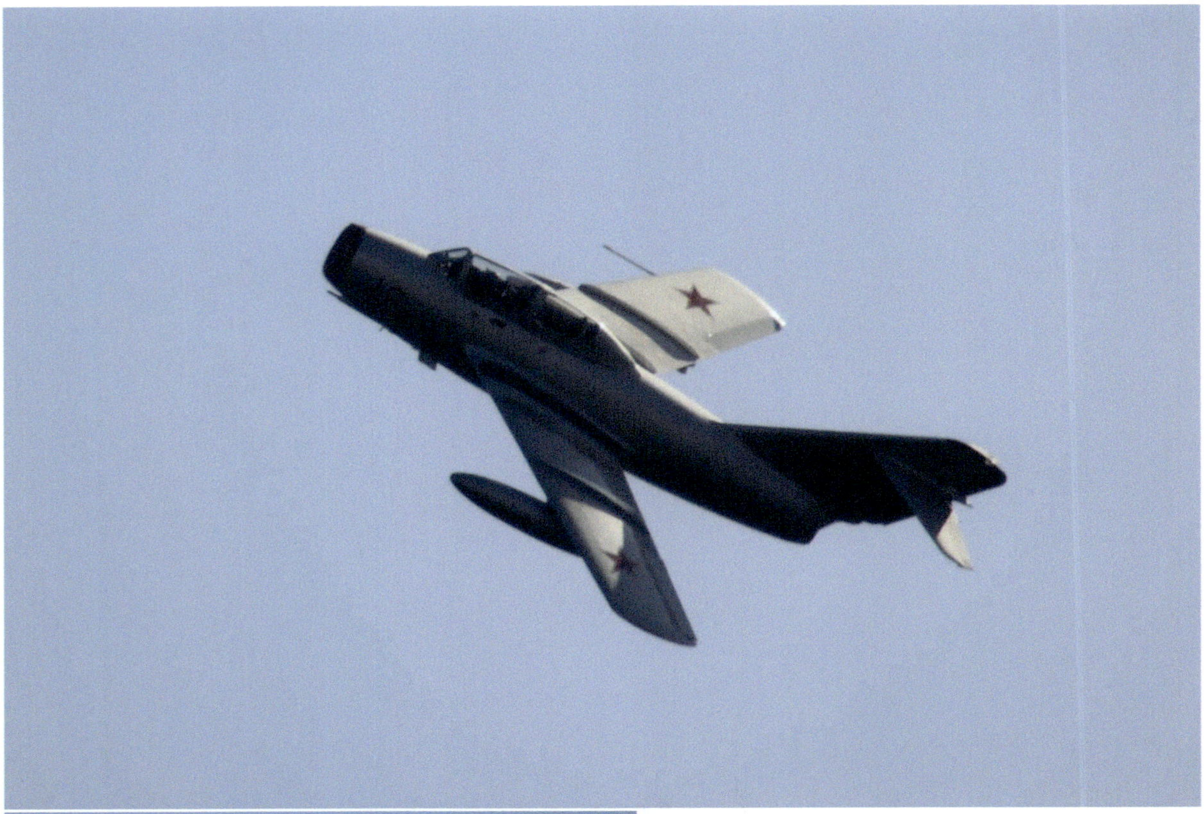

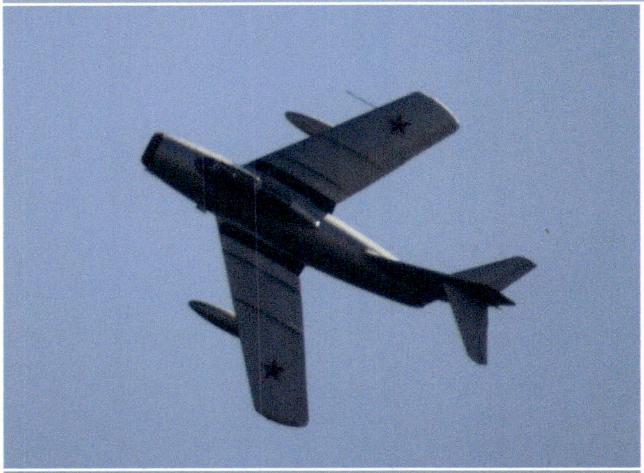

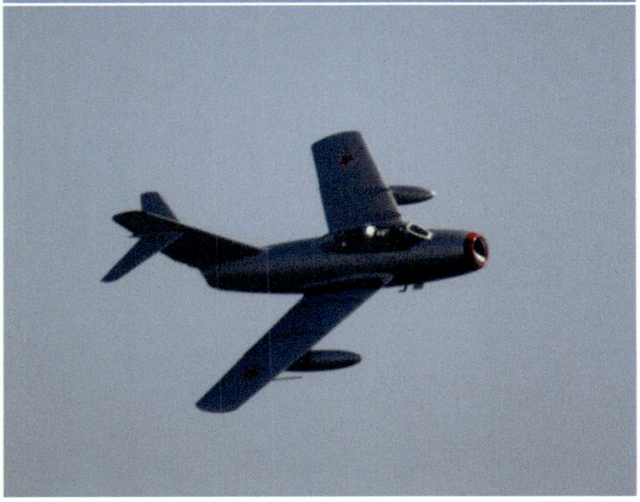

Quick Facts

Length: 10.10 m (33 feet, 2 in)

Wing Span: 10.08 m (33 feet, 1 in)

Height: 3.7 m (12 feet, 2 in)

Powerplant: 1 x Klimov VK-1 turbojet engine developing 5,952 lb of thrust.

Maximum Speed: 567 KIAS (1,050 km/h) or 0.92 Mach

Maximum Range: 1,156miles (1,860 km)

Service Ceiling: 50,853 ft (15,500m; 9.6 miles)

Rate-of-Climb: 11,480 feet-per-minute (3,499 m/min)

Max Load Factor: Clean: 8 G

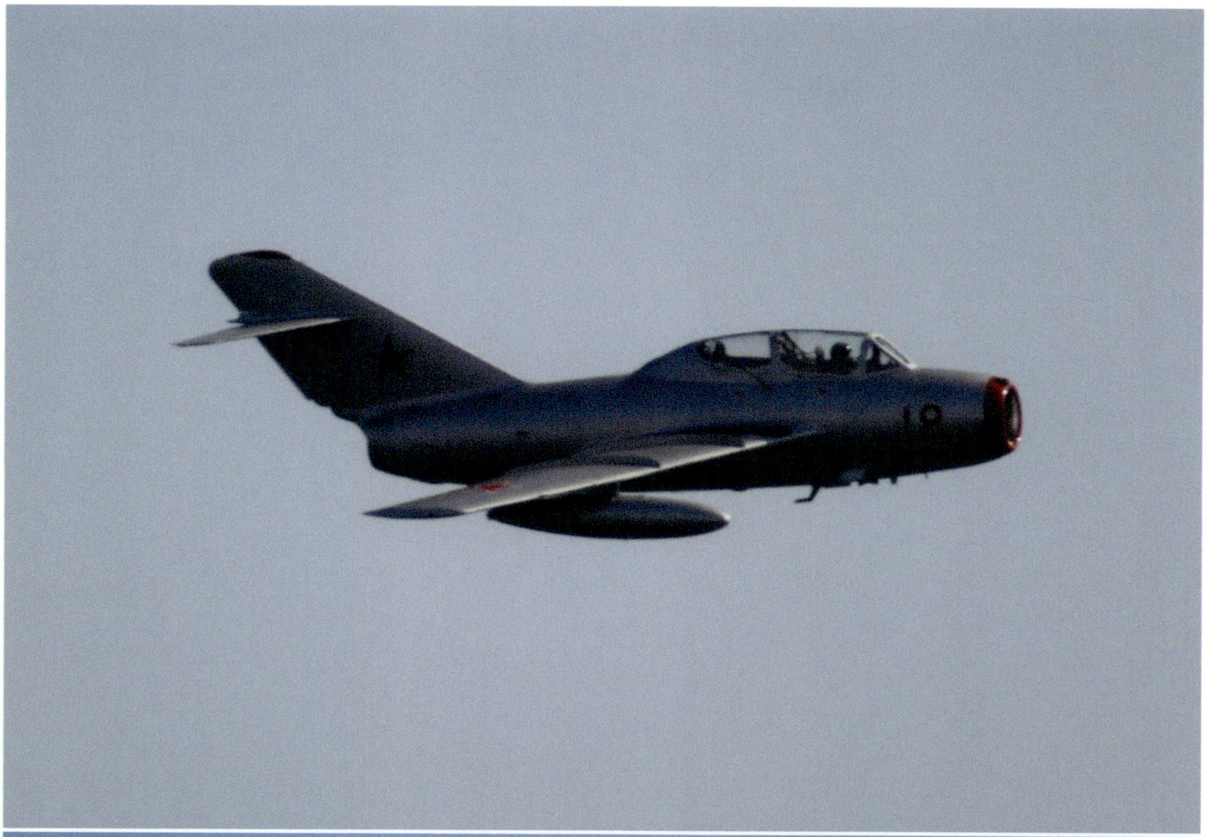

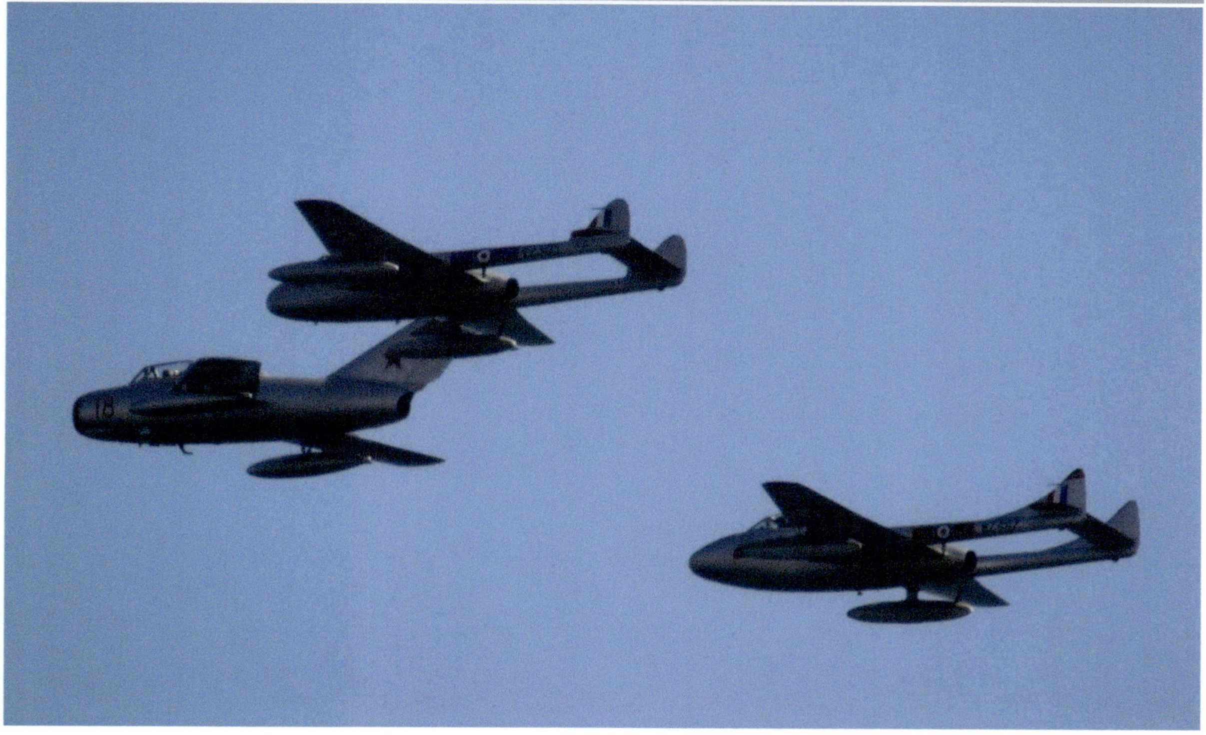

Canadair T-33 Silver Star

The Canadair CT-133 Silver Star was the Canadian version of the Lockheed T-33 Shooting Star jet trainer aircraft, produced under license by Canadair from 1951 to 2005. Unlike the original T-33, the CT-133 was powered by the Rolls-Royce Nene 10 turbojet instead of the Allison J33 engine. The CT-133 had a distinctive appearance due to the large fuel tanks usually carried on each wingtip. In total, Canadair built 656 of these Canadian Silver Star aircraft for the Royal Canadian Air Force, where they served as jet trainers from the 1950s until their retirement in 2005.

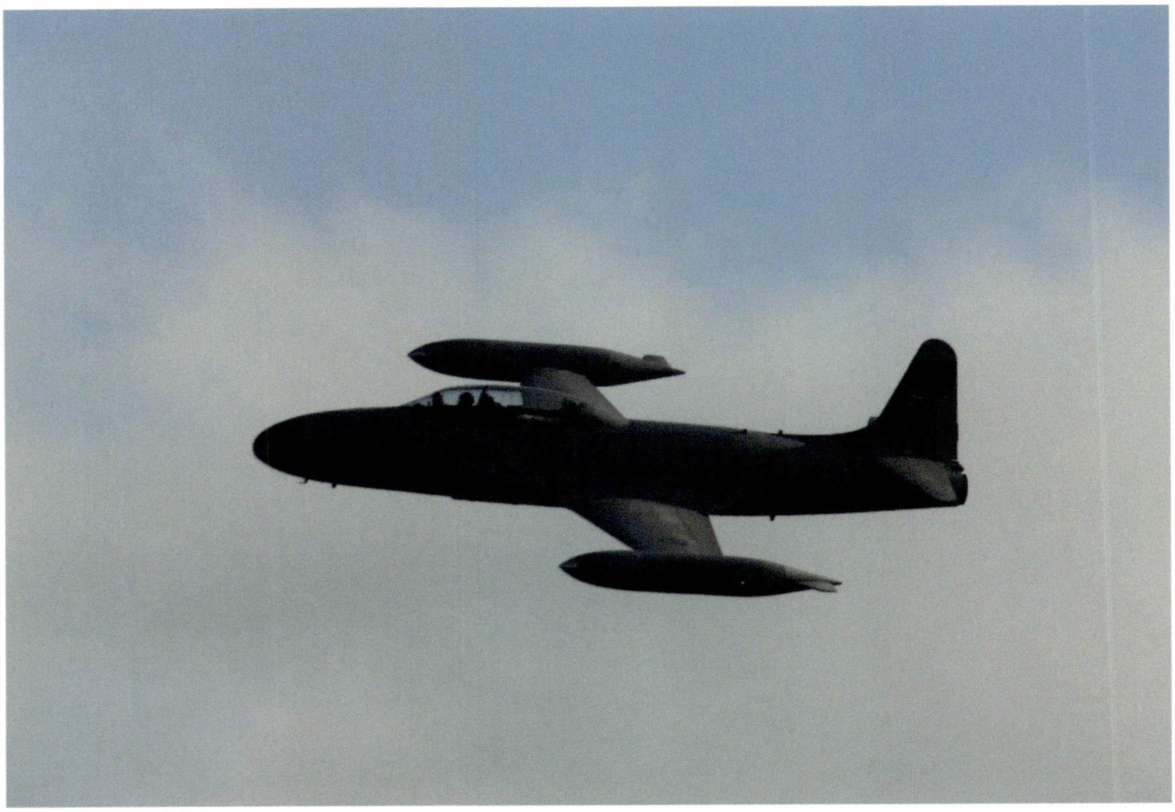

The T-33 was a reliable aircraft with forgiving flight characteristics, enabling it to have an extremely long service life in the Royal Canadian Air Force (later the Canadian Forces). One of its more unusual roles was as an aerobatic demonstration aircraft called the Red Knight. Although the T-33 stopped being used as a trainer in 1976, over 50 of the aircraft remained in the Canadian Forces inventory as late as 1995.

The T-33 on display at the 2019 Bournemouth Air Festival is part of the Norwegian Air Force Historical Squadron. In addition to performing a solo flight demonstration, the T-33 made several flypasts accompanied by the Squadron's MiG-15.

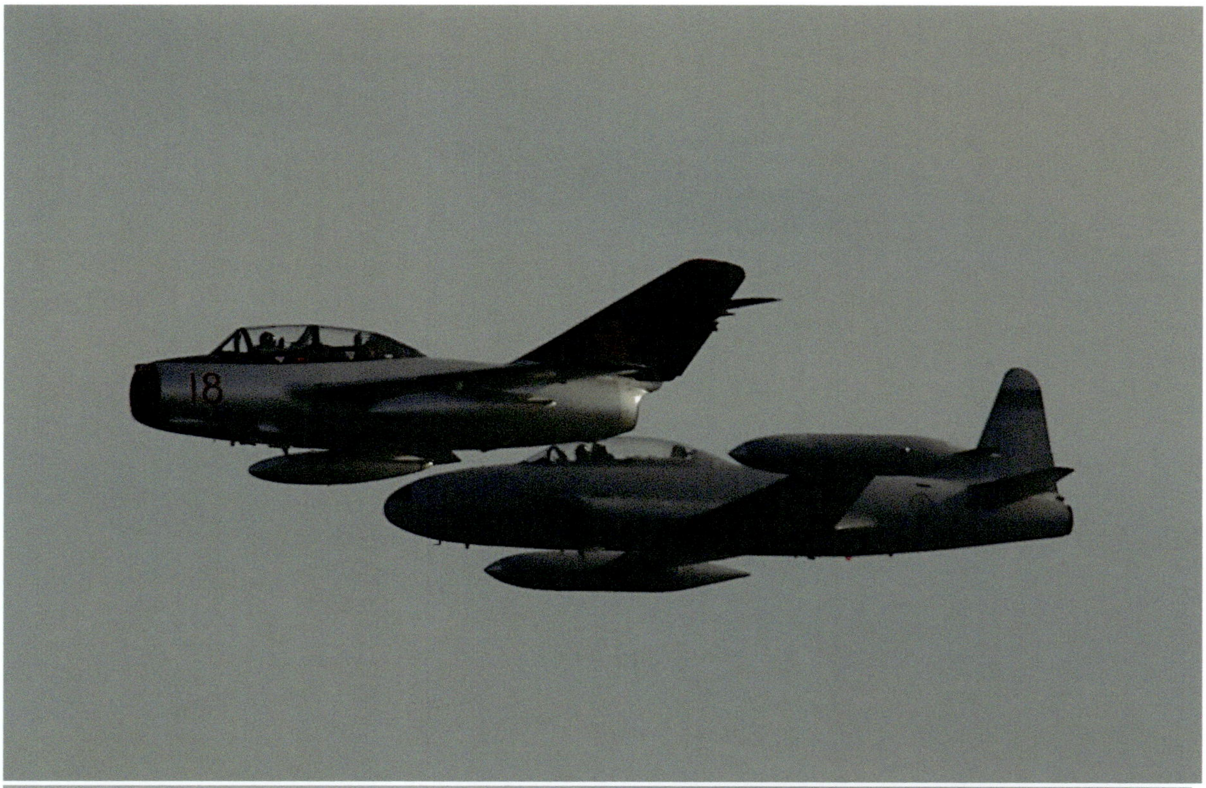

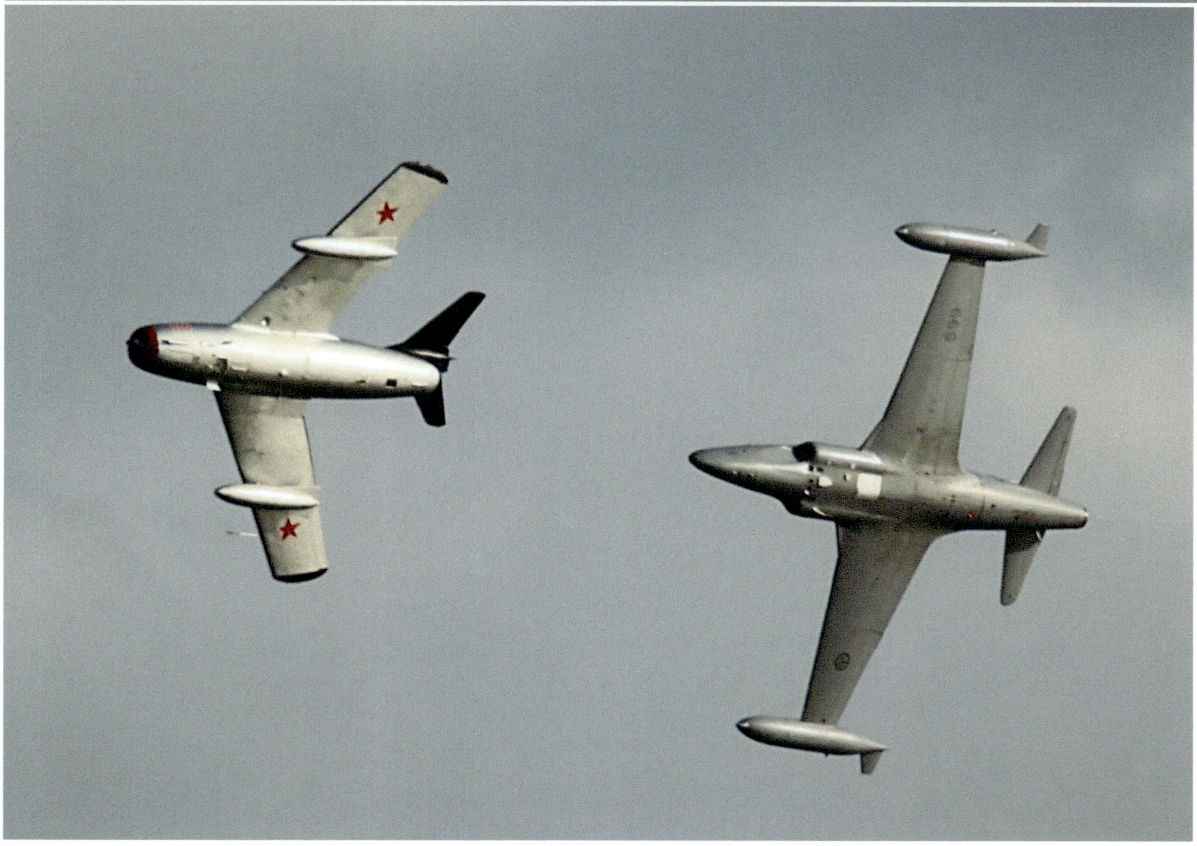

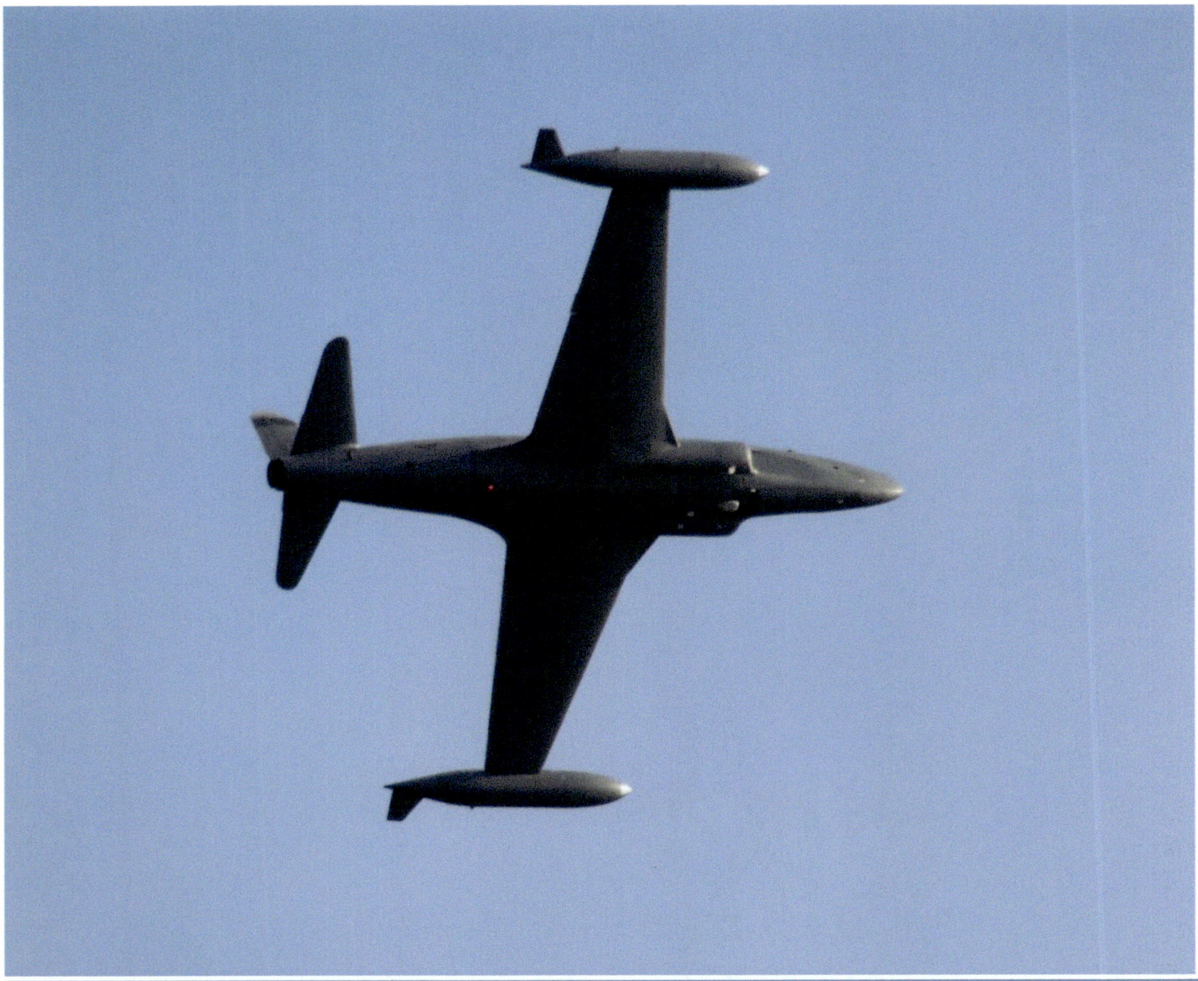

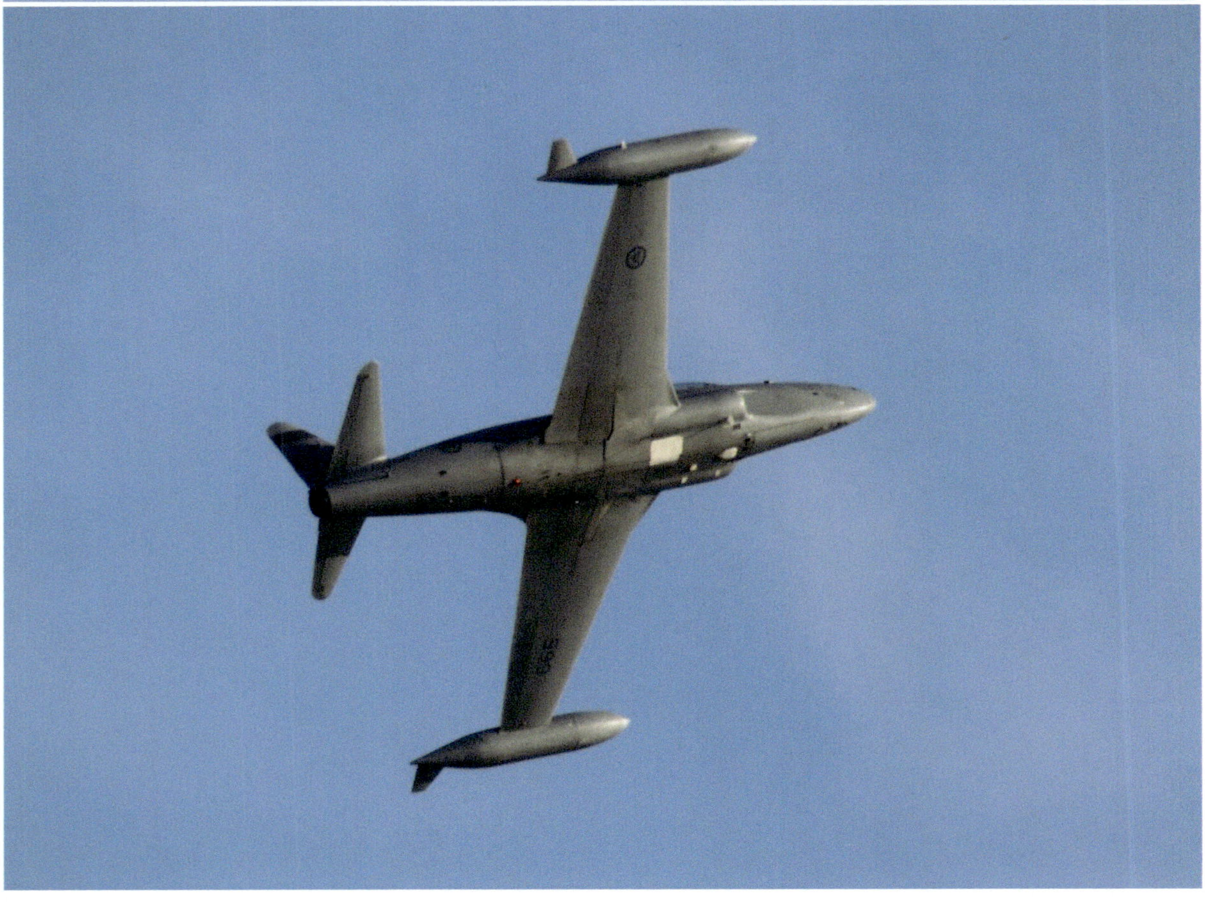

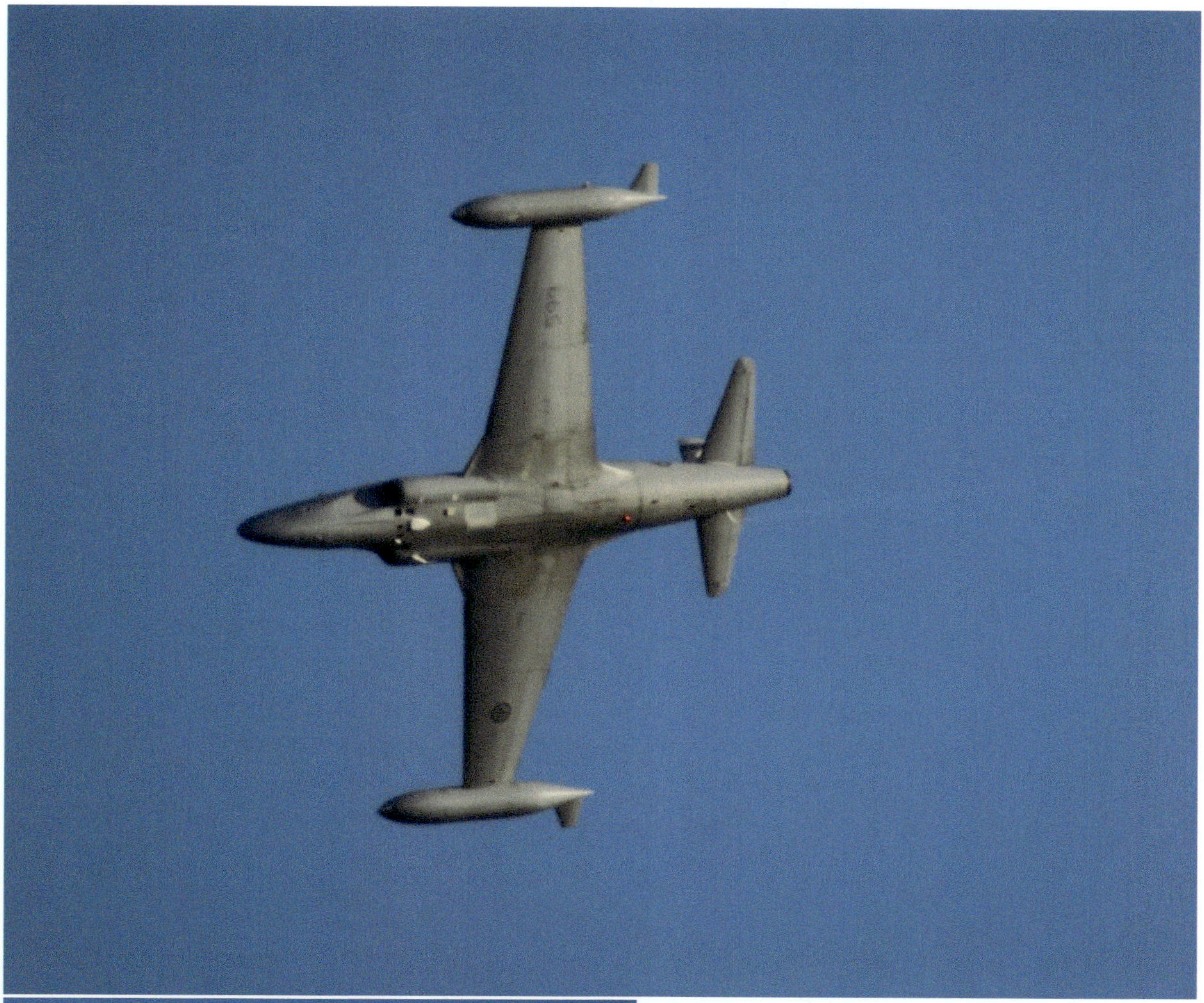

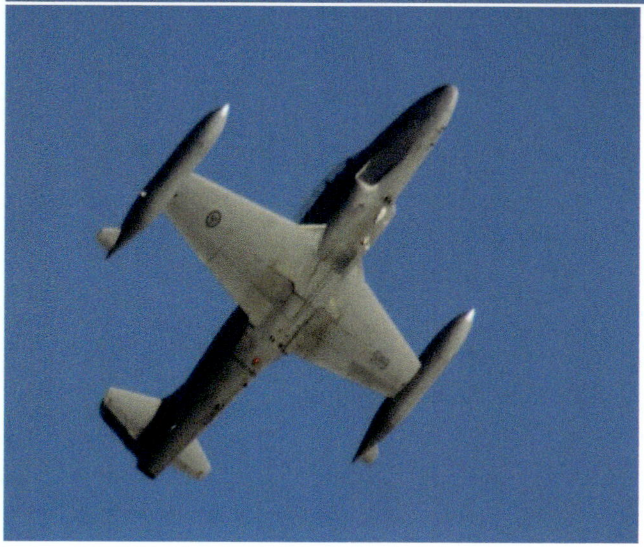

Quick Facts

Crew: 1–2

Length: 11.48 m (37 ft 8 in)

Wingspan: 12.93 m (42 ft 5 in)

Height: 3.55 m (11 ft 8 in)

Empty weight: 3830 kg (8440 lb)

Max. take-off weight: 7630 kg (16800 lb)

Powerplant: 1 × Rolls-Royce Nene 10 turbojet, 22 kN (5000 lb)

Maximum speed: 920 km/h (500 kts, 570 mi/h)

Service ceiling: 14000 m (47000 ft)

Hawker Hunter

The Hawker Hunter was a British jet fighter with swept wings, developed by Hawker Aircraft for the Royal Air Force in the late 1940s and early 1950s. Powered by the newly developed Rolls-Royce Avon turbojet engine, it was Hawker's first jet aircraft procured by the RAF. On September 7, 1953, the modified prototype set a new world airspeed record of 727.63 mph, breaking the sound barrier in level flight.

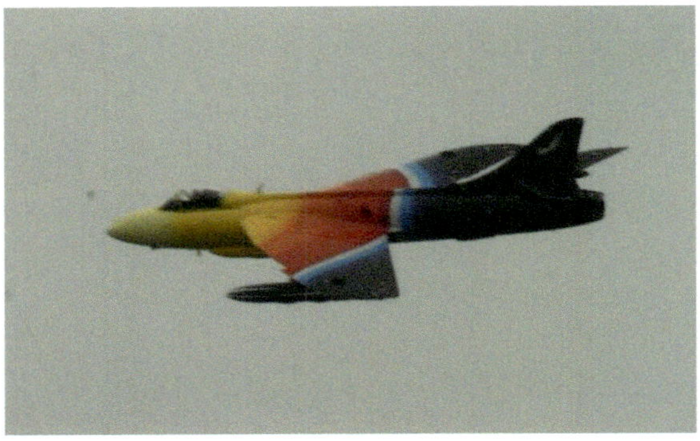

From the outset it was clear that the type had exceptional performance, being the first RAF aircraft capable of effectively matching the English Electric Canberra bomber. The Hunter also set numerous aviation records, including absolute speed records. The type was also lauded for its quick turnaround time, enabled by features such as its removable gun pack and pressurised fuelling system, and for its easy handling in flight.

To facilitate production and reduce vulnerability to attack, the airframe of the Hunter consists of six major interchangeable sections that can be assembled individually: the forward fuselage (containing the cockpit and armament pack), centre fuselage (with integral wing roots and air duct intakes), rear fuselage, tail unit, and two wings made separately.

The Hunter F.1, the Royal Air Force's first high-speed jet fighter equipped with radar and fully powered flight controls, entered service in July 1954. Replacing the Gloster Meteor, Canadair Sabre, and de Havilland Venom in RAF service, the Hunter overcame initial challenges like limited fuel capacity and engine surging. Early models were restricted to only about an hour of flight time by their low fuel capacity. The Avon engines also encountered surging and stalling issues. Later Hunter variants solved these problems, with the Sapphire-powered F.2 eliminating the engine defects. Other necessary modifications included diverting cannon gas emissions to prevent fuselage damage and redesigning the ejected cannon ammunition links that had struck the underside of the fuselage.

Miss Demeanour

Originally built as an F.4 for the RAF, XF947 retired in 1996 and was sold to a new UK owner who ferried it to Dunsfold. Jonathan Whaley purchased the aircraft in 1997 and ferried it to Hurn, where he completely restored it and re-registered it as G-PSST (Personal Super Sonic Transport). By mid-1998, the restoration was finished. Carried out in December 1998-January 1999, Whaley opted for an unusual civilian paint scheme rather than keeping the military markings. This colourful 're-entry' paintjob made the jet a favourite at airshows for years. Renamed Miss Demeanour, the jet toured airshows nearly nonstop from 1999-2015. One of its most memorable displays was at the 2014 Bournemouth Air Festival, when it flew in formation with a Sea Vixen and Canberra, allowing for great photos of the three stunning jets.

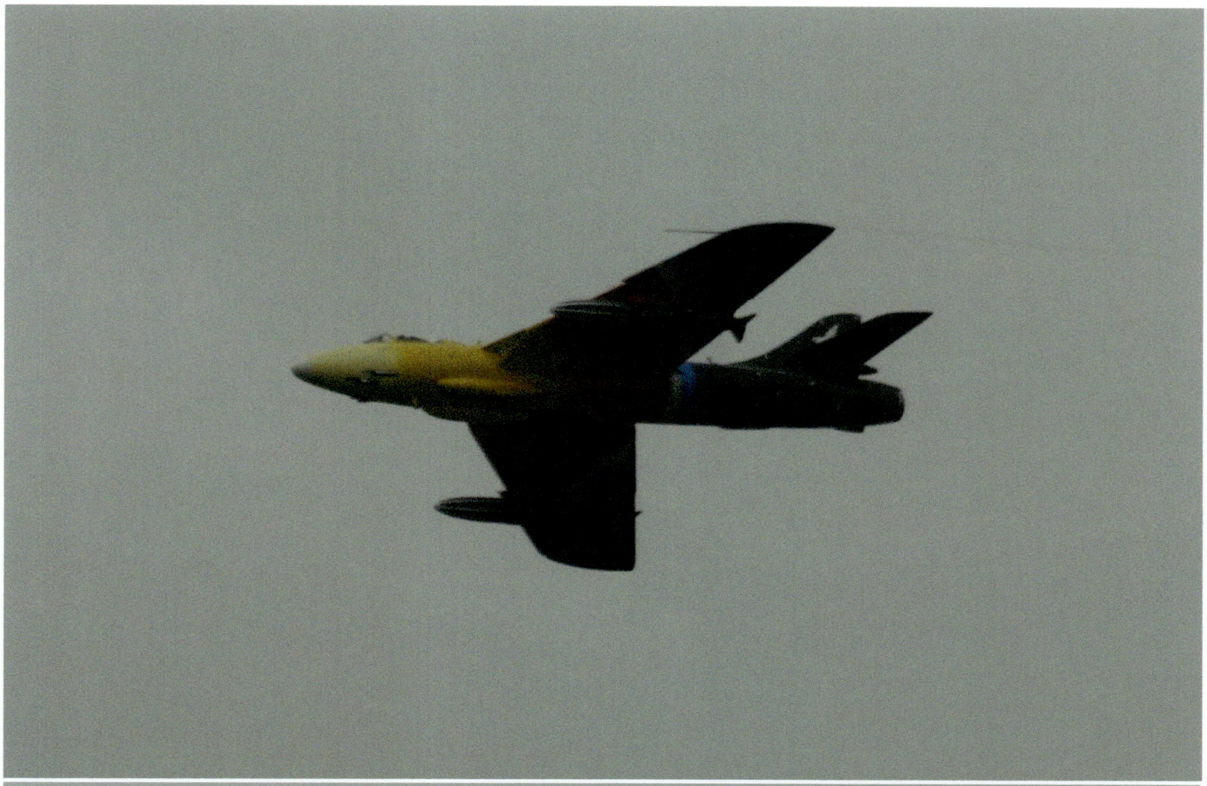

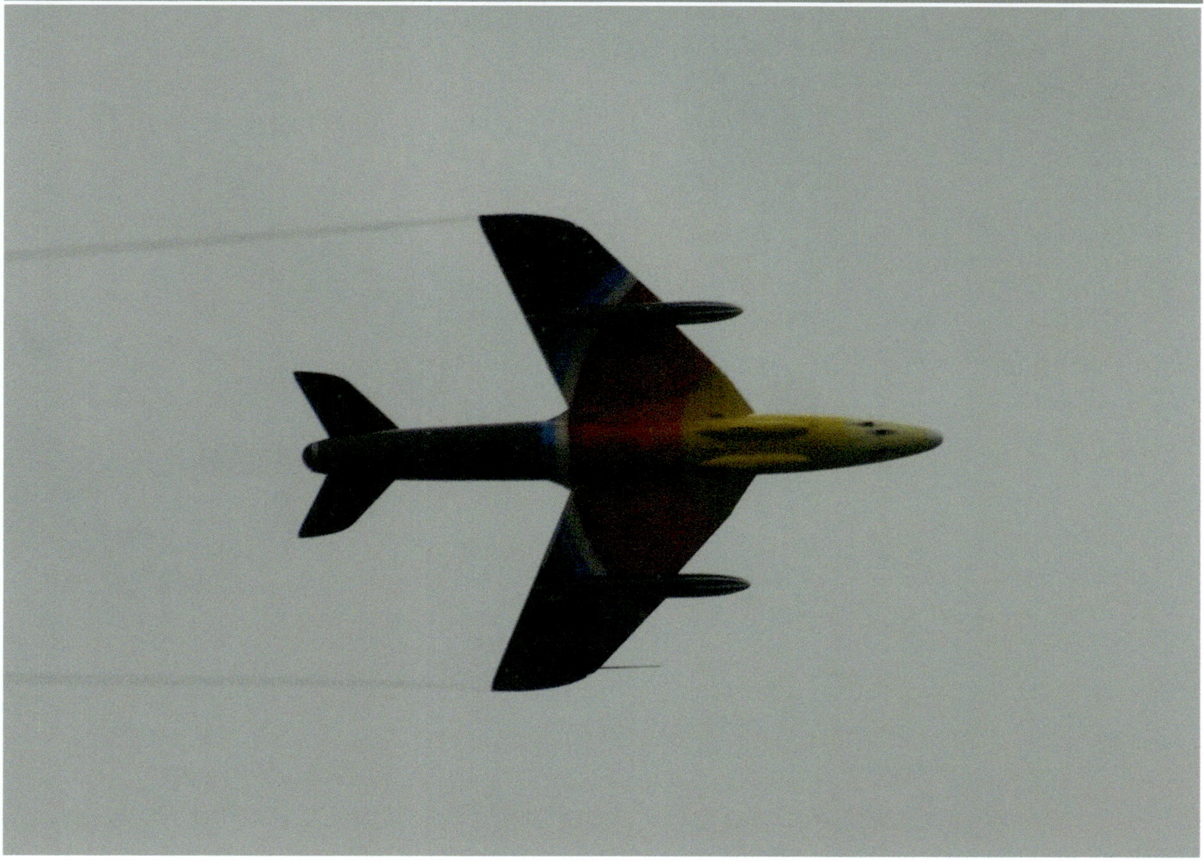

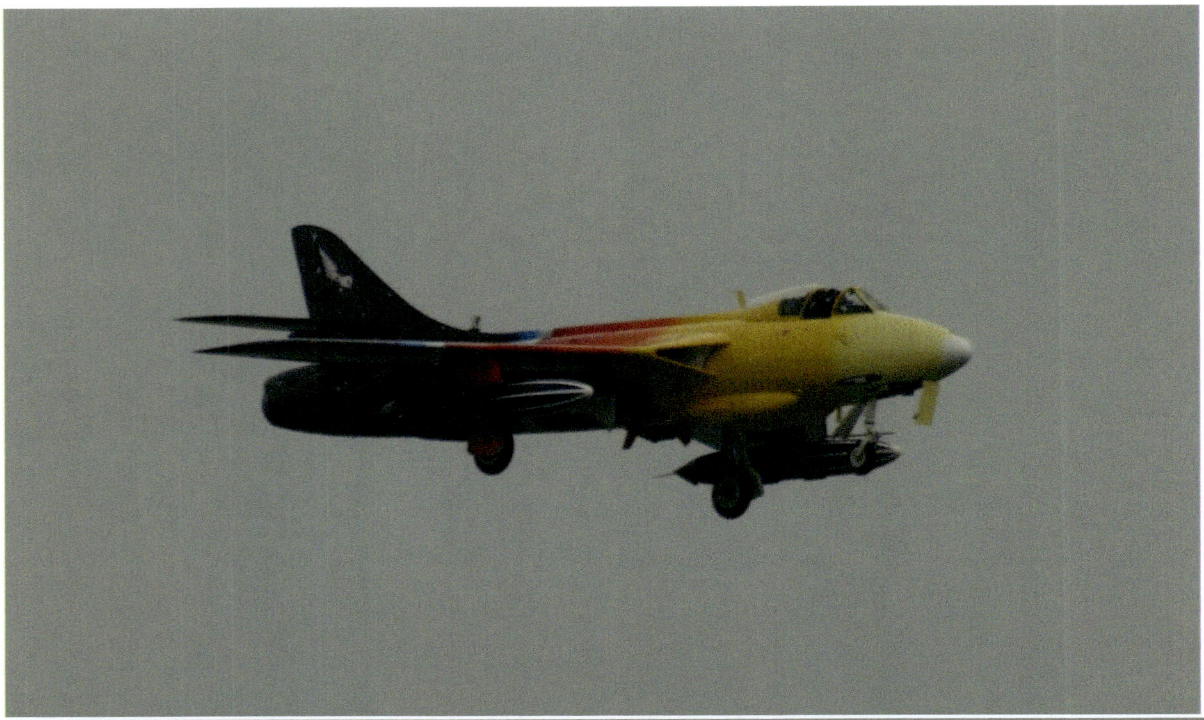

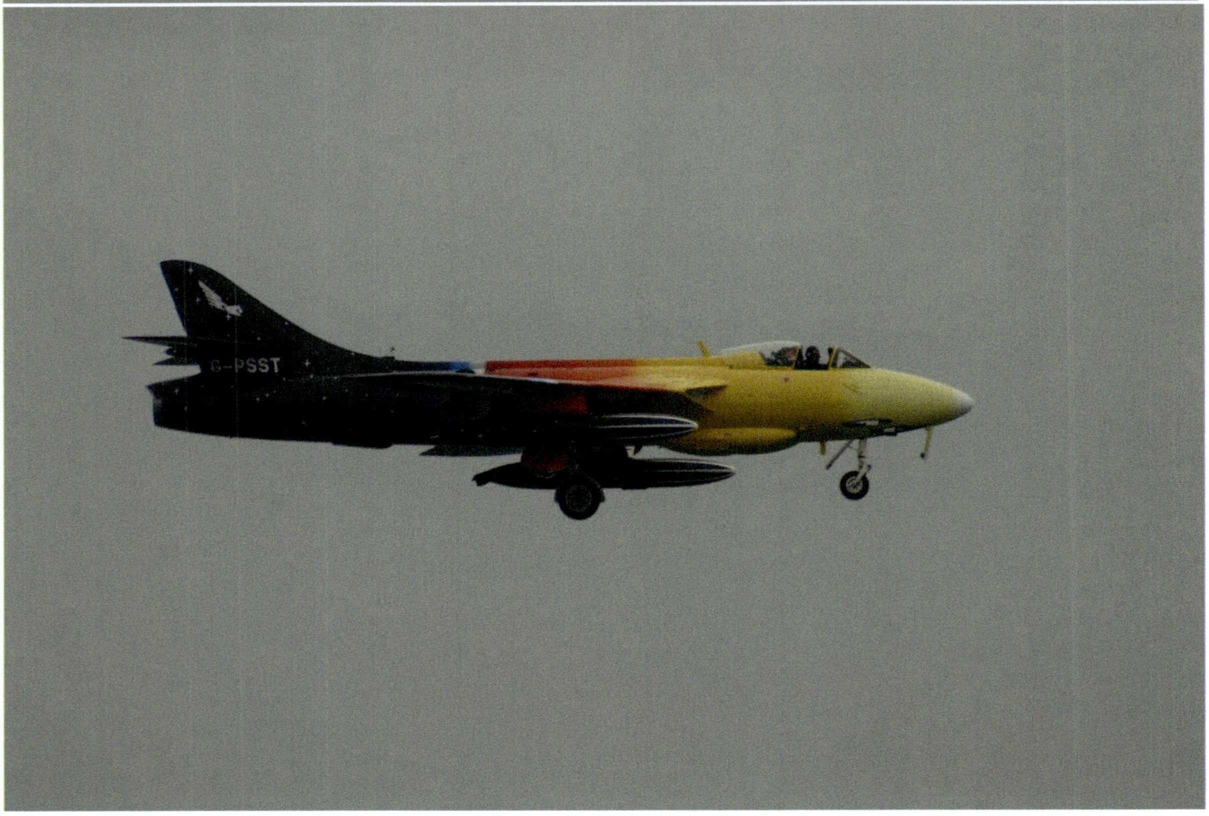
G-PSST

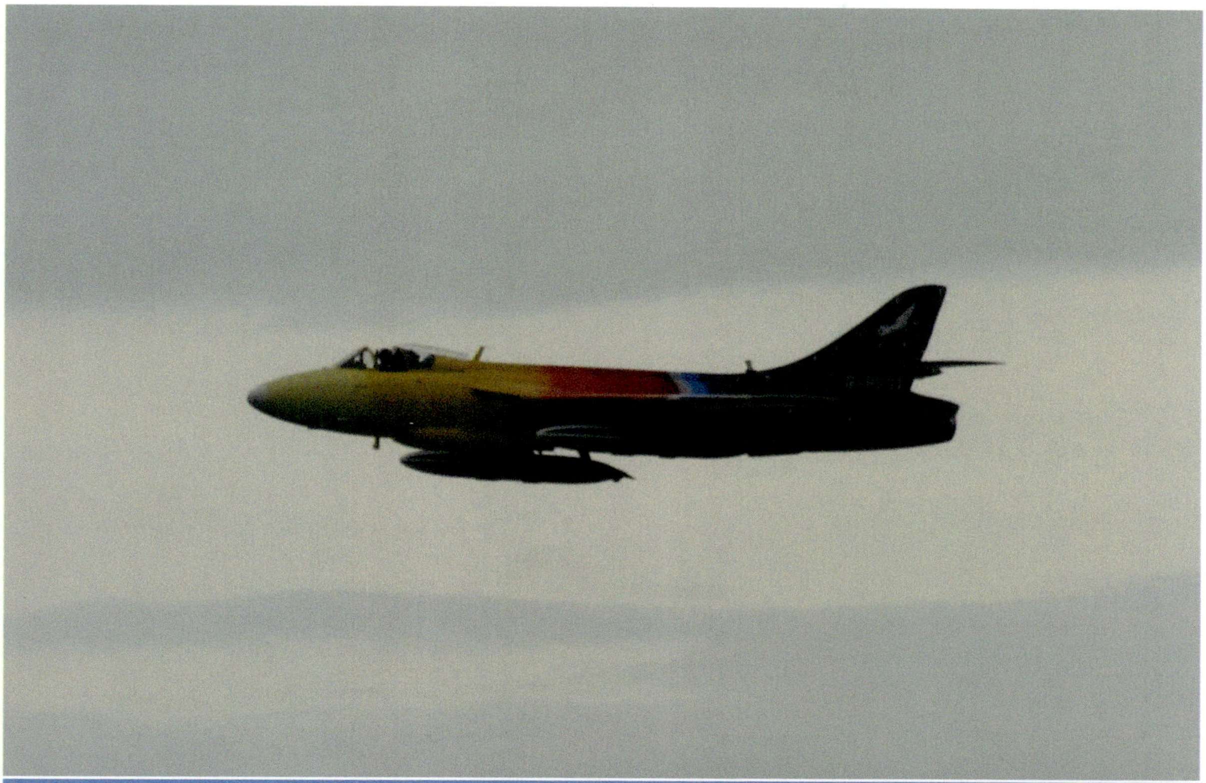

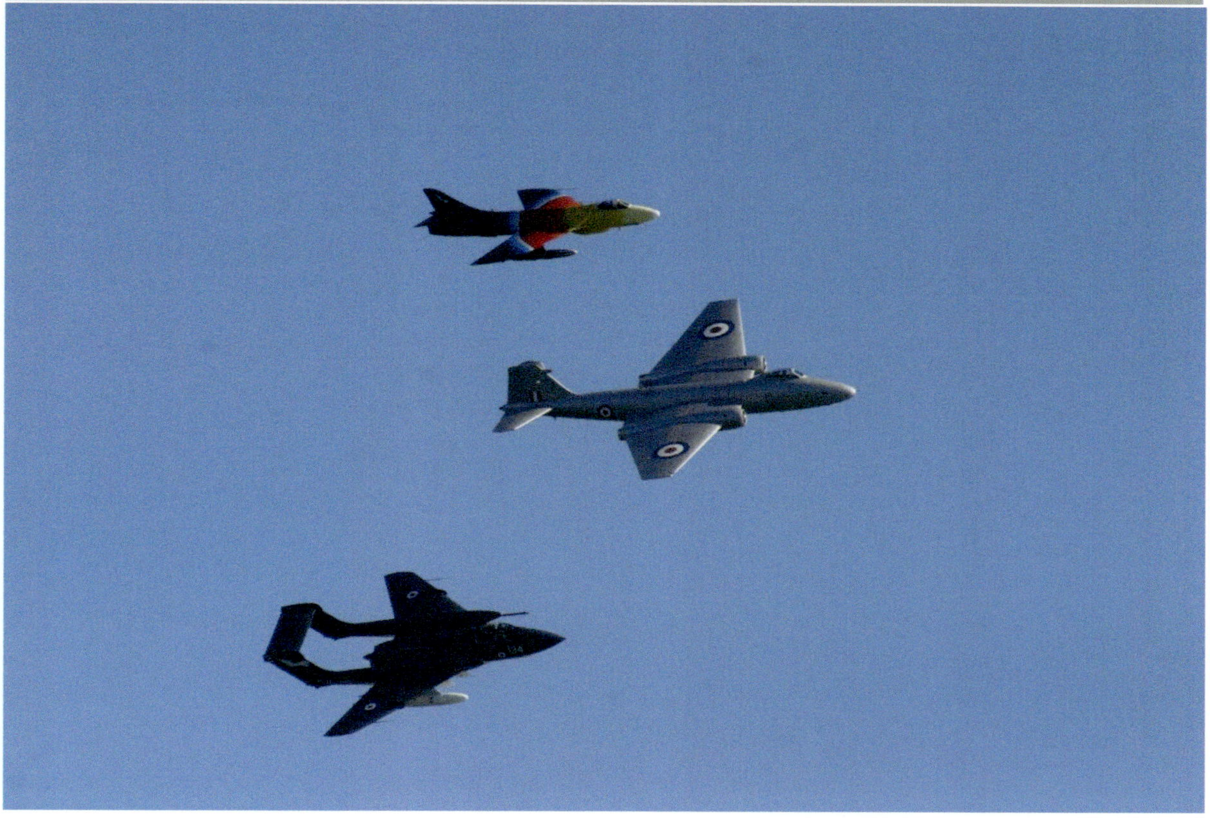

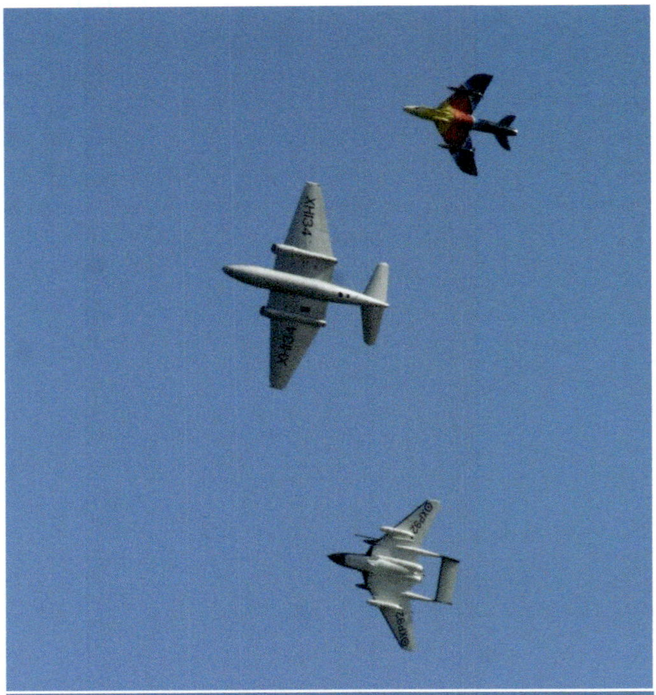

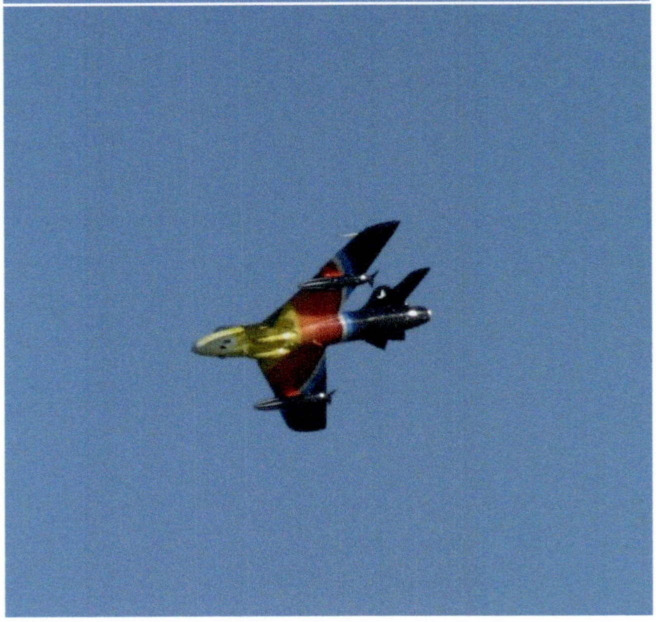

Quick Facts

General

Crew: 1

Length: 45 ft 10.5 in (13.983 m)

Wingspan: 33 ft 8 in (10.26 m)

Height: 13 ft 2 in (4.01 m)

Max take-off weight: 24,600 lb (11,158 kg)

Powerplant: 1 × Rolls-Royce Avon 207 turbojet engine, 10,145 lbf

Performance

Maximum speed: 623 mph at 36,000 ft (11,000 m), 715 mph) at sea level

Maximum speed: Mach 0.94

Combat range: 385 mi (620 km, 335 nmi)

Ferry range: 1,900 mi (3,100 km, 1,700 nmi) maximum external fuel

Service ceiling: 50,000 ft (15,000 m)

Armament

Guns: 4× 30 mm (1.18 in) ADEN revolver cannon in a removable gun pack

Rockets: 4× Matra rocket pods (each with 18 × SNEB 68 mm (2.68 in) rockets)

Missiles: 4× AIM-9 Sidewinder Air-to-air missiles

de Havilland Sea Vixen

The Sea Vixen was a twin-engine, twin boom-tailed fighter jet designed by the de Havilland Aircraft Company in the late 1940s and flown by the Royal Navy's Fleet Air Arm from the 1950s to early 1970s. Originally developed from de Havilland's earlier jet fighters, this two-seat, carrier-based aircraft was built to serve as a fleet air-defence fighter. After de Havilland was acquired by Hawker Siddeley in 1960, the Sea Vixen was later known as the Hawker Siddeley Sea Vixen.

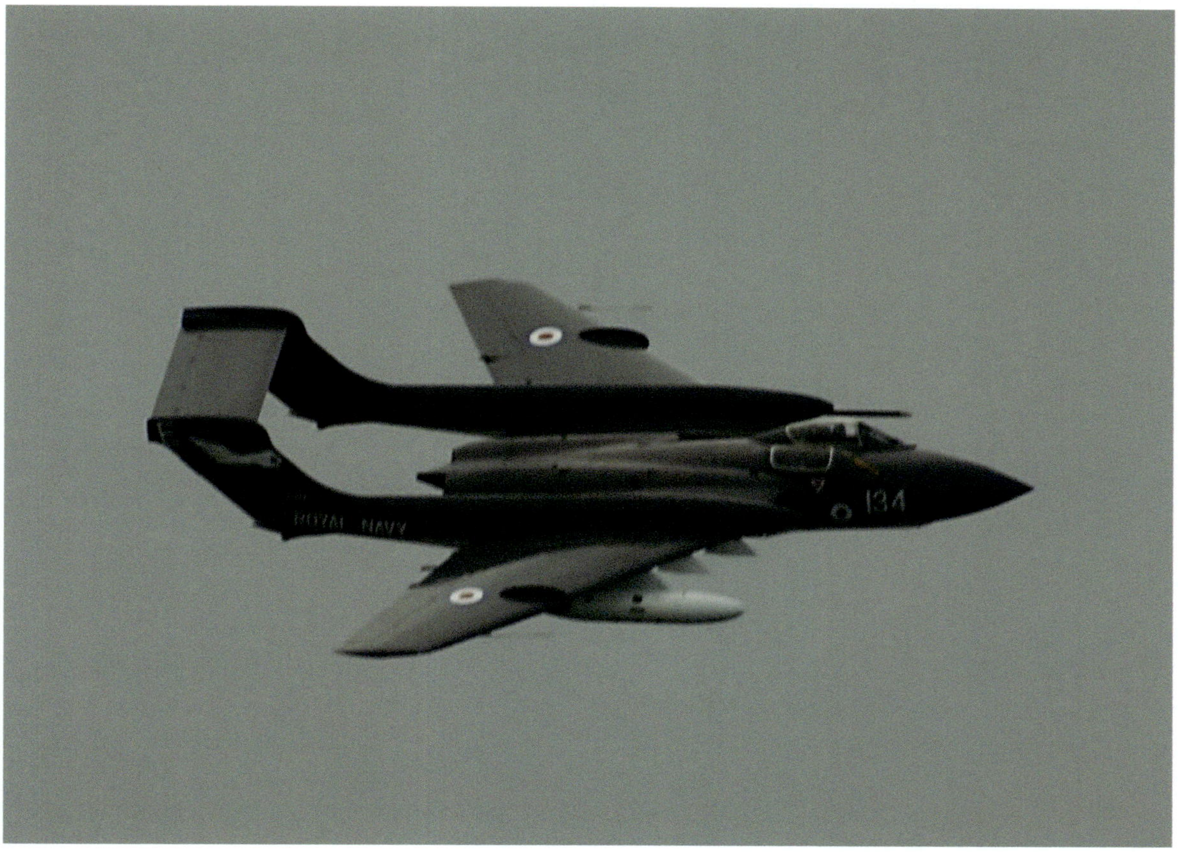

In 1946, the de Havilland Aircraft Company conferred with the British Admiralty to determine their requirements for a future jet-powered, all-weather fighter equipped with radar. The discussions made clear that the fighter would need a two-person crew to operate the radar and navigation systems in addition to flying the aircraft. Further, two engines were deemed necessary for safety during over-ocean flights, and swept wings were seen as desirable.

The DH 110 prototype had a twin-boom, all-metal fuselage and 45-degree swept wings, similar to earlier de Havilland designs like the Vampire and Venom. Powered by two Rolls-Royce Avon turbojets capable of 7,500 lbf thrust each, the DH 110 became the first British two-seat combat aircraft to break the sound barrier in a shallow dive. Its armament consisted of four 30mm ADEN cannons.

The de Havilland Sea Vixen was a crowd favourite during the early years of the Bournemouth Air Festival.

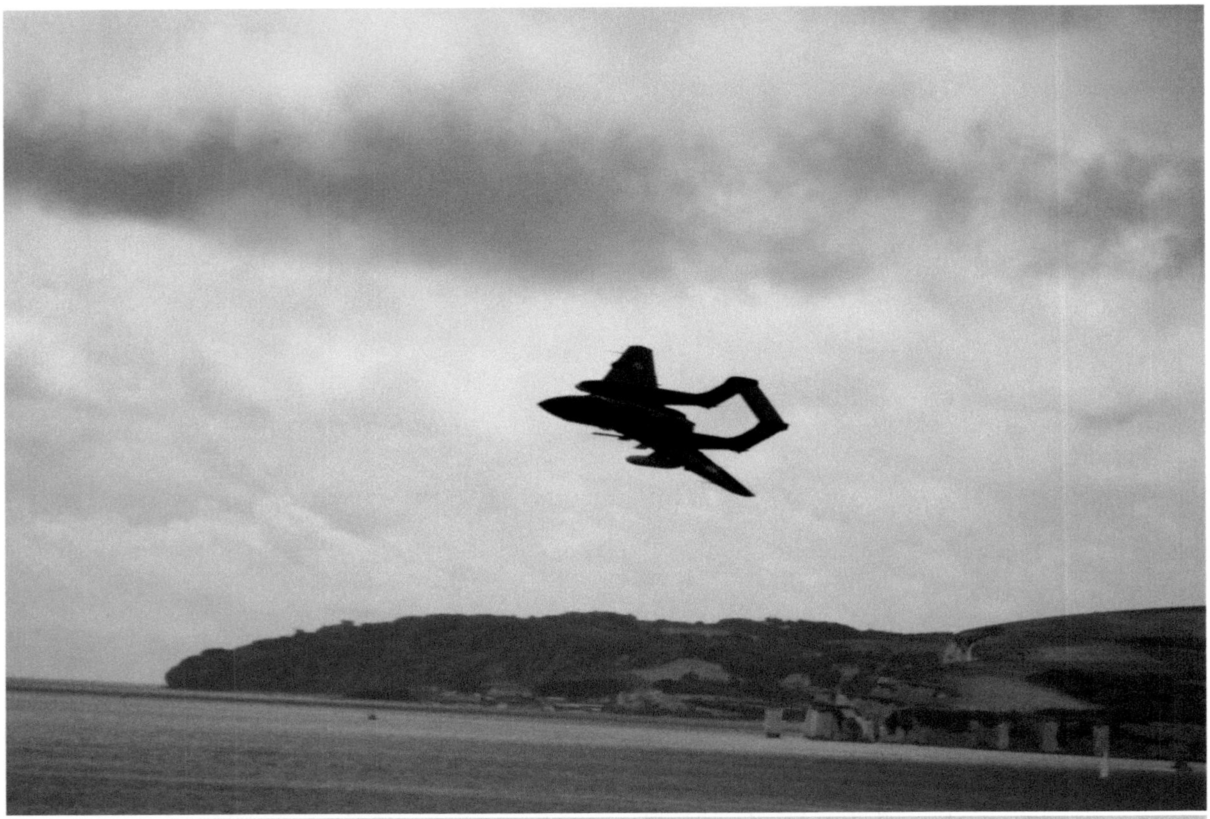

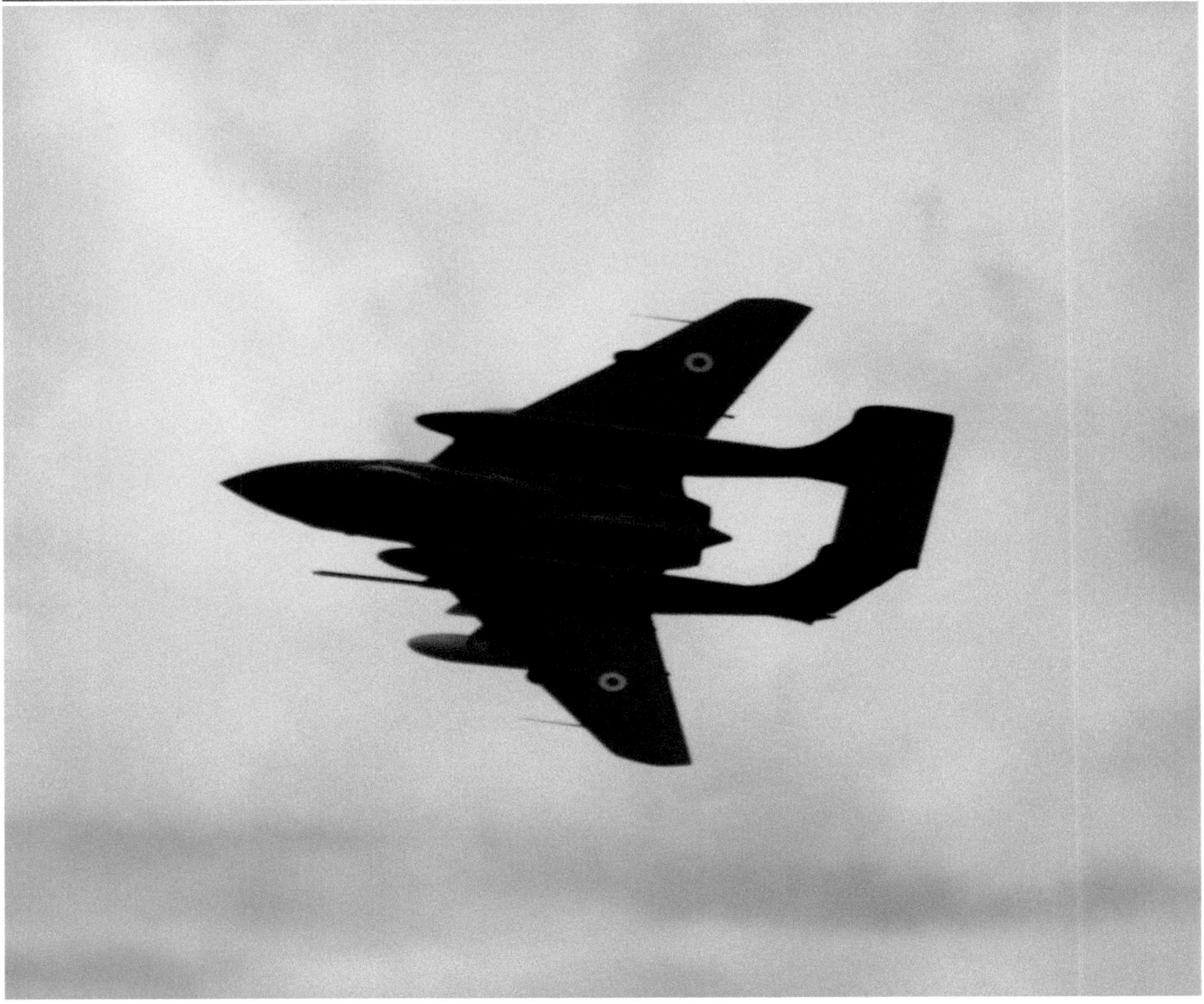

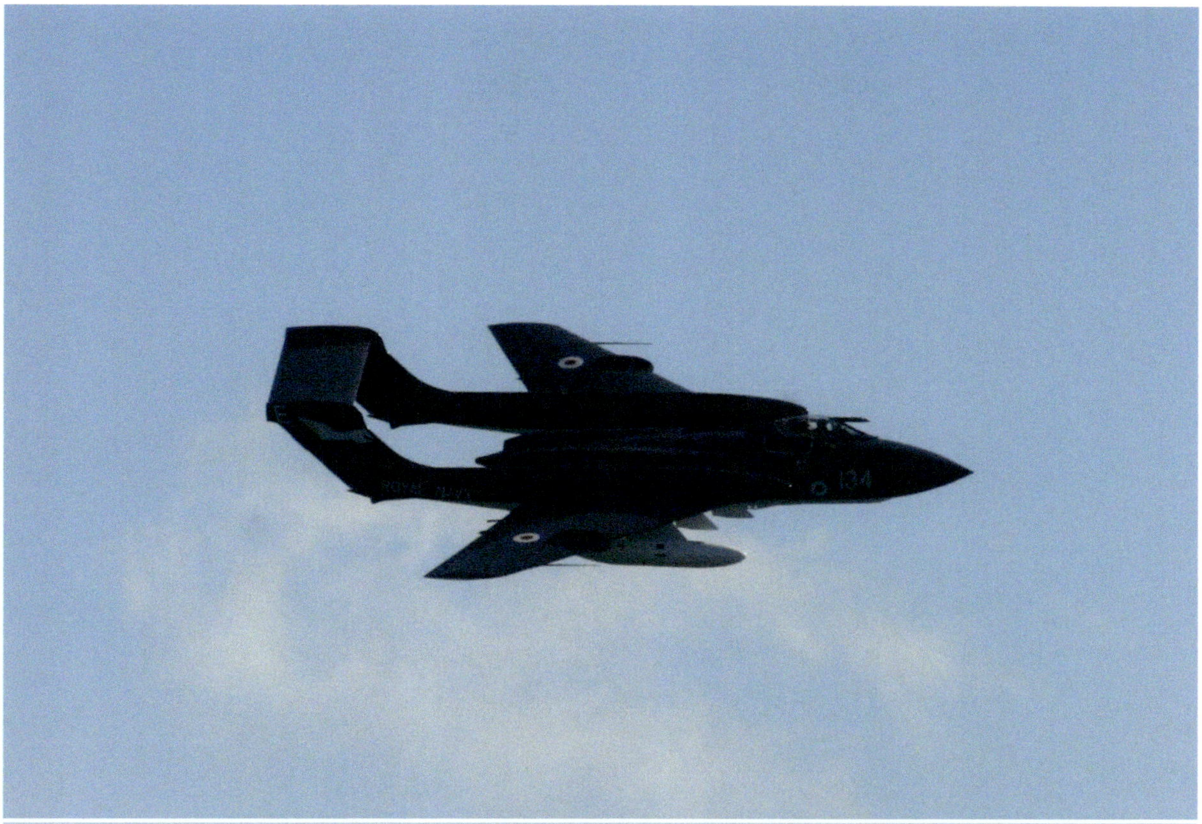
ROYAL NAVY
134

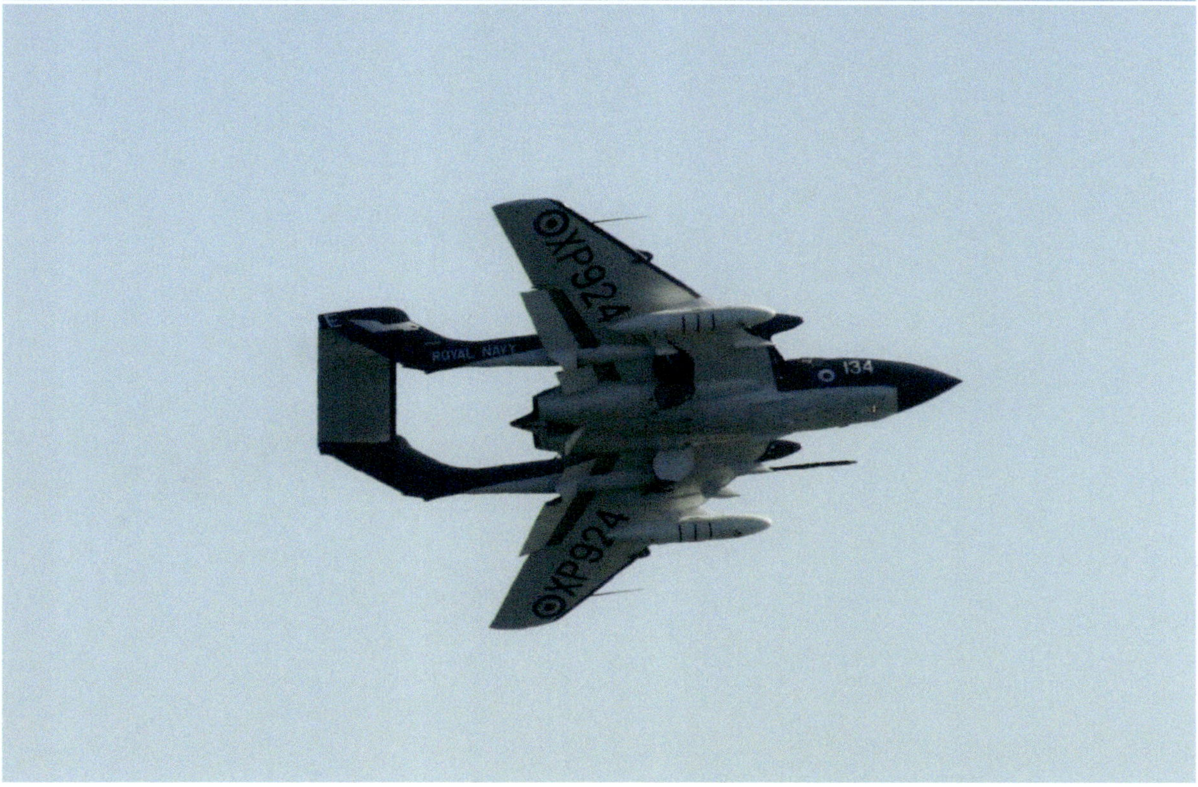
XP924
ROYAL NAVY
134
XP924

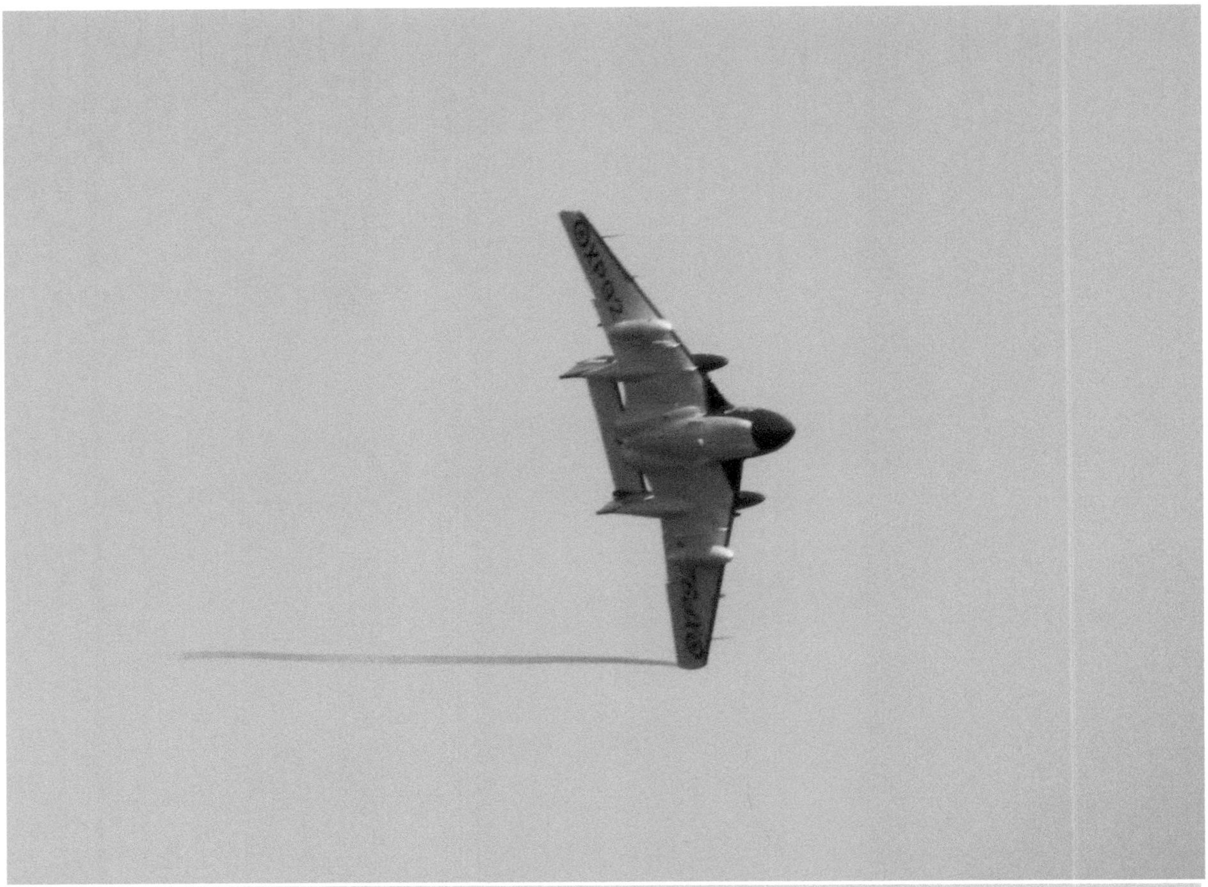
XP924

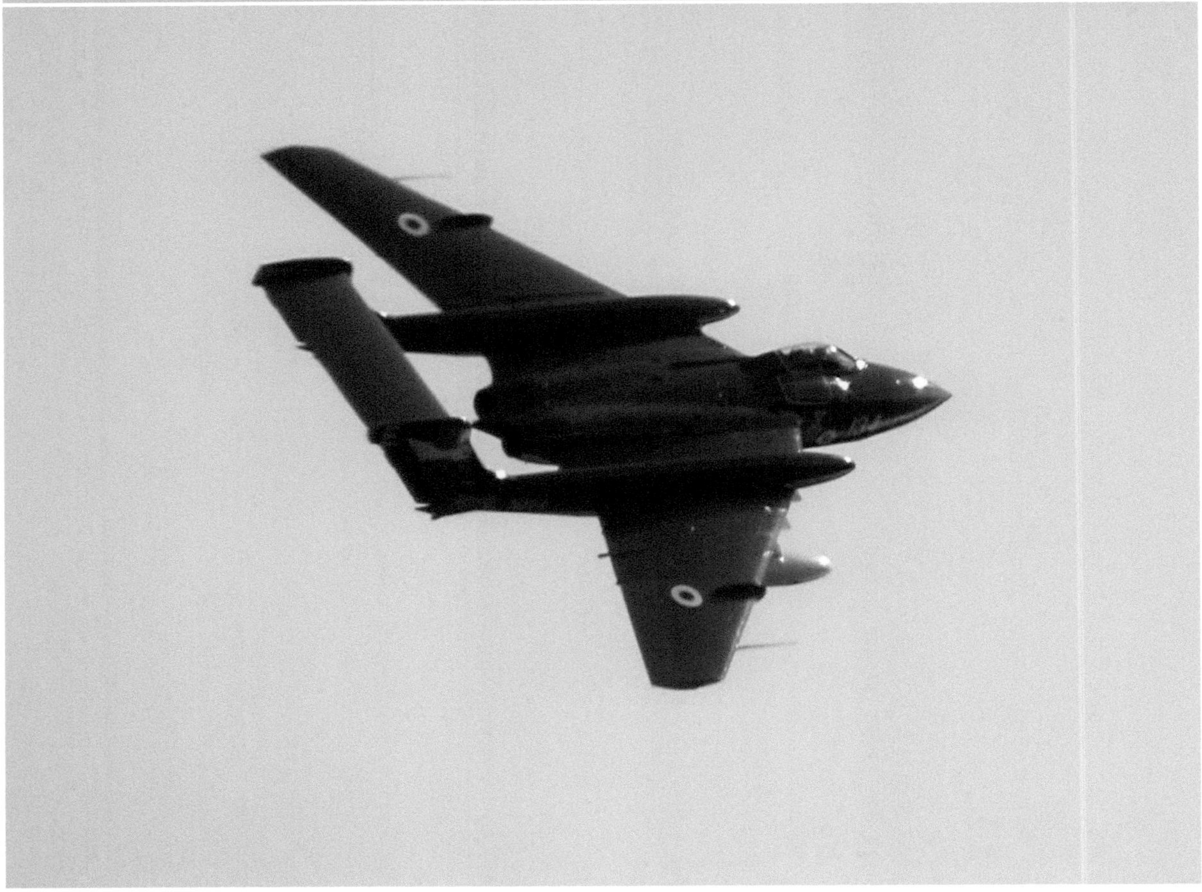

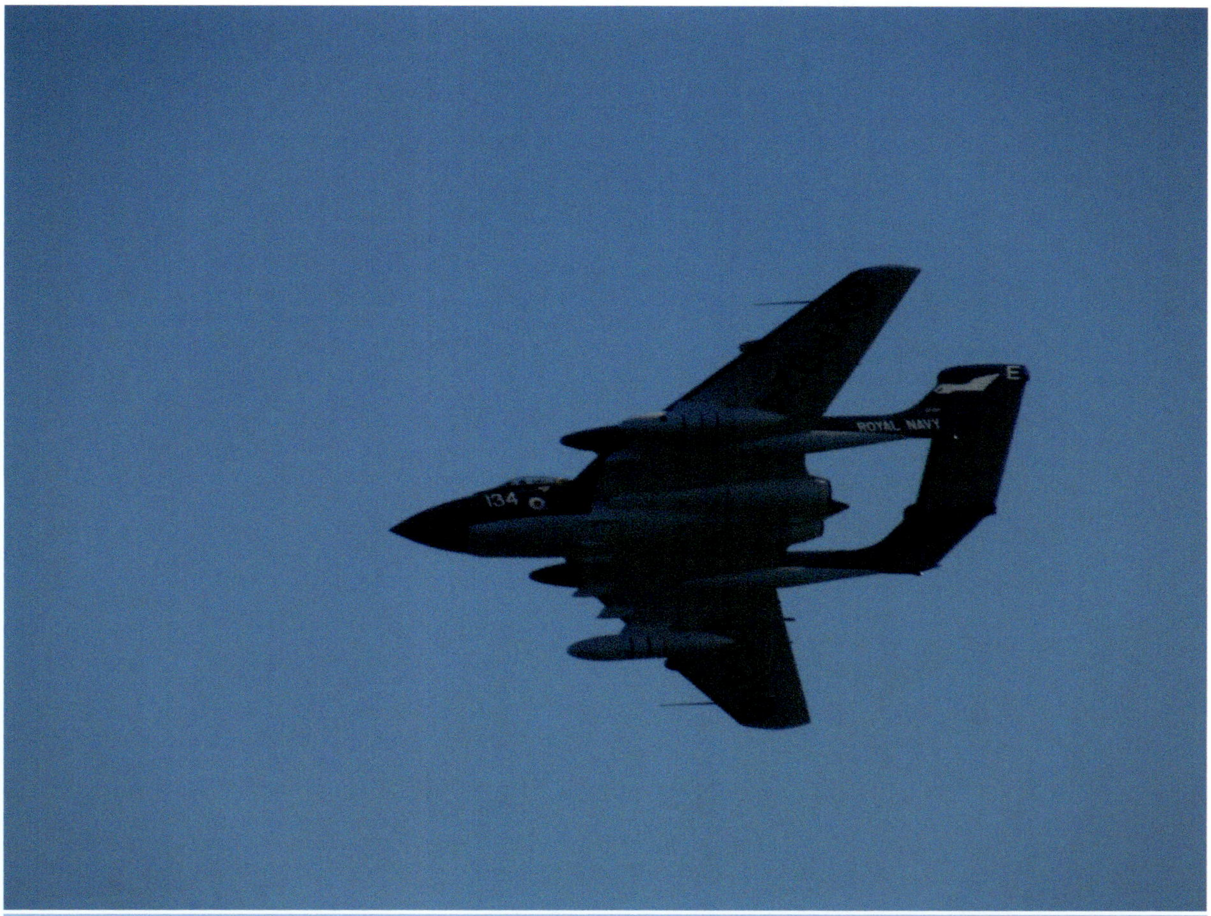
134
ROYAL NAVY
E

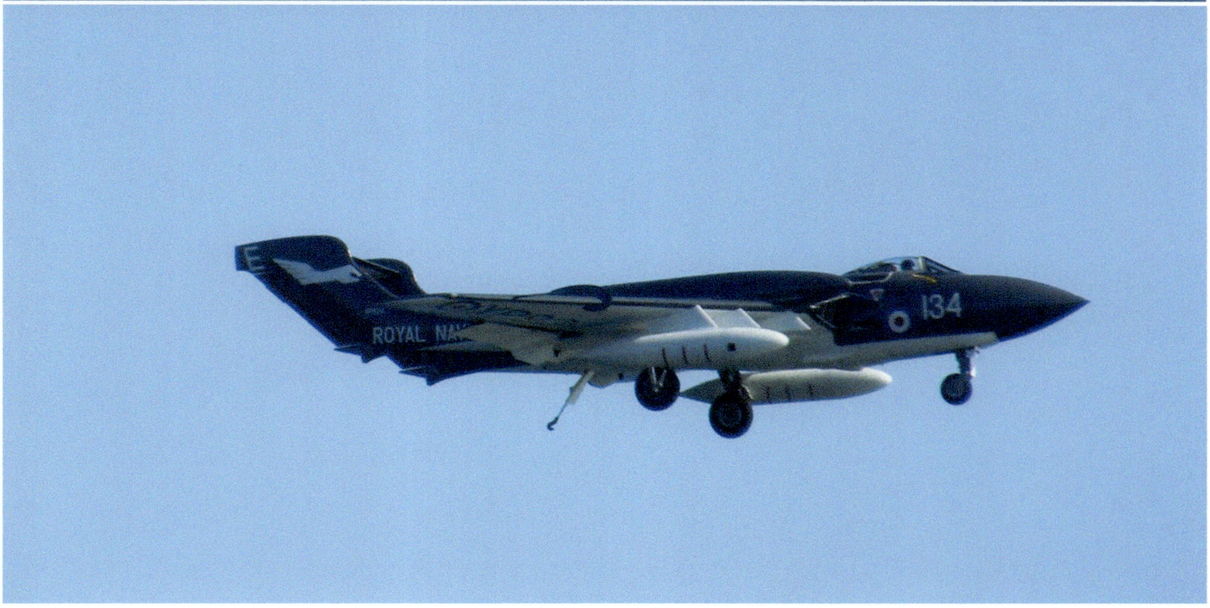
E
ROYAL NA
134

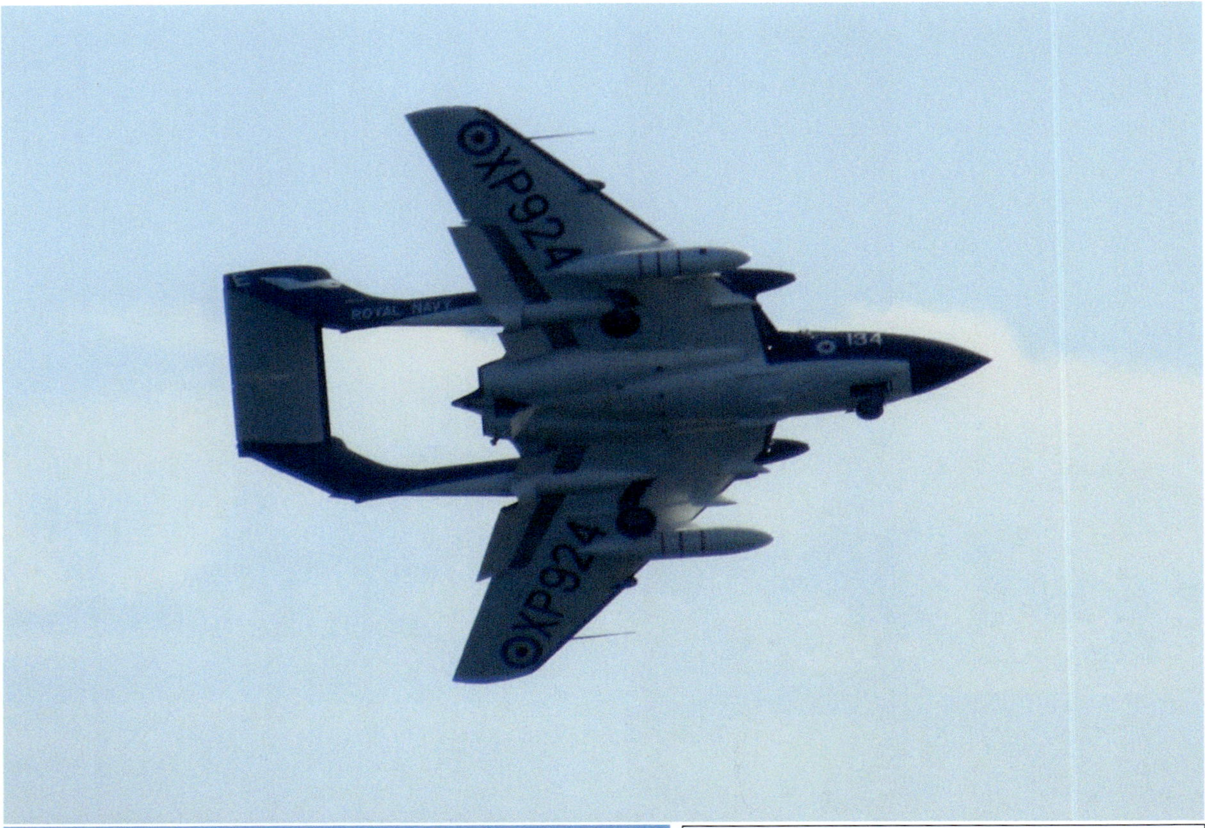

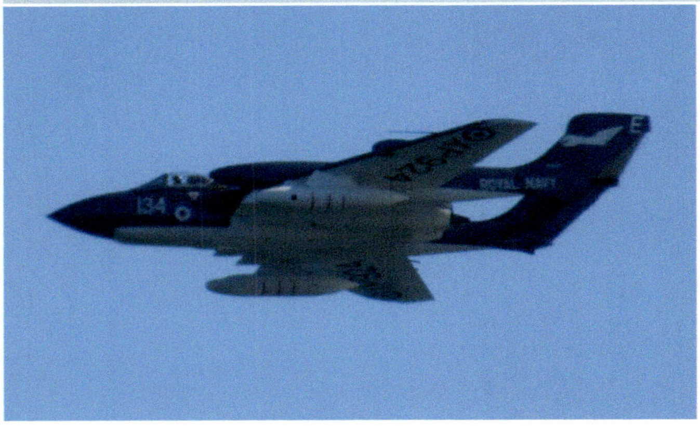

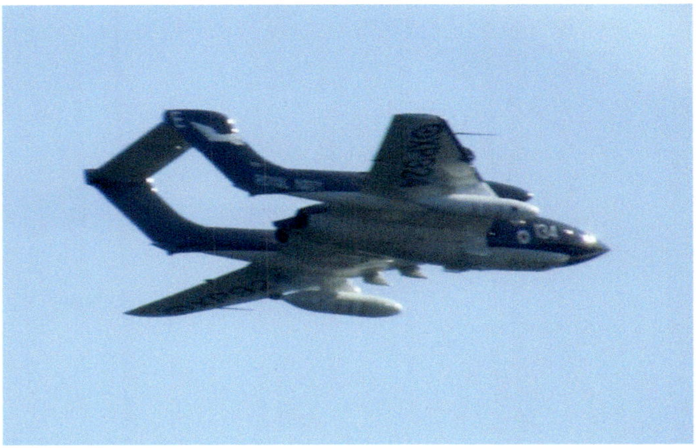

Quick Facts

General

Crew: 2

Length: 55 ft 7 in (16.94 m)

Wingspan: 51 ft 0 in (15.54 m)

Height: 10 ft 9 in (3.28 m)

Powerplant: 2 × Rolls-Royce Avon 208 turbojet engines

Performance

Maximum speed: 690 mph / Mach 0.91

Range: 790 mi (1,270 km, 690 nmi)

Service ceiling: 48,000 ft

Armament

Hardpoints: 6 , with provisions to carry combinations of: Rockets, Missiles and Bombs

English Electric Canberra

The English Electric Canberra, developed in the late 1940s, was the first jet-powered bomber to enter service with the Royal Air Force and became one of the most successful and enduring military aircraft ever. Designed to meet the RAF's need for a high-altitude, high-speed bomber, the Canberra served in bombing and reconnaissance roles for decades, establishing itself as a versatile and adaptable jet.

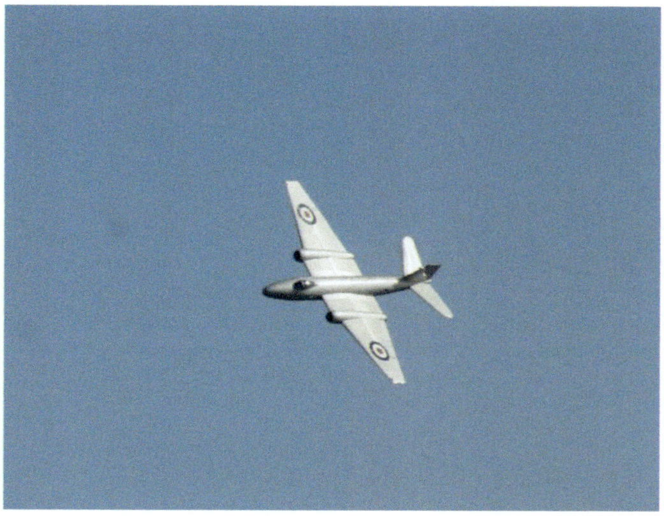

In February 1951, a Canberra set a world record when it became the first jet aircraft to make a nonstop transatlantic flight. Throughout most of the 1950s, the Canberra could fly at a higher altitude than any other aircraft in the world, and in 1957, a Canberra established a world altitude record of 70,310 feet.

The Canberra served for more than 50 years with some operators. In June 2006, the RAF retired the last three of its Canberra's 57 years after its first flight. Three of the Martin B-57 variant remain in service, performing meteorological and re-entry tracking work for NASA.

The Canberra's overall design is simple, somewhat resembling an enlarged Gloster Meteor fighter but with a mid-wing instead. Its main difference from previous piston-powered bombers was the use of twin Rolls-Royce Avon turbojet engines.

The Canberra bomber had a two-man crew seated in tandem on Martin-Baker ejection seats within a fighter-style cabin featuring a large blown canopy. However, delays developing the planned automatic radar bombsight required adding a bombardier's position housed in the nose.

The Canberra B.2 began entering service with 101 Squadron in January 1951. By May, 101 Squadron was fully equipped with the aircraft. Later that year, No. 9 Squadron also started receiving Canberra's. Production of the Canberra accelerated after the outbreak of the Korean War. Orders for the aircraft increased, surpassing production capacity. The Canberra was designated a "super priority" aircraft as a result.

The Canberra made its appearance at the 2014 Bournemouth Air Festival, where it also formed a three-ship formation with the Hawker Hunter and Sea Vixen providing a unique photographic opportunity for keen photographers.

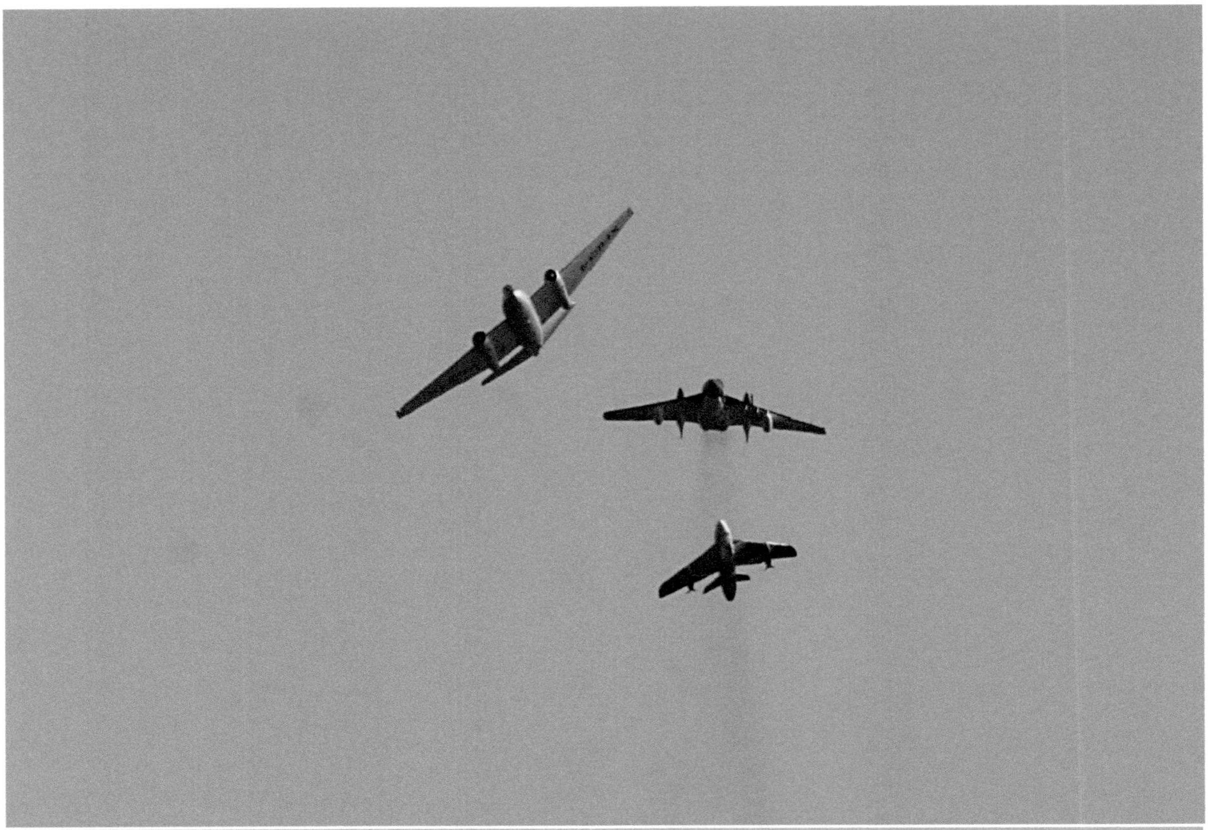

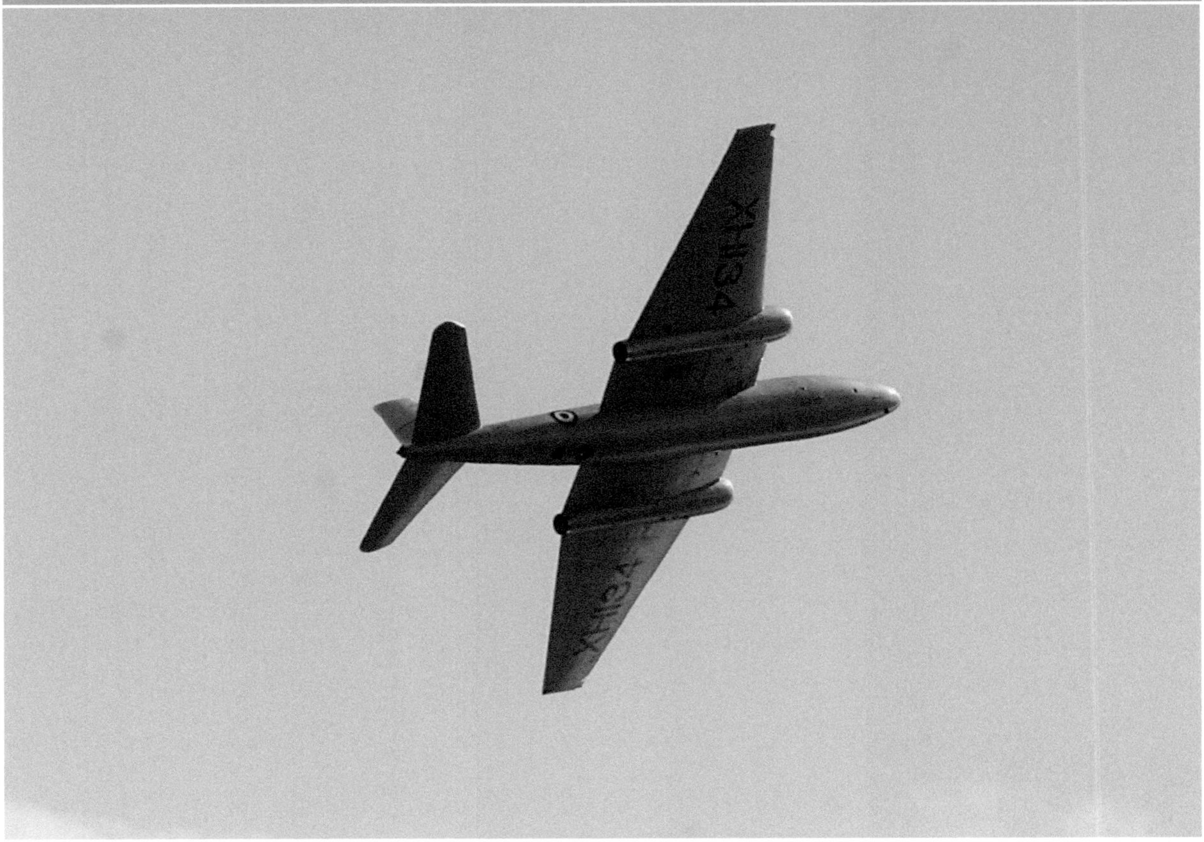
XH134

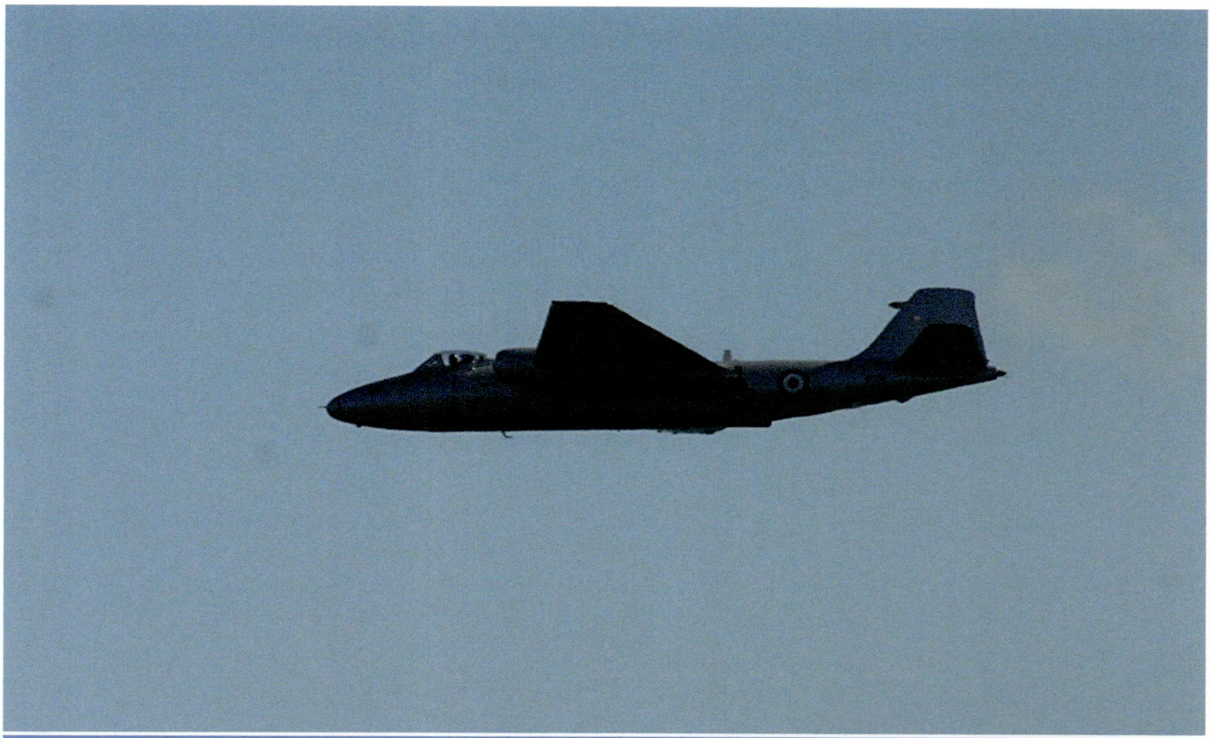

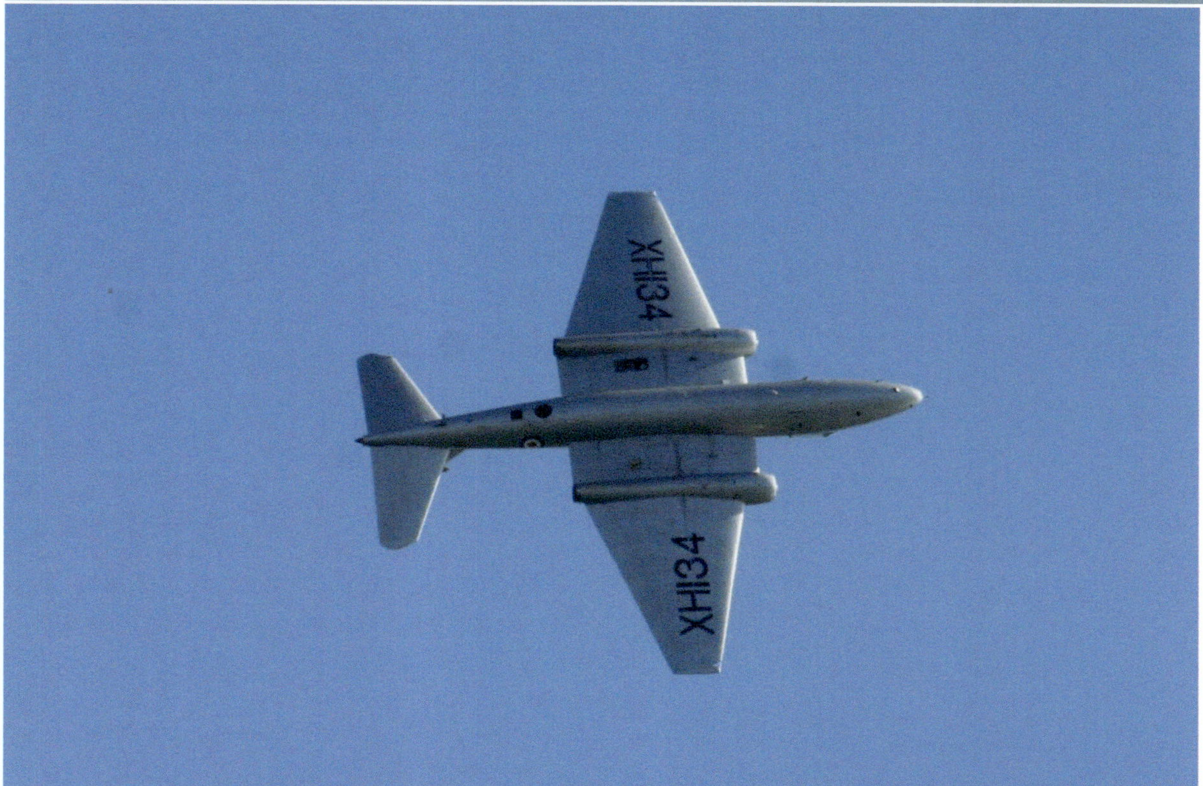
XH134
XH134

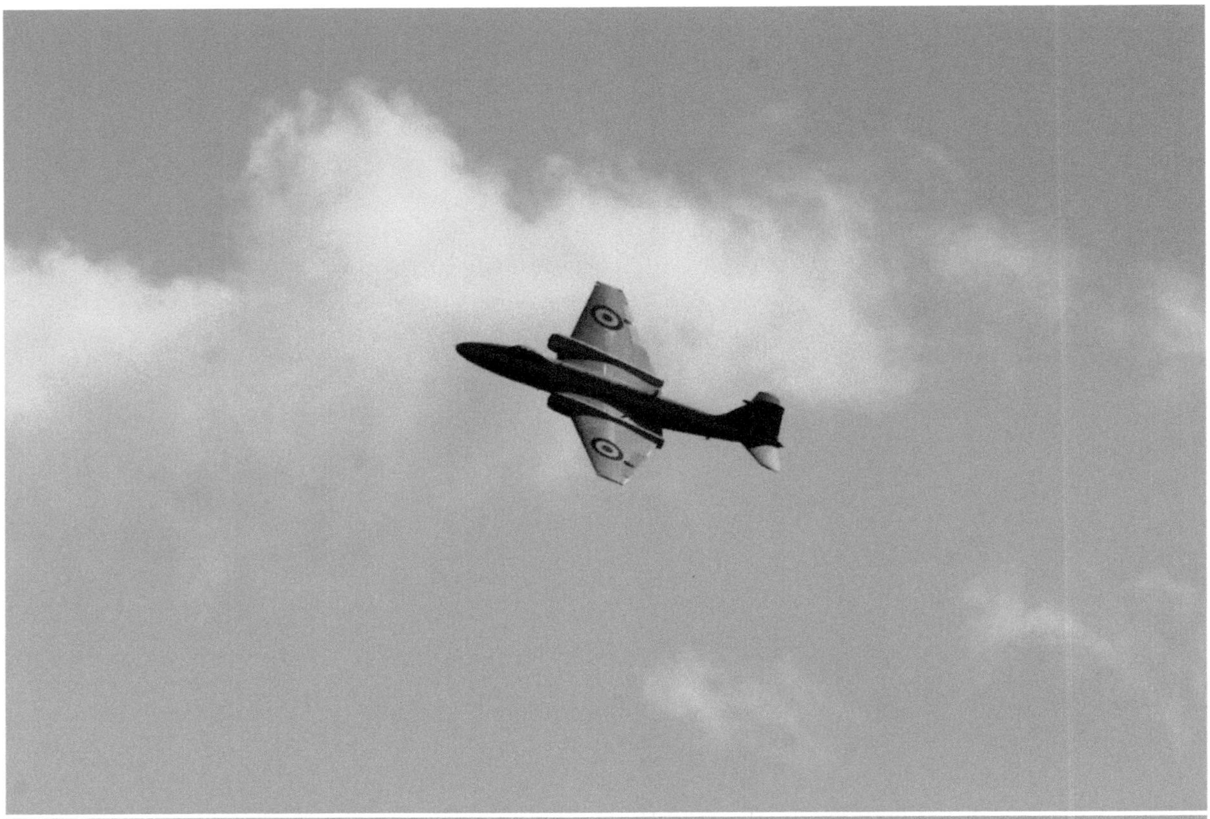

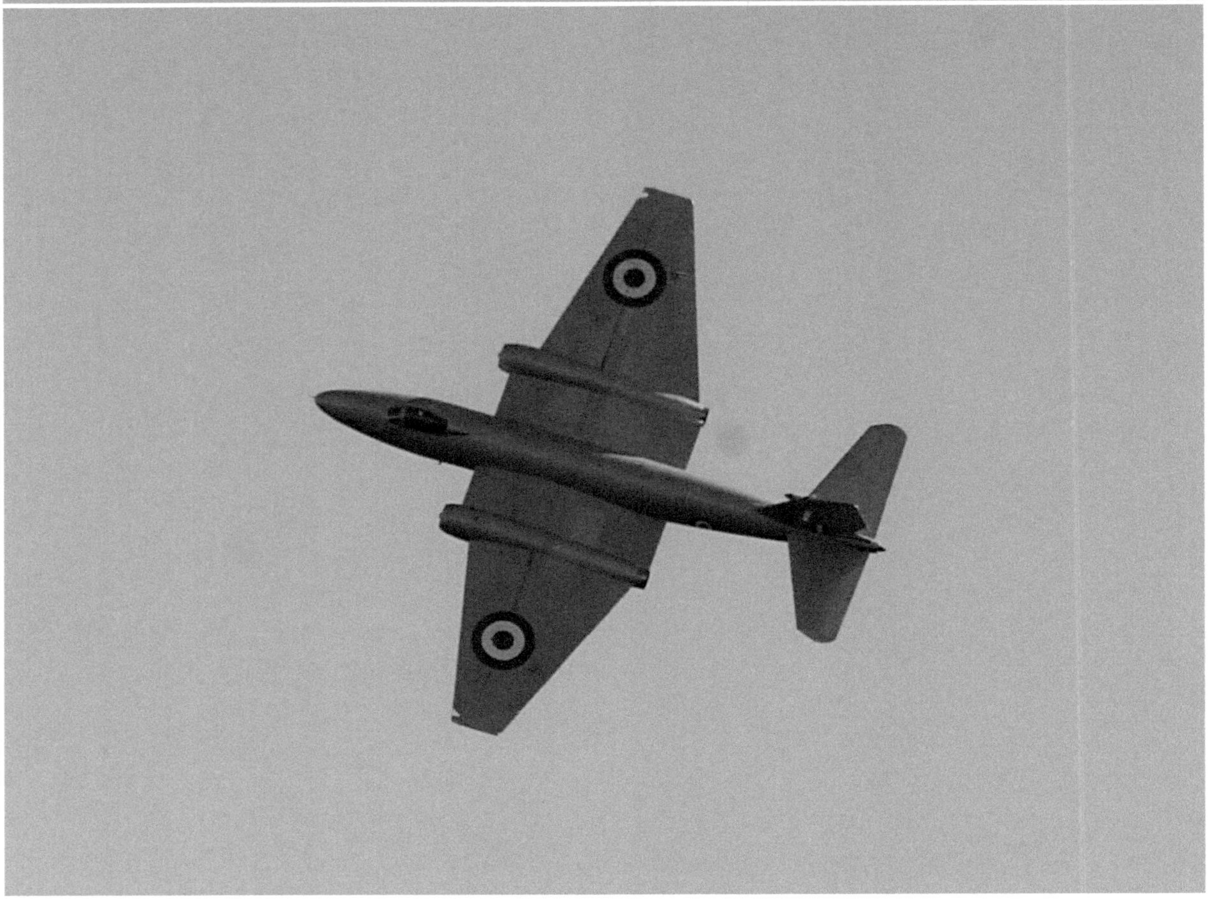

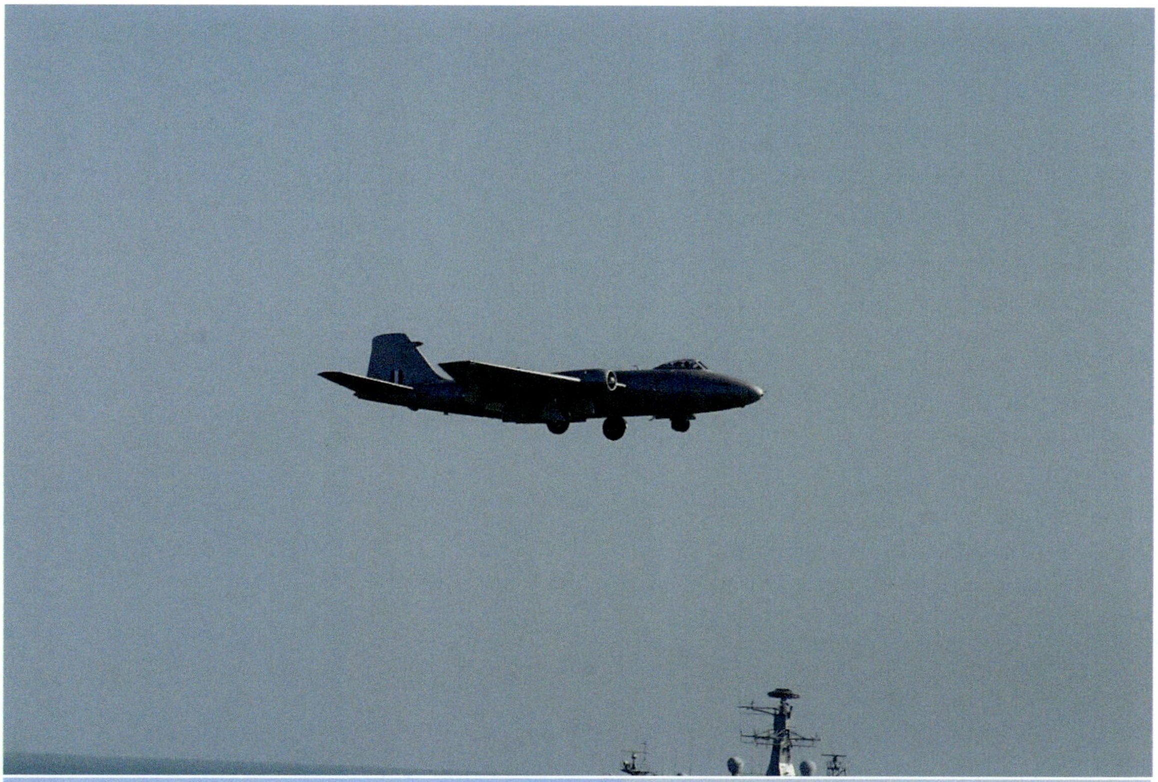

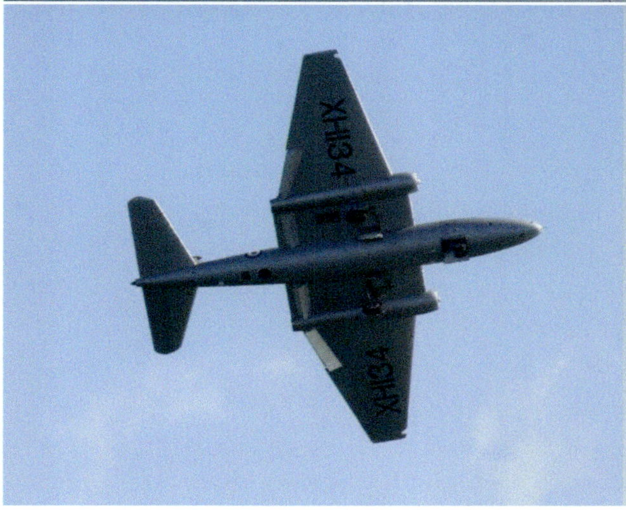

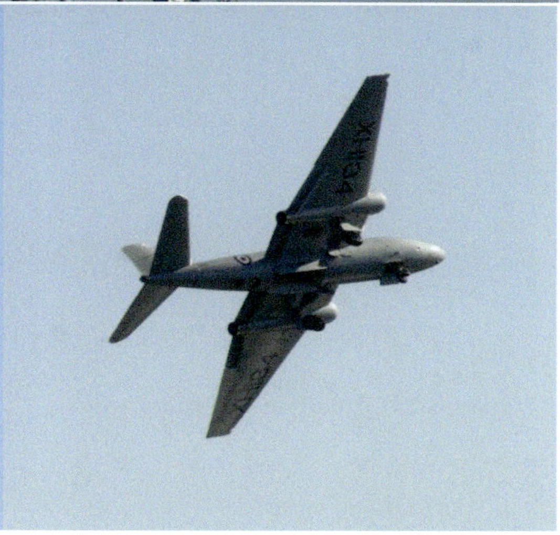

Quick Facts

Crew: 3
Length: 65 ft 6 in (19.96 m)
Wingspan: 64 ft 0 in (19.51 m)
Height: 15 ft 8 in (4.78 m)

Maximum speed: 580 mph at 40,000 ft
Maximum speed: Mach 0.88
Combat range: 810 miles

Guns: 4 × 20 mm Hispano Mk.V cannon mounted in rear bomb bay
Rockets: 2 × unguided rocket pods
Bombs: Total of 8,000 lb (3,628 kg) of payload can be mounted inside the internal bomb bay

Royal Netherlands Air Force F-16 Demo Team

The F-16 Fighting Falcon, originally developed by General Dynamics for the United States Air Force, is a successful American single-engine supersonic multirole fighter aircraft. Designed initially as an air superiority day fighter, the aircraft has evolved since 1976 into an all-weather multirole fighter, with over 4,600 built to date.

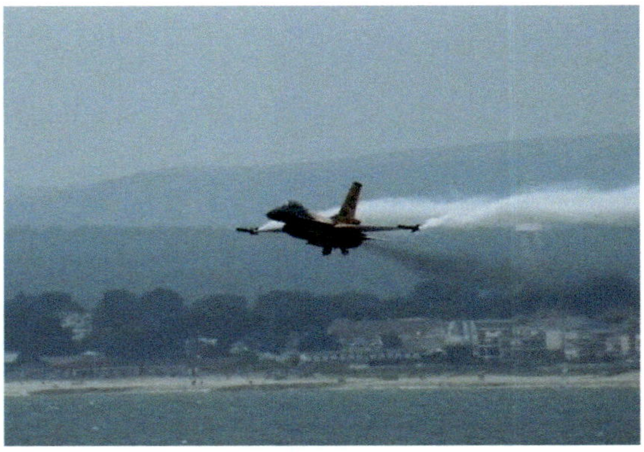

The Fighting Falcon's key features include a frameless bubble canopy for enhanced cockpit visibility, a side-mounted control stick to ease control while manoeuvring, an ejection seat reclined 30 degrees from vertical to reduce the effect of g-forces on the pilot, and the first use of a relaxed static stability/fly-by-wire flight control system that helps to make it an agile aircraft. The F-16 has an internal M61 Vulcan cannon and 11 hardpoints.

The F-16 jet fighter has a cropped-delta wing that blends into the fuselage and incorporates forebody strakes for vortex control. It has a fixed, underslung air intake for its single turbofan engine, a conventional three-surface tail with all-moving horizontal stabilators, a pair of ventral fins under the rear fuselage, and tricycle landing gear with the nose gear retracting into the fuselage just behind the air intake.

Early versions of the F-16 fighter jet could carry up to six AIM-9 Sidewinder heat-seeking, short-range air-to-air missiles by using rail launchers on each wingtip. These early F-16s were also armed with radar-guided, medium-range AIM-7 Sparrow missiles. More recent F-16 variants are equipped to carry the AIM-120 AMRAAM missile. To reduce wing flutter, these newer F-16s often mount the AIM-120 on the wingtips instead of at other hardpoints.

First International Military Participation

The 2010 Bournemouth Air Festival marked the first international military participants when the Royal Netherlands Air Force F-16 Demo Team took to the skies. The striking black-orange F-16 displayed an orange lion on its back and underside, representing the Coat of Arms of the Dutch Royal Family. For five years, this vividly painted aircraft has been the star attraction of the RNLAF airshows.

The F-16 Demo Team aimed to dazzle the crowd as soon as they entered the display area. Trailing smoke from its winglets, the F-16 performed a series of rolls, climbs, and inverted passes that demonstrated the aircraft's agility. The routine culminated in a dramatic low pass followed by a steep climb, with flares dispensing along the way. This breathtaking F-16 demo was a highlight of the 2010 Air Festival and paved the way for more international participation in future Air Festivals.

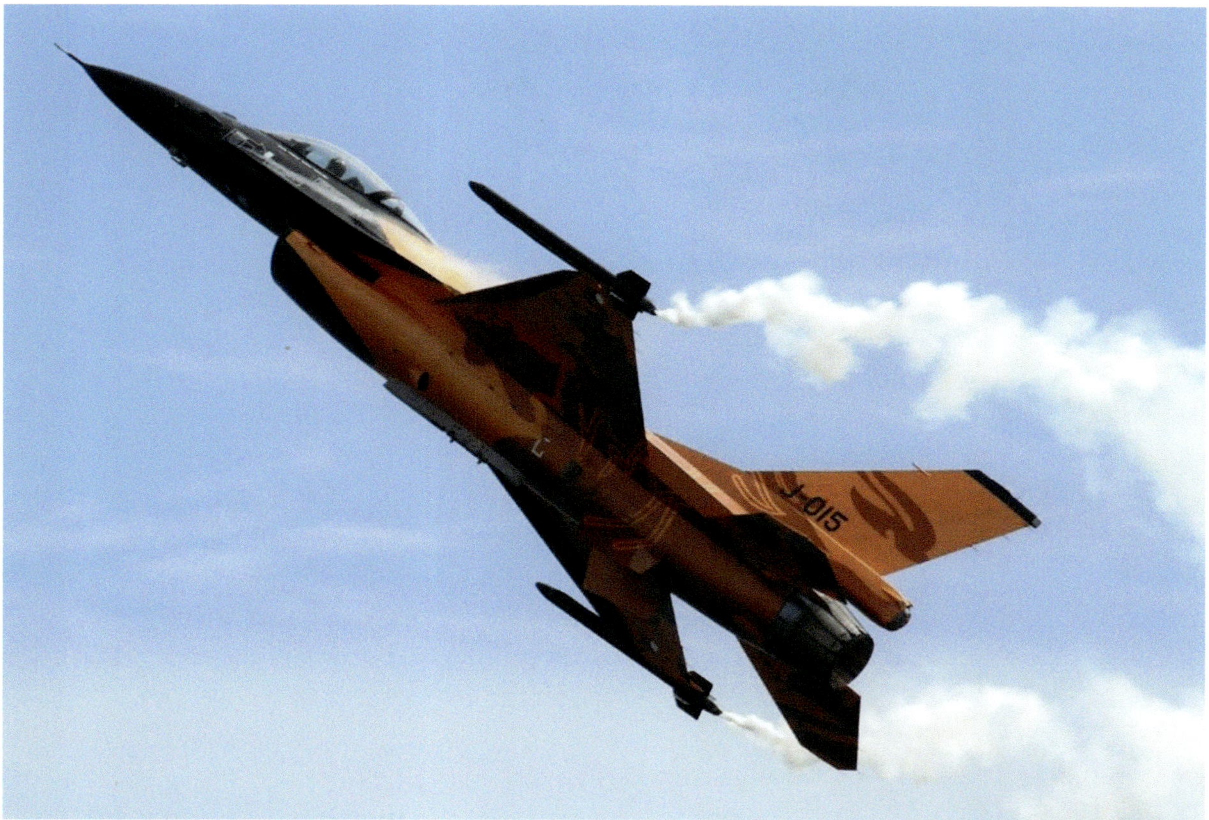
J-015

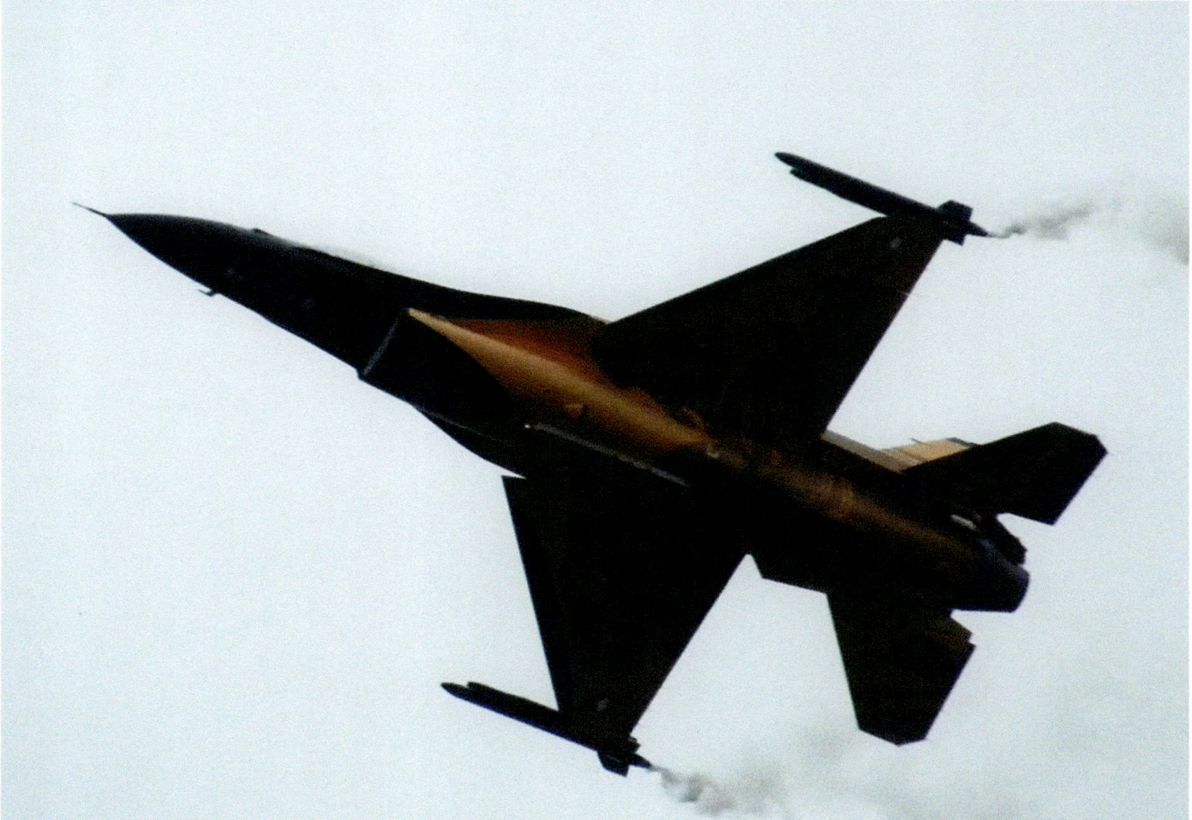

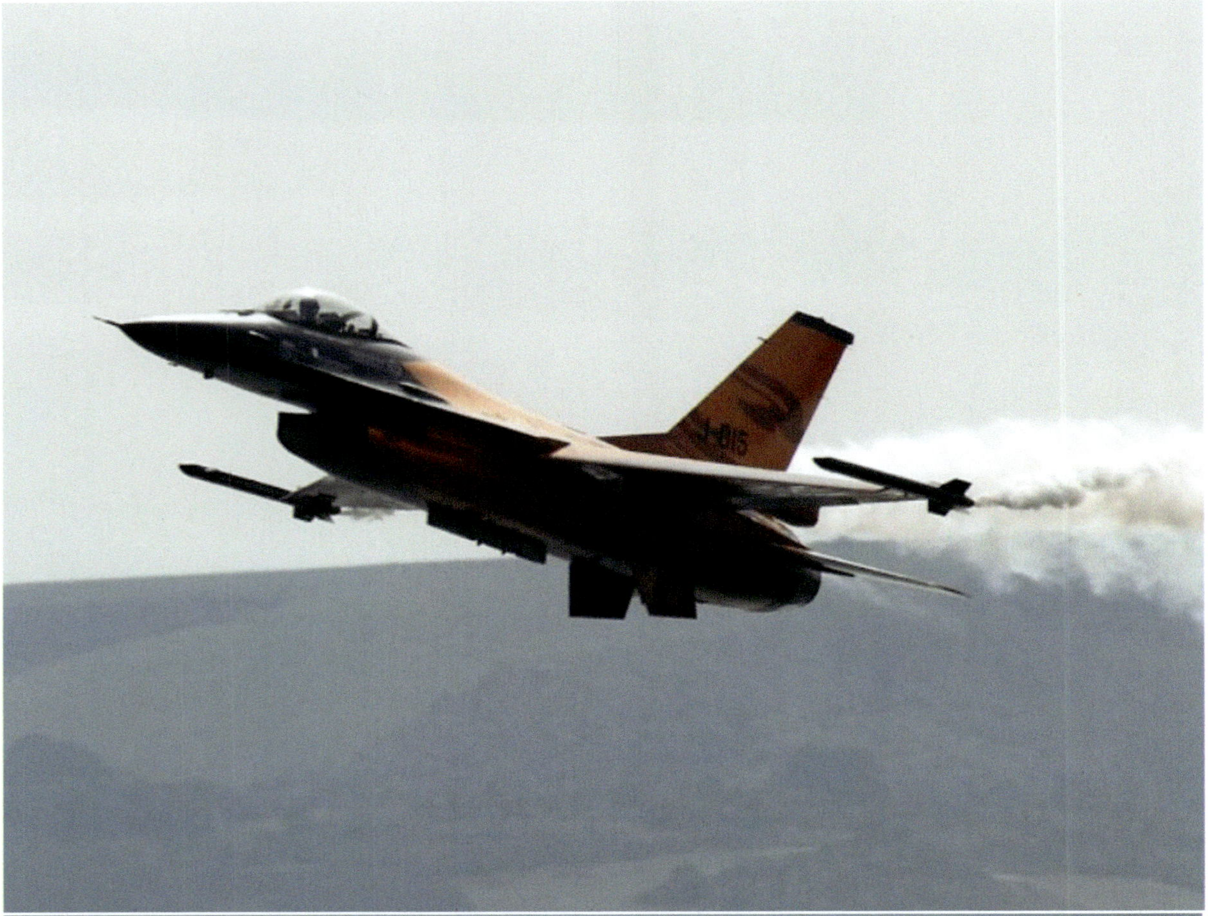

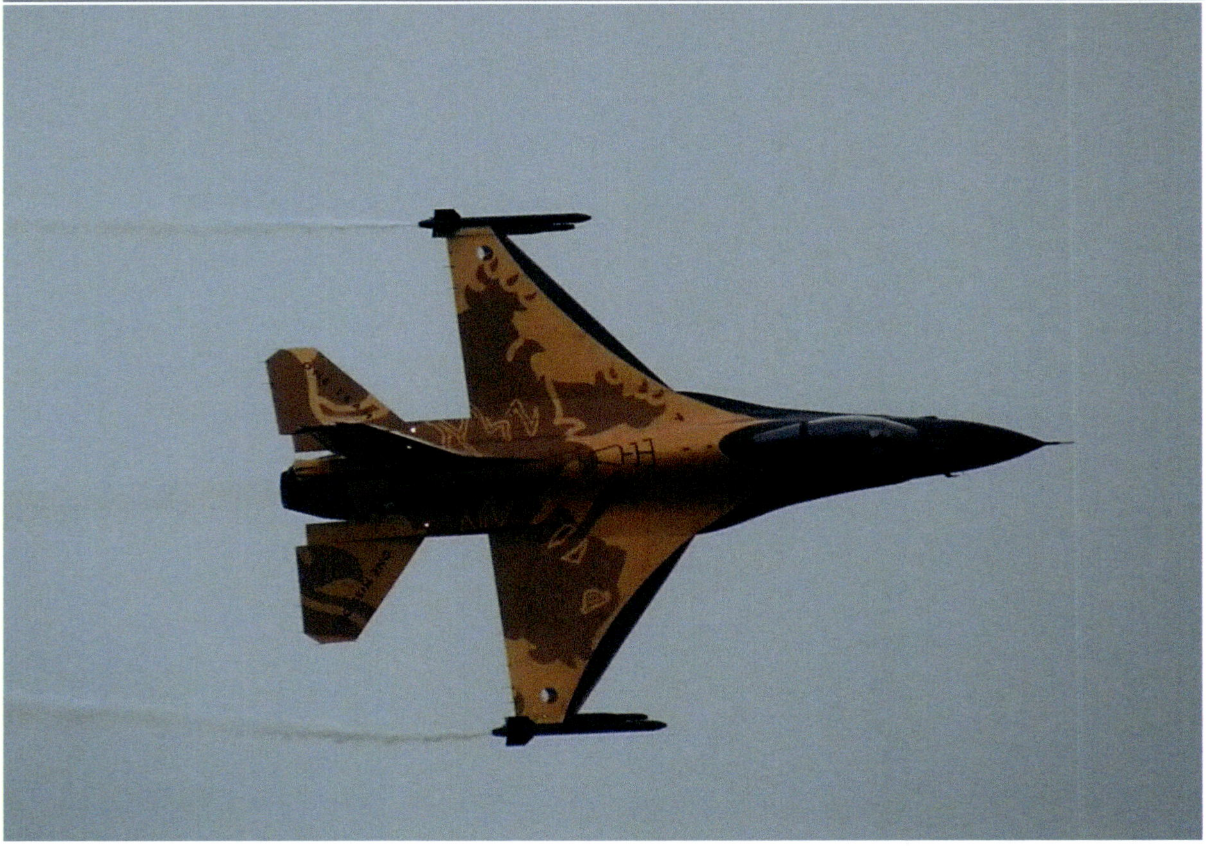

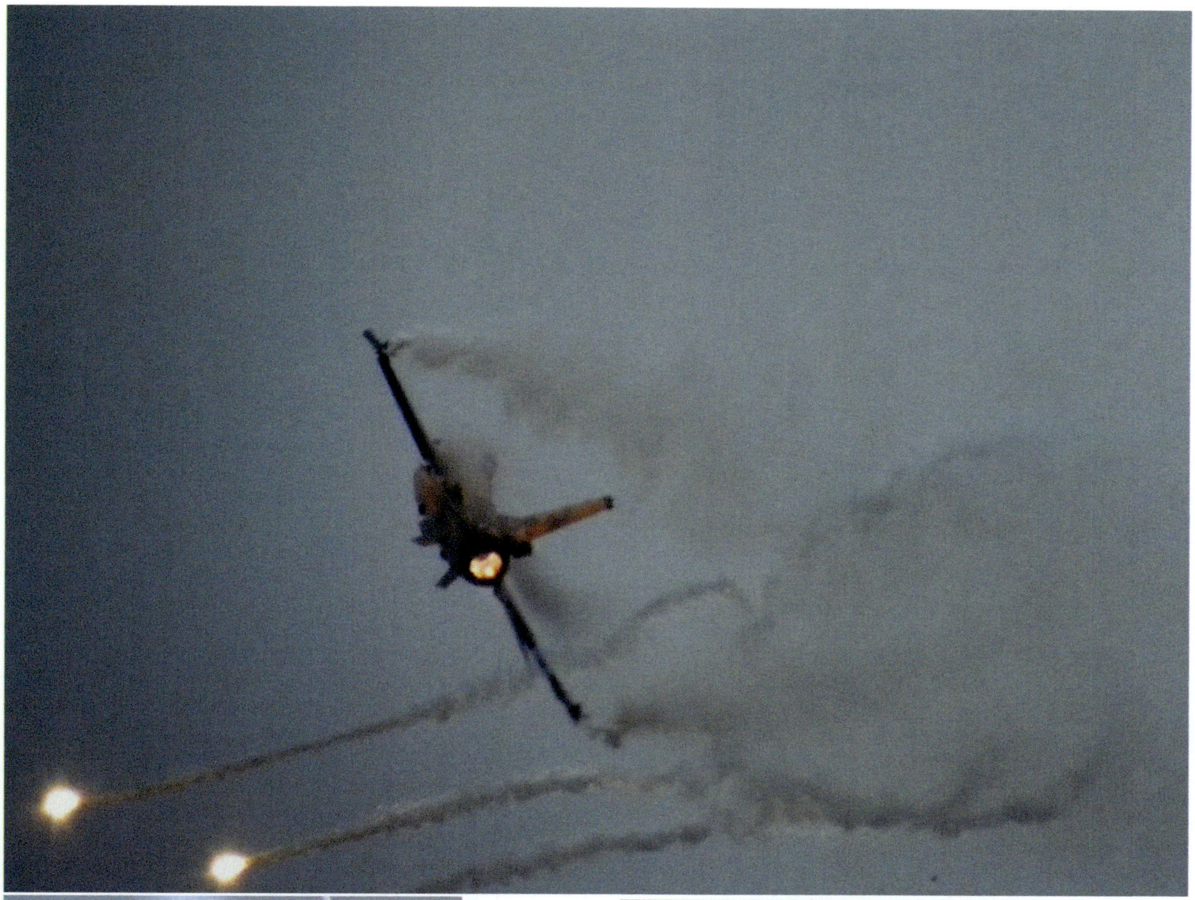

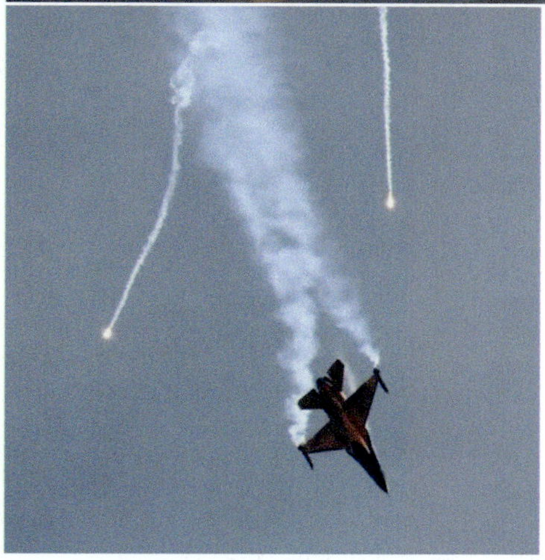

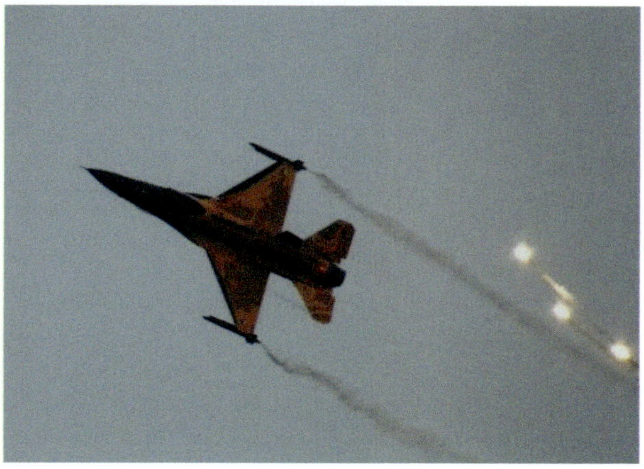

Quick Facts

General

Crew: 1

Length: 49 ft 5 in (15.06 m)

Wingspan: 32 ft 8 in (9.96 m)

Height: 16 ft (4.9 m)

Powerplant: 1 × General Electric F110-GE-129

Performance

Maximum speed: Mach 2.05, 1,176 kn (1,353 mph; 2,178 km/h)

Combat range: 295 nmi (339 mi, 546 km)

Armament

Guns: 1 × 20 mm (0.787 in) M61A1 Vulcan 6-barrel rotary cannon

Missiles: Multiple Air to Air and Air to Surface

Tornado GR4

The Panavia Tornado was a multirole combat aircraft developed and built by Panavia Aircraft GmbH, a consortium consisting of aerospace companies from Britain, West Germany, and Italy. First flying in 1974, the Tornado entered service with several European air forces in the late 1970s and early 1980s, replacing a wide range of aging aircraft types.

The first prototype of the Tornado aircraft, nicknamed the "Tonka" by the British, made its maiden flight on 30 October 1974 from BAC Warton. The first full production Tornado GR1 (ZA319) took off on its inaugural flight on 10 July 1979 from Warton. The Royal Air Force received its first two Tornados (ZA320 and ZA322) on 1 July 1980 at the Tornado Training and Trials Establishment (TTTE) at RAF Cottesmore. Crews that qualified at the TTTE proceeded to the Tornado Weapons Conversion Unit (TWCU), formed on 1 August 1981 at RAF Honington, before assignment to a front-line squadron.

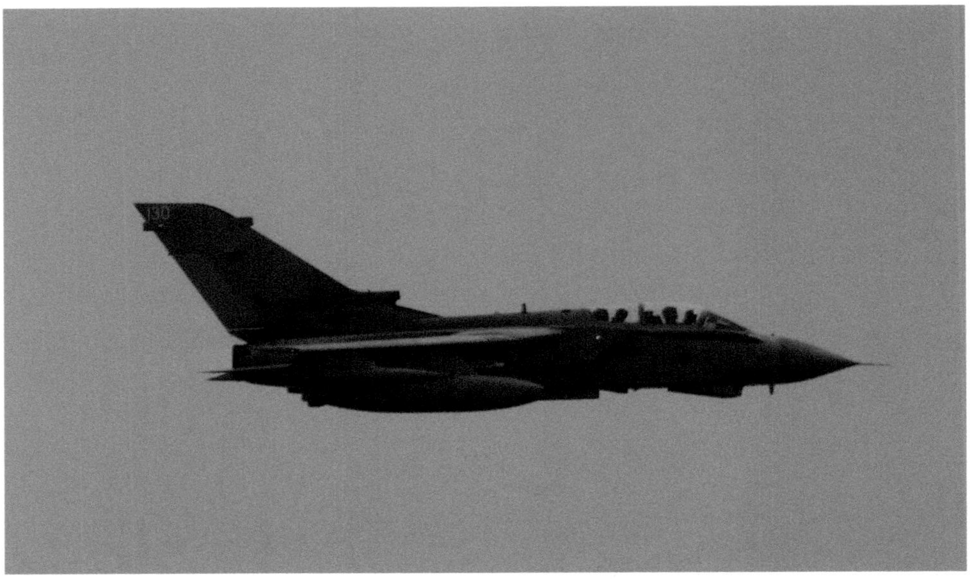

The RAF's GR1 fleet underwent extensive upgrades to become the Tornado GR4, which featured multiple improvements including a forward looking infrared system, a wide-angle head-up display, enhanced cockpit displays, night vision capabilities, new avionics, and GPS. These upgrades facilitated the integration of newly purchased armaments and sensors such as the Storm Shadow cruise missile, Brimstone anti-tank missile, Paveway III laser-guided bombs, and the RAPTOR reconnaissance pod.

To operate effectively at both high and low speeds, the Tornado employs a variable-sweep wing. Typically, swept or delta wings are used for high-speed performance but are inefficient at low speeds. However, the Tornado needs to excel as a low-level supersonic strike aircraft, requiring good characteristics in both high-speed and low-speed flight. The variable-sweep wing allows it to achieve this desired balance of performance.

The Tornado can carry most air-launched weapons used by NATO, including unguided bombs, laser-guided bombs, anti-ship missiles, anti-radiation missiles, anti-personnel mines, and runway attack munitions. To improve its survivability in combat, the Tornado has countermeasures like flare and chaff dispensers and electronic countermeasure pods that mount under the wings.

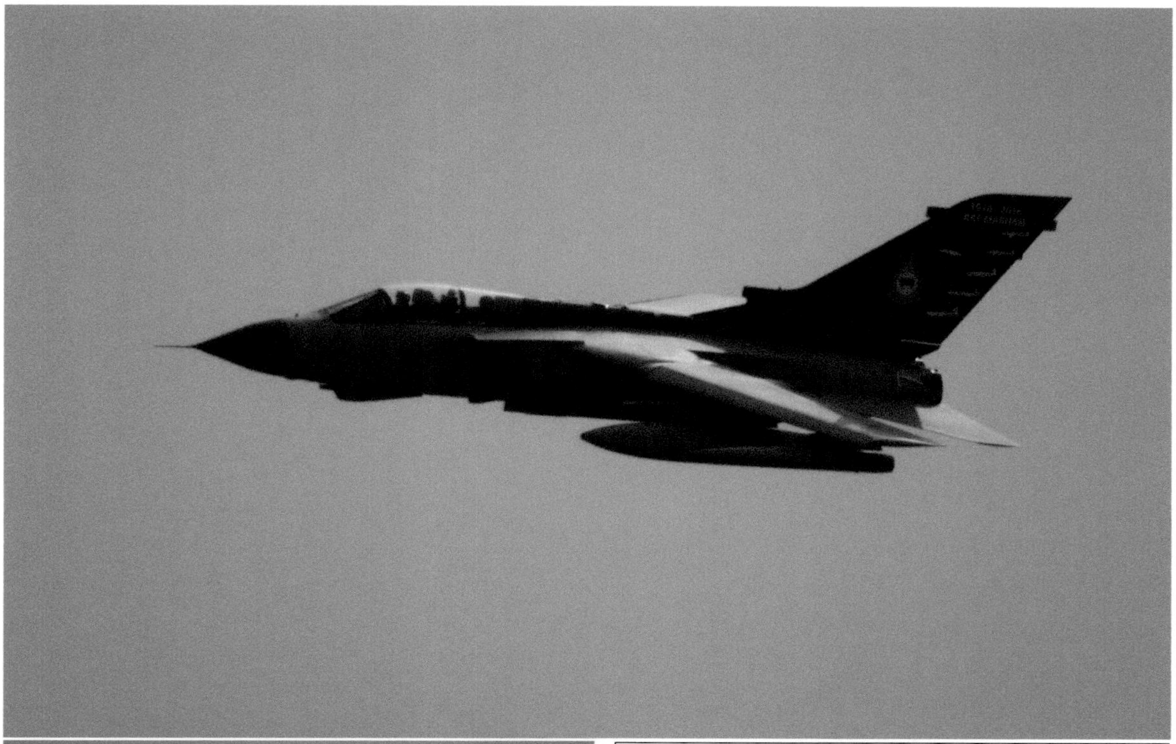

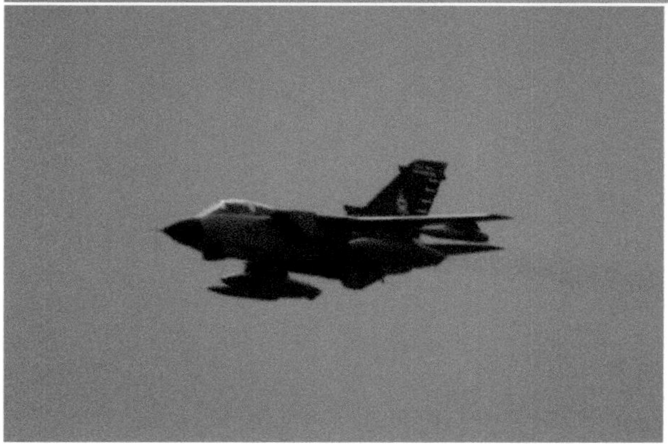

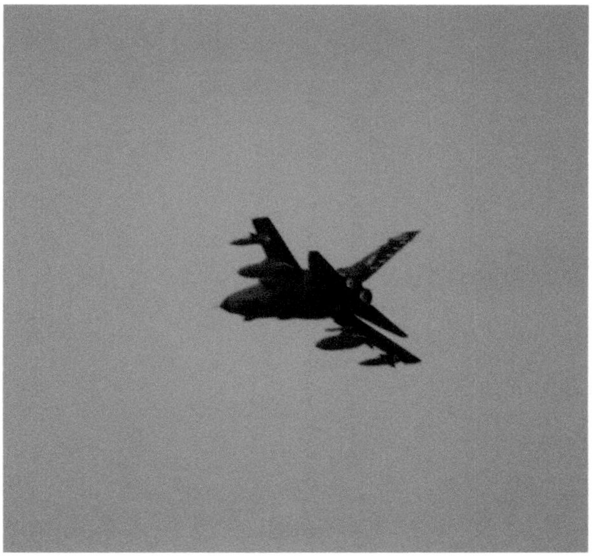

Quick Facts

General

Crew: 2

Length: 16.72 m (54 ft 10 in)

Wingspan: 13.91 m (45 ft 8 in) at 25° sweep

Swept wingspan: 8.60 m (28 ft 3 in) swept at 67° sweep

Height: 5.95 m (19 ft 6 in)

Powerplant: 2 × Turbo-Union RB199-34R Mk 103 afterburning 3-spool turbofan

Performance

Maximum speed: 2,400 km/h (1,500 mph) at 9,000 m (30,000 ft) 1,482 km/h (921 mph; 800 kn) IAS near sea level

Maximum speed: Mach 2.2

Range: 1,390 km (860 mi, 750 nmi)

Armament

Guns: 1 × 27 mm (1.06 in) Mauser BK-27 revolver cannon

Hardpoints: 3 × under-fuselage and 4 × under-wing pylon stations with a capacity of 9,000 kg (19,800 lb)

Saab 35 Draken

The Saab 35 Draken, meaning 'The Kite' or 'The Dragon' in Swedish, was a fighter-interceptor developed and manufactured by the Swedish aerospace company Svenska Aeroplan Aktiebolaget (SAAB) from 1955 to 1974. The Swedish Air Force intended the Draken to replace the Saab 29 Tunnan day fighter and Saab 32B Lansen night fighter, both of which were also under development at the time. Work on the Draken began in 1948 as part of this next-generation fighter program.

The Saab 35 Draken entered aviation history with its many "firsts." It was the first Western European combat aircraft with true supersonic capability to enter service, as well as the first fully supersonic aircraft deployed in Western Europe.

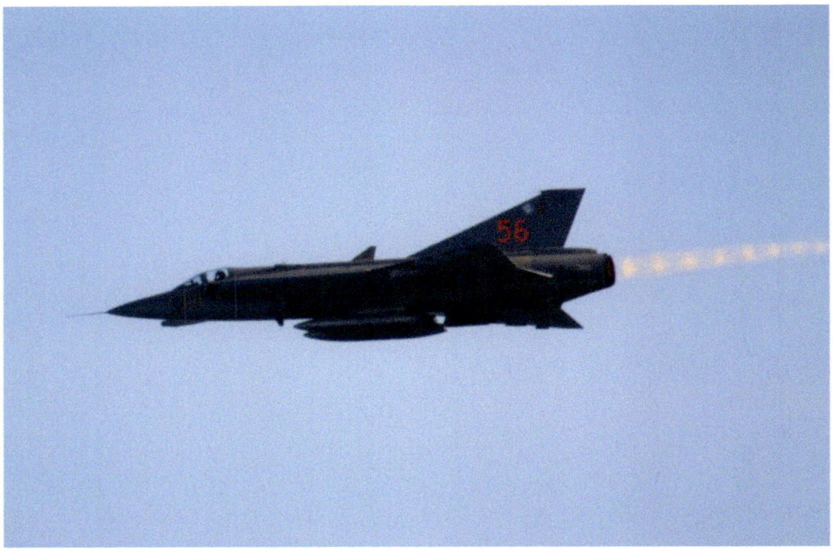

One of the first combat aircraft with an unconventional double delta wing design, it was drawn up by early 1950. This wing design enabled it to become the first known aircraft capable of performing the Cobra manoeuvre.

The Saab 35 Draken fighter jet features a unique double delta wing design that blends seamlessly with the fuselage, creating a smooth, blended wing-body appearance. According to Flight International, the Draken's seamless fuselage-wing integration makes it difficult to visually distinguish where one ends and the other begins. The futuristic design foreshadowed the later "blended wing-body" concept. The Draken's circular fuselage leads into a large inboard wing surface that extends nearly to the engine intakes.

Propulsion was provided by a single Svenska Flygmotor RM6B/C turbojet engine, which was a license-built model of the Rolls-Royce Avon 200/300 engine (also known as the Avon Mk.48A and Mk.60). To provide emergency power, a ram turbine was positioned under the aircraft's nose. The engine also had a built-in emergency starter unit.

In 1987, the Swedish government began modifying 67 of its J 35F2 fighter jets to the improved J 35J standard, a process that continued through 1991. The upgrades extended the aircraft's lifespan and modernized its electronics, cannon, and pylons for two additional AIM-9 Sidewinder missiles under the intakes. Fuel capacity was also increased.

During the 2019 Bournemouth Air Festival, the Swedish Air Force Historic Flight's single-seat Saab Draken J-35J made its first flying display appearance on the UK mainland. With its slick double delta wings and extraordinary flame of reheat paired with thunderous noise, the Draken commanded everyone's attention, rivalling even the impressive Typhoon.

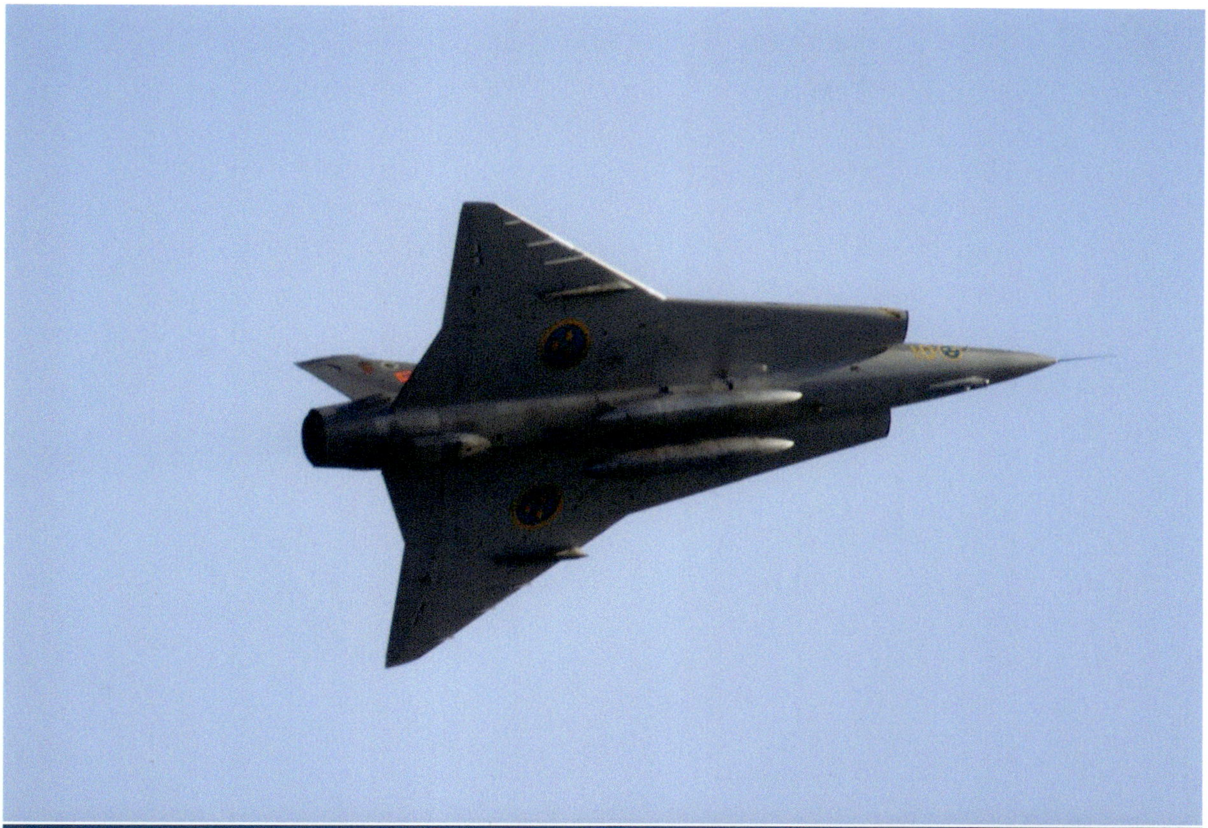

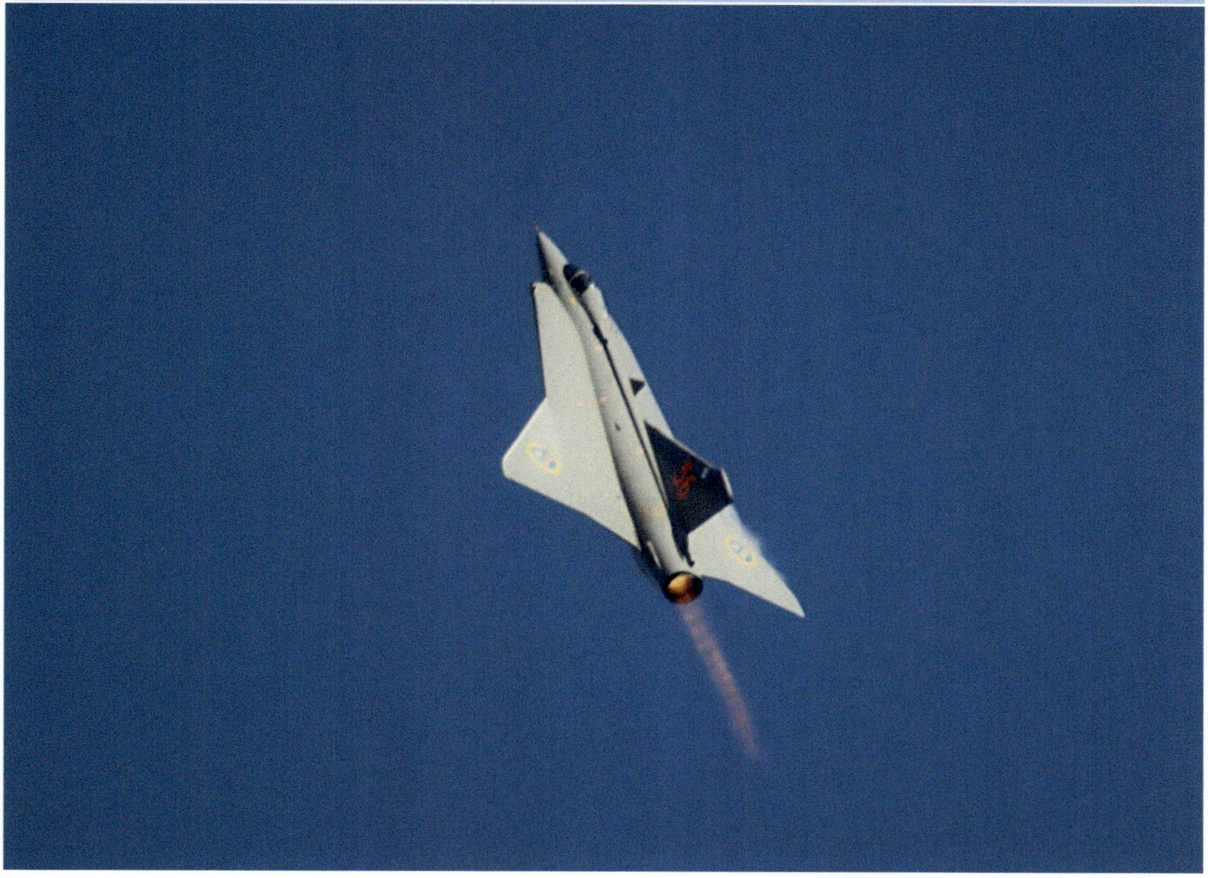

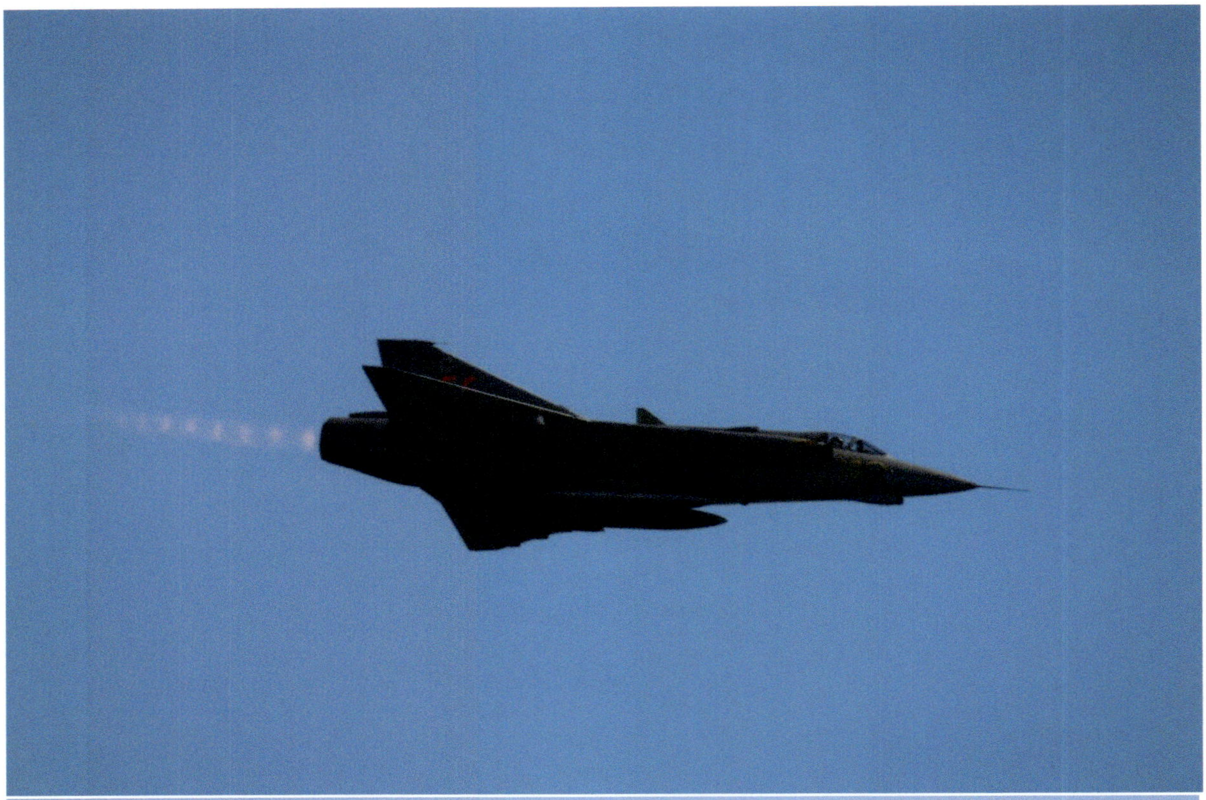

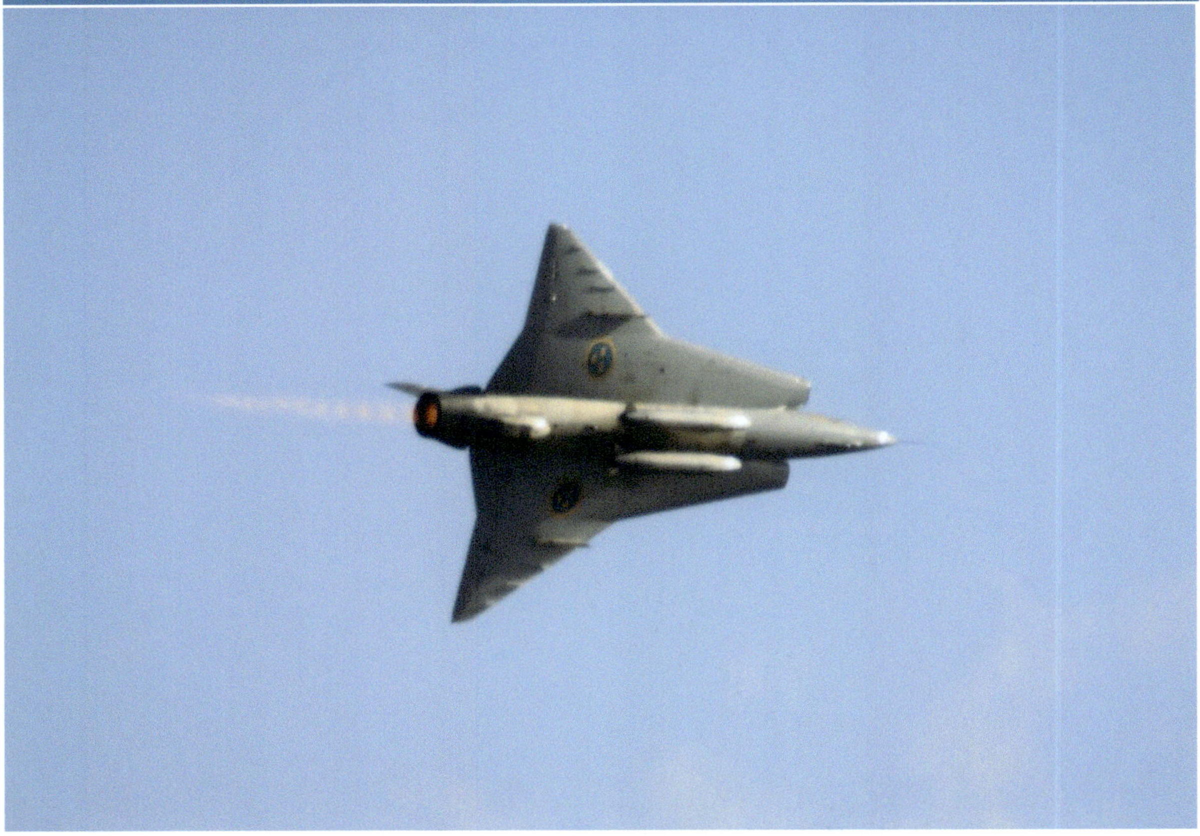

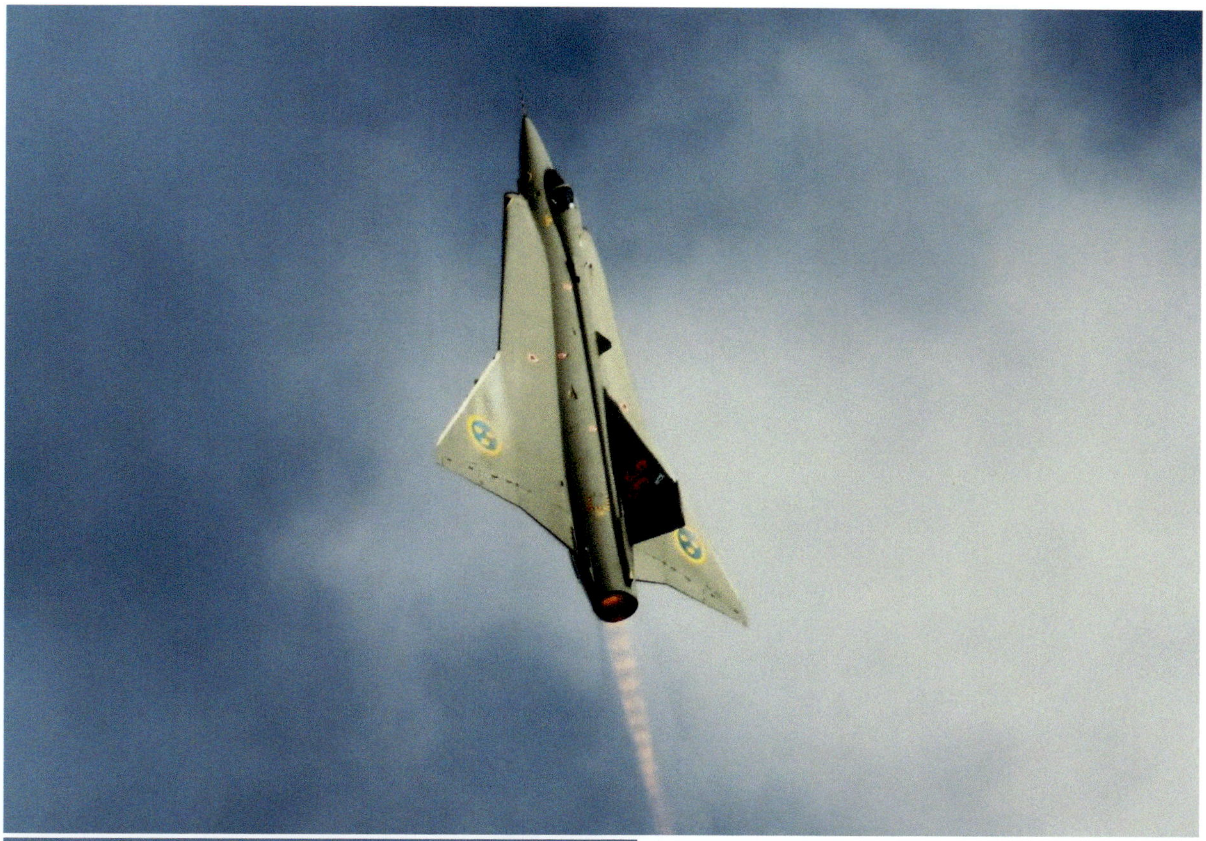

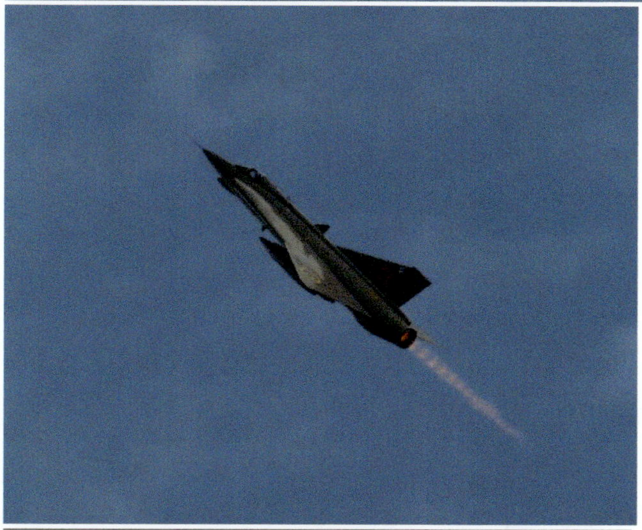

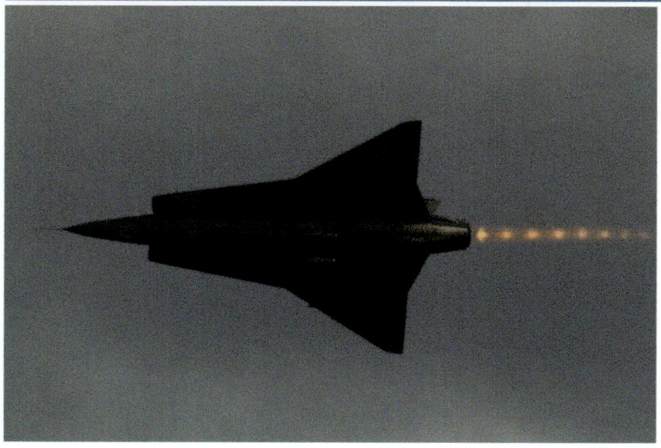

Quick Facts

General

Crew: 1

Length: 15.35 m (50 ft 4 in)

Wingspan: 9.42 m (30 ft 11 in)

Height: 3.89 m (12 ft 9 in)

Powerplant: 1 × Svenska Flygmotor RM6C afterburning turbojet engine

Performance

Maximum speed: 2,450 km/h (1,520 mph)

Service ceiling: 20,000 m (66,000 ft)

Armament

Guns: 1× or 2× 30 mm akan m/55 ADEN cannon with 100 rounds per gun

Hardpoints: Six for ordnance, or drop tanks on the bottom two hardpoints, with provisions to carry combinations of Rockets, Missiles and Bombs

Boeing P-8 Poseidon

The Boeing P-8 Poseidon, an American maritime patrol and reconnaissance aircraft, was developed and produced by Boeing Defence, Space & Security using the civilian Boeing 737-800 as its base. Originally designed for the U.S. Navy to serve in an anti-submarine detection role, the P-8 can now deploy Mark 54 torpedoes as glide bombs from up to 30,000 feet by utilizing the High-Altitude Anti-Submarine Warfare Weapon Capability Air Launch Accessory.

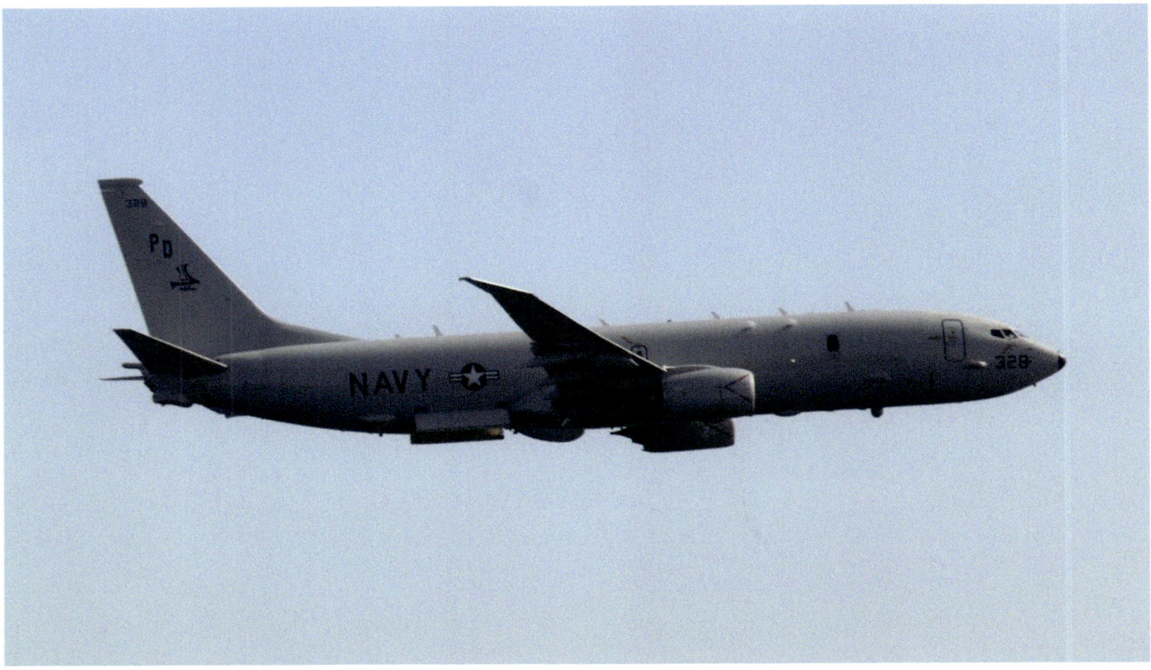

At the 2019 Airfestival, a US Navy P-8 Poseidon maritime surveillance aircraft made its debut with two flypasts on Friday. This aircraft belongs to Commander Task Force 67, headquartered at the Sigonella base on Sicily.

The UK announced on November 23, 2015 that it intended to order nine P-8 Poseidon aircraft as part of the Strategic Defence and Security Review 2015, following the cancellation of the Nimrod MRA4 program. The Royal Air Force's Poseidon's, which are based at RAF Lossiemouth in Scotland, will protect the UK's nuclear deterrent and aircraft carriers in addition to conducting search-and-rescue and overland reconnaissance missions.

The Royal Air Force operates Poseidon MRA Mk1 aircraft, which have the service name Poseidon MRA Mk1. These maritime patrol aircraft are flown by No. 120 Squadron and No. 201 Squadron of the RAF. The first Poseidon MRA Mk1, with serial number ZP801, made its maiden flight on July 13, 2019. The United Kingdom took delivery of its first Poseidon, named Pride of Moray, at Boeing's Seattle facility on October 29. This aircraft arrived at Kinloss Barracks in February 2020 before being relocated to RAF Lossiemouth in October 2020.

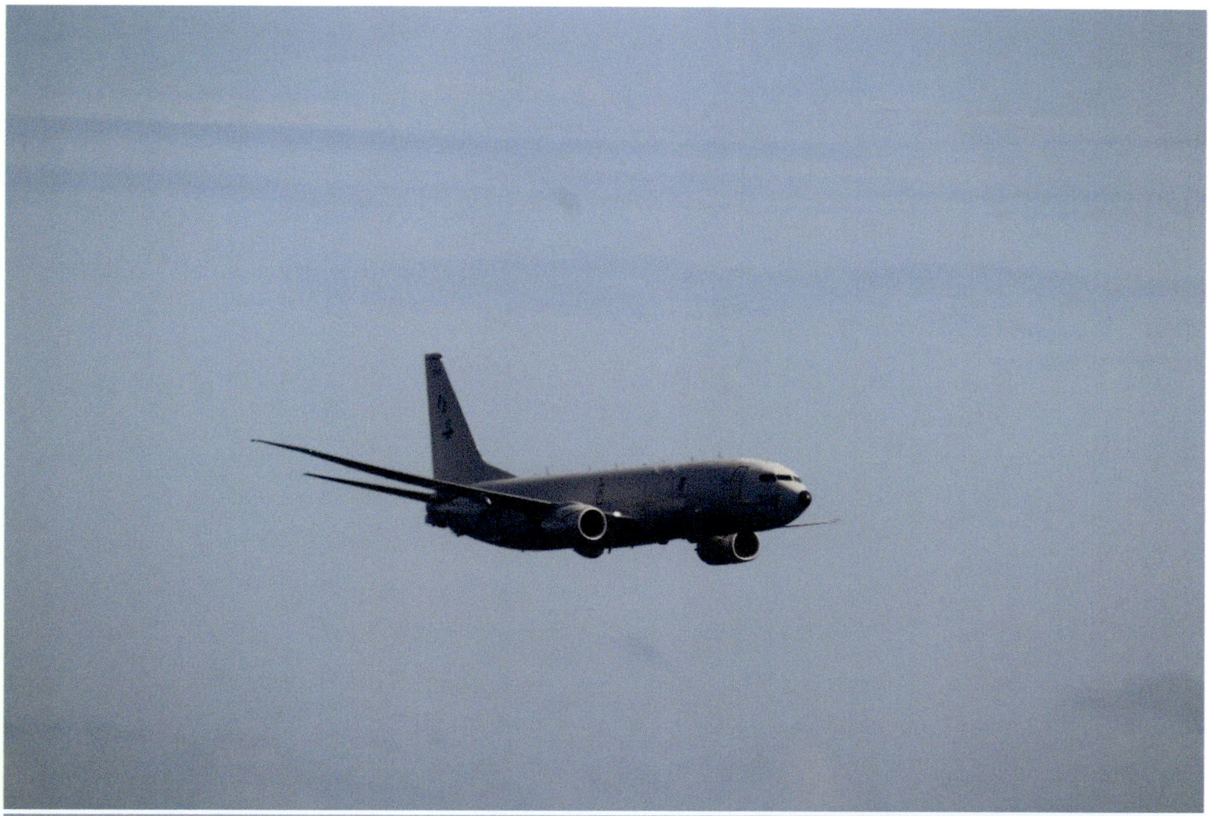

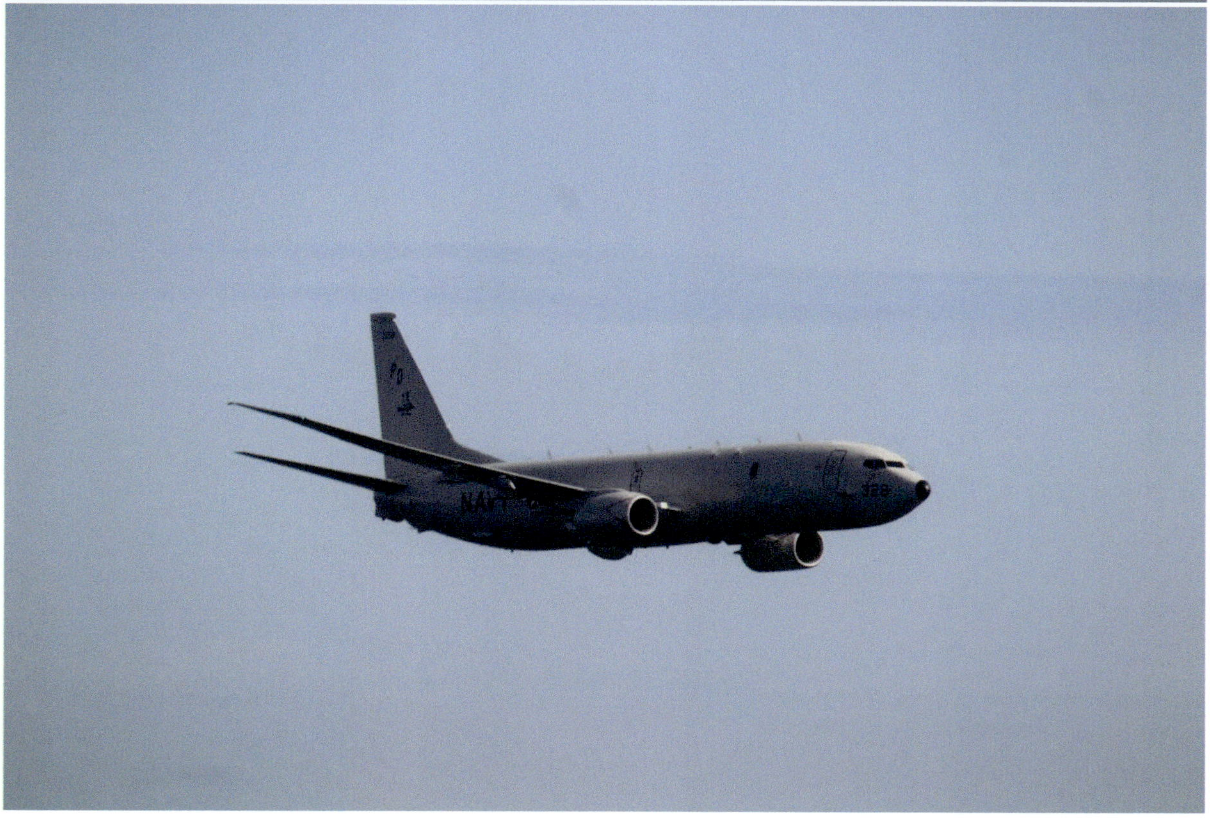

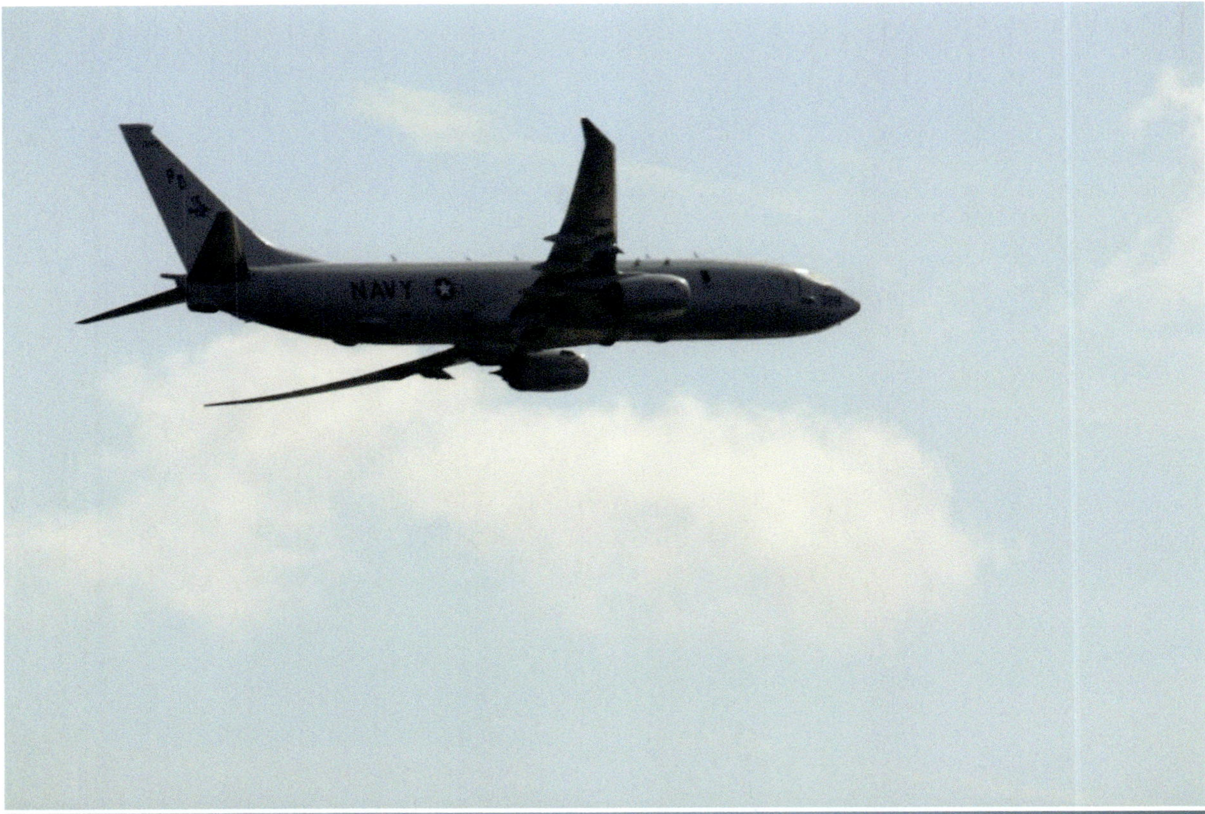
NAVY

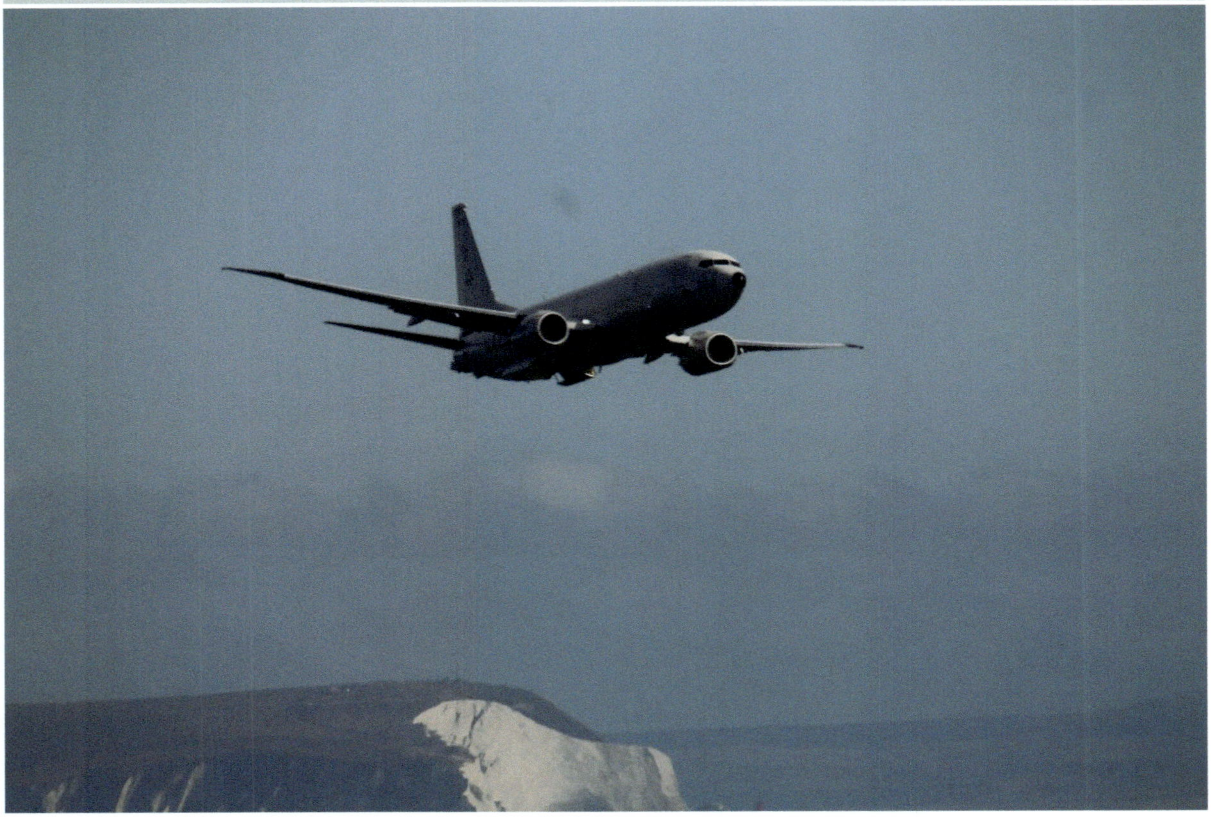

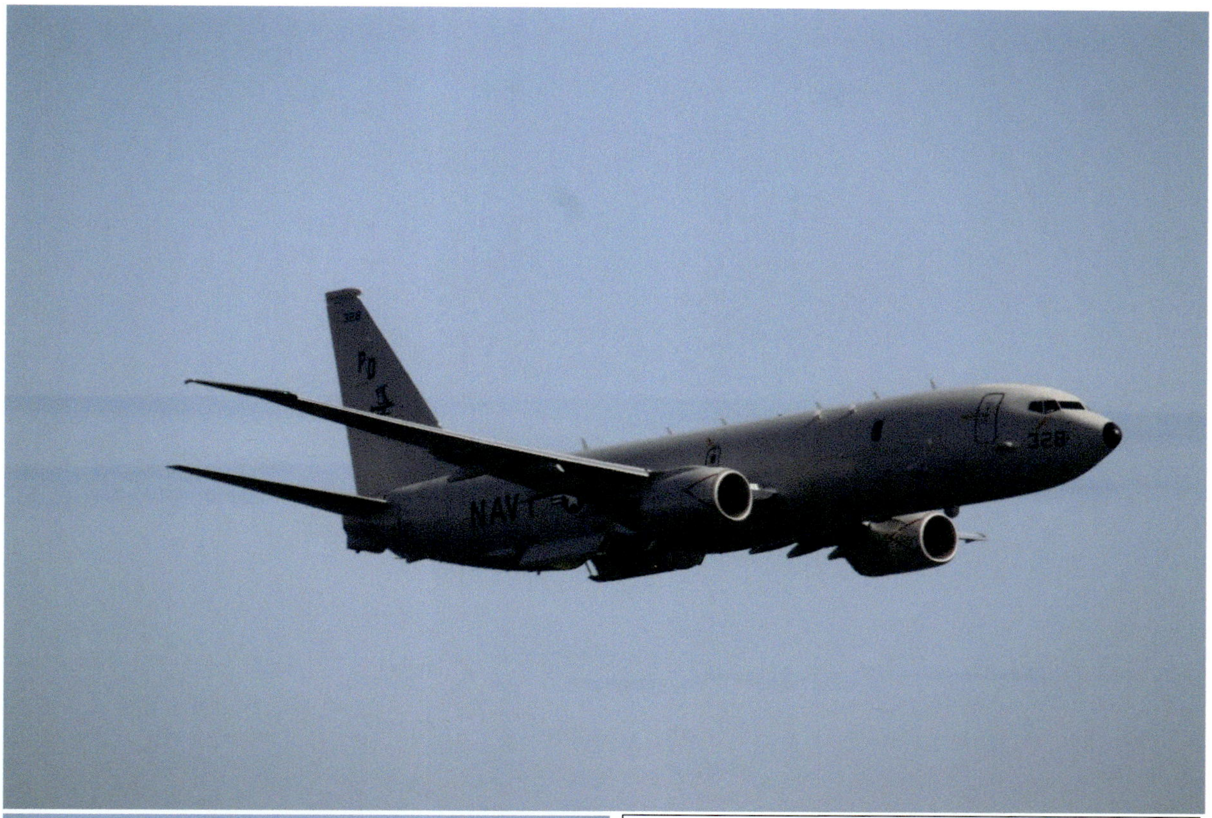

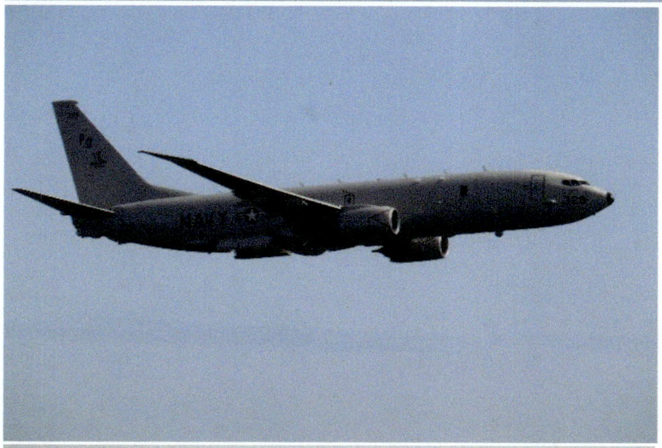

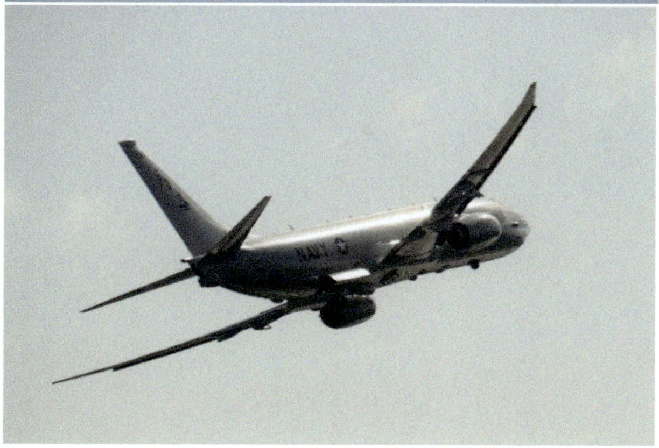

Quick Facts

General

Crew: Flight: two; **Mission:** seven

Capacity: 19,800 lb (9,000 kg)

Length: 129 ft 5 in (39.47 m)

Wingspan: 123 ft 6 in (37.64 m)

Height: 42 ft 1 in (12.83 m)

Powerplant: 2 × CFM56-7B27A turbofans

Armament

Hardpoints: 11 total, Internal Bay with 5 hardpoints and 6 external hardpoints for a variety of conventional weapons such as AGM-84 Harpoon, AGM-84H/K SLAM-ER, AGM-88 AARGM-ER, AGM-158C LRASM, Mark 54 torpedo, Sting Ray torpedo

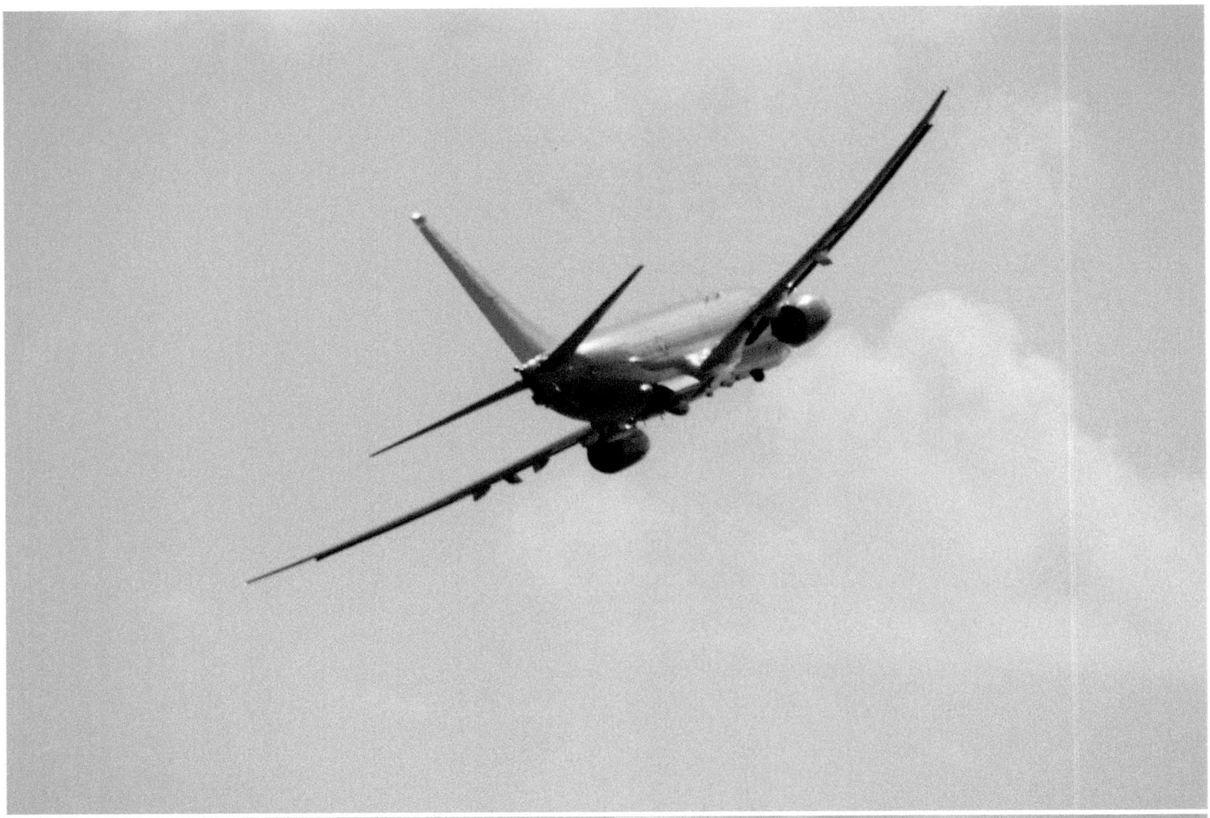

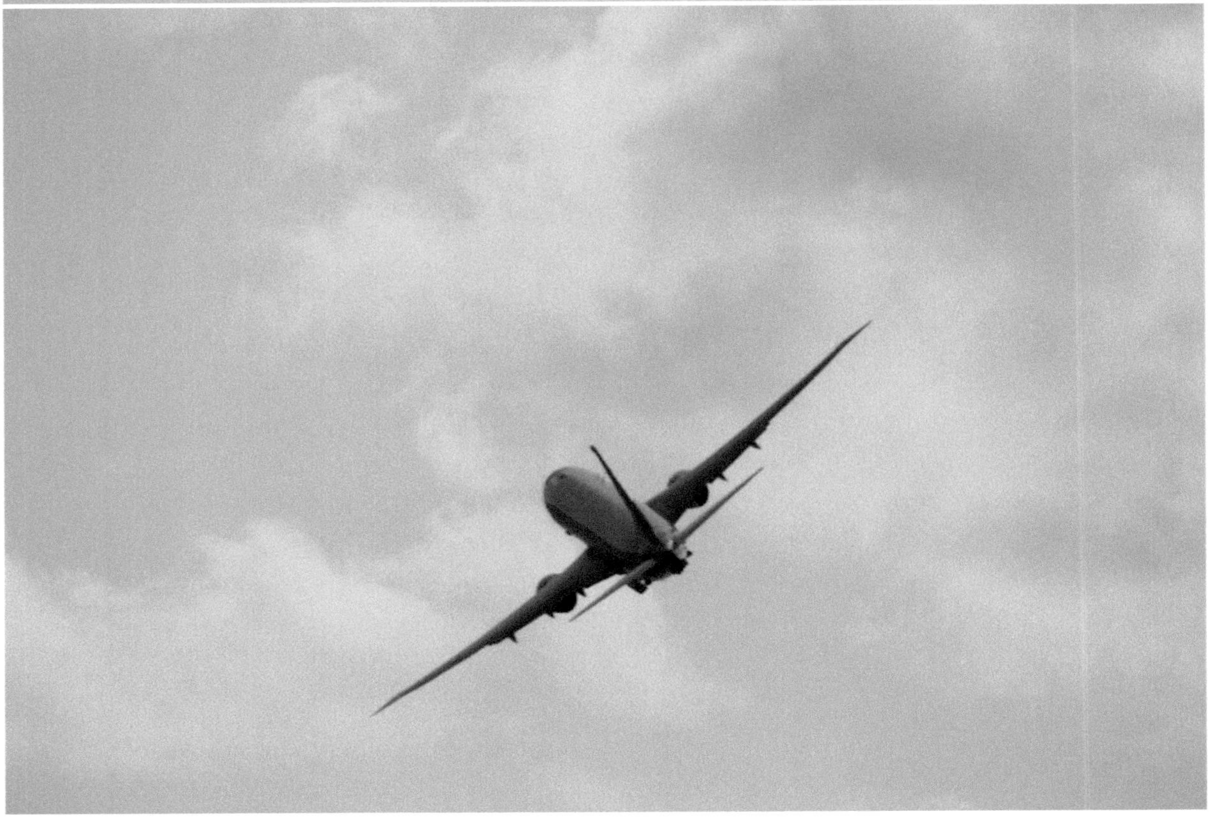

Boeing B-52 Stratofortress

The Boeing B-52 Stratofortress, designed and built by Boeing which continues to support it, is an American long-range, subsonic, jet-powered strategic bomber that has been operated by the United States Air Force since the 1950s and NASA for over 40 years. Capable of carrying up to 70,000 pounds of weapons, the B-52 has a typical combat range of approximately 8,800 miles.

The B-52 shared many technological similarities with the preceding B-47 Stratojet strategic bomber. The two aircraft used the same basic design, such as swept wings and podded jet engines, and the cabin included the crew ejection systems.

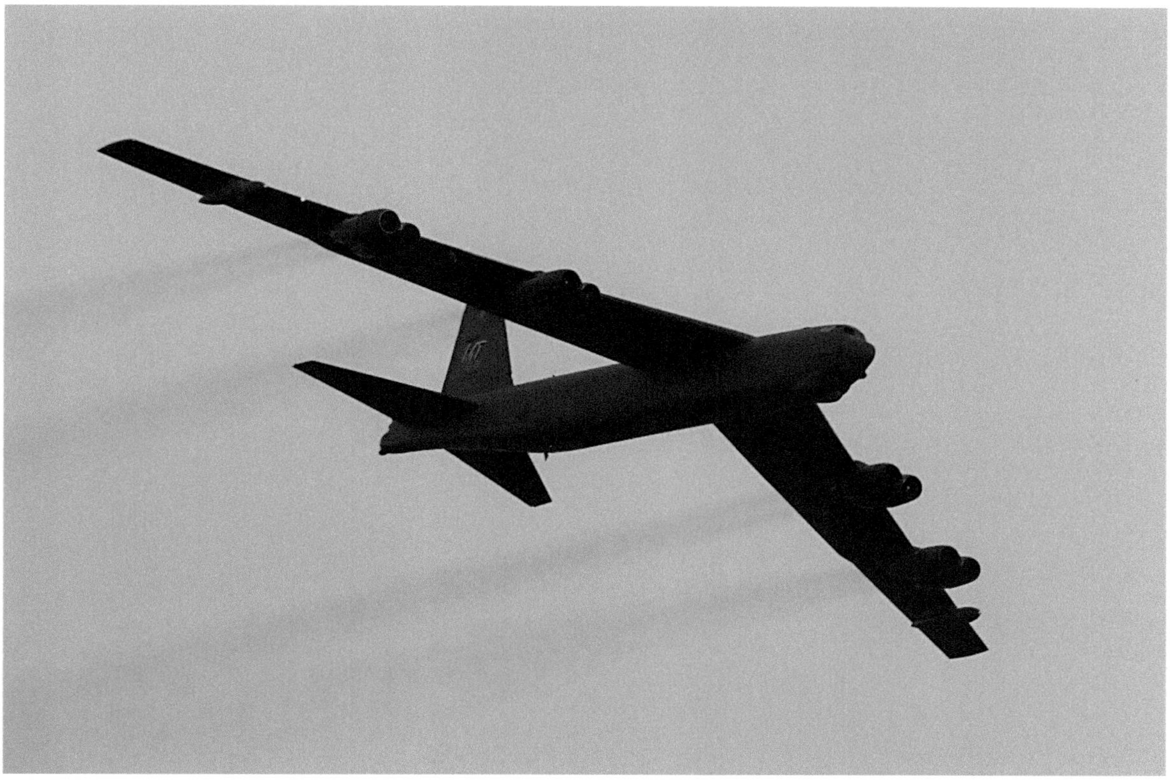

The eight engines of the B-52 bomber were arranged in four pods, each pod hanging from a pylon beneath and ahead of the wings' leading edges. This careful placement of the pylons enabled them to act as wing fences, delaying stall. The first two prototypes, the XB-52 and YB-52, were powered by experimental Pratt & Whitney YJ57-P-3 turbojet engines, each providing 8,700 pounds of static thrust.

During the 2022 Airfestival, a United States Air Force Boeing B-52H Stratofortress from North Dakota's Minot Air Force Base 23rd Bomb Squadron flew past the event. The flypast occurred as the aircraft returned to its temporary base at RAF Fairford, Gloucestershire from NATO exercises across Europe. As part of the Bomber Task Force regularly deployed to Fairford, the B-52H had spent the day on a training sortie.

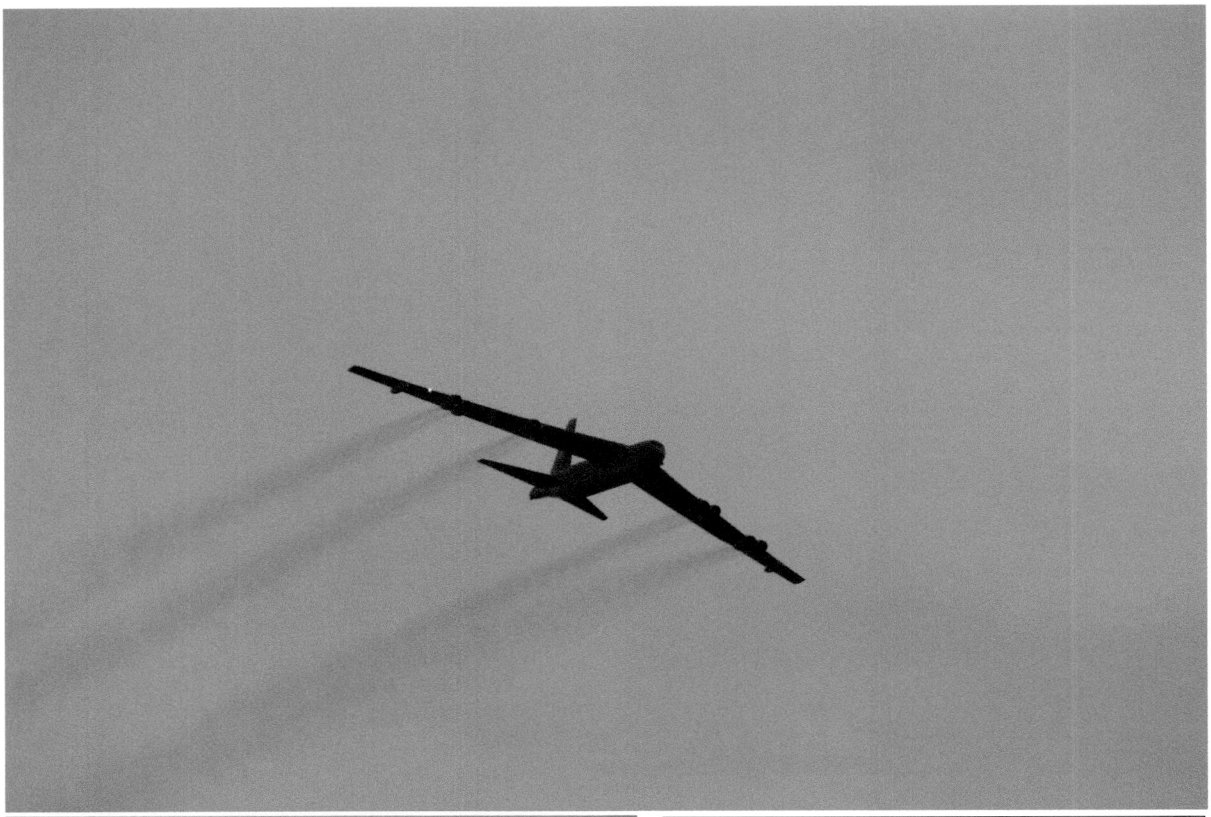

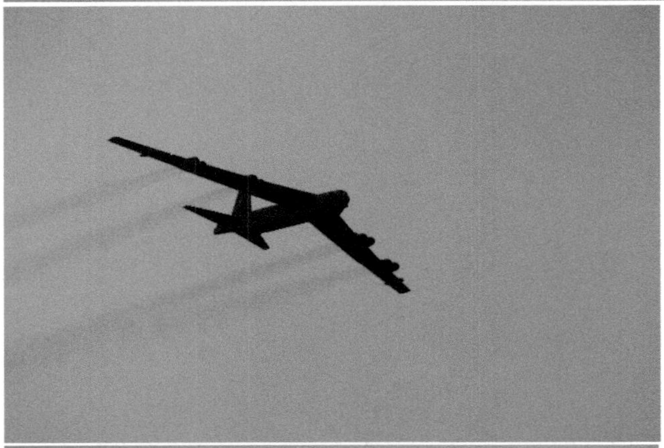

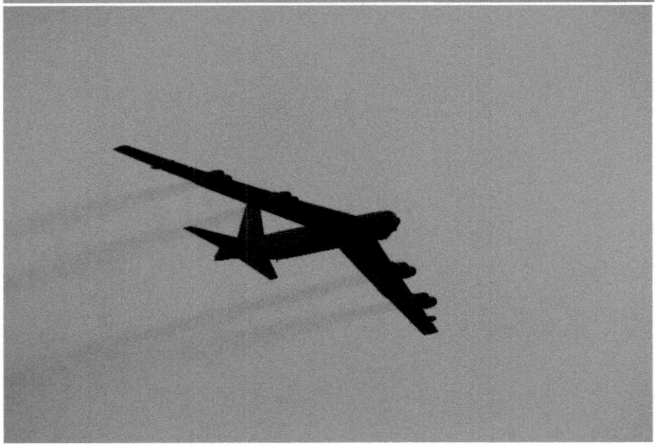

Quick Facts

General

Crew: 5 (pilot, copilot, weapon systems officer, navigator, electronic warfare officer)

Length: 159 ft 4 in (48.5 m)

Wingspan: 185 ft 0 in (56.4 m)

Height: 40 ft 8 in (12.4 m)

Performance

Maximum speed: 650 mph (1,050 km/h, 560 kn)

Cruise speed: 509 mph (819 km/h, 442 kn)

Combat range: 8,800 mi (14,200 km)

Armament

Guns: 1× 20 mm (0.787 in)

Bombs: Approximately 70,000 pounds (32,000 kg)

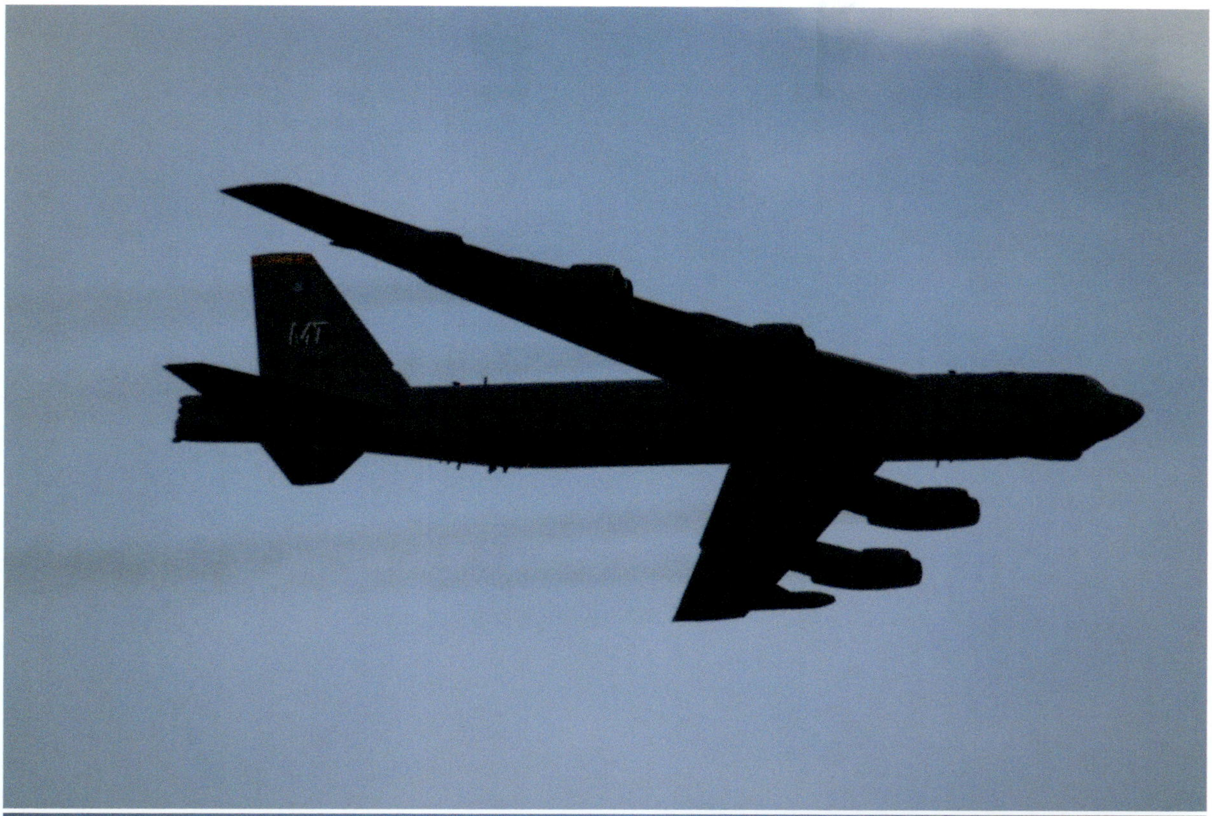

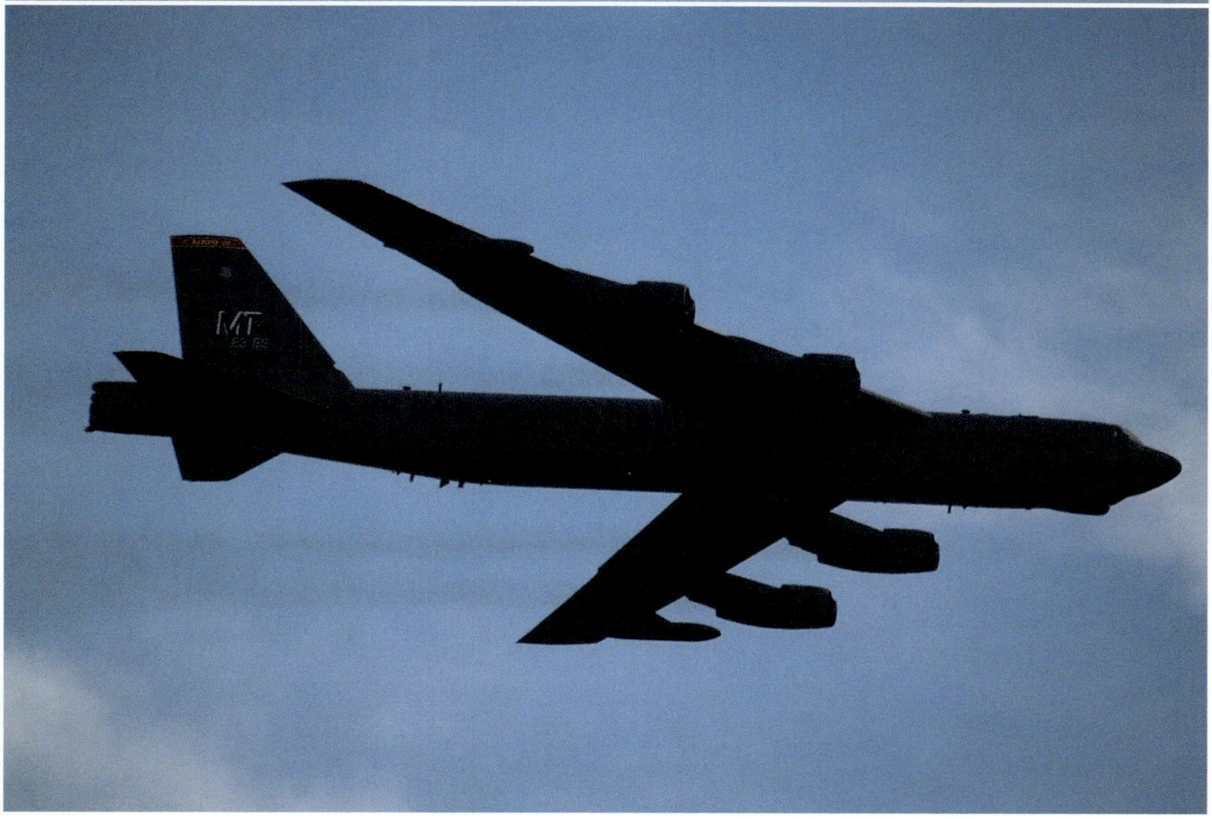

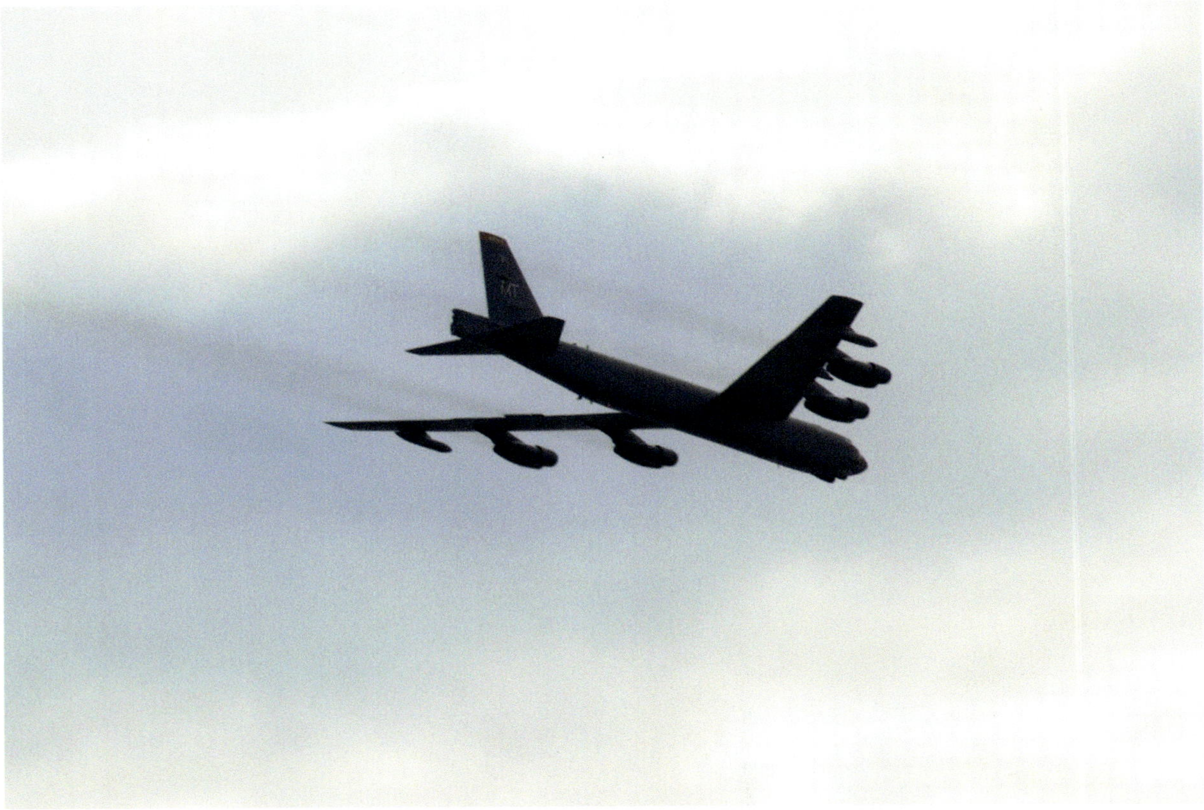

Avro Vulcan – XH558

The Avro Vulcan XH558, nicknamed "Spirit of Great Britain", was the last flying example of the Royal Air Force's 136 Avro Vulcan bombers that served during the Cold War. Bearing the military serial number XH558 and civil registration G-VLCN, this delta-winged jet was the final Vulcan in RAF service and the last one airborne after the fleet's retirement in 1986. First flown in 1960, XH558 was converted to a maritime reconnaissance aircraft in 1973, then an air-to-air refuelling tanker in 1982. After its withdrawal from service in 1984, it flew with the RAF's Vulcan Display Flight until 1992. On 28 October 2015, more than 50 years after its maiden flight, XH558 took to the skies for the final time.

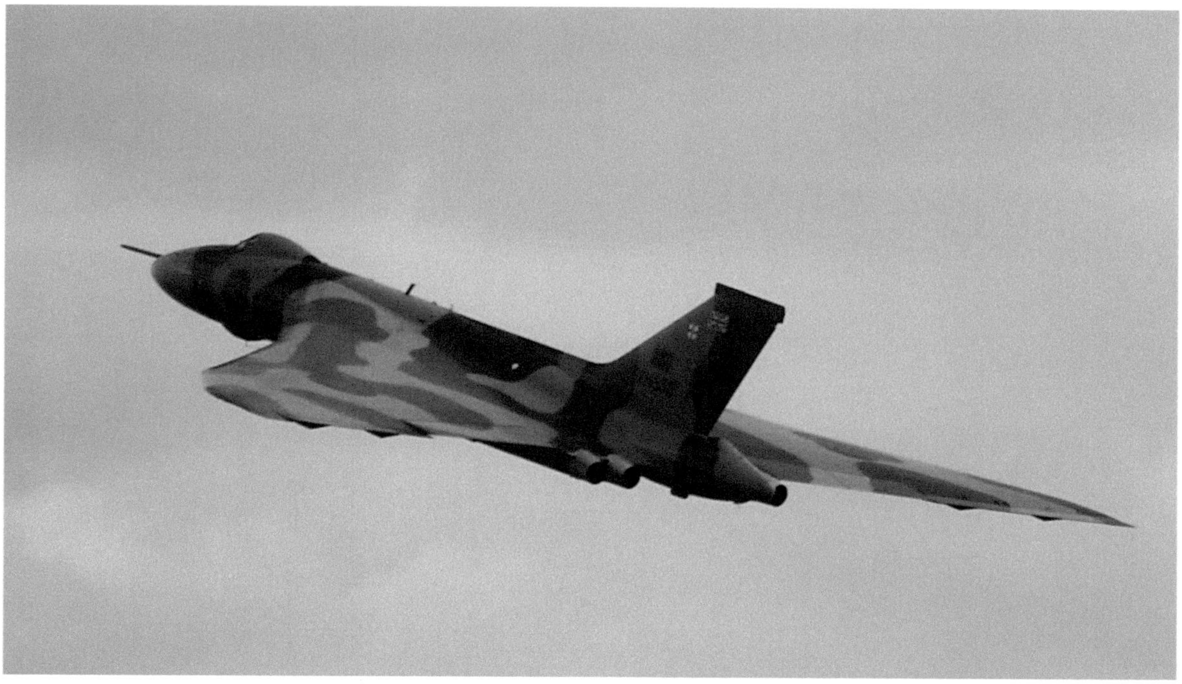

XH558 A Brief History

The Vulcan was produced at Woodford Aerodrome between 1956 and 1965, with 136 aircraft built in total. The first Vulcan entered operational service with the RAF on 20 May 1957. XH558, the first upgraded B2 model, made its inaugural flight from Woodford on 25 May 1960. It was then delivered to the RAF's No. 230 Operational Conversion Unit at Waddington, Lincolnshire on 1 July 1960.

In August 1973, XH558 was one of nine Vulcan bombers converted to a maritime radar reconnaissance configuration for use by No. 27 Squadron. By 1979, the Vulcan was deemed redundant, and the first aircraft was scrapped in December 1980. In 1982, XH558 became one of six Vulcans converted into aerial refuelling tankers, temporarily filling gaps in the RAF's tanker fleet caused by the Falklands War. XH558 was finally withdrawn from service on September 17, 1984.

XH558 was then chosen to perform display flights with the Royal Air Force's Vulcan Display Flight at Waddington Air Force Base. In 1985, it was restored to its original B2 configuration and made its first appearance at an airshow in Bournemouth in May of that year. XH558 flew with the Vulcan Display Flight for seven years until its final flight at Cranfield in September 1992.

Through public donations and lottery funding, the Vulcan To The Sky Trust restored the Vulcan bomber XH558 to airworthy condition. The Trust returned XH558 to flight on October 18, 2007, after raising £6.5 million in donations. XH558 resumed its airshow career in 2008, funded by ongoing donations of £2 million annually for operating costs. After extending its flying lifespan by two years, XH558 made its final flight on May 15, 2015 when the companies maintaining it withdrew support. Since retiring from flight, XH558 is now maintained in taxiable condition along with two other surviving Vulcan bombers, XL426 and XM655.

The majestic XH558 plane delighted crowds at the Bournemouth Air Festival, but its 2015 show marked an emotional finale - the vintage jet's last flight over Bournemouth on August 23rd left fans mourning the end of an era as that would be the last time we see XH558 in our skyline.

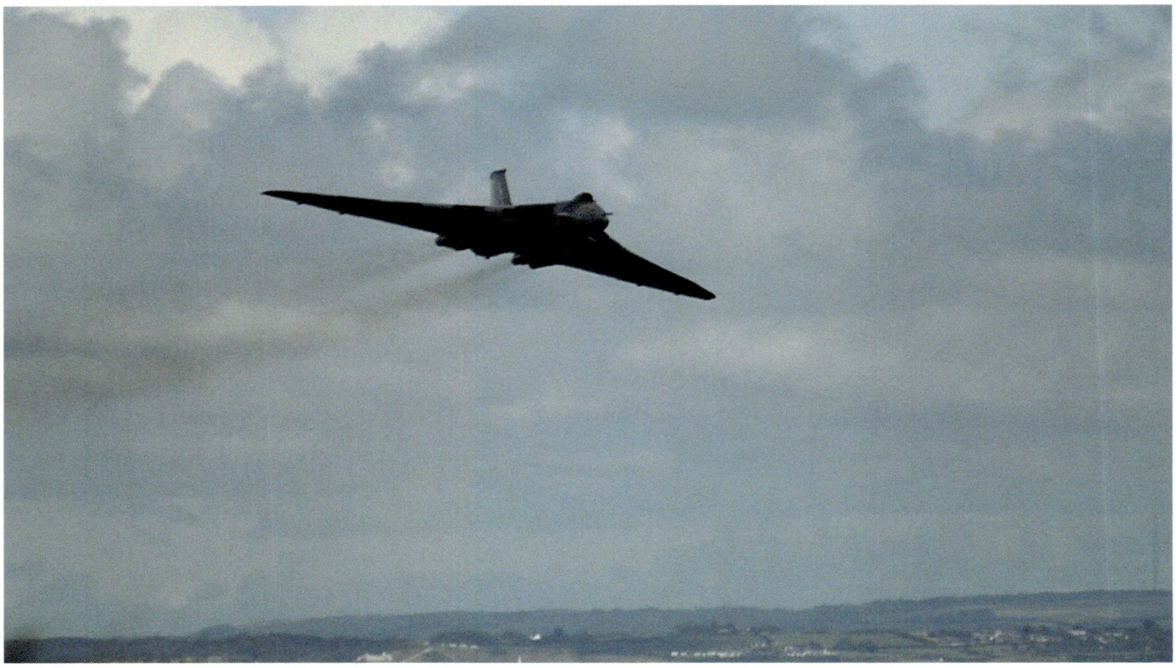

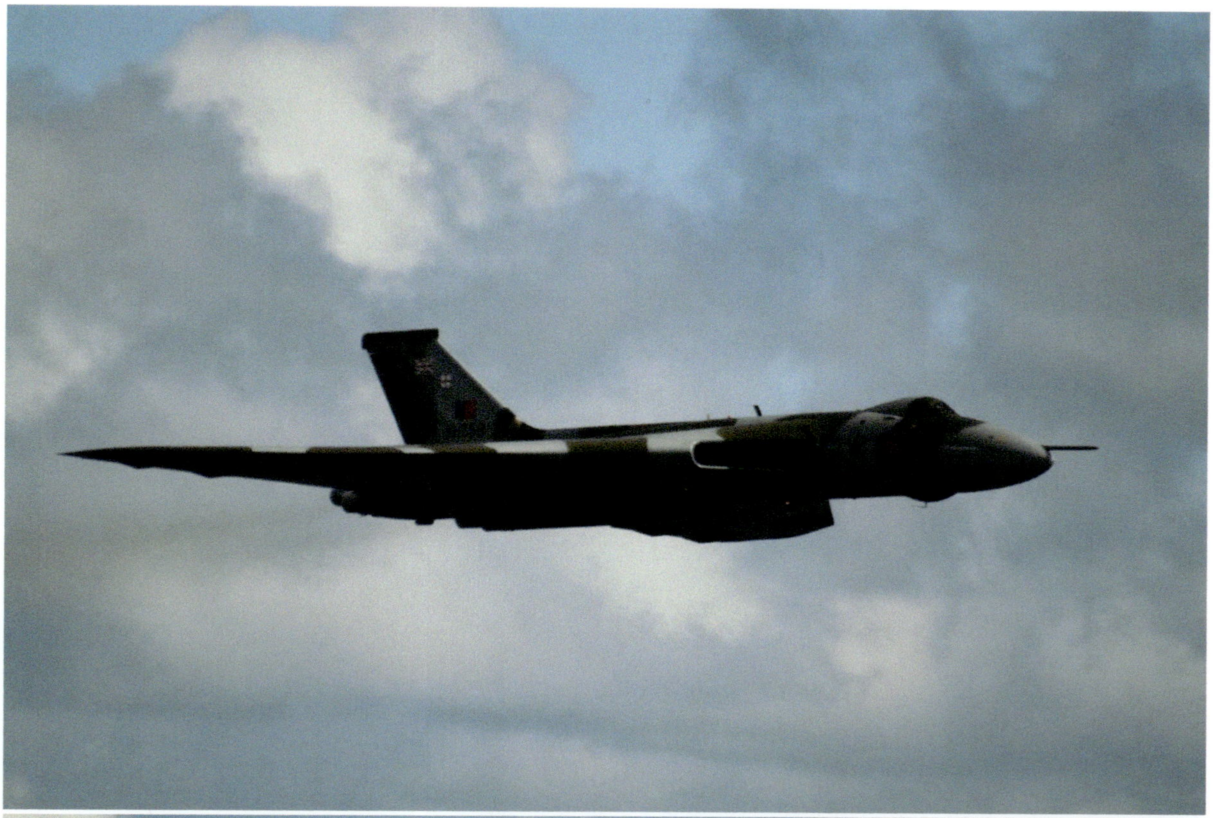

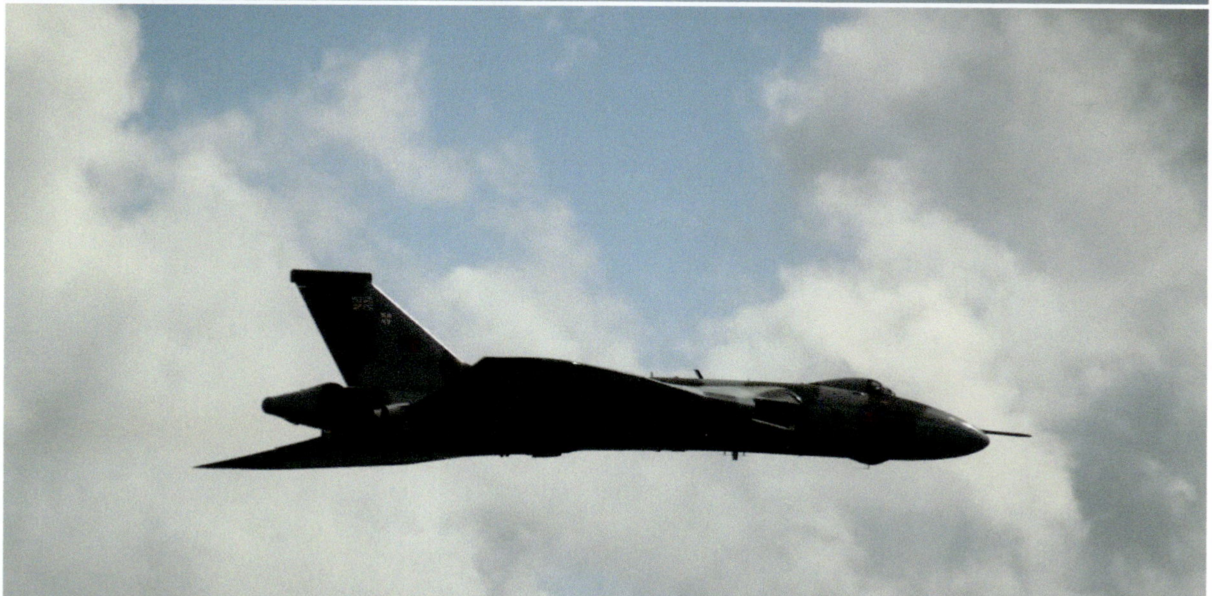

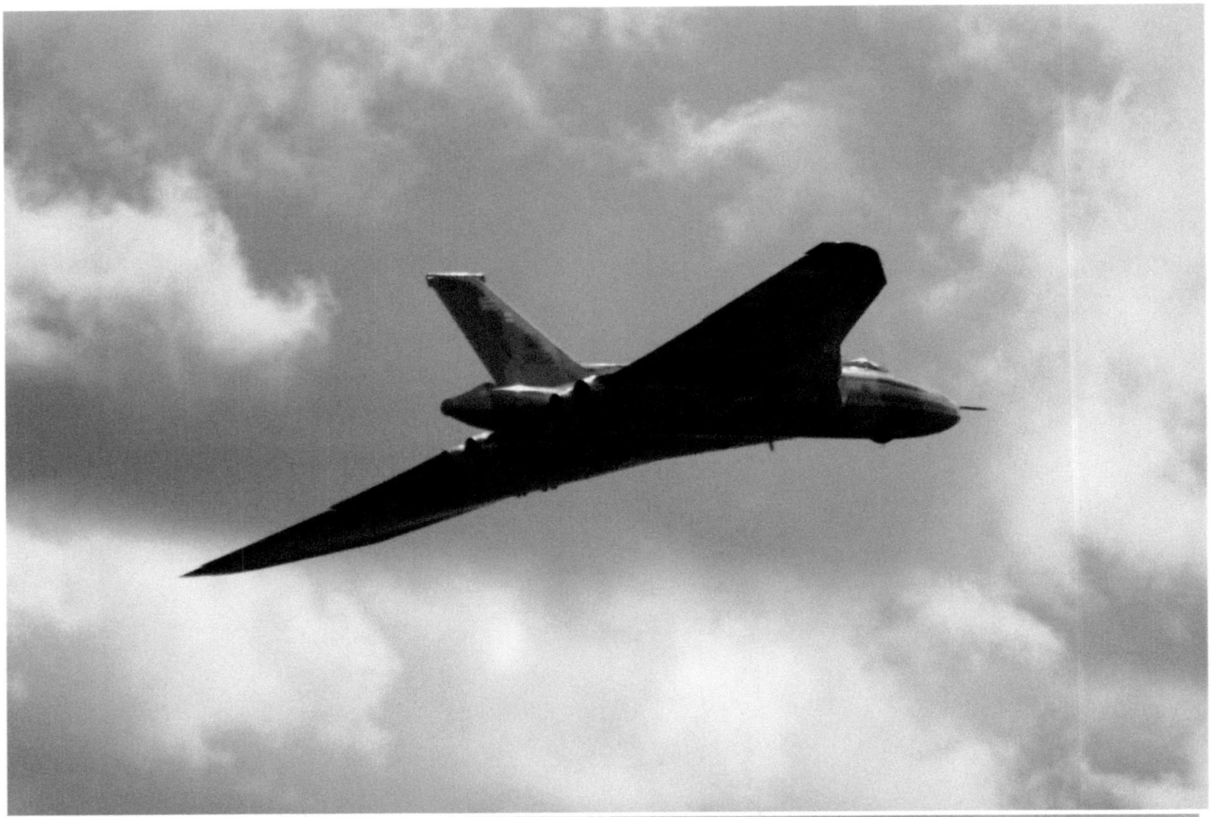

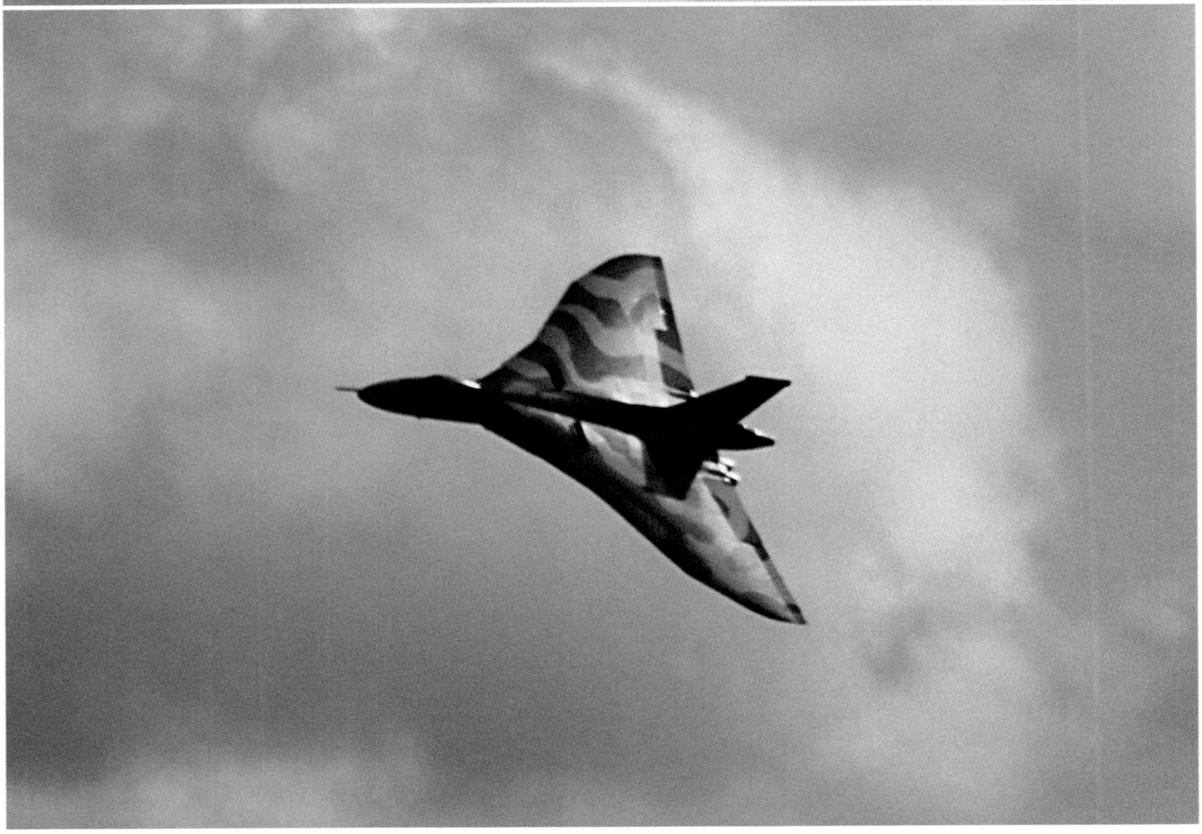

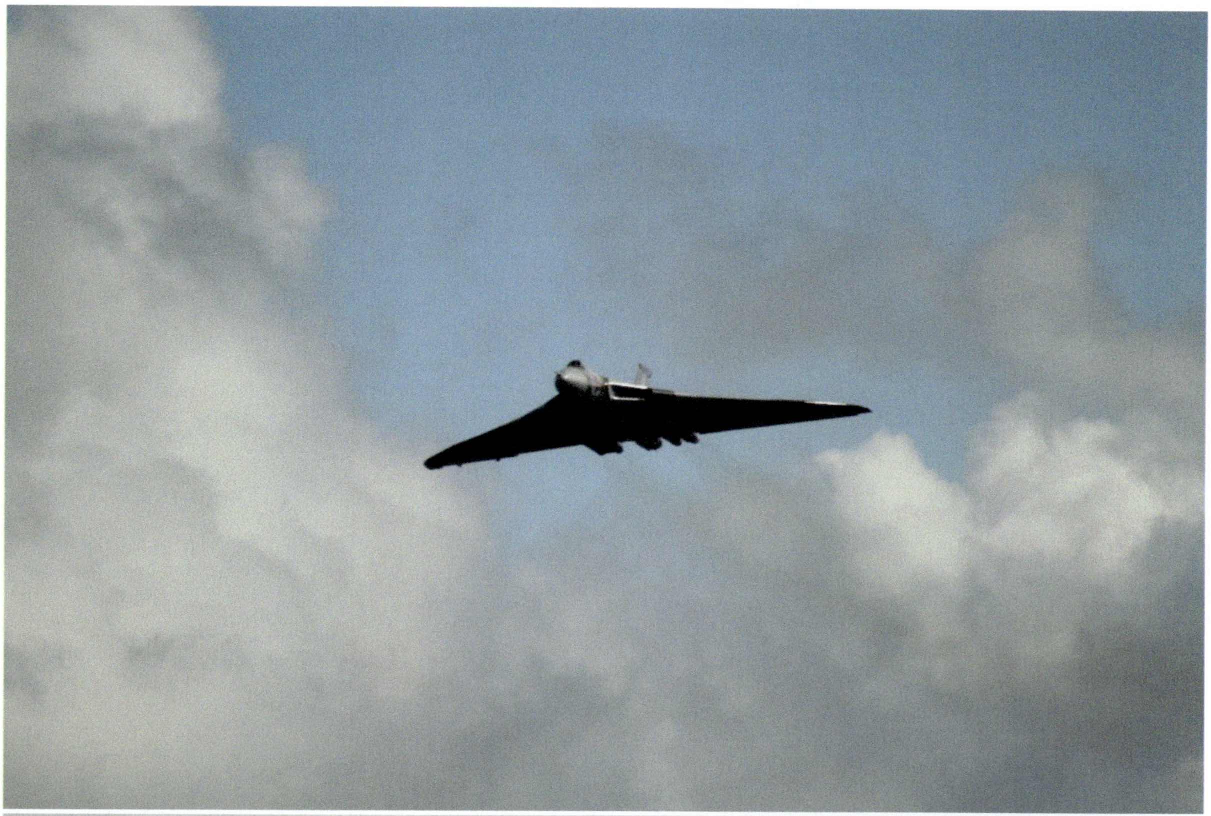

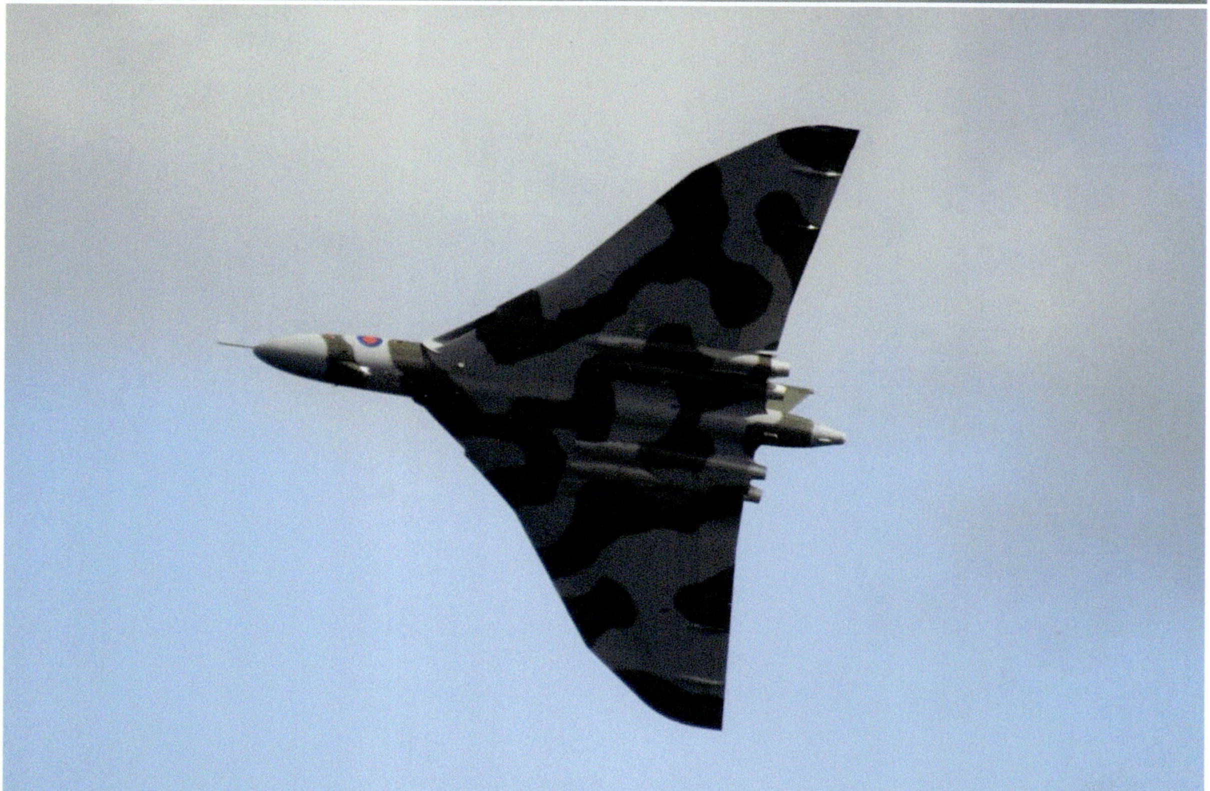

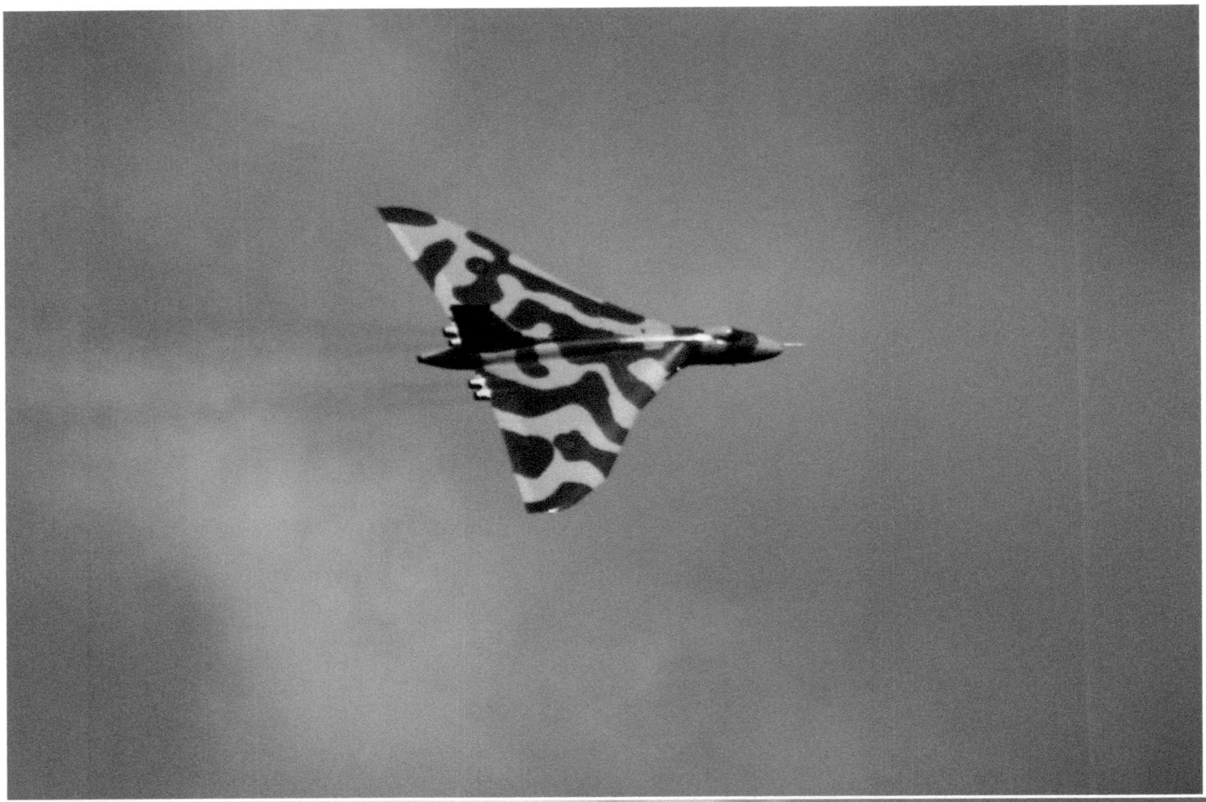

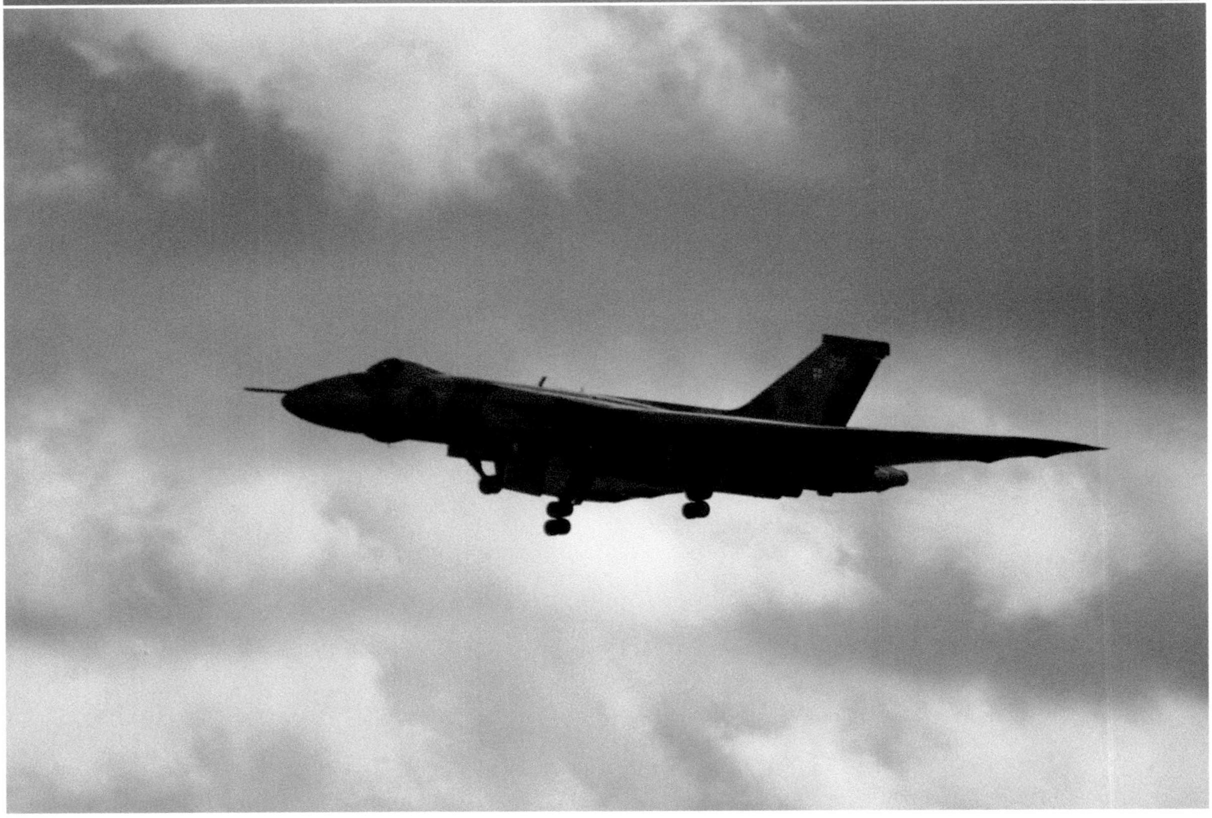

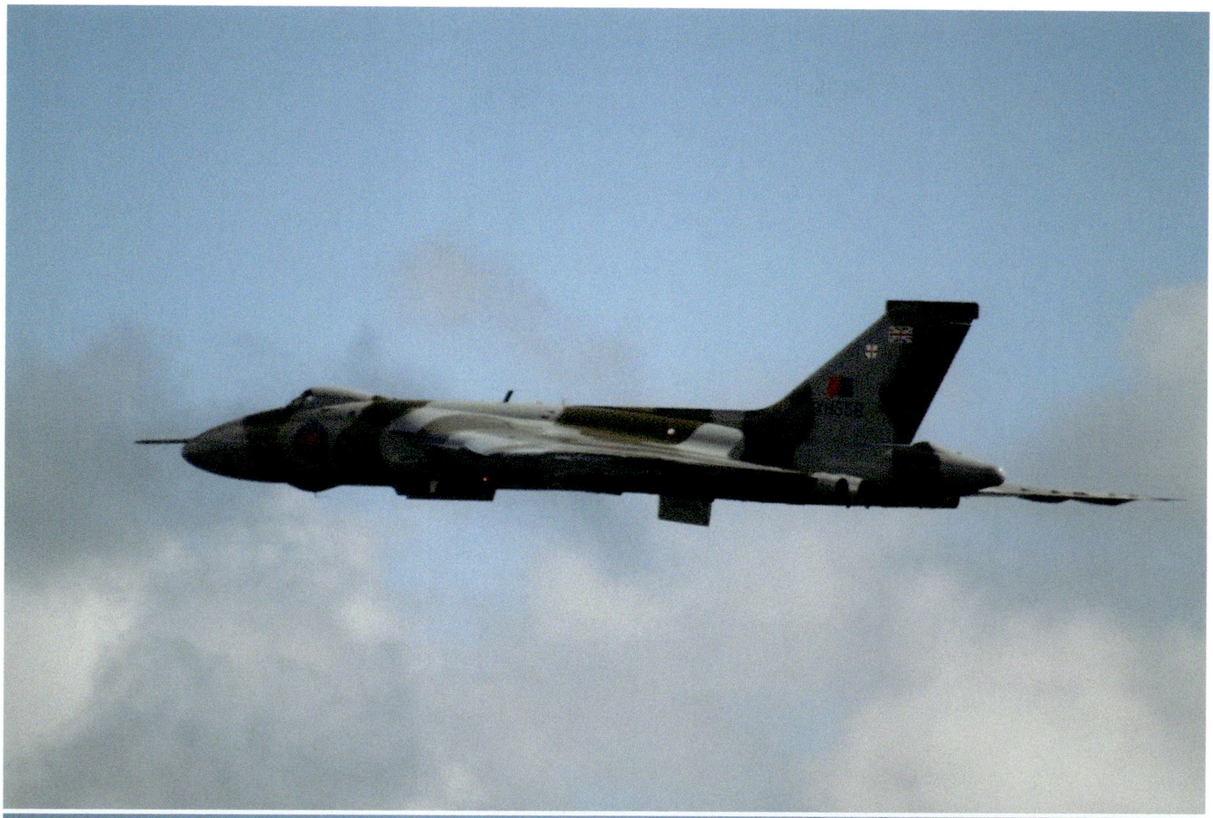

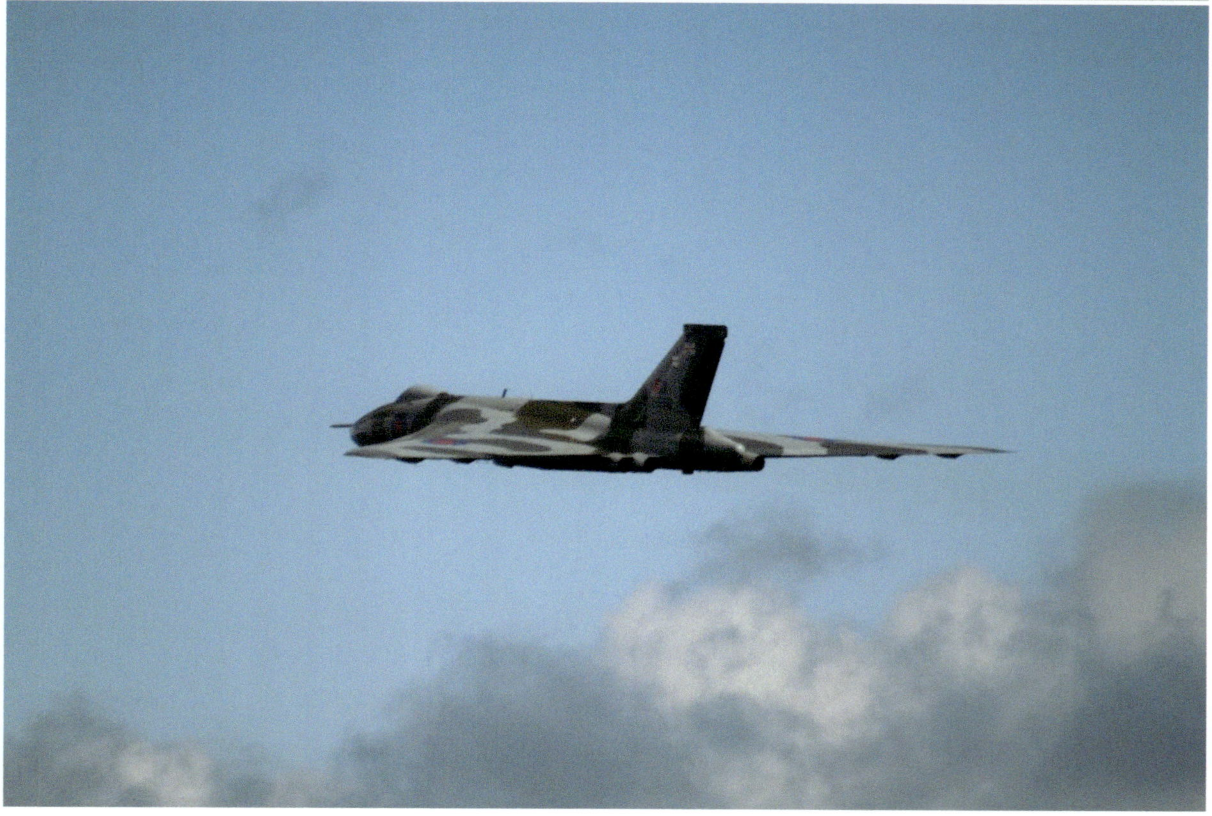

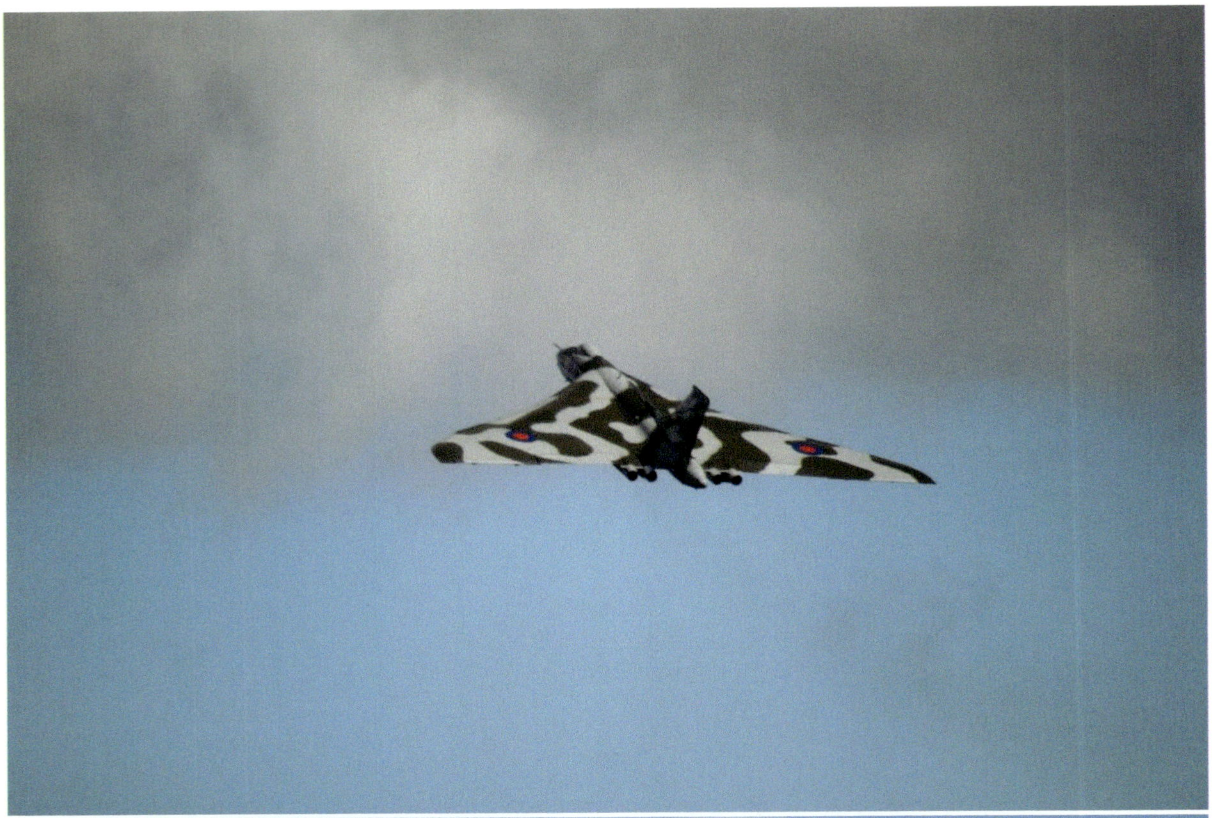

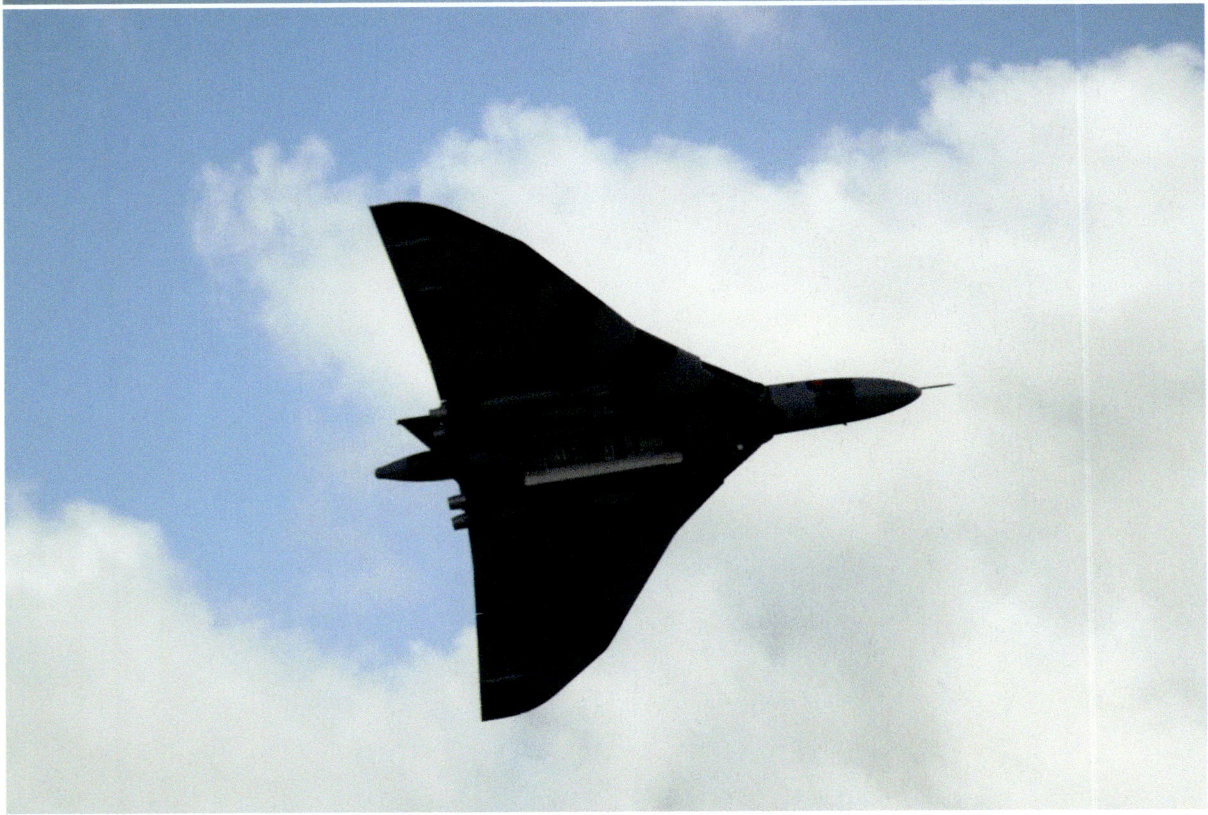

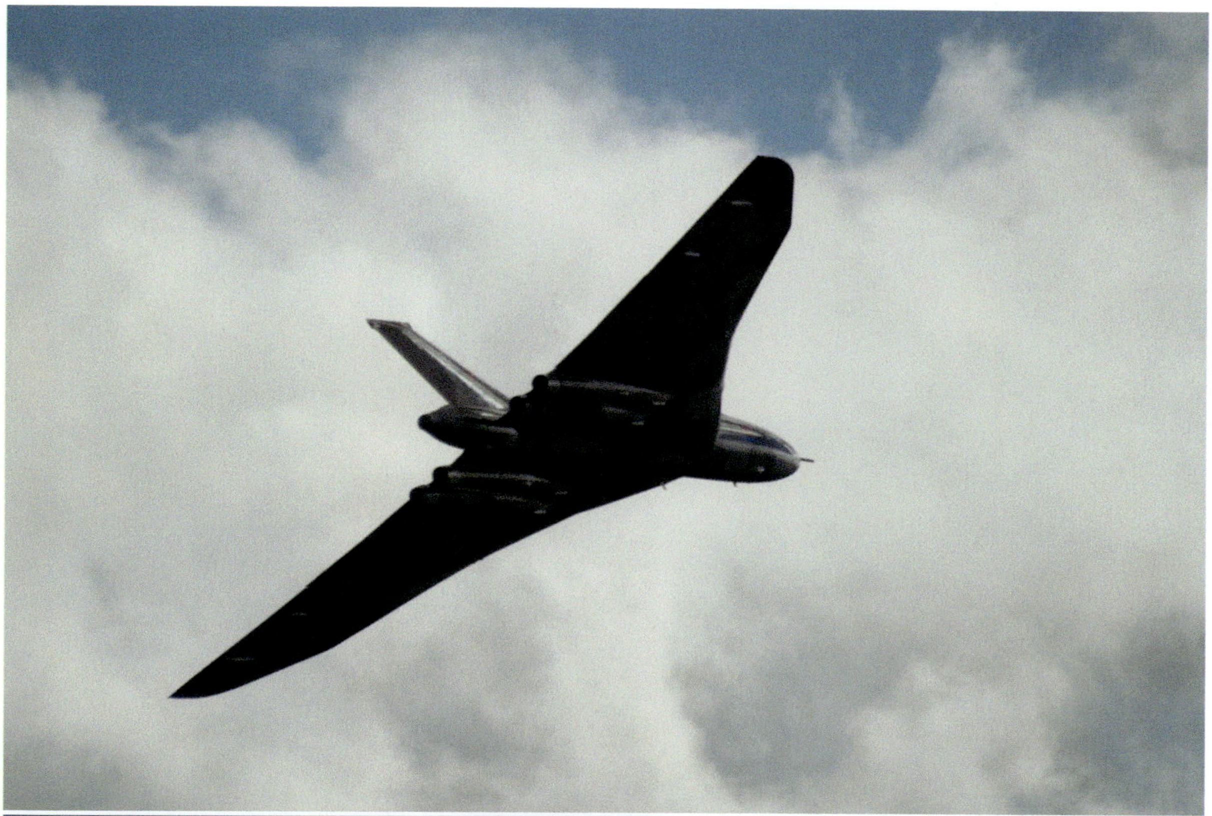

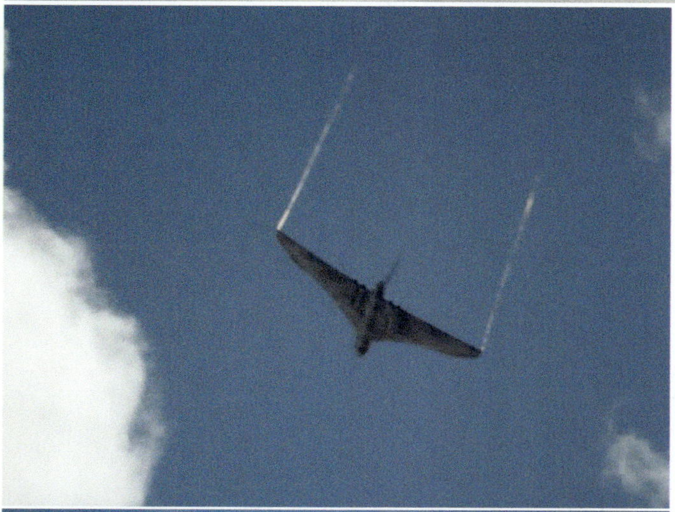

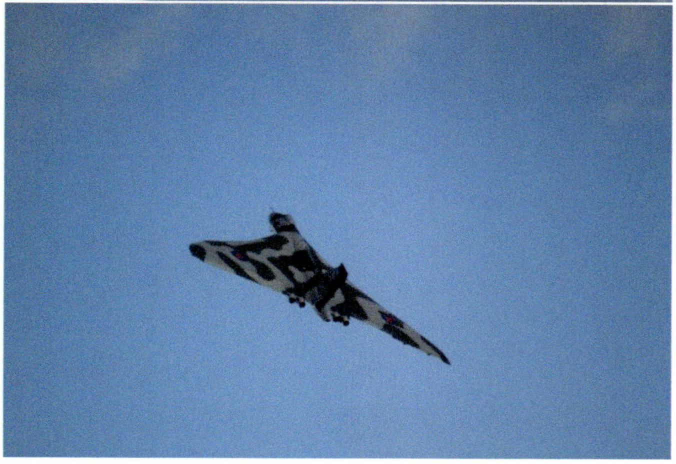

Quick Facts

General

Crew: 5 (pilot, co-pilot, AEO, navigator radar, navigator plotter)

Length: 97 ft 1 in (29.59 m)

Wingspan: 99 ft 5 in (30.30 m)

Height: 26 ft 6 in (8.08 m)

Performance

Maximum speed: (646 mph, 1,039 km/h)

Maximum speed: Mach 0.96

Cruise speed: (567 mph, 913 km/h)

Armament

21 × 1,000 pounds (454 kg) of conventional bombs

1 × Blue Danube nuclear gravity bomb

1 × Violet Club 400 kt nuclear gravity bomb

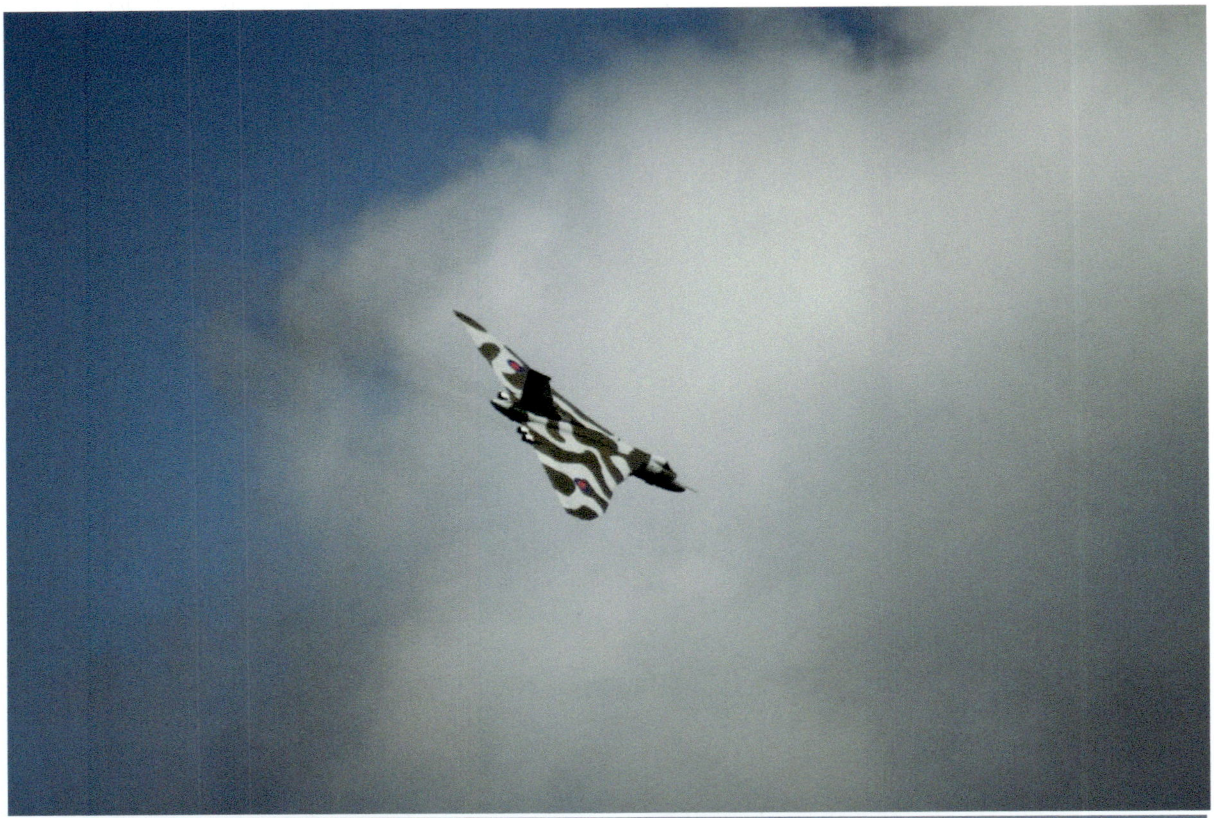

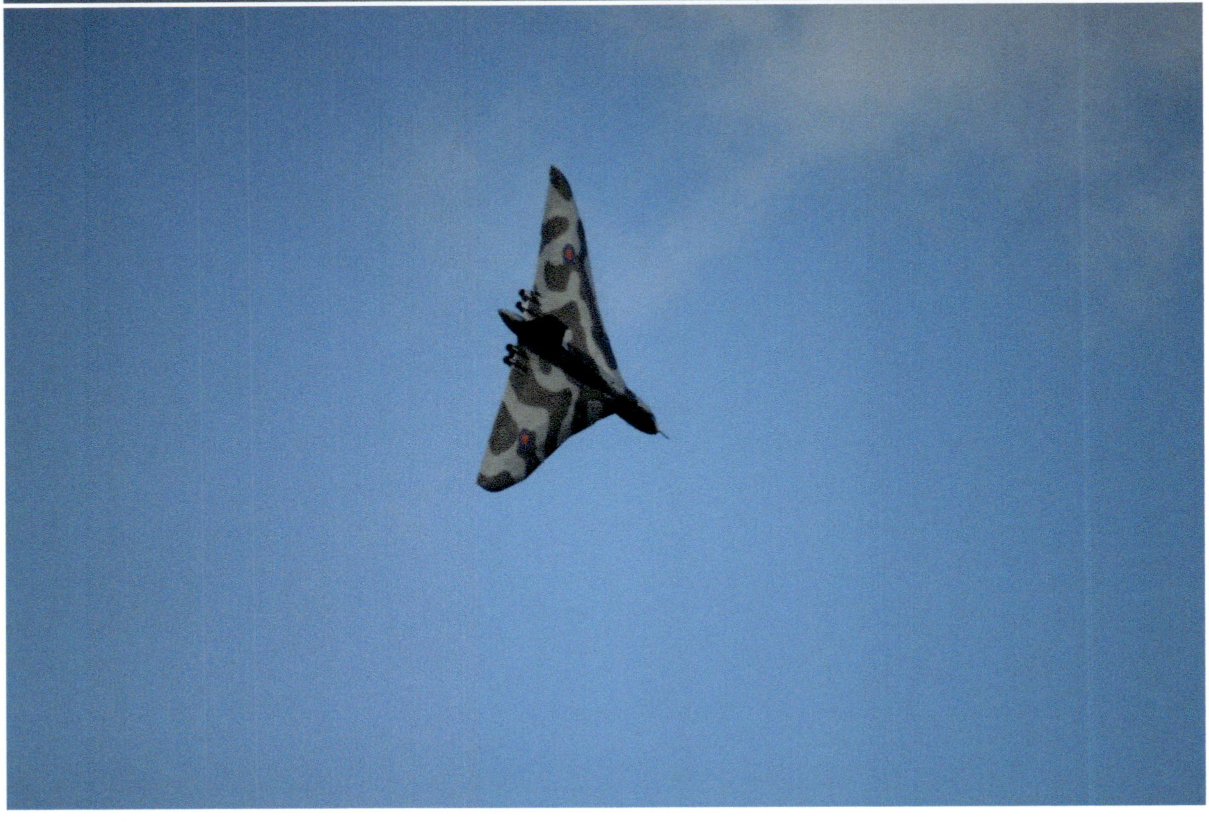

Breitling Jet Team

Established in 2003 by a group of experienced French military pilots, the Breitling Jet Team started with four L-39 Albatros aircraft before expanding to a seven-jet formation. The planes feature distinctive Breitling livery, reflecting the Swiss luxury watchmaker's sponsorship of and partnership with the team.

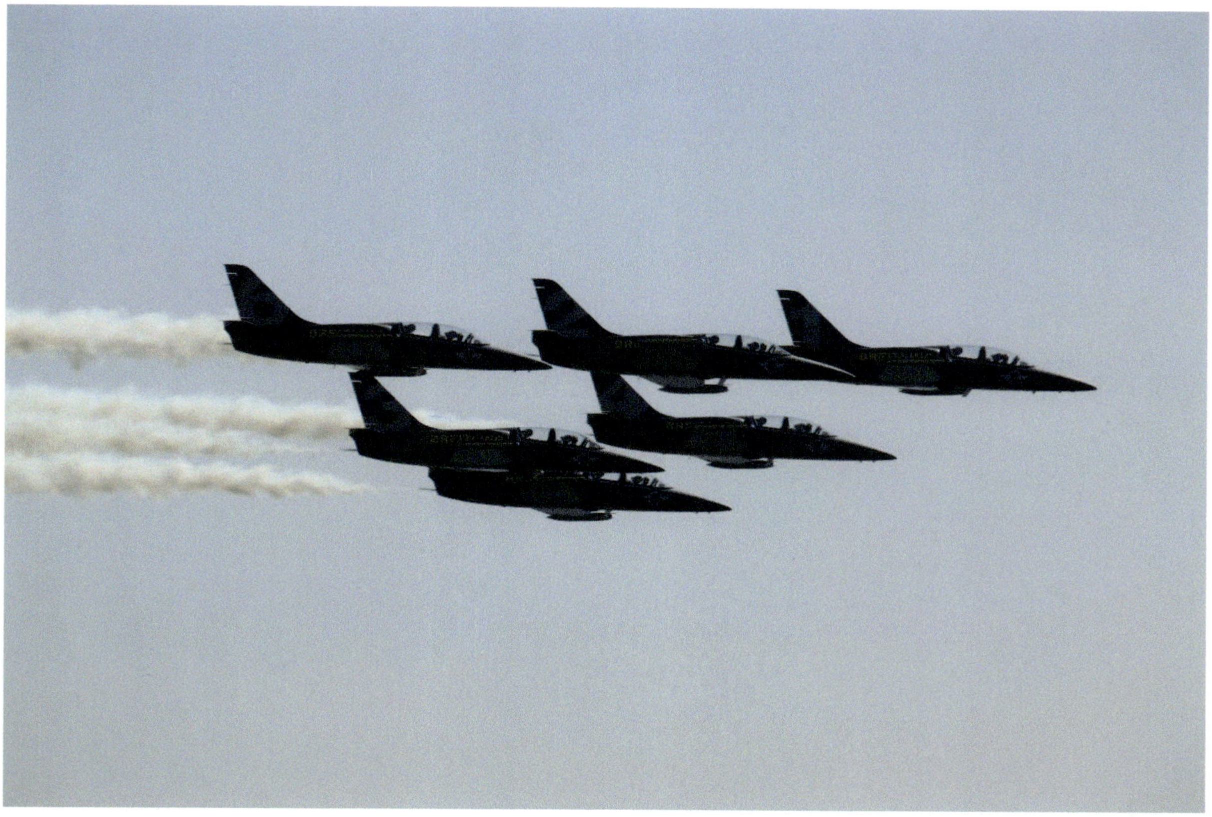

The Breitling Jet Team made their debut at the 2018 Bournemouth Airfestival, performing their display from Friday to Sunday. This marked both their first and unfortunately last appearance at the Airfestival, as Breitling withdrew sponsorship in 2019, leading the team to subsequently discontinue performances.

L-39 Albatros

The Aero L-39 Albatros, designed and produced in Czechoslovakia by Aero Vodochody, is the world's most widely used jet trainer. In addition to its primary roles of basic and advanced pilot training, the high-performance L-39 has also flown combat missions in a light attack capacity.

The L-39 Albatros was designed to be a cost-effective jet-powered trainer aircraft that can also conduct ground attack missions. To maximize operational flexibility, simplicity, and affordability, most onboard systems were simplified to reduce maintenance needs and minimize damage from mishandling by inexperienced aircrews.

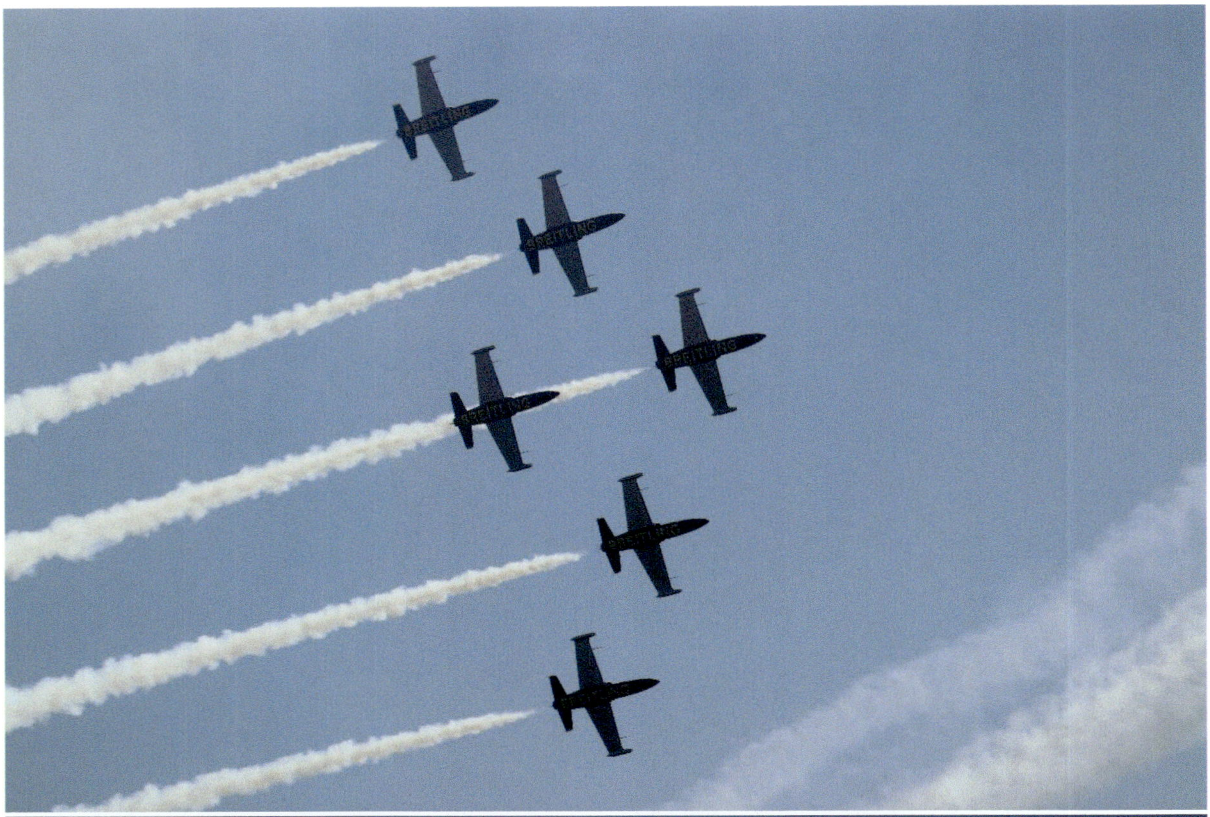
BREITLING

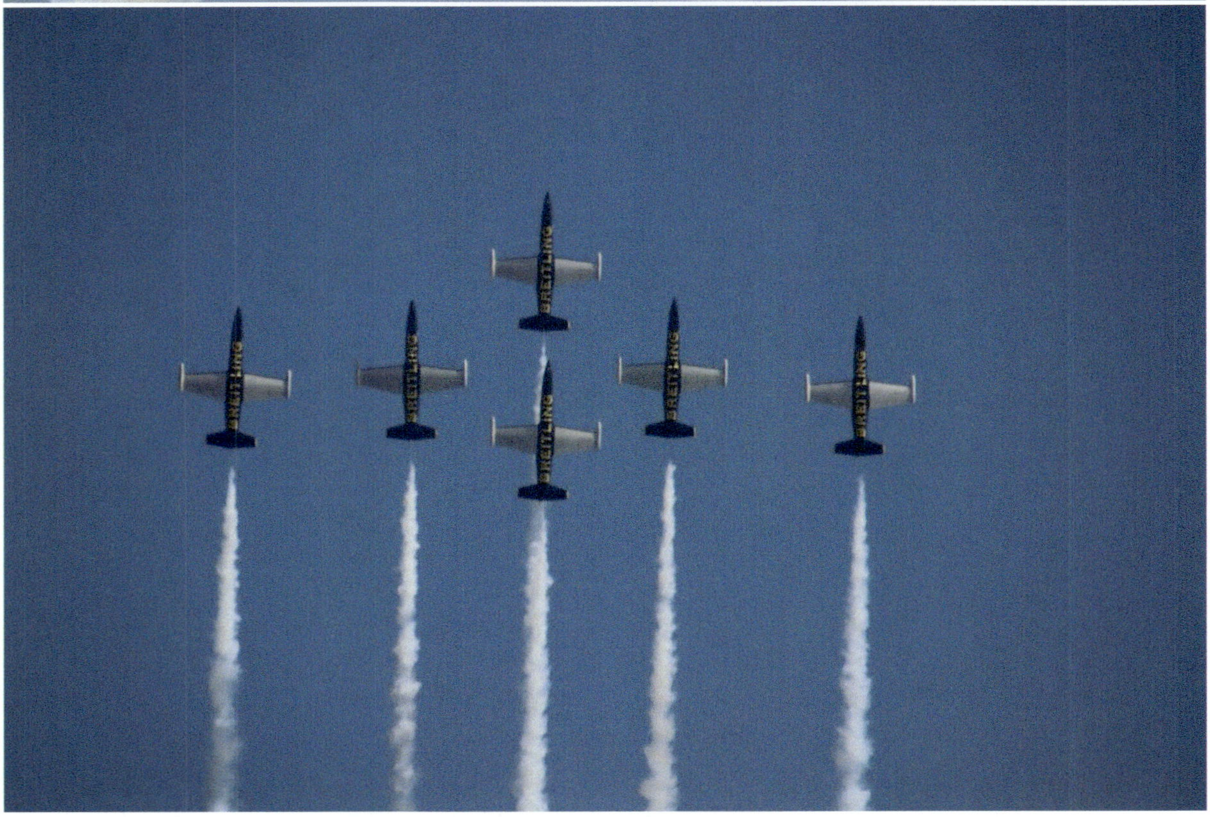
BREITLING

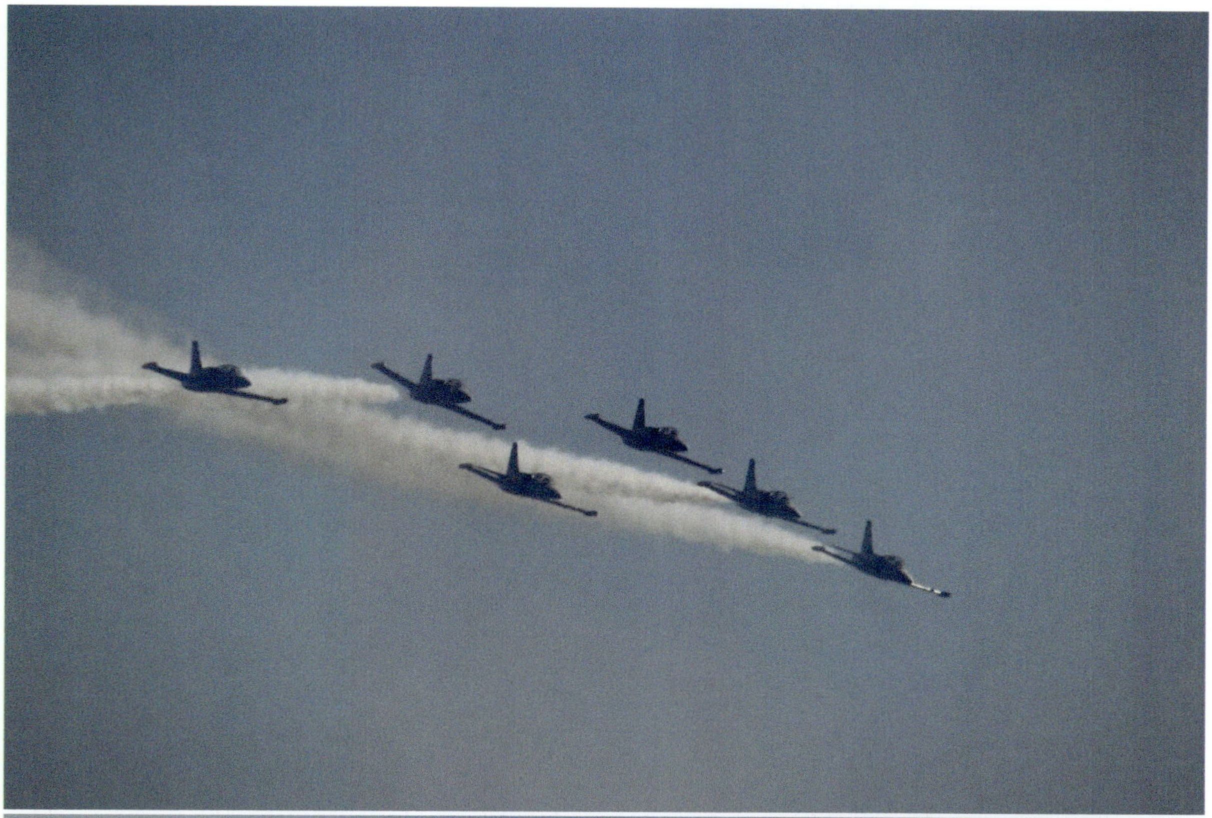

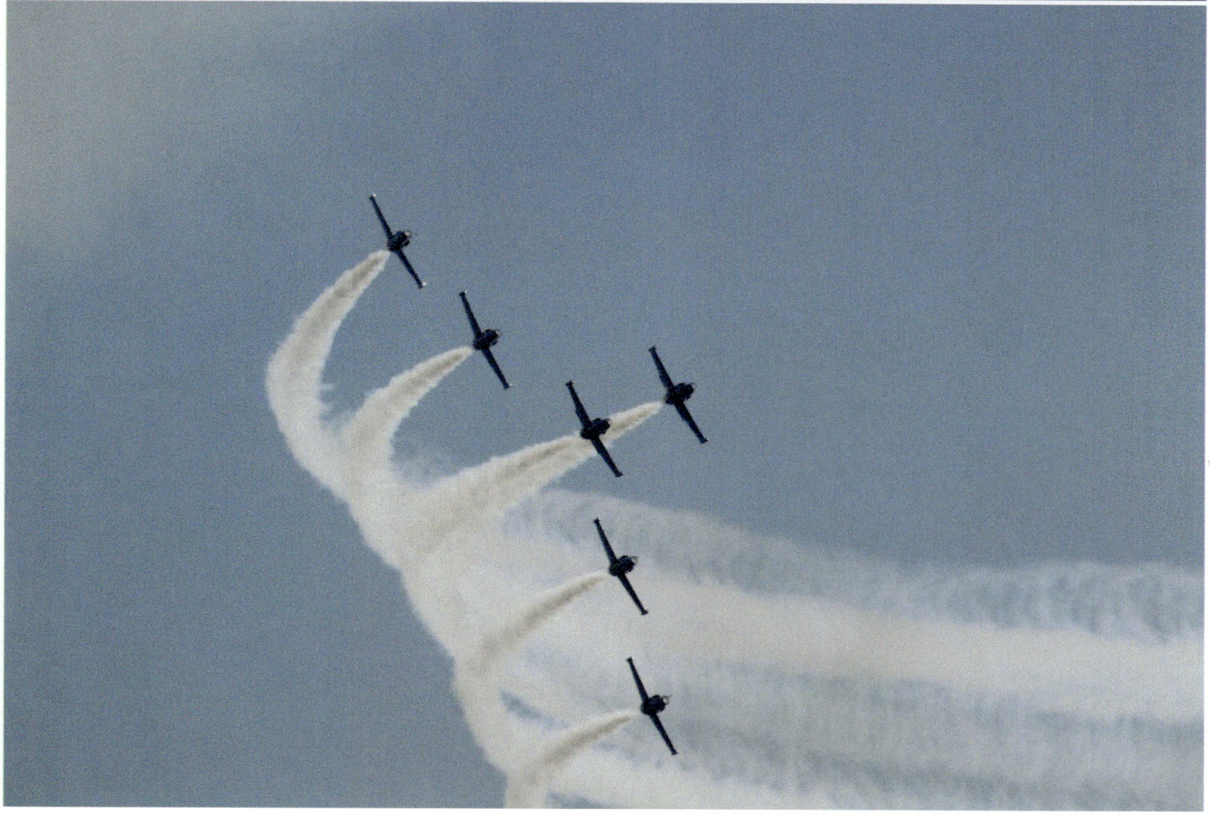

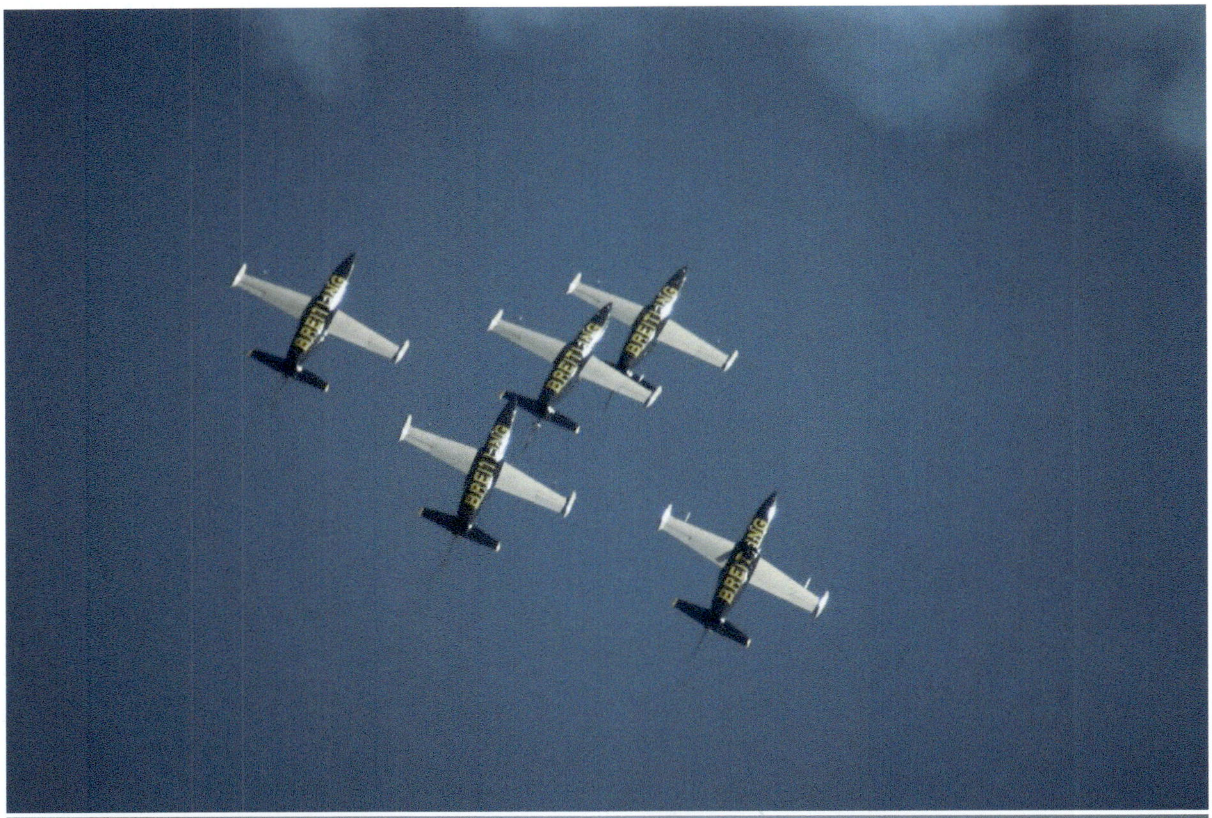
BREITLING

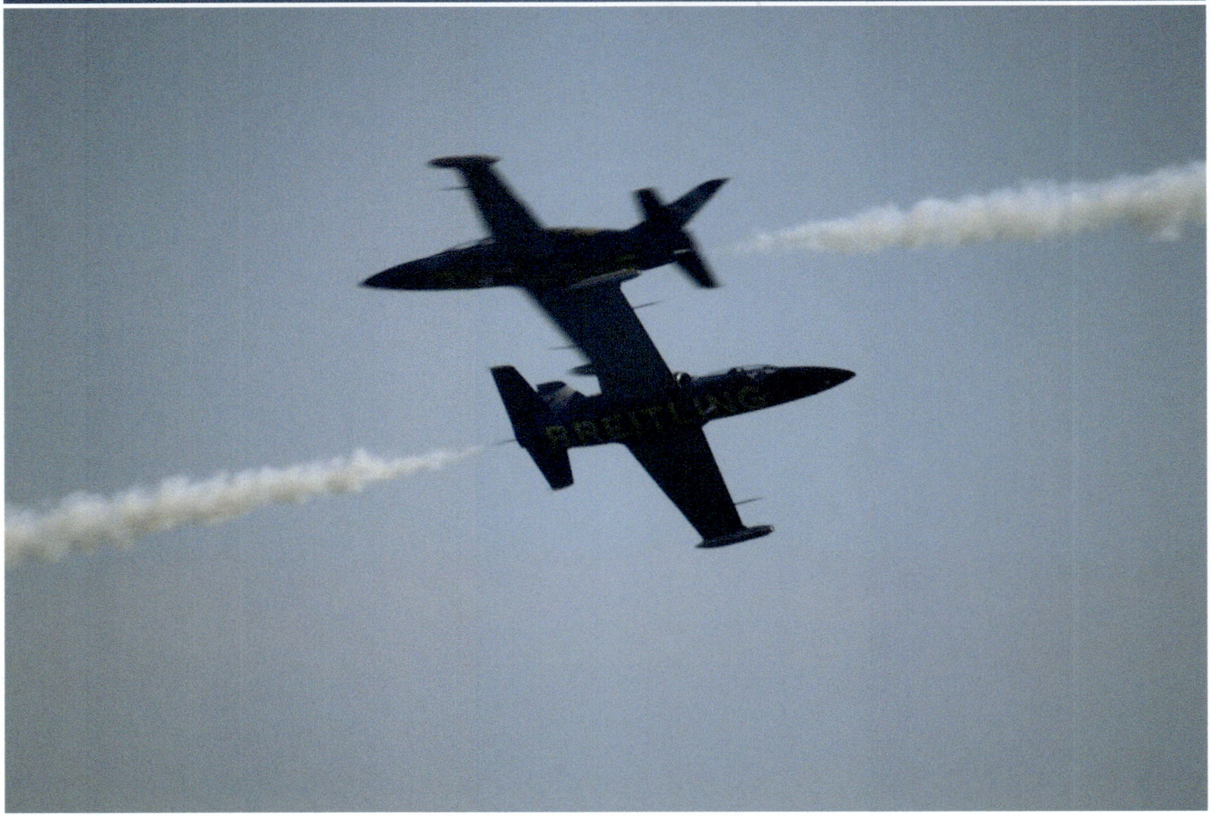
BREITLING

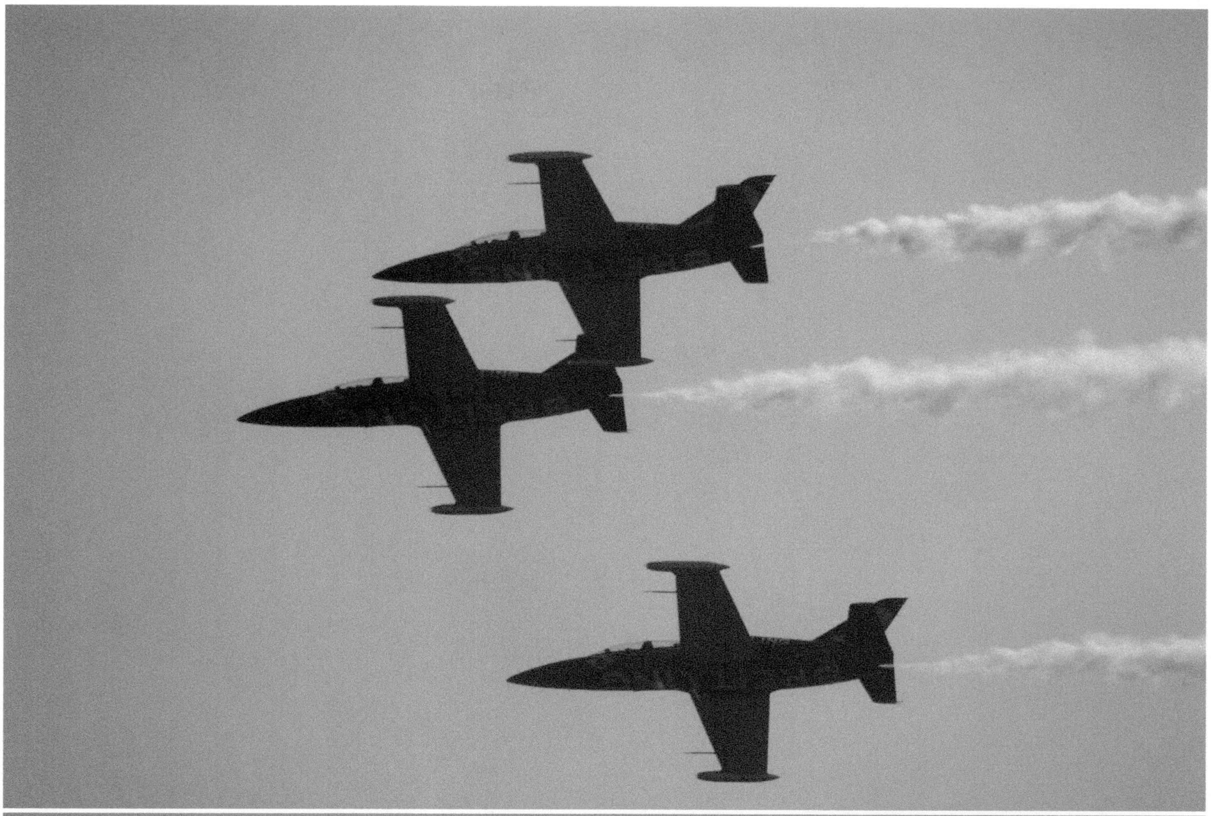

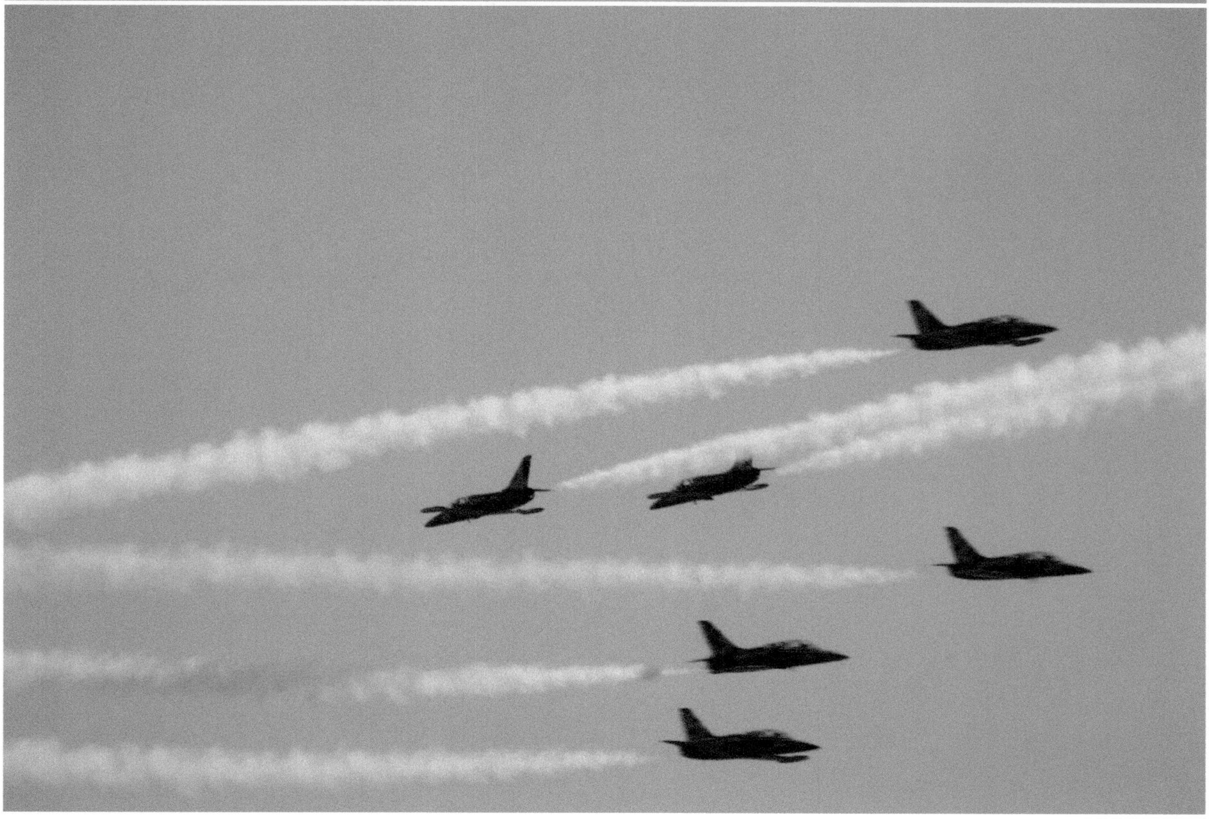

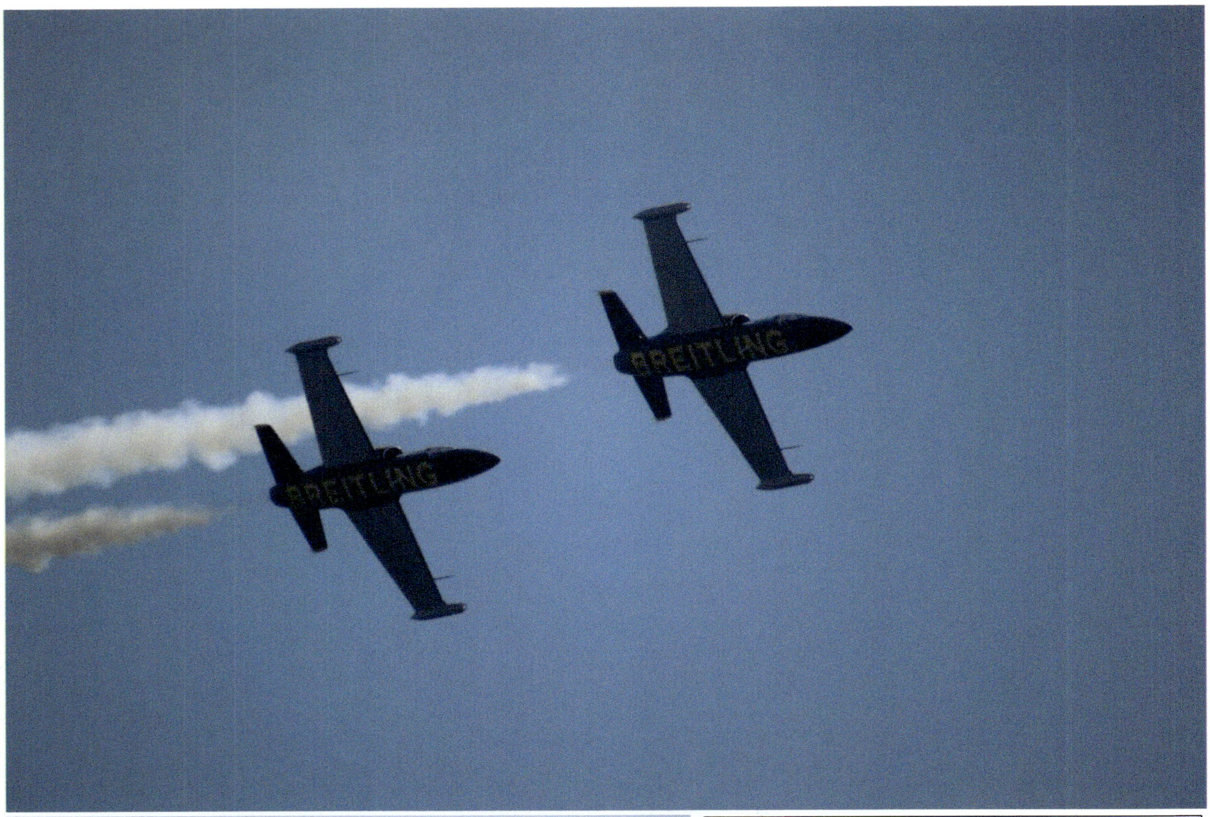

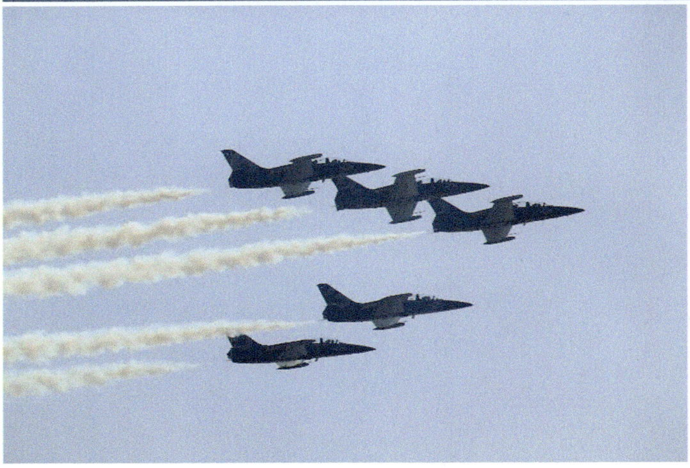

Quick Facts

General

Crew: 2

Length: 12.13 m (39 ft 10 in)

Wingspan: 9.46 m (31 ft 0 in)

Height: 4.77 m (15 ft 8 in)

Performance

Maximum speed: 750 km/h (470 mph)

Range: 1,100 km (680 mi)

Armament

Up to 2,425 pounds of weapons on four underwing hardpoints, including bombs, 57- or 130-mm rocket pods, gun pods.

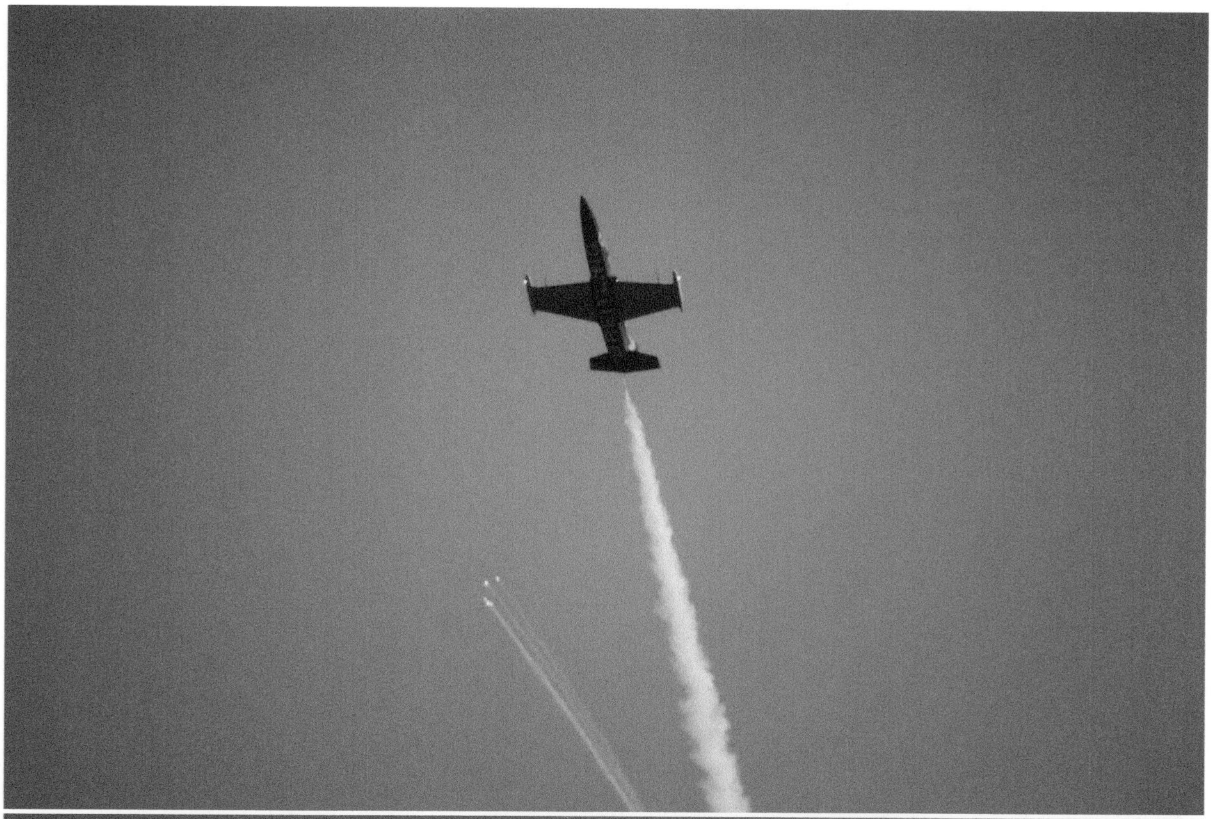

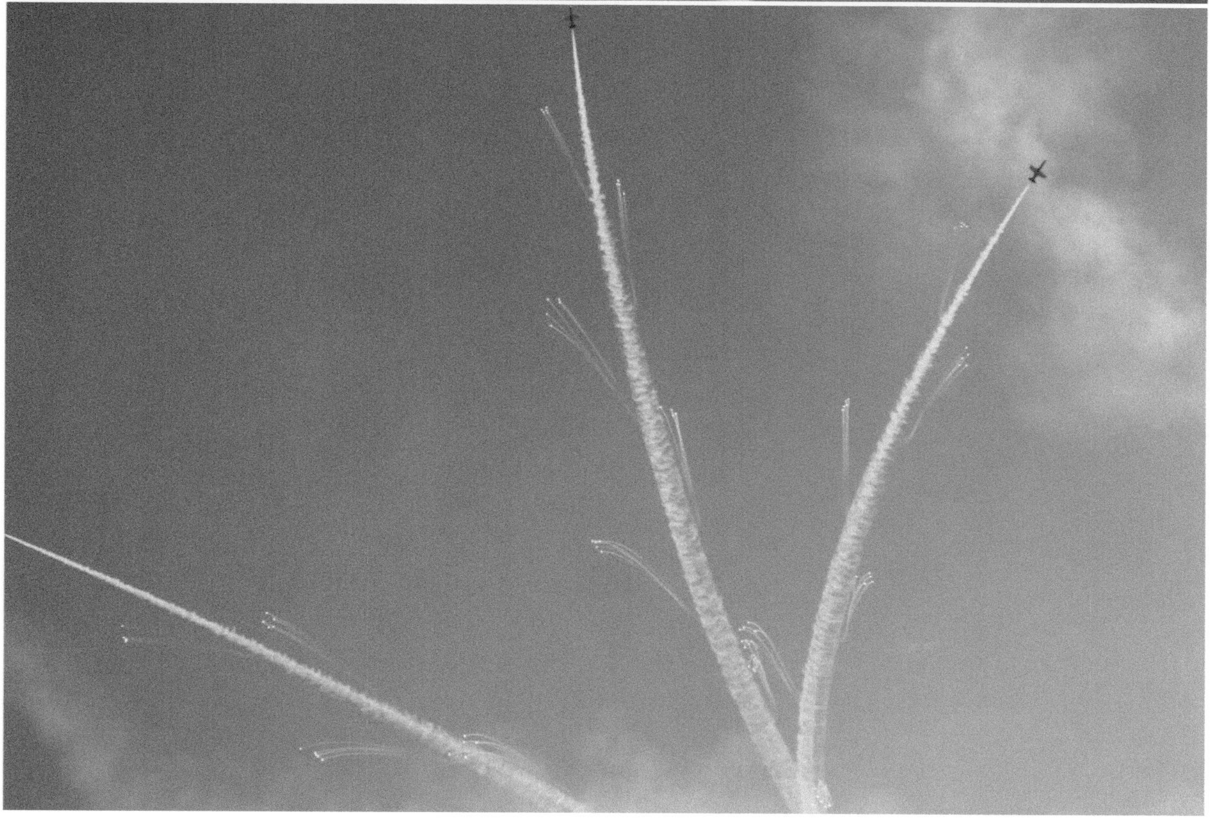

Tigers Army Parachute Display Team

The 9-member Princess of Wales's Royal Regiment Tigers Freefall Army Parachute Display Team was established in 1986. The team performs daytime and nighttime parachute displays over water, land, and into stadia from various heights. Their routines utilize massive 2000 sq ft flags, smoke, and specialised techniques for jumping into tight spaces.

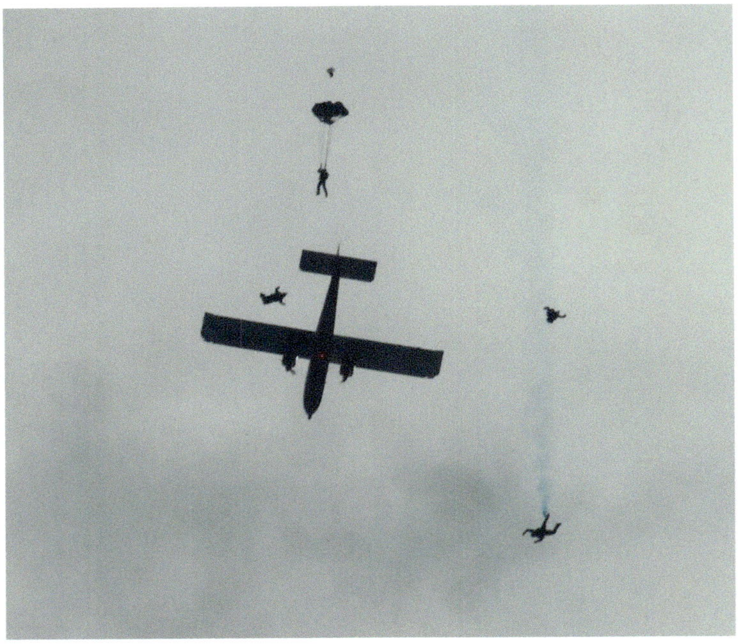

All members of The Tigers are active service persons and provide the thrilling displays of freefall and parachuting in their spare time. The Tigers are a firm favourite of the Airfestival and have performed at every Airfestival since its inception.

The team feels a strong sense of competition, as those who land closest to the orange target on the beach are deemed the best jumpers. When preparing to leap from 15,000 feet or higher, the tiny target and coastal winds pose significant challenges.

The Tigers perform different routines with their jump and bring variety to the Airfestival. Over the years we have seen freefall, connection of three parachutists before braking into their landing formation. One team member also wore a wingsuit and hurtled towards the ground over the heads on the crowd before deploying their parachute at the last possible moment.

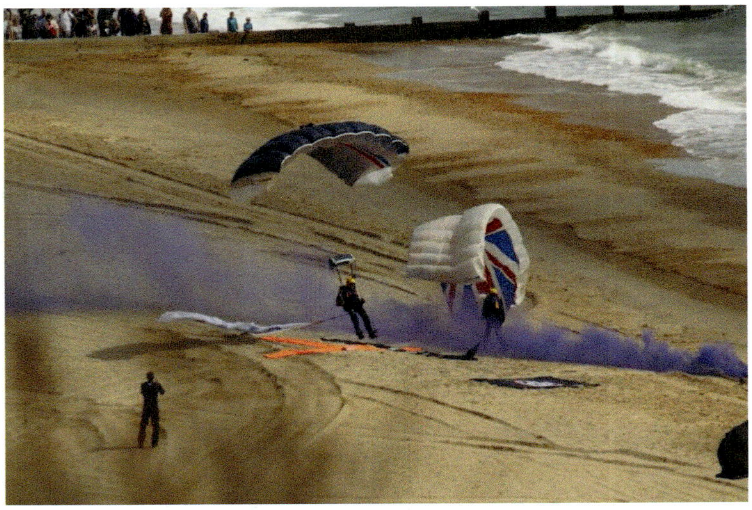

One of the most gripping displays during the day was when a team member deployed their parachute then proceeded to cut the chute free, before deploying their reserve chute. This was to demonstrate the procedure to follow should the first chute fail or get tangled up, this was definitely a jaw dropping moment.

The team have smoke pods on their boots, which also add to the dramatic displays performed by The Tiger. They also deploy flags from their boots to promote the Army and the work of the team and also their charitable partners and sponsors. The largest flag to date was at the 2023 Airfestival, this was a 2000 sq ft Army flag. They also perform dusk jumps with pyrotechnics and glowing jumpsuits.

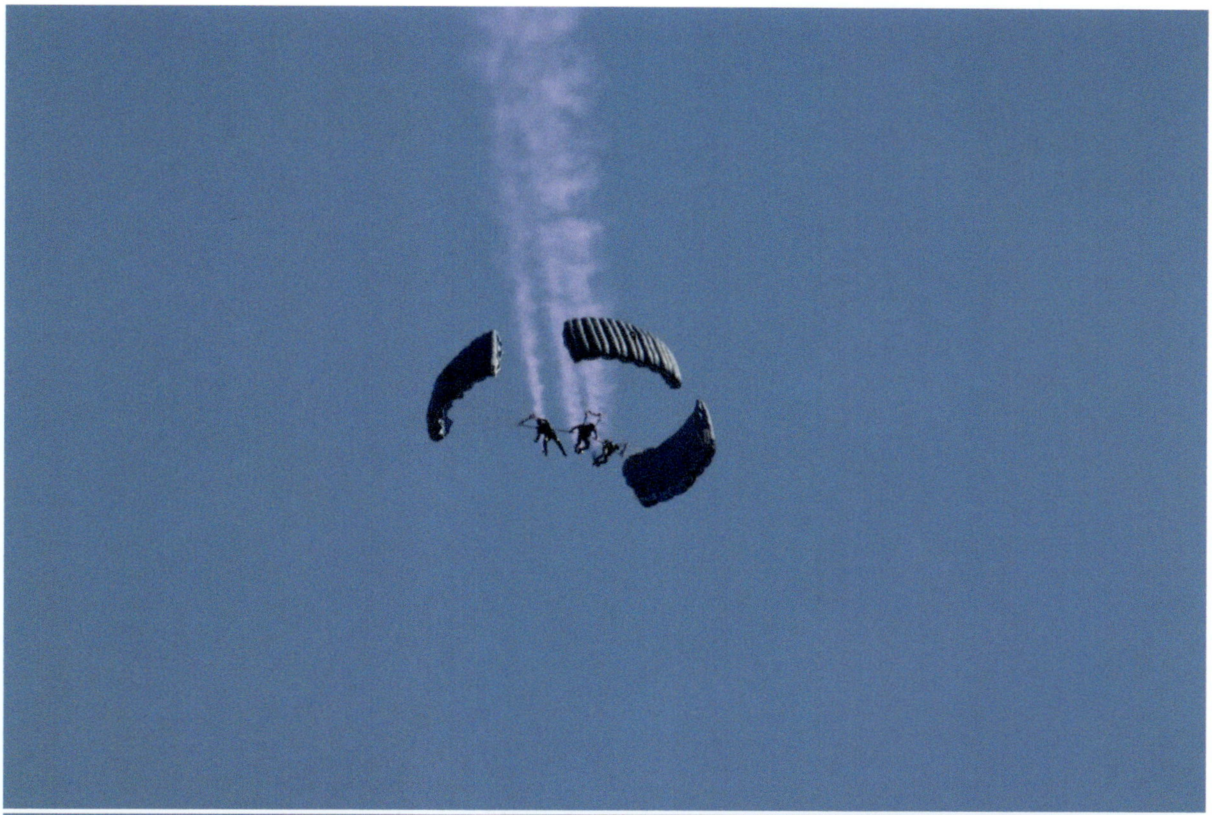

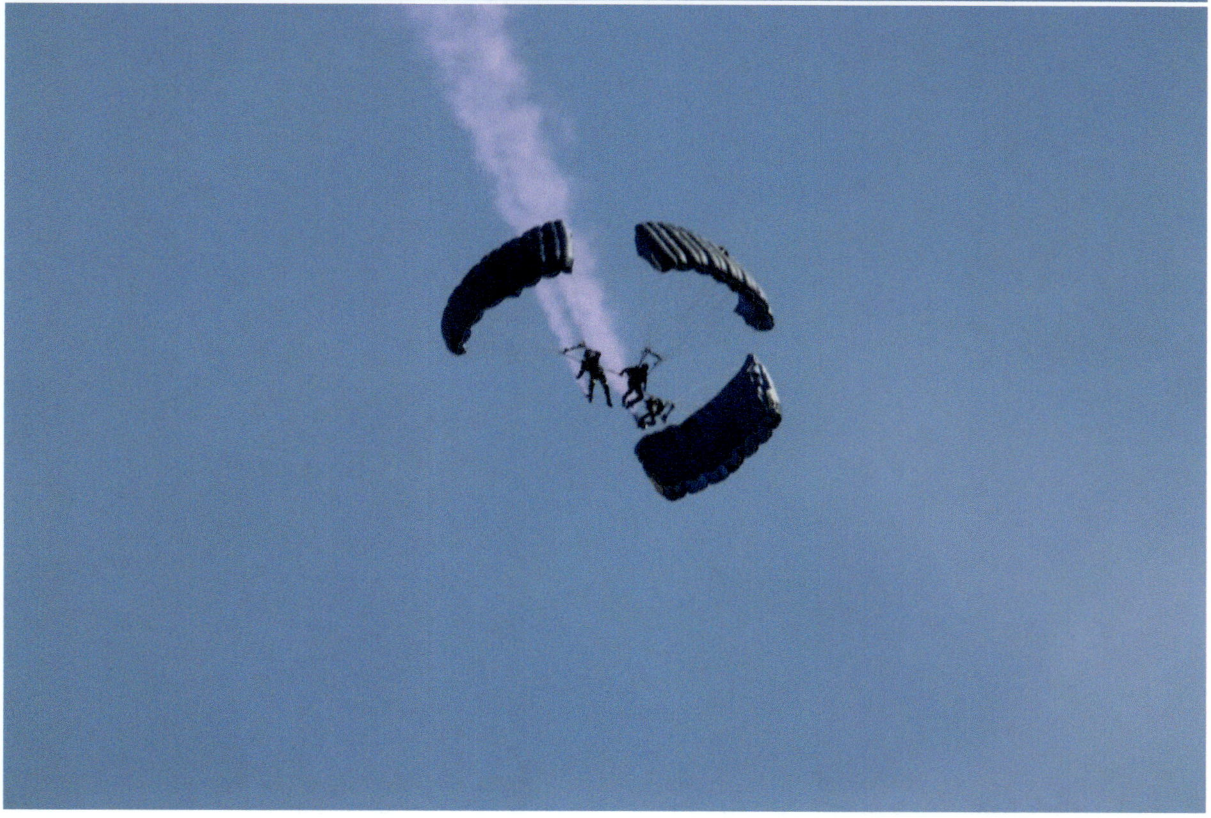

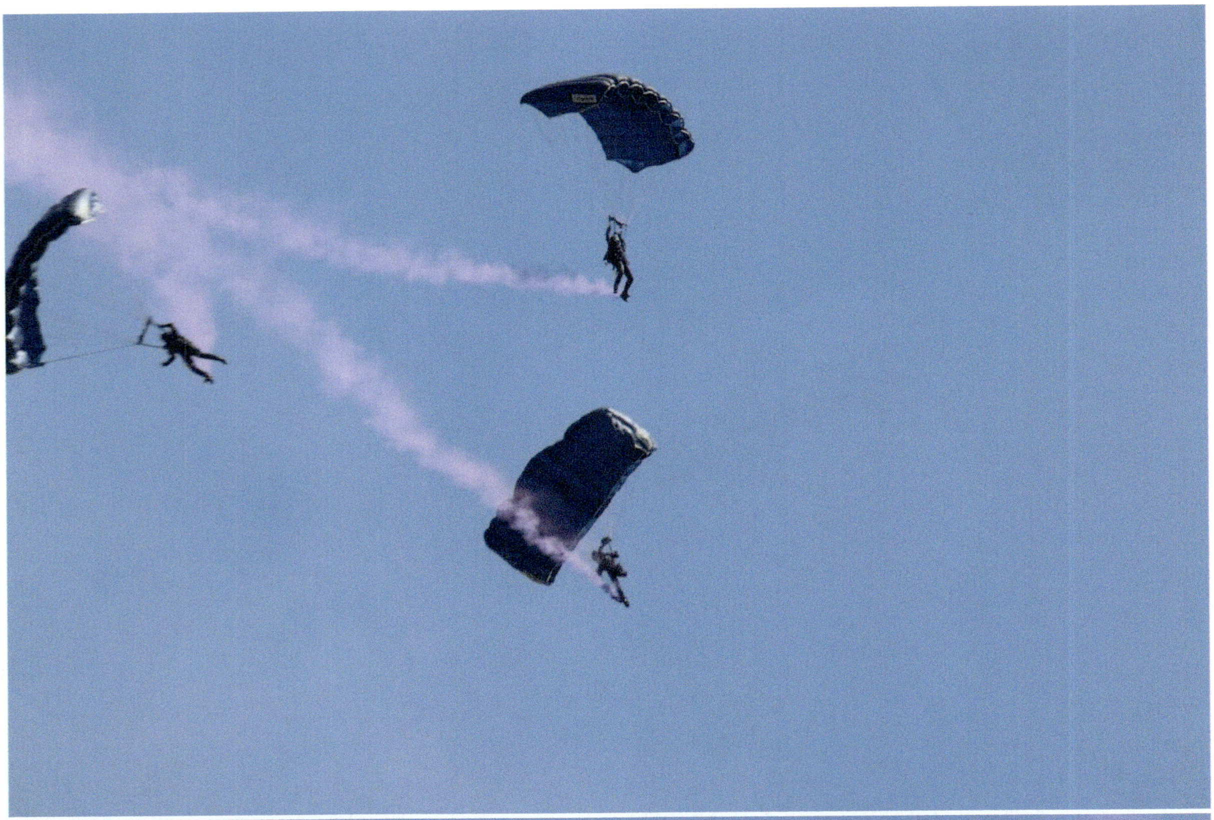

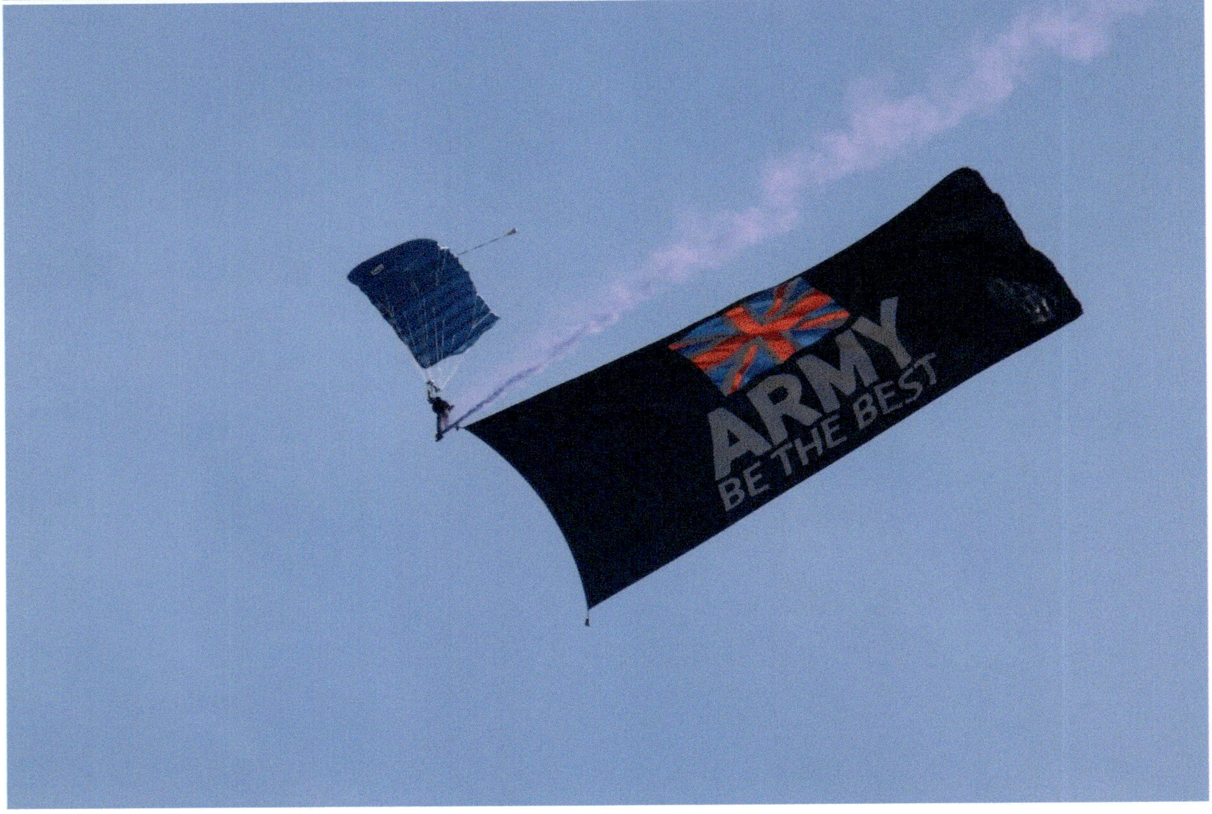
ARMY
BE THE BEST

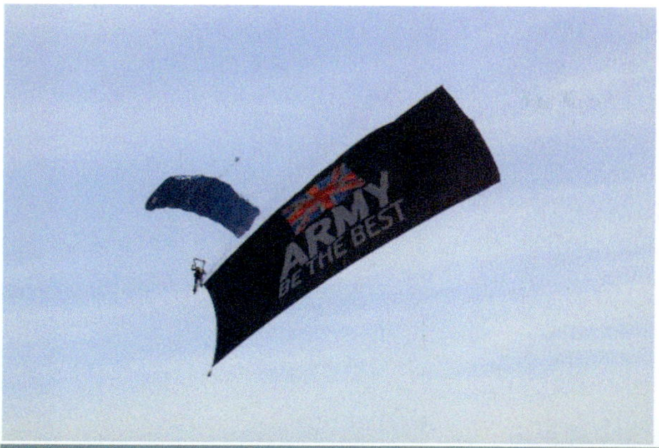
ARMY
BE THE BEST

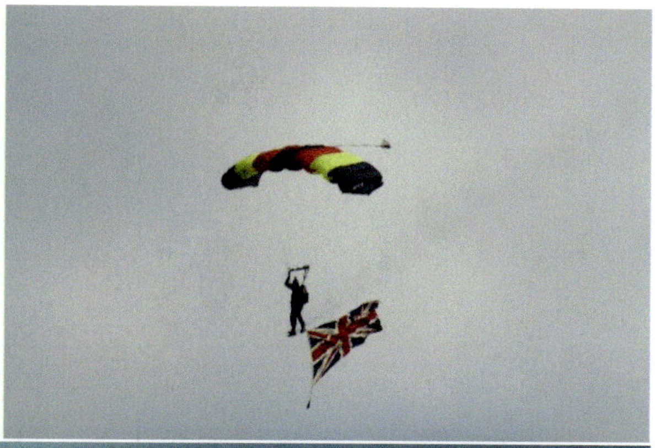

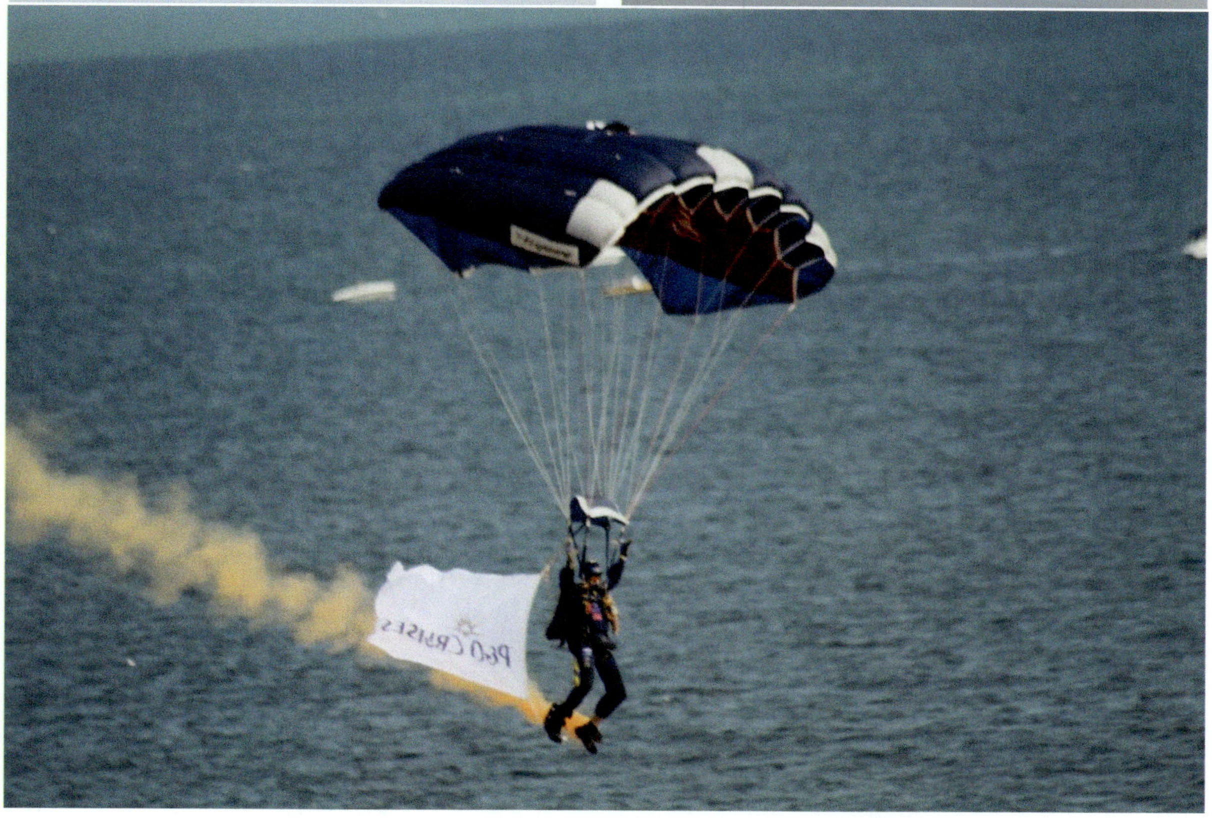

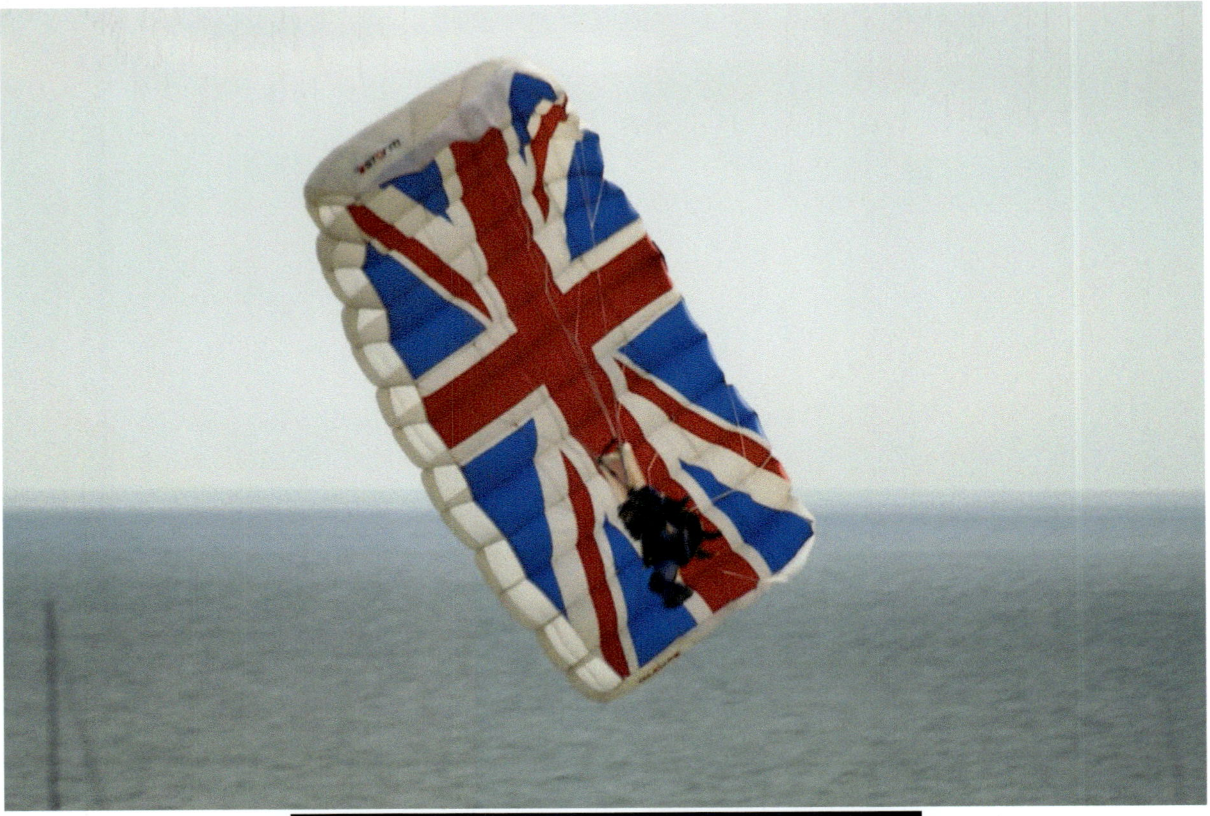

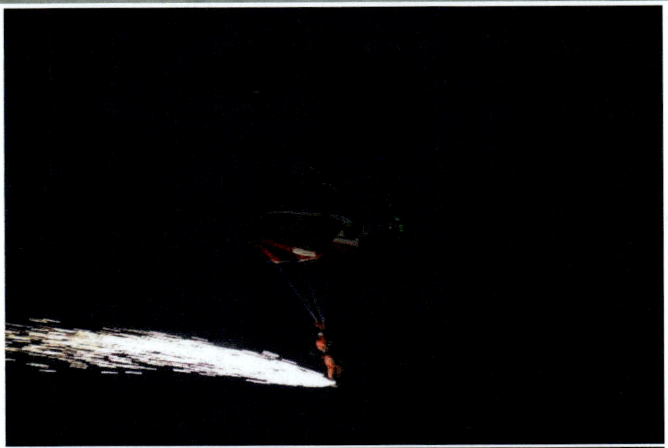

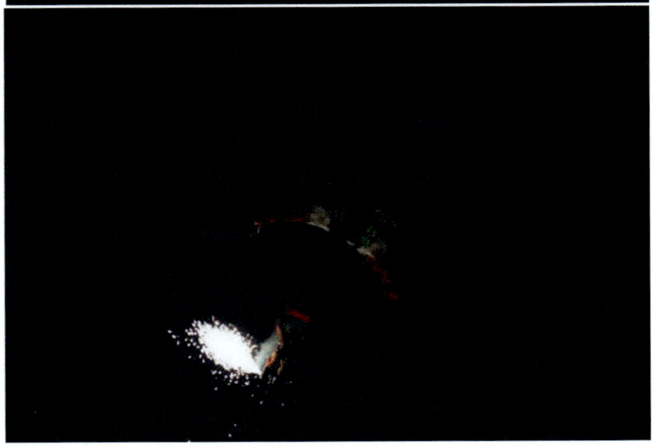

Typhoon Display Team

The RAF Typhoon Display Team represents the formidable power and advanced technology of the Eurofighter Typhoon in today's military aviation scene. Since its formation, the team's jaw-dropping aerial displays have come to epitomize the Typhoon's phenomenal capabilities, wowing crowds with the fighter jet's incredible manoeuvrability and brute force.

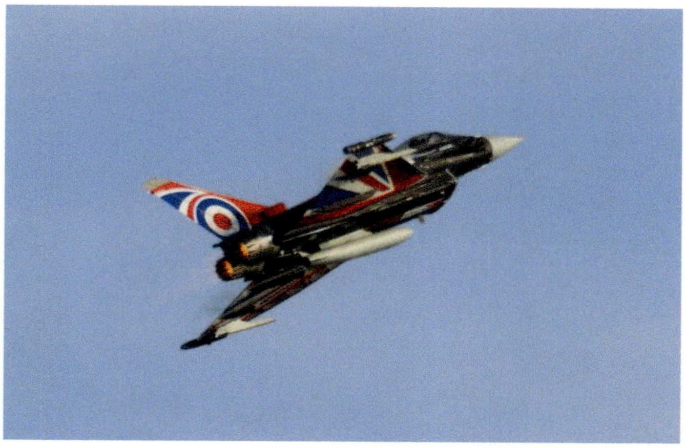

Each year the Team selects a new pilot to showcase the capabilities of the Typhoon, each pilot brings their own routine which keep the Teams displays unique and refreshing, but what they do have in common is delivering high octane manoeuvres whilst also demonstrating the agility of the aircraft.

The Typhoon Display Team has been a crowd favourite over the years, drawing spectators from across the country. One thing with the Typhoon is that you hear it before you see it, thanks its two Eurojet EJ200 engines which thunder across the sky.

The Typhoon Display Team has performed its displays in aircraft with different paint schemes, ranging from a basic grey called "Triple X" to a camouflaged Typhoon nicknamed "GiNA." The most popular is the black Typhoon with Union Jack markings known as "Black Jack"—a true representation of the Royal Air Force that delights crowds.

Eurofighter Typhoon.

The Eurofighter Typhoon is a twin-engine, supersonic multirole fighter jet developed and manufactured by a European consortium of Airbus, BAE Systems, and Leonardo. Originally intended as an air superiority fighter, the Typhoon has a canard delta wing design and originated from the 1983 multinational Future European Fighter Aircraft program between the UK, Germany, France, Italy, and Spain - nations which had previously collaborated on the Panavia Tornado combat aircraft.

The Typhoon is a highly manoeuvrable aircraft at both supersonic and low speeds. This agility stems from an intentionally unstable design stabilized by a quadruplex digital fly-by-wire control system. The fly-by-wire system prevents the pilot from exceeding safe operating limits and provides the artificial stability needed to compensate for the Typhoon's inherent instability. Additionally, the Typhoon features a lightweight construction with 82% composites, including 70% carbon fibre and 12% glass fibre. This lightweight build gives the Typhoon an estimated lifespan of 6,000 flight hours.

In order to reduce its radar cross section, measures were taken to make the Typhoon stealthier, though it was not designated a stealth fighter. For example, the Typhoon has jet inlets that conceal the engines' front (a strong radar target) from detection.

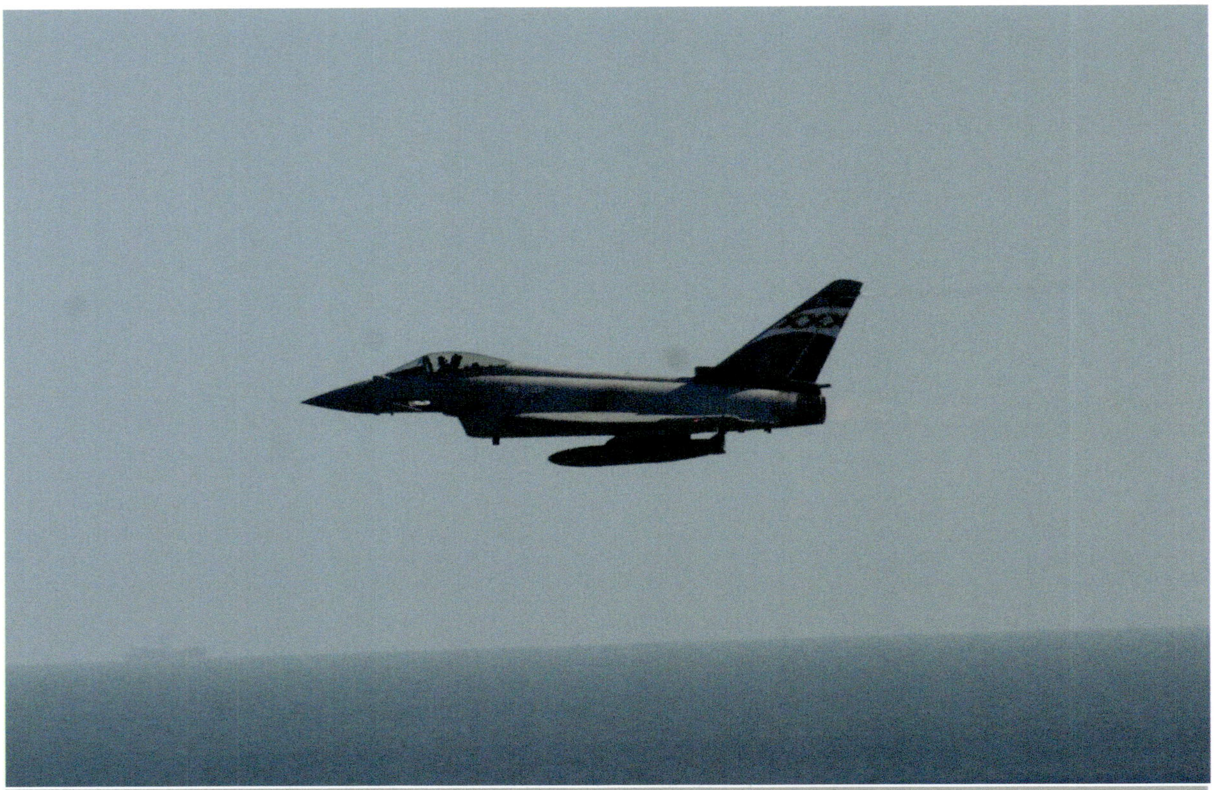

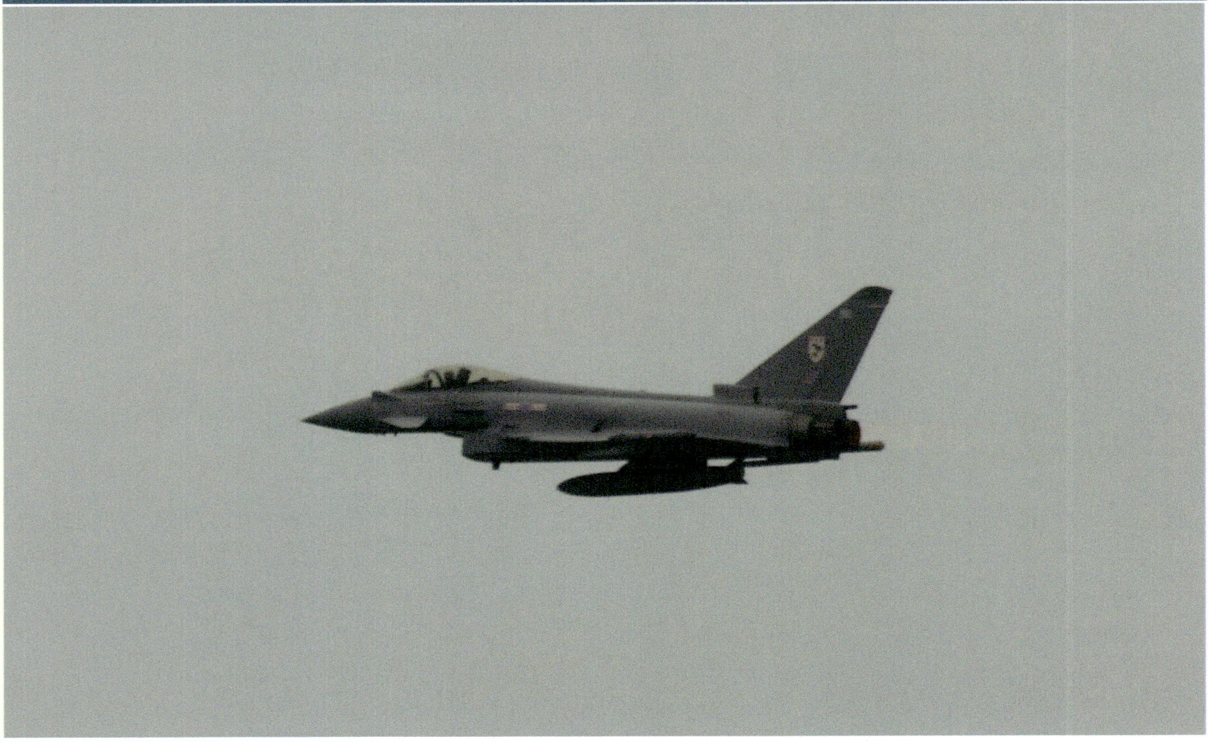

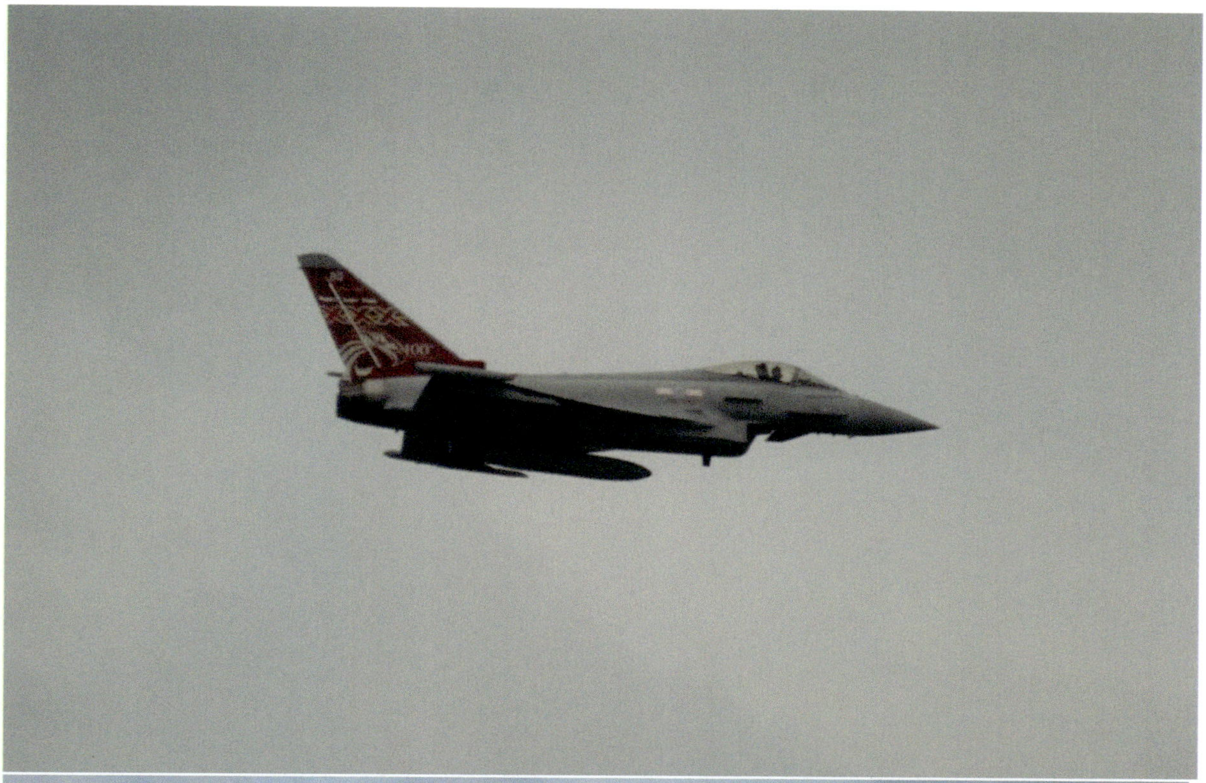

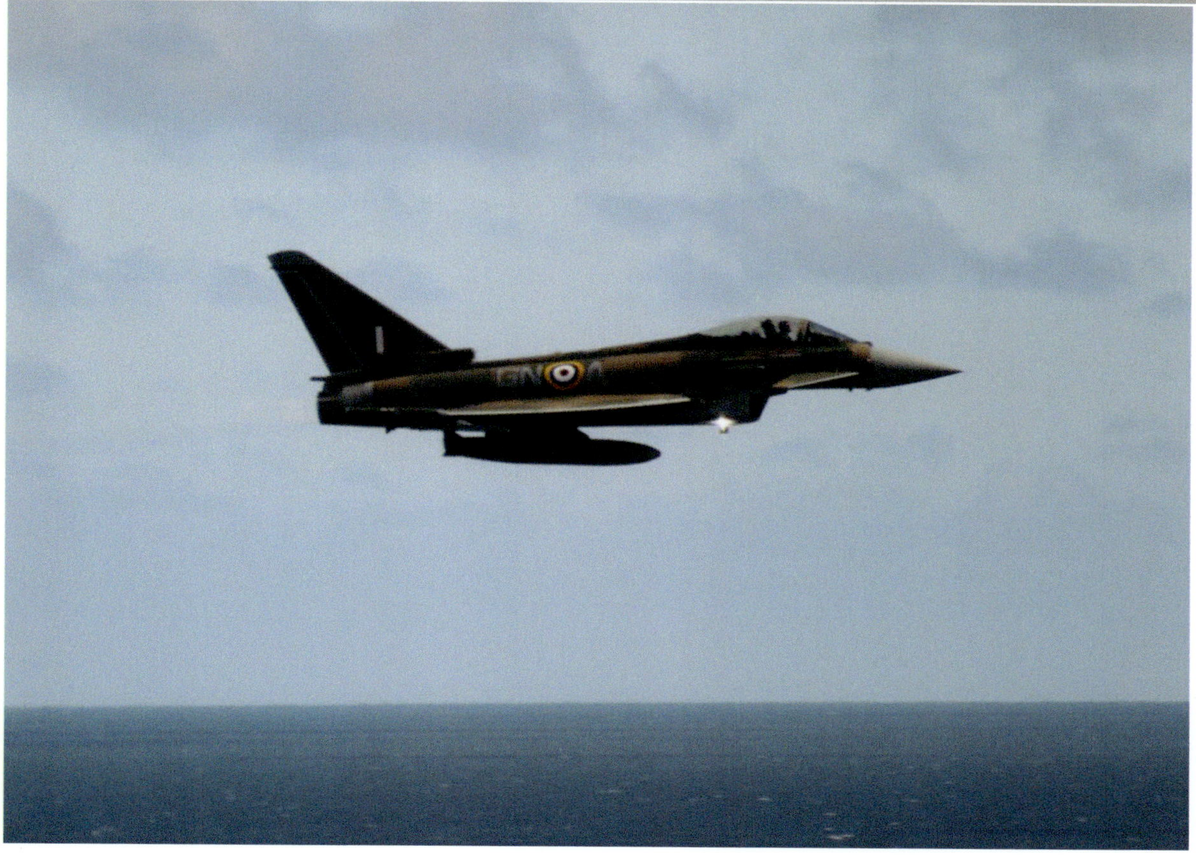

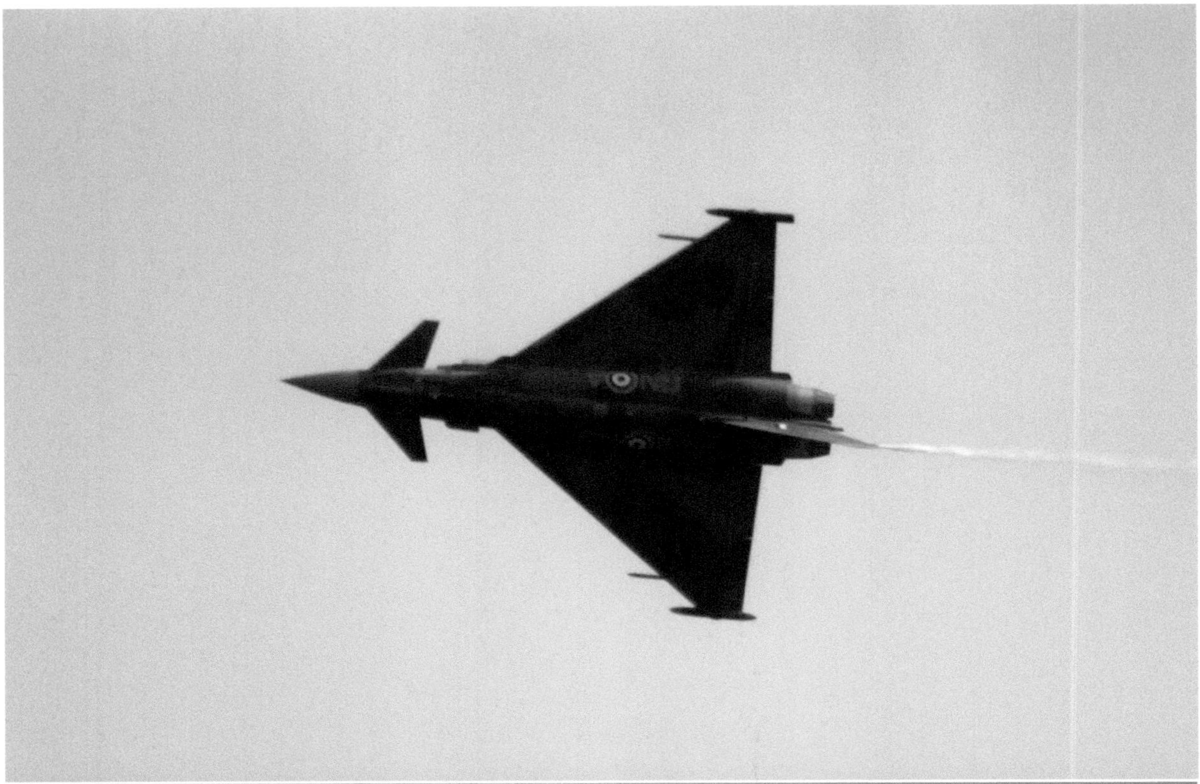

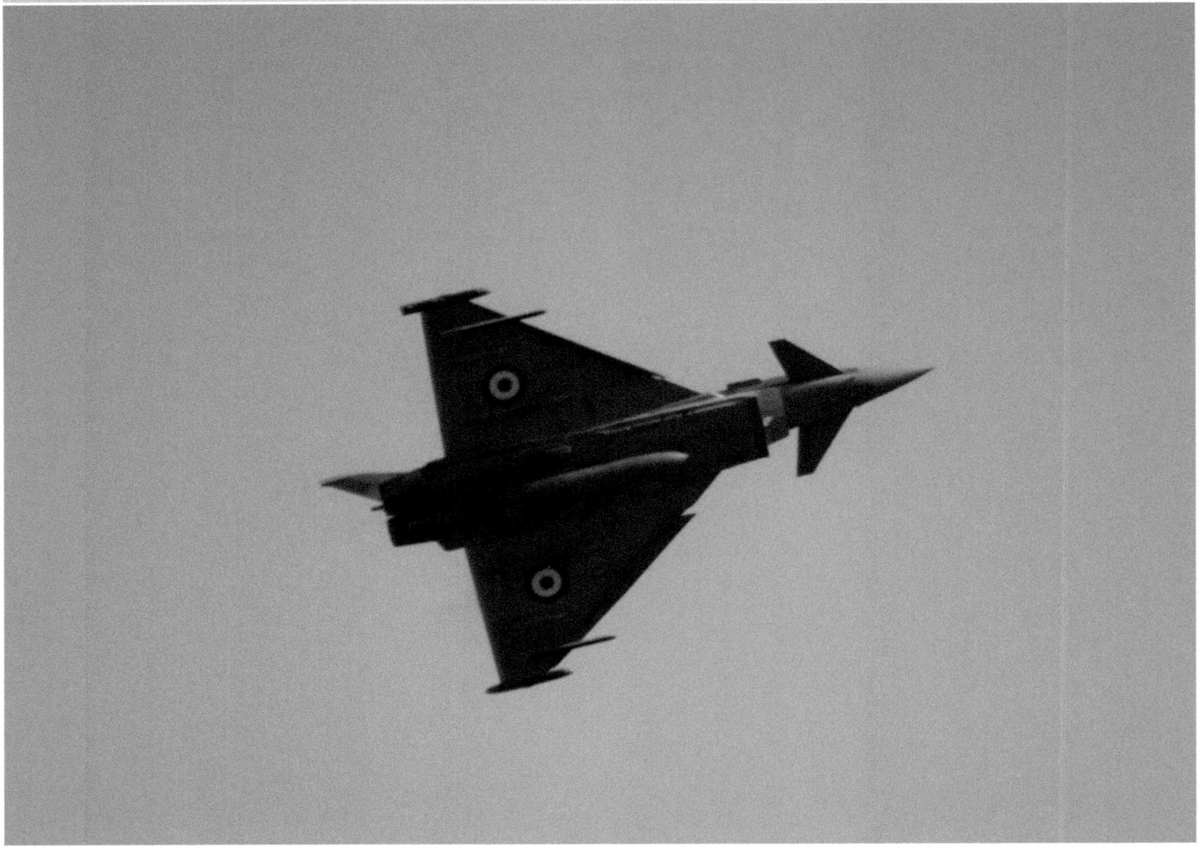

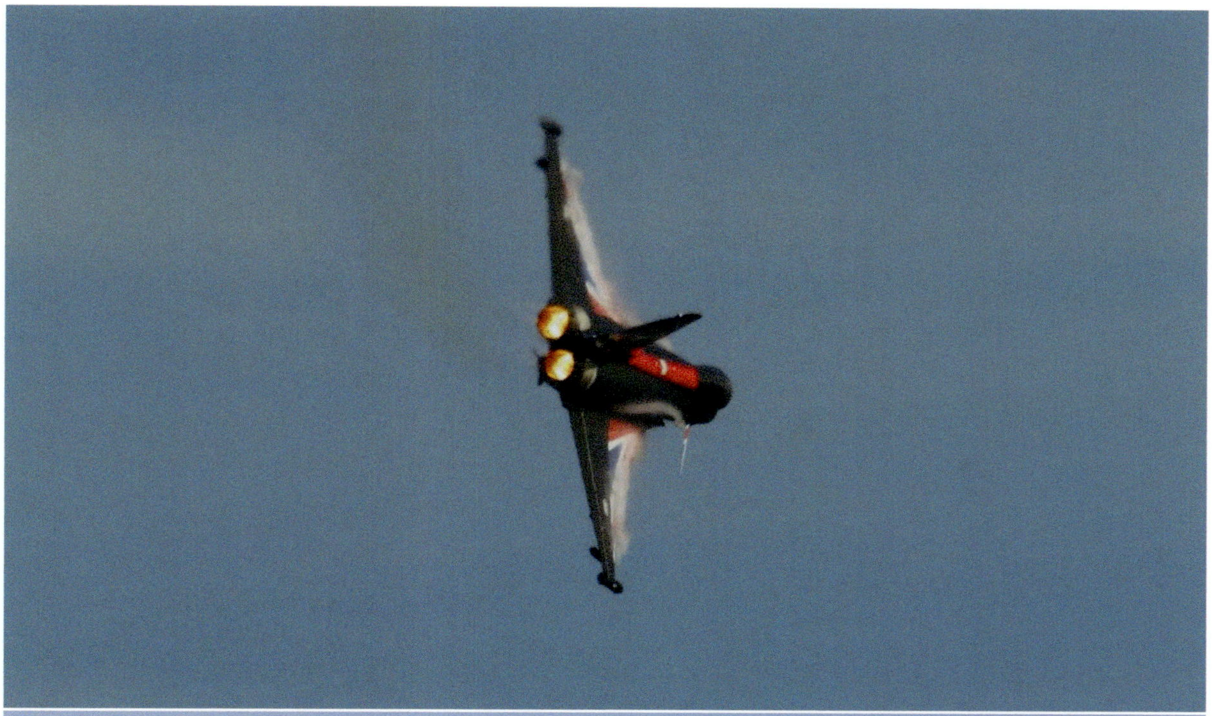

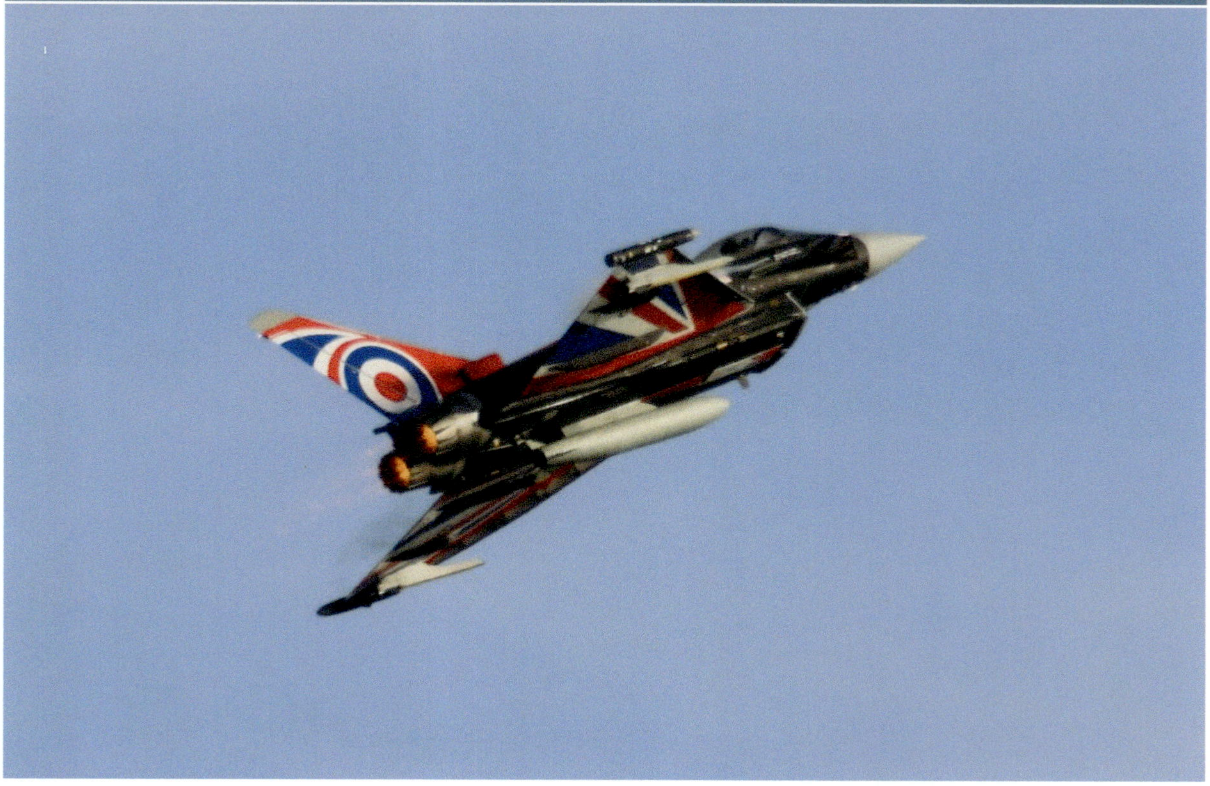

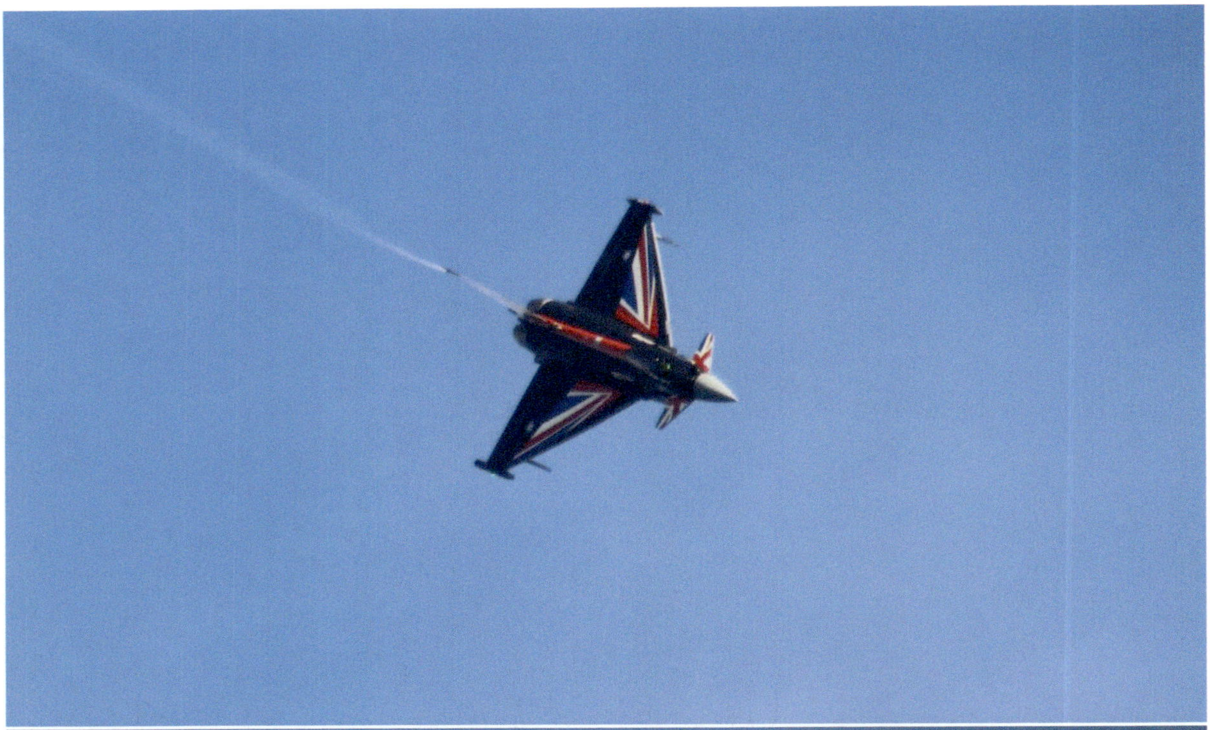

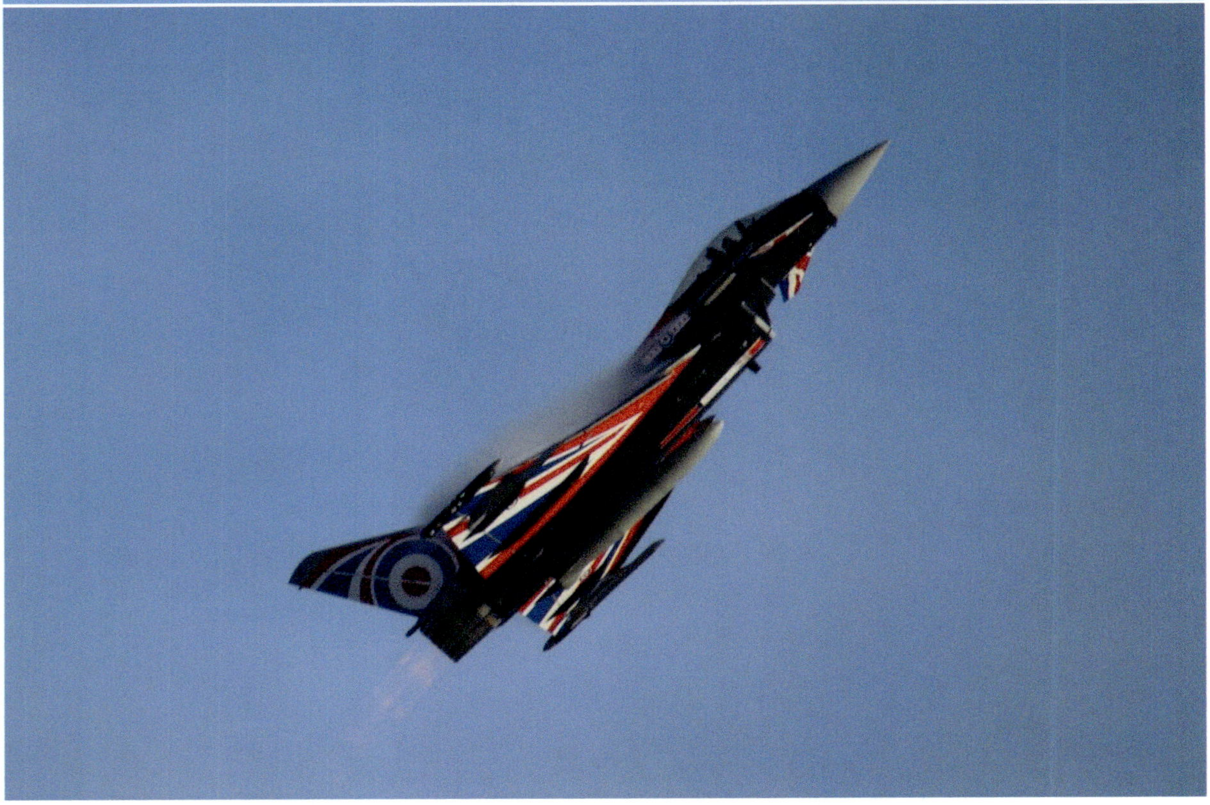

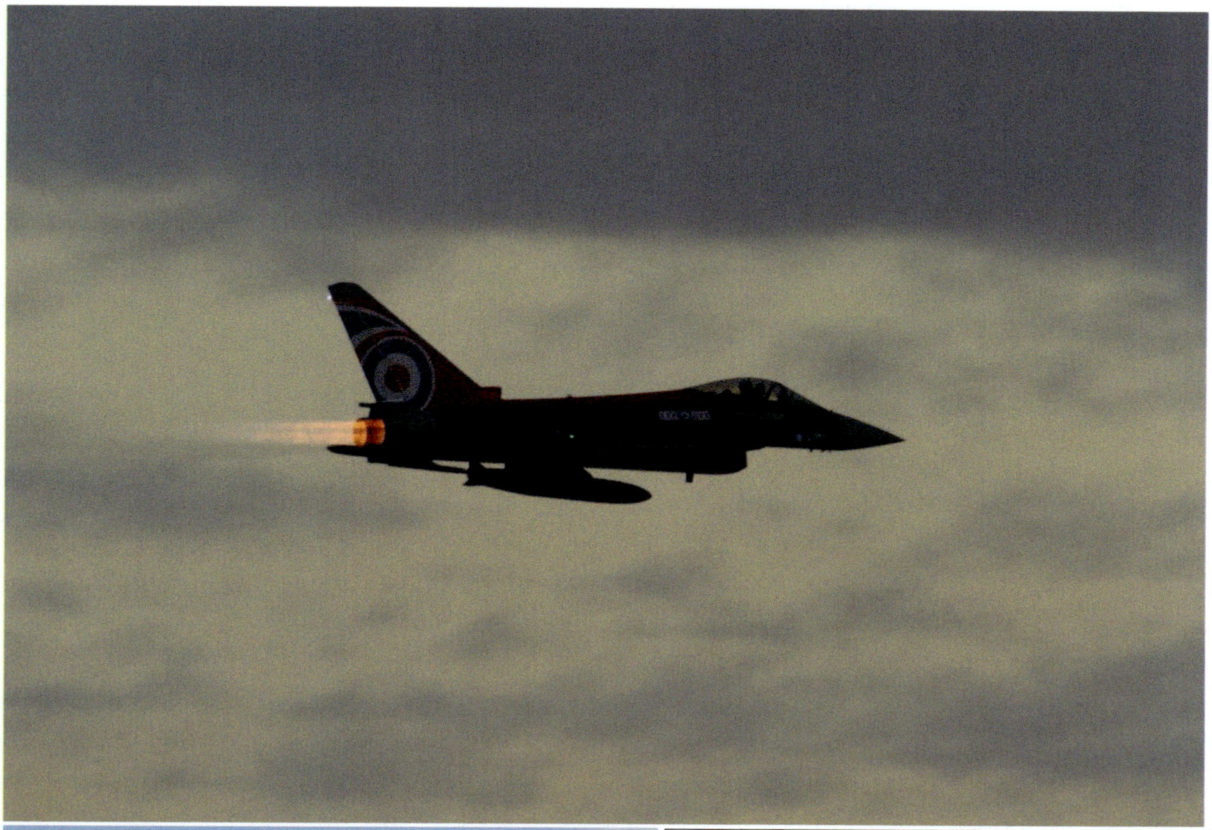

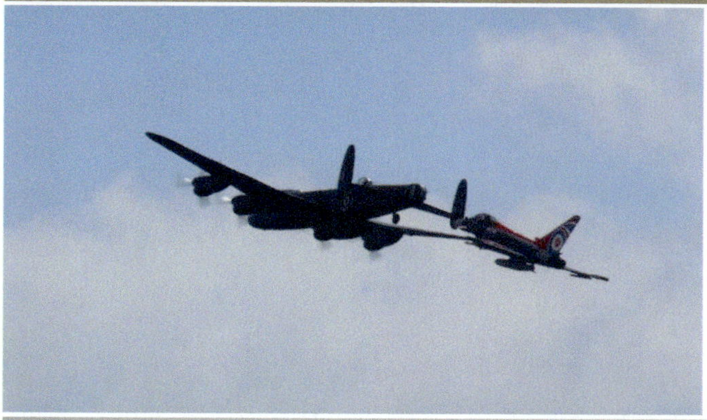

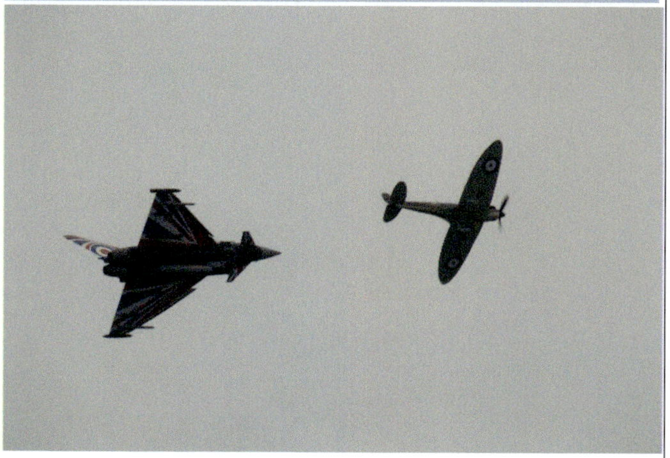

Quick Facts

General

Crew: 1 or 2

Length: 15.96 m (52 ft 4 in)

Wingspan: 10.95 m (35 ft 11 in)

Height: 5.28 m (17 ft 4 in)

Performance

Maximum speed: 2,125 km/h (1,320 mph)

Brakes-off to Take-off acceleration: <8s

Brakes-off to supersonic acceleration: <30s

Brakes-off to Mach 1.6 at 11,000 m: <150s

Armament

Guns: 1 × 27 mm

Hardpoints: 13 – ability to carry various missiles and bombs

Royal Air Force Aerobatic Team – The Red Arrows

The Royal Air Force Aerobatic Team, known as the Red Arrows, is the aerobatics display squadron of the Royal Air Force based at RAF Waddington. Formed in 1964 to replace unofficial display teams, the Red Arrows have become icons of British culture, performing their signature diamond nine formation at summer events across the UK. Their badge features the aircraft in their famous formation along with the motto "Éclat," meaning "brilliance" in French.

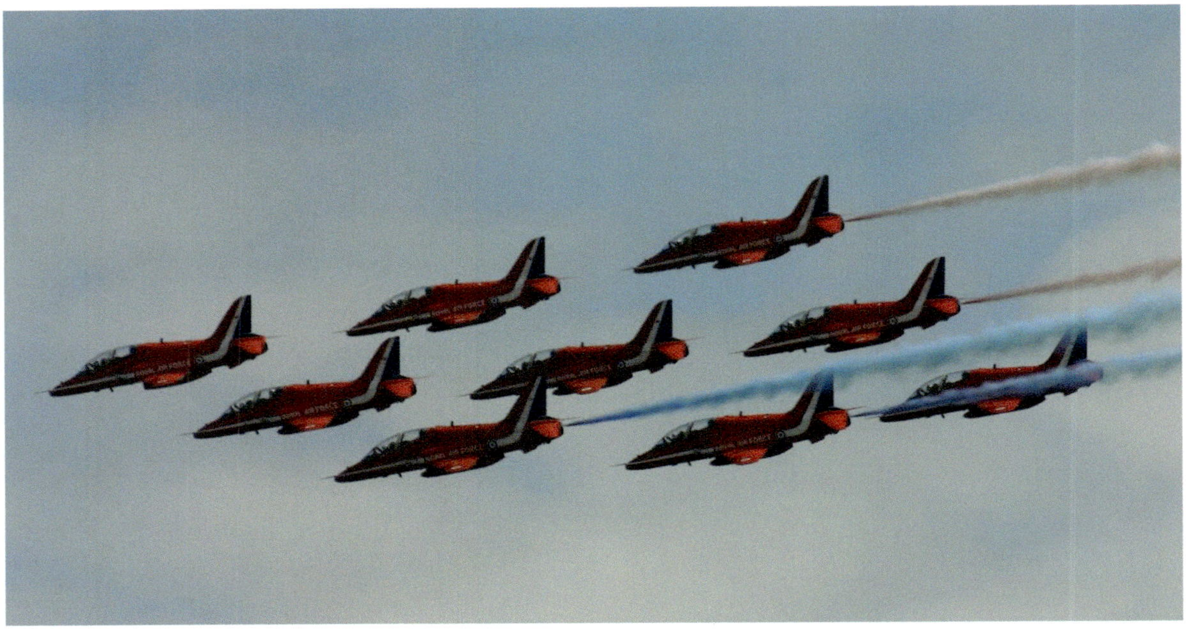

The team was initially equipped with seven Folland Gnats, a more economical aircraft to operate than front-line fighters. In their first season performing aerobatic displays, the Red Arrows flew at 65 shows across Europe. The team expanded to nine pilots in 1966, allowing them to develop their signature Diamond Nine formation. In late 1979, they switched to the BAE Hawk trainer aircraft. To date, the Red Arrows have performed over 4,800 displays in 57 countries worldwide.

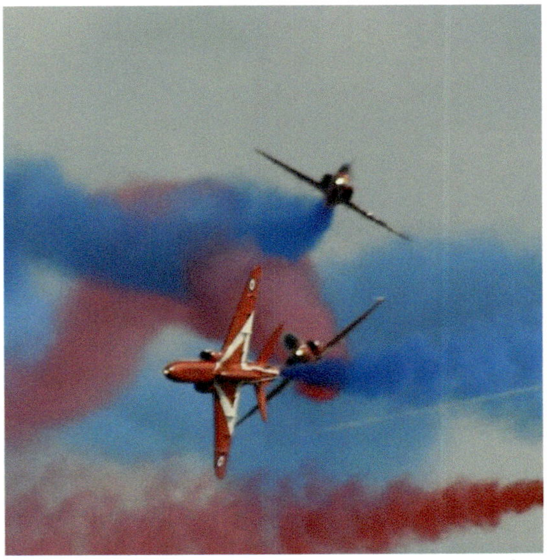

The Red Arrows began operations at RAF Little Rissington in Gloucestershire, home of the Central Flying School. In 1966, they relocated to RAF Kemble when RAF Fairford became the testing site for the Concorde airliner. The team moved again in 1983 to RAF Scampton, which had become the new headquarters of the Central Flying School. After Scampton's closure in 1995, the Red Arrows were temporarily stationed at nearby RAF Cranwell but continued using Scampton's airspace and runways. In 2000, the team returned to RAF Scampton until its closure in October 2022, prompting another move to their current home at RAF Waddington. The Red Arrows also use RAF Akrotiri in Cyprus during winter months for training in ideal weather conditions.

The Red Arrow has three aerial display routines that vary based on the cloud ceiling at show time: a Full Looping Display requiring a minimum cloud ceiling of 5,500 feet (1,700 m), a Rolling Display with wingovers and rolls flown between 2,500 and 5,500 feet (760 and 1,700 m), and a low-altitude Flat Display of flypasts and steep turns flown below 2,500 feet (760 m).

In 2014, the Red Arrows celebrated 50 years of aerobatic history as a display team. For the entire 2014 display season, the aircraft carried special 50th anniversary markings on their tails instead of just the red, white and blue stripes. 2024 now marks the Red Arrows' 60th anniversary, also known as their Diamond year.

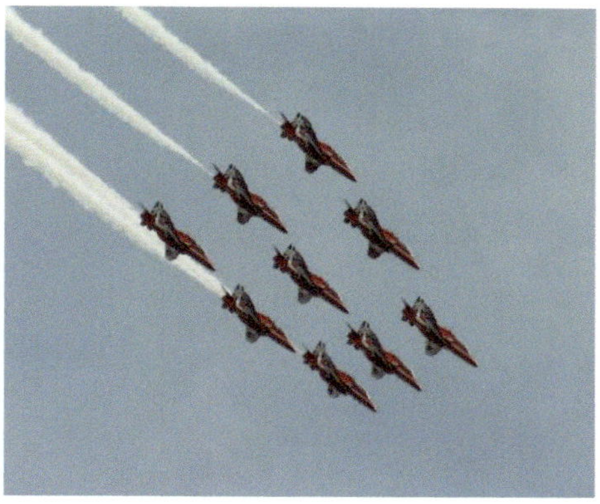

The Red Arrows are famous for their vibrant vapor trails, often called "the smoke," which are crucial for flight safety during the team's displays. These vapor trails allow the Lead Pilot to judge wind speed and direction. They also enable the distant aircraft to locate each other in the second half of the show when sections of the formation spread miles apart. The smoke system uses 10 imperial gallons (45 L) per minute, so each plane can trail coloured smoke for 7 minutes total: 5 minutes of white, 1 minute of blue, and 1 minute of red.

The vivid, colourful smoke trails also enhance the visual impact of the airshow when viewed from the ground. Well-known manoeuvres like the heart, rollbacks, and carousel would lack visual appeal without the dramatic smoke effects.

The Reds' formation is divided into two sections. The front section, called Enid after the famous British children's author Enid Blyton who wrote the Famous Five series, is comprised of Reds 1 through 5. The rear section, named Hanna in honour of one of the team's founding pilots and early leaders, includes Reds 6 through 9. This rear section features the Synchro Pair, Reds 6 and 7, who execute the highly popular opposition manoeuvres during the latter part of the airshow. All of the manoeuvres have names such as The Vixen Roll, Apollo Loop and Twist, Tornado, Detonator, Cyclone, and the crowd favourite, The Red Arrow Heart.

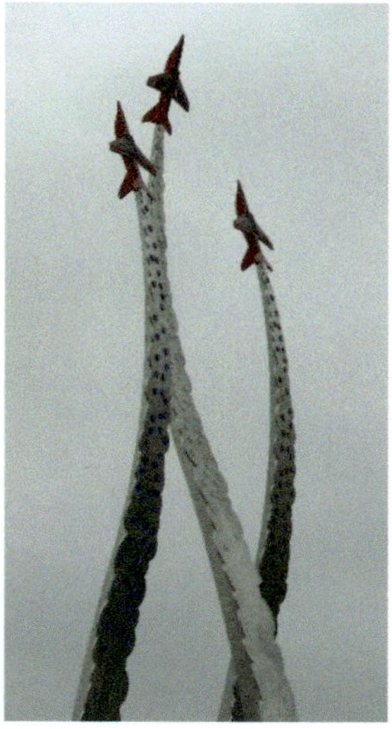

During the 2011 Bournemouth Air Festival on Saturday, a Red Arrow crashed into a field near Throop Mill, one mile from Bournemouth Airport, after the plane's air show performance. The pilot of Red 4 (XX179), Flt Lt Jon Egging, died in the accident. A memorial honouring Egging was originally unveiled in 2012 at East Cliff in Bournemouth, before being relocated nearby in 2017 due to a landslide.

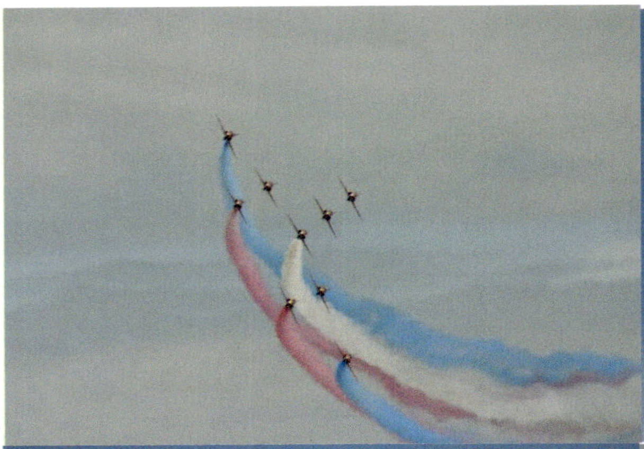
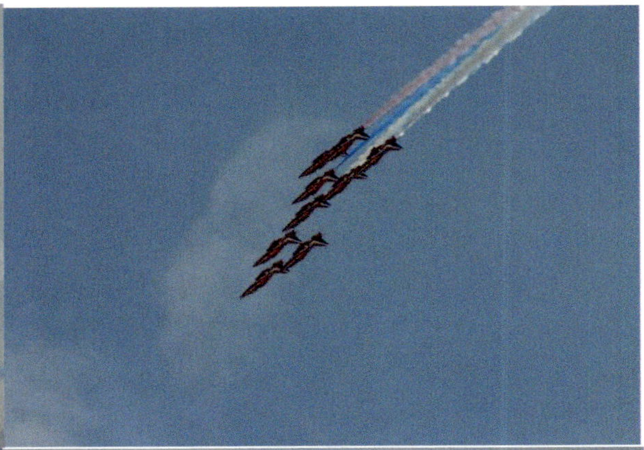
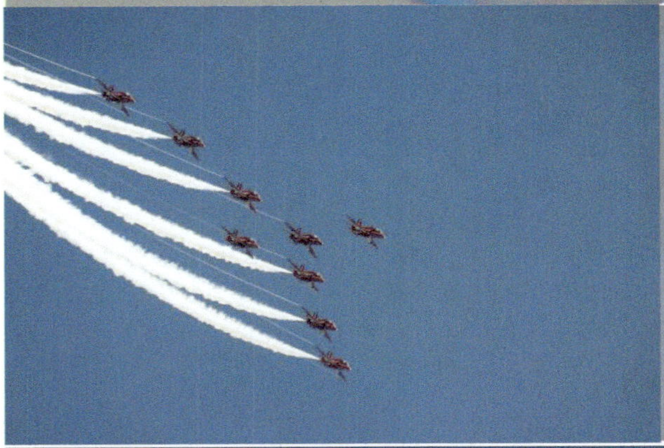
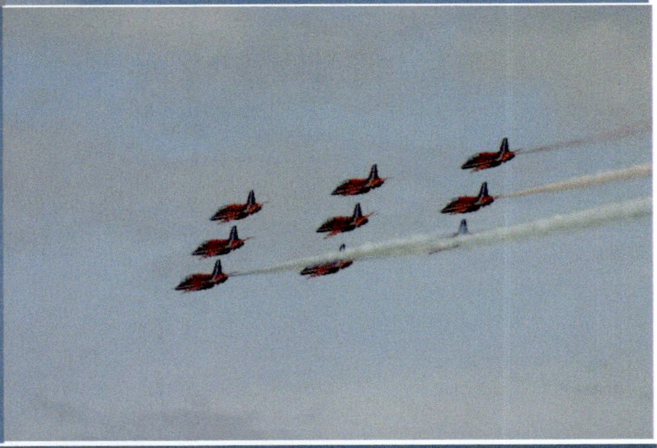
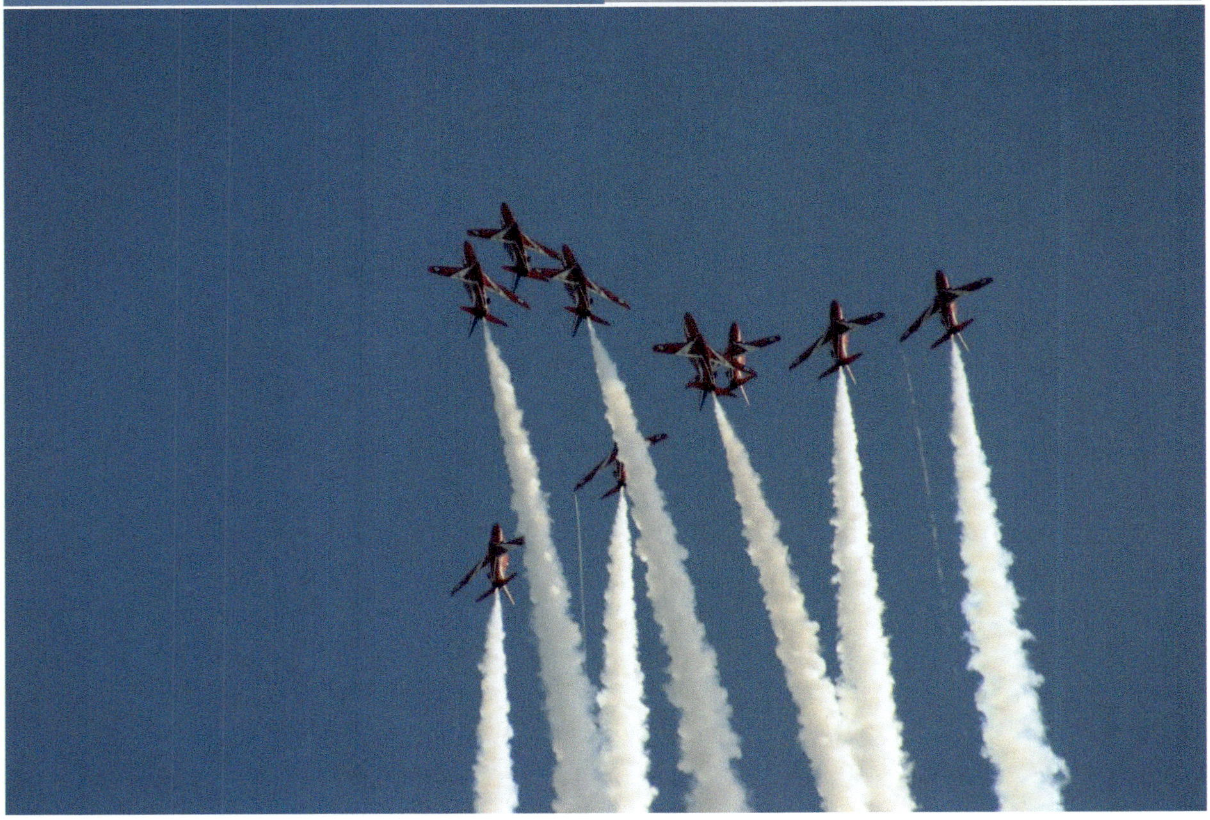

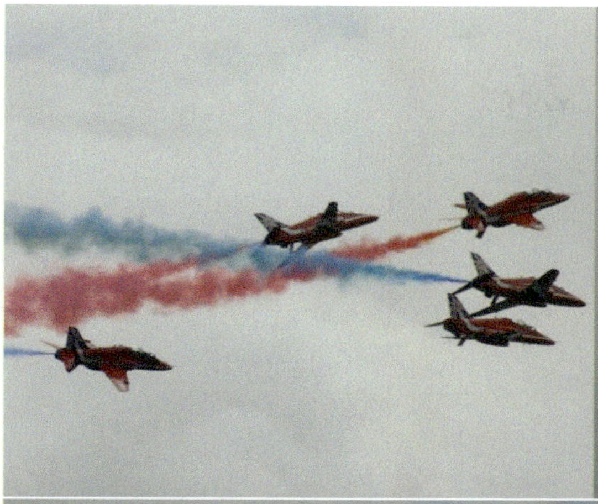
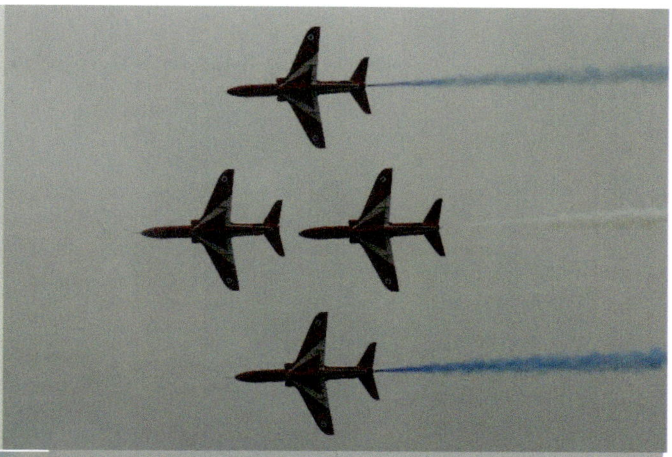
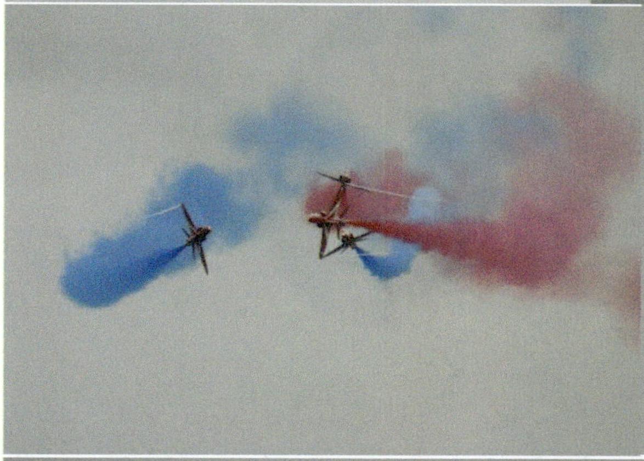
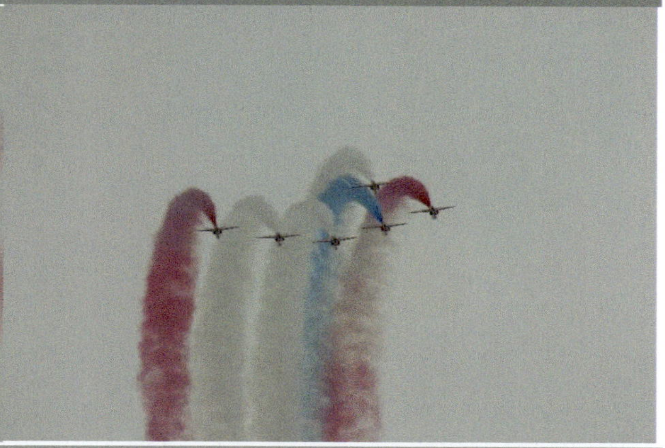
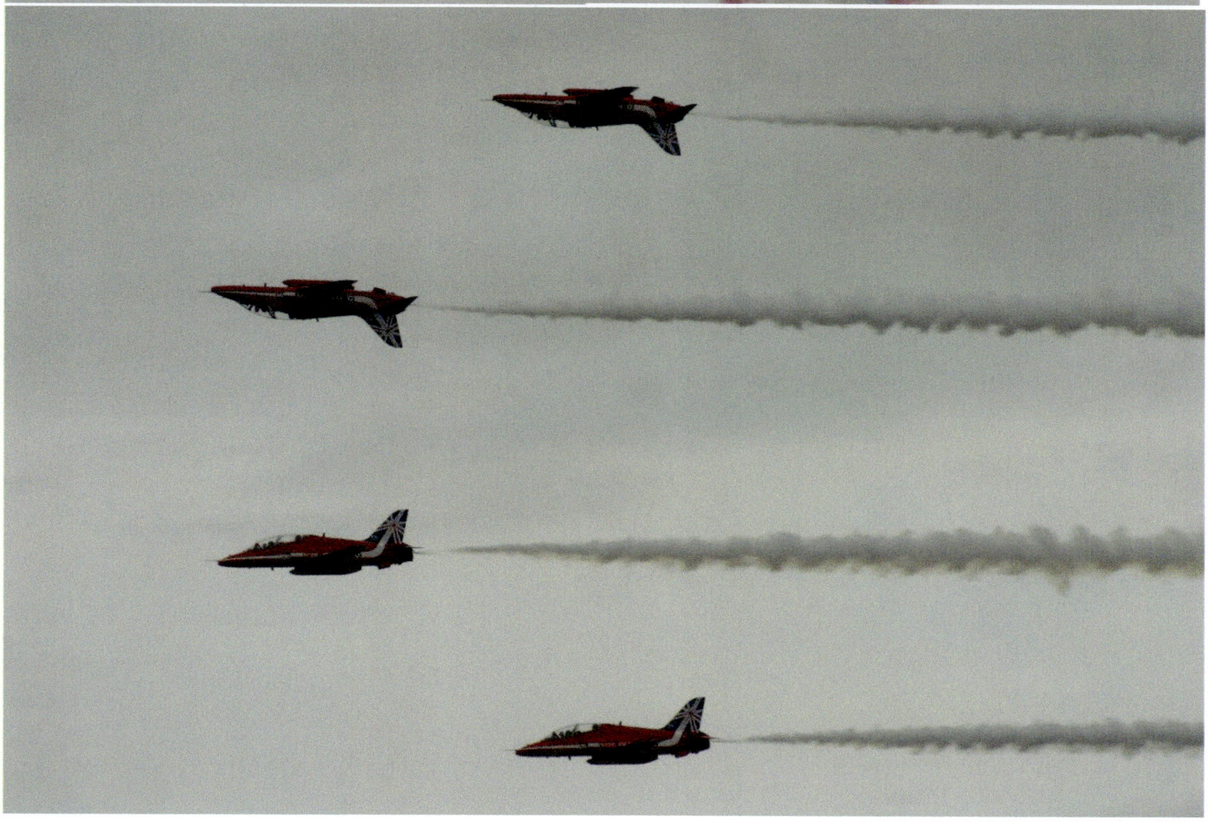

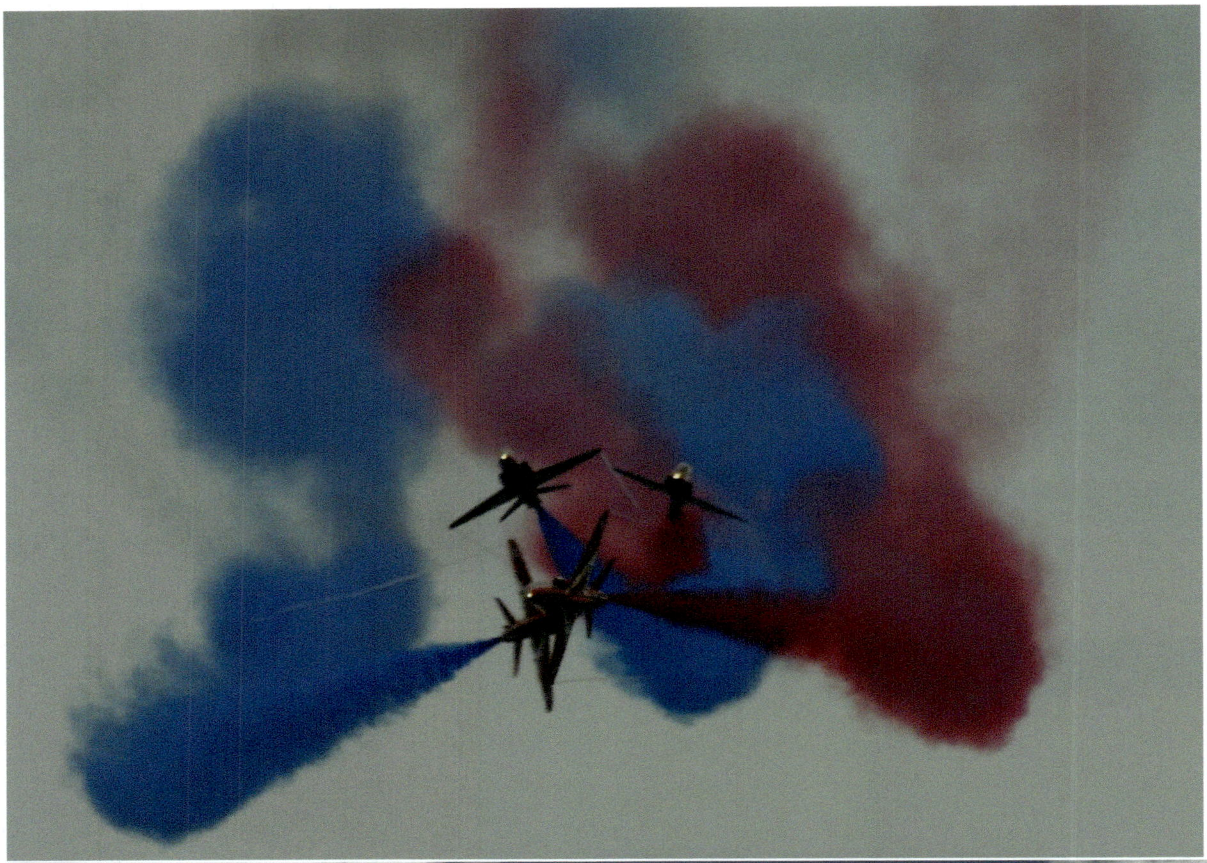

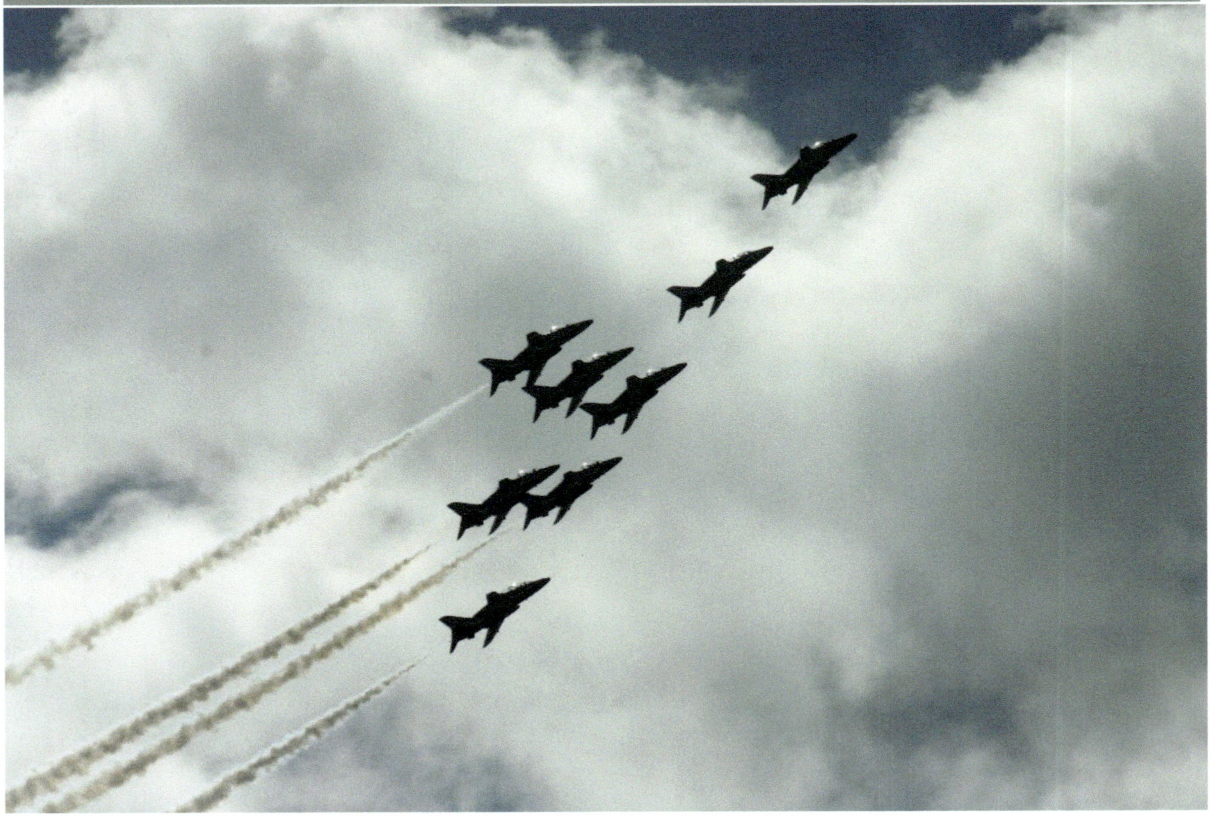

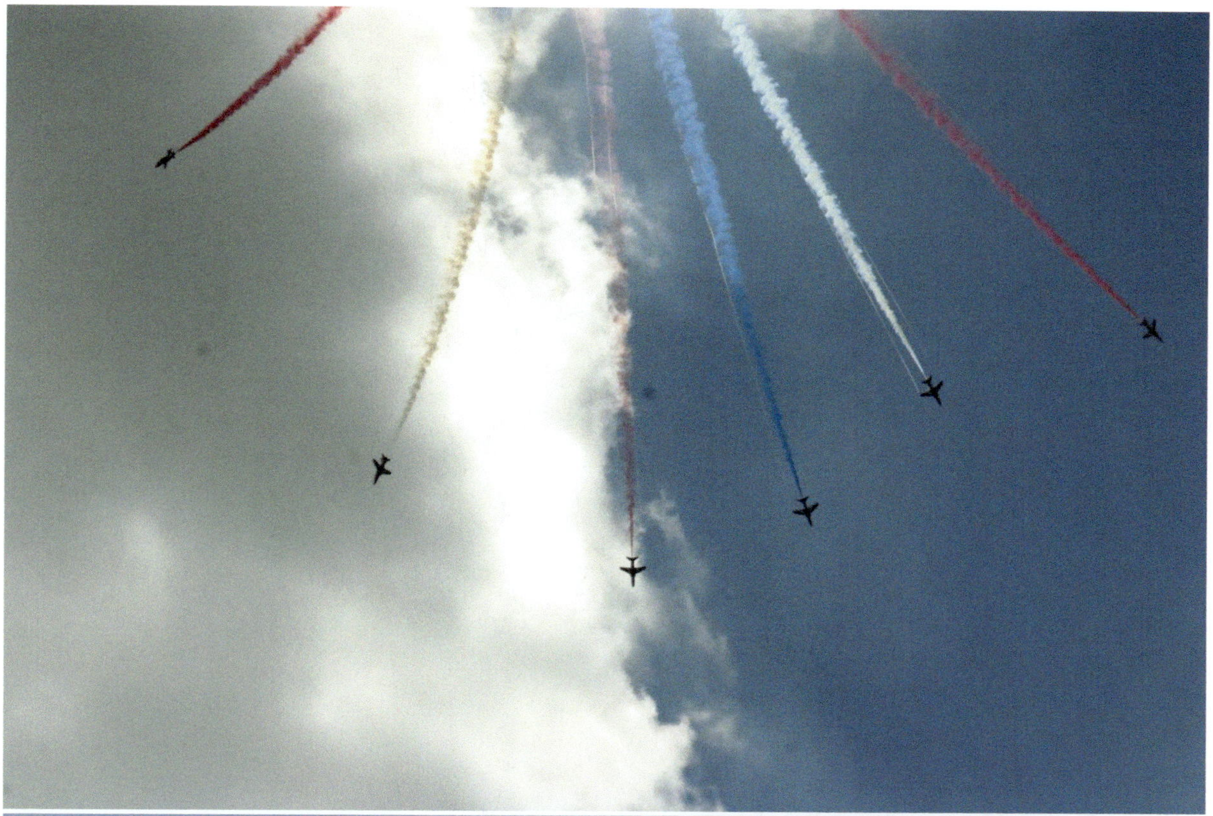

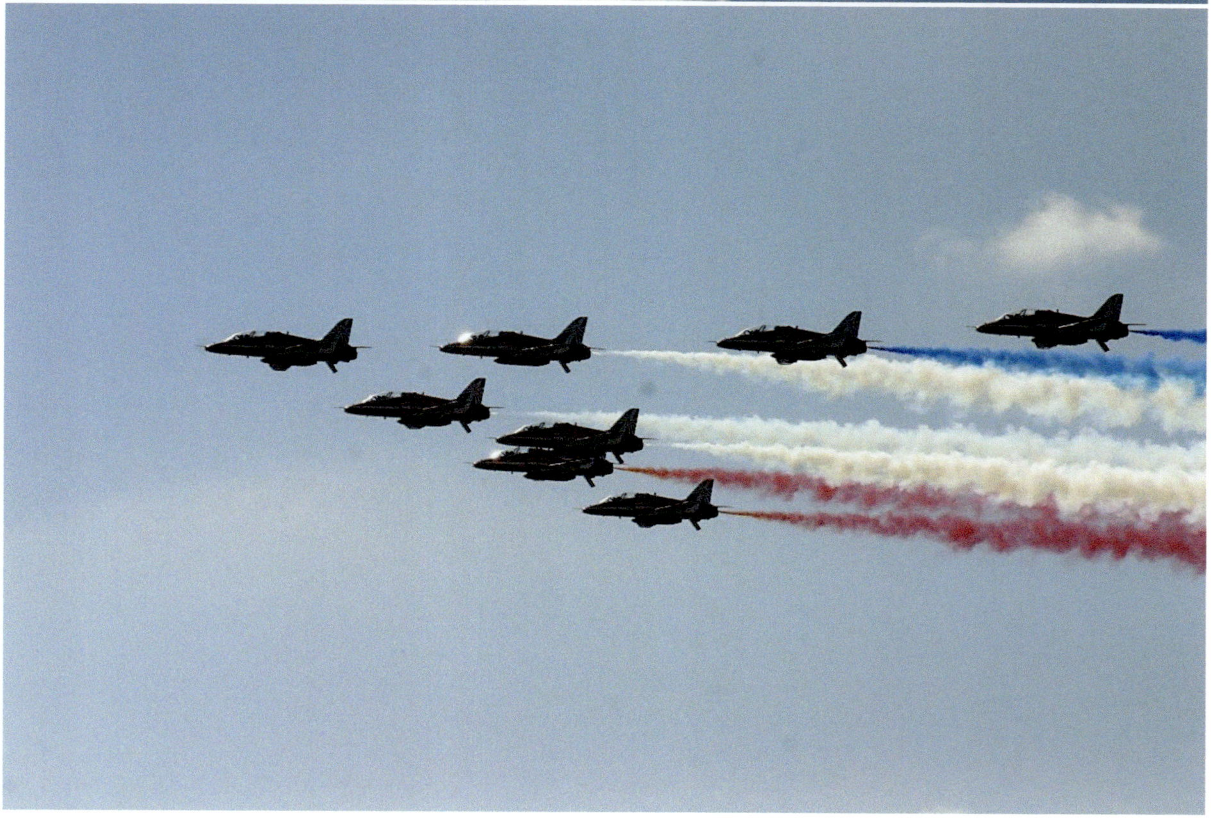

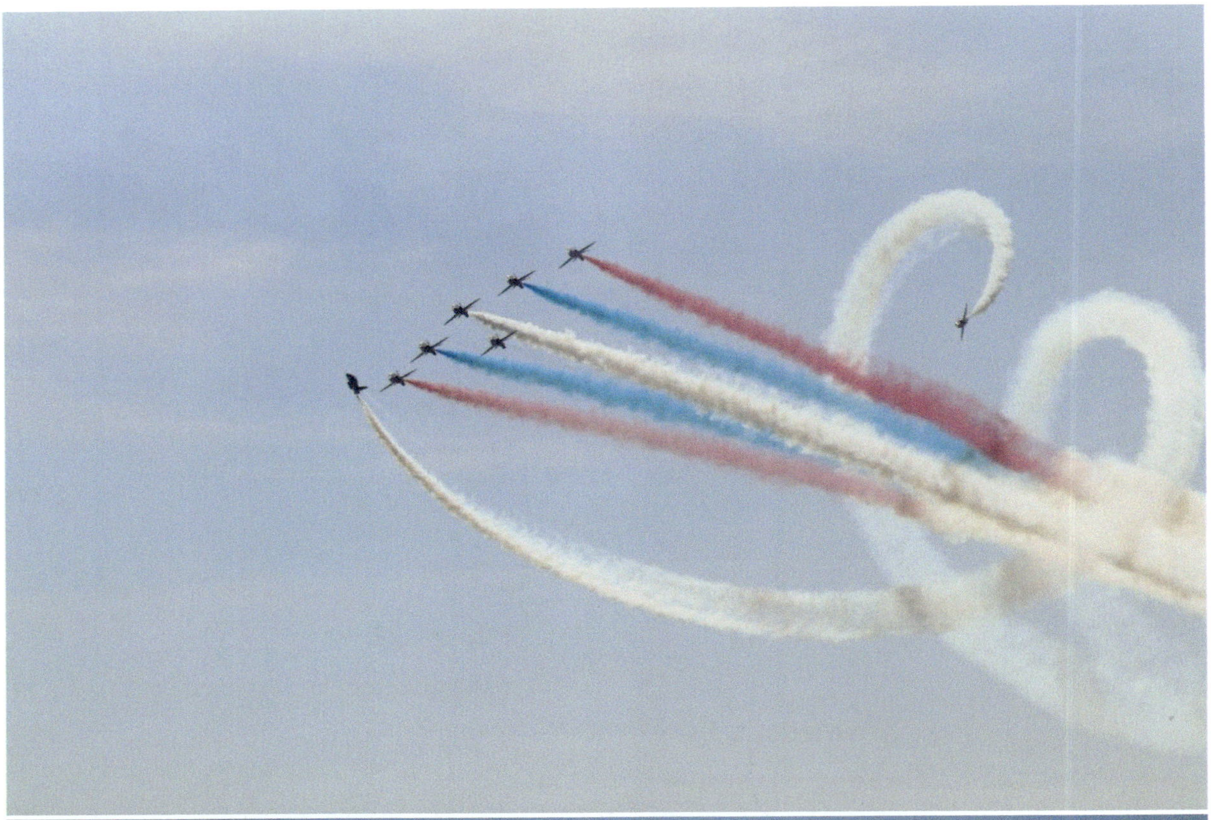

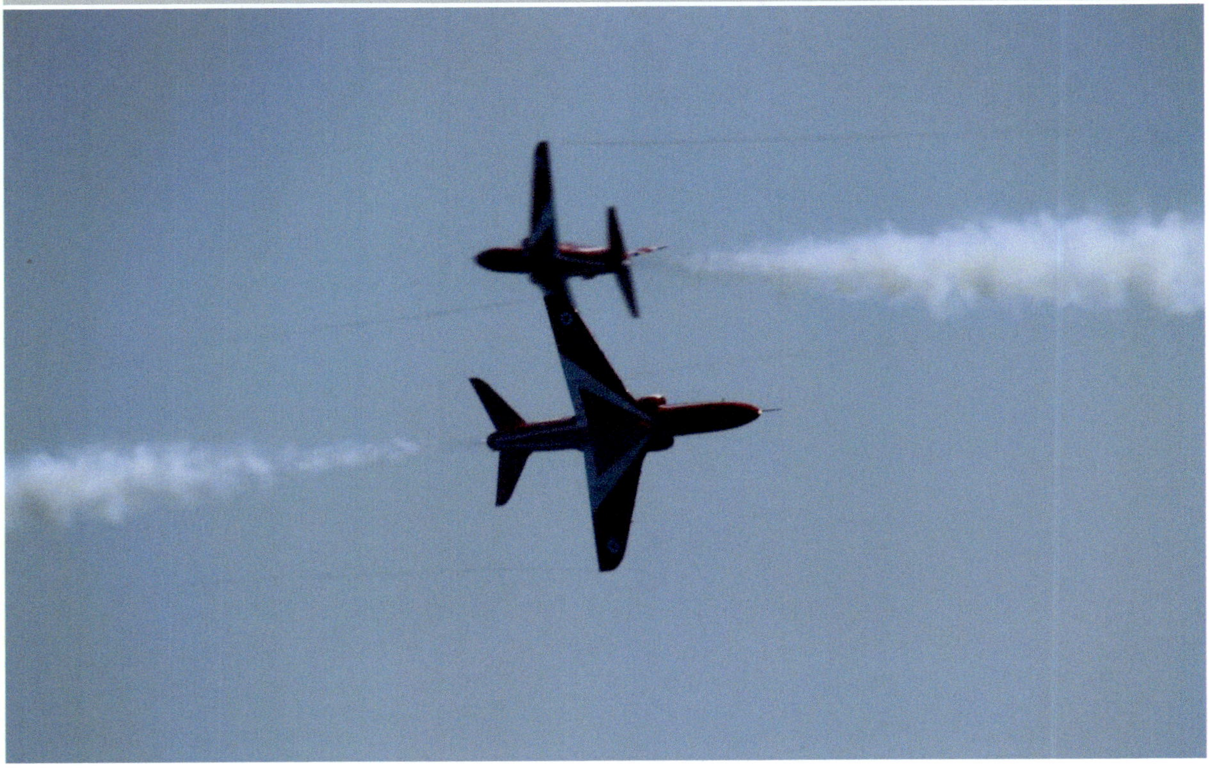

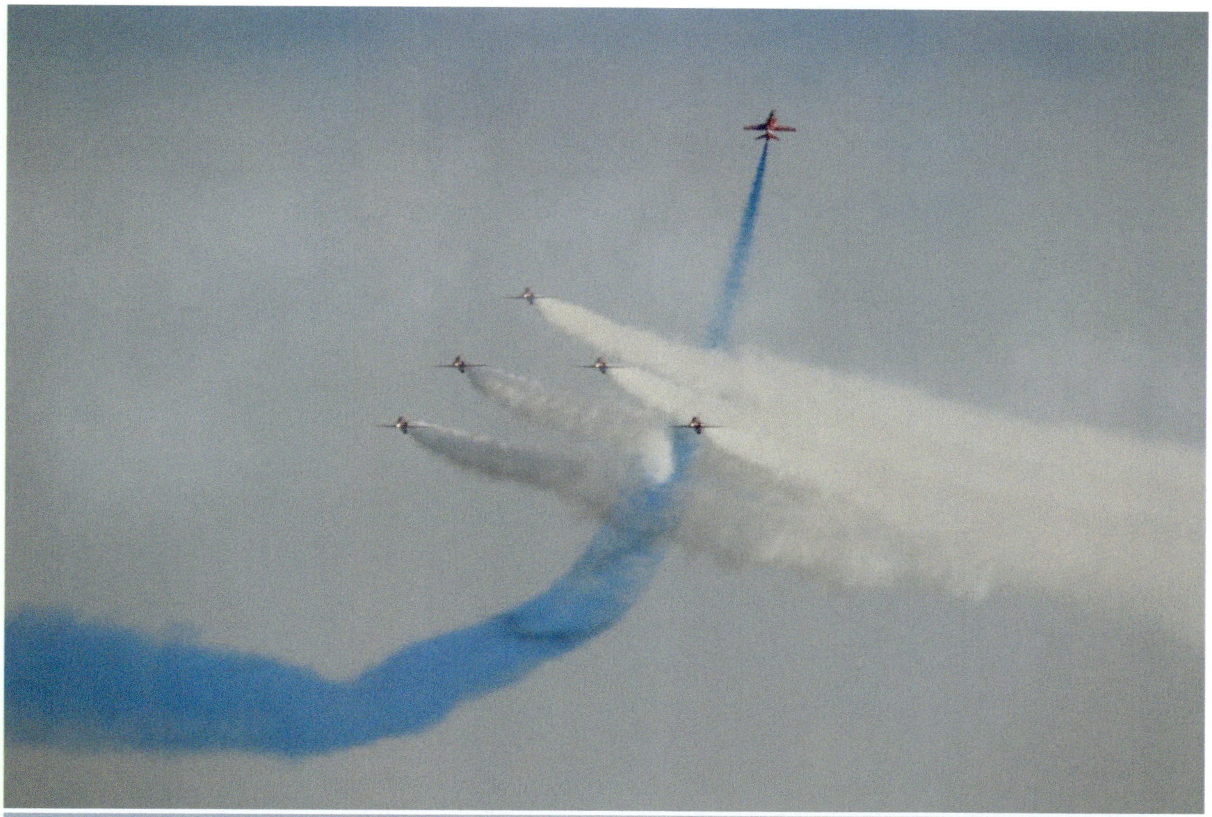

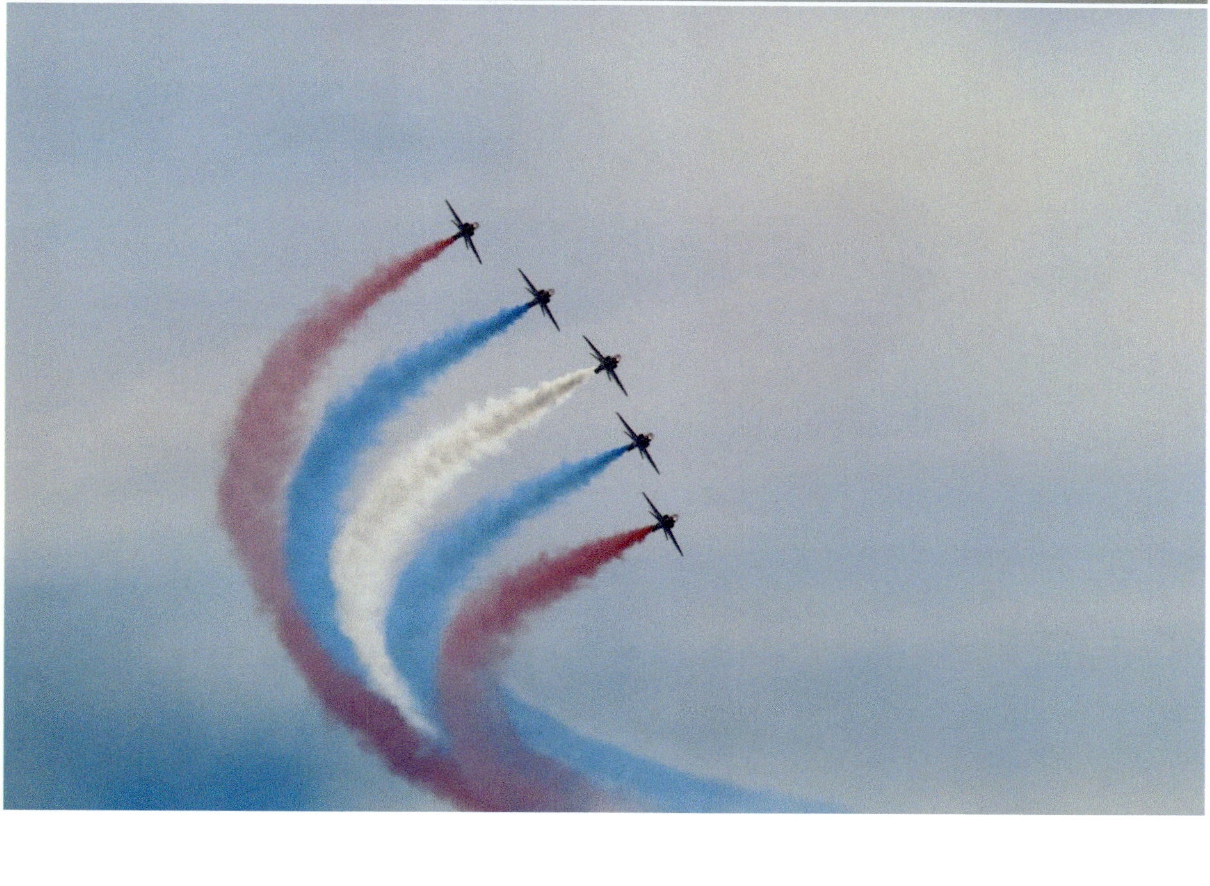

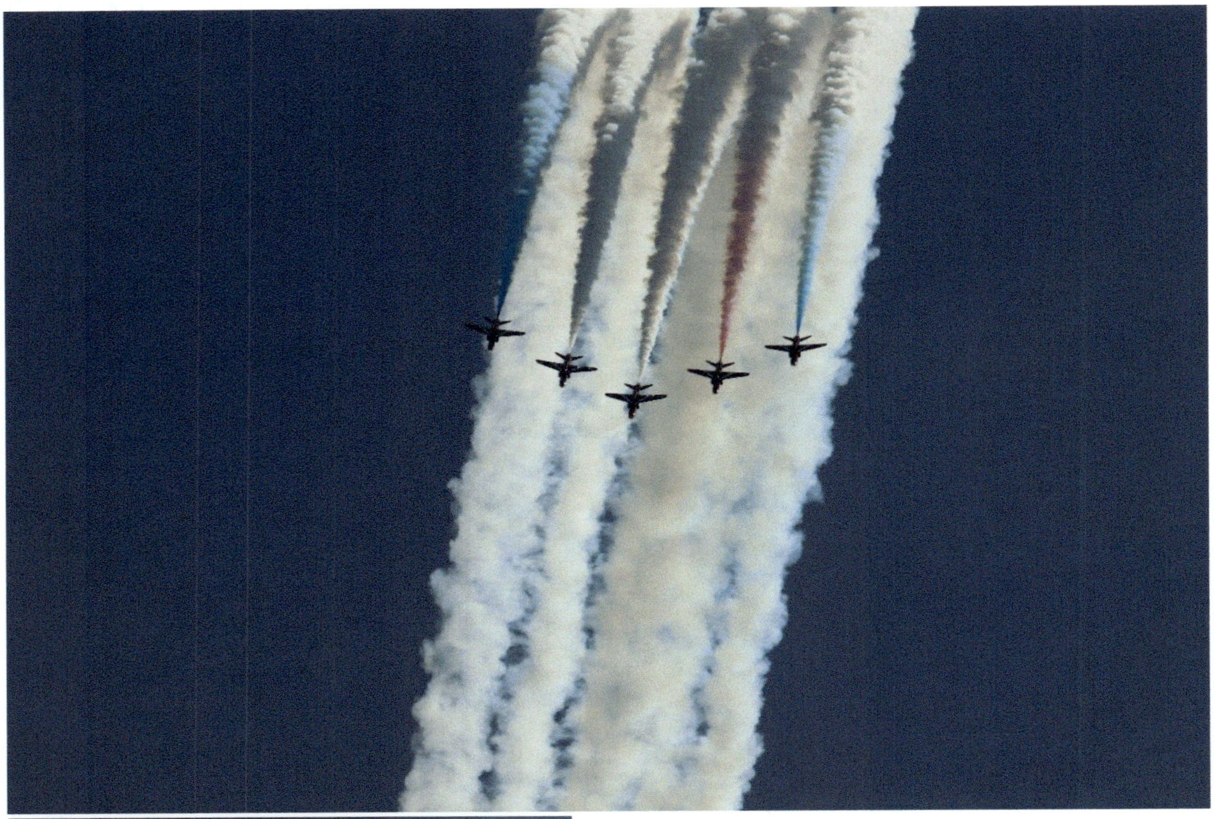

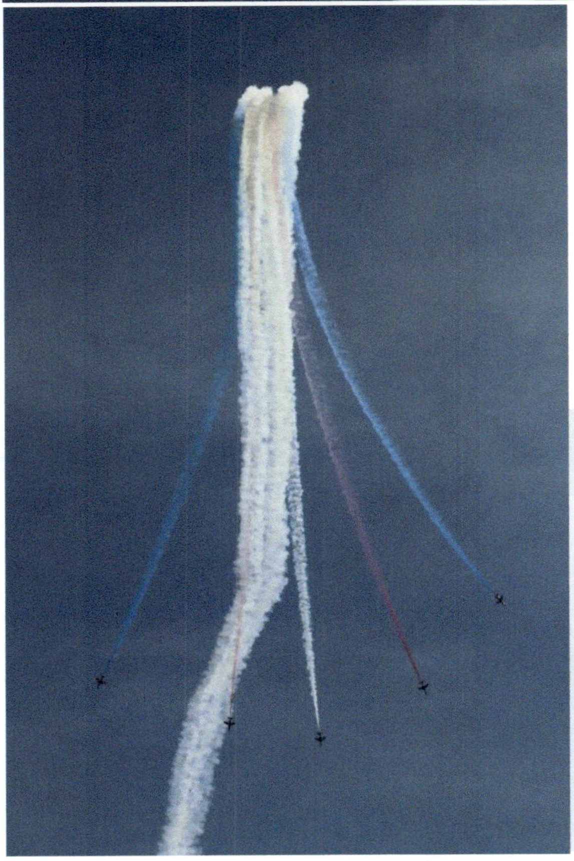

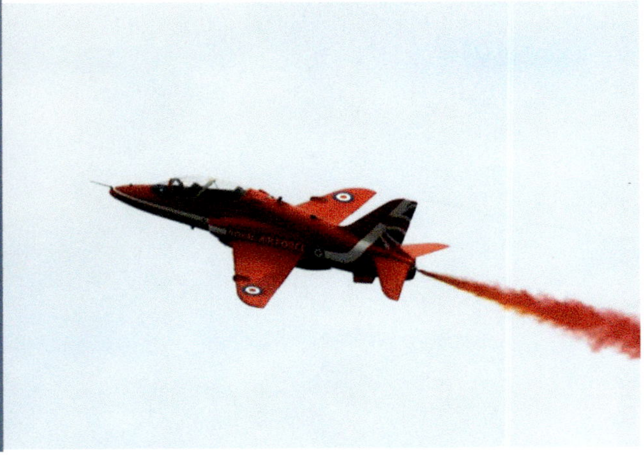

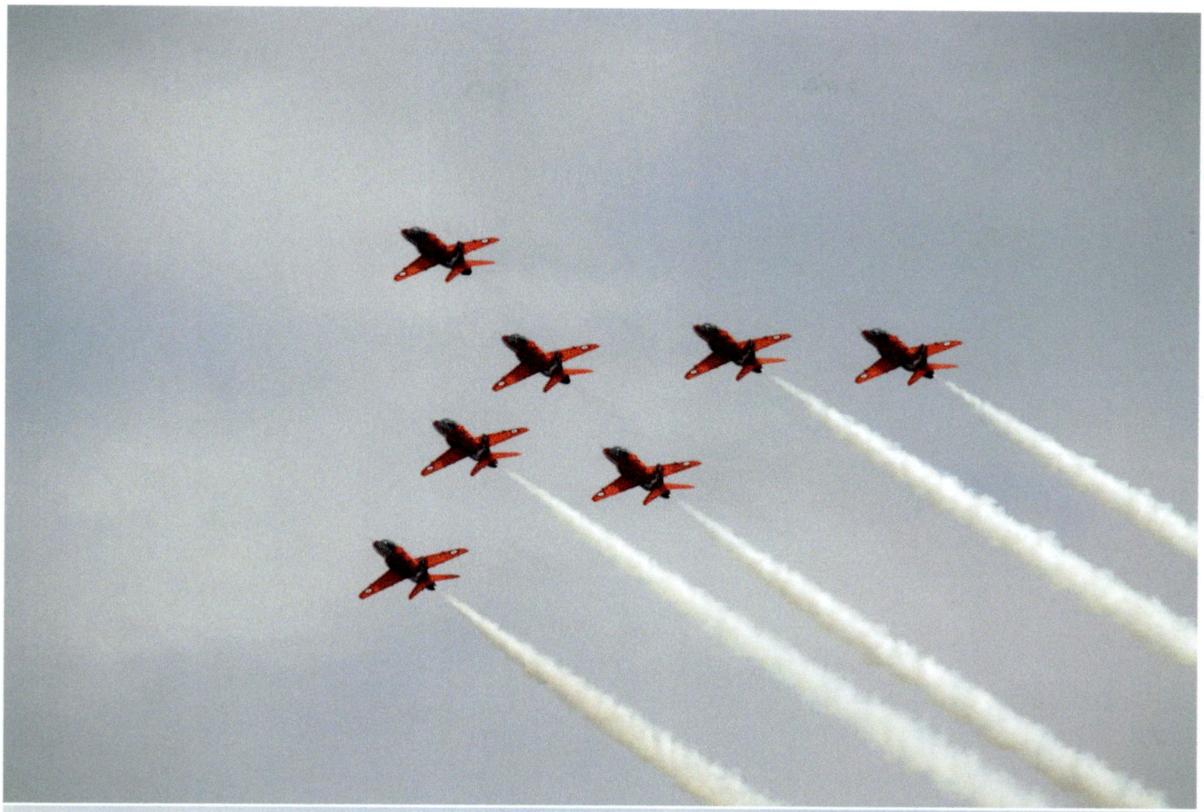

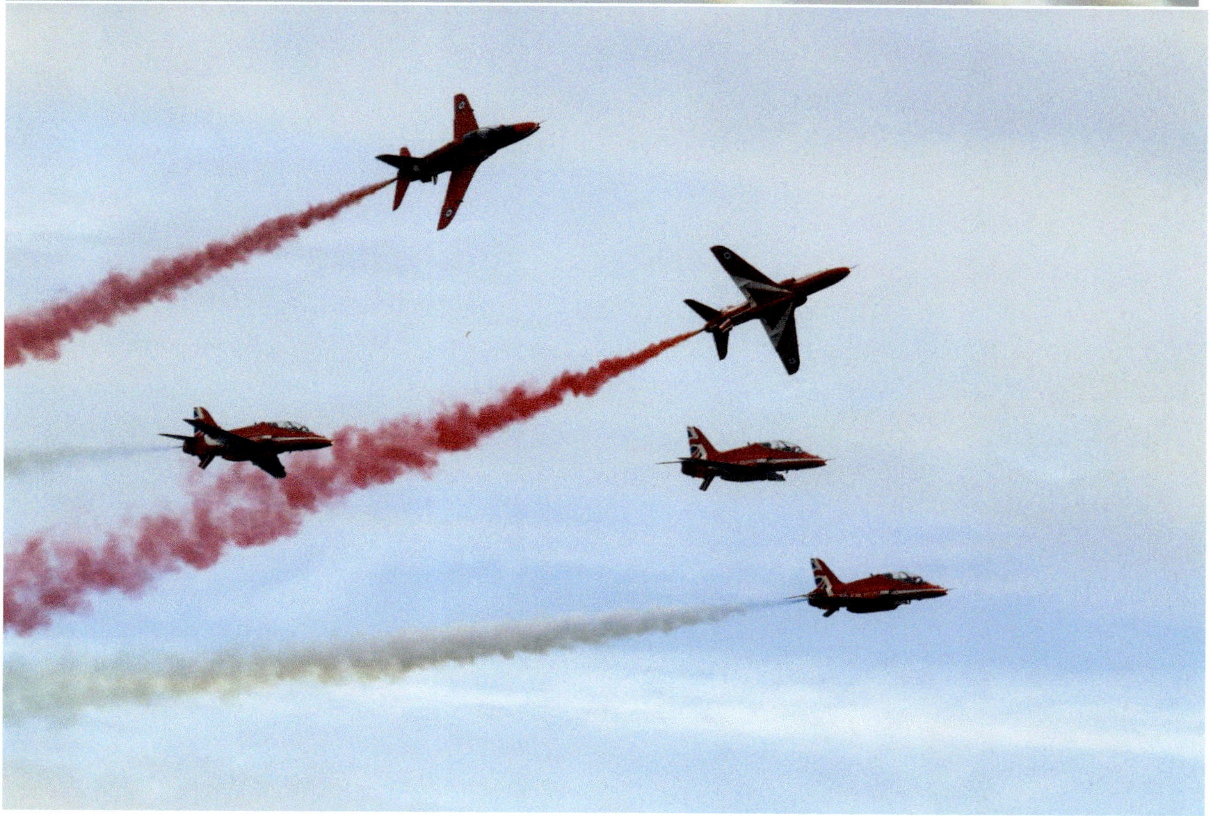

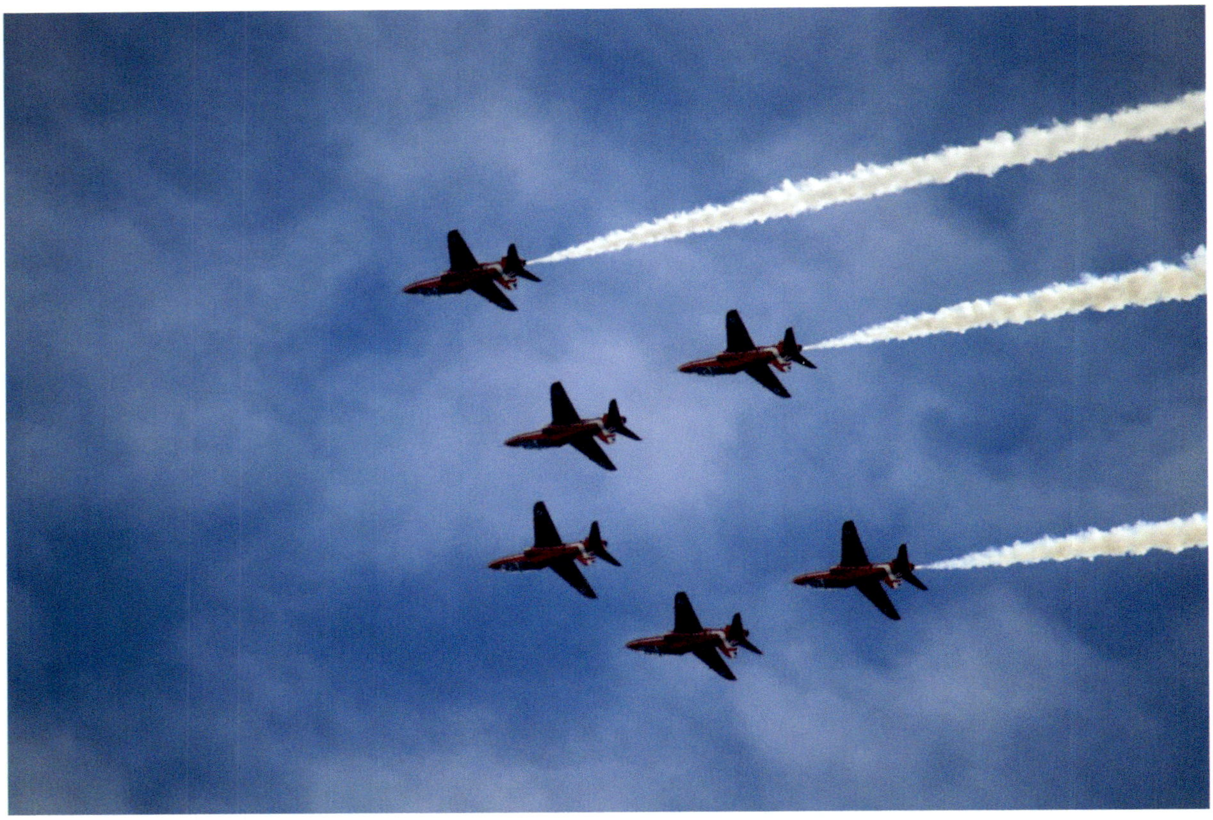

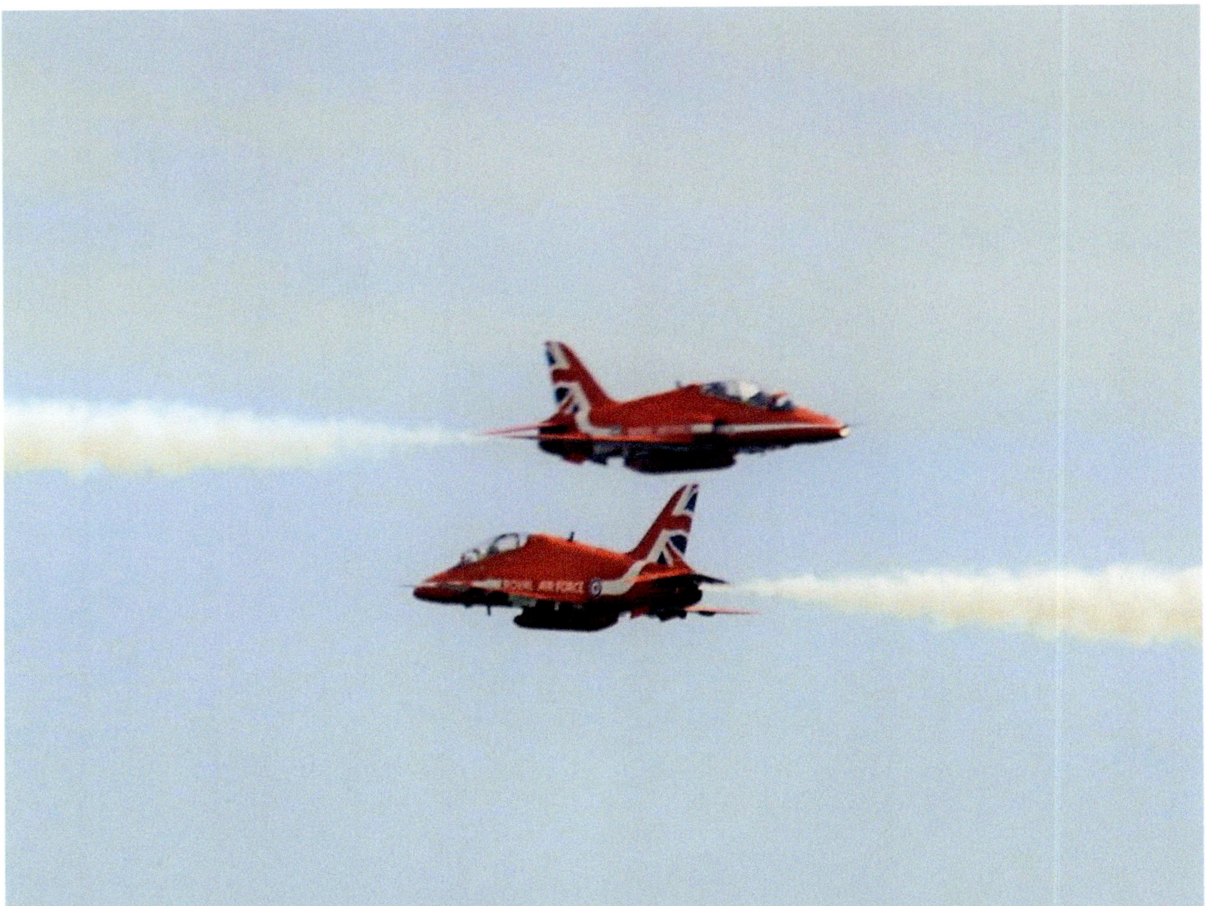
ROYAL AIR FORCE

Rotary Wing Aircraft

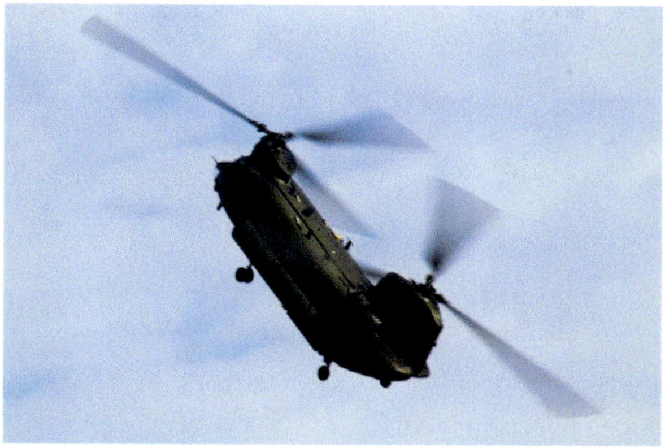

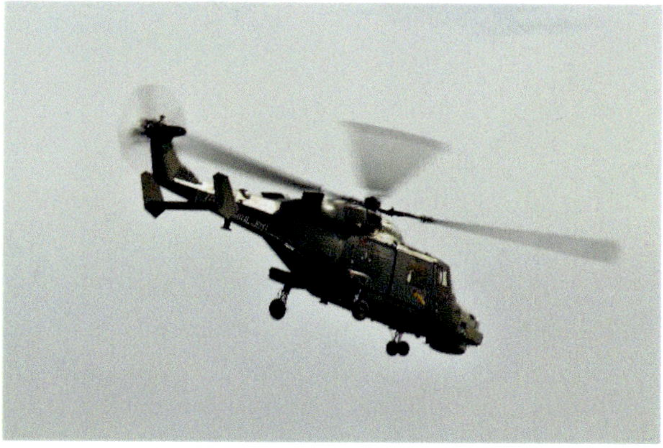

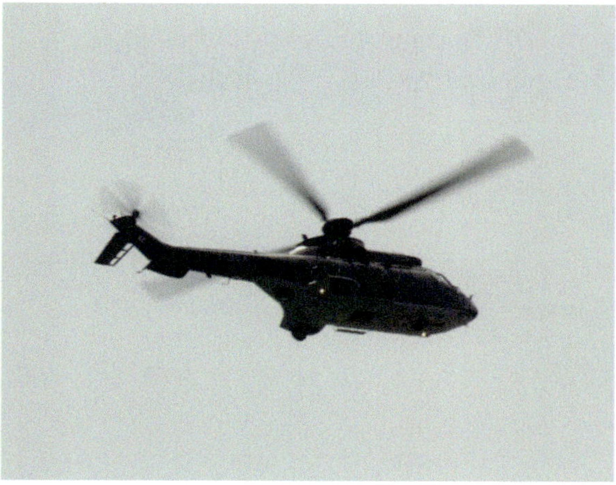

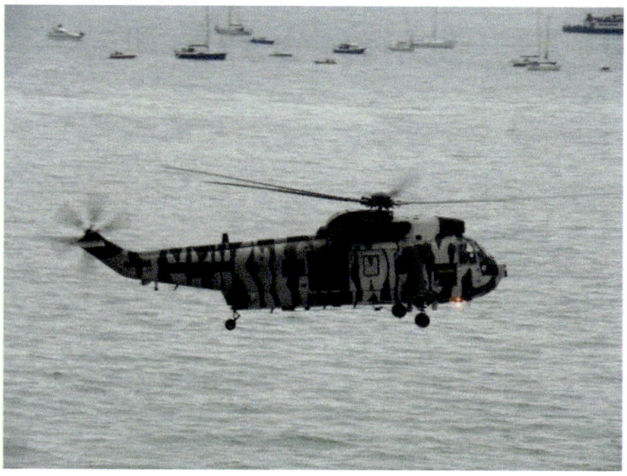

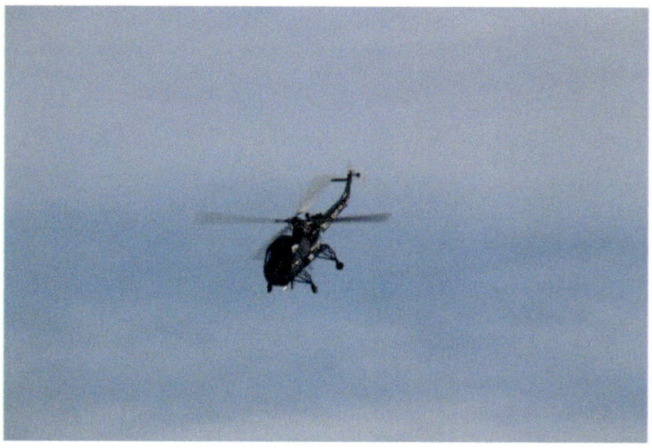

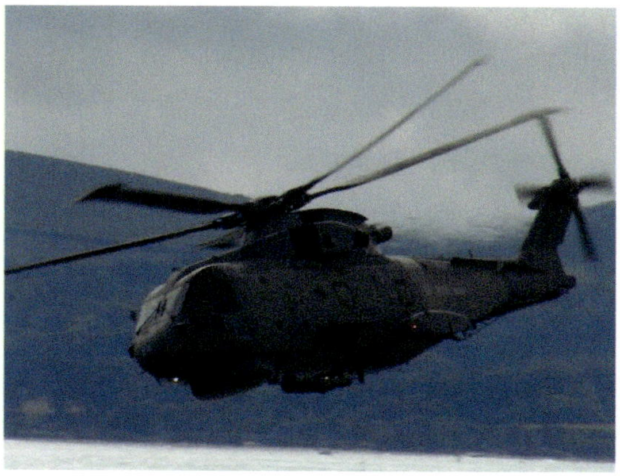

Westland Wasp

The Westland Wasp is a small British anti-submarine helicopter from the 1960s. Designed by Westland Helicopters, it originated from the Saunders-Roe P.531 program, which also produced the Westland Scout for the British Army. Based on the earlier piston-engine Saunders-Roe Skeeter, the Wasp has a turbine engine and is small enough to land on frigate decks. It was made to meet the Royal Navy's need for a helicopter that could carry two homing torpedoes.

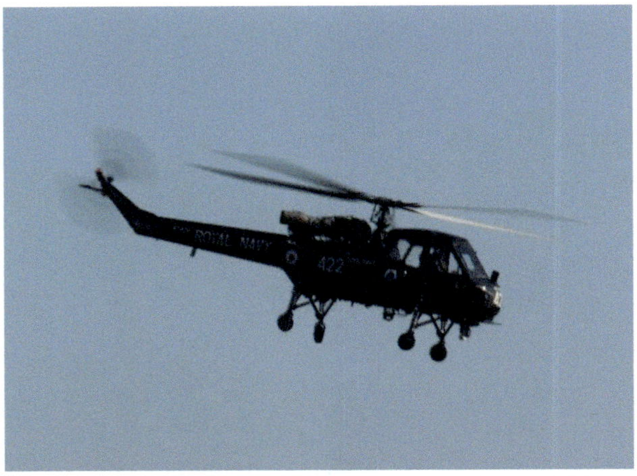

The increasing speed and attack range of the submarine threat, and the increased range at which this threat could be detected led to a Royal Navy requirement for a "Manned Torpedo-Carrying Helicopter" (MATCH).

The Wasp HAS.1 entered service in 1964 for small ship operations after extensive trials from June 1963 to March 1964 by the 700(W) Intensive Flying Trials Unit. The aircraft was primarily used by the 829 Naval Air Squadron, but also served to train crews for frontline duty with the 706 Naval Air Squadron from 1965-1967 and the 703 Naval Air Squadron from 1972-1981.

The Royal Naval Air Station Portland was one of the busiest air stations on the South Coast between 1959 and 1999. It was home to the Royal Navy's Wasp helicopter which, with its folding tail and rotor blades, quadricycle undercarriage with castoring wheels, and compact size, was well-suited for operating off the small decks of naval warships of that era. The pioneering Wasp made vital contributions to solving the challenges of maritime helicopter operations.

A total of 133 Wasps were produced after its first flight in October 1962. These helicopters were used primarily for anti-submarine operations, launching from frigates and other vessels. The Wasp could carry two homing torpedoes but lacked its own submarine detection system. Instead, it relied heavily on target guidance from other aircraft or ships equipped with sonar.

The Navy Wings Heritage Flight brought the Wasp helicopter to the 2023 Bournemouth Air Festival to showcase the early era aircraft's capabilities. The Wasp made a series of passes across the seafront, including steep turns, that provided ample photographic opportunities. It also partnered with the Fairey Swordfish biplane, another part of the Navy Wings Heritage Flight, to make formation passes over the crowds.

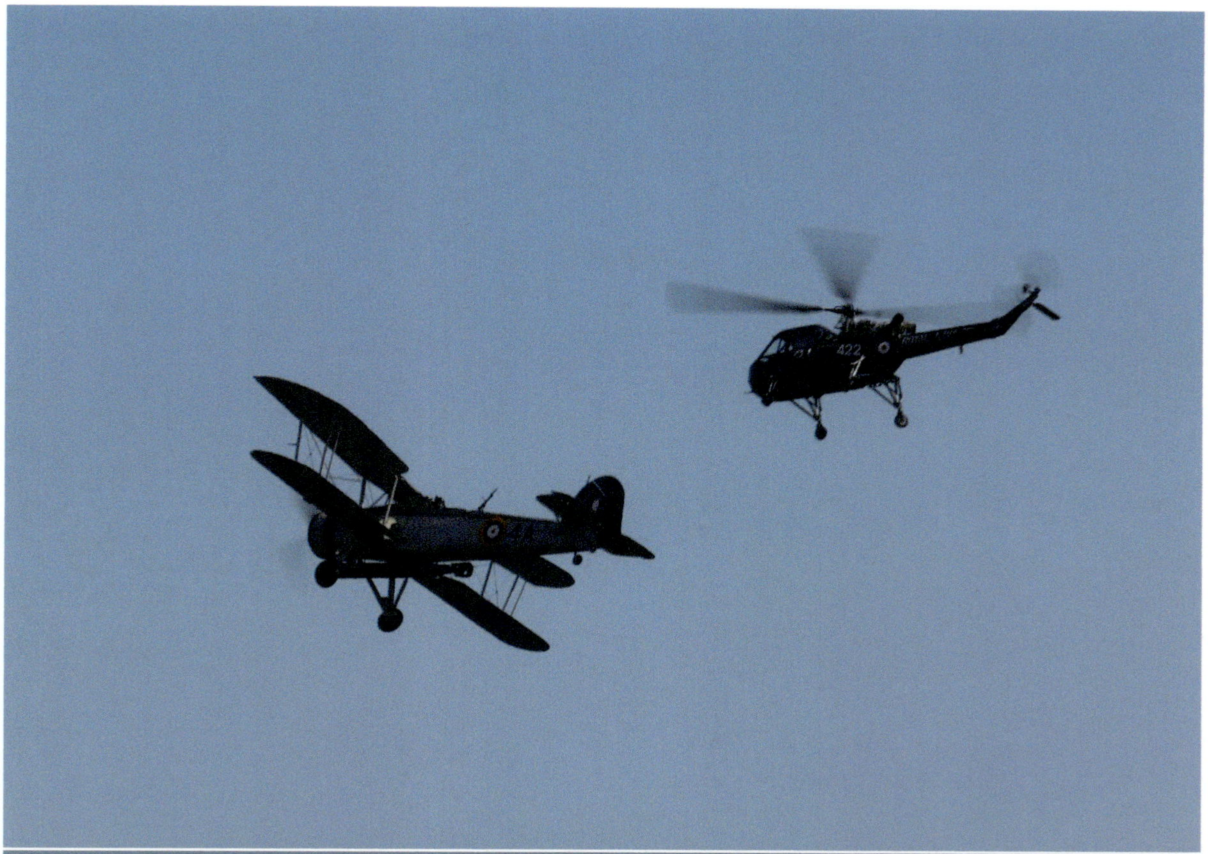

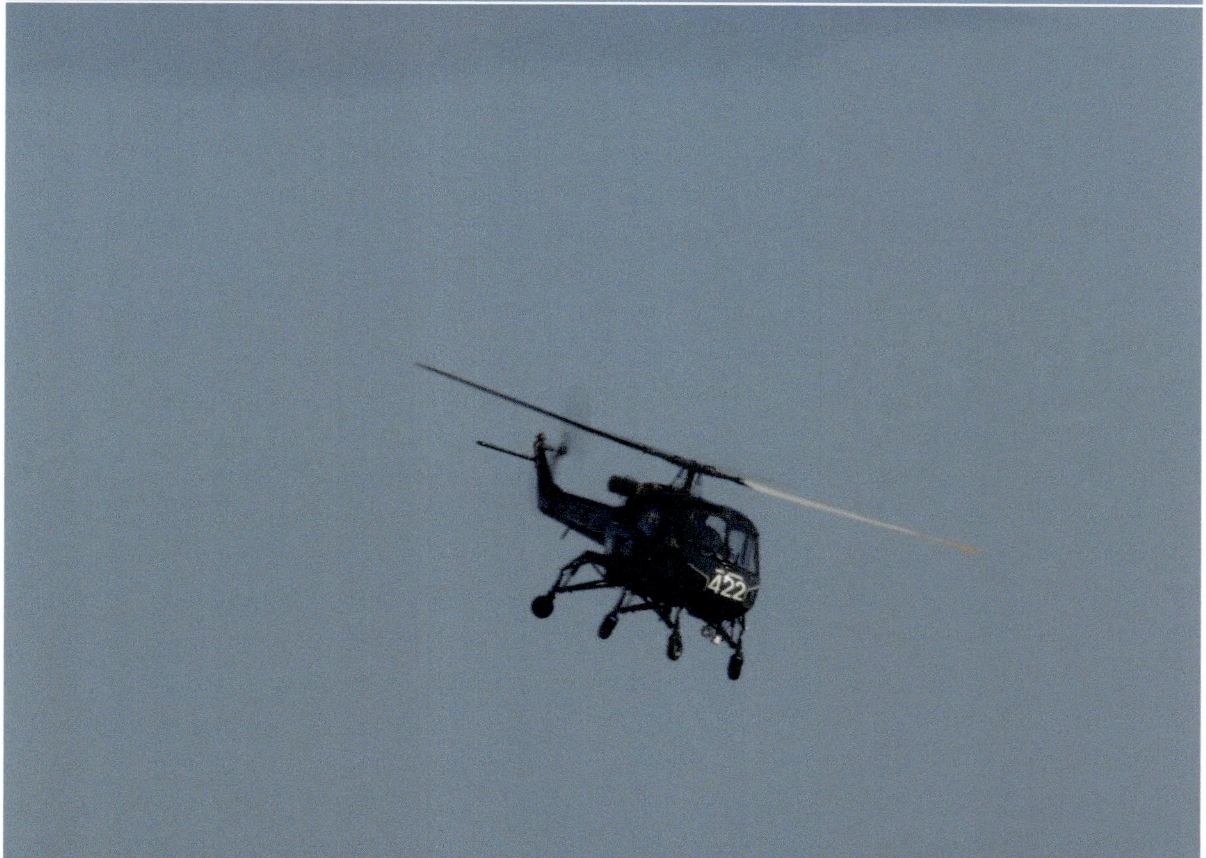

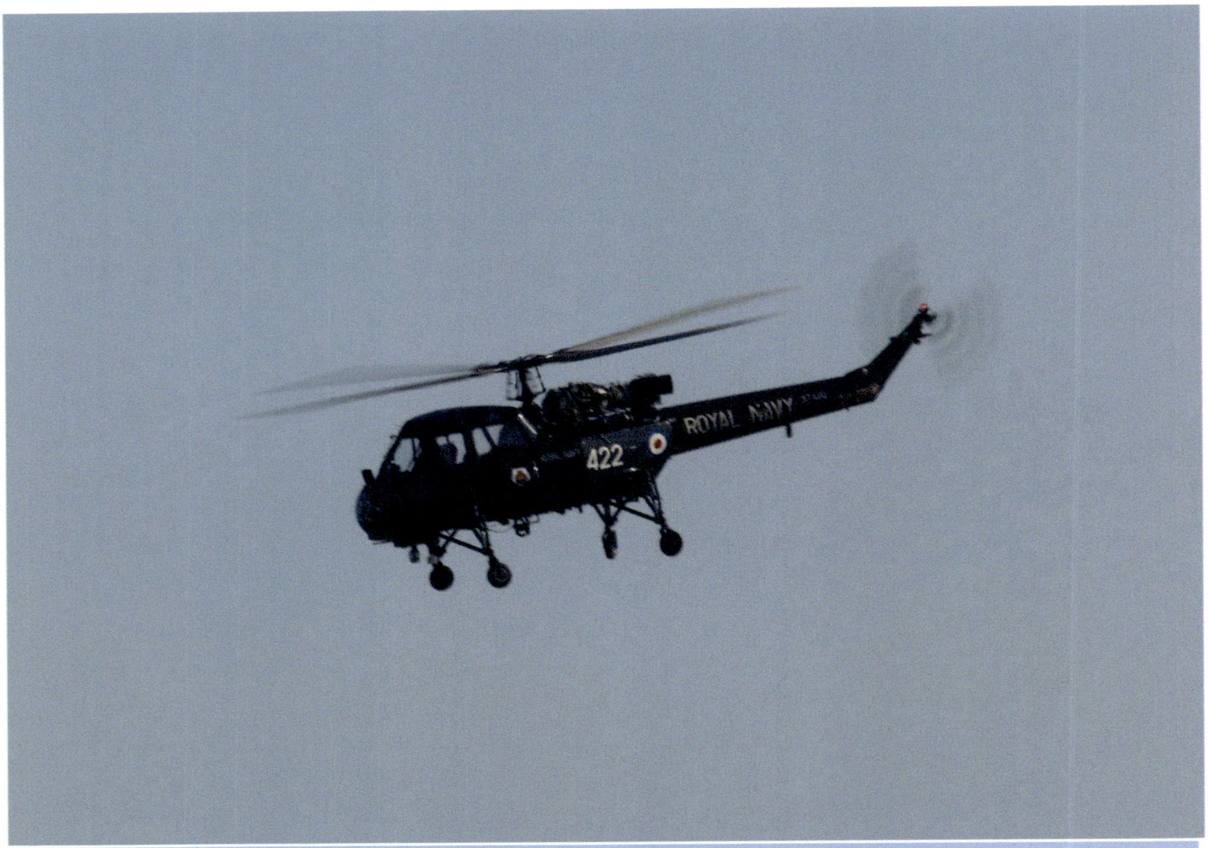
ROYAL NAVY
422

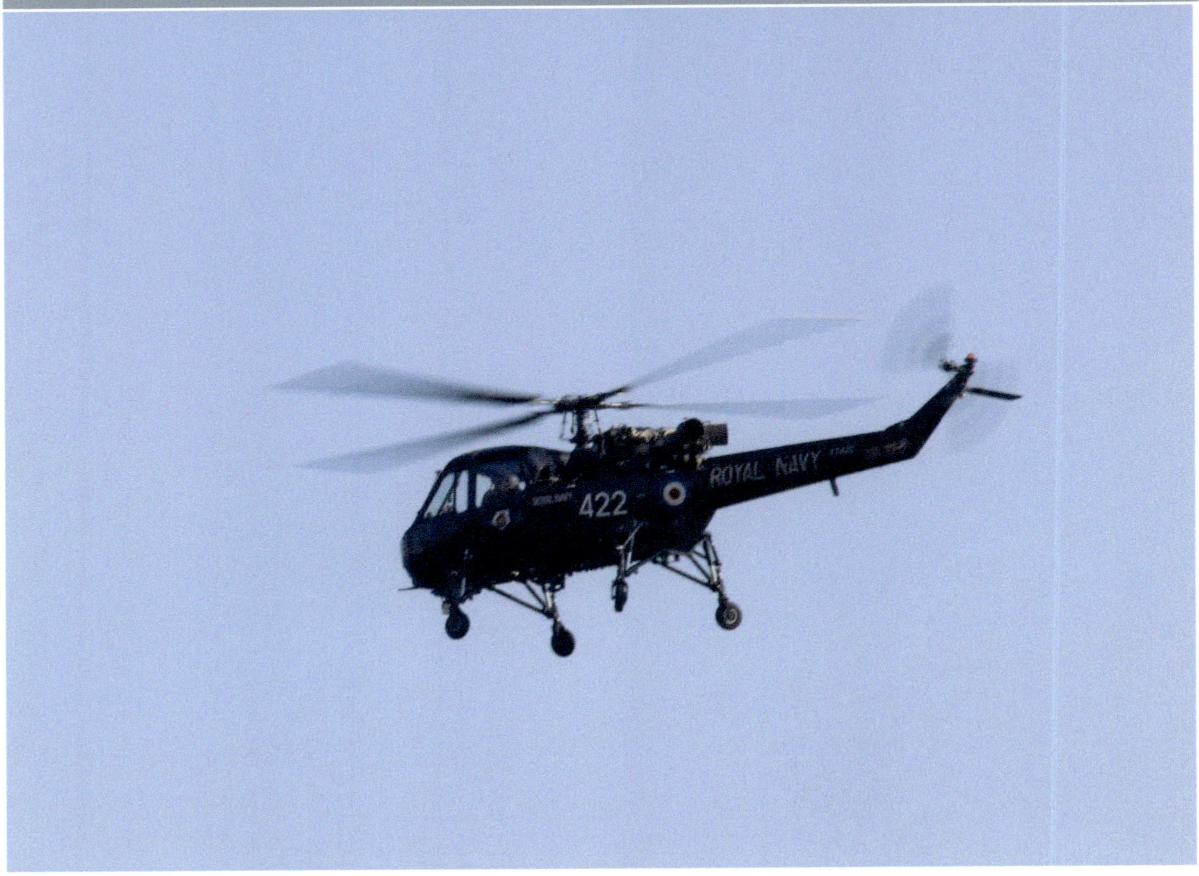
ROYAL NAVY
422

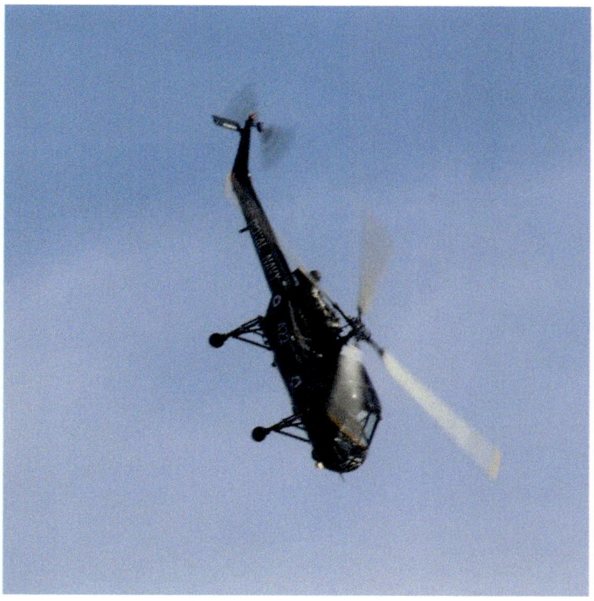

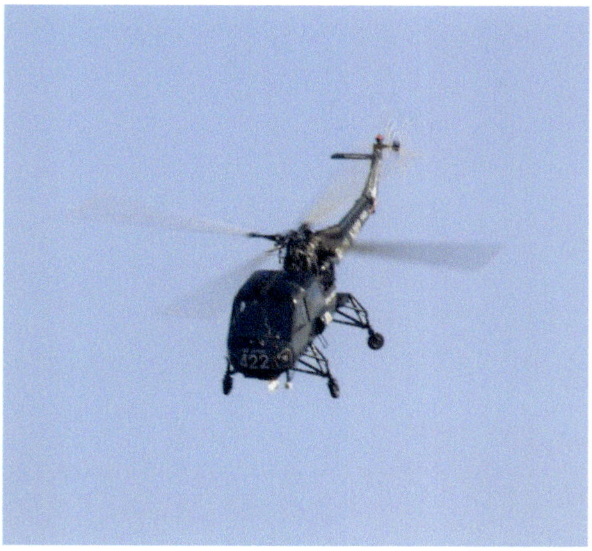

Quick Facts

General

Crew: 1 pilot, 1 Aircrewman

Capacity: up to 4 passengers

Length: 40 ft 4 in (12.29 m) overall, 30 ft 4 in (9.24 m) fuselage only

Height: 8 ft 11 in (2.72 m)

Powerplant: 1 × Rolls-Royce Nimbus 103 turboshaft engine

Performance

Maximum speed: 104 kn (120 mph, 193 km/h)

Cruise speed: 96 kn (110 mph, 178 km/h)

Range: 263 nmi (303 mi, 487 km)

Service ceiling: 12,200 ft (3,700 m)

Armament

2 x Mk 44 or 1 x Mk 46 torpedo or 2 x Mk 44 depth charges or WE.177 600lb Nuclear Depth Bomb.[28][29]

4 x SS.11 or 2 x AS.12 missiles.

L7 GPMG, 4.5 Flares, Smoke/flame floats.

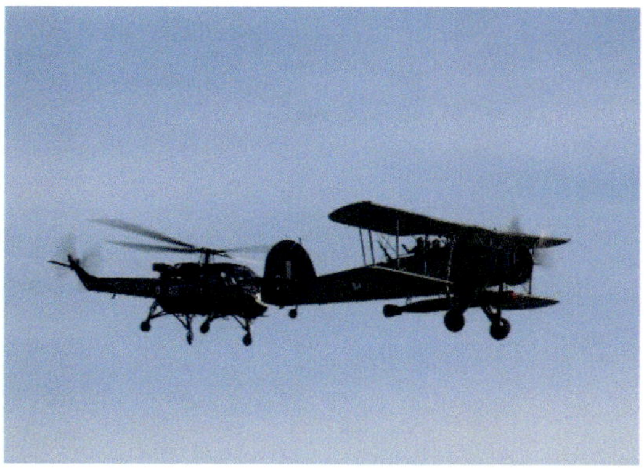

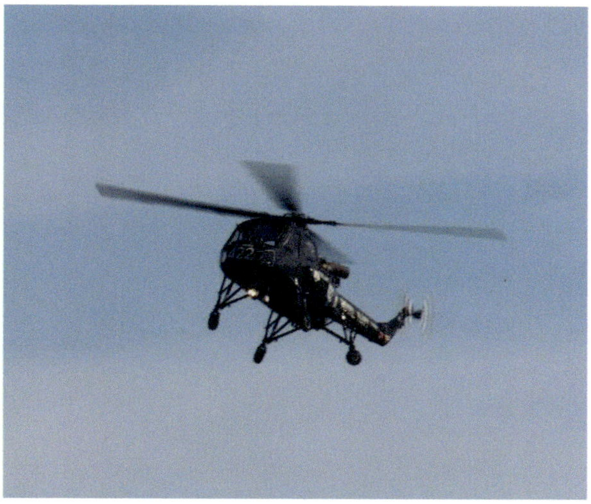

Super Puma

The Eurocopter AS332 Super Puma is a medium-sized utility helicopter powered by two Turbomeca Makila 1A1 turboshaft engines. These engines drive the four-bladed main rotor and five-bladed tail rotor, as well as two independent hydraulic systems and two electrical alternators. Six internal fuel tanks provide the basic fuel supply, while additional auxiliary and external tanks can extend flight endurance. For safety, the Super Puma utilizes crashworthy fuel tank plumbing along with fire detection and suppression systems in the engine bay.

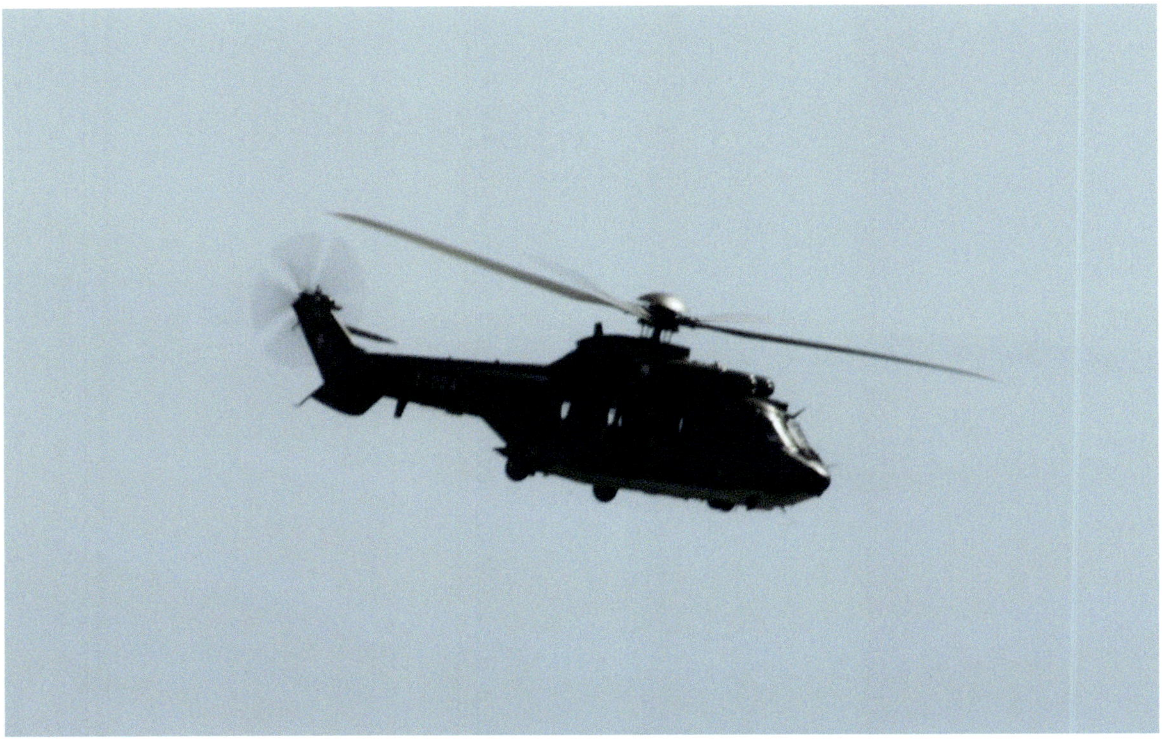

The Super Puma's main cabin can be accessed through sliding plug doors and has a reconfigurable floor plan that allows for different passenger seating or cargo layouts, including specialized medical configurations. According to Airbus Helicopters, the short-fuselage AS332 model seats up to 15 passengers plus 2 pilots, while the stretched AS332 fits up to 20 passengers plus 2 pilots comfortably.

During the 2016 Bournemouth Airfestival the Swiss Air Force presented the Super Puma Display Team who fly a dramatic routine in the large helicopter which at times is nearly aerobatic. The specially trained pilots of the Super Puma Display Team showcase the dynamics and some of the capabilities of the Super Puma with their demonstration and the display last for approximately eight minutes.

The 2016 display was the first and last time the Super Puma Display Team appeared at the Bournemouth Air Festival.

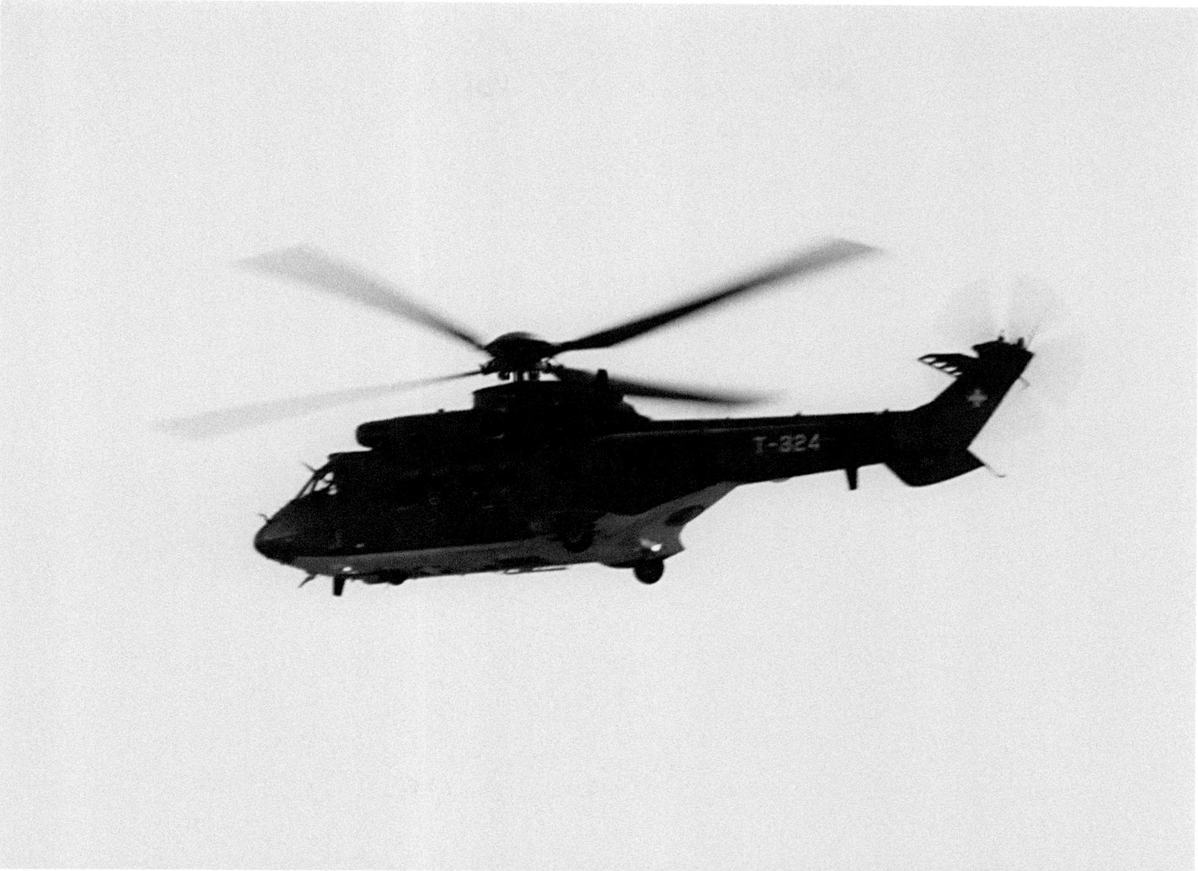
T-324

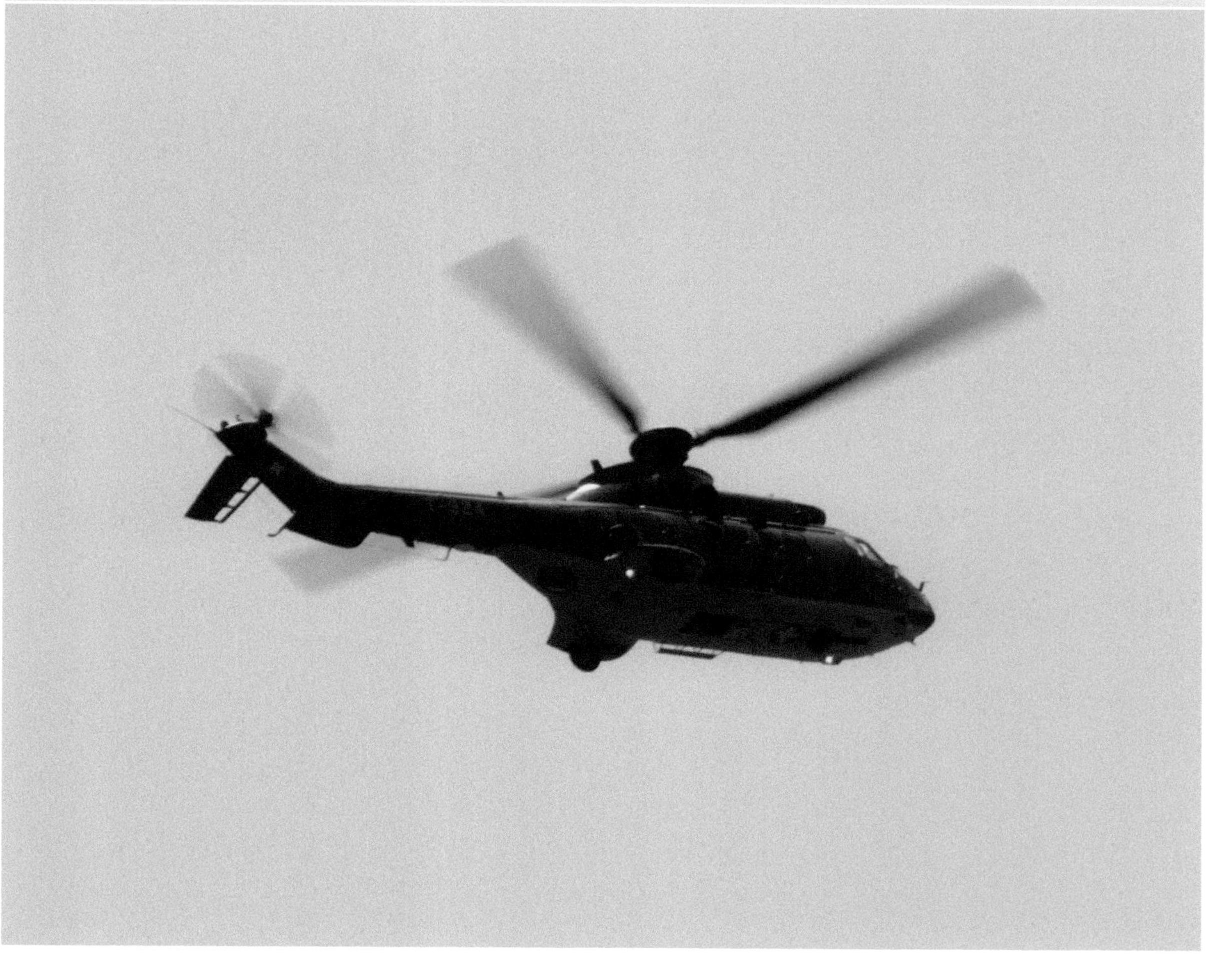

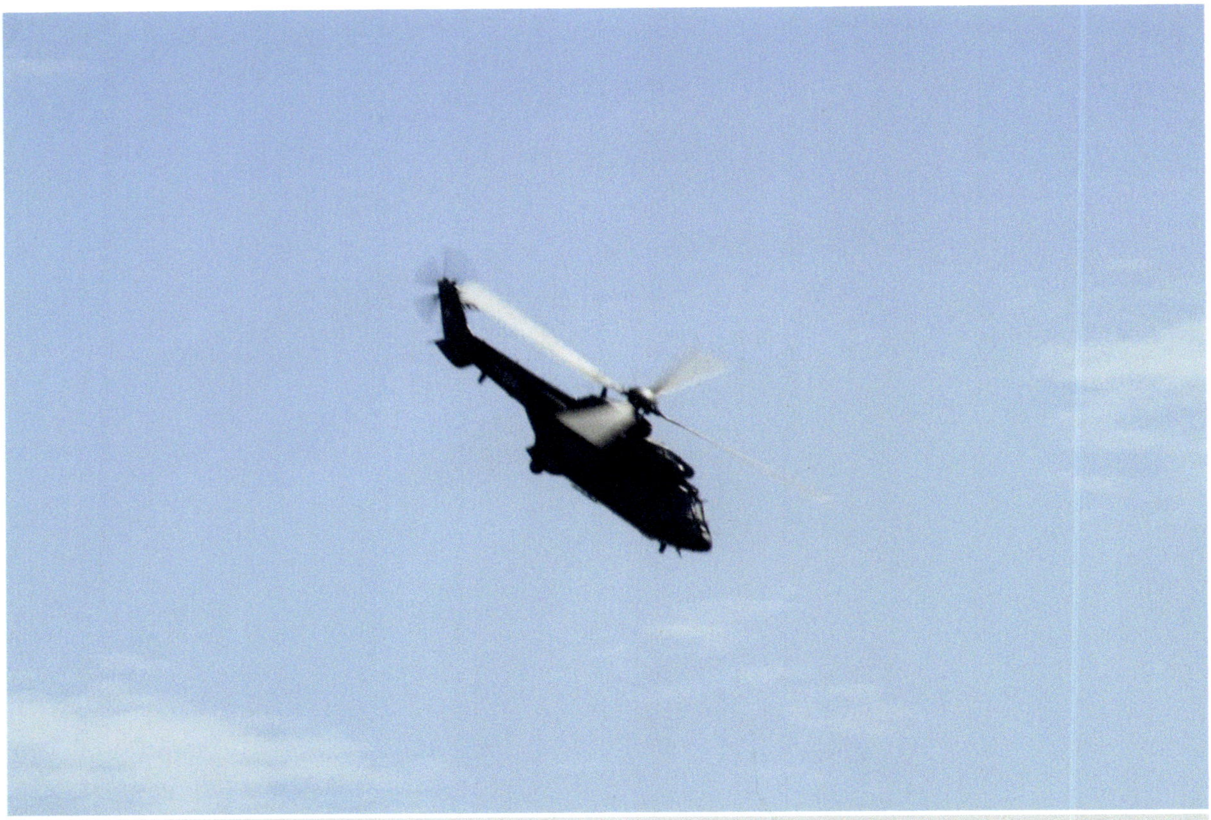

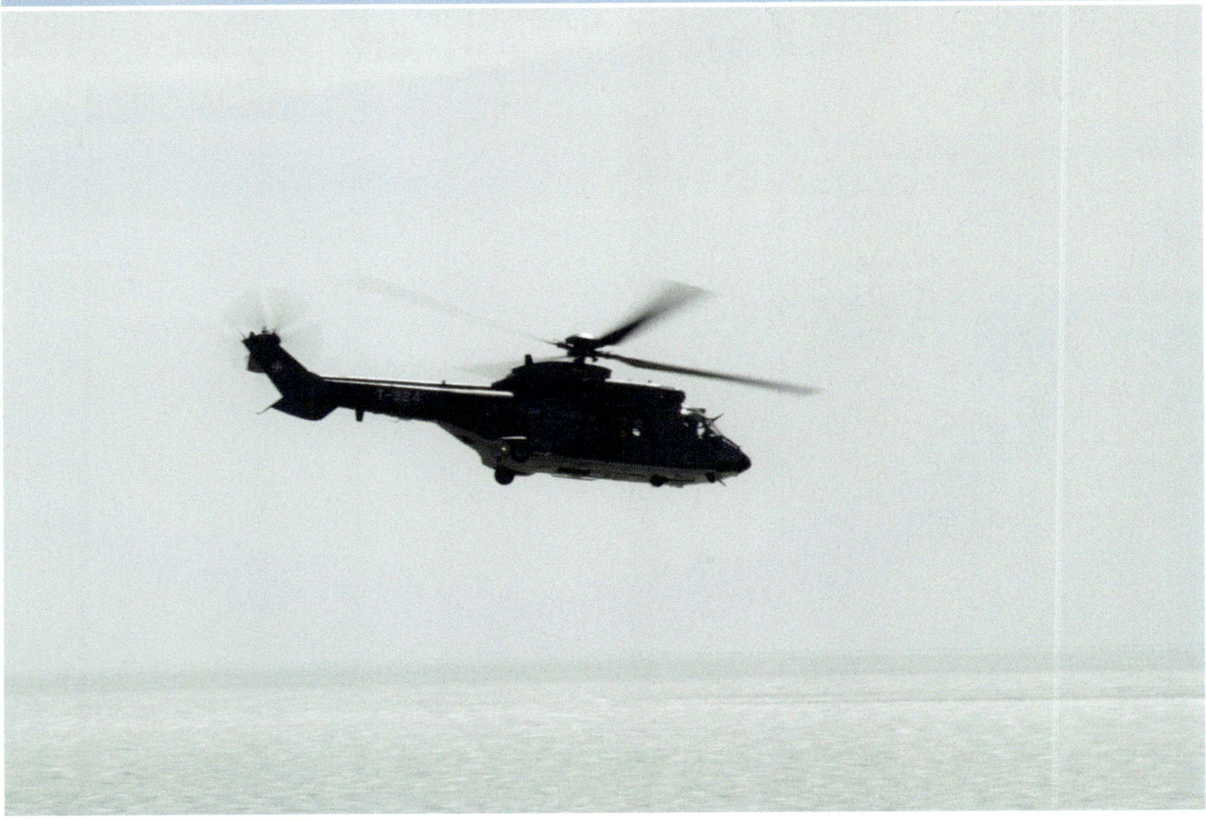

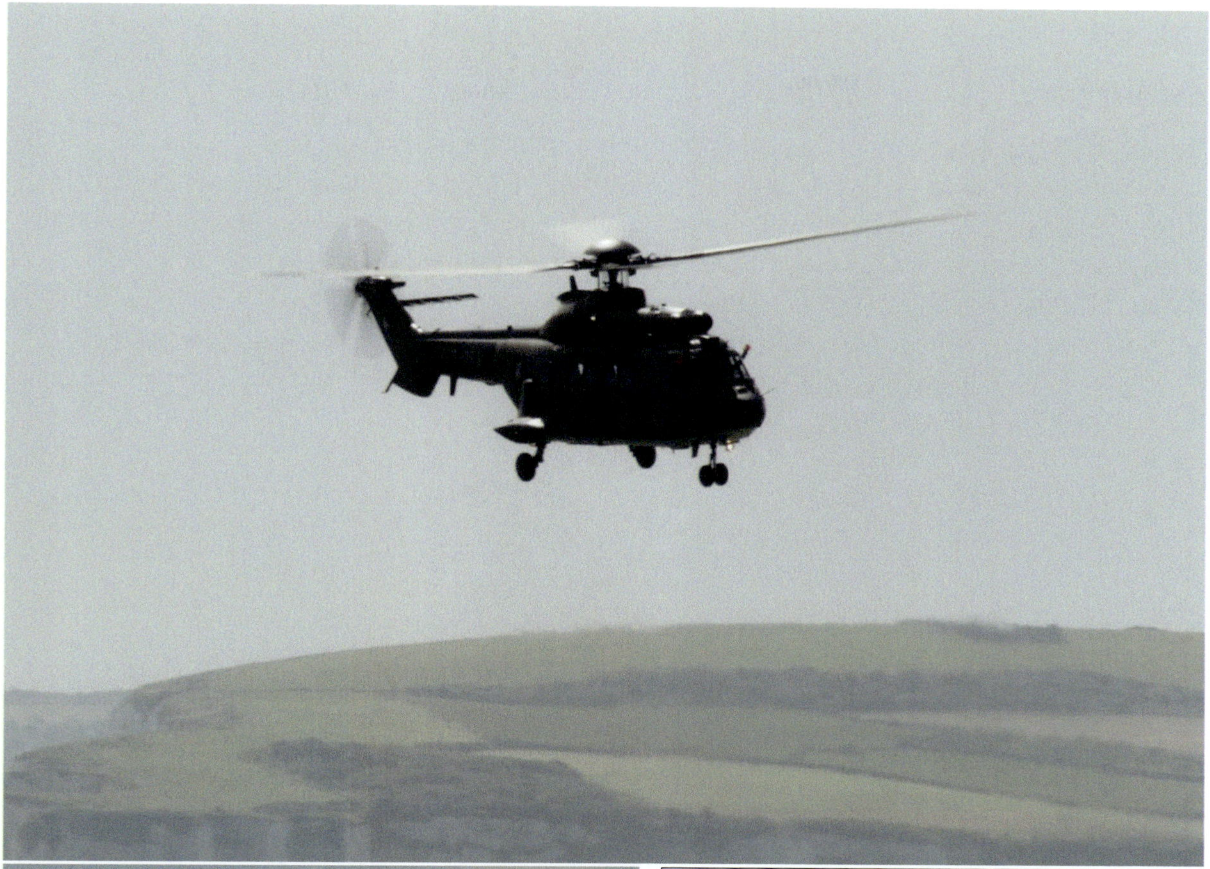

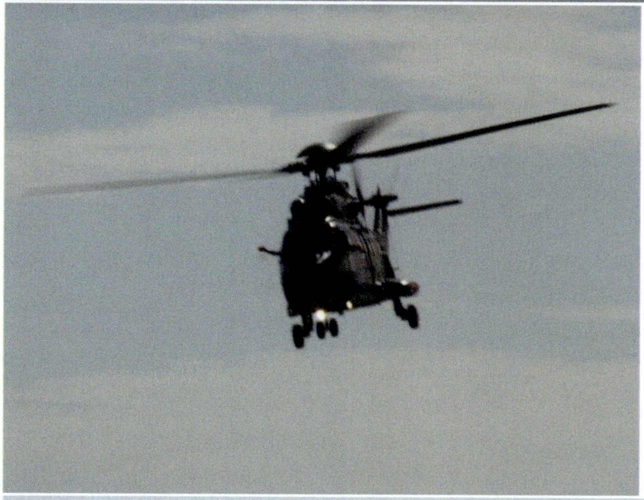

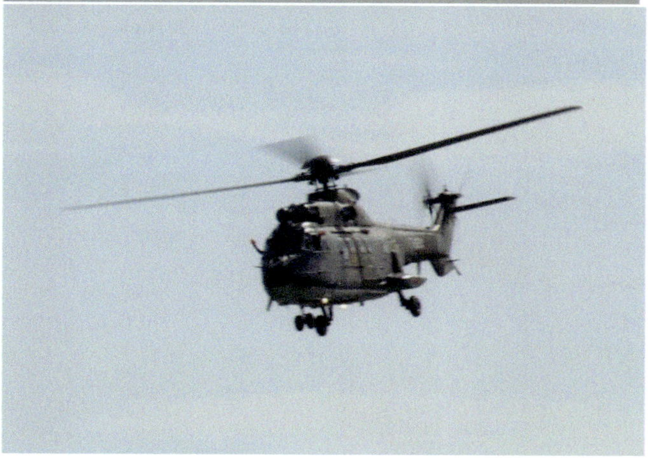

Quick Facts

General

Crew: 2

Length: 16.79 m (55 ft 1 in) fuselage

18.7 m (61 ft) rotor turning

Height: 4.97 m (16 ft 4 in)

Powerplant: 2 × Turbomeca Makila 1A2 turboshaft

Performance

Cruise speed: 277 km/h (172 mph, 150 kn)

Range: 851 km (529 mi, 460 nmi)

Service ceiling: 5,180 m (16,990 ft)

Rate of climb: 7.4 m/s (1,460 ft/min)

Westland Sea King

Westland Helicopters, which had a long-standing licensing agreement with Sikorsky Aircraft to build Sikorsky helicopters, extended the agreement to include the Sikorsky SH-3 Sea King soon after the Sea King's first flight in 1969. Westland then independently developed the Sea King, integrating many components from British suppliers. Key changes were the use of twin Rolls-Royce Gnome turboshaft engines and an automatic flight control system. Designed primarily for anti-submarine warfare and search and rescue missions, the Sea King spawned a troop transport variant called the Commando, developed by Westland.

To replace the Westland Wessex, the Royal Navy chose the Sea King to fulfil the need for an anti-submarine warfare helicopter, ordering 60 SH-3D Sea Kings from Westland in June 1966. Sikorsky built the prototype and three pre-production models at its Stratford, Connecticut facility before shipping them to the United Kingdom to serve as trials and pattern aircraft.

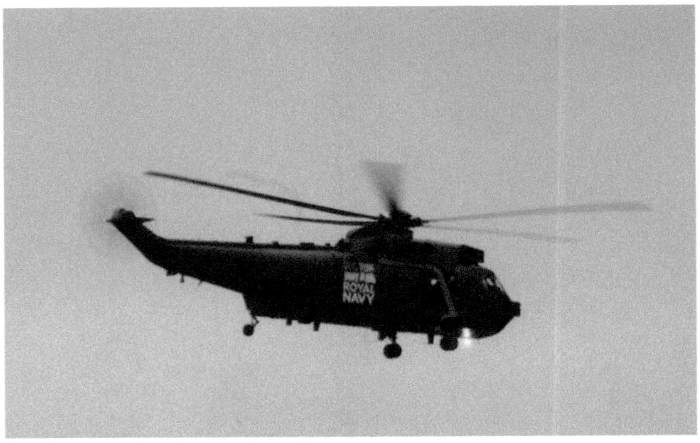

The first Westland-built Sea King helicopter, designated HAS1, took its inaugural flight on May 7, 1969 in Yeovil. Westland and the Aeroplane and Armament Experimental Establishment used the first two helicopters for trials and evaluations. Afterward, Westland began delivering subsequent production Sea Kings to the Royal Navy's 700 Naval Air Squadron starting in August 1969. By 1979, to meet anti-submarine and secondary anti-ship requirements, the Royal Navy had ordered 56 HAS1s and 21 HAS2s. One of the most extensively modified Sea King variants was the Royal Navy's Westland Commando HC4, which could carry up to 28 fully-equipped troops.

The 2011 Airfestival featured a Royal Marine Sea King helicopter participating in a beach landing demonstration. The distinctive Sea King sported a zebra-striped livery. In 2015, two Navy Sea Kings made appearances, each displaying Royal Navy insignia flags on their side doors. During routines both years, troops descended ropes from the hovering Sea Kings into waiting boats below, demonstrating the helicopter's capabilities and crews' skills in deploying troops onto vessels when needed.

On 26 September 2018, the Royal Navy retired the last of its Sea King helicopters, marking the end of this aircraft's long service. Most Sea King operators have already replaced, or plan to replace, these aging helicopters with more modern models like the NH90 and AW101. The exception is Heli Operations, which continues flying three Sea King Mk 5s out of RNAS Portland to train German Navy pilots.

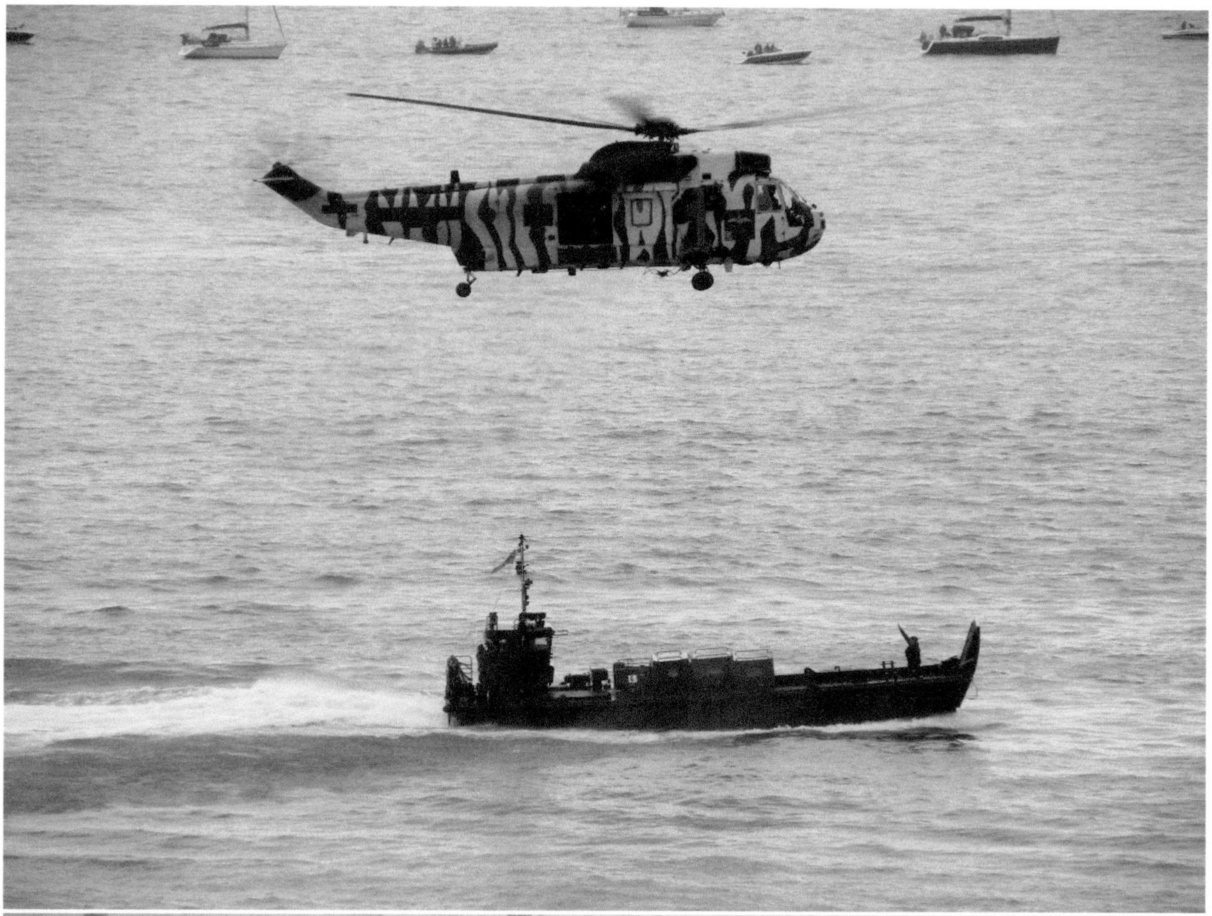

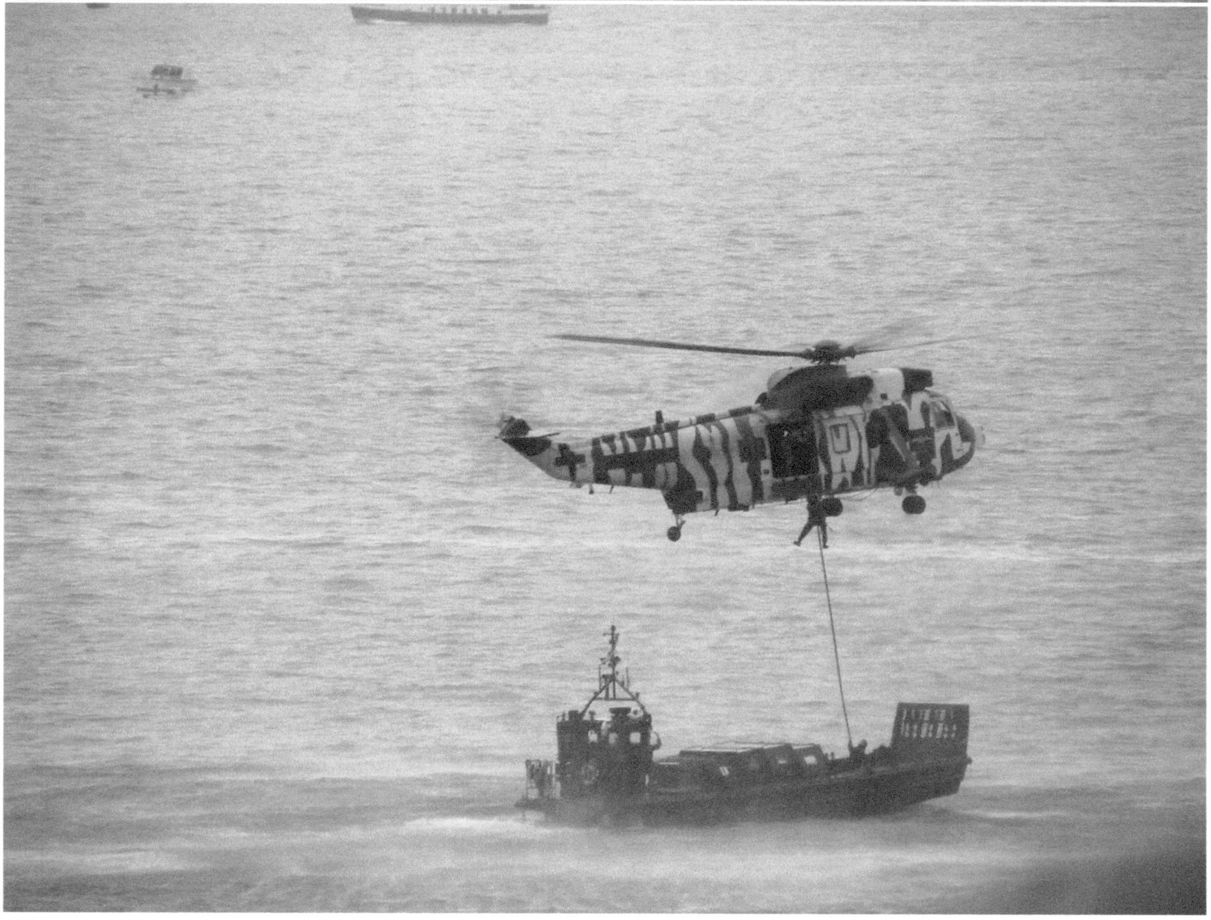

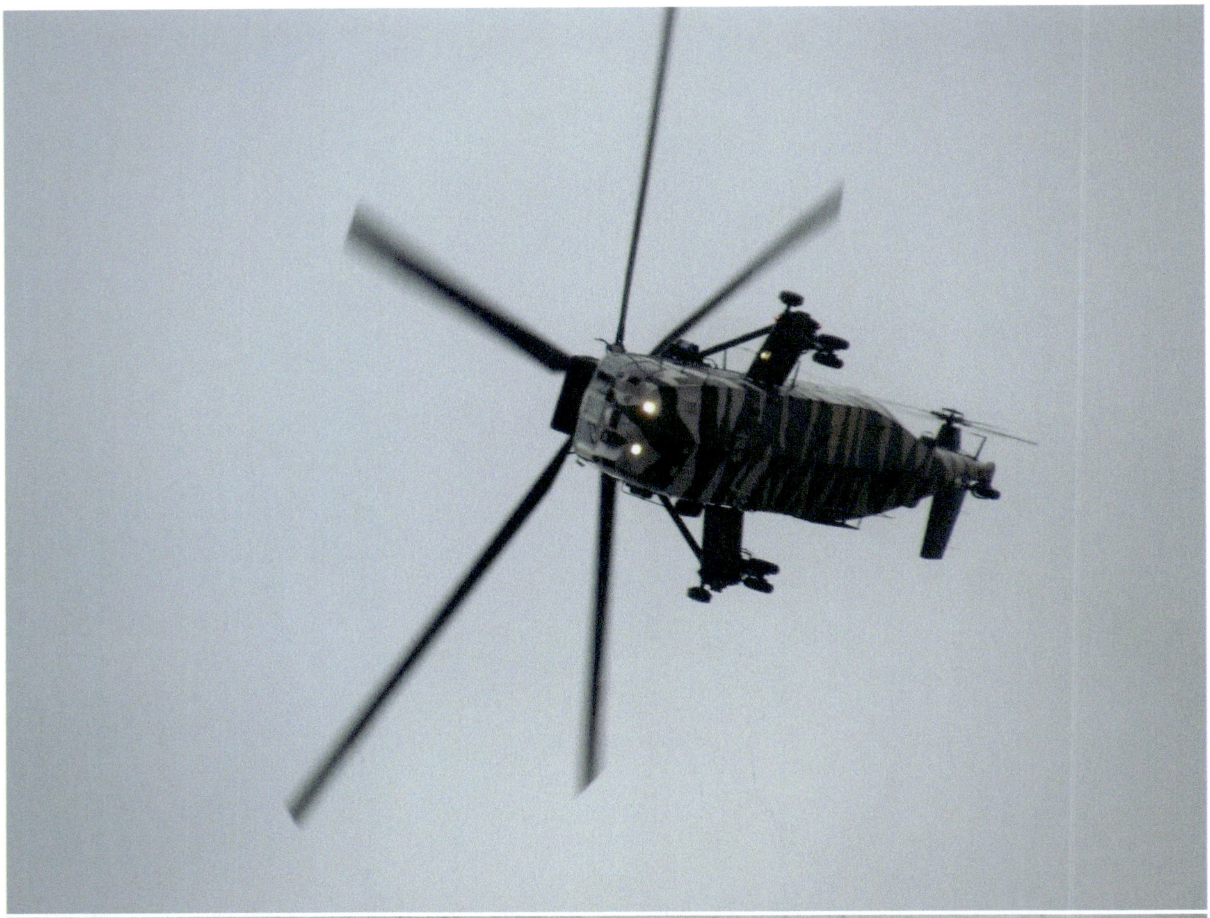

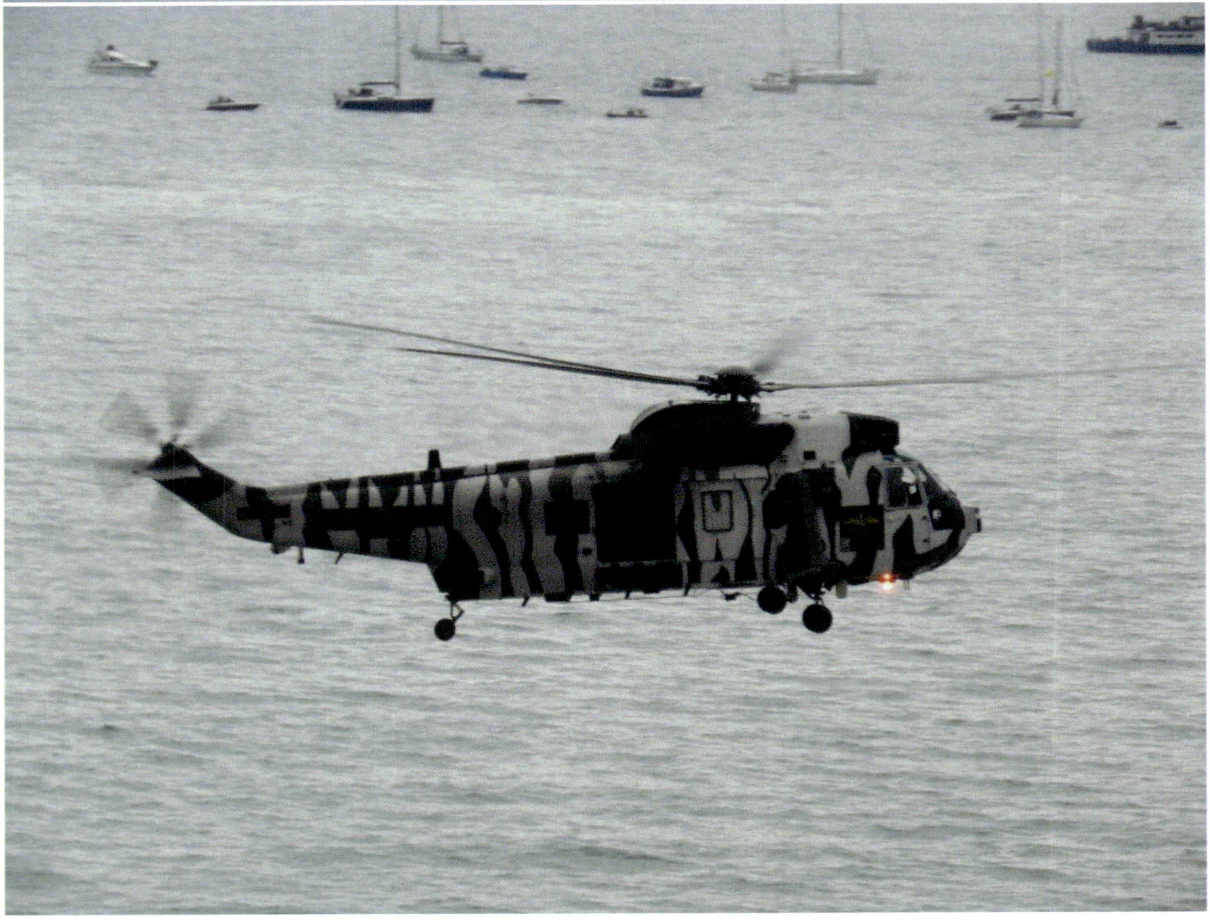

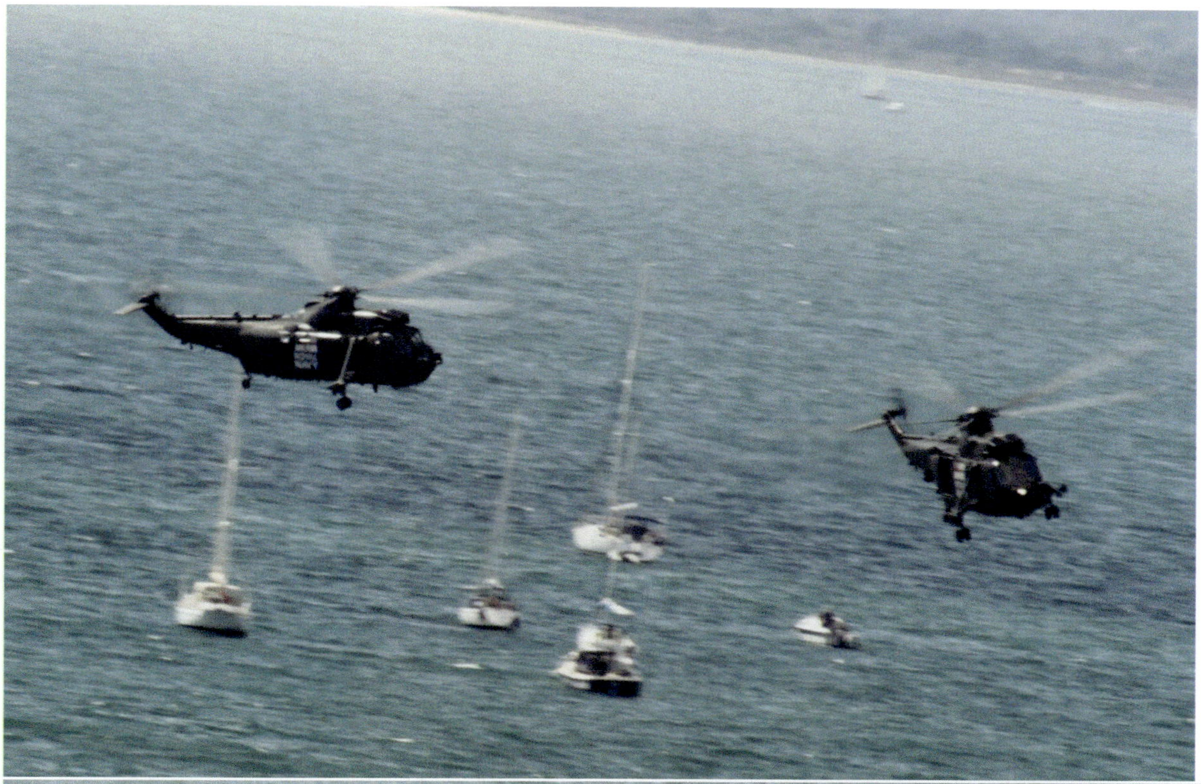

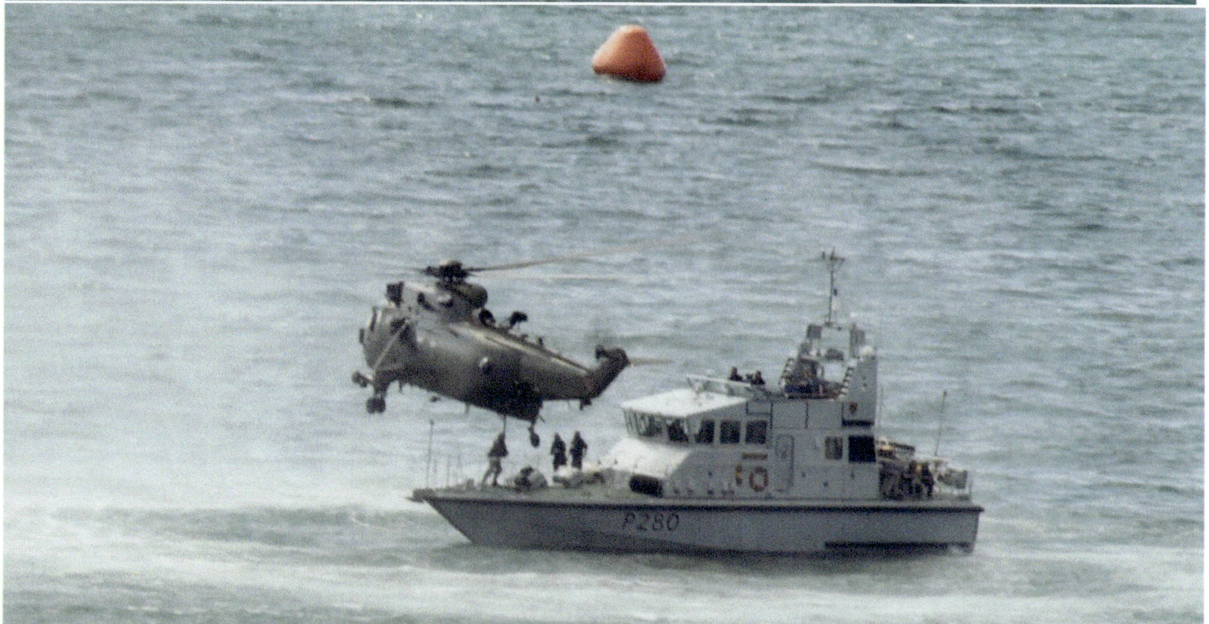
P280

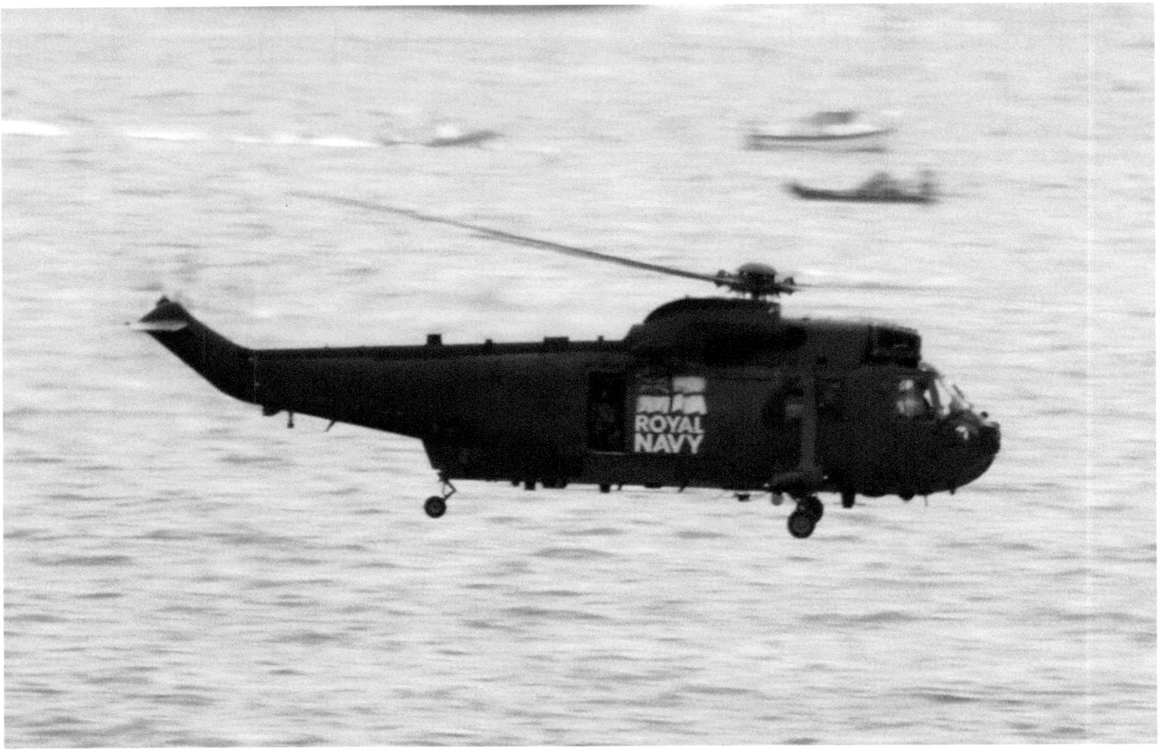

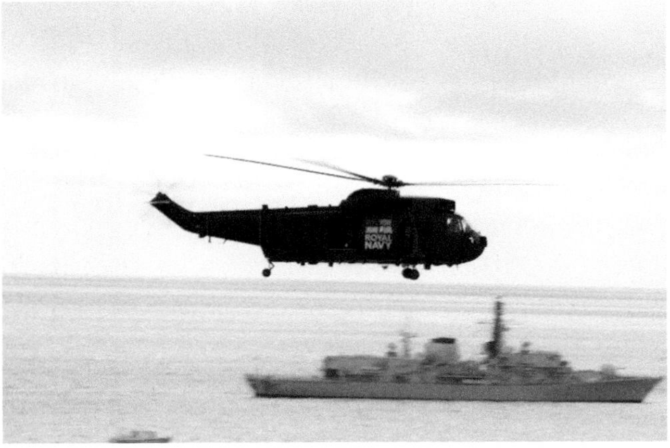

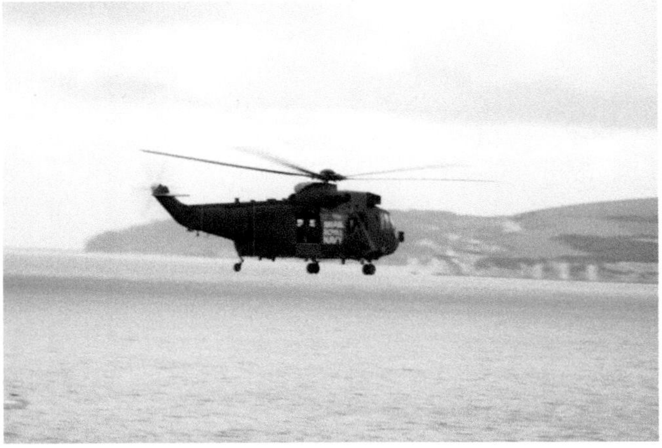

Quick Facts

General

Crew: 2-4

Length: 55 ft 10 in (17.02 m)

Height: 16 ft 10 in (5.13 m)

Powerplant: 2 × Rolls-Royce H.1400-2 Gnome turboshaft engines

Performance

Cruise speed: 112 kn (129 mph, 207 km/h)

Range: 664 nmi (764 mi, 1,230 km)

Rate of climb: 2,020 ft/min

Armament

4× Mark 44, Mark 46 or Sting Ray torpedoes, or 4× Depth charges

Provision for a door mounted machine gun – various calibres installable

Agusta Westland AW101 – Merlin

The AgustaWestland AW101 is a medium-lift military and civil helicopter first flown in 1987. Developed through a joint venture between Westland Helicopters in the United Kingdom and Agusta in Italy to meet national requirements for a modern naval utility aircraft, the Royal Navy calls the Agusta Westland AW101 the Merlin. It is manufactured in Yeovil, England and Vergiate, Italy.

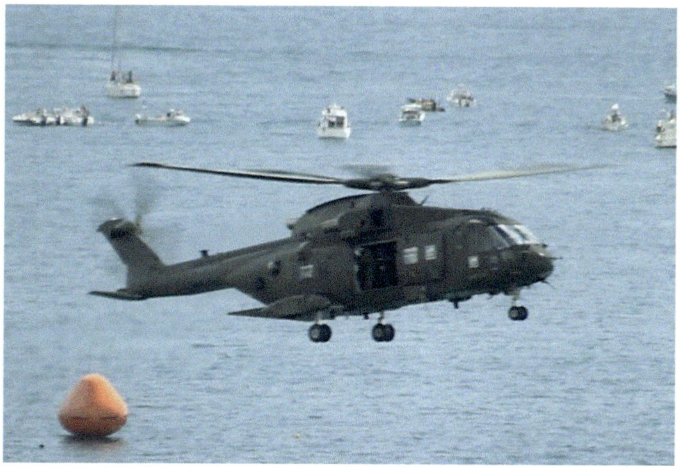

In 1977, the UK Ministry of Defence issued a requirement for an anti-submarine warfare (ASW) helicopter to replace the Royal Navy's Westland Sea Kings, which were becoming inadequate in the face of advances in Soviet submarine technology.

Agusta and Westland signed an agreement to collaborate on the project. They formed a new joint venture company called EH Industries Limited (EHI) to develop and market the new helicopter. On June 12, 1981, the UK government confirmed its participation in the project. It allocated an initial budget of £20 million to develop nine pre-production prototypes.

The AW101 Merlin helicopter utilizes a conventional design but incorporates advanced technologies like rotor blades, avionics, and composites. The lightweight yet damage-resistant fuselage uses modular aluminium-lithium alloy construction. An active vibration control system called the active control of structural response system decreases airframe vibration by up to 80%. This enhances crew comfort and reduces airframe stress. Armoured seats provide protection for the cockpit crew.

Most versions of the AW101 helicopter come equipped with self-defence systems like chaff and flare launchers, infrared countermeasures jammers, electronic support and threat detection equipment, and a laser warning system. British AW101s feature added armour plating to protect against small arms fire.

The British Royal Navy originally ordered 44 anti-submarine warfare aircraft called the Merlin HAS.1 (Helicopter, Anti-Submarine Mark 1), but soon renamed them the Merlin HM1 (Helicopter, Maritime Mark 1). The Navy received the first fully operational Merlin on May 17, 1997, and the helicopter entered service on June 2, 2000. Separately, the Royal Air Force ordered 22 Merlin HC3 helicopters for transport missions. The first of these entered service in January 2001 with No. 28 Squadron RAF at RAF Benson. The versatile Merlin is frequently used to transport troops and bulky cargo, either internally or underslung, including vehicles and artillery.

Over the years, the Merlin helicopter has repeatedly made appearances at the Bournemouth Air Festival, where it has showcased its impressive manoeuvrability. During the festival, the Merlin's crew has also demonstrated their skills by dangling from the hovering helicopter above the sea.

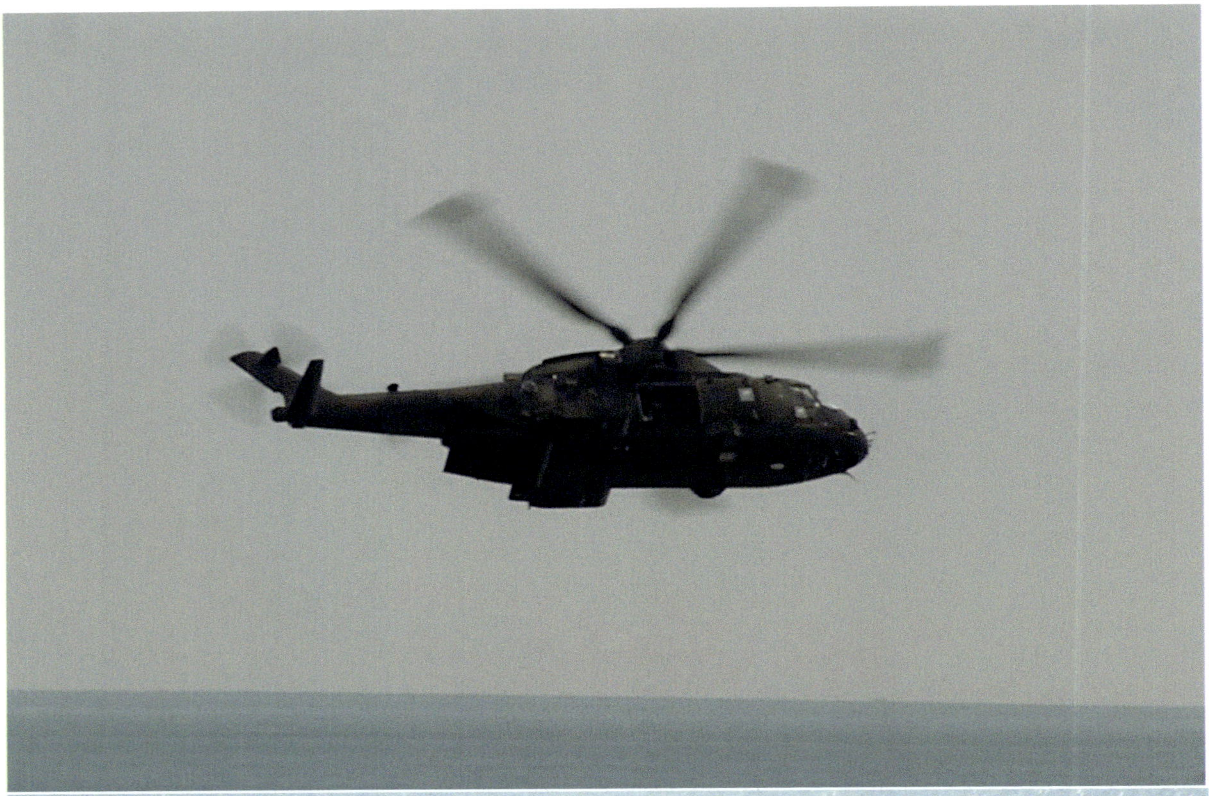

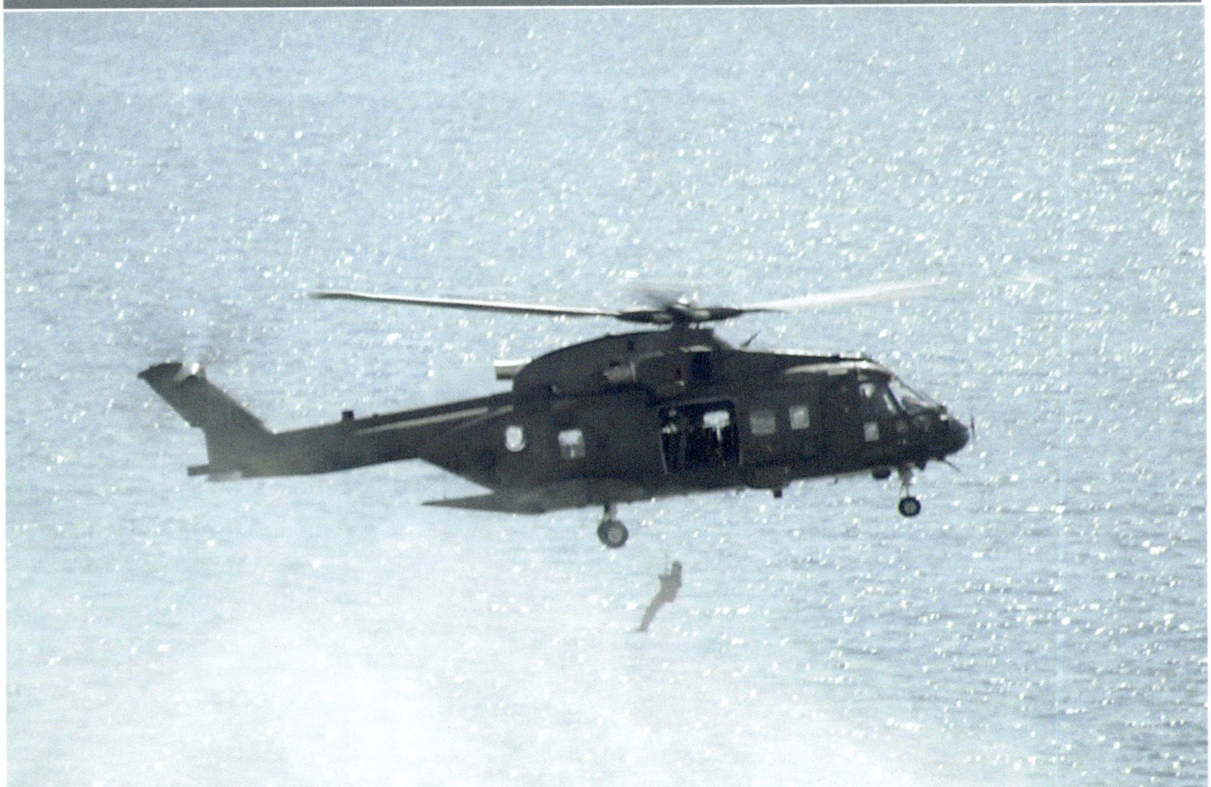

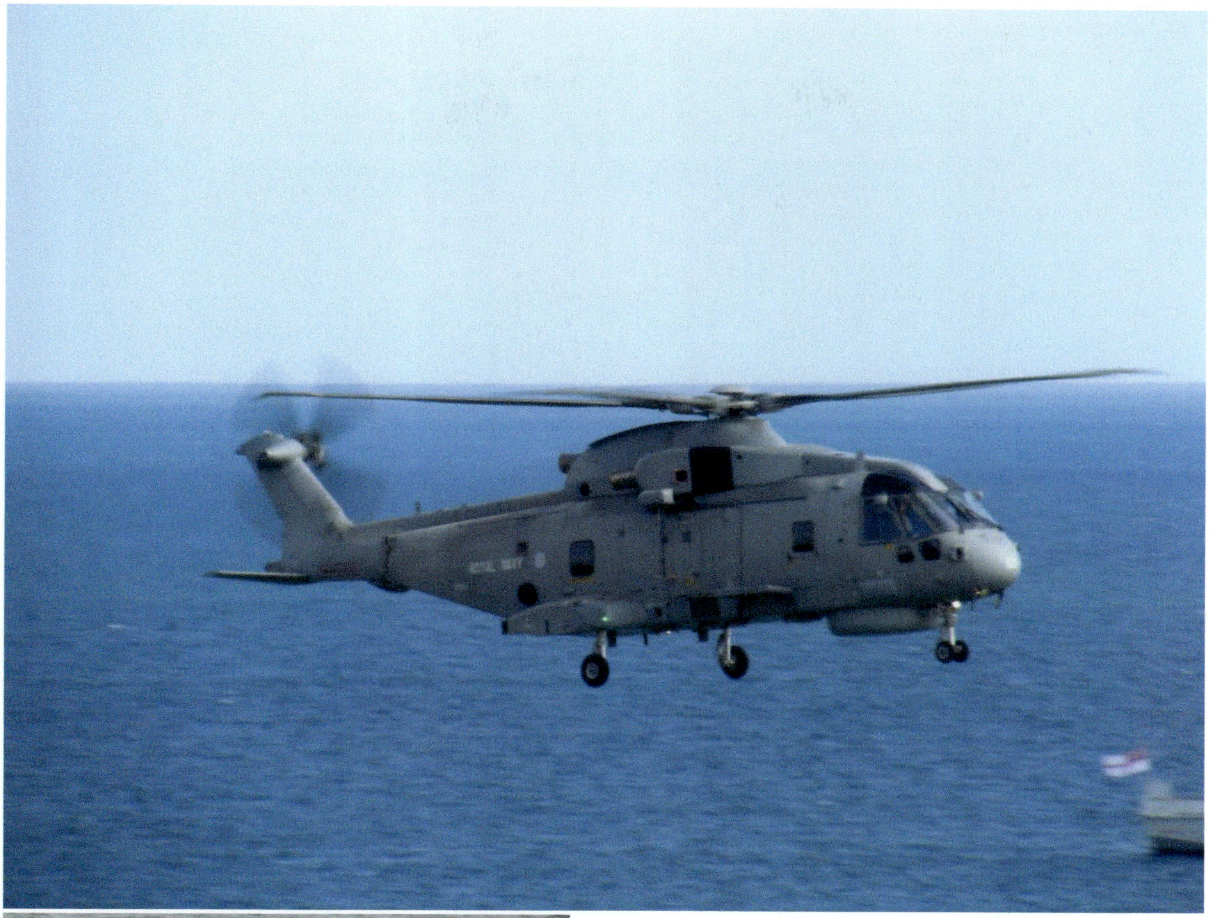

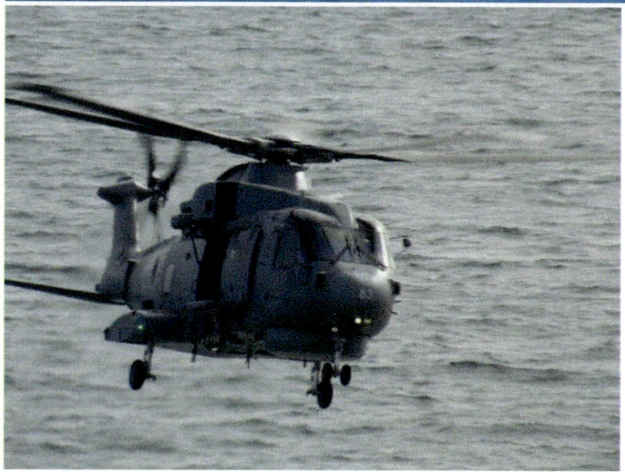

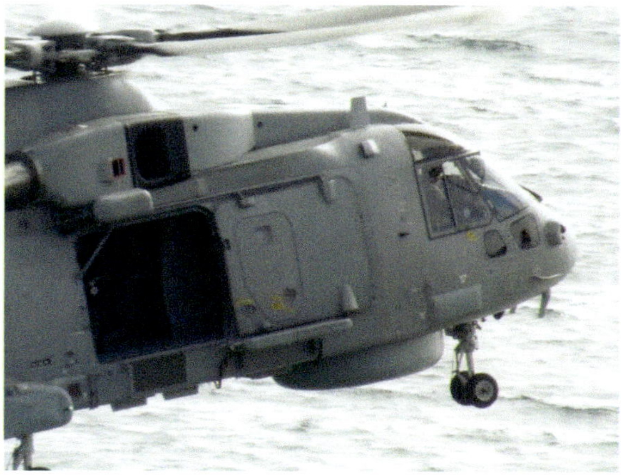

Quick Facts

General

Crew: 3–4

Capacity: 26 troops (38 passengers) or 5 tonnes of payload or 4 stretchers (with sonar array removed)

Length: 19.53 m (64 ft 1 in) fuselage

Height: 6.62 m (21 ft 9 in)

Powerplant: 3 × Rolls-Royce Turbomeca RTM322-01 turboshaft engines

Performance

Cruise speed: 278 km/h (173 mph, 150 kn)

Range: 1,389 km (863 mi, 750 nmi)

Endurance: 5 hours

Armament

Bombs: 4× Sting Ray homing torpedoes or Mk 11 depth charges

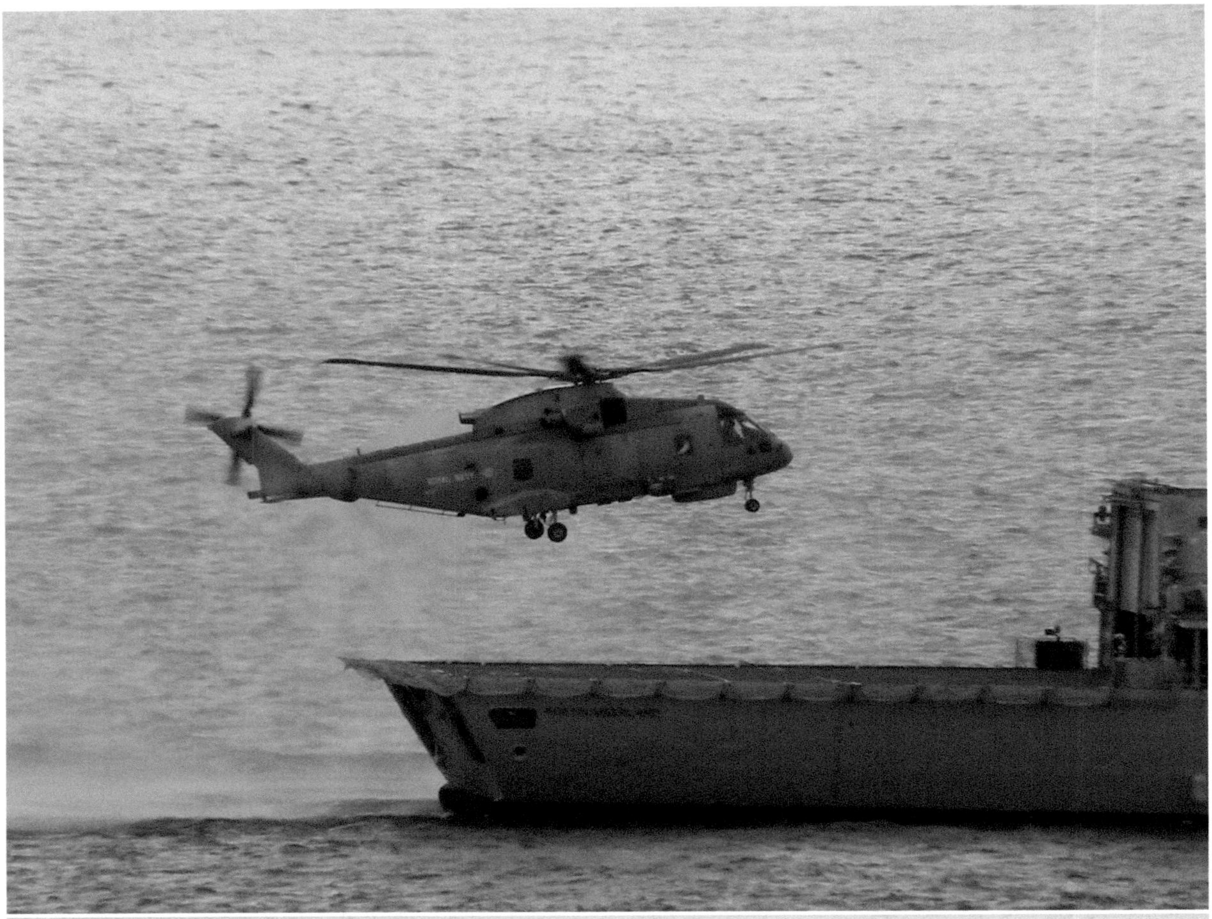

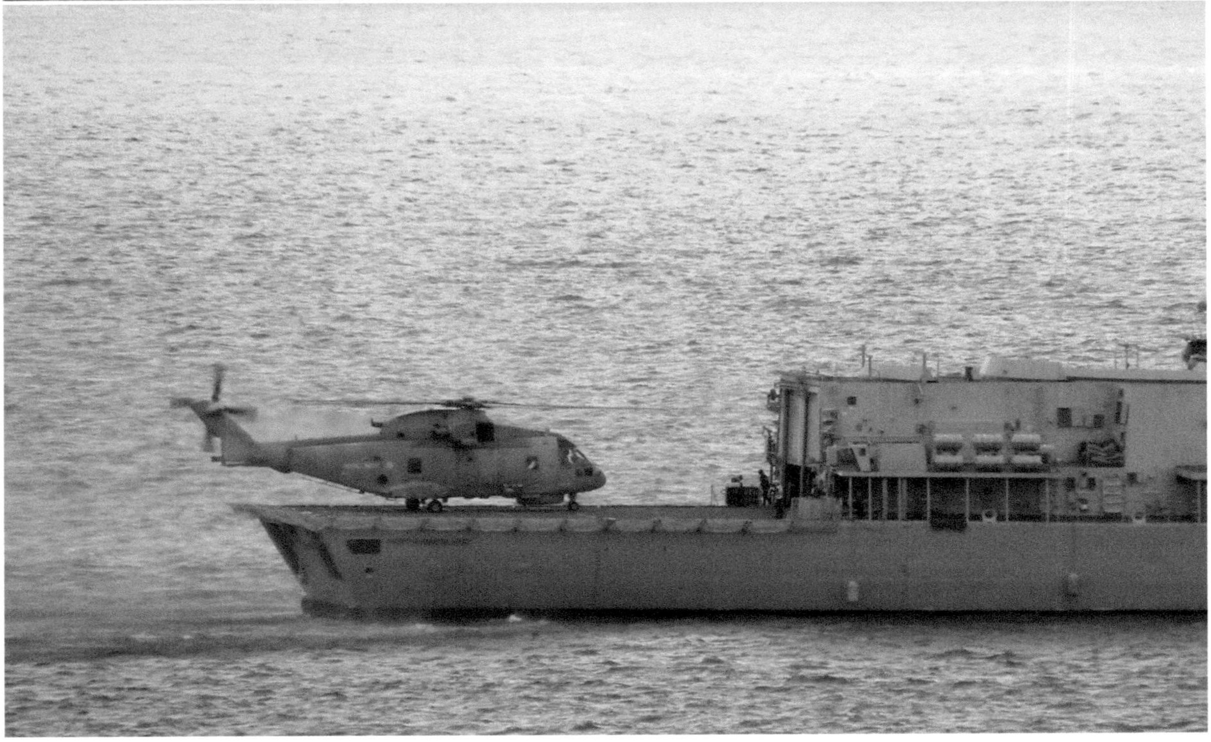

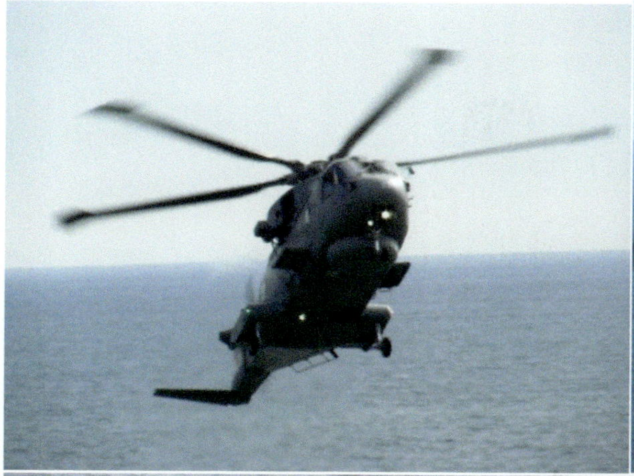

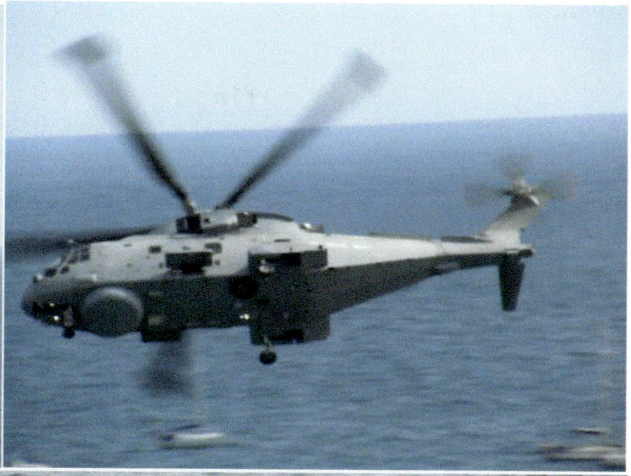

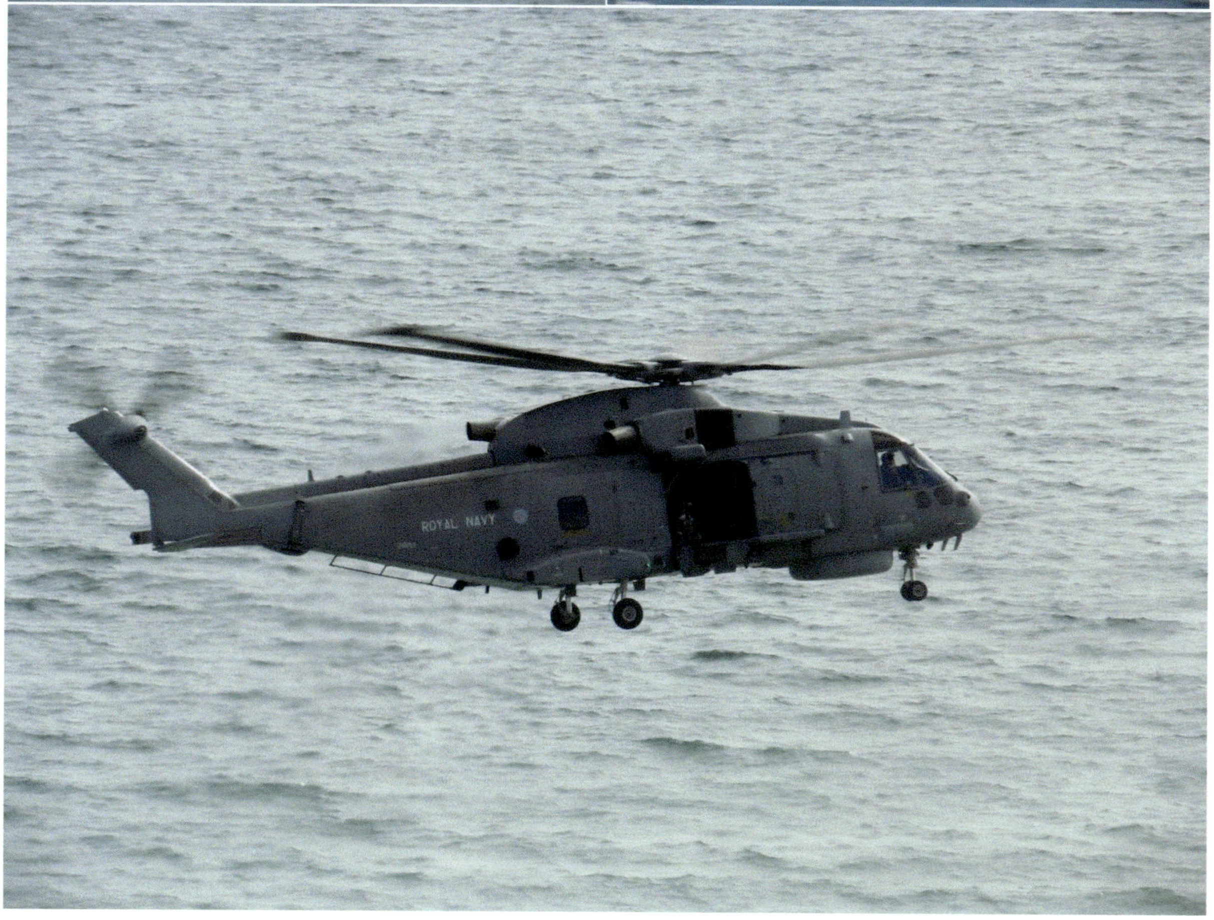
ROYAL NAVY

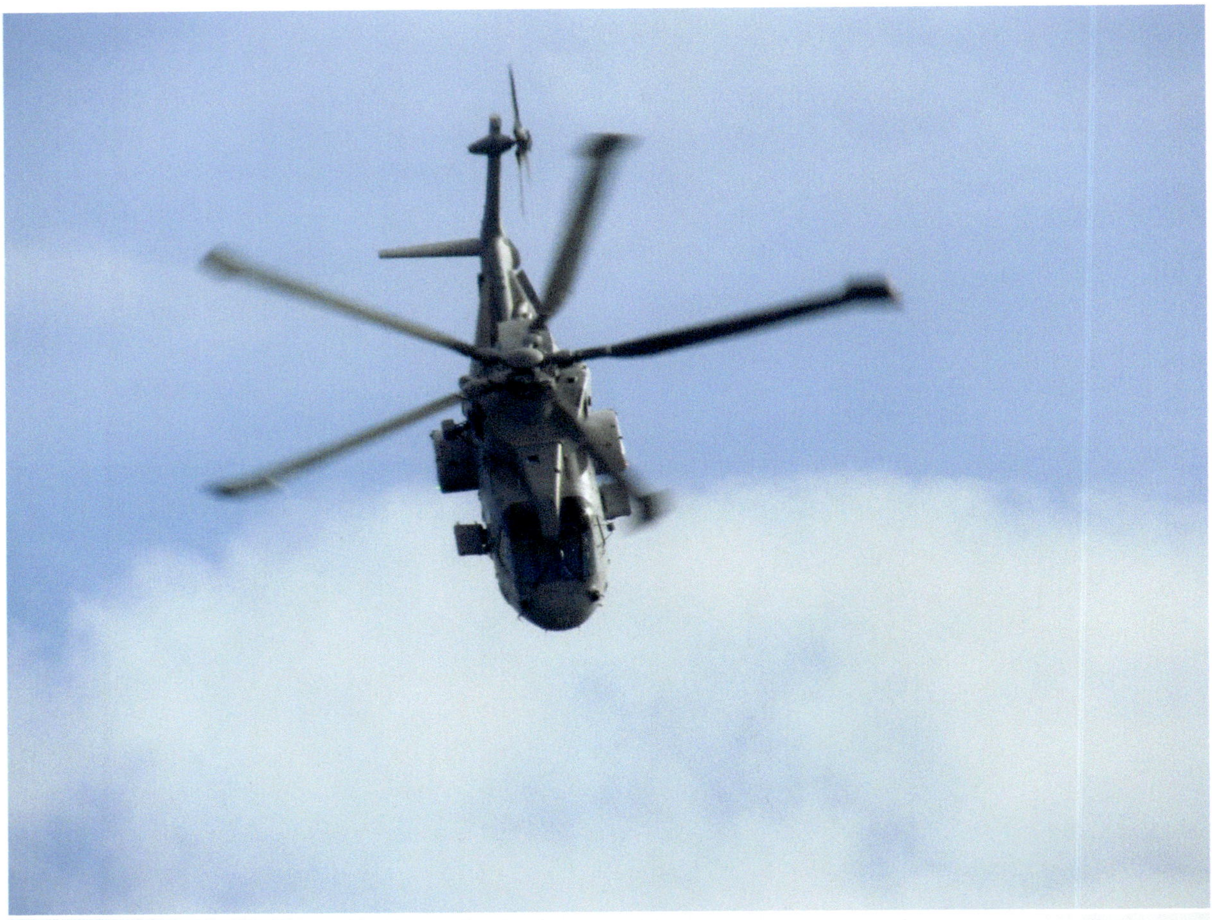

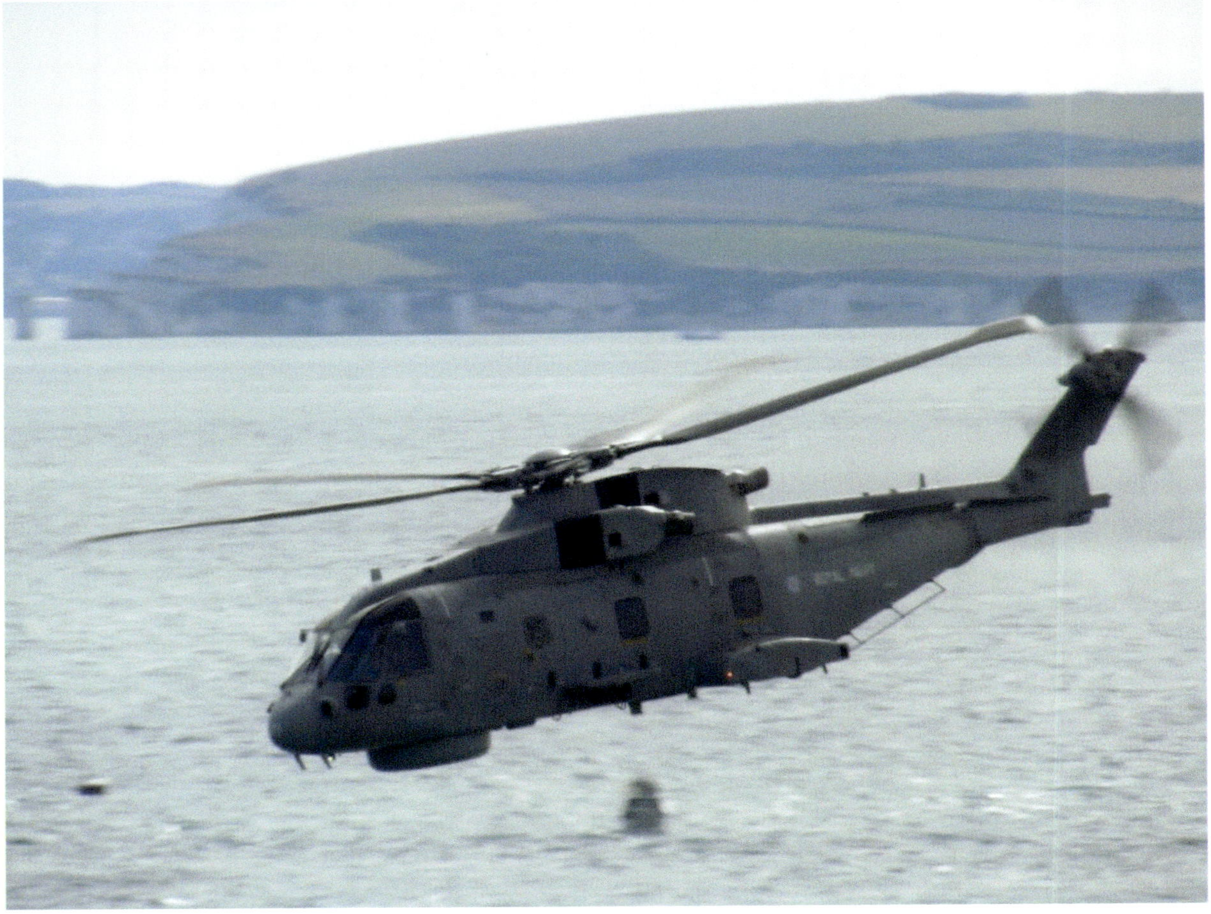

Army Air Corps - Westland Lynx

The Westland Lynx is a British military helicopter designed and manufactured by Westland Helicopters in Yeovil, England. Originally intended for civil and naval use, the twin-engine Lynx was later developed into battlefield and naval variants due to military interest. First entering service in 1977, the Lynx is a fully aerobatic helicopter capable of performing loops and rolls. In 1986, a modified Lynx set the official helicopter airspeed record at 400.87 km/h (249.09 mph).

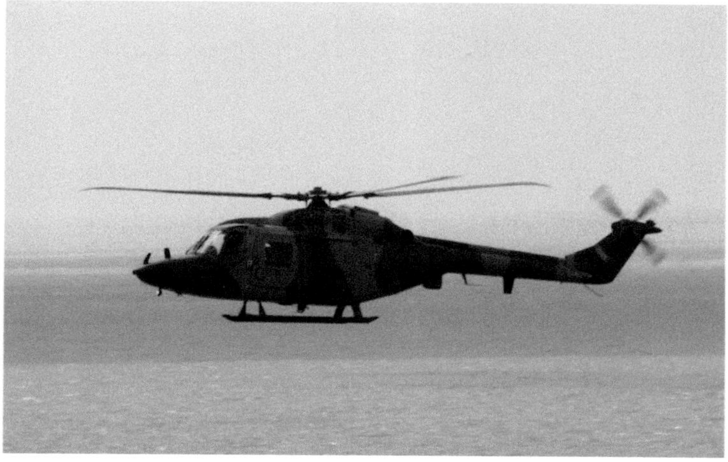

The Westland Scout and Wasp helicopters were slated for replacement in the mid-1960s, so designers began work on a more advanced successor to the UH-1 Iroquois. The new design would be powered by twin Bristol Siddeley BS.360 turboshaft engines.

The first Lynx prototype took its maiden flight on 21 March 1971. Impressed with the helicopter's capabilities, the British Army soon ordered over 100 Lynx helicopters. Designated as Lynx AH.1 (Army Helicopter Mark 1), the fleet would serve the British Army in numerous roles, including transport, armed escort, anti-tank warfare, reconnaissance, and evacuation missions.

Early versions of the Lynx helicopter used skids for landing gear, while later models were outfitted with wheels to enable ground handling on warship decks. This distinction in undercarriage reflects the Lynx's adaptation over time for both land and naval warfare through specialized variants developed for the Army and Navy.

The Lynx helicopter has a two-person cockpit where the pilot and co-pilot sit side-by-side. Although it was designed for a two-person crew, the British Army typically flies the Lynx with a three-person crew that includes a door gunner. The cabin behind the cockpit is accessed through large sliding doors on both sides of the fuselage. Depending on the seating configuration, the cabin can hold up to ten fully equipped troops.

The British Army's Army Air Corps (AAC) began operating the Lynx AH.1 helicopter in 1979, followed by the Fleet Air Arm (FAA) adopting the Lynx HAS.2 in 1981. During the 1980s, the FAA upgraded its fleet to the Lynx HAS.3 standard and further improved to the HMA.8 standard in the 1990s. The Army upgraded most of its aircraft to the Lynx AH.7 and later AH.9/AH.9A standards for use as utility helicopters. The Lynx has also been utilized by the Royal Marines' 3 Commando Brigade Air Squadron and later the Commando Helicopter Force, serving as reconnaissance and attack/utility helicopters in support of the Royal Marines.

The Army Air Corps demonstrated the full capabilities of their Lynx helicopter during the 2012 and 2014 Air Festivals, stunning crowds with tight manoeuvres. The most mesmerising moment was seeing the Lynx perform a full backflip, as no one expects to see a helicopter briefly fly upside down. This incredible feat showed the tremendous skill of the pilot and the agility of the inspiring Lynx helicopter. Since its retirement, the Lynx and its jaw-dropping aerial displays will be sorely missed at the Bournemouth Air Festival and events across the country.

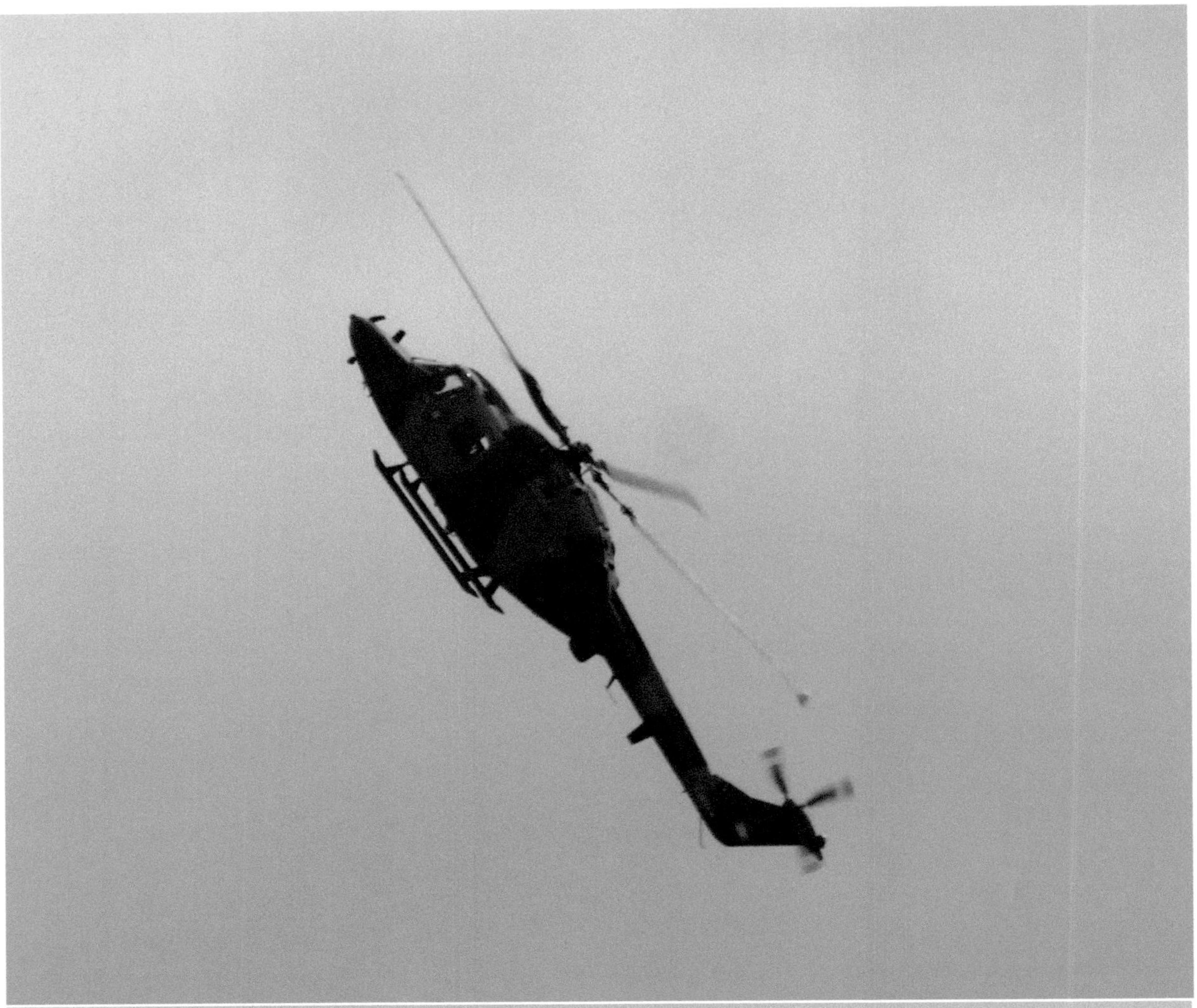

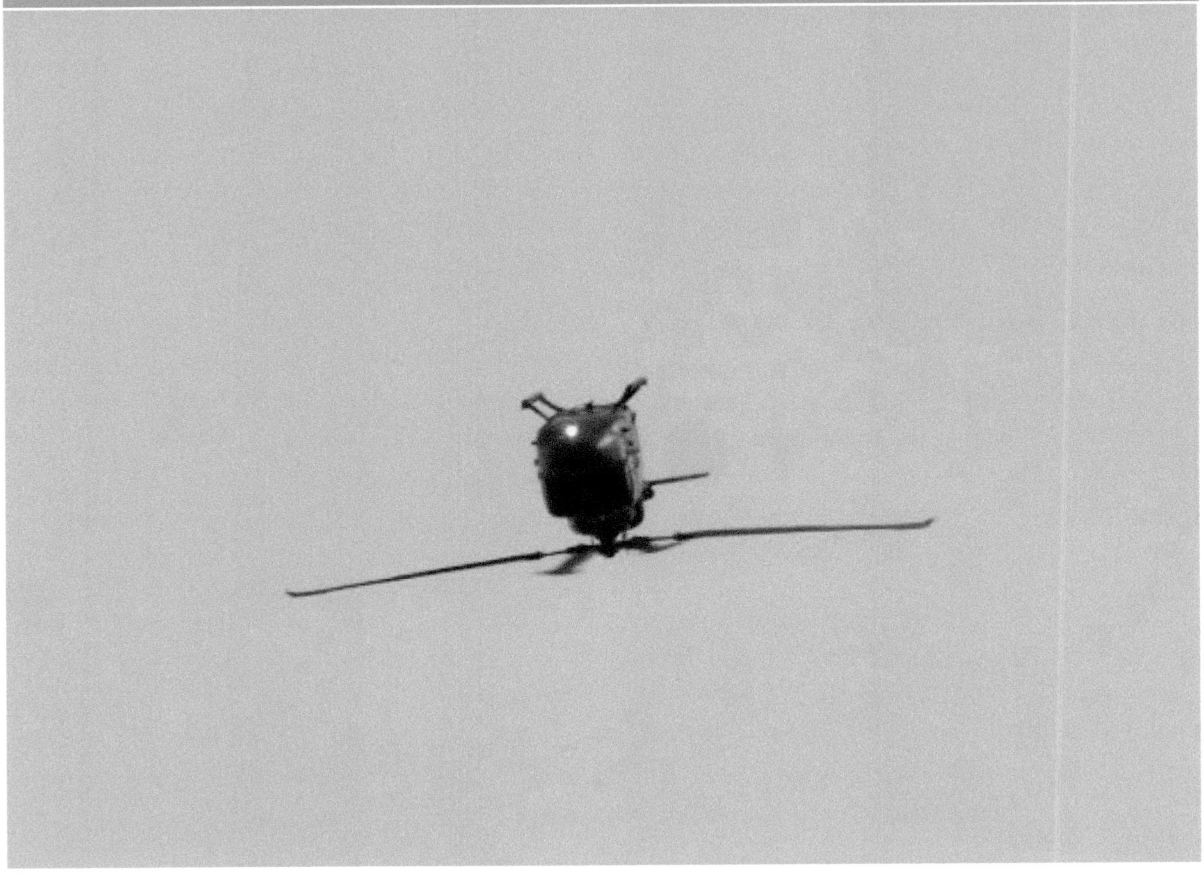

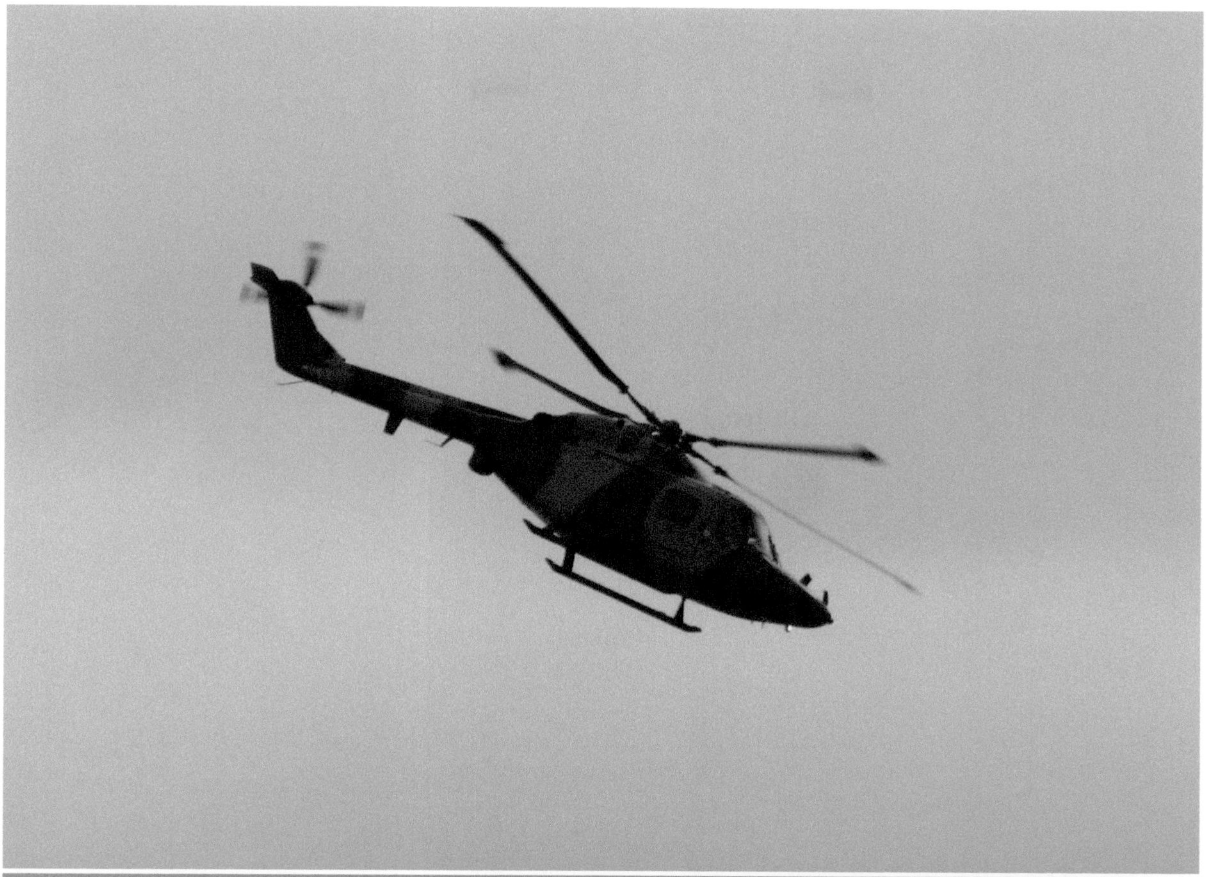

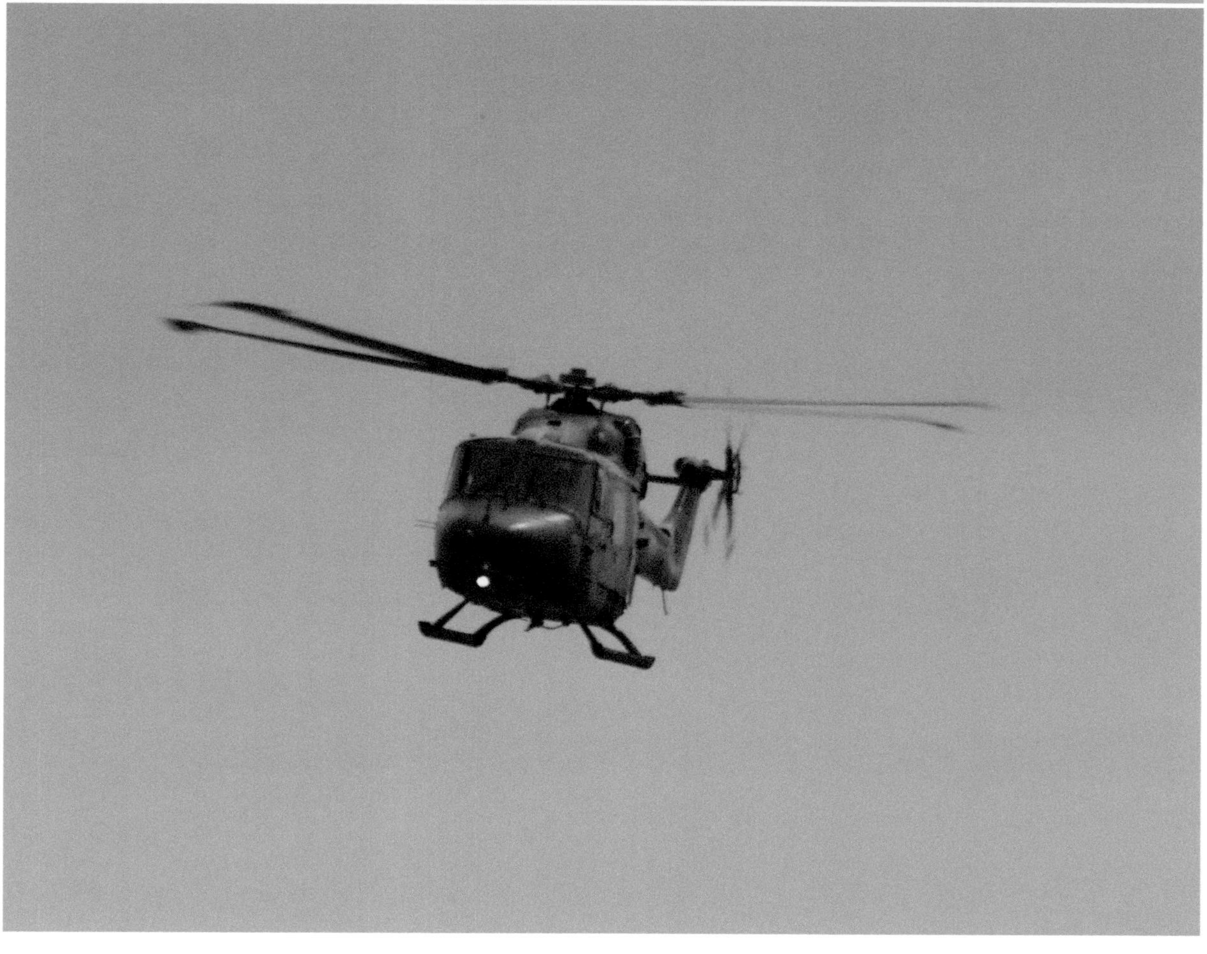

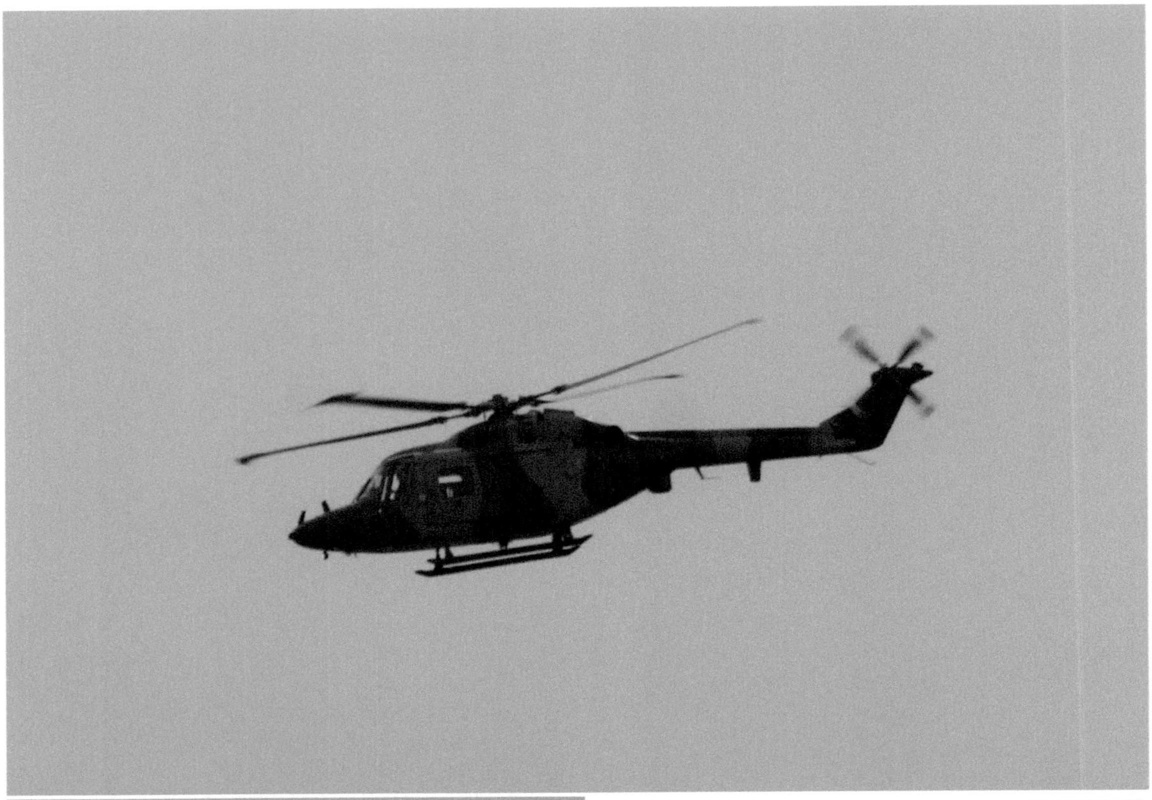

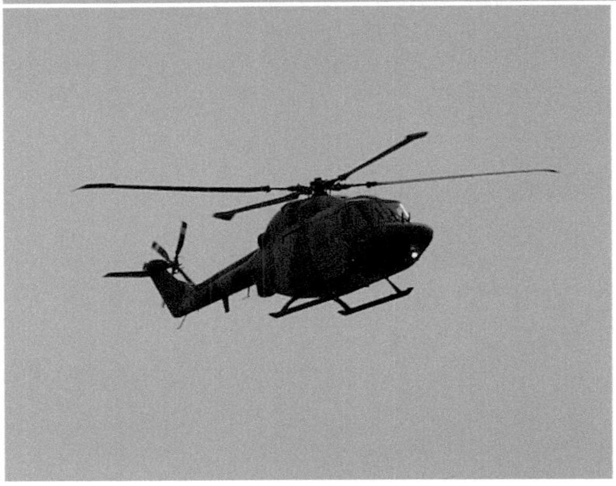

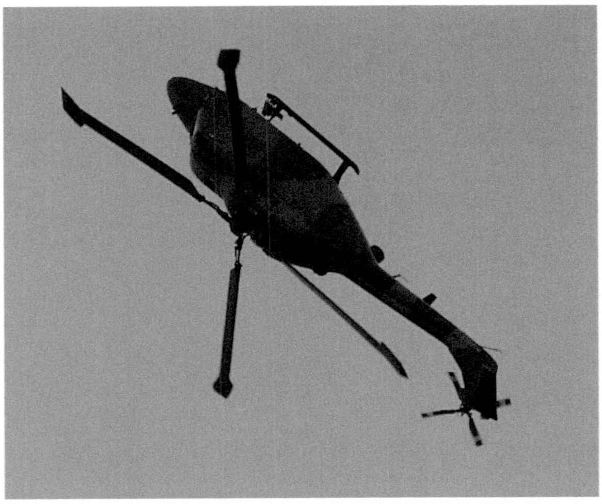

Quick Facts

General

Crew: 2-3

Capacity: 8 troops / 3,000 lb (1,361 kg)

Length overall: 50 ft (15.24 m)

Width folded: 9 ft 7.75 in (2.94 m)

Height: 12 ft 0.5 in (3.670 m) including tail-rotor

Powerplant: 2 × LHTEC CTS800-4N turboshaft engines

Performance

Maximum speed: 175 kn (201 mph, 324 km/h)

Range: 285 nmi (328 mi, 528 km)

Armament

Naval: 2 x torpedoes or 4x Sea Skua missiles or 2 x depth charges

Attack: 1 x 20mm Oerlikon cannon, 2 x 70mm rocket pods CRV7, 8 x TOW ATGM

Wildcat Demo Team (Black Cats)

The Wildcat Demo Team (Black Cats) are the Royal Navy's helicopter display team. The team is composed of two AgustaWestland Wildcat HMA.2 anti-submarine and anti-shipping helicopters, with the aircraft and crews drawn from 825 Naval Air Squadron based at RNAS Yeovilton in Somerset.

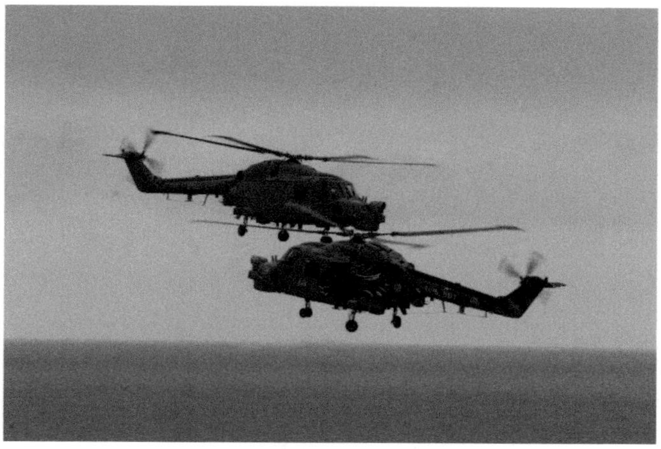

The Black Cats aerobatic display team was originally known as the 'Lynx Pair' when they first performed with the Westland Lynx helicopters in 2001. After their first three display seasons, the team adopted the name 'Black Cats' in 2004, which was inspired by the emblem of the now disbanded 702 Naval Air Squadron depicting a fierce black cat. The term 'blackcatting' in naval slang refers to one-upmanship, so the new name signified the team's aspiration to perform daring aerial manoeuvres that would surpass other display teams.

Beginning in 2019, the Black Cats rebranded as the 'Wildcat Demo Team' and now operate only one aircraft. The team confirmed that for shows in 2020 and beyond, their displays would feature a solo Wildcat rather than the pair of aircraft that audiences had grown accustomed to seeing over the years.

The Wildcat Demo Team has performed at numerous Air Festivals over the years. We have had the pleasure of seeing the pair of Black Cats executing close formation flypasts, tight pirouetting manoeuvres, and thrilling crossovers—an amazing sight as two helicopters cross paths at close range. Since 2020, the Wildcat's solo displays have also been inspirational, with talented pilots putting the Wildcat through its paces and demonstrating the helicopter's true capabilities.

The AW159 Wildcat is a further development of the Westland Lynx. While the AW159 shares broad similarities in appearance to the Lynx, it has significant design differences and is heavily modernised and adapted to gain new attributes and functionality. The AW159 comprises 95% new components; the remaining 5%, consisting of such items as the fuel system and main rotor gearbox, are interchangeable with the Lynx AH7 and HMA8 variants.

The Wildcat helicopter has a larger payload capacity and longer range compared to the previous Super Lynx model. It is designed to carry up to 8 Future Anti-Surface Guided Weapons and travel up to 185 kilometres from a host ship while remaining on station for one hour. The Wildcat is able to perform aerial reconnaissance, anti-submarine warfare, anti-surface warfare, utility transport, fire control, command and control, and troop transport missions.

On 29 August 2014, the Wildcat AH1 helicopter officially joined the Army Air Corps fleet. The Royal Navy began using its first Wildcat HMA2 in operational deployments on 23 March 2015 aboard the HMS Lancaster. By September 2015, the British Armed Forces had taken delivery of 48 Wildcat helicopters total for the Army and Navy.

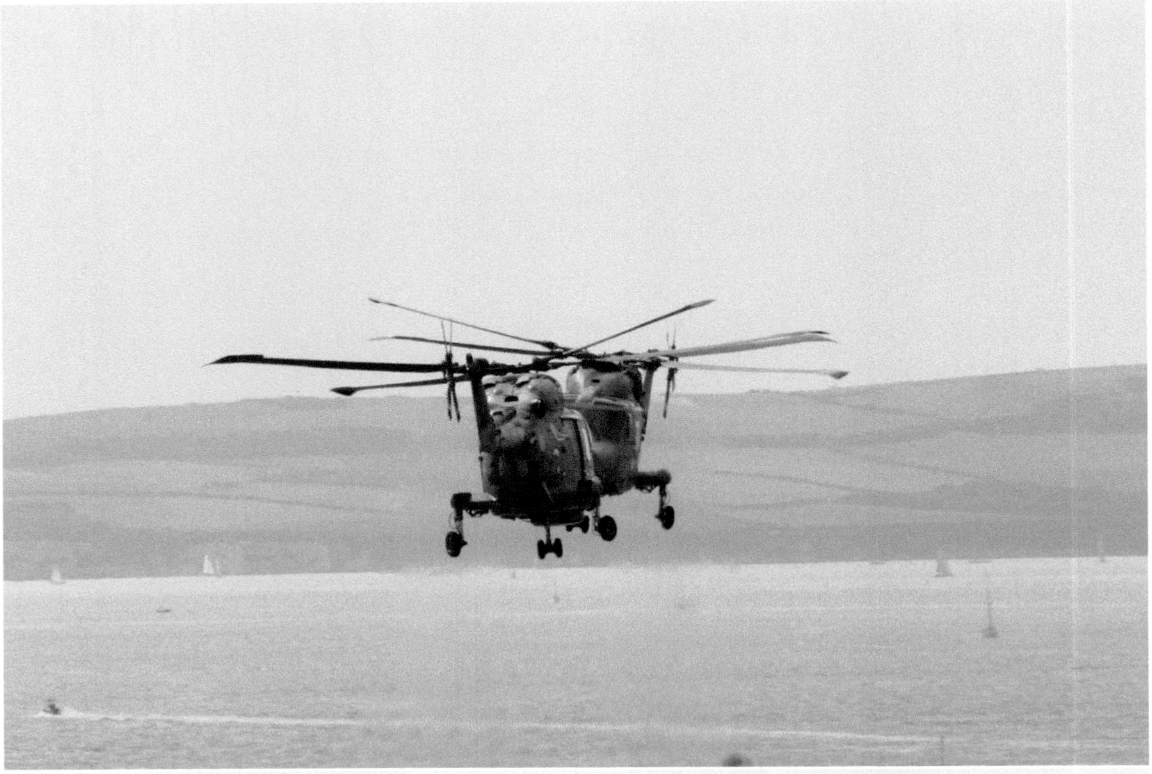

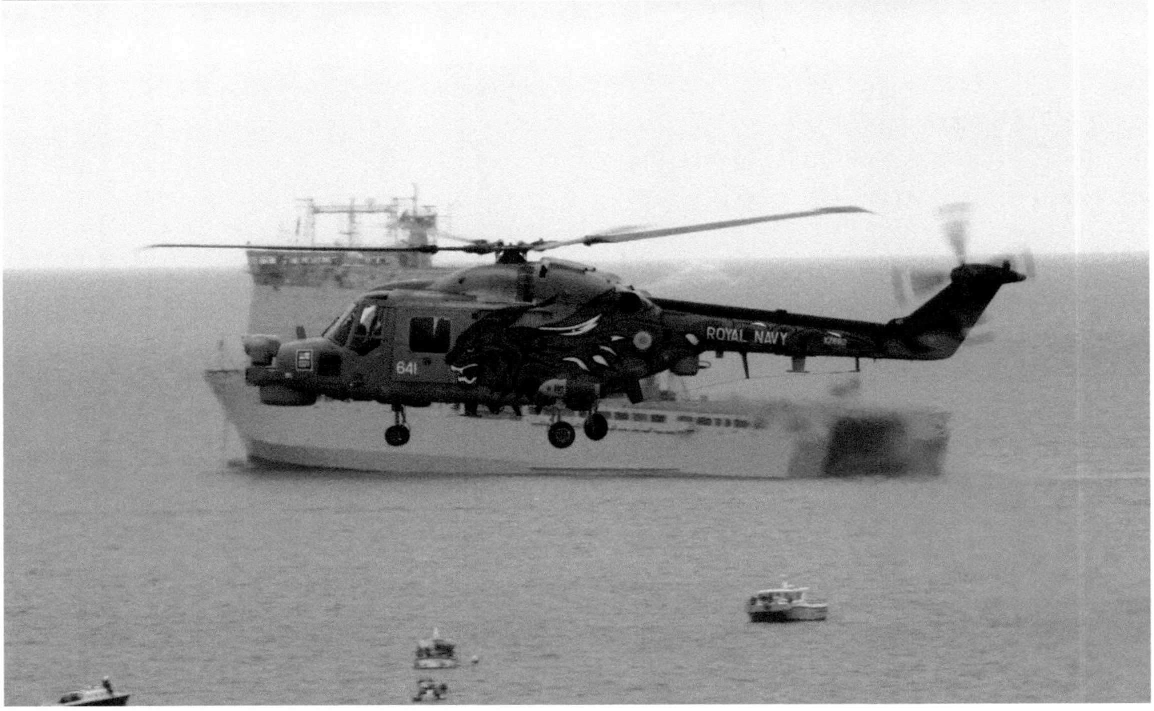
ROYAL NAVY
641

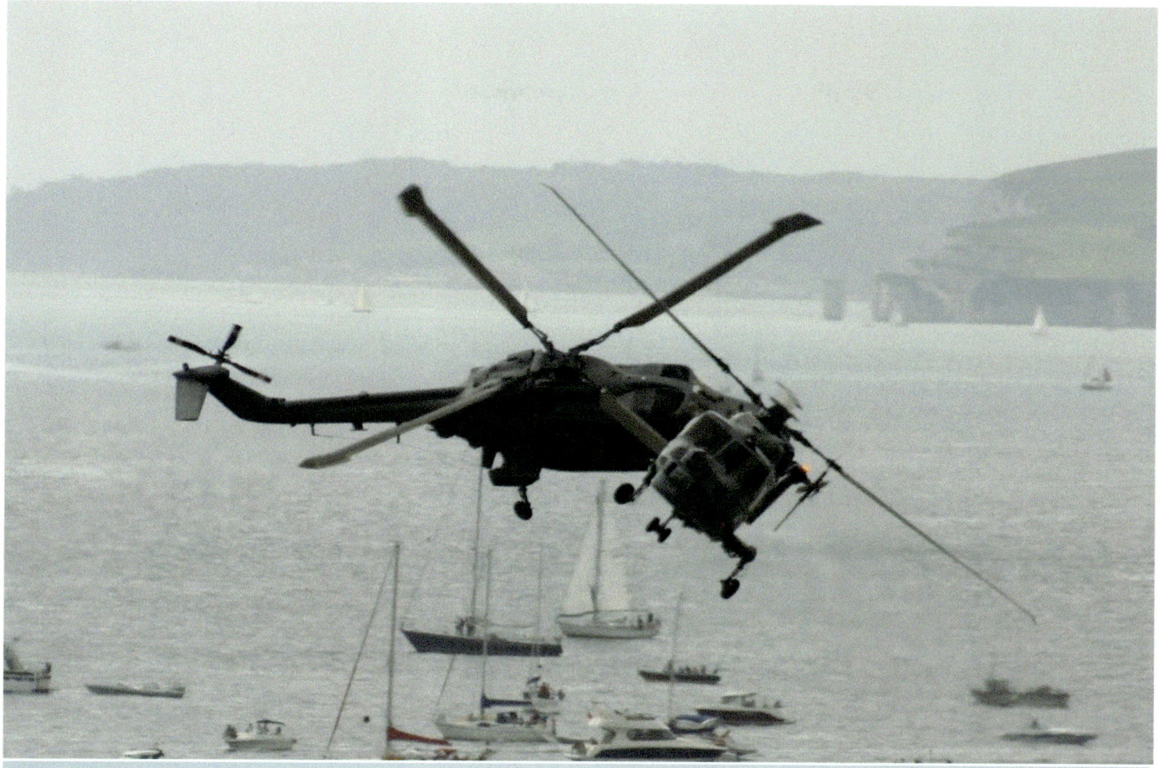

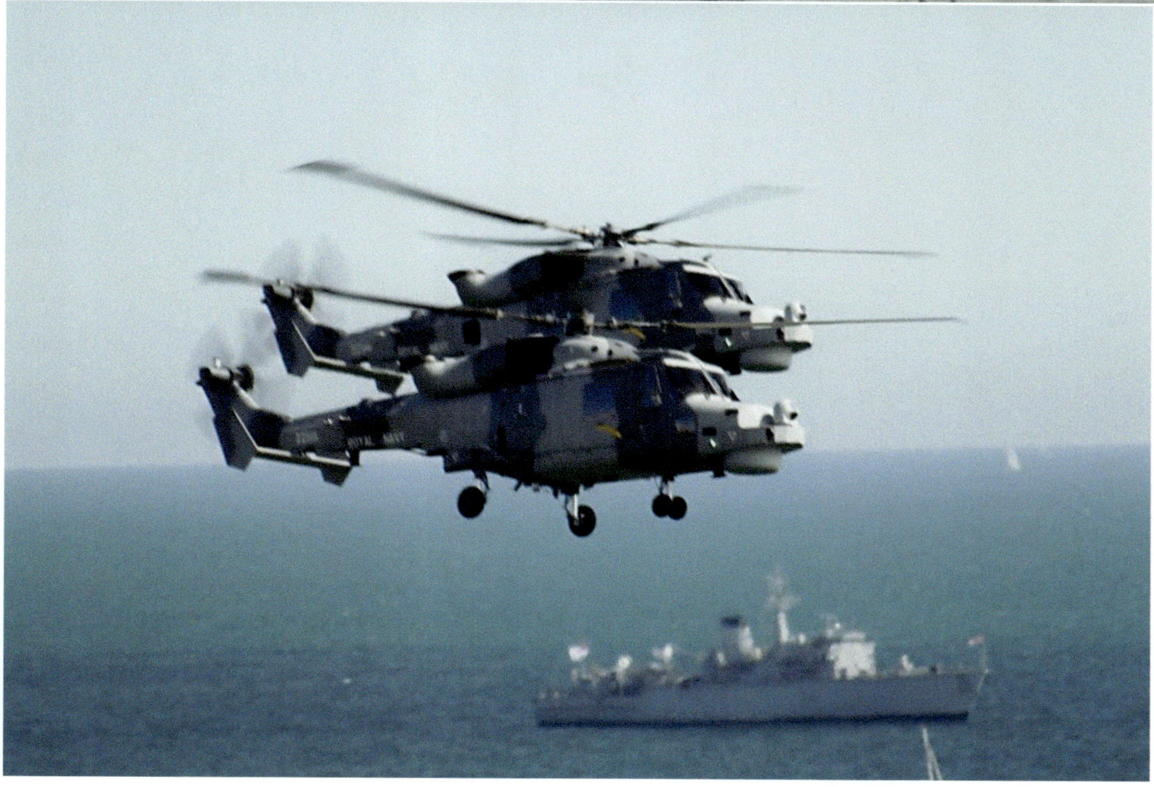

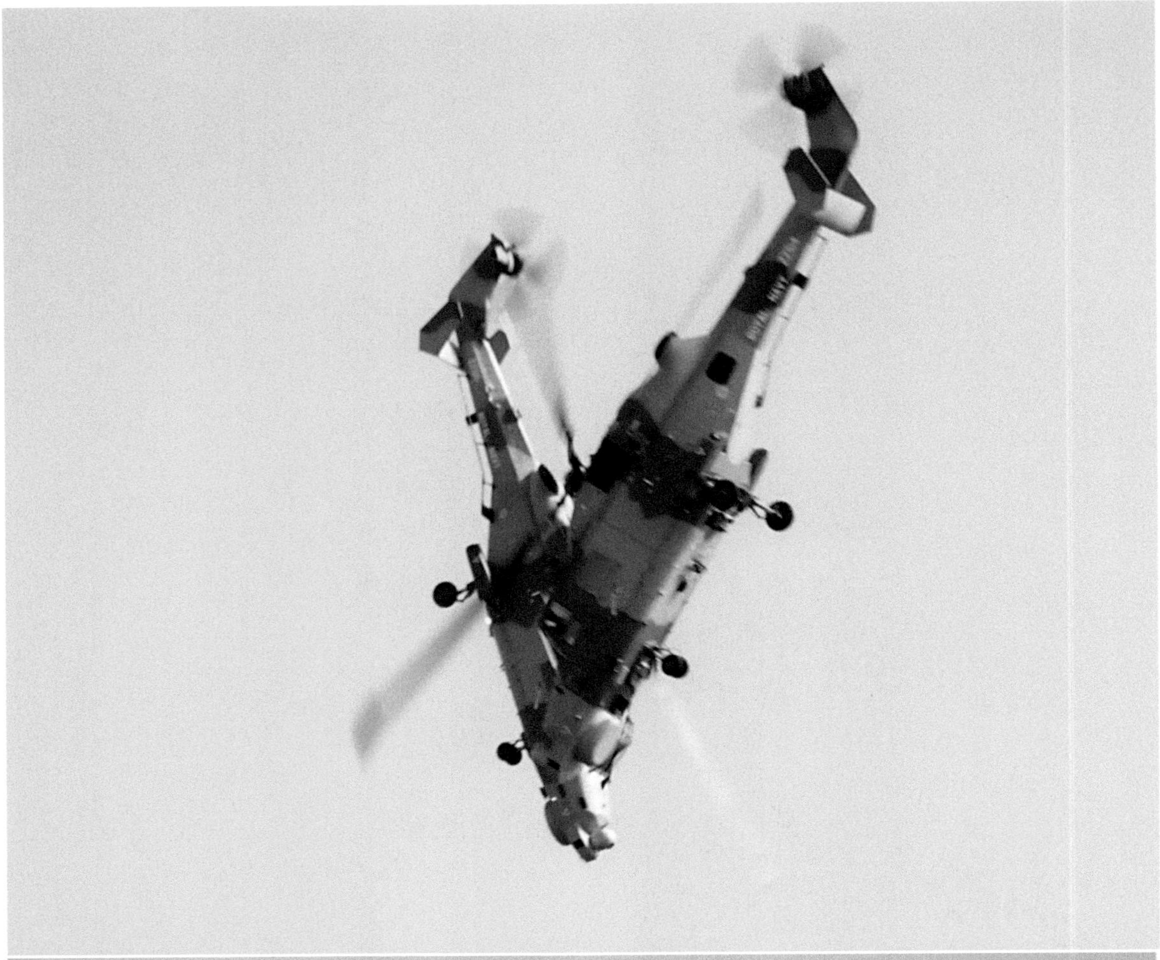

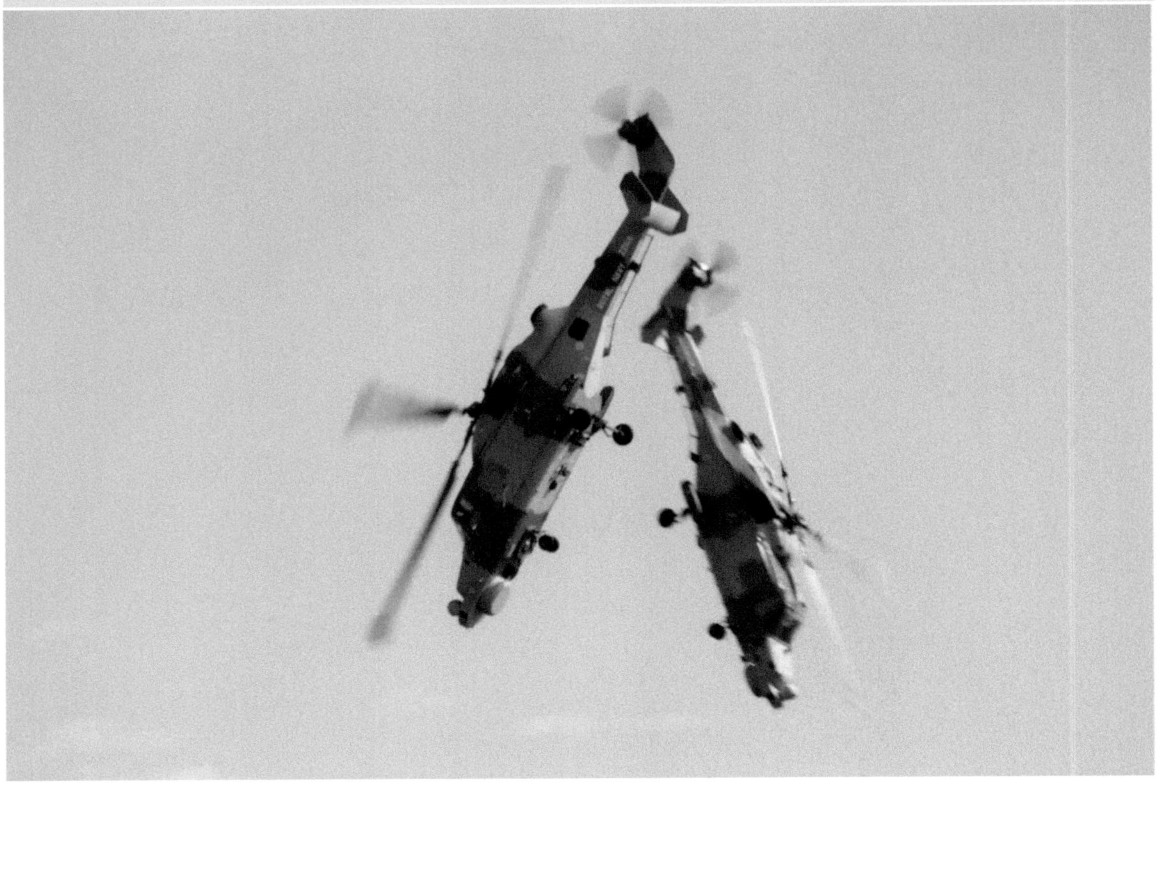

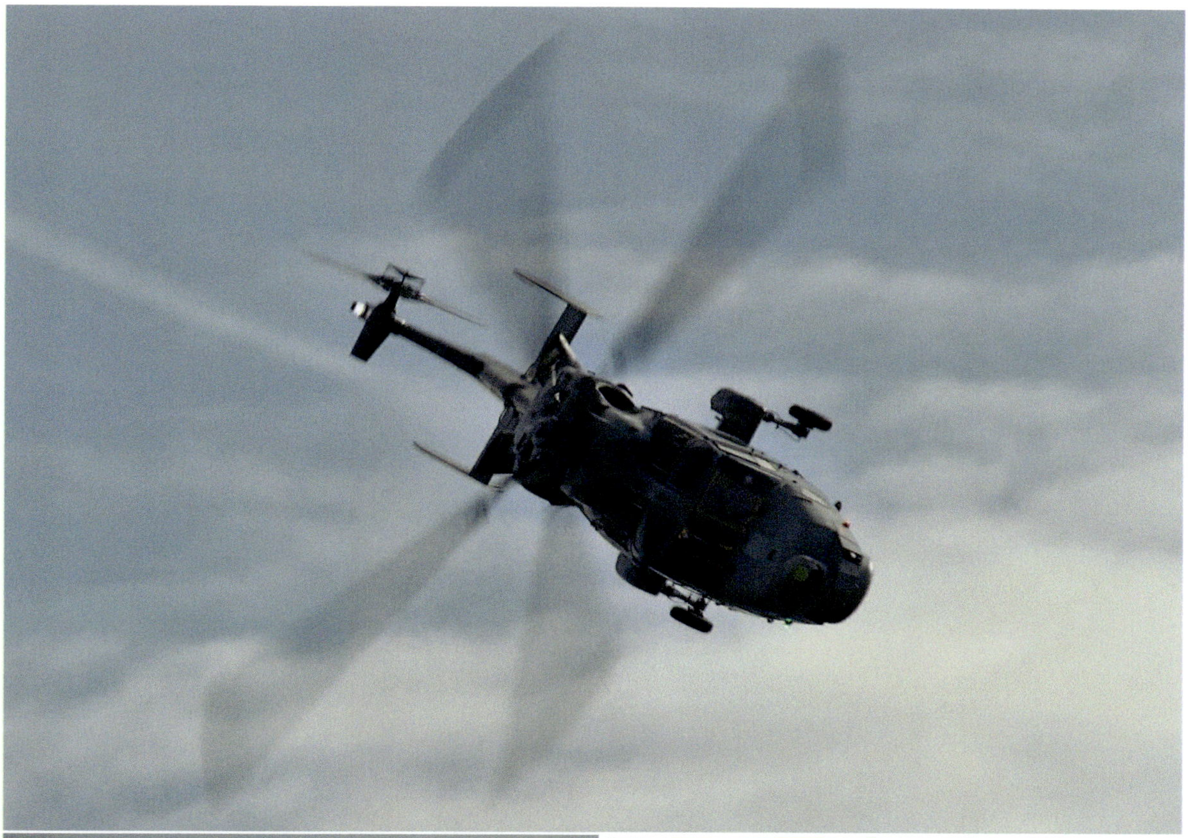

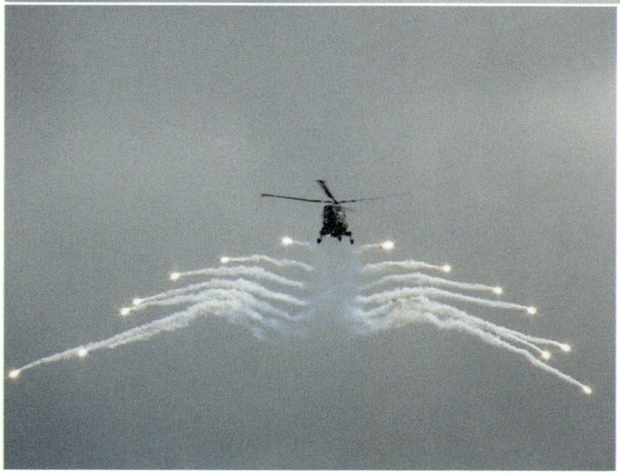

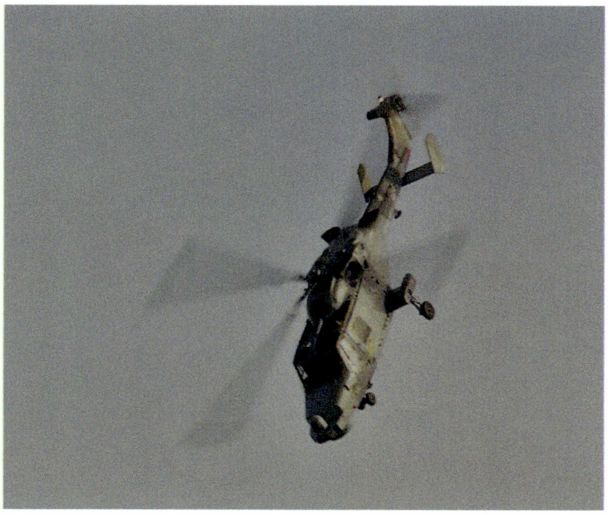

Quick Facts

General

Crew: 2 pilots

Capacity: 6 passengers, including door gunner

Length: 15.24 m (50 ft 0 in)

Height: 3.73 m (12 ft 3 in)

Performance

Maximum speed: 311 km/h (193 mph)

Range: 777 km (483 mi, 420 nmi)

Armament

Pintle-mounted machine gun

Multiple Air-to-surface missile systems and ASW weapons

Sting Ray torpedo and Mk.11 depth charges

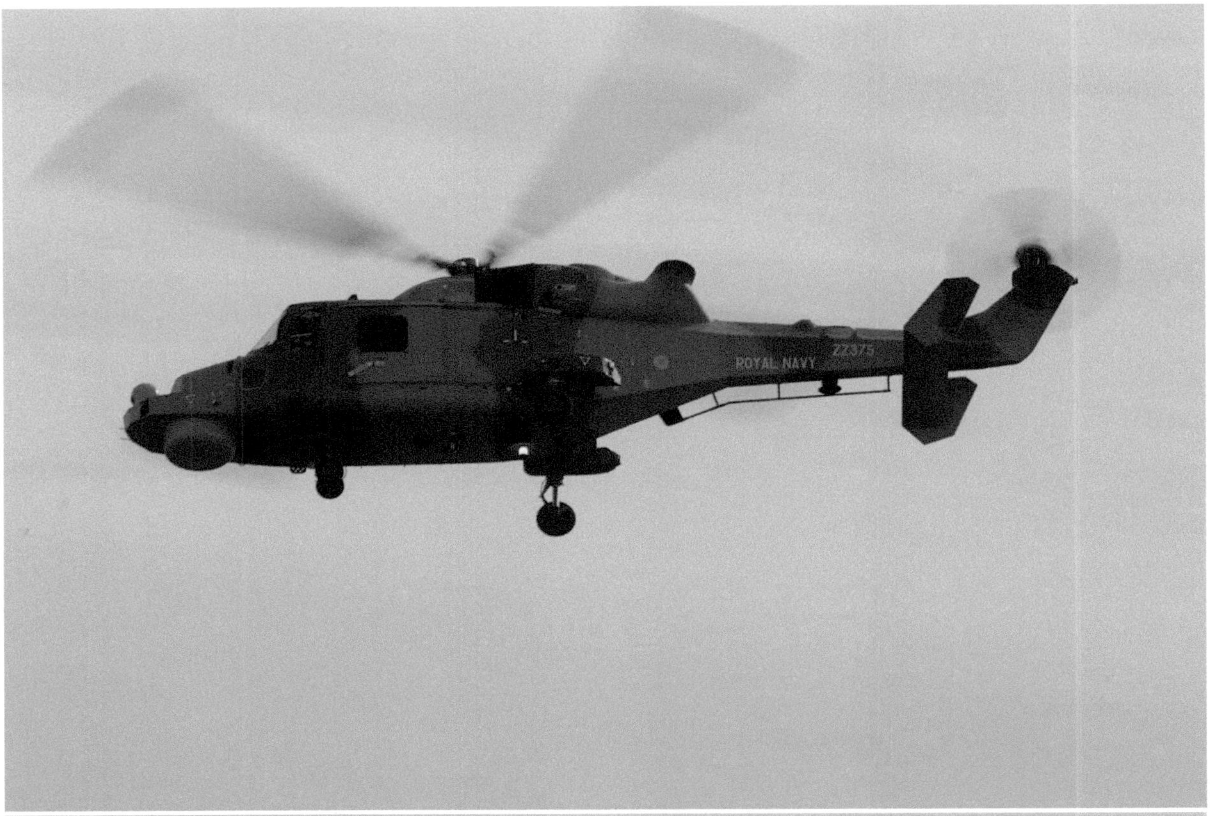
ROYAL NAVY
ZZ375

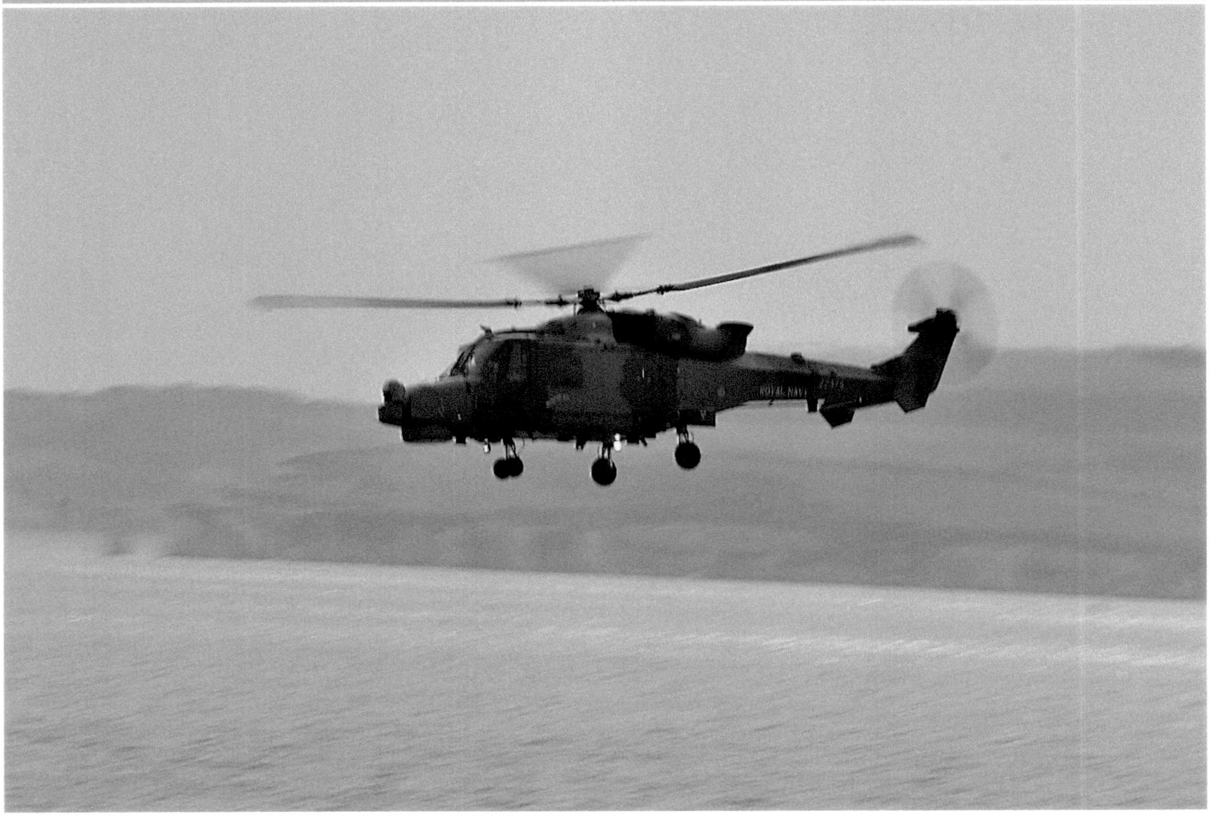
ROYAL NAVY

Chinook Display Team

The Chinook Display Team, an aerobatic display group that flies the Boeing CH-47 Chinook helicopter, performs at air shows across the United Kingdom. Based at RAF Odiham and composed of Royal Air Force volunteers, the team trains for exhibitions during breaks from military duties. Their skilful manoeuvres in the iconic twin-rotor Chinook delight airshow crowds who appreciate both the aircraft's capabilities and its vital role in UK defence.

After a 12-year absence, solo Chinook helicopter displays returned to the UK airshow circuit in 2004 and have since become a regular highlight of the Bournemouth Air Festival. During these breathtaking displays, the pilots push the Chinook to its limits, the distinctive 'wokka wokka' sound of the engines and rotors filling the air along with the thunderous 'blade slap' generated by rotor manoeuvres. The displays also feature great crowd interaction, with the open rear ramp providing views of the crew waving their giant orange gloves as they fly past sideways.

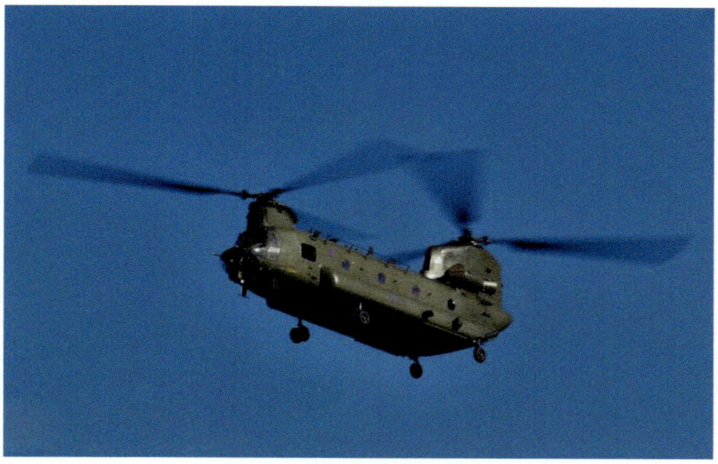

The Boeing CH-47 Chinook is a large, tandem rotor helicopter and the backbone of British heavy-lift aviation. Operated by the Royal Air Force, the Chinook is the largest fleet of its kind outside the United States. Based on variants of the U.S. Army's Chinook, RAF Chinooks have seen extensive service worldwide in conflicts including the Falklands War, Balkans, Northern Ireland, Iraq, and Afghanistan. Normally operating from RAF Odiham in England, the versatile Chinook provides vital transport and logistics support across all British armed forces branches. The Chinook entered RAF service on March 23, 1980 and is expected to remain active until the 2040s.

The Chinook helicopter was deployed by the UK throughout its two decades of operations in Afghanistan. The aircraft's rear ramp allows troops to quickly embark and disembark, while its quick loading capabilities enable vehicles to drive on and off. Special forces and commandos can also fast rope from the rear ramp, belly hatch, or side cabin doorways.

One Chinook helicopter, identified by its original squadron code Bravo November, has gained widespread fame for its exceptional service record. This remarkable aircraft has participated in every major Royal Air Force operation involving helicopters over the past 40 years, including missions in the Falklands, Lebanon, Germany, Northern Ireland, Iraq, and Afghanistan.

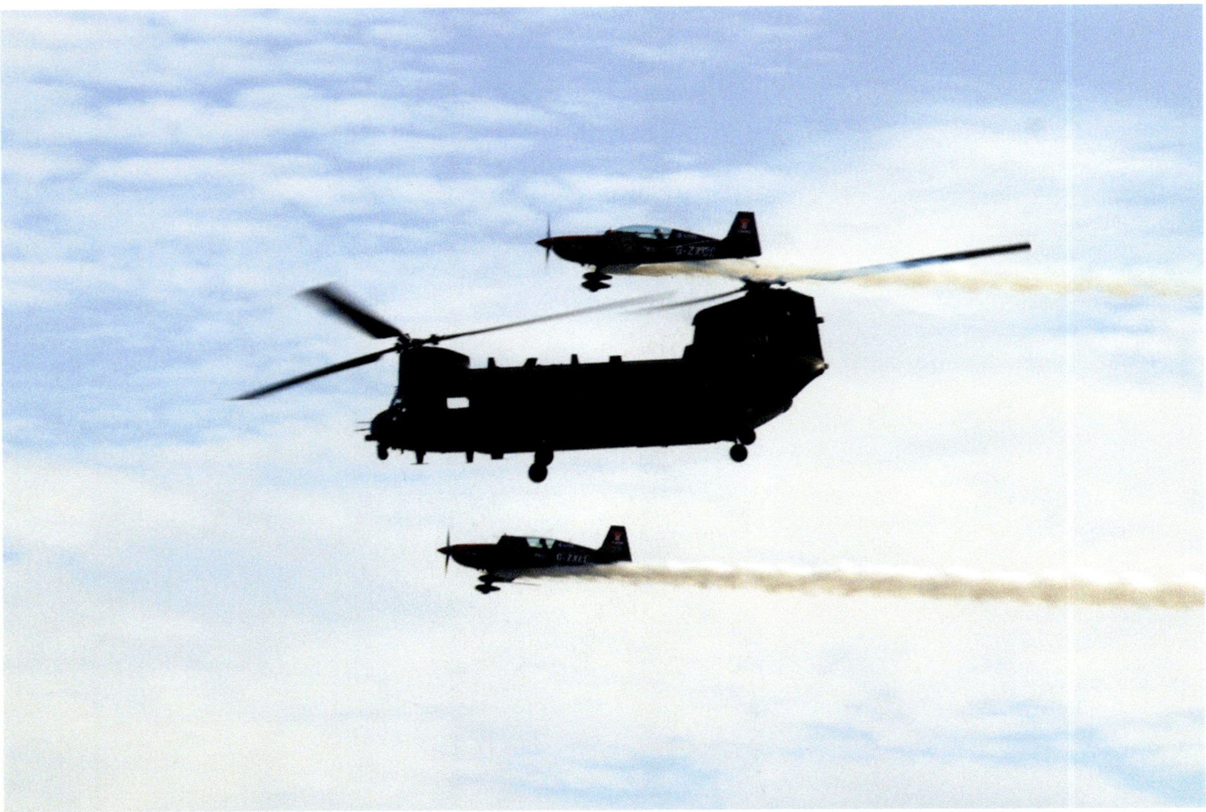

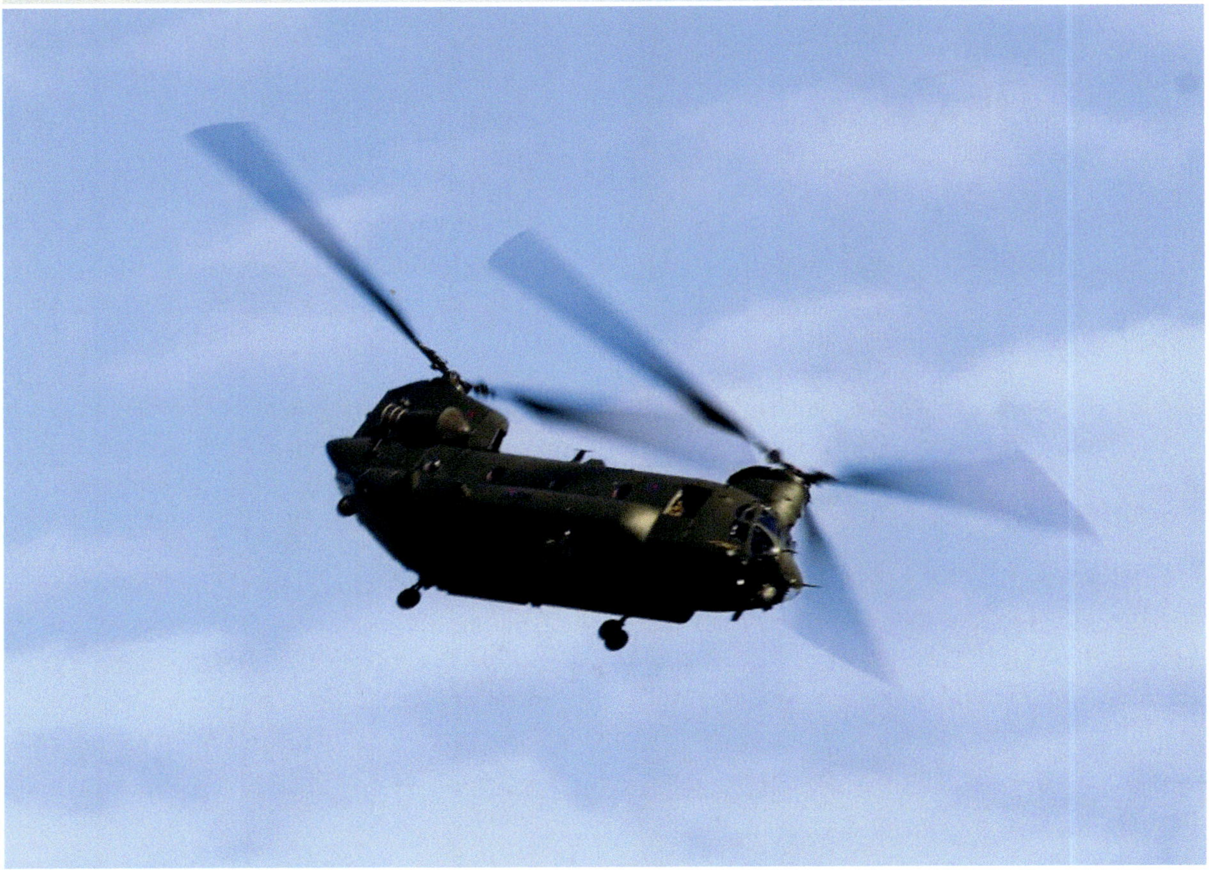

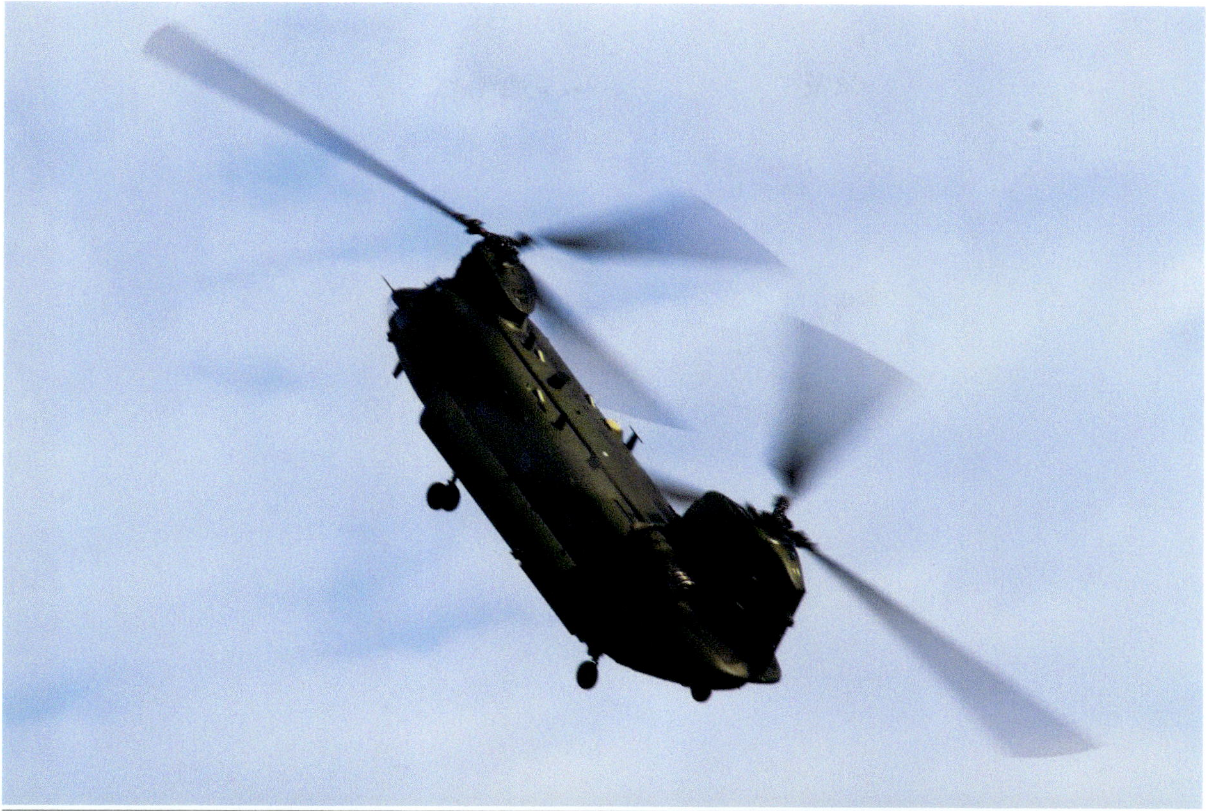

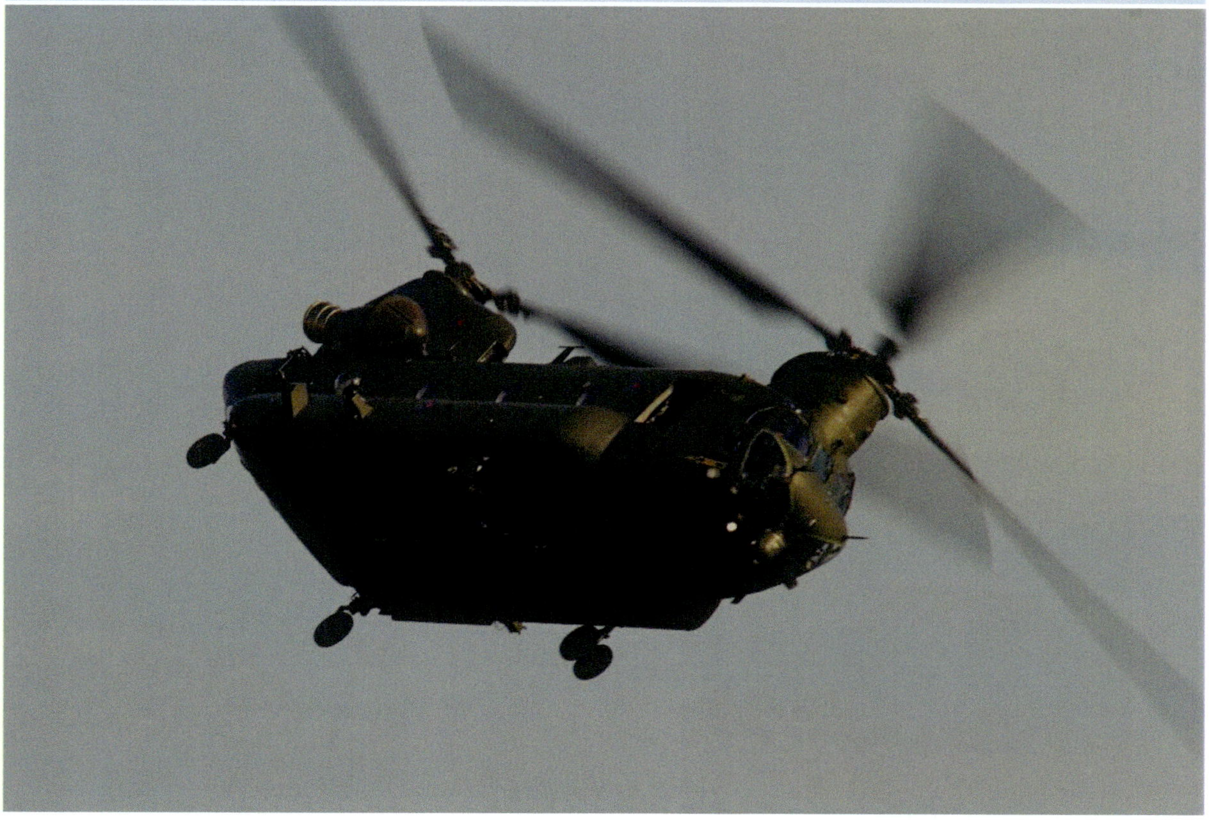

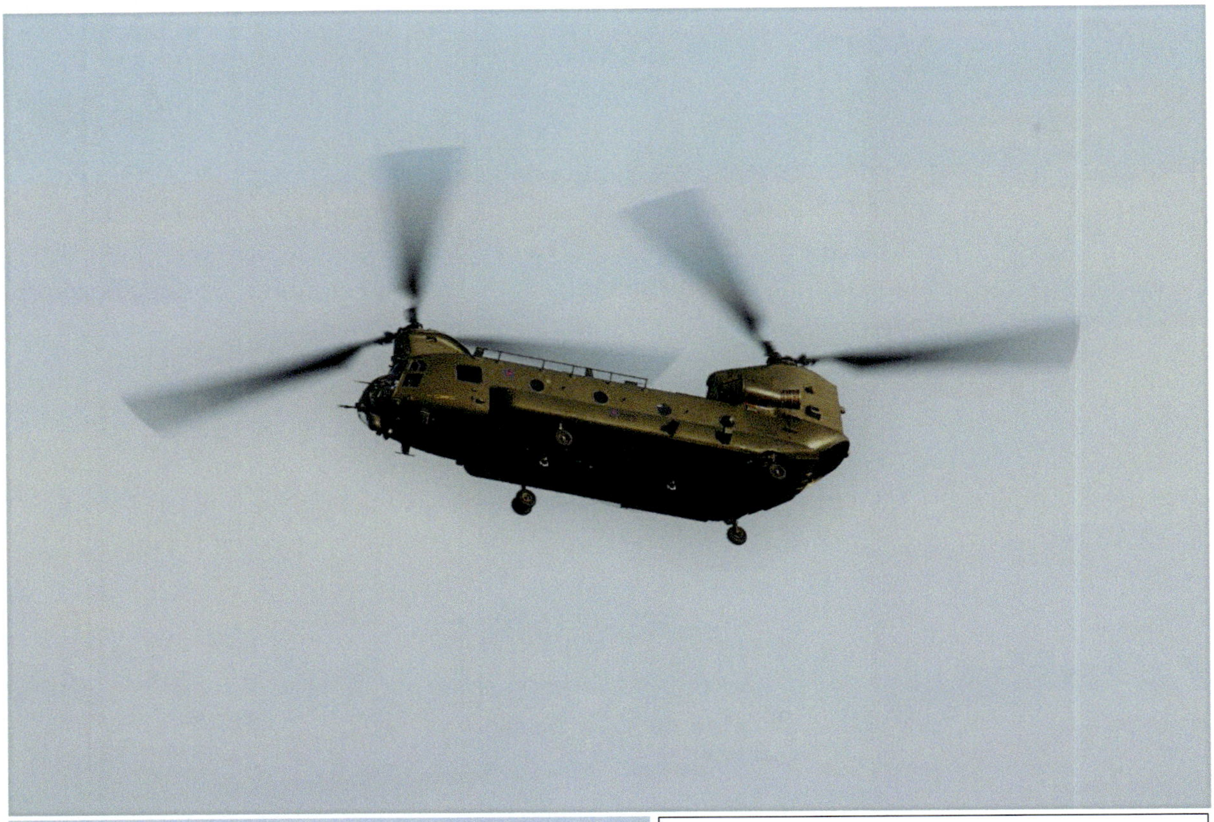

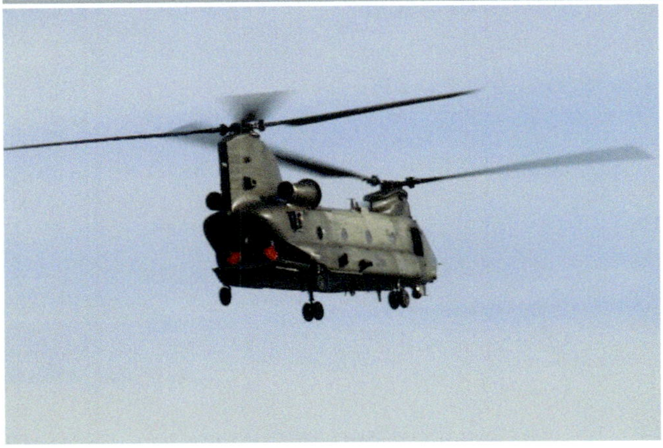

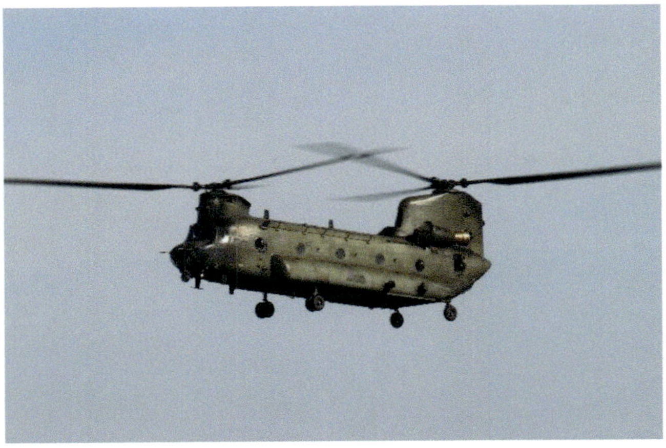

Quick Facts

General

Crew: 3–4 (pilot, copilot, one or two air loadmasters depending on aircraft role)

Capacity: 55 soldiers and equipment

Length: 98 ft 9 in (30.10 m)

Height: 18 ft 8 in (5.69 m)

Powerplant: 2 × Honeywell T55-GA-712 turboshaft engines

Performance

Maximum speed: 159 kn (183 mph, 294 km/h)

Service ceiling: 18,500 ft (5,600 m)

Rate of climb: 1,980 ft/min

Armament

Guns: 2× M134 Miniguns and 1× M60 machine gun

Final Thoughts

We have now reached the end of my memories of the aircraft at the Bournemouth Air Festival over the years. I hope you have enjoyed the photos and learned something about the planes. As you can see, there has been a wide variety of aircraft and display teams throughout the festival's history. Revisiting my photo archives let me unearth some forgotten one-time visitors and share this diverse collection with you.

While the pilots flying thrilling air shows command the spotlight, we must not forget the ground crews whose tireless work makes these displays possible. Without the many support staff inspecting, maintaining, and preparing the aircraft before and after each performance, there would be no breathtaking stunts in the sky. The pilots may be the stars of the show, but the ground crews are the backbone enabling air displays to entertain audiences across the UK and around the world.

The Air Festival has created fond memories and lifelong friendships for many residents and visitors over the years. As a visitor, I hope this book has evoked those wonderful memories for you as well. This beloved community event has brought incredible joy to all for free. I sincerely hope the Air Festival continues beyond 2024.

I often get asked, "Why do you go back every year when it's the same?" I have two responses. First, although some aircraft return, there are always exciting newcomers and special joint flypasts, like the Typhoon with the Spitfire in 2022 and the Lancaster in 2023, and the Hunter, Sea Vixen and Canberra flying in formation. Second, as an avid aviation photographer, I aim to improve my skills and photos each time while studying the routines to capture that ideal moment.

If any young people are reading this, I hope this book has sparked your interest in aviation and photography. My advice is to visit air shows, appreciate the aircraft and pilots, but also engage with the ground crews. With hard work, you could become a future display pilot or support staff member.

As I bid you my final farewell, I want to again thank my amazing parents for making time to take me to RAF Coltishall, where my interest in aviation photography began. The 2015 Air Festival will also hold special memories for me, as it was the last Bournemouth Air Festival my parents attended together before my Dad passed away a couple weeks after the event.

I want to give a huge thank you to my wife, son, and daughter for their continued support of my passion for aviation photography and for patiently looking through the hundreds of photos I eagerly share with them after every Air Festival.

9781836022183
WS - #0070 - 190625 - C269 - 297/210/19 - PB - 9781836022183 - Gloss Lamination